MW00667213

Still the Arena of Civil War

Violence and Turmoil in Reconstruction Texas, 1865–1874

Edited by
Kenneth W. Howell

UNT PRESS

University of North Texas Press
Denton, Texas

©2012 University of North Texas Press

All rights reserved.

Printed in the United States of America.

10 9 8 7 6 5 4 3 2 1

Permissions:
University of North Texas Press
1155 Union Circle #311336
Denton, TX 76203-5017

The paper used in this book meets the minimum requirements
of the American National Standard for Permanence
of Paper for Printed Library Materials, z39.48.1984.
Binding materials have been chosen for durability.

Library of Congress Cataloging-in-Publication Data

Still the arena of Civil War : violence and turmoil in Reconstruction Texas, 1865/1874 / edited by Kenneth Wayne Howell.—1st ed.
p. cm.
Includes bibliographical references and index.
ISBN 978-1-57441-449-3 (cloth : alk. paper)
ISBN 978-1-57441-457-8 (e-book)
1. Reconstruction (U.S. history, 1865-1877)—Texas. 2. Violence—Texas—History—19th century. 3. Frontier and pioneer life—Texas. 4. Texas—Race relations—History—19th century. 5. Minorities—Violence against—Texas—History—19th century. 6. Texas—Politics and government—1865–1950. I. Howell, Kenneth Wayne, 1967–
F391.S855 2012
976.4′06—dc23

2011042256

For Felesha, the love of my life

Contents

List of Maps

List of Illustrations

Preface

The Reconstruction era represents one of America's great paradoxes. It was a period of expanded liberty and democracy: two of America's most sacred principles. It should have been a period of exuberance and celebration. However, the post-Civil War era was in many ways a period of disappointment and missed opportunities. Instead of accepting the end of slavery and the expansion of suffrage rights for African American males, most white Southerners looked longingly to the past and exerted all their efforts to maintain the spirit of the antebellum era. As a result, southern landowners created an oppressive labor system in sharecropping, fought federal efforts to expand voting rights to southern blacks, and engaged in continual political warfare against Republicans for control of their state governments. To accomplish their goals, the white Southerners initiated a relentless campaign of violence against the freedpeople and their white allies. In essence, the people of the South continued to fight the Civil War after 1865 and did not relent until they won what had turned into a true war of attrition: the War of Reconstruction.

This study examines Reconstruction violence in Texas, focusing on the years between 1865 and 1874. In the pages that follow, readers will learn about the hardships that black Texans and their white allies suffered at the hands of ex-Confederates, former Secessionists, and conservative Democrats. Additionally, scholars will recognize that Texas was unique among the southern states during the post-Civil War years. Indian depredations, continuing problems between whites and Tejanos in South Texas, and ex-Confederate attacks on blacks served to make Texas the most violent place in all the former Confederate states. These circumstances added to the difficult task that federal authorities already experienced in reconstructing the Lone Star State. These circumstances alone make this study important to all who study this tumultuous period in United States and Texas history.

I first became interested in Reconstruction Texas after taking a class with Dr. James M. Smallwood at the University of Texas-Tyler in 1990. Since taking his course on Civil War and Reconstruction, I and Dr. Smallwood have become close friends and have shared many conversations on the successes and failures of the Reconstruction era. Over the years, we have come to the general conclusion that violence played a significant role in bringing an end to Reconstruction in Texas. In fact, we have concluded that the same could be said for most of the former

Confederate states. One night about five years ago during one of our regular late-night telephone conversations, I mentioned that I wanted to edit a volume on Reconstruction Texas. As I discussed various topics that I wanted to include in the book, Dr. Smallwood suggested that I consider delaying the Reconstruction project and instead edit a volume on the Civil War, especially since the sesquicentennial of the war was quickly approaching. During the weeks that followed, I came to the conclusion that my mentor was correct and began to work on *Seventh Star of the Confederacy: Texas during the Civil War*. I am now glad that I took Dr. Smallwood's advice as *Seventh Star* has been well received by scholars and students. However, I knew if I were going to provide a more thorough understanding of the Civil War era in Texas, I would need to return to my original project, especially considering that the Civil War did not end in 1865 for most Texans.

While this is not a complete history of the Reconstruction era in Texas, I believe it is the most comprehensive examination of violence in the state between 1865 and 1874. Readers will realize fairly quickly that the story of Reconstruction Texas was a frightful tale of blood—a story of violence that is unsurpassed in the annals of American history. Like most edited volumes, however, this study does not examine every aspect of the topic covered, but it is my sincere hope that it will provide greater understanding of the role violence played in Reconstruction Texas, and that the chapters presented here might serve as a catalyst for future studies.

Kenneth W. Howell
College Station, Texas

Acknowledgments

I owe a great debt to many people who have helped with the completion of this work. First and foremost, I would like to express my gratitude to my contributors. Each worked diligently to make all deadlines and was patient with me as I worked through the editing and publishing process, even during unexpected delays. This study would not have been possible without their tireless efforts.

On a more personal note, I owe Dr. James M. Smallwood a special debt of gratitude. Over the years, he has been my biggest supporter, and has listened for more hours than I can count to my ideas about Reconstruction Texas, sometimes agreeing with me and other times gently moving me back on the correct path when my ideas strayed too far from what facts would support. He continues to serve as a constant inspiration, and as an ideal model for what a scholar should be. In many ways, he has been more a father to me than a mentor. For all that he has done for me, I want to thank him from the bottom of my heart.

Also, I would like to thank many of my closest professional and personal friends (members of the Victoria Secrets, or as I like to affectionately refer to them, the Texas History Mafia) who have continued to encourage me to complete this project. Some of them were even gracious enough to make a contribution to this volume. Of this group, I am especially grateful to Charles and Pat Spurlin, Mary Jo O'Rear, Bruce Glasrud, Cary Wintz, Doug Kubicek, Carroll Scogin-Brincefield, Charles Grear, Henry and Linda Wolf, George Cooper, Donaly Brice, Harold Weiss, and Chuck and Pat Parsons. Thank you all for listening to my ideas on the War of Reconstruction.

I also owe a debt of gratitude to my colleagues at Prairie View A&M University, especially Walle Engedayehu, Michael Nojeim, Ron Goodwin, James Jones, and Dean Danny Kelley. They are always supportive of my research endeavors, and on many occasions have expressed interest in my publications. They have been and remain a daily source of inspiration. Furthermore, I would like to thank my students at Prairie View A&M University. Their enthusiasm for history and willingness to listen to my ideas on Reconstruction in various courses over the years have helped to sustain my research efforts and have aided me in developing my own thoughts on the Reconstruction era. As is often the case, I believe that I learned as much from their questions as they did from my lectures.

Also, I greatly appreciate the staff and editors at University of North Texas Press, especially Ron Chrisman. Ron's belief in this project and his professionalism gave me solace during the publication process. In addition, I want to thank Patrick Williams who read every word of the manuscript and offered invaluable insights for its improvement, especially the introduction. Patrick's suggestions improved this work. Finally, I want to thank my copy editor Karen DeVinney for improving the overall readability of the original manuscript. Despite all the professional assistance that I received while editing this work, I accept full responsibility for all errors of fact, faulty interpretations, and mistaken conclusions.

Finally, I want to express my gratitude to my family for all their support and encouragement. They never complained about the many hours that I spent working on this project, which would not have been possible without them by my side.

K.W.H.

Introduction

The Elusive Story of Violence in Reconstruction Texas, 1865–1874

by

Kenneth W. Howell

The American Civil War was one of the most significant events in the history of the United States. In four years more than six hundred thousand men died, Unionism triumphed, and slavery was abolished, but peace remained elusive. Amazingly, the victors showed extreme leniency toward the vanquished, a circumstance that allowed white Southerners after a brief time of reconstruction to regain control of the South's social, political, and economic institutions. Perhaps even more ironic, the vanquished for nearly a decade following the Civil War committed an untold number of violent acts against the victors. Throughout the South individuals and terrorist groups intimidated, beat, and murdered freedpeople, Republicans, and federal troops. By the end of the Reconstruction era, Southerners were able to achieve through violence what they had not been able to achieve during the Civil War: the liberty to preserve white supremacy in their society.

In some ways, violence in Texas was similar to that experienced in other southern states. As in other former Confederate states, black Texans were murdered in public as well as in their homes—victims of ex-Confederates, guerrilla and outlaw bands, and Democratic politicians who turned a blind eye to their plight. White Unionists, who supported the federal government and sometimes even favored equal rights for the newly freed slaves, were also vulnerable to attacks from the same groups. Even though scholars have examined violence committed against blacks and their white allies in detail and have clearly revealed that white supremacists in the South used violence to undermine the federal government's mission of reconstructing the political, economic, and social structure of the Old South, the subject of violence in the postwar South remains an elusive topic. By focusing almost exclusively on the violence committed by southern whites against blacks and federal authorities, scholars have perhaps oversimplified the hostilities that actually existed in Texas between 1865 and 1876. In essence, these scholars have only looked at one dimension of violent acts committed in the state and therefore have failed to fully understand the broader implications that violence played in Reconstruction Texas. There is no doubt that white on black violence was widespread and played a vital role in stalling federal efforts in the state, but very few attempts have been made to categorize these hostile acts within the context of time and space, thus providing a more complete picture of how such malevolent behaviors influenced the history of the Lone Star State.

Two of the earliest studies that examined Reconstruction violence in Texas were the 1866 report of the Congressional Joint Committee on Reconstruction and the 1868 report of the Special Committee on Lawlessness. The Congressional Joint Committee on Reconstruction produced the more extensive of the two reports, covering the conditions of the entire South. Members of the Joint Committee on Reconstruction interviewed military personnel who served in the southern states during the early days of Reconstruction, as well as a select group of Southerners, including both Unionists and former Secessionists. The primary objective of the Joint Committee was to more fully understand the current state of affairs in the former Confederate states in order to make recommendations to the House and Senate regarding future legislation to restore the South to its proper place within the Union. One of the most noticeable conclusions of the Committee's investigation was that white Southerners were violently attacking white Unionists and freedpeople.[1]

The "Report of the Special Committee on Lawlessness and Violence in Texas" focused specifically on the violence in the Lone Star State. Members of this committee submitted their findings to both the 1868 Constitutional Convention in Texas and the United States Congress. The committee reported exclusively on the number of homicides between 1865 and 1868. Similar to the findings of the Joint Committee on Reconstruction, the figures included in the Report of the Special Committee reveal "a frightful story of blood." The members stated that their report represented "stubborn facts, which cannot be suppressed by denials or by denouncing them as fabricated for political effect; and whoever attempts it is not only unfaithful to history, not only an apologist for crime, but may be justly charged as an accessory to the wickedness itself, as encouraging and abetting murders, and as equally guilty with them." They concluded, "We cannot shut our eyes upon these appalling scenes of bloodshed; and, instead of attempting to conceal them, it becomes us to face them honestly, and address ourselves to the duty of discovering the cause and locating the responsibility of this slaughter of our fellow citizens." The report detailed how ex-Confederates, outlaws, and other miscreants terrorized Unionists in the state and how they thwarted federal policies.[2]

Based on these reports as well as others, historians have attempted to recount the story of Reconstruction and to place violence within its proper context.[3] Perhaps more than at any time in American history, the historical record of Reconstruction has become a controversial battle ground for academics of widely divergent views regarding violence and its causes. Beginning in the early twentieth century, professional historians often claimed that the violent actions of terrorist groups, such as the Ku Klux Klan, were no different from those of Republican organizations such as the Union Loyal Leagues who vied for political control of the South. According to early scholars, the Klan and similar terrorist groups were initially honorable organizations that attempted to save the white South by challenging "Negro Rule," which had been established by federal troops, "carpetbaggers," and "scalawags." Such scholars claimed that these "noble" associations were taken over by outlaws who used them to support their own efforts at plunder. Once the outlaws seized control of the organizations, responsible southern leaders officially disbanded the groups.

One of the earliest professional historians to espouse such views was William A. Dunning. Writing at the turn of the twentieth century and reflecting a view commonly held by white Americans of his generation, Dunning suggested that federal efforts at Reconstruction had been misguided. He argued that Radical Republicans in Congress had imposed an idealistic and hostile regimen of civil and political reform on the South that was doomed to failure from the beginning. Dunning accepted the commonly held perception among white Southerners that blacks were inherently incapable of participating in democratic governments in the southern states. Like most white Southerners, Dunning celebrated the collapse of the Republican state governments in the South.[4]

In the late 1920s, scholars continued to blame the failures of Reconstruction on Congressional Republican policies. Supported by twentieth-century racism, historians argued that Northerners' hatred of the South permitted Republicans to use the federal government to defeat the political ideal of states' rights and to crush the social construct of white supremacy. Most scholars writing during this era concluded that President Andrew Johnson was a champion of the common man, while they represented Republican leaders as anti-democratic and wealthy elitists. In particular, Claude Bowers's *The Tragic Era: The Revolution after Lincoln* argued that the Republican rule in the South led to corruption and black equality. According to Bowers, "Negro Rule" was justification enough for white Southerners' use of violence to redeem the South from the misguided and unwanted Republican governments.[5]

With the onset of the Great Depression, scholars writing in the 1930s began to examine the Reconstruction era from an economic perspective. Howard Beale's *The Critical Year: A Study of Andrew Johnson and Reconstruction* argued that northern business interests used the chaotic era of Reconstruction to take control and use the federal government to further capitalism in the country. W. E. B. Du Bois, a noted African American scholar who adhered to the Marxist view of history, took an opposing position in *Black Reconstruction.* Du Bois argued that northern capitalists formed an alliance with the freedpeople and poor whites of the South, who were attempting to create a democratic society in the southern states. During the early 1870s, northern businessmen abandoned this alliance and formed a new one with white southern elites, who agreed to accept northern capitalists' domination of the federal government in exchange for control of their state governments.[6] Even though economic interpretations provided new insights into the era, they did little to explain the widespread violence in the southern states between 1865 and 1877.

Reconstruction historiography experienced few interpretive changes during the 1940s and 1950s. However, in varying degrees during the 1960s historians began to challenge the original interpretations of the Reconstruction era. It was these revisionist scholars who revived the reputation of the Republican Party, as well as the freedpeople, and highlighted the destructive forces of white Southerners' adherence to states' rights and white supremacy. Influenced by the civil rights movement of their own generation, the revisionists viewed Reconstruction as the initial movement to establish racial, civil, and political equality. At the same time, the revisionists focused less on accusations of corruption among southern Republican governments, choosing instead to stress the progressive nature of their policies. These scholars often found that the violence taking place in the southern states, including Texas, resulted from political struggles for control of state and local governments and from the federal government's push to secure black equality.[7]

In the 1970s and 1980s, the primary focus of Reconstruction scholars was to analyze the success and failures of the Republican Party. These studies often revealed a division between conservative and radical Republican leaders. Scholars found that moderate and Radical Republicans worked together because they feared that President Johnson was placing the South back in the hands of ex-Confederates and former Secessionists. They also argued that most Republicans were sincere about securing basic rights for black Southerners, but many conservatives and radicals in the party often disagreed on the limits of black rights. Some revisionist historians laid the failure of Reconstruction at the feet of President Johnson, while others blamed the conservative nature of Congress. Still other scholars argued that the collapse of Republican Reconstruction policy occurred during President Ulysses S. Grant's administration. While most, if not all, revisionists mentioned that numerous violent episodes occurred in the southern states, some examined southern violence within a political context and primarily focused their analysis on how hostilities impacted the Republican Party.[8] As such, students of the era were left with an incomplete understanding of southern violence during the Reconstruction period.

Other historians writing in the 1970s and 1980s tended to focus more directly on how terrorism and violence shaped southern society, economically and politically. George Rable and Allen Trelease were leading figures among this group of scholars. Rable's *But There Was No Peace* offers one of the better explanations for southern violence. He examines multiple causes underlying the South's reaction to defeat in the Civil War and to Republican rule, including the impact of the physical destruction of the South; the powerlessness that Southerners felt at the beginning of the postwar years; southern politicians' need to control their states' readmission to the Union and to accept as few changes as possible in the antebellum political structure; the refusal to admit guilt for the war and justification of the Lost Cause; the fear of northern Republicans as arbiters of change; the rage associated with frustrations of delayed national reunification; the resentment toward federal troops in the South; and the prevalence of white supremacist ideology. Rable also mentions that the South was a haven for outlaws and desperadoes, men who had perfected the art of killing during the war and who now used those skills to wrest plunder from helpless victims in their home region. The victims often were those who were afforded the least protection in society: blacks and white Unionists. Such outlaw gangs proved resistant to federal efforts to bring them to justice because they gained favor with the general populace by professing loyalty to the "Lost Cause" and the Democratic Party. In fact, many of these outlaws became folk heroes in their region of the South.[9]

According to Rable, postwar violence in the South can be divided into three phases: racial confrontations between 1865 and 1866, a counter-revolution initiated by terrorist groups against Congressional Reconstruction beginning in 1868, and the Democrats' mobilization of their state party organizations to coordinate with terrorist groups to defeat Republican candidates during state elections between 1874 and 1876. During the first phase, the South witnessed racial riots in Memphis and New Orleans in 1866. In the second phase, the Klan served as an "instrument of redemption" for the South, but ultimately declined when it failed to achieve its central objective of overthrowing Republican state governments in the South. Finally, in Alabama, Mississippi, and South Carolina, the Democratic Party organized white supremacy campaigns and used terrorism to intimidate Republican voters and their party candidates. Better organized than the earlier Klan, this new form of political violence proved more effective in squashing the black vote and thereby removing the last vestige of Republican state governments in the South. Therefore, Rable convincingly argues that violence was a critical element in bringing an end to Reconstruction, and he is correct when he states that "peace became war carried on by other means."[10]

Allen W. Trelease's *White Terror: The Ku Klux Klan Conspiracy and Southern Reconstruction* describes southern violence during the Reconstruction era. Unlike historians who supported Dunning's sympathetic view of the Klan, Trelease argues that the Klan members initiated a reign of terror that primarily targeted freedpeople, whom they "whipped, shot, hanged, robbed, raped, and otherwise outraged."[11] The primary goal of the Klan, as well as similar terrorist organizations, was to suppress the freedpeople and to restore white supremacy in the southern states. After 1867, the Klansmen focused their efforts on preventing the establishment of new Republican governments by obstructing the election process. When their efforts did not produce adequate results, the terrorists initiated efforts to destabilize and undermine Republicans once they took office. The Klan was particularly active in areas where "the two parties [Democratic and Republican] or the two races [whites and blacks] were nearly equal, or where there was a white majority large enough to intimidate the freedmen."[12] But this pattern was not universal because, as Trelease notes, the Klan also operated in some areas where the freedpeople outnumbered whites, and conversely in some areas where the white population was predominant. While acts of terror against blacks often occurred without any direct relation to politics, Trelease argues that white violence was also designed to weaken the Republican authority in the southern states. In this regard, the Klan was extremely effective, but

Trelease finds that not so much that it could be "credited with overthrowing Republican control." However, these groups were "clearly instrumental in breaking up the Union League and local Republican organization in many counties."[13]

Revisionist scholars such as Rable and Trelease have attempted to explain the significance of violence in the Reconstruction South, but what about Texas? Although Trelease provides significant insights into the violence that was perpetrated in the Lone Star State, he focuses only on Klan activities after 1868. Finding that at least twenty East Texas counties witnessed Klan terror, Trelease reveals that these Ku Klux groups, like those in other southern states, attempted to secure white supremacist ideology by attacking and intimidating the freedpeople, and challenged Republican rule by attacking the party's political leaders at both the local and state level. He concludes that the Klan diminished in strength after Republican Governor Edmund J. Davis asked the legislature to create a state police and a militia, and to vest him with the power to declare martial law. The legislature created the state police, which began to sweep the state of disguised bands. Trelease argues that by 1872, Davis's use of martial law and the state police began to curb Klan violence, but did not end it. Perhaps more importantly, he finds that local lawmen and jurists prosecuted very few of the accused Klansmen for their crimes and convicted even fewer.[14]

Trelease differs sharply from early Texas historians who shared Dunning's views. In *Reconstruction in Texas*, Charles W. Ramsdell states that the Klan emerged because of the "continuous and peculiarly offensive activity of branches of the Union League and the Grand Army of the Republic among the negroes with the view of securing political control through the black vote." Further, he mentions that the Klan was not "very extensive" and that it did not "deserve the sinister reputation that it later acquired." For Ramsdell, the Klan and other terrorist groups were upstanding southern citizens who banded together to save the South from the "abuses" of the Radical Republicans.[15] In describing the Klan's activities, Ramsdell finds that "Bands of Ku Klux made their appearance in nearly all parts of the state, especially where the Loyal Union League had produced restlessness among the blacks. Sometimes giant horsemen, shrouded in ghostly white, some of them headless, passed at midnight through the negro settlements, disarming and frightening the superstitious freedmen out of their senses, but otherwise doing no harm." He continues, "Sometimes, however, the matter did not stop with these comparatively harmless pranks. Now and then the negroes and Radical whites, whose political activity made them particularly obnoxious, received written warnings couched in mysterious and sanguinary terms, and embellished with fearful symbols." Ramsdell at least admits that the Klan was violent when their warnings were ignored, stating that "the offender was likely to be taken out and whipped, or even murdered." Yet, he also argued that "in many cases the guilty parties proved to be reckless and irresponsible persons masquerading under the name of Ku Klux; and they only helped to bring the name of the organization into disrepute and to furnish campaign material to the Radicals." In the end, Ramsdell faulted black Texans and Radicals for causing the violence perpetrated against them by terrorist groups, or simply blamed the violence on sinister outlaws.[16] Until the civil rights revolution of the 1960s, other Texas scholars who published accounts of Reconstruction tended to accept Ramsdell's overall interpretation.[17]

Texas scholars who lived through the 1960s civil rights movement began to challenge Ramsdell's interpretation of Reconstruction Texas, especially in regards to violence. Although these scholars did not always agree about the particulars, they all claimed that the outcome of the Civil War left psychological scars on society. Historians such as James Smallwood, Barry Crouch, Carl Moneyhon, and William Richter provided new approaches to understanding the motivations behind the violence in Reconstruction Texas. Smallwood found that the main cause of violence against blacks during this era was whites' desire to maintain white supremacy and secure control of state and local politics. Crouch generally agreed with Smallwood's assessment, but also added that politically motivated violence had been oversimplified and that racial conflicts between whites and blacks often arose from a wide range of economic and social causes. Richter tended to focus more on how violence affected federal military authorities and Bureau agents operating in Texas. While finding that the federal authorities operating in Texas made an honest effort to bring law and order to the state, they often found that they had little, sometimes no, support from Congress and their superiors, who either did not fully understand the conditions on the ground or were incompetent. Publishing the first modern history of Reconstruction Texas, Moneyhon provided a synthesis of these scholarly works, focusing on the political developments in the state. His work is one of the best single-volume studies of Texas during this era.[18]

As a synthesis, Moneyhon's *Texas after the Civil War: The Struggle of Reconstruction* provides readers a glimpse of Reconstruction violence, finding that most hostilities in Texas primarily resulted from social, economic, and political issues. Moneyhon contends that the "Republican party threatened the very survival of the state's antebellum Democratic political leadership, plantation interests, and the racist attitudes that supported both." As such, Democrats and their supporters "used every means at hand to defeat the new party." He states that "violence, intimidation, election fraud, and blatant appeals to racial fears were coupled to more traditional campaign tactics of misinformation and misrepresentation to create a white majority, ultimately organized in the Democratic party, opposed to the state's Republican government." Standing against such an ominous force, Republicans "found themselves unable to respond to their opponents in a manner capable of defeating them. . . . They could have done little short of engaging in full-scale civil and racial war to succeed." Moneyhon concludes that "antebellum leaders, not the whole of the people, kept the state on its old road, leaving Texans a legacy of a single-crop agriculture system that dominated the economy and racial repression that lasted into the next century."[19] Though Moneyhon adequately examines violent actions of white Texans within a political and economic context, scholars are still left with an incomplete understanding of the social complexities of hostilities occurring in the state.[20]

Influenced by the writings of revisionists, especially Moneyhon, Gregg Cantrell has also made valuable contributions to our understanding of Reconstruction violence. Generally agreeing with the revisionist assessments of this volatile era, Cantrell argues that violence resulted from "an expression of hostility to political conditions" and was "closely associated with political developments." He found that violence peaked in the years following the passage of the Reconstruction Acts of 1867, which secured black suffrage and political participation in the southern states, including Texas. Cantrell argued that by asserting themselves in a variety of ways, the freedpeople became the "most available symbol of the South's defeat and of Northern 'aggression,' and thus served as a convenient scapegoat" for white Texans.[21]

Just as they did in the broader South, ex-Confederates, guerillas, and outlaw bands made life miserable for the freedpeople in Texas. As mentioned above, revisionist historians have provided detailed examinations of this type of violence. Additionally, they have demonstrated that Democrats were unsympathetic to the suffering of blacks in the state. [22] These scholars have illustrated particularly well how white supremacists disrupted the Reconstruction process by thwarting the efforts of Radical Republicans in Texas. However, by focusing primarily on the crimes that whites committed against blacks and federal officials, the revisionists have overlooked some of the nuances of violence in the state between 1865 and 1874. Thus, despite all the efforts of revisionist historians, Reconstruction violence in Texas still remains an elusive topic.

While Cantrell, Moneyhon, and other revisionists have made important discoveries about white-on-black and white-on-white violence, there are other questions that must be considered in order to have a more complete picture of how violence influenced the history of the Lone Star State. For example, did frontier violence impact the administration of federal Reconstruction policies? Were there acts of violence that had little relation to the Reconstruction efforts of the federal government? Did all areas in the state experience violent outbreaks against federal authority? If not, what made those areas experiencing less violence different from the regions overwhelmed by terrorist groups bent on preserving white supremacy? To what degree did violence impact the political development of the state? Before we can fully understand the violence present in the Lone Star State during the Reconstruction period, we must address these, as well as other, important questions.

Though many questions remain unanswered, scholars can identify several general trends associated with Reconstruction violence in Texas. First, and perhaps the most obvious, is that there was a violent political war waged in Texas between Democrats and Republicans. In 1866, Bvt. Maj. Gen. George Armstrong Custer testified before the Joint Committee on Reconstruction, casting light on the political mood of the state. Custer, like many of those who testified before the committee, reinforced the idea that certain areas in Texas were still in a virtual state of war. Custer stated that "in Texas it would hardly be possible to find a man who has been strictly faithful to the Union, and remained in the South, during the war. [The rebels] forced all who were truly Union men to leave the state. Those who did not were murdered. The people of the north have no conception of the number of murders that have been committed in that state during and since the war." Custer was certain that it would not be "safe for a loyal man to remain in Texas . . . after the [federal] troops were withdrawn. I have within my possession letters from prominent Union men in the State, saying that if the troops were to be withdrawn they wished to be informed of it for the purpose of making arrangements to leave when the troops did; that it would be unsafe and unwise for them to remain." He continued, "In many parts of Texas Union men dare not express their sentiments as regards loyalty to the general government. Their lives would be endangered by so doing. Union men are being murdered there to this day."[23]

When asked if he knew of any organizations in the state that were attempting to thwart the actions of the federal government, Custer answered that "it was reported to me frequently that such organizations did exist, and I have no doubt in my mind that they have existed in the northern part of the state. I was so thoroughly convinced of the fact that I sent a considerable force into that section of the state to disperse them. The fact that such organizations did exist was confirmed by the statements, written and oral, of loyal men, and by the reports of officers sent there on duty." Perhaps the most revealing moment of Custer's testimony came when the Joint Committee inquired whether Texans, if offered the opportunity to secede without war, would stay in the Union or leave. Custer simply replied, "I think they would prefer to go out."[24] Custer's insights were correct. Ex-Confederates, former Secessionists, and conservative Democrats wanted to remain as far removed from federal control as possible, and many were willing to wage a guerrilla war to accomplish their purpose.

Beginning in December 1865, Congressional Republicans declared Presidential Reconstruction a failure and took steps to seize control of the reconstruction process from Johnson by passing the Civil Rights Act of 1866 and the Freedmen's Bureau Act over the president's veto. Additionally, Congress also secured the passage of the Fourteenth Amendment. In an effort to solidify their control of Reconstruction, Congress next passed the Reconstruction Acts. The first of these acts passed on March 2, 1867, and declared that Congress now viewed the existing state governments in former Confederate states as provisional, except in Tennessee where the state legislature had already ratified the Fourteenth Amendment. Subsequent legislation divided the southern states into five military districts, instituted martial law, disenfranchised former Confederate leaders, and established procedures by which the southern states would create new constitutions that ensured the protection of black civil rights. Texas and Louisiana made up the Fifth Military District. As Congressional Republicans gained control of the Reconstruction process and made clear their resolve to protect the political and civil rights of black Southerners, terrorist organizations in Texas gained strength. By 1868, the most infamous was the Ku Klux Klan.[25]

Republicans also began to gain power in state governments throughout the South, including Texas. As Republicans moved to solidify that state for their party, violence against their supporters not only escalated, but also became organized, with numerous terrorist groups emerging, especially in areas with larger populations of freedmen. Gen. Joseph

Reynolds reported to the Secretary of War in 1868 that "armed organizations, generally known as 'Ku-Klux Klans,' exist, independently or in concert with other armed bands, in many parts of Texas, but are most numerous, bold, and aggressive east of the Trinity River. The precise objects of the organization cannot be readily explained, but seem, in this State, to be to disarm, rob, and, in many cases, murder Union men and negroes, and, as occasion may offer, murder United States officers and soldiers." Reynolds also stated that the Ku Kluxers intimidated "every one who knows anything of the organization, but will not join it."[26]

General Reynolds speculated about the motives of these terrorist groups. He stated, "What political end, if any, is aimed at by these bands I cannot say, but they attend in large bodies the political meetings (barbecues) which have been and are still being held in various parts of this State, under the auspices of the democratic clubs of the different counties." Furthermore, Reynolds claimed that "the speakers encourage their attendance, and in several counties men have been indicated by name from the speaker's stand as those selected for murder. The men thus pointed out have no course left them but to leave their homes or be murdered on the first convenient opportunity. The murder of negroes is so common as to render it impossible to keep accurate account of them."[27]

General Reynolds was not the only one to report on violence occurring in the state after 1868. Writing for the *Cincinnati Commercial* in 1869, a traveling correspondent commented on conditions in Texas. He wrote:

> You cannot pick up a paper in East Texas without reading of murder, assassinations, and robbery . . . and yet not a fourth part of the truth has been told; not one in ten is reported. Go where you will, and you will hear of fresh murders and violence . . . The civil authorities is powerless—the military insufficient in number, while hell has transferred its capital from Pandemonium to Jefferson, and the devil is holding high carnival in Gilmer, Tyler, Canton, Quitman, Boston, Marshall and other places in Texas.[28]

It is certain that the Klan and other terrorist groups were responsible for the murder and mayhem that plagued the state. Despite the best efforts of the Republican government in Texas, these groups continued to wreak havoc on blacks and white Unionists. In time, the Klan would become a paramilitary force that the Democratic Party used to overwhelm their Republican adversaries, especially in local politics.[29]

The alignment between Democratic leaders and terrorist groups was most visible in areas with large black populations, where both groups coordinated the use of massive violence prior to elections in an effort to intimidate African American voters and their white allies. For example, on April 11, 1871, the editor of the Austin *Daily State Journal* wrote a telling article about discordant Texas Democrats, stating that "they do not concede that the negro is lawfully a voter, with civil and political rights equal to their own. They do not regard the thirteenth, fourteenth, and fifteenth amendments to the federal constitution as valid and binding; but confidently expect to override and nullify them whenever they shall have triumphed in the restoration of the Democratic party to power." The editorial concluded by claiming that "the South is still the arena of civil war."[30]

By 1874, the Republican Party lost control of the Texas state government to the Democrats. However, violence perpetrated against Republicans who were engaged in local politics did not disappear. In 1875, J. N. Baughman, a Republican member of the state legislature from Wharton County, wrote "on last Thursday, the 7th of January, I was waited on by an armed mob, composed of the leading democrats of the county, and ordered to leave the county or they would kill me." He continued, "I asked them what their objections were to me staying there; their answer was, 'You are a d__d radical,' and they did not want any of my sort in the county, and they did not intend to let me stay there, me or any other damned radical; and they took the vote on it, and every one (the sheriff and his deputy among the crowd) voted that I should not stay." Believing that the rule of law might still prevail, Baughman approached the sheriff for protection against his persecutors. The sheriff bluntly stated that "he could not give [him] any, as [he] was a damned radical, and he with the rest did not want [him] there."[31]

Baughman decided to remain forted up in his office, staying off the street out of fear of being killed. Sometime later, six men came to his office with guns in hand, vowing that they were there to murder him. Fortunately, Baughman was able to evade them and to seek the protection of a neighbor, who hid him until nightfall. In the meantime, his pursuers discovered where he was hiding and came to the door, threatening to break it down. Even though the sheriff made an effort to stop them, the gunmen paid no attention and were about to follow through on their threat of forced entry when the neighbor's wife appeared and begged them to desist. Moved by the woman's plea and perhaps the sheriff's protest, the men abandoned their efforts. Fearing that the men would return, Baughman left his neighbor's home under the cover of darkness and traveled to Austin, making a formal complaint to Governor Coke and asking him for protection. The governor refused, stating that he had no authority to act in the matter. In his report to the United States Attorney General, Baughman reflected on why the men had threatened him: "It seems what started them this particular day, we were having an election for justice of the peace to fill a vacancy, and I was issuing tickets for the republican party at my store, and the first time the crowd waited on me they gave me orders to issue no more tickets. I was a soldier in the Union Army—served four years—is another objection they have to me."[32]

Governor Davis, who forwarded Baughman's account to the United States Attorney General, revealed that similar problems were occurring at Grand Saline in Van Zandt County. According to Davis, S. J. Richardson, who owned the saline and hired freedpeople to work for him, reported that "a number of colored have been killed, the last act of the sort being the forcing open the colored man's mouth and shooting their pistols into it by the disguised mob." Davis continued, "There are other localities where similar outrages have been perpetrated on colored people with a few months past. As the state authorities *practically* refuse to take action in such cases as these of Captain Baughman and Mr. Richardson, the question arises as to where they are to seek help. I suppose citizens of the United States are entitled to protection from *some* source." Davis concluded, "Those of one class of politics or color cannot, it seems, get it from our State authorities. Such persons have no rights that anybody here (who differs with them politically) is bound to respect. Can they, then, get it from the United States authorities? If from neither, it occurs to me that the war for the Union was very much of a farce."[33] Unfortunately for Baughman, the federal government failed to answer Davis's call for help. Baughman was murdered in his own home more than a year later. Apparently, thirty men surrounded his house, broke in his door, and "riddled his body with bullets" while he lay in bed too sick to get up.[34]

Even as late as 1876, violence and murder continued to plague Unionists and African Americans. Writing to President Grant from Austin, Texas, Mrs. Elizabeth Schobey detailed how her husband was gunned downed by two desperadoes in Bastrop County. Although she was not present at the time of the murder, she recalled what witnesses had told her: "the men rode up to his home and called him to the door he invited them to come in they said they could not stop that they only wanted to see him a few minutes he walked about twelve steps from the door when they both shot him through the heart they fired three times either shot would have killed him." Mrs. Schobey speculated on why her husband was killed, saying that "Mr. Schobey was a Republican a firm friend of Governor Davis and the Republicans were running him as Candidate for the Legislature it is said that he had secured the Majority of the votes in Fayitte and Bastrop Countys he has been Teaching Colored school for several years along with myself and has also been a successful lawer." She continued, "He had made several speeches that did not please the opposite party and was shot down like a dog in his own yard without one word of warning he lived about 1-1/2 hours after they shot." Reportedly, Mr. Schobey's dying words were instructions for his wife and two sons to leave the country as soon as possible, stating that if they stayed they would be murdered also.[35]

Based just on the accounts above, there can be no question that Texans were engaged in a violent and bloody war for control of state and local politics. However, we are still left with several important questions: Were the terrorists in Texas any different from those in other southern states? Did they have the same impact on political realignment as terrorist groups operating in the Lower South (Mississippi, Alabama, Georgia, or South Carolina) during the late 1860s and 1870s? Generally speaking, the evidence suggests that terrorists in the Lone Star State were very similar to those in other regions of the South, especially at the county level. Like their southern counterparts, Texas terrorists embraced the same tactics, preyed upon the same victims, embraced the same objectives of restoring political and social control to the Democratic Party, and remained dedicated to the idea of white supremacy and black inferiority.

Some historians emphasize the natural advantages Democrats enjoyed statewide. A huge migration of white Southerners to Texas after the war, they stress, swelled the party's ranks and allowed Democrats to vote themselves back into power. But, while numerical superiority would eventually contribute to their taking control of the state government beginning in 1871, a statewide majority among registered voters did not guarantee that whites could gain control of local and county politics, especially in regions where blacks represented a significant part of the population.[36]

Between 1867 and 1871, white conservatives perceived that they were living under the oppressive thumb of the Radical Republicans, whose rule might continue at least for the remainder of their lifetimes. Under such conditions, individuals turned to violent behaviors to obstruct the Republican government in their state. In fact, they continued to embrace violence as a tactical means of preserving their political and social beliefs until it was clear that Democrats would regain control of the local, county, and state governments. Beginning in 1871, when Texans realized that conservative Democrats would regain political control of the state, they no longer saw the need or validity of terrorist activities. Their enemies had been defeated; they had essentially won the "War of Reconstruction." Nevertheless, violence at the local level continued, especially in areas where the black population was equal to or larger than that of whites. In most cases, whites used violence to reinforce social and political dominance over their black neighbors. The primary difference, however, was that they could engage in violent activities without fear of reprisal from state authorities. As these individuals banded together

Illustration 1. Death at the polls, and free from "federal interference" by Thomas Nast. Illustration first appeared in *Harper's Weekly*, Oct. 18, 1879. (Courtesy of Library of Congress)

in organized units, they aided the Democratic Party's return to power in 1873. The terrorists' primary targets were Radical Republicans and loyal Unionists, especially African Americans, who represented the largest block of Republican supporters in the state.[37]

A second generalization regarding Reconstruction violence in Texas is that a violent race war was waged against people of color. By the late spring and the summer of 1865, whites were beating, whipping, and killing black Texans even more than they had during the years of slavery. Most of the freedpeople became victims of crimes because of their new status in society. In many cases the perpetrators were young men who had fought in the Civil War. They hated the Yankees and the outcome of the war, and in their frustration, they targeted freedpeople and white Unionists, the very groups that supported federal Reconstruction policies and who were least able to protect themselves. One historian listed the reasons why Anglos killed freedmen:

> [F]reedman did not remove hat when he passed him [a white man]; Negro would not allow himself to be whipped; freedman would not allow his wife to be whipped by a white man; he [a freedman] was carrying a letter to a Freedmen's Bureau official; [one murderer killed] Negroes just to see them kick; [one white killed] because he wanted to thin out niggers a little; [freedman] did not hand over his money quick enough; [freedman] would not give up his whiskey flask.[38]

Even though rational minds today consider these justifications absurd, the majority of white Texans during the late nineteenth century believed in the absolute right of white supremacy. In an atmosphere of racial hatred where the least provocation could lead to an uncontrollable riot, whites waged war against black Texans and their white allies.

Contemporaries often commented about the treatment of freedpeople. In 1865 from Paris, Texas, Mrs. L. E. Potts wrote to President Andrew Johnson, providing personal testimony about events unfolding in her area of the state. She reported, "I wish that my poor pen could tell you of their [freedpeople] persecutions here. They are now just out of slavery only a few months, and their masters are so angry to lose them that they are trying to persecute them back into slavery." She continued by stating that "there have never been any federal troops in here, and everything savors of rebellion. I wish we could have a few soldiers here just for a while, to let these rebels know that they have been whipped." Mrs. Potts concluded her letter with a plea for the president to take action to save the freedpeople, stating that "your good heart and wise head know best what to do. I have stated only facts; the negroes need protection here. When they work they scarcely ever get any pay; and what are they to do?" Mrs. Potts, however, placed too much faith in Johnson, because he simply turned the matter over to Maj. Gen. Oliver Otis Howard, the head of the Bureau of Refugees, Freedmen, and Abandoned Lands, giving little more thought to the suffering African Americans in Texas.[39]

At about the same time that Mrs. Potts wrote her letter, Custer was giving his testimony before the Joint Committee on Reconstruction.[40] Custer made lengthy comments regarding the conditions of freedpeople in Texas, stating that "there is a very strong feeling of hostility towards the freedmen as a general thing." The general continued, "There are exceptions, of course; but the great mass of the people there seem to look upon the freedmen as being connected with, or as being the cause of, their present condition, and they do not hesitate to improve every opportunity to inflict injuries upon [them] in order, seemingly, to punish [them] for this." According to Custer, freedpeople could not find justice in Texas courts. He testified that whites frequently murdered ex-slaves for the slightest provocations, or for no provocation at all. The murderers were rarely brought before the courts for their heinous crimes. Even in the cases where the killers were tried, white juries acquitted them. Because of such harsh treatment, Custer surmised that the freedpeople would remain "loyal without a single exception" to the federal government. The general stated that "they realize, as all Union men in the state do, that their only safety and protection lies in the general government; and they realize too, that if the troops are withdrawn, they will be still more exposed than they are now."[41]

In 1866, Bvt. Maj. Gen. William E. Strong, who served as Inspector General of the Bureau of Refugees, Freedmen, and Abandoned Lands, also testified before the Joint Committee on Reconstruction. He reported that conditions in the larger cities of Texas were relatively peaceful, but in "in the interior of the state, one or two hundred miles from the prominent cities, away from the influence of federal troops and federal bayonets, at points where our army has never penetrated, and where the citizens have but little fear of arrest and punishment for crimes committed, I assure you there is a fearful state of things; the freedmen are in a worse condition than they ever were as slaves." Strong continued by explaining that the freedmen were "frequently beaten unmercifully, and shot down like wild beasts, without any provocation, followed with hounds, and maltreated in every possible way. It is the same old story of cruelty only there is more of it in Texas than any southern State that I have visited."[42]

While there were circumstances of blacks engaged in violent acts against whites, the majority of race-related incidents in Texas between 1865 and 1874 were whites attacking African American citizens. This violence resulted from whites' irrational hatred of blacks and their opposition to the social changes that challenged the belief of white supremacy. In the early phases of Reconstruction, individuals or small gangs were primarily responsible. However, well-organized terrorist groups began to emerge in response to political changes in Texas, especially after Congress took a more active role in directing the affairs of the southern states.

By 1868, the Ku Klux Klan as well as other terrorist organizations openly operated in the state. The Klan's violent intentions were often hidden by claims that the terrorist groups acted out of self-defense, chivalry, and honor. Frequently, the Klansmen stated that they were merely protecting white Texans from incipient black uprisings or that they were fighting rampant black crime, a problem that the authorities, especially Republican officials, were accused of ignoring. Klan members also claimed that they disciplined recalcitrant black laborers to the benefit of white employers. Such activities were designed to keep blacks docile and on the job, but often resulted in laborers leaving their jobs and in the disruption of white landowners' economic stability. As an agent of social control, the Klan enjoyed greater success. In an attempt to keep African Americans within their defined social bounds, the terrorists attempted to prevent them from owning and renting land, lynched black men who cohabitated with white women, punished individuals who supported the idea of black social equality, beat or killed African Americans accused of insolence toward whites, and conducted vendettas against the teachers of black schools. Beginning as early as 1867, the Klan-like terrorist organizations developed strong opposition to the Radical Republicans and their agenda that supported African American suffrage.

In early 1871 during a speech before Congress, Benjamin F. Butler commented on the type of justice that blacks could expect to receive in Texas. Butler reported that a freedman by the name of Jenkins "had some difficulty with a planter, upon whose estate he was a laborer. Two friends of the planter therefore most unmercifully whipped Jenkins until nearly dead, and then told him he would be killed if he went before the grand jury." Butler continued, "In the effort of Jenkins to obtain justice he was called before the grand jury, whereupon he was followed from the court-house and murdered by four men, two of whom had assaulted him before, and his opponent, who meanwhile had wounded another man by mistake for Jenkins; whereupon the judge of the county court issued his warrant for the arrest of the four murderers." The men were apprehended, brought before the judge, and prosecuted for the unprovoked murder. However, before the accused could be removed from the courtroom, a gun battle broke out between the outlaws, who had managed to obtain weapons from their friends who attended the court proceedings, and the local sheriff. Before the battle ended, several people were wounded; the judge and district attorney barely escaped with their lives; and at least one individual was killed. Butler reported that "twenty or thirty confederates, armed with shot-guns, with horses ready, greeted the murderers with cheers; then mounting their horses and firing their pistols, yelling like savages, the prisoners, followed by their friends, made good their escape from town."[43]

Such accounts as those found above suggest that a violent race war of whites against African Americans had engulfed Texas in the post-Civil War years. However, African Americans were not the only to suffer at the hands of white Texans. Tejanos in South Texas also were victims of white supremacists. While not typically included in the story of Reconstruction, the racial confrontations between whites and Tejanos are a vital part of the state's history during this era. This is not to say that scholars have completely ignored hostilities against Tejanos during the Reconstruction era. Arnoldo De León's *They Called Them Greasers: Anglo Attitudes toward Mexicans in Texas, 1821–1900* is perhaps one of the more informative examinations of white violence inflicted against Tejanos. De León states that "after 1865, whites sounded repeated alarms manifesting old fears. Even more than before, they conjured up visions of Mexicans doing to them what they were doing to Mexicans and imagined terrors that evolved into exaggerated fantasies far more frightening than the actual threat." Furthermore, "any assault on the white racial order, any disturbance involving Mexicans was classified" as uprisings, insurgencies, or riots. All incidents were placed in a context of a possible massacre of whites. De León is one of the few scholars who suggest that the violence committed against Tejanos was connected to hostilities carried out in other regions of the state. He contends that "in part, this was a reflection of the era, the most violent in Texas history. During this time, Central Texas was embroiled in a wide variety of violent episodes growing out of troubles from the Civil War and Reconstruction, outlaw activity, vigilantism, community feuds, agrarian radicalism, and political agitation."

De León further comments that at the same time "Anglos throughout the state faced the most severe resistance from colored people—by riotous and uppity blacks in the old plantation region, by intransigent Indians making their last stand in the western frontier, and by unneighborly Mexicans. It was in this era that the colored thread of multiracial society posed the greatest challenge to the white racial order."[44]

Another generalization regarding violence in the Reconstruction Texas is that hostilities often resulted from economic changes. Moneyhon's *Texas after the Civil War* is particularly informative about violent episodes that were related to economic and labor issues. Moneyhon contends that "economic reasons may have underlay a large portion of the increased violence as individual landlords and whole communities tried to gain greater control over the freedmen and their labor." He reveals that landowners who faced falling cotton prices in 1865 often tried to cheat their workers (sharecroppers) out of their fair share of the harvest. In areas outside of the reach of military authorities, landowners often "drove their workers away from their farms and then claimed the freedmen had broken their contracts and did not have to be paid. Some may even have used local gangs to raid their own plantations, where they beat workers and threatened even-more-dire violence to secure the planter's goal." In these cases, "any worker who resisted intimidation might well end up dead. In the first year of freedom, bureau officials catalogued the murder of some thirty-eight freedmen."[45] These types of incidents were common in the plantation regions of the state throughout the Reconstruction era.

Yet there were areas in Texas in which economic changes produced a calming effect. Some towns, particularly along the coast, even welcomed federal troops, because they often stimulated the local economy. Also, in many of these regions, the black population was significantly less than the white population. Thus, white fear of "Negro Rule" was less than in other areas of the state where the black population was near equal or greater than that of whites. Regardless, few scholars have examined in detail this aspect of Reconstruction.

A fourth generalization is that outlaw gangs were responsible for many of the violent incidents occurring in Reconstruction Texas. Numerous outlaw bands operated in the confused and chaotic days of Reconstruction, benefitting from the absence of effective law enforcement and using the "Lost Cause" ideology to shield themselves from prosecution in the courts. Former Confederates and Democratic supporters tended to look the other way as long as these gangs targeted freedpeople, native Unionists, and Union soldiers. In Northeast Texas alone, gangs formed around such personalities as Benjamin Bickerstaff, Cullen Montgomery Baker, Bob Lee, Elisha Guest, Ben Griffith, Henry Farrar, John "Pomp" Duty, "Indian Bill" English, and others. Every one of these men claimed loyalty to the "Lost Cause." One of the more infamous of the desperadoes, Bob Lee, was once heard to say that he would fight to remove the Yankee invaders "from the thickets and canebrakes of Texas for a hundred years if necessary."[46] Despite their claims, the vast majority of these outlaw bands simply engaged in violence for the purpose of pillaging the weaker and unprotected citizens in society: freedpeople and Unionists. As long as their activities remained focused on these groups, the majority of the white citizenry remained indifferent to their crimes.

Next, scholars can generalize that frontier violence significantly impacted the Reconstruction process. Texas, unlike the rest of the South, was still a frontier state during the Reconstruction era and had to contend with a unique set of problems. For example, Native American raids on frontier settlements escalated in the months following the war because of a lack of troops stationed in frontier fortifications. Initially, the Texans living in counties located on the frontier line were left to fend for themselves. Following the end of the Civil War, no civil government in Austin could provide aid. Even after a new state constitution had been created and a new state government had been elected in 1866, federal policies prevented the state government from taking actions against Native American warriors in the western counties of the state. Gov. James Webb Throckmorton, who had lived most of his life on the North Texas frontier and had witnessed Indian depredations first hand, promised to do all in his power to protect the frontier settlers. The governor's efforts to make good on his promise drove a wedge between his administration and federal military authorities. Though the state legislature was willing to create frontier ranging companies to deal with the Indian problem, federal authorities were not willing to allow the legislature to arm a frontier force that might later be ordered to the interior of the state where they could challenge the authority of federal troops. In fact, some federal commanders believed that Texas officials were exaggerating the violence on the frontier to lure federal authorities into removing their troops from the interior of the state where they were providing protection to the freedpeople. State leaders viewed the circumstances differently, claiming that the federal military was more concerned with protecting the rights of African Americans than providing relief to whites living on the frontier line. As a result, harsh feelings developed. In this heated atmosphere, the federal military found it increasingly difficult to serve in Texas. Eventually, the troops were moved to the frontier, but only after frontier violence had divided state and federal authorities.[47]

Finally, and perhaps most importantly, scholars can generalize that the Civil War did not end in 1865. Traditionally, historians have viewed the American Civil War (1861–1865) and the Reconstruction era (1865–1877) as two distinct and separate periods in United States history. Though this approach provides a convenient way to understand two very complex eras, it tends to skew the general understanding of the violence that became commonplace in the South during Reconstruction. Scholarly celebrations of the Union victory in the Civil War tend to ignore the fact that the United States government ultimately failed to reconstruct southern society in the decades following the war. A more constructive way to study these two periods of American history is to examine the eras as two distinct phases of a continuous conflict between the northern and southern states, which lasted from 1861 to 1877.

In the first phase of the war (1861–1865), the United States and Confederate governments used conventional military forces to achieve their respective goals: The federal troops fought to preserve the Union and, after the Emancipation Proclamation went into effect in January 1863, to end slavery. The Confederate military fought to win southern independence and to preserve the institution of slavery. The larger population of the northern states, greater industrial capabilities, and naval superiority dictated almost from the very beginning that the Union would win a war of attrition. Even though it is true that the South, including Texas, would be forever changed during the first phase of the war with the end of slavery, a war primarily fought for political control of the southern states and the preservation of white supremacy continued.

During the second phase of the war (1865–1877), which can be referred to as the War of Reconstruction, southern whites organized terrorist groups and initiated a prolonged guerrilla war against Republican governments in the southern states that sought to force political and social change on the South.[48] Beginning in 1866, Republicans in Congress demanded that southern legislatures recognize the new status of the freedpeople (ex-slaves) to whom they had granted suffrage rights and equal protection under the law. The idea of providing former slaves with civil rights challenged the traditional social and political structure of the Old South and proved unacceptable to the majority of white Texans. This is not surprising considering that whites in the state had seceded from the

Union and fought a bloody civil war to preserve an institution of chattel slavery, an institution built on the ideological concept of black inferiority. Because white Texans continued to wage a guerrilla war against federal authorities after 1865, especially in areas with significant black populations, scholars are forced to address an important question: Can the Reconstruction era simply be viewed as a continuation of the Civil War? In part, evidence from Reconstruction Texas suggests that the answer to this question is a definitive "YES"!

* * * * * * * *

This edited volume examines in detail the violence and turmoil in Reconstruction Texas, focusing on the years between 1865 and 1874. The chapters survey various forms of disorder, cruelty, and bloodshed and identify the social, political, and economic impact on the Texas citizenry. This study also explains why certain regions in Texas tended to be more violent than others, as well as illustrates that frontier violence made Texas unique among the southern states in the post-Civil War years. Readers will undoubtedly see overlapping stories in the various chapters. In some ways this could not be helped. The editor made a conscious decision early in the project to allow his contributors to set the stage for each of their individual topics. In this way, each chapter can stand alone as an individual work. However, the editor believes that collectively the essays presented in this chapter represent the most comprehensive examination of violence in Reconstruction Texas to date.

The book is divided into four sections: Part One: Representatives of Change: Soldiers, Bureau Agents, and Lawmen deals with violence as witnessed by federal military personnel, agents of the Freedmen's Bureau, and the Texas State Police that was activated during Governor Davis's administration. The essays included in this section provide a greater understanding of the role of the peacekeepers. Christopher Bean challenges the idea that all Bureau agents faced death and peril around every corner. Although he recognizes that many agents lived and worked in hostile environments, he also points out that other agents were assigned to areas where there were no violent outbreaks. For these agents, their time in Texas proved uneventful. William Richter, however, reminds us that many Bureau agents, especially those serving in Northeast Texas, faced many trials and tribulations. In some cases, the agents paid the ultimate price when confronting terrorist groups operating in Texas. Such was the case of William Kirkman. Additionally, Richter convincingly discusses the historiographical differences between his own interpretations of the facts surrounding the murder of Kirkman with that of other revisionist historians who have examined the murder. The study of history itself is sometimes a "bloody" battle. Richter holds no punches in challenging other scholarly interpretations. Those who are familiar with the Reconstruction historiography of Texas realize that other revisionist scholars have been critical of certain aspects of Richter scholarship over the last twenty-five years, and in this volume he has been given the wide latitude to address his critics.

Charles D. Spurlin, Richard McCaslin, and Dale Baum provide us with new perspectives regarding the peacekeepers. In agreement with Bean's general conclusion that some areas were not as violent as others, Spurlin argues that the citizens in Victoria and Calhoun counties accepted and even welcomed the arrival of the United States military. As he suggests, the citizens benefited economically from the military's presence. The violent incidents that did erupt in the county primarily resulted from tensions that developed between a small contingent of local whites and a select number of black troops stationed in Victoria County as well as a temporary breakdown in military command.

While many of the peacekeepers were committed to their mission and attempted to bring real reform to the state in most cases, others engaged in more questionable activities. McCaslin reveals that some Bureau agents abused their position and took advantage of the citizens in their charge. Such was the case with William Longworth. While Longworth was not killed in the line of duty, his story reveals another side of the tensions between conservative citizens and local Bureau agents. There is little doubt that Longworth contributed to the turmoil of the state. Other Unionists, such as Ben Brown in Robertson County, used extralegal methods to protect freedpeople and white Unionists. Unfortunately, as Baum reveals, these tactics eventually corrupted Brown and his vigilante gang, causing the freedpeople as well as the Republican Party more harm than good during the Reconstruction era.

Finally in this section, Donaly Brice traces the evolution of the Texas State Police and their efforts to curb violence during Davis's tenure as governor. Brice illustrates particularly well the type of violence that confronted the Republican government of Texas. In part, violence explains why the Davis administration failed to retain control. The governor's efforts to protect Republicans and African Americans against violent attacks by the terrorist groups drained the state coffers, which were already stretched to the limits by programs designed to improve the lives of all

Texans, including designs for the state's first attempt at public education. As a result, the Republican legislature was forced to raise taxes, a prospect that fueled the Democratic Party's campaign rhetoric against Davis and other Republican politicians.

Part Two: The Insurgents and Their Allies: Texas Terrorists, Politicians, and Newspaper Editors focuses on the years between 1865 and 1872. James Smallwood provides insight into the emergence of terrorist groups in the state and reveals how their violent tactics helped to bring an end to federal Reconstruction efforts in the state. According to Smallwood, violence was one of the single most important factors contributing to the failure of Reconstruction in the Lone Star State. Carl Moneyhon focuses more on the relationship between the most visible of the terrorist groups, the Ku Klux Klan, and their relationship to the Democratic Party. Moneyhon makes a convincing argument that the Democrats were primarily responsible for the emergence of the Klan in Texas. However, he questions how effective the Klan was in bringing an end to the Republican governments. By the beginning of 1869, he argues that the Klan became ineffective in shaping the outcome of state and national elections. Readers will note that Smallwood in contradiction to Moneyhon finds evidence of the Klan operating in Texas prior to the spring of 1867. The reason for this difference is that Smallwood identifies one terrorist group operating in an East Texas county that referred to itself as the Klan, while Moneyhon examines the emergence of the Ku Klux Klan as a statewide organization. Regardless of when the Klan first emerged in Texas, both scholars' points are poignant: no matter what the terrorists called themselves, they began operation in the state in a matter of months following the Civil War and continued their terroristic activities well after the Democrats regained control of the state government.

Mary Jo O'Rear examines how Texas newspaper editors reported the news of violent events. Looking at the coverage of violence inside and outside of the state, editors generally reflected the views of their subscribers. As such, it is obvious that Texas readers were bombarded with news that favored the perspective of ex-Confederates and conservative Democrats. In many cases, editors justified violence against blacks and Unionists, dismissing it as the natural result of northerners' faulty social and political adjustments. In other words, the majority of editors tended to support the white supremacist argument that violence in the South, including Texas, occurred because the federal government provided social and political equality to blacks. While the views of the editors also provide insights into the various regions where their papers circulated, this essay has been included in this section because it speaks to the direct views of the editors, who often supported the activities of terrorist groups and conservative Democrats. In many ways, they accomplished with the pen what the terrorist raiders did with a gun.

Part Three: The Victims: Minorities and Women discusses in detail how African Americans experienced violence in Reconstruction Texas. Using the WPA Slave Narratives, Ronald Goodwin revisits the experiences of both men and women between 1865 and 1874. Goodwin reveals that blacks who challenged the traditional social and political conventions that were still in practice in the postwar years often became victims of white terrorist groups. Some scholars will undoubtedly question Goodwin's dependence on WPA records, arguing that some of the individuals who were interviewed were not held as slaves in Texas prior to the war, or that they came to the state later in the Reconstruction era. Even if they were latecomers, their experiences in Texas during Reconstruction remain valid. Additionally, despite all the hazards of using the WPA records, they still remain a viable source for understanding the African American experience during this era. Rebecca Kosary's essay reveals the torment and anguish that black women endured during this time. Kosary reveals how black women coped with the emotional and physical abuse experienced at the hands of white men, especially the brutal crime of rape.

Also in this section, in perhaps the most significant work in this volume Andrés Tijerina examines the experiences of Tejanos during Reconstruction. Few scholars have attempted to place violence committed against the Tejano community within the context of the Reconstruction era. This essay examines the motives behind Anglo violence against established Mexican Americans in South Texas. Tijerina reveals that Anglos resumed a war against Tejano landholders that predated the Civil War, a program of ethnic cleansing designed to strike fear in the hearts of Tejano landowners and force them to leave their ancestral lands forever. Once the Tejanos were gone, Anglos claimed the abandoned lands. While governmental attention was primarily focused on curbing other aspects of violence, state and federal politicians paid little or no attention to the plight of the Tejano community during the Reconstruction years.

In Part Four: Regional Perspectives: The Frontier, the Interior, and Places in Between Kenneth Howell's essay explains how frontier violence created an atmosphere of distrust between federal authorities and the state government that eventually led to Gov. James Webb Throckmorton's removal from office. In many ways, Howell's essay reinforces the idea that frontier conditions made Texas unique among the southern states. Also in Part Four, Doug Kubicek and Carroll Scogin-Brincefield examine local violence in Lavaca County. They reveal that the violence was not only a continuation of the Civil War, but also a result of long-standing divisions within the county. The authors also describe how the county experienced a false calm when federal troops were present. Unfortunately, troops were rarely stationed in the region for any length of time, providing ex-Confederates and outlaw gangs ample opportunity to operate without fear of reprisal. Finally, John Gorman examines counties along the lower Brazos River and explains that violence was in direct relation to the large African American population. By examining a select group of counties, Gorman identifies that violent acts against the black community occurred more frequently and more intensely in the Lower Brazos River, a region where African Americans significantly outnumbered whites.

Despite the fact that this compilation of essays provides significant insights into Reconstruction violence, the editor realizes that this is in no way the final word on this subject. In fact, it is the editor's hope that this study will revive interest in the Reconstruction era and will be a catalyst for future research. It was during this era that Texans, and to larger degree the South, continued to wage war against the federal government. If scholars can agree that the Civil War lasted beyond 1865, it opens new interpretive challenges—the greatest of which is that the South actually won a war of attrition. While this perspective will undoubtedly remain controversial, one fact cannot be denied: Texas was one of the most violent places in the South after the Civil War.

ENDNOTES

1. United States Congress, *Report of the Joint Committee on Reconstruction at the First Session Thirty-Ninth Congress* (Washington, D.C.: Government Printing Office, 1866), Part IV.

2. *Journal of Reconstruction Convention, Which Met at Austin, Texas, June 1, A.D. 1868* (Austin, 1870). This report was submitted to and printed by U.S. Senate, Committee on the Judiciary, 40th Congress, 2nd Session, Miscellaneous Document No. 109 (Serial 1319), 3–8. One of the best analyses of this report is Barry A. Crouch's "A Spirit of Lawlessness: White Violence, Texas Blacks, 1865–1868," *Journal of Social History* 18 (December 1984): 217–32.

3. Another extensive document is the *Criminal Offences Committed in State of Texas*, assistant commissioner, Austin, vols. 11–13, Records

of the Bureau of Freedmen, Refugees, and Abandoned Lands, Texas, Record Group 105, National Archives. A brief description of these records is found in Barry A. Crouch, "Hidden Sources of Black History: The Texas Freedmen's Bureau Records as a Case Study," *Southwestern Historical Quarterly* 83 (1980): 224–25. Also see Richard M. Brown, *Strain of Violence: Historical Studies of American Violence and Vigilantism* (New York: Oxford University Press, 1975); Richard M. Brown, "The Archives of Violence," *American Archivist* 41 (1978): 431–43.

4. William A. Dunning, *Reconstruction: Political and Economic* (New York: Harper & Brothers, 1907); William A. Dunning, *Essays on the Civil War and Reconstruction* (New York: Macmillan, 1897).

5. Claude G. Bowers, *The Tragic Era: The Revolution after Lincoln* (Boston: Houghton Mifflin, 1929); Also see George F. Milton, *The Age of Hate: Andrew Johnson and the Radicals* (New York: Coward McCan, 1930).

6. Howard K. Beale, *The Critical Year: A Study of Andrew Johnson and Reconstruction* (New York: Harcourt Brace, 1930); W. E. B. Du Bois, *Black Reconstruction: An Essay Toward a History of the Part Which Black Folk Played in the Attempt to Reconstruct Democracy in America, 1860–1880* (New York: Harcourt Brace, 1935, reprinted as *Black Reconstruction in America* [Cleveland: World, 1964] and [New York: Atheneum, 1992]).

7. Two of the best examples of the views of early revisionist scholars are Kenneth M. Stampp, *The Era of Reconstruction, 1865–1879* (New York: Knopf, 1965) and John Hope Franklin, *Reconstruction: After the Civil War* (Chicago: University of Chicago Press, 1961).

8. For more on the divisions among Republican leadership, see Herman Belz, *Reconstructing the Union: Theory and Policy During the Civil War* (Ithaca: Cornell University Press, 1969); Michael Les Benedict, *The Fruits of Victory: Alternatives in Restoring the Union, 1865–1877* (Philadelphia: Lippincott, 1975); William Gillette, *Retreat from Reconstruction, 1869–1879* (Baton Rouge: Louisiana State University Press, 1979); Michael Perman, *The Road to Redemption: Southern Politics, 1869–1879* (Chapel Hill: University of North Carolina Press, 1984); and Mark W. Summers, *Railroads, Reconstruction, and the Gospel of Prosperity: Aid under the Radical Republicans, 1865–1877* (Princeton: Princeton University Press, 1984).

9. George C. Rable, *But There Was No Peace: The Role of Violence in the Politics of Reconstruction* (1984; repr. Athens: University of Georgia Press, 2007), 1–17.

10. Ibid., 15, 101; Ford, *A Companion to the Civil War and Reconstruction*, 338–39.

11. Allen Trelease, *White Terror: The Ku Klux Klan Conspiracy and Southern Reconstruction* (New York: Harper and Row, 1971; repr. Baton Rouge: Louisiana State University Press, 1999), xi.

12. Ibid., 64.

13. Ibid., 419; Ford, *A Companion to the Civil War and Reconstruction*, 338.

14. Trelease, *White Terror*, 137–48.

15. Charles W. Ramsdell, *Reconstruction in Texas* (New York: Columbia University Press, 1910; reprinted Austin: University of Texas Press, 1970), 192. Ramsdell was a student of William A. Dunning.

16. Ibid., 232.

17. For other scholarly accounts that followed Ramsdell's model, see Ernest Wallace, *Texas in Turmoil* (Austin: Stech-Vaughn Company, 1965) and William C. Nunn, *Texas Under the Carpetbaggers* (Austin: University of Texas Press, 1962).

18. For the best examples of early revisionist scholarship see James M. Smallwood, *Time of Hope, Time of Despair: Black Texans During Reconstruction* (New York: Kennikat Press, 1981); Barry A. Crouch, *The Freedmen's Bureau and Black Texans* (Austin: University of Texas Press, 1992); William L. Richter, *The Army in Texas During Reconstruction, 1865–1870* (College Station: Texas A&M University Press, 1987); William L. Richter, *Overreached on All Sides: The Freedmen's Bureau Administrators in Texas, 1865–1868* (College Station: Texas A&M University Press, 1991); Carl H. Moneyhon, *Republicanism in Reconstruction Texas* (Austin: University of Texas Press, 1980; reprinted College Station: Texas A&M University Press, 2001).

19. Carl Moneyhon, *Texas after the Civil War: The Struggle of Reconstruction* (College Station: Texas A&M University Press, 2004), 4–5.

20. For additional perspectives on political Reconstruction in Texas see Randolph B. Campbell, *Grass-Roots Reconstruction in Texas, 1865–1880* (Baton Rouge: Louisiana State University Press, 1997); Dale Baum, *The Shattering of Texas Unionism: Politics in the Lone Star State During the Civil War Era* (Baton Rouge: Louisiana State University Press, 1998). For studies that reflect briefly on Reconstruction politics and examine in detail the aftermath of Reconstruction see Patrick G. Williams, *Beyond Redemption: Texas Democrats After*

Reconstruction (College Station: Texas A&M University Press, 2007); Alwyn Barr, *Reconstruction to Reform: Texas Politics, 1876–1906* (Austin: University of Texas Press, 1971; repr. Dallas: Southern Methodist University Press, 2000).

21. Gregg Cantrell, "Racial Violence and Reconstruction Politics in Texas, 1867–1868," *Southwestern Historical Quarterly* 93 (January 1990): 333–55.

22. For more on the rampant violence against black Texans and their white allies see, James M. Smallwood, Barry A. Crouch, and Larry Peacock, *Murder and Mayhem: The War of Reconstruction in Texas* (College Station: Texas A&M University Press, 2003), Barry A. Crouch and Donaly Brice, *Cullen Montgomery Baker: Reconstruction Desperado* (Baton Rouge: Louisiana State University Press, 1997), James M. Smallwood and Kenneth W. Howell, *The Devil's Triangle: Ben Bickerstaff, Northeast Texans, and the War of Reconstruction in Texas* (Lufkin, TX: Best of East Texas Publishers, 2007), James M. Smallwood, *The Feud That Wasn't: The Taylor Ring, Bill Sutton, John Wesley Hardin, and Violence in Texas* (College Station: Texas A&M University Press, 2008).

23. United States Congress, *Report of the Joint Committee on Reconstruction at the First Session Thirty-Ninth Congress* (Washington, D.C.: Government Printing Office, 1866), Part IV, 72–78.

24. Ibid.

25. For more on the Klan in Texas see Trelease, *White Terror*.

26. Robert M. Fogelson and Richard E. Rubenstein, eds., *Affairs in the Late Insurrectionary States*, Mass Violence in America Series (New York: Arno Press & The New York Times, 1969), 19.

27. Ibid.

28. *Cincinnati Commercial*, quoted in the *Montgomery Alabama State Journal*, January 30, 1869.

29. For more on Klan violence in Northeast Texas see Smallwood, Crouch, and Peacock, *Murder and Mayhem.*

30. *Daily State Journal* (Austin, Texas), April 11, 1871.

31. Robert M. Fogelson and Richard E. Rubenstein, eds., *Use of the Army in Certain of the Southern States*, Mass Violence in America Series (New York: Arno Press & The New York Times, 1969), 133–34.

32. Ibid., 134.

33. Ibid.

34. Ibid., 143.

35. Ibid., 134–37.

36. For more on how demographic shifts affected state politics see Williams, *Beyond Redemption* and Barr, *Reconstruction to Reform.*

37. For more on the violence in Texas, especially in the northern and eastern part of the state, see Governor Andrew J. Hamilton to President Andrew Johnson, March 1, 1866, Andrew Johnson Papers, Archives, Manuscript Division, Library of Congress, Washington, D.C.; Bvt. Capt. Charles S. Roberts to Assistant Adjutant General, August 12, November 12, 1867, Assistant Commissioner, Texas, Letters Received, Bureau of Refugee, Freedman, and Abandoned Lands, Record Group 105, National Archives; Capt. Samuel H. Starr to Lt. Charles E. Morse, AAAG, February 9, 1868, LR, DT, 5MD, RG 393, NA; James M. Smallwood, "When the Klan Rode," *Journal of the West* 25 (October 1986), 4-13; Smallwood, *Time of Hope, Time of Despair*; Richter, *The Army in Texas During Reconstruction*; Richter, *Overreached on All Sides*; Charles V. Keener, "Racial Turmoil in Texas, 1865–1871" (M. A. thesis, North Texas State University, 1971); Rebecca A. Kosary, "Regression to Barbarism in Reconstruction Texas: An Analysis of White Violence against African-Americans from the Texas Freedmen's Bureau Records, 1865–1868" (M. A. thesis, Southwest Texas State University, 1999).

38. Claude Elliott, "The Freedmen's Bureau in Texas," *Southwestern Historical Quarterly* 56 (July 1952): 6.

39. United States House of Representatives, "Conditions of Affairs in Texas," *House Executive Documents, Doc. No. 61*, Thirty-ninth Congress. 2nd session (Washington: Government Printing Office, 1866).

40. Richter, *The Army in Texas During Reconstruction*, 19. For a brief account of Custer's career, including his time in Texas, see Brian W. Dippie, "George Armstrong Custer," *New Handbook of Texas,* 2:460; for more depth, see John M. Carroll, ed., *Custer in Texas: An Uninterrupted Narrative* (New York: Sol Lewis/Liveright, 1975).

41. United States Congress, *Report of the Joint Committee on Reconstruction*, Part IV, 72–78.

42. Ibid., 35–39.

43. House of Representatives, *To Protect Loyal and Peaceable Citizens of the United States*, report submitted by Mr. B. F. Butler on February 20, 1871, 41st Congress, 3rd sess., Report No. 37, 2.

44. Arnoldo De León, *They Called Them Greasers: Anglo Attitudes toward Mexicans in Texas, 1821–1900* (Austin: University of Texas Press, 1983), 87.

45. Moneyhon, *Texas After the Civil War*, 35–36.

46. Smallwood, Crouch, and Peacock, *Murder and Mayhem*, 33.

47. Kenneth W. Howell, *Texas Confederate, Reconstruction Governor: James Webb Throckmorton* (College Station, Texas A&M University Press, 2008), 119–28.

48. See Smallwood, Crouch, and Peacock, *Murder and Mayhem*.

Part One

Representatives of Change: Soldiers, Bureau Agents, and Lawmen

CHAPTER 1

The Post of Greatest Peril?: The Freedmen's Bureau Subassistant Commissioners and Reconstruction Violence in Texas, 1865–1869

by

Christopher Bean

Following the Civil War, federal authorities often described Texas as a bastion of unconquered former Confederates and violence-prone frontiersmen. Many northerners viewed Texas as an unpleasant place—in many cases, a deadly one, especially for Unionists and freedmen who either worked for or supported the federal government and the Republican Party. During the early postwar years, white Texans were particularly concerned about subassistant commissioners (SAC) of the Bureau of Refugees, Freedmen, and Abandoned Lands (more commonly referred to as the Freedmen's Bureau), a select group of men who were entrusted to oversee the former slaves' transition from bondage to freedom and who proved a biting reminder of the South's recent defeat. Even the commissioner of the Bureau, Oliver Otis Howard, wrote in his autobiography that Texas was "the post of greatest peril." Given that contemporaries viewed Texas in such negative terms, it is not surprising that scholars examining the Reconstruction era have emphasized the role that violence played in obstructing the Bureau's activities in the state. In fact, during the last fifty years within academia, violence against members of the Freedmen's Bureau has become a self-evident truth, something all Bureau men experienced in the performance of their duties. However, scholars have failed to produce a comprehensive study of the violence waged against Bureau men in the Lone Star State. As such, this essay will examine the frequency and intensity of violent acts perpetrated against SACs in Texas as described by the Bureau agents themselves.[1]

Although the Bureau entered the state in September 1865, major resistance to the organization and its agents did not occur until the spring

Illustration 2. The Freedmen's Bureau by Alfred Rudolph Waud. Illustration first appeared in *Harper's Weekly*, July 25, 1868. (Courtesy of Library of Congress)

and summer of 1866. As they recovered from the shock of defeat, white Texans "awakened" with a clearer idea about what the Radical Republicans wanted to achieve with their Reconstruction agenda. Compared with this agenda, which most white Texans found unacceptable, President Andrew Johnson's plan for Reconstruction was more acceptable, if not more lenient, one that allowed them to retain control of their states with little control and interference from the national government. Once the newly elected state legislature "met" benchmarks set down by Johnson, and he declared Reconstruction complete, white Texans quickly moved to reassert greater autonomy over their own affairs. The recently elected governor, James W. Throckmorton, a prewar Unionist but a man imbued with racial beliefs similar to those of the most ardent fire-eating Democrat, was a fierce opponent of federal intervention in state matters. The governor resented the Freedmen's Bureau, which he sarcastically called "one of the grand Institutions of the country." Throckmorton announced that he would not "countenance any wrong or outrage" arising from the Bureau's activities, which included any actions taken by agents other than caring for black indigents. His belligerent stance not only caused conflict between ex-Confederates and

Bureau men, but also emboldened some local officials to resist all federal authority.[2]

Although superiors reminded subordinates that "you must not pay any attention to any action" from the local officials, these words were of little consolation to those in the field. When written appeals for redress—both to state executives and Bureau officials—proved ineffective, local officials resorted to more forceful maneuvers, i.e., attempted arrest and detainment of SACs. Crockett officials indicted Stanton Weaver for interfering with a freedman's arrest, while the Harris County sheriff issued an arrest warrant for Bryon Porter. Backed by the local post commander, however, Porter ignored the writ. Jacob C. DeGress also feared arrest if not for the local garrison's presence. A simple "reminder" that an agent's power rested in federal authority defused the situation, but on rare occasions that reminder had to come armed with bayonets.[3]

Conflict between SACs and civil officials often arose when state officials refused to abide by state or federal law, such as providing aid to refugees and the poor in their counties regardless of color. In a few instances, however, disputes arose due to the actions of belligerent or obtuse SACs. The cases of William Longworth and Samuel A. Craig are instructive. These two agents had great difficulties—for differing reasons—with local officials. Although born in New York, Longworth was considered by white Texans to be a "scalawag," since he lived in the state for many years prior to the war. Due to his Unionism, Longworth claimed to be the most persecuted man in West Texas. This Unionism and persecution helped win his appointment as chief justice of Wilson County in the administration of Throckmorton's predecessor, Governor A. J. Hamilton and in the Bureau. Longworth exuded confidence in his abilities. "I think I am equal to the extent of the whole territory asked for," he boldly wrote, "and am in the bosom of almost every individual within the same."[4]

Almost immediately, Longworth got into problems with citizens about apprenticeship, which was an established practice prior to the war to alleviate suffering, but one subject to abuse after the war. Used to procure labor for planters, the practice could easily transition into "legalized kidnapping" or a "cruel injustice." As an agent, Longworth had first-hand knowledge of such abuse, since black parents often came to him wanting help to get back their children. Moved by these pleas, he believed apprenticing was simply slavery in a new form; thus he refused to apprentice freed children and returned those already apprenticed to their parents or guardians. For example, wanting to make a point, Longworth ordered James L. Dial to return two freed children apprenticed to him and fined the man ninety dollars as well as charged him with kidnapping and false imprisonment and had him detained. The incensed defendant believed Longworth had disgraced "and continues to disgrace" his position as a federal officer and petitioned Bureau headquarters, but found little support.[5]

The story might have ended there if not for Longworth's confrontation with William C. Wiseman, judge of Guadalupe County. Believing the agent had exceeded his authority, Wiseman not only issued a writ of *habeas corpus* in order to retrieve the two freed children, but also ordered Longworth's arrest, something the agent successfully avoided. The saga, however, did not end there. Angry citizens flooded Bureau headquarters with letters decrying what they called illegal and heavy-handed tactics by Longworth. To Longworth, these attacks only confirmed the justness of his course. "Where is the man, from Abraham Lincoln, down to myself that has not been hardened" by people like these, he wrote, for with these people "Christ himself would find persecutors and slanderors [*sic*]. . . ."[6]

Although Longworth thought his course sound, officials at Bureau headquarters in Galveston began to wonder. He received a letter enumerating the many complaints about his conduct. Admitting only timidity in fining whites to the maximum, Longworth dismissed the charges, calling them "false, absolutely and unqualifiedly false" and "transparent." For having to answer them, in fact, he even chided superiors for wasting the agency's already scarce paper. In response to his critics, Longworth reminded his superiors that "I was sent here to counteract and keep in check" these very people and asked for a court martial to clear his name.[7]

Superiors assured him that a court martial was unnecessary, news Longworth expressed disappointment about, for he believed that such an inquiry would embarrass those, both in and out of the Bureau, who doubted him. And doubt was exactly what many at headquarters felt toward him. Wanting certainty, headquarters dispatched William H. Sinclair, the Bureau's inspector in the state, to get to the bottom of the matter. But in a surprise move, Assistant Commissioner J. B. Kiddoo decided not to wait for the inspector's report. Whether due to his "unnecessary" actions against the white citizens in his district or his generally abrasive and insulting manner toward the staff at headquarters, Longworth was relieved. The official explanation was that Kiddoo desired to replace civilian agents with army officers, but most certainly, Longworth precipitated his own removal. This statement is supported by Sinclair's report, which confirmed many of the white citizens' accusations and Bureau officials' suspicions: Longworth caused much unnecessary strife by exceeding his authority and engaging in arbitrary justice. In fact, Sinclair was so angered by the agent's actions, he recommended he be turned over to civil authorities for questioning, something Bureau officials declined to do.[8]

Longworth's successor, Samuel A. Craig, entered this tense situation as the problems between white residents and former agent Longworth were still unfolding. Longworth, now a private citizen and smarting after his removal, told Bureau officials he fully expected—"it is inevitable"—to have to answer to a "rebel jury" for his actions when he was subassistant commissioner. Despite belittling his successor, Longworth nonetheless appealed to Craig for protection, especially after Guadalupe County (Seguin) officials arrested the former agent for "illegal" acts committed when he was agent. Kiddoo ordered Craig to secure Longworth's release and seize all papers relating to the former agent's arrest. Although some at headquarters believed he deserved his current fate, the actions of the local authorities could not be allowed to stand, for the ramifications would be detrimental to all other Bureau agents. Craig, accompanied by some soldiers, freed Longworth from jail.[9]

Craig's stern course drew praise from his superiors and enmity from civil officials. The district judge for the area, John Ireland, a former Confederate, was livid at Craig's actions and wanted to "make short work of the Bureau." Ireland issued a warrant for Craig's arrest, but the sheriff feared U.S. soldiers still in the county and refused to arrest him. By early 1867, however, the soldiers had left the county and Ireland once again moved against the SAC. Craig recalled later that the sheriff arrived at a pool hall where he was playing. He knew the reason for the sheriff's arrival. "I slowly with my cue in hand, backed toward the door and found it locked," Craig later wrote. "The sheriff came over near as tho[ugh] watching the game . . . Soon he took out the warrant and commenced to read it to me." The agent quickly realized resistance was futile. Six men had arrived to help the sheriff with the arrest; he added, "all were loaded [with] six, six shooters to my one, it was no use to resist." Military officials ordered the recently departed detail back to Guadalupe County, and they released the imprisoned agent. The ordeal, however, took its toll on Craig and shortly after his release he left the Bureau.[10]

Events in Washington, D.C., only exacerbated problems. In early 1866 Bureau officials in Washington and Texas warned field personnel to expect trouble as Congress moved to renew the Freedmen's Bureau. President Johnson's actions and words proved these officials quite prescient, for they greatly influenced white Texans' resistance. Through his proclamations and vetoes, including the second Bureau bill and Civil Rights Act, President Johnson resisted congressional influence in reconstructing the former Confederate states. With "a friend in Washington," white Texans were encouraged to resist the Radicals' plan, particularly the renewal of the hated Bureau. A planter from southeast Texas spoke for many whites when he applauded the president's veto of "that most rascally Freedmen's Bureau Bill." Many SACs reported to headquarters the "increased spirit of hostility manifested" by the president's stance. As one of them noted, "We suppose [Johnson] had leaned southward by this time."[11]

A good many of these reports of increased hostility were valid, while some were not. Agents assigned in Texas could easily have been influenced by the state's reputation and the numerous stories from the northern press about murder and mayhem. Before these men ever assumed their positions or set foot in their subdistricts, they "expected" the worst, for it was widely reported that Union men and federal agents were never safe in the Lone Star State. For some, it was as bad as they thought. For a few, however, it was not. Consider the cases of Bureau agents Thomas H. Baker, Louis W. Stevenson, and James P. Butler. At Lockhart, Thomas H. Baker arrived at his post in May 1868 and immediately requested troops, claiming that the feeling of the white people "is any thing else but good either by words or actions." He further admitted that the "freed people can get but little or no protection outside" the Bureau agent's office. Within two months of being at his post, however, Baker notified superiors that "for the present the free people can manage to get along without them." For the rest of the year, he reported the same, even remarking in October that "I get along with my business to use a common saying as a lasy [sic] as an old Shoe." Louis W. Stevenson at Columbus reported that local law enforcement was to carry out the execution of a freedman and that he needed a detachment of soldiers. He worried that "certain bad white men may take advantage of the event to cause a disturbance which is evidently desired." Stevenson even suggested that the governor commute the man's sentence, believing this would prevent the expected "emergency." The next month, after the execution had "passed off quietly," Stevenson wrote that "I see no real necessity for troops." For the first half of 1868, James P. Butler at Huntsville wrote superiors that he needed troops and expected trouble and could not do his duty without them. "There are no troops stationed at this post," he stated in March 1868, "the necessity for their presence is very obvious to you and it would be almost superfluous for me to report that I have so often embraced in my former reports in regard to their necessity. One thing very evident they give tone and force to the existence of a Bureau." By the late spring of 1868, however, Butler admitted he still did not have troops but "they are not much needed," and he labored "under no difficulties . . ., everything is progressing peaceably and amicably."[12]

To say violence did not exist or that the Reconstruction Texas experienced little violence would also be clearly wrong, for the works of George C. Rable and Allen W. Trelease show otherwise. But not all claims are trustworthy. For example, the "scalawag" Bureau agent Philip Howard at Meridian, Bosque County, believed his life threatened throughout the spring and summer of 1866. He thanked "the Supreme ruler for my preservation in my laborious and arderous [*sic*] duties I have done with no force to protect me, things but few men would [have] attempted and has won general esteem for my firm and mild course with these people." A few months later in July 1866, Howard further commented on his impending assassination. "I have run great risk of my life in holding this office," he observed. "I am old and they cannot cheat me out of many years if the[y] kill me, I have done what I considered was my duty under the surrounding circumstances." Howard heard about a fray in Waco, believing the incident would result in an assault against him and informed his superiors that he awaited his turn. "[T]he Rebs are getting moore [*sic*] bold every day and I do not know when they may attack me." Before his anticipated demise could come, however, Howard, "tired of the risk" and frustrated that he "can do nothing with them without help," asked to be relieved of duty in late 1866. Kiddoo personally thanked Howard for his service in the Bureau. Having "escaped" with his life, Howard was doubtless thankful to be rid of the job and its responsibilities. In fact, he was so "thankful" that he returned to Bureau service in 1867, accepting the position as SAC at Meridian and remaining there until early the next year. Ironically, after his tenure, he apparently set aside whatever "fears" he had of the people who supposedly wanted to kill him and married a local girl. The two lived in the same county until at least 1880 when he disappeared from the census.[13]

By 1867, President Johnson's vision of Reconstruction had been discredited in the eyes of most Northerners. They saw it as too lenient, causing many of the problems reported throughout the South. In response, Congress took the reins of power and moved to implement their own Reconstruction plan, one more harsh and punitive than the president's. In early 1867, as Congress wrested control of Reconstruction from the president, the Freedmen's Bureau in Texas soon came under the leadership

Illustration 3. Gen. Charles Griffin. (Courtesy of Library of Congress)

of the military, and its new assistant commissioner, Charles Griffin. Authorized under the Reconstruction Act of 1867, which invalidated the governments created under presidents Abraham Lincoln and Andrew Johnson and placed the former Confederate states (except Tennessee) under military rule, Griffin issued several orders for field agents that had an immediate effect. Griffin delegated more responsibility to the civil authorities and ordered agents to observe that local authorities carried out these responsibilities. The general also consolidated the Bureau and the military under one central command in Texas. Agents would no longer be assigned to remote areas with little protection against white outrages.

In fact, throughout Texas, Bureau agents reported race relations that ranged from "very bitter" and "apathetic" to "honest," "well disposed," and "quiet," if not completely "amicable." In a few places, it was nothing short of "good." It was so "good," in fact, that some wrote they did not need troops. Although those agents who were stationed along the Mexican border and the Texas frontier reported that they did not need troops to protect the freedmen against white violence (mainly because there were so few freedmen in their subdistricts), more than a few in the interior, especially those stationed in coastal counties, said the same. In all, seventeen counties were quiet enough that those stationed there reported no need for troops. Generally speaking, all but four of the seventeen counties were located near or on the Texas coast (Upshur, Kaufman, Leon, and Bosque were exceptions). These counties where SACs reported no need for troops generally had either higher percentages of freedmen or much lower percentages of freedmen compared to non-coastal counties and the state as a whole. For examples, in Wharton and Refugio Counties freedpeople represented 84 percent and 10 percent of the total population in these counties, respectively. Nearly two-thirds of the counties in which agents reported no need for troops had freedmen populations either below 30 percent or above 50 percent. Thus, it appears the freedmen population in a county affected the level of violence.[14]

A former colored regiment officer and one of the most respected Bureau agents in Texas, William H. Rock, had no troops in his district. Throughout the spring and summer of 1867 and continuing into 1868, the Richmond agent and native of Canada claimed their presence was unnecessary, since local officials cooperated with him. An Ohioan and officer in the 35th Infantry Regiment, J. R. Fitch, observed that white attitudes toward the freedpeople ranged from "indifferent" to "kindly disposed" and "friendly" in Refugio, a coastal county north of Corpus Christi. Although he encountered little difficulty during registration, he believed troops necessary as a show of force. With voter registration's conclusion, Fitch no longer thought a detachment of soldiers necessary in his district. "I do not think there would be any difficulty," Finch wrote. Should officials appoint a good magistrate, he suggested the man "should also be the Sub Asst Comm." and that "would be all that is necessary and be much more efficacious than a military comdr." A. H. Mayer gleefully wrote that few whites in Liberty have "Slave on the brain." As a result, Mayer did not need troops until perhaps when registration began.[15]

In the spring and summer of 1867 Hiram Clark, a "carpetbagger" from Illinois, had very little trouble in his subdistrict, which comprised the counties of DeWitt, Karnes, and Victoria. "I have no troops and think none are necessary," he reported that July. "The people seem to realize the condition they are in and promptly comply with all requests and obey all orders." This continued throughout the rest of the year. In La Grange, Isaac Johnson, a native Pennsylvanian and late captain in the 114th U.S.C.T., had no troops at his post. Despite acknowledging a hostile disposition by the whites, which was in the form of words not actions, Johnson admitted that "I can get along without them until the settlement [time]." Edward Miller, an agent who impressed superiors enough that after his muster out they reappointed him as a civilian agent, credited the calm situation in Bryan City, Brazos County, to the Reconstruction Act of 1867. The carpetbagger from New York and Veteran Reserve Corps (partially disabled or incapacitated soldiers, who performed duties to free up more able-bodied troops) officer believed "there is no necessity" for troops in Bryan City. The officer often repeated in subsequent reports that the civil authorities "are always willing to assist me in the execution of my duties."[16]

At Huntsville, James P. Butler, who appeared surprised by the good race relations in his area, reported throughout the spring and early summer that local officials impartially administered justice. He believed his presence in the district was all that was required to keep the situation calm and admitted the only need for troops was the "unavoidable pleasure" of arresting those "unreconstructed" parties. A similar situation existed in Beaumont. John H. Archer, an Englishman, routinely submitted terse reports, seeing no need for troops throughout the second half of 1867. He attributed the situation to a cooperative civil government. Bureau agent Philip Howard, however, experienced a different situation in his subdistrict. "I can say they [would be better to] never have been freed than to remove the troops," he reported from Meridian in June 1867. Despite his worrisome nature at times, the "scalawag" agent was considered by one assistant commissioner one of the best civilian agents to have served the agency in Texas. By the end of the year, Howard had changed his opinion, even after the troops in the area had been withdrawn. With one exception in October (due to voter registration), Howard reported good race relations and few complaints by freedmen. Race relations were good enough for Howard to report to superiors that he did not "kneed" any troops. He even believed there would be no need for the Freedmen's Bureau if the entire county was run by loyal men.[17]

Instances when agents reported they did not need troops continued until the agency left the state in late 1868. Even as the Bureau wound down its operations and violence increased throughout the state in 1868, there were districts that remained orderly enough not to necessitate troops. In the summer of 1868 A. K. Foster had a very cooperative and effective sheriff in Hallettsville. Foster repeatedly informed superiors that he had no troops "nor can I say that there is a necessity for any." According to Fred W. Reinhard, he needed no troops in mid-summer 1868 because the "civil authorities in [the county] do their duty." In Columbus, New Yorker Louis W. Stevenson admitted "generally as expressed, the feeling [between the races] is good." As a result, he often stated in the spring and summer of 1868 that he did not need troops. At Lockhart, Thomas H. Baker, throughout the summer and fall of 1868, informed superiors that he thought troops unnecessary in his district. Other SACs, such Hamilton C. Peterson, Thomas C. Griffin, Hiram Clark, and William Holt, also reported no need for troops in 1868.[18]

These claims might be dismissed by some historians as evidence that some Bureau men painted an overly optimistic picture for those at headquarters in order to hide their misdeeds. For example, historian John A. Carpenter concluded that the "monthly reports provide the best way of sizing up the officer, what his prejudices and reactions were, what kind of job he was doing." But when the reports contain virtually no information or when the agent month after month wrote briefly that all was going very well, then it must be concluded either that the agent was careless in making out his reports, or, more likely, was not doing a conscientious job. It is always possible that their reports reflected the true situation, yet, with other agents reporting atrocities, unfair treatment, and other forms of hostility to the freedmen, the objective observer can only assume that some of these agents were lax in the performance of their duty.[19]

Not wanting to be accused by superiors of incompetence, these men also could have believed it better to have reported all was good. So it is possible that all who stated they did not need or did not want troops were "lying." But this does not hold up to further scrutiny. Just as historians have begun to discover that "the South," "southerners," "Confederates," and even "freedmen" are narrow definitions implying consensus and conformity, with little difference and diversity, so too are the claims about violence within all subdistricts and experienced by all SACs. Violence toward agents was influenced by many factors, such as political events from Austin and Washington, D.C., economic forces, like a bad crop, the number of freedpeople residing the district, the presence of U.S. troops, and even the actions and demeanor of the agent. As most of these aspects differed and fluctuated throughout the state month to month and year to year, it should be expected that so too would the level of violence and resistance reported by agents during the Bureau's existence in Texas.[20]

Furthermore, such claims do not consider the attitudes of many at headquarters in Galveston: suspicion toward the former Rebel community and belief that Texas was wrought with violence. Thus, it would not make sense to report something contradicting that. This was because any agent who reported that he did not need troops would be in stark contrast to what many superiors expected and contrary to pleas from others, who reported deteriorating conditions. Any agent who reported he did not need troops, considering the numerous requests by others, would definitely have raised some questions from superiors about that subordinate's competence. If agents "lied" or "exaggerated" every time they claimed troops were unnecessary in their subdistricts, this would have been discovered with routine inspections. But no instance of inspectors finding field agents "doctoring" their reports can be found in the extensive Bureau records. These men took pride in their work, and the thought of shirking their responsibilities as agents was not an option for many of them and very difficult to accept when compared to the reactions when their job performance was, in their judgment, unfairly questioned.

This is not to say all claims of violence were misleading, for many were quite accurate. From threats to physical assaults to murders, Bureau agents personally experienced white anger about freedmen's new -found freedom. The latter part of 1867 was a difficult and violent time for many of them. More than a few agents believed their lives threatened, and others actually escaped attempted assaults or murder plots. Albert Evans at Sherman was "fully satisfied" that bushwhackers "plotted against" his life. The lack of troops, Evans noted, literally paralyzed operations in Sherman to the extent that he could hardly leave his office. This was also a problem for his successor, Thomas Murray Tolman. H. S. Johnson, who admitted to superiors in Galveston that he could do nothing more than give those who committed violent acts "a good scare," worried after ordering the arrest of a white man for attacking a freedman. "I think they will put him through," Johnson wrote, "and perhaps when I return [from a tour] he will attempt to do me the same favor." Albert A. Metzner at San Augustine, who many times had described the chaotic conditions in Shelby County in his district, wrote that he had received death threats from whites in that county. "I have received three or four messages that I would be hung whenever I showed myself there," he declared, "I shall leave for Shelby tomorrow to try it."[21]

Some suffered physical assaults as well as verbal threats, actions rarely occurring prior to 1867. Unknown whites, who James Lowrie believed were part of a serenading party that went throughout town, shot him in the thigh while he slept in his room at Jasper. As he lay in his bed wounded, Lowrie dispatched his roommate to bring troops immediately. The post commander and agent at Livingston, Louis Sanger, arrived with his men but found the attacking party had dispersed. With a few troops to protect him, things remained quiet for Lowrie as he healed. Yet he still feared another assassination attempt. The order brought about by the troops ended when Lowrie arrested the sheriff for murder. According to Lowrie, he had to release the sheriff from custody "owing to excitement and armed people threatening to rescue him." Although he promised he would remain in the county, the sheriff quickly fled the area. Bureau officials ordered the Bureau agent in Beaumont, John H. Archer, to Jasper to investigate the shooting of Lowrie. "[T]he only way to prove who are the guilty parties," Lowrie concluded after discovering the extent of citizen involvement, "is to arrest the whole town. . . . "[22]

A similar situation was experienced by Charles F. Rand in Clarksville. Rand noted his inability to travel his subdistrict safely. To calm the situation, he prohibited the carrying of firearms within the city's limits, an order that one citizen, John Henderson, disregarded. Rand confronted Henderson, ordering him to relinquish his gun. Henderson refused, and Rand ordered the sheriff, whom the agent was talking with at the time, to arrest the man. But before the sheriff could move to arrest Henderson, he lunged at Rand with a club. With the use of only one arm due to an injury during the war, Rand still was able to deflect the blow, only to stare down the barrel of Henderson's revolver. Defying his "invalid status," the agent quickly dived into an empty room to evade the gun-wielding man. Henderson fled the scene.[23]

Rand's troubles were far from over, however. Throughout the summer of 1868, desperadoes routinely entered Clarksville and threatened white Unionists and freedmen. Fearful that he would be assassinated, Rand did not take these offenses lying down, and, invoking a memorable statement during the Overland Campaign in the war, promised superiors to "fight it out on that line." He would not have to wait long for that fight, because Ben Griffith, a former Confederate cavalryman, arrived in the city with trouble on his mind. Having recently escaped from federal officials, Griffith returned to the city with hopes of exacting revenge. After bragging about his exploits to a crowd of local whites, Griffith mounted his horse and made his way out of town. Outside of town, he stopped to torment a teenage black male. A bystander witnessed the assault and ran back to town and reported the incident to Rand. The Bureau man immediately gathered a posse to capture Griffith. They found the desperado a mile outside of town. When Rand yelled for him to halt, Griffith tried to escape. He did not get far before the posse riddled him with bullets. Griffith's death only worsened the situation in the county for Rand, as the whites in the town turned their anger against him, threatening his life daily. The intrepid man was at a loss what to do. To stay in town, he noted, with no troops for sixty miles "and [Confederate] sympathizers all around, is to say the least very unpleasant." He reported that he had packed up his papers and sent them to Marshall. "I am worn out from exhaustion occasioned by constant anxiety both day and night," Rand told his superiors. Military officials dispatched troops to Clarksville, and under cover of night they sneaked Rand out of the "blood-thirsty hole." The military sent a detachment of troops to replace the departed Rand.[24]

In late 1867, Charles E. Culver experienced the ultimate hostility of white citizens in Cotton Gin. In fact, Culver, as he described the conditions in his subdistrict, expressed an opinion held by more than a few agents. "You who are so far away from this scene cannot see the picture as it is," he said, "nor can I write so as to give you an adequate idea." Although as "good natured as the day is long" and not easily "aggravated into imposing" on the white locals, Culver had every reason to worry. A religious man, Culver entered Bureau service to help the less fortunate. On more than one occasion, Culver had to get his point across through the barrel of his gun. His zeal, incorruptibility, and steadfastness were intolerable to many whites in the area. While at a July 4th celebration in Corsicana, one white citizen referred to Culver as "that damned Yankee Bureau man" in a speech. This only encouraged the rest of the crowd to join in on the verbal attacks against him. For the rest of the day, they verbally accosted him, bragging about their resiliency in resisting the Union cause. They showed their "resiliency" in late 1867, when they gunned down and killed Culver in the streets of Cotton Gin as he tried to enforce a local ordinance.[25]

Including Culver, three subassistant commissioners were murdered in the line of duty. The other men were felled in 1868. On his way to Dallas to replace William H. Horton, George Eber was robbed and murdered. His murderer(s) were never found. While at Boston, near the border with Oklahoma Territory, William G. Kirkman received death threats and was indicted for murder in September 1868 for shooting a prisoner who tried to escape. During his time at Boston, Kirkman simply lived day to day, but his luck ran out. With things deteriorating in Northeast Texas in late 1868, headquarters began recalling field personnel from the area, including Kirkman. As the agent busied himself collecting and organizing the office records, Cullen Baker and his gang arrived in town. Kirkman noticed their arrival and tried to make it to a nearby house to make a stand. Before he made it to the house, however, he was shot down in the street.[26]

From its inception until its demise, the Freedmen's Bureau was a controversial organization. While many Northerners resisted its creation on constitutional grounds, most southerners resisted it on racial grounds, seeing the organization not only as benefiting the former slaves, but seeing it as a painful reminder of defeat and emancipation. Resistance against the agency in Texas, however, did not really begin until spring and summer 1866 as white Texans reawakened from the shock of defeat. Continuing throughout 1867 and 1868, the resistance and violence toward it ebbed and flowed, often times increasing due to events coming out of Washington. The performance of individual Bureau agents also influenced resistance and violence. To be certain, many experienced resistance and violence because of their presence, regardless of a wise and prudent course. But for others, it can be argued they created unnecessary problems with vindictive and unwise approaches.

Furthermore, violence against SACs in Texas was not the norm as generally argued. Yes, violence could happen at a moment's notice. And yes, there were regions in the state that were unsafe for any member of the federal government. But the evidence does not hold this to be true all the time and throughout the state. In their own words, many Bureau men stated that they either did not need the troops stationed within their subdistricts, or believed no troops were needed to be assigned within their subdistricts in order to perform their duties. With such contradictions, it is an opportune time to reexamine violence and the Freedmen's Bureau in Texas.

ENDNOTES

1. The Bureau of Refugees, Freedmen, and Abandoned Lands was the nation's first welfare organization. Created in March 1865, the Freedmen's Bureau's responsibilities were in its namesake. The organization was to deal with the problems created by the war and emancipation in the former Confederacy and slave-holding states. The organization was headed by a commissioner in Washington, who had subordinate assistant commissioners below him. Each assistant commissioner generally oversaw the operations of the Bureau within a state. In Texas the assistant commissioner established his headquarters first in Galveston and later in Austin. Below the assistant commissioner were subassistant commissioners assigned to subdistricts throughout each former slave-holding state. These men were the Bureau's field agents and were the direct contacts with the former slaves and white citizens. O. O. Howard, *Autobiography of Oliver Otis Howard*, 2 vols. (New York: The Baker and Taylor Company, 1908), 2:218. For works on the Freedmen's Bureau in

Texas and violence against it, see William L. Richter, *Overreached on All Sides: The Freedmen's Bureau Administrators in Texas, 1865–1868* (College Station: Texas A&M University Press, 1991); William L. Richter, "' This Blood-Thirsty Hole': The Freedmen's Bureau Agency at Clarksville, Texas, 1867–1868," *Civil War History* 38 (March 1992): 51–77; William L. Richter, "' The Revolver Rules the Day!': Colonel DeWitt C. Brown and the Freedmen's Bureau in Paris, Texas, 1867–1868," *Southwestern Historical Quarterly* 93 (January 1990): 302–32; William L. Richter, "Tyrant and Reformer: General Griffin Reconstructs Texas, 1865–1866," *Prologue* 10 (Winter 1978): 225–41; William L. Richter, "Who Was the Real Head of the Texas Freedmen's Bureau?: The Role of Brevet Colonel William H. Sinclair as Acting Assistant Inspector General," *Military History of the Southwest* 20 (Fall 1990): 121–56; Barry A. Crouch, *The Freedmen's Bureau and Black Texans* (Austin: University of Texas Press, 1992); Barry A. Crouch, "The 'Chords of Love': Legalizing Black Marital and Family Rights in Postwar Texas," *Journal of Negro History* 79 (Autumn 1994): 334–51; Barry A. Crouch, "Guardian of the Freedpeople: Texas Freedmen Bureau Agents and the Black Community," *Southern Studies: An Interdisciplinary Journal of the South* 3 (Fall 1992): 185–201; Barry Crouch, "Spirit of Lawlessness: White Violence, Texas Blacks, 1865–1868," *Journal of Social History* 48 (Winter 1984): 217–32. For other specific studies of the Freedmen's Bureau outside of Texas that highlight the violence the organization experienced, see Martin Abbott, *The Freedmen's Bureau in South Carolina, 1865–1872* (Chapel Hill: University of North Carolina Press, 1967); John A. Carpenter, *The Sword and the Olive Branch: Oliver Otis Howard* (Pittsburgh: University of Pittsburgh Press, 1964); Paul A. Cimbala, *Under the Guardianship of the Nation: The Freedmen's Bureau and the Reconstruction of Georgia, 1865–1870* (Athens: University of Georgia Press, 1997); Randy Finley, *From Slavery to Uncertain Freedom: The Freedmen's Bureau in Arkansas, 1865–1869* (Fayetteville: University of Arkansas Press, 1996); and William S. McFeely, *Yankee Stepfather: General O. O. Howard and the Freedmen* (New York: W. W. Norton & Company, 1968).

2. J. W. Throckmorton to J. B. Kiddoo, August 30, 1866, Letters Received, 1866–1867, Records of the Assistant Commissioner for the State of Texas, Bureau of Refugees, Freedmen, and Abandoned Lands, 1865–1869, Record Group 105, National Archives and Records Administration, Washington, D.C. (Microfilm M821, reel 9), hereafter cited as AC; J. W. Throckmorton to Louis T. Wigfall, December 30, 1866, James W. Throckmorton Papers, Letterbook, 1866–1867, Center for American

History, Austin, Texas; Philip H. Sheridan, *Personal Memoirs of Philip Sheridan* (London: Chatto and Windus Piccadilly, 1888), 232.

3. Endorsement of letter from H. W. Allen, Hempstead, to William H. Sinclair, A.A.G., June 2, 1866, AC, Endorsements Sent, April 1866–September 1867, reel 2; Stanton Weaver, Crockett, to Judge Cooper, February 28, 1867, AC, Unregistered Letters Received, 1865–1866, reel 17; Byron Porter, Houston, to Lemuel K. Morton, A.A.A.G., September 12, 1866, AC, Letters Received, 1866–1867, reel 7; Jacob C. DeGress, Houston, to Henry A. Ellis, A.A.A.G., December 14, 1866, AC, Letters Received, 1866–1867, reel 5.

4. William Longworth to Secretary of the Freedmen's Bureau for the State of Texas, June 30, 1865, AC, Letters Received, September 1865–March 1867, reel 7; William Longworth, Sutherland Springs, to [E. M. Gregory], January 15, 1866, AC, Unregistered Letters Received, 1865–1866, reel 17; Ron Tyler, ed., *The New Handbook of Texas*, 6 vols. (Austin: Texas State Historical Association, 1996), 3:458–59; Special Orders No. 18, December 28, 1865, AC, Issuances and Rosters of Bureau Personnel and Special Orders Received, October 1865–April 1869, reel 19; William Longworth to A. J. Hamilton, October 9, 1865, Hamilton Governor Correspondences; William Longworth to A. J. Hamilton, October 10, 1865, Hamilton Governor Correspondences.

5. Leon Litwack, *Been in the Storm So Long: The Aftermath of Slavery* (New York: Alfred K. Knopf, 1979), 237; Mary Farmer-Kaiser, "With a Weight of Circumstances Like Millstones About their Necks: Freedwomen, Federal Relief, and the Benevolent Guardianship of the Freedmen's Bureau," *Virginia Magazine of History and Biography* 115 (2007): 431; William Longworth, Sutherland Springs, to [E. M. Gregory], March 9, 1866, AC, Letters Received, 1866–1867, reel 6; James L. Dial to [J. B.] Kiddoo, June 6, 1866, AC, Letters Received, 1866–1867, reel 5; William H. Sinclair, A.A.G., to William Longworth, Sutherland Springs, March 23, 1866, AC, Letters Sent, September 1865–March 1867, reel 1; James L. Dial to E. M. Gregory, February 10, 1866, AC, Letters Received, 1866–1867, reel 5; R. H. Brahan to [Headquarters], May 8, 1866, AC, Letters Received, 1866–1867, reel 6; William H. Sinclair, A.A.G., to James L. Dial, March 19, 1866, AC, Letters Sent, September 1865–March 1867, reel 1.

6. William Longworth, Seguin, to [William H. Sinclair, A.A.G.], May 27, 1866, AC, Letters Received, 1866–1867, reel 6; William Longworth, Sutherland Springs, to William H. Sinclair, A.A.G., May 1, 1866, AC, Letters Received, 1866–1867, reel 6; William Longworth,

Sutherland Springs, to William H. Sinclair, A.A.G., April 25, 1866, AC, Letters Received, 1866–1867, reel 6; [William C.] Wiseman to [William] Longworth, Seguin, May 18, 1866, AC, Unregistered Letters Received, 1865–1866, reel 17; William H. Sinclair, A.A.G., to William Longworth, Sutherland Springs, May 2, 1866, AC, Letters Sent, September 1865–March 1867, reel 1. For the letters from citizens, see S. J. Pickett to A. J. Hamilton, [January 1866], Hamilton Governor Correspondences; Samuel Gilmore to William H. Sinclair, A.A.G., May 18, 1866, AC, Letters Received, 1866–1867, reel 5; S. Wright to Colonel Sherwood Neil, [1866], AC, Letters Received, 1866–1867, reel 9.

7. William Longworth, Seguin, to William H. Sinclair, A.A.G., May 30, 1866, AC, Letters Received, 1866–1867, reel 6; William Longworth, Seguin, to William H. Sinclair, A.A.G., June 25, 1866, AC, Letters Received, 1866–1867, reel 6.

8. William H. Sinclair, A.A.G., to William Longworth, Seguin, June 9, 1866, and July 27, 1866, AC, Letters Sent, September 1865–March 1867, reel 1; William Longworth, Seguin, to J. B. Kiddoo, June 21, 1866, Letters Received, 1866–1867, reel 6; Special Orders No. 95, AC, Issuances and Rosters of Bureau Personnel and Special Orders Received, October 1865–April 1869, reel 19; Henry A. Ellis, A.A.A.G., to Maj. Gen. Philip Sheridan, Commander, Department of the Gulf, November 10, 1866, AC, Letters Sent, September 1865–March 1867, reel 1; O. O. Howard to General, February 23, 1866, AC, Unregistered Letters Received, 1865–1866, reel 17; William H. Sinclair, Inspector, to Henry Ellis, A.A.A.G., October 7, 1866, AC, Letters Received, 1866–1867, reel 5.

9. William Longworth to [J. B.] Kiddoo, November 12, 1866, AC, Letters Received, 1866–1867, reel 6; Henry A. Ellis, A.A.A.G, to William Longworth, September 19, 1866, AC, Letters Sent, September 1865–March 1867, reel 1; Endorsement of letter from William Longworth to J. B. Kiddoo, September 17, 1866, AC, Endorsements Sent, April 1866–September 1867, reel 2; J. B. Kiddoo to William Longworth, September 21, 1866, AC, Letters Sent, September 1865–March 1867, reel 1; Henry A. Ellis, A.A.A.G., to Samuel A. Craig, Seguin, September 28, 1866, AC, Letters Sent, September 1865–March 1867, reel 1; Samuel A. Craig, Seguin, to William H. Sinclair, A.A.G., October 21, 1866, AC, Letters Received, 1866–1867, reel 4.

10. James B. Moore, Seguin, to Colonel, August 6, 1866, AC, Letters Received, 1866-1867, reel 7; Samuel A. Craig, "Memoirs of Civil War and Reconstruction," *Civil War Times Illustrated Collection of Civil War Papers* (Carlisle Barracks, PA: U.S. Army Military History Institute),

89–91; William H. Sinclair, Inspector, to J. T. Kirkman, A.A.A.G., May 29, 1867, AC, Letters Received, 1866-1867, reel 7; Samuel A. Craig, Seguin, to William H. Sinclair, A.A.G., October 21, 1866, AC, Letters Received, 1866–1867, reel 4; Tyler, *New Handbook of Texas*, 3:867; Samuel A. Craig, Seguin, to Henry A. Ellis, A.A.G., December 6, 8, and 11, 1866, AC, Letters Received, 1866–1867, reel 4; Endorsement of letter from T. S. Leason to J. B. Kiddoo, December 21, 1866, AC, Endorsements Sent, April 1866–September 1867, reel 2; Special Orders No. 148, December 14, 1866, and No. 154, December 25, 1866, AC, Issuances and Rosters of Bureau Personnel and Special Orders Received, October 1865–April 1869, reel 19.

11. James L. Roark, *Masters Without Slaves: Southern Planters in the Civil War and Reconstruction* (New York: W. W. Norton & Company, 1977), 139; Craig, "Memoirs," 82; James D. Richardson, ed., *A Compilation of the Messages and Papers of the Presidents, 1789–1897*, 10 vols. (Washington, D.C.: Government Printing Office, 1897), 6:398–405, 422–26; O. O. Howard to General, February 23, 1866, AC, Unregistered Letters Received, 1865–1866, reel 17; Circular No. 7, March 6, 1866, AC, Issuances and Rosters of Bureau Personnel and Special Orders Received, October 1865-April 1869, reel 19; Dan T. Carter, *When the War Was Over: The Failure of Self-Reconstruction in the South, 1865–1867* (Baton Rouge: Louisiana State University Press, 1985), 54; E. D. Townsend, A.A.G., to Brvt. Maj. Gen. P. M. Brannan, Commander, Department of Georgia, April 9, 1866, AC, Issuances and Rosters of Bureau Personnel and Special Orders Received, reel 19. For the showdown between President Andrew Johnson and the Radical Republicans about various Reconstruction issues like the Freedmen's Bureau, see LaWanda Cox and John H. Cox, *Politics, Principle, and Prejudice 1865–1866: Dilemma of Reconstruction America* (London: The Free Press of Glencoe, 1963). For reports associating the president's words and actions with increased hostility, see Byron Porter, Houston, to William H. Sinclair, A.A.G., May 3, 1866, AC, Letters Received, 1866–1867, reel 7; F. D. Inge, Leona, to [E. M.] Gregory, March 22, 1866, AC, Letters Received, 1866–1867, reel 6; John H. Archer, Hempstead, to J. B. Kiddoo, January 10, 1867, AC, December 1866–May 1867, reel 20; Philip Howard, Meridian, to E. M. Gregory, March 22, 1866, and Philip Howard, Meridian, to [J. B. Kiddoo], July 31, 1866, and William Longworth, Sutherland Springs, to William H. Sinclair, May 1, 1866, and William Longworth, Sutherland Springs, to General, March 9, 1866, all AC, Letters Received, 1866–1867, reel 6; Camp Carter, Sterling, to [J. B. Kiddoo], May 21,

1866, AC, Letters Received, 1866–1867, reel 4. For agents in other states and their opinions about President Andrew Johnson, see William F. Mugleston, ed., "The Freedmen's Bureau and Reconstruction in Virginia: The Diary of Marcus Sterling Hopkins, a Union Officer," *Virginia Magazine of History and Biography* 86 (January 1978): 49.

12. Thomas H. Baker, Lockhart, to Charles A. Vernou, A.A.A.G., May 31, 1868, and June 30, 1868, AC, Reports of Operations and Conditions, May–July, 1868, reel 25; Thomas H. Baker, Lockhart, to Charles A. Vernou, A.A.A.G., July 31, 1868, AC, Reports of Operations and Conditions, May–July, 1868, reel 26; Thomas H. Baker, Lockhart, to C. S. Roberts, A.A.A.G., October 31, 1868, AC, Reports of Operations and Conditions, August–October, 1868, reel 27; Louis W. Stevenson, Columbus, to Charles A. Vernou, A.A.A.G., November 30, 1868, and December 31, 1868, AC, Reports of Operations and Conditions, November–December, 1868, reel 28; James P. Butler, Huntsville, to J. P. Richardson, A.A.A.G., March 1, 1868, AC, Reports of Operations and Conditions, March–August, 1868, reel 25; James P. Butler, Huntsville, to J. P. Richardson, A.A.A.G., March 2, 1868, AC, Reports of Operations and Conditions, March–April, 1868, reel 25; James P. Butler, to J. P. Richardson, A.A.A.G., May 31, 1868, AC, Reports of Operations and Conditions, May–July, 1868, reel 26. For the reports of Thomas H. Baker, see Thomas H. Baker, Lockhart, to Charles S. Morse, A.A.A.G., August, 31, 1868, AC; Thomas H. Baker, Lockhart, to C. S. Roberts, A.A.A.G., September 5, 1868, and October 31, 1868, AC; Thomas H. Baker, Lockhart, to Charles A. Vernou, A.A.A.G., November 30, 1868, and December 31, 1868, AC (all in Reports of Operations and Conditions, reels 27–28). For the reports of James P. Butler, see James P. Butler, Huntsville, to J. P. Richardson, A.A.A.G., AC, Reports of Operations and Conditions, January–February, 1868, reel 24; James P. Butler, Huntsville, to J. P. Richardson, A.A.A.G., February 29, 1868, AC, Reports of Operations and Conditions, January–February, 1868, reel 24. For examples of exaggerated reports, see Croushore and Potter, eds., *A Union Officer in the Reconstruction*, 110-112; Richter, "Revolver Rules the Day!" 325; George Bentley, *A History of the Freedmen's Bureau* (Philadelphia: University of Pennsylvania Press, 1955), 100; and Paul David Philips, "Freedmen's Bureau in Tennessee" (Ph. D. diss., Vanderbilt University, 1966), 324.

13. Philip Howard, Meridian, to [E. M.] Gregory, April 1, 1866, AC, Letters Received, 1866-1867, reel 6; Philip Howard, Meridian, to [J. B. Kiddoo], July 10, 1866, AC, Letters Received, 1866–1867, reel 6; Philip

Howard, Meridian, to William H. Sinclair, A.A.G., August 22, 1866, AC, Letters Received, 1866–1867, reel 6; Special Orders No. 128, October 27, 1866, AC, Issuances and Rosters of Bureau Personnel and Special Orders Received, October 1865–April 1869; Special Orders No. 96, October 31, 1867, and No. 6, January 25, 1868, AC, Issuances and Rosters of Bureau Personnel and Special Orders Received, October 1865–April 1869, reel 19; For the works on violence, see George C. Rable, *But There Was No Peace: The Role of Violence in the Politics of Reconstruction* (Athens: University of Georgia Press, 1984); Barry A. Crouch, "Spirit of Lawlessness: White Violence, Texas Blacks, 1865–1868," *Journal of Social History* 48 (Winter 1984): 217–32; William L. Richter, *The Army in Texas During Reconstruction, 1865–1870* (College Station: Texas A&M University Press, 1987); and Allen W. Trelease, *White Terror: The Ku Klux Klan Conspiracy and Southern Reconstruction* (Baton Rouge: Louisiana State University Press, 1999).

14. Bureau agents on the frontier and Mexican border often described good relations between whites and the freedmen. Race relations were so good that a few agents even admitted there was no need for the Bureau along the border. This was partly because the whites needed the black population to help protect against Indians and partly because of the few numbers of either whites or blacks to cause race problems. See Lewis G. Brown, Rio Grande City, to J. T. Kirkman, A.A.A.G., June 6, 1867, AC, Letters Received, 1866–1867, reel 4; Charles C. Cresson, San Antonio, to Charles A. Vernou, A.A.A.G., September 2, 1868, AC, Reports of Operations and Conditions, August–October, 1868, reel 27; John W. Eckles, San Antonio, to Charles A. Vernou, A.A.A.G., September 30, 1868, AC, Reports of Operations and Conditions, August–October, 1868, reel 27; J. R. Fitch, San Antonio, to Charles A. Vernou, A.A.A.G., November 30, 1868, AC, Reports of Operations and Conditions, November–December, 1868, reel 28; P. E. Holcomb, Goliad, to [Headquarters], July 15, 1867, AC, Letters Received, 1866–1867, reel 6; Ranald S. Mackenzie, Brownsville, to J. P. Richardson, A.A.A.G., December 20, 1867, and A. M. Randol, Brownsville, to J. P. Richardson, A.A.A.G., January 7, 1868, AC, Reports of Operations and Conditions, November–December 1867, reel 23; S. B. Hayman, Fort Griffin, to Charles A. Vernou, July 3, 1868, AC, Reports of Operations and Conditions, May–July 1868, reel 26; Charles Steelhammer, Weatherford, to J. P. Richardson, A.A.A.G., February 1, 1868, and George C. Cram, Camp Verde, to J. P. Richardson, A.A.A.G., February 8, 1868, AC, Reports of Operations and Conditions, January-February 1868, reel 24; A. M. D. McCook, Brownsville, to Charles A.

Vernou, A.A.A.G., August 31, 1868, AC, Reports of Operations and Conditions, August-October, 1868, reel 27; P. E. Holcomb, Fort Mason, to J. P. Richardson, A.A.A.G., May 1, 1868, AC, Reports of Operations and Conditions, March-April, 1868, reel 25.

15. J. R. Fitch, Refugio, to J. P. Richardson, A.A.A.G., January 31, 1867, AC, Reports of Operations and Conditions, January–February 1868, reel 24; A. H. Mayer, Liberty, to J. T. Kirkman, A.A.A.G., May 1, 1867, and William H. Rock, Richmond, to J. T. Kirkman, A.A.A.G., March 6, 1867, AC, Reports of Operations and Conditions, December 1866-May 1867, reel 20; William H. Rock, Richmond, to Charles A. Vernou, A.A.A.G., July 15, 1868, AC, Reports of Operations and Conditions, May–July, 1868, reel 26; William H. Rock, Richmond, to Charles A. Vernou, A.A.A.G., November 8, 1868, AC, Reports of Operations and Conditions, August–October, 1868, reel 27; J. R. Fitch, Refugio, to J. T. Kirkman, A.A.A.G., August 31, 1867, AC, Reports of Operations and Conditions, June–August, 1867, reel 21; J. R. Fitch, Refugio, to Charles Garretson, A.A.A.G., October 1, 1867, AC, Reports of Operations and Conditions, September–October, 1867, reel 22; J. R. Fitch, Refugio, to Charles Garretson, A.A.A.G., November 1, 1867, and to J. P. Richardson, A.A.A.G., December 1, 1867, AC, Reports of Operations and Conditions, November–December 1867, reel 23; A. H. Mayer, Liberty, to J. T. Kirkman, A.A.A.G., June 2, 1867, AC, Reports of Operations and Conditions, December 1866–May 1867, reel 20.

16. Hiram Clark, Clinton, to [J. T. Kirkman, A.A.A.G.], July 5, 1867, and P. E. Holcomb, Goliad, to J. T. Kirkman, A.A.A.G., August 21, 1867, AC, Reports of Operations and Conditions, June-August, 1867, reel 21; Isaac Johnson, La Grange, to J. T. Kirkman, A.A.A.G., September 3, 1867, and Edward Miller, Millican, to J. T. Kirkman, A.A.A.G., March 31, 1867 and May 31, 1867, AC, Reports of Operations and Conditions, December 1866–May 1867, reel 20; Edward Miller, Bryan City, to J. P. Richardson, A.A.A.G., November 30, 1867, AC, Reports of Operations and Conditions, November-December, 1867, reel 23; Hiram Clark, Clinton, to [J. T. Kirkman, A.A.A.G.], May 28, 1867, AC, Reports of Operations and Conditions, December 1866-May 1867, reel 20; Hiram Clark, Clinton, to Charles Garretson, A.A.A.G., September 30, 1867, and to J. P. Richardson, A.A.A.G., October 31, 1867, AC, Reports of Operations and Conditions, September-October, 1867, reel 22; Hiram Clark, Clinton, to J. P. Richardson, A.A.A.G., [December 1867], AC, Reports of Operations and Conditions, November-December, 1867, reel 23.

17. James P. Butler, Huntsville, to J. T. Kirkman, A.A.A.G., May 31, 1867, and May 25, 1867, AC, Reports of Operations and Conditions, December 1866–May 1867, reel 20; Philip Howard, Meridian, to [Headquarters], June 30, 1867, AC, Reports of Operations and Conditions, June-August, 1867, reel 21; Philip Howard, Meridian, to J. P. Richardson, A.A.A.G., November 30, 1867, AC, Reports of Operations and Conditions, September-October, 1867, reel 22; James P. Butler, Huntsville, to J. T. Kirkman, A.A.A.G., June 30, 1867, and Philip Howard, Meridian, to J. T. Kirkman, A.A.A.G., August 31, 1867, AC, Reports of Operations and Conditions, June-August, 1867, reel 21; John H. Archer, Beaumont, to J. T. Kirkman, A.A.A.G., AC, Reports of Operations and Conditions, December 1866-May 1867, reel 22; John H. Archer, Beaumont, to J. P. Richardson, A.A.A.G., November 1, 1867, and Philip Howard, Meridian, to Charles Garretson, A.A.A.G., October 31, 1867, AC, Reports of Operations and Conditions, September-October, 1867, reel 22; Philip Howard, Meridian, to J. P. Richardson, A.A.A.G., December 31, 1867, AC, Reports of Operations and Conditions, November–December 1867, reel 23; Philip Howard, Meridian, to J. P. Richardson, A.A.A.G., January 31, 1867, AC, Reports of Operations and Conditions, January–February 1868, reel 24; Philip Howard, Meridian, to Charles Garretson, A.A.A.G., September 30, 1867, AC, Reports of Operations and Conditions, September–October 1867, reel 22.

18. A. K. Foster, Hallettsville, to Charles A. Vernou, A.A.A.G., July 1 and July 31, 1868, and Louis W. Stevenson, Columbus, to Charles A. Vernou, A.A.A.G., May 31, 1868, and Fred W. Reinhard, Centreville, to Charles A. Vernou, A.A.A.G., July 10, 1868, and A. K. Foster, Hallettsville, to Charles A. Vernou, A.A.A.G., May 31, 1868, all found in AC, Reports of Operations and Conditions, May–July, 1868, reel 26; Hamilton C. Peterson, Lockhart, to J. P. Richardson, A.A.A.G., March 31, 1868, AC, Reports of Operations and Conditions, March-April, 1868, reel 25; A. K. Foster, Hallettsville, to Charles A. Vernou, A.A.A.G., August 31, 1868, and September 30, 1868, and October 31, 1868, AC, Reports of Operations and Conditions, August-October, 1868, reel 27; A. K. Foster, Hallettsville, to Charles A. Vernou, A.A.A.G., November 30, 1868, and December 2, 1868, AC, Reports of Operations and Conditions, November-December, 1868, reel 28; Louis W. Stevenson, Columbus, to J. P. Richardson, A.A.A.G., April 30, 1868, AC, Reports of Operations and Conditions, March–April, 1868, reel 25; Louis W. Stevenson, Columbus, to Charles A. Vernou, A.A.A.G., June 30, 1868, and July 31, 1868, AC, Reports of Operations and Conditions, May-July, 1868, reel

26; Thomas H. Baker, Lockhart, to Charles A. Vernou, A.A.A.G., July 31, 1868, AC, Reports of Operations and Conditions, May–July 1868, reel 26; Thomas H. Baker, Lockhart, to Charles S. Morse, A.A.A.G., August 31, 1868, AC, Reports of Operations and Conditions, August-October, 1868, reel 27; Thomas H. Baker, Lockhart, to C. S. Roberts, A.A.A.G., October 31, 1868, and September 30, 1868, AC, Reports of Operations and Conditions, August–October 1868, reel 27; Thomas H. Baker, Lockhart, to Charles A. Vernou, A.A.A.G., November 30, 1868, AC, Reports of Operations and Conditions, November-December, 1868, reel 28; Thomas H. Baker, Lockhart, to Charles A. Vernou, A.A.A.G., December 31, 1868, AC, Reports of Operations and Conditions, November–December 1868, reel 28. For the reports of Peterson, Griffin, Clark, and Holt, see Hamilton C. Peterson, Lockhart, to J. P. Richardson, A.A.A.G., April 30, 1868, AC, Reports of Operations and Conditions, March–April 1868, reel 25; Thomas C. Griffin, Kaufman, to Charles A. Vernou, A.A.A.G., December 1, 1868, AC, Reports of Operations and Conditions, November–December 1868, reel 28; Hiram Clark, Clinton, to Charles A. Vernou, A.A.A.G., July 2, 1868, AC, Reports of Operations and Conditions, May–July 1868, reel 26; Hiram Clark, Victoria, to [Charles A. Vernou, A.A.A.G.], November 3, 1868, AC, Reports of Operations and Conditions, August–October, 1868, reel 27; Hiram Clark, Clinton, to J. P. Richardson, A.A.A.G., January 2, 1868, AC, Reports of Operations and Conditions, November–December, 1867, reel 23; Hiram Clark, Clinton, to J. P. Richardson, A.A.A.G, March 3, 1868, AC, Reports of Operations and Conditions, January-February, 1868, reel 24; Hiram Clark, Clinton, to Charles A. Vernou, A.A.A.G., September 2, 1868, AC, Reports of Operations and Conditions, August-October, 1868, reel 27; William Holt, La Grange, to C. S. Roberts, A.A.A.G., October, 31, 1868, and September 30, 1868, AC, Reports of Operations and Conditions, August-October, 1868, reel 27.

19. John A. Carpenter, "Agents of the Freedmen's Bureau," John A. Carpenter Papers, New York Public Library, New York, 118–19.

20. For the study that found the discrepancy, see Mugleston, ed., "The Freedmen's Bureau and Reconstruction in Virginia," 49.

21. Albert Evans, Sherman, to S. H. Lathrop, A.A.A.G., February 14, 1867, AC, Reports of Operations and Conditions, December 1866–May 1867, reel 20; H. S. Johnson, Sumpter, to J. T. Kirkman, A.A.A.G., August 20, 1867, and May 8, 1867, AC, Letters Received, 1866–1867, reel 6; Albert A. Metzner, San Augustine, to J. T. Kirkman, A.A.A.G., July 31, 1867, AC, June–August, 1867, reel 21; Albert Evans, Sherman,

to J. T. Kirkman, A.A.A.G., February 28, 1867, AC, December 1866–May 1867, reel 20; Thomas M. Tolman, Sherman, to [Headquarters], March 31, 1867, AC, Reports of Operations and Conditions, December 1866–May 1867, reel 20. For another example, see Byron Porter, Bastrop, to J. P. Richardson, A.A.A.G., November 17, 1867, AC, Letters Received, 1867–1869, reel 14; Byron Porter, Bastrop, to J. T. Kirkman, A.A.A.G., April 18, 1867, SAC, Letters Sent, February 1867–February 1868, reel 13; and Byron Porter, Bastrop, to J. T. Kirkman, A.A.A.G., August 28, 1867, AC, Letters Received, 1867–1869, reel 14.

22. James Lowrie, Jasper, to Charles Garretson, A.A.A.G., September 30, 1867, AC, Reports of Operations and Conditions, September-October, 1867, reel 22; John H. Archer, Beaumont, to J. T. Kirkman, A.A.A.G., August 14, 1867, AC, Letters Received, 1866–1867, reel 4; James Lowrie, Jasper, to J. T. Kirkman, A.A.A.G., August 31, 1867, and July 31, 1867, AC, Report of Operations and Conditions, June–August, 1867, reel 21; James Lowrie, Jasper, to J. J. Reynolds, October 22, 1867, AC, Unregistered Letters Received, 1867–1869 and Undated, reel 18.

23. DeWitt C. Brown, Paris, to J. P. Richardson, A.A.A.G., December 1, 1867, AC, Reports of Operations and Conditions, November–December, 1867, reel 23; J. P. Richardson, A.A.A.G., to Charles F. Rand, Clarksville, February 14, 1868, and C. S. Roberts, A.A.A.G., to Gregory Barrett, Tyler, August 28, 1868, AC, Letters Sent, March 1867–May 1869, reel 1; Charles F. Rand, Clarksville, to J. P. Richardson, A.A.A.G., February 4, 1868, AC, Letters Received, 1867–1869, reel 14; Richter, "This Blood-Thirsty Hole," 64–66; Charles F. Rand, Clarksville, to C. S. Roberts, A.A.A.G., April 20, 1868, AC, Letters Received, 1867–1868, reel 14; Charles F. Rand, Clarksville, to C. S. Roberts, A.A.A.G., April 30, 1868, AC, Reports of Operations and Conditions, March–April, 1868, reel 25. For other examples of Bureau agents issuing firearms orders that Bureau officials countermanded, see Endorsement of letter from Edward Miller, Millican, to J. T. Kirkman, A.A.A.G., June 14, 1867, and Endorsement of letter from James P. Butler, Huntsville, to J. T. Kirkman, A.A.A.G., June 17, 1867, AC, Endorsements Sent, April 1866–September 1867, reel 2. For another example, see William H. Rock, Richmond, to J. T. Kirkman, A.A.A.G., August 12, 1867, AC, Reports of Operations and Conditions, June-August, 1867, reel 21; William H. Rock, Richmond, to J. D. O'Connell, Houston, August 30, 1867, AC, Letters Received, 1867-1869, reel 14; Charles Griffin to O. O. Howard, June 15, 1867, AC, Unregistered Letters Received, 1867–1869 and Undated,

reel 18; William H. Rock, Richmond, to Charles Garretson, A.A.A.G., September 20, 1867, AC, Reports of Operations and Conditions, June-August, 1867, reel 21; and *Field Record of Officers of the Veteran Reserve Corps, from the Commencement to the Close of the Rebellion* (Washington, D.C.: Scriver & Swing, n.d.), 28.

24. Richter, "This Blood-Thirsty Hole," 66-70; Charles F. Rand, Clarksville, to Charles A. Vernou, A.A.A.G., July 21, 1868, July 18, 1868, and August 2, 1868, M752C, Letters Received, July-August, 1868, reel 60; Charles F. Rand, Clarksville, to Charles A. Vernou, A.A.A.G., July 31, 1868, AC, Reports of Operations and Conditions, May–July, 1868, reel 26; Richter, "Revolver Rules the Day," 317–19; Endorsement of letter from DeWitt C. Brown, Paris, to J. P. Richardson, A.A.A.G., December 2, 1867, AC, Endorsements Sent, September 1867–May 1869, reel 2; William L. Richter, "' Oh God, Let Us Have Revenge': Ben Griffith and His Family during the Civil War and Reconstruction," *Arkansas Historical Quarterly* 57 (Autumn 1998): 274; Charles F. Rand, Marshall, to E. D. Morgan, U.S. Senator, September 11, 1868, AC, Letters Received, 1867–1869, reel 13; Tyler, ed., *New Handbook of Texas*, 5:496; Julius Hayden, Marshall, to Charles A. Vernou, A.A.A.G., September 2, 1868, AC, Letters Received, 1867–1869, reel 12; James M. Smallwood, Kenneth W. Howell, and Carol C. Taylor, *The Devil's Triangle: Ben Bickerstaff, Northeast Texans, and the War of Reconstruction in Texas* (Lufkin: The Best of East Texas Publishers, 2007), 84–85.

25. Charles E. Culver, Corsicana, to J. T. Kirkman, A.A.A.G., July 22, 1867, AC, Letters Received, 1866–1867, reel 4; Charles E. Culver, Cotton Gin, to Charles Garretson, A.A.A.G., October 10, 1867, AC, Letters Received, 1867–1869, reel 10; Charles E. Culver, Cotton Gin, to J. T. Kirkman, A.A.A.G., July 24, 1867, and June 26, 1867, AC, Letters Received, 1866–1867, reel 4; James M. Smallwood, "Charles E. Culver, A Reconstruction Agent in Texas: The Work of Local Freedmen's Bureau Agents and the Black Community," *Civil War History* 27 (December 1981): 357–58, 360–61; Charles E. Culver, Cotton Gin, to J. T. Kirkman, A.A.A.G., June 30, 1867, AC, Reports of Operations and Conditions, June–August, 1867, reel 21; Charles E. Culver, Cotton Gin, to Charles Garretson, A.A.A.G., September 20, 1867, and November 1, 1867, AC, Reports of Operations and Conditions, September–October, 1867, reel 22.

26. William G. Kirkman, Boston, to C. S. Roberts, A.A.A.G., September 18, 1868, AC, Letters Received, 1867–1869, reel 13; N. B. Anderson to [J. J. Reynolds], September 13, 1868, AC, Letters Received,

1867–1869, reel 13; Richter, "This Blood-Thirsty Hole," 71; George S. Shorkley, Clarksville, to C. S. Roberts, A.A.A.G., October 15, 1868, AC, Letters Received, 1867–1869, reel 15; Thomas C. Griffin, Kaufman, to J. P. Richardson, A.A.A.G., April 11, 1868, AC, Letters Received, 1867–1869, reel 11; J. J. Reynolds to O. O. Howard, March 21, 1868, and September 18, 1868, AC, Letters Received, 1867–1869, reel 16.

CHAPTER 2

"Shoot or Get Out of the Way!": The Murder of Texas Freedmen's Bureau Agent William G. Kirkman by Cullen Baker—and the Historians

by

William L. Richter

Deep in the northeast corner of Texas dominated by the misty swamps that form the Sulphur River lies Bowie County, named after the famous knife-wielding frontiersman who died at the Alamo. Created in 1841, Bowie County had a pre-Civil War white population dominated by planters who emigrated from the Deep South. Steeped in the slavery system of antebellum Dixie, these whites voted overwhelmingly (96 percent) to secede twenty years later. As if to taunt the whites for their miscalculation in supporting the Lost Cause, newly freed slaves made up a majority (64 percent) of the citizens of Bowie County in 1865 and registered voters (55 percent) in 1867. Even the name of the county seat, Boston, has a strange Yankee-like ring that continues to mock its rich southern heritage. Nowadays some do claim that the town was actually named after the New England metropolis by its first settlers, the Burnam brothers. Other more-unreconstructed souls insist just as vehemently that it received its seemingly-out-of-place appellation from the surname of an early store owner.[1]

Be that as it may, the Sulphur area's claim to fame now revolves around reports that it is reputedly haunted by the apparition of the Fouke monster, or the Skunk Ape, a southern version of the legendary Big Foot. But 125 years ago different ghosts roamed the swamps and byways of Bowie County. These shadowy figures were the white-robed members of the Ku Klux Klan, the infamous masked regulators of white supremacy, who fought a violent guerrilla war against their perceived enemies. The "Kluckers," as the Klansmen were known locally, sought to stymie those who aided in the Reconstruction of Texas: the formation of a loyal Union state government and the enfranchisement of the recently freed slaves.

Through very inflammatory adjectives, the Kluckers stereotyped their opponents: "blue-coated dogs of despotism," Union soldiers who occupied the defeated Confederacy; "Scalawags," southern whites who stayed loyal to the federal cause; "Carpetbaggers," Yankee civilian newcomers; and "free niggers," the ex-slaves who dared to believe in the promises of Emancipation.[2] Most of all, the Kluckers targeted the activities of those whom they ridiculed as "the drawers of the bureau" the agents of the Bureau of Refugees, Freedmen and Abandoned Lands. This was the quasi-military federal agency charged with the tasks of easing and speeding the transition of the former slaves into free American citizens endowed with equal civil rights, administering plantation lands abandoned during the war, and assisting loyal refugees to return home for a new start.[3]

Although technically a part of the War Department, the Bureau possessed an independent command system consisting of a commissioner, Bvt. Maj. Gen. Oliver Otis Howard; twelve assistant commissioners, who controlled activities in sixteen states (including Texas) and two territories below the Mason-Dixon line; and numerous subassistant commissioners, the agents who were in direct contact with the blacks on the local level. By 1867, there were sixty-nine such agents in Texas alone, who operated in fifty-nine subdistricts in the area east of the hundredth meridian, a zone about the size of Alabama and Mississippi combined.[4]

As the Bureau agent assigned to Boston and Bowie County, Subassistant Commissioner William Gilbert Kirkman's Reconstruction operations have drawn inordinate attention from historians.[5] This is quite understandable. Kirkman's records are among the most complete of any Bureau agent who served in Texas, extending down to actual field orders and judicial proceedings, giving the current scholar easy access to how agents operated and leading to two biographical treatments in the last twenty-five years.

Unfortunately neither study has fully explored Kirkman's sojourn in Boston faithfully nor completely. Each erroneously treats the Bureau agent as an isolated part of the Reconstruction process in northeastern Texas and southern Arkansas. James Smallwood's 1970 article in *Texana*, for example, portrays Kirkman as a dedicated, Protestant social reformer, checked on all fronts by violence or the threat of violence, valiantly struggling to improve local conditions for the black people, finally shot down in a street gun battle by his vicious opponents. But he may argue beyond the evidence in Kirkman's motivation for reform and he completely misconstrues the events surrounding the Bureau man's death.

On the other hand, in his book, *The Freedmen's Bureau and Black Texans*, Barry A. Crouch gets the circumstances of Kirkman's death more or less correct, but makes him a highly successful agent who brought significant change to the lives of his black charges, compounding an exaggeration that Smallwood also makes. Crouch goes on to portray Kirkman as some prescient, noble vanguard for late twentieth-century political correctness—a problem that haunts every page of his revisionist study of the Bureau as a whole. Kirkman's description in his own words of his often cold feelings towards both blacks and women belies this assessment, as does the common historical error of turning someone from a previous time into a modern thinker and doer.

Crouch also conveniently dismisses every historian who preceded him as irrelevant and misguided in a manner that at best can be described as fatuous.[6] He is not unique in his perusal of local Bureau records as he claims. Smallwood preceded him, as did Robert W. Shook on a lesser basis. And for a self-professed complete researcher, he completely ignores the Bureau's education efforts in Bowie County, Kirkman's most successful program, which nonetheless collapsed almost as fast as it began, as was noted correctly by Smallwood.

Kirkman's portrait as well as a sketch that would fill out information Crouch finds missing elsewhere appears in a century-old history of the 39th Illinois Volunteer Infantry, which Crouch credits but utilizes selectively. Crouch magnifies Smallwood's brief mention of the violence that checkmated Kirkman's progress, to present a more or less accurate portrayal of conditions in Bowie County, overall.[7]

But white opposition was of a far more pervasive, subtle nature than either of these scholars represents. With some notable exceptions, primarily the presence of the noted brigand Cullen Baker, it is comprised of oral threats and massive foot-dragging—waiting out the Bureau until its demise at the end of 1868. As will be seen, Kirkman received lots of threats, but experienced actual physical violence only three times: when brigands attacked his command once in Boston, when he and his patrol were ambushed on the road, and when he was murdered.

Most of the violence in Bowie County was directed against those blacks who tried to assert their rights as free laborers and voters. There were forty-five crimes reported to the Bureau from July 1867 to October 1868, including the death of a white soldier and Kirkman himself, and forty-two reported to the army, which duplicated the Bureau list exactly in thirty-six cases. The rest of the difference in the lists came from the fact that Kirkman reported certain crimes (arson, shooting at and wounding or missing, whippings, verbal threat, and maltreatment) separately, while the army lumped them all into simple assaults and battery. This averages out to three murders or assaults a month (using the army's simpler definitions) for the fifteen months of Kirkman's service.[8]

It is not hard to fathom why unreconstructed Bowie County whites so hated Bureau policy, for in performing his duties, Kirkman challenged the very assumptions upon which southern society had rested for centuries. His murder was not only a senseless, traumatic affair that illustrates the adverse conditions under which Bureau men operated in Texas, but the events leading up to his death show the scope of the opposition that plagued the whole federal agenda for reconstructing Texas, and point out the inadequate program of the U. S. Congress, the hesitant actions of the loyal state government, and the lack of cooperation between Bureau and army commands in combating it.

Born in Jacksonville, Illinois, Kirkman had enlisted in the Union army as a private in 1861 at age sixteen, where he soon established a reputation as a "enthusiastic and plucky soldier." He served his three years and returned to Chicago where he resumed his prewar trade as a telegrapher. By 1867, he decided to go to Texas as a Bureau representative. Kirkman's older brother, Joel, also a Civil War volunteer (Captain, 21st Illinois Infantry, a regiment trained by then-Colonel U.S. Grant) had transferred to the regular army after the war and was now an officer in the 17th Infantry and an acting assistant adjutant general at headquarters in Galveston, the right hand man of Bvt. Maj. Gen. Charles Griffin, who commanded both the army and Bureau staffs in Texas by 1867. It was through his brother's influence, along with a recommendation from his old regimental commander, Bvt. Brig. Gen. Thomas O. Osborn, that William Kirkman received his initial appointment.[9]

Hired on at one-hundred dollars a month, a standard amount for Texas agents at that time, Kirkman began work upon his arrival in Boston on July 5, 1867.[10] Although this was two years after the Bureau's advent in the state, he was the first and only agent for Bowie County. He was also one of the few agents who served long enough in a single agency to obtain a more than superficial knowledge of his command area.[11]

Since there were neither abandoned lands nor loyal refugees in the area when Kirkman received his appointment, his duties were strictly focused on the plight of the African Americans in his subdistrict, and revealed just how little reconstructing had been done in outlying parts of the state.

Kirkman correctly saw the main problem facing blacks to be their second-class status in society. The issue came to a head in four broad categories, all of which Smallwood and Crouch cover to some degree or another: the general mistreatment of African Americans,[12] labor contract disputes,[13] the denial of black access to education,[14] and the opposition of the white power structure expressed through legal and extralegal means.[15]

The Bureau referred to the poor treatment of the newly freed slaves under the term "outrages," which covered many wrongs, some of which were legal under the slave regime, others of which were not. A common complaint of blacks, for example, Kirkman said, was that white employers whipped them as if they were still slaves and not free laborers. Blacks were beaten with revolver butts, chains, whips, broad leather straps, and pieces of wood for a multitude of mistakes, such as arguing, disobeying a direct order, breaking a piece of equipment, or violating or disputing the terms of contract. Planters told Kirkman that the free labor policy had totally ruined the freed slaves as field hands. Many claimed that they would not employ blacks the following year—but they always did.[16]

The crops had done poorly in Bowie County during 1867, Kirkman discovered, and the planters blamed it all on what they perceived to be the lackadaisical approach of the freedmen to field labor. Although Kirkman agreed that "the colored people in many instances are not working as they should," he ascribed it to their distrust of planters who had defrauded them of the past two years' wages, compounded by lousy weather. In his assessment, Agent Kirkman reflected the attitude of the new Assistant Commissioner of Texas, Bvt. Maj. Gen. Joseph Jones Reynolds, who lamented that the freedpeople as a class worked faithfully, but "their ignorance, their idleness, and their follies" were the theme of every tongue. Kirkman admitted that "in a majority of cases, the [white] people are willing to give them their rights," but he found that "in many cases, [whites] certainly do not hold their contracts and the fear of the [A]lmighty before their eyes as they should."[17]

One case typified the attitude of dissenters in Kirkman's eyes. Henry Bivins had refused to come in for trial after taking a pot-shot at a black woman (who claimed to be living as his wife) during a personal dispute. In his defense the Confederate veteran told Kirkman that he thought that the war was over, "the Yankies [*sic*] had all gone home, and [we] could do as [we] pleased." No one could have put the feelings of Bowie County's whites better.[18]

About half of Kirkman's cases were assaults and batteries. Many of these crimes went unreported, according to Kirkman, because whites would lie in the woods and shoot those freedmen with the temerity to come into his office. Indeed the subassistant commissioner did not learn of a single case of a white murdering a Negro until November 11, four months after he took office. The actual shooting had taken place fourteen months earlier. A black woman, Rachel Leeper, had refused to carry her bag of seed from the edge of the field after a hard day of sowing cotton. Her employer, William Jones, ordered it done. Rachel refused again. Jones left the field, and returned with his revolver. When Rachel refused a third time he shot her. She died a few days later.

Jones fled to Arkansas and was still at large. In an understated comment, Kirkman said that the incident had "been kept very quiet, and the freedmen advised to keep it a secret, or they might be hurt." The agent recommended that Jones be hunted down (Kirkman suspected that he was living in Washington County with his father) and tried by a military commission. He concluded that failure "to place this case . . . before the civil law, would . . . certainly insure the escape of the criminal."[19]

Up to now, Kirkman had been using the local courts to decide cases reported to him, in accordance to instructions from Bureau Inspector DeWitt C. Brown, currently operating out of Tyler and soon to become subassistant commissioner at nearby Paris, Texas. Kirkman disliked this practice, believing that even when the county court found on behalf of black litigants, the decisions were not as severe as they should have been. But headquarters confirmed Brown's guidelines, and told Kirkman to recommend removals of those officials who failed to do justice and to recommend appointments of those who would. Kirkman continued to report numerous murders of freedmen later in his term, but was hindered in his investigations as many victims as well as witnesses of the crimes disappeared without a trace.[20]

Kirkman believed that such incidents showed that full emancipation was still an unachieved ideal in his subdistrict. He kept an especially jaundiced eye on the operation of the state apprenticeship law, which allowed the county court to bind black minor and orphan children to white guardians until they reached adulthood. Kirkman carefully reviewed the many complaints he received, as he considered apprenticeship to be a guise for continued slavery. Although he generally ordered black children given up to parents or relatives, Kirkman was not above approving an existing apprenticeship, particularly if the guardian were amenable to depositing a higher bond as security for good treatment.[21]

To make the often-fragmented black family a more attractive unit (by his own northern, white Protestant standards) in which to place these children, Kirkman engaged in a small moral crusade of the sanctity of marriage, which he saw as "very loosely conducted" among the blacks. He asked headquarters for guidance, and was referred to Circular No. 9, promulgated March 23, 1866, with the concurrence of the state government. Basically this order placed all blacks under state law regulating marriages and divorce, and recognized those former slaves "cohabiting together or associating as man and wife" as being legally married. Kirkman worked with the local courts, brought suits against blacks for adultery, abandonment, bigamy, and spousal mistreatment, all in an effort to strengthen the institution of marriage.[22]

But perhaps the most numerous cases that Kirkman adjudicated under the Freedmen's Bureau Act of 1866 were those involving labor contracts. Freedmen professed to be cheated out of wages, not only for the present growing season, but also for the two previous years. Most claims revolved around a system of legal deductions assessed by whites under the state labor code of 1866. Although the Texas laws were based upon earlier Freedmen's Bureau directives, there were important, subtle differences. The contract law called for fines for "disobedience," loss of double pay for any feigned sickness, and double indemnity for any theft. All fines were assessed by employers, with appeal to the county court, which was staffed by the same planter class. Especially offensive was the requirement that black laborers be on call twenty-four hours a day, and "to be especially civil and polite to their employer, his family, and guests." Of course, transgressions meant more salary deductions.[23]

To combat these Black Codes, which Bureau headquarters had supposedly declared inoperative six months earlier (such technicalities had a way of getting lost in the vast Texas backcountry), Kirkman ordered the county judge to stop enforcing the state regulation. He then called on local blacks to file their complaints of unfair wage deductions and nonpayment of wages with his office. Usually the subassistant commissioner merely sent a summons to the parties involved to appear in his office at Boston for a hearing. The process became more complicated when whites denied his authority by refusing to obey the agent's summons. Kirkman responded to such defiance by setting another appointment and compelled appearance with a troop escort. Recalcitrant whites were then assessed a fine for contempt. Often the offenders would appeal the fine to state Bureau headquarters in Austin or the army district headquarters in New Orleans, which was their prerogative. Very few obtained a reprieve, however, although Kirkman was not above reducing a fine, especially if the defendant were short of cash.

Kirkman filled every monthly report with cases involving labor disputes. A typical suit was the one against A. R. Moores, fined for contempt after losing a wage dispute. Moores appealed the fine to Austin headquarters and threatened a civil suit against Kirkman if the fine were not remitted. Kirkman, in turn, accused Moores of disloyalty and the illegal use of corporal punishment and abusive language to his freedmen. Headquarters ultimately sustained Kirkman, but the process dragged on for eight months. One Bureau historian includes Bowie among those agencies he sampled that "almost always found in favor of Negroes." But given the lack of proper procedure and the want of a Bureau agent in the years previous to Kirkman's arrival, this might rather show the difficulties under which blacks lived, rather than any overt prejudice on Kirkman's part.[24]

The frustration Kirkman faced in gaining justice for black laborers manifested itself in early November 1867. The agent argued that the reluctance of planters to bring in the contracts for the past year for approval meant that they would have to be "forced to comply with the law." The subassistant commissioner admitted that "there is no doubt but what the freedmen have been injudicious and done wrong in running themselves in debt so heavily," and he righteously thought many blacks deserved to suffer the consequences.

But Kirkman feared that the poor crop of 1867 would lead to unparalleled fraud by planters desiring to show a profit by any means possible. He believed that if the planters did justice to their employees, and the freedmen worked hard, the lack of profit in 1867 might be made up the following year. Kirkman also wished to bind both planters and freedmen for the coming year, instead of the usual practice of binding freedmen alone, because of the lack of cash and credit in the region.[25]

As a temporary solution to the problem, Kirkman issued a circular order requesting twenty-six planters by name, and everyone else in general, to appear before him, the county judge, a justice of the peace, the county clerk, or any notary before November 20, and draw up or have approved labor contracts for 1867. No settlement with hands for the past year would be allowed without a written, properly approved contract. Kirkman warned that no planter would be allowed to discharge any employee before the end of the year. This was a favorite ploy of planters, who fired freedmen on some pretense to deprive them of their whole years' wages, after all the work had been done. To further prevent fraud, planters were to present their books to Kirkman for audit before any final settlement.

In his order, Kirkman listed not only the usual "rebels" who would plague him throughout his tenure (Runnels, Moores, Hooks, Rosser, and

Griffith), but even loyalists like Judge John Garland. Especially defiant defendants, like H. C. Jones, found Kirkman not the least bit hesitant to seize their whole year's crops until an agreement was reached on the wages owed the black laborers. The subassistant commissioner held Jones' cotton and corn crop in lieu of wages owed for both 1866 and 1867. It took Kirkman five days to straighten out the debacle on the Jones plantation. Yet for all of his trouble, he only managed to secure a final settlement of fifty cents on the dollar for the laborers.[26]

To ease the contract process for 1868, Kirkman, by now six months into his tenure and more fully conversant with the ins and outs of his subdistrict, instituted some fresh policies. On January 27, he issued a new circular on the labor contract process. In it, he repeated much of the content of his November order concerning the approval of contracts by certain legal entities. Planters were given to the end of February to submit all contracts for approval. But the subassistant commissioner also had a warning for the black labor force. "Negroes will not be allowed or permitted to congregate in large numbers," Kirkman said, "where they have no means of making a honest living." Any freedperson not contracting by the middle of February would be declared a vagrant and forcibly hired out by the Bureau agent. Kirkman gratuitously advised blacks not to contract with any white who had not settled fairly with his hands in any previous year.[27]

The planters ignored Kirkman's edict through a massive campaign of passive resistance. One month after the deadline for submitting contracts for approval, the Bureau agent issued a new order. He repeated his admonitions of January, and tacked on a fine of one dollar for each freedmen a planter employed without the benefit of an approved contract after March 31. On April 10, the fine would be raised to five dollars per hand for resistant planters. He also extended the scope of his operations into Davis (now Cass) County, which had recently been transferred to his jurisdiction.

On the deadline, as promised, Kirkman initiated his policy of fines for late contracts. At first he refused to be swayed by protests, but on April 6, he suspended the fines for plantations located over twenty miles from Boston. The planters, however, went over the subassistant commissioner's head and obtained a complete reprieve from headquarters. Kirkman's superior forced him to remit all monies collected and suspend all punitive parts of his circular.

Despite this setback, Kirkman was pleased with the overall results in the new year's contracts, which he considered "a great deal more liberal, systematic, and just" than previous ones. However, one affected plantation manager, N. M. Campbell, was especially irritated because he had cooperated with Kirkman on earlier contract matters. When former Texas governor H. R. Runnels claimed a lien against all crops until the Fowler and Campbell Co., his lessees, paid their rent, Kirkman denied him the right to put a lien on the one-third of the crop that was contracted to pay the freedmen's wages. Instead, Kirkman redrew the contracts with a special clause denying the lien, and ordered Runnels to sign them. The ex-governor refused. Kirkman then said he would require Runnels to put up a bond to guarantee the freedmen's share. Again Runnels refused. The impasse was broken only when Fowler and Campbell graciously offered to deposit a $5,000-bond to guarantee the laborers' wages, which Kirkman accepted. There had been no violence, but much resentment was evident.[28]

Like the contract issue, the creation of schools for blacks started off promisingly, only to end in some disappointment. In August 1867, "a large number of colored people" met at Myrtle Springs, a few miles northeast of Boston, and voted to organize a school. They elected a board of trustees consisting of freedmen Forrest Hooks, Major Halloway, and Henry Fort, whom Kirkman confirmed with Bureau appointments. A local white planter, Warren Hooks (a man ordinarily not noted for his fair treatment of free black laborers with eight known assaults on his record), offered a free land grant, and about two hundred dollars was raised by subscription to erect a building for church and school purposes. About one hundred pupils were expected to enroll in classes. Kirkman described the blacks as full of "good feeling" over education and "willing to exert themselves" to assure its success. There was, however, "a considerable degree of prejudice among the white citizens against organizing colored schools," Kirkman feared.[29]

Initially, white opposition confined itself to planters miffed that they had not been as smart as Warren Hooks and got the school located on their plantations, as its presence was a good draw for signing up future laborers. Their muffled enthusiasm caused Kirkman to opine hopefully that "there will be, I think, no opposition in this county, now, to the establishment of Freedmen's schools." A second subscription drive was gotten up and, with the assistance of two-hundred dollars in Bureau school money, a building measuring thirty by fifty-two feet was constructed by the blacks themselves in their spare time. Kirkman also applied to headquarters for a teacher, and began negotiations for another plot of land in Boston for a second school district. Dr. I. M. Ball ultimately donated a town plot to the black board of trustees, but the local freedmen lacked the money to construct another schoolhouse. Although unwilling to help finance black education, the oral support among planters remained constant.[30]

That winter, however, the attitude of whites toward education began to harden. At one meeting that Kirkman was to attend but decided not to go to at the last minute, two whites rode up with shotguns, looking for the subassistant commissioner. Not finding Kirkman, they told the crowd that if they ever got hold of the agent, they "would shoot [his] head off." Efforts to start the school system continued, nonetheless, although trustees were disappointed to find that no teacher was available from the Bureau or benevolent associations. Kirkman decided to forge on and support as instructor a local black leader currently serving on the board of trustees, Forrest Hooks, whom he described as a preacher and a "colored (yellow) man" who could read and write.[31]

By March 1868, Kirkman had secured Hooks' appointment as a Bureau teacher at ten dollars a month, one-fourth the usual salary of a white instructor. The school had thirty-six day students and fifty-six Sunday scholars at its high point in September 1868. "The pupils are learning Spelling and Reading," Hooks reported. "Eight are making figures." But Hooks doubted that the school could continue much longer. He was receiving daily threats and frequent visits from those whom he tactfully referred to as "the out side party," the local Ku Klux Klan. "The threatens [*sic*] are so heavy that I dont [*sic*] know what to do and I would like Soon to hear from the Bureau, and learn from you what to do," Hooks implored. Kirkman promised, "I will give Forrest Hooks suitable instruction" as to school security, but the situation soon worsened and the school seems to have closed. Hooks experienced "truble," as he spelled it, with the Ku Klux all summer; scary, but no one was reported as beaten or killed.[32]

Although Kirkman's main responsibility revolved around the condition of Bowie County's black population, it quickly brought him into contact with the white power structure, comprised of men who were resentful at the loss of the recent war and its social/economic results. And here, violence came increasingly into play. Typical in this respect was the attitude of County Judge A. G. Haskins. When Kirkman asked the county to provide assistance for "one or two" indigent freedmen, the judge refused. According to Kirkman, the judge stated "that the South had been ruined (or words to that effect) by the Gov't and he thought they ought to provide for the pauper f[reed]m[en]." Kirkman went to a higher court and obtained a writ of mandamus ordering Haskins to accede to the agent's original request.[33]

Haskins' sentiment was a fairly common attitude among Bowie County whites after the war, and Kirkman realized that unless he worked to alleviate this bitterness "by all practicable and just means," Reconstruction's effect would be minimal. He never succeeded in this. "The feelings of the white people can hardly be described," the agent said. He noted that whites and blacks "have but little sympathy for each other—a feeling, in my judgment, that must change for the better . . . if they . . . are to . . . have any quiet or peace." Although Kirkman believed that much of the onus lay with whites, he perceived that the "black people also have very many opinions that are erroneous and unjust."[34]

The subassistant commissioner was "of the opinion that reconstruction . . . will have to begin at the heart of those who are now so biased and warped in their views," and to that end, Kirkman promised to act "in a spirit of *kindness*, *justice*, and *firmness*, and upon the principle to *forgive* some of their errors" and thus provide "a nucleus around which to assemble the feelings and interests of the people." After all, said Kirkman, "there are those (who I think were earnest in the cause of the South), who warmly assist me, with sympathy and influence." This contrasted favorably with the "cold shoulder" which "presented itself from a good many sides," when the subassistant commissioner arrived in Boston. Whites who cooperate, concluded the agent sagaciously, "should be encouraged, whatever their *war* principles may have been."[35]

Throughout the spring of 1868, Kirkman believed that both races exhibited "a more liberal feeling, more quiet." And although he still learned "of rare occurrences where a person feels aggrieved for being reported to the Bureau," the subassistant commissioner maintained that "generally, the disposition is to get along as quietly and peacefully as possible." By May Kirkman felt good enough to take a few days off, "absent recreating," as he described it.

But there were lingering racial problems, which the agent attributed to a few men who did "not feel disposed to give the freedmen the benefit of the reconstruction acts," particularly the freedmen's new right to vote. The subassistant commissioner named specifically A. R. Moores, who made "very bitter remarks" about what he would do if blacks voted, and former Texas governor H. R. Runnels, who allegedly fired a hand who did vote. Kirkman also accused Runnels of hiring Ben Griffith, a local tough, to shoot another freedman in Arkansas at Christmas 1865, but lacked sufficient proof to prosecute. But there were plenty of other cases.[36]

The sullen hostility of these few key community leaders, combined with the antics of a group of professional miscreants, at first made Kirkman's life miserable, and then tenuous. It was no wonder that the local white leaders disliked Kirkman. They viewed him as an outsider, young, brash, full of the certainty of youth, and a general Yankee know-it-all concerning the immorality of slavery and the postwar management of Negroes. Such assessments did not bode well with the elder men of the county who had dominated blacks all of their lives and were reluctant to change despite the loss of the late war.[37]

Worse yet, during Kirkman's tenure and under his tutelage, a whole new political structure had been established in Bowie County, based upon the few men, "traitors" to local whites, who had stayed loyal to the Union during the war. These men were put into office under a policy of military removals and appointments, initiated by General Griffin at headquarters in Galveston and continued after his death from yellow fever in September 1867 by his successor, Bvt. Maj. Gen. Joseph J. Reynolds, who had recently transferred both the army and Bureau headquarters to Austin.[38]

As both army commander and Bureau assistant commissioner for Texas, Reynolds depended upon the subassistant commissioners' active intervention in local politics to keep him informed. Agent Kirkman was equal to the task. Although his appointees often declined to serve, because of ill-health or intimidation, the Boston Bureau agent never hesitated to recommend others to headquarters in his effort to "purify" politics in his subdistrict. Kirkman also issued permits to carry firearms to loyal men, but was unable to prevent those beyond the pale from doing the same without his approval. Through contact with his brother Joel, the acting assistant adjutant general at Texas Bureau headquarters, Kirkman influenced headquarters decisions. For example, he managed to get Edwin Finch, a casual drinking acquaintance, appointed the agent at Milford, between Dallas and Waco. When his wife, Lucy, died of yellow fever in late August 1867, however, Joel Kirkman received a leave and eventual transfer back to his regiment now stationed in the Rio Grande Valley, and William Kirkman's influence with headquarters declined accordingly.[39]

Typical of the political quarrels that Kirkman became involved with was his incessant battle with the county sheriff, W. E. Duke. Elected under the long-gone Conservative government in 1866, Duke was too flippant in his concept of his duties to suit the aggressive subassistant commissioner. The sheriff first attracted Kirkman's attention when he had refused to intervene in a small street melee. As twenty-five shots ricocheted down the street, and one man was severely beaten, Duke sat motionless in a chair in front of a store and watched the whole thing. Other similar incidents would follow.

It was not that Duke lacked nerve (he would arrest any soldier for misconduct); he just never moved upon families of influence from the days of slavery. Kirkman recommended Duke's removal a half-dozen times, but failed because headquarters wanted a replacement guaranteed first. Finally, in June 1868, Kirkman got Thomas A. Morrow to agree to accept the military appointment. But headquarters delayed confirming Morrow to consult with state convention members as to Morrow's "political purity," and by the time the appointment came through, the thoroughly disgusted Morrow declined to serve. Kirkman stated the obvious in his disappointment: "the state needs good reliable men in the offices." But the net result of Kirkman's struggle was that Bowie County was left without any law enforcement officer at all by October 1868, except himself.[40]

Part of Kirkman's complaint about Sheriff Duke emanated from the arrest, indictment, and trial of John Sullivan, whom the subassistant commissioner described as "a desperate and reckless looking character" from Tennessee. Sullivan habitually carried a knife up his sleeve, and used it to threaten a 6th Cavalry private, Francis P. Davis. The trooper left the barroom where this happened, but Sullivan swore to track him down and kill him.

Following Davis to a second liquor parlor, Sullivan casually apologized for the earlier ruckus and insisted that everyone have a drink. But as Davis lifted his glass, Sullivan lunged at the trooper with knife drawn. Davis managed to parry the blow, taking the knife in his arm "near the rist," as Kirkman misspelled it. The crowd held Sullivan for arrest, and Kirkman threw him into the recently renovated county jail. The county grand jury immediately indicted Sullivan, the district court tried and convicted him, and the malefactor faced two years in the state penitentiary. So far, so good.

Then things began to go wrong. Sullivan's attorney, W. B. Wright of Clarksville, who had a big reputation for defending anyone in northeastern Texas in trouble with the army or Bureau, appealed the case to the state supreme court. He claimed that Sullivan's full name was not on the original indictment, and that the trial judge had erred in allowing the prosecutor time to amend it during the proceedings. Meanwhile Kirkman believed that Sullivan and another man arrested with him were possibly deserters from the 6th Cavalry, and had tried to kill Davis, who recognized them, to silence him. Kirkman sent Sullivan's compatriot to the 6th Cavalry outpost at Mount Pleasant for possible identification, but nothing came of it.

Sullivan languished in the Bowie County jail five months, pending the results of his appeal. Then he decided to take matters into his own hands. On February 20, Sullivan and a fellow inmate tried to escape by burning a hole in the foot-thick wooden floor. This stupid act nearly asphyxiated them. Three days later, the two men dismantled the wall around a rear door and fled. Sheriff Duke made a half-hearted attempt to follow the trail, but returned empty-handed. After all, Sullivan had merely tried to kill a Yankee soldier, figured Duke. Kirkman made another complaint about the sheriff to headquarters.[41]

Since Sullivan was an outsider, few in town really cared about his fate. But this was not so with other bad men Kirkman faced. Many of them had relatives and friends scattered all over Texas and Arkansas who would rally to their aid if threatened by a Bureau agent. Take Ben Griffith, for example, a known killer of freedpeople and local hero, wanted in both Texas and Arkansas, and whose brother John ran a plantation (the accounts of which were ever in arrears much to Kirkman's disgust) in Bowie County. In October 1867, Kirkman spent several days with his Arkansas counterpart, 1st Lt. Hiram Willis, the subassistant commissioner at Rocky Comfort, "among the almost impenetrable canebreaks" of the Little River basin searching for Griffith. Local whites warned Griffith of the agents' approach, and all they found was a cold camp. It was probably just as well. Months later, when Charles Rand, the Bureau agent at Clarksville, gunned down Griffith for resisting arrest, Rand would have to flee for his life from the wrath of Griffith's kin and supporters.[42]

As Kirkman soon discovered, northeastern Texas after the Civil War was full of "desperate characters" like Griffith and Sullivan. Local civil authorities proved unable to maintain law and order, and the area along the Red River was the most lawless. Violent men slipped between Missouri, Arkansas, Louisiana, the Indian Nations, and Texas, committing crimes in one area, and hiding out among friends and terrified citizens in another "in the midst of canebreaks and abandoned fields overgrown with Cockle Burr," as Kirkman vividly described it.

The Bureau estimated that these interrelated, yet competing, gangs had over one hundred gunmen, whom they could assemble to overawe zealous county officials, or perform murders to keep authorities impotent. The names of their leaders—Griffith, Elisha Guest, "Indian Bill" English, Benjamin F. Bickerstaff, Bob Lee, Henry Ferrar, and, worst of all, Cullen Montgomery Baker, the "Swamp Fox of the Sulphur River"—were enough to put fear in the hearts of the staunchest law-and-order advocates.[43]

Of these brigands, Cullen Baker became Kirkman's special nemesis. A deserter from the Confederate army, Baker had begun his marauding during the war. He claimed to be pro-southern, but he was not adverse to killing anyone, friend or foe, who got in his way. Some blamed his almost psychotic desire to kill upon grief he suffered upon the death of his wife. In any case, he soon gave up a failing ferry business for the more profitable life of crime. He was wanted for the murder of Unionists and freedmen, and specialized in making fools of the soldiers sent to arrest him. Once, surrounded by a military patrol, Baker turned and charged the stupefied soldiers. Six-guns blazing, Baker cut his way through the trap, getting away unharmed, leaving three bluecoats dead in his wake. The patrol commander escaped death only because Baker's revolver misfired. Baker now flaunted a new, deadlier sobriquet: "Yankee Killer."[44]

Although Kirkman had heard of a man he described as "Col. Baker" (people-in-the-know often referred to Cullen as "Cul" which Yankee Bureau men mistakenly thought was an abbreviated military rank) on his trip to Boston to take command, he did not meet up with Baker until shortly after assuming the position of subassistant commissioner in July 1867. The Bureau agent had a tip that Baker was in Davis County to the south of Boston, where the outlaw often visited his sisters' families. Taking his escort, a half dozen mounted men, Kirkman spent a futile day searching for the elusive "Swamp Fox." As the weary party returned to Boston, Kirkman noticed that they were being followed. The patrol warily dismounted and entered the courthouse.

Suddenly, the subassistant commissioner and his men were hailed from the street by an angry Baker. Audaciously, he sent in a note demanding Kirkman's surrender. Kirkman refused. Baker disappeared from the street. Soon after, an unknown sharpshooter blasted Private Albert E. Titus. The street grew quiet; Baker was gone. Kirkman managed to gain a warrant based on the fact Baker had carried two or three revolvers and a shotgun, and Titus was killed by a shotgun blast. Kirkman called on Major Ira Claflin at nearby Mount Pleasant for aid, and the major responded with a platoon of the 6th Cavalry. But when the force approached the outlaw's suspected hideout in Davis County, the cavalrymen heard a shot and the blowing of a horn. Entering the "Swamp Fox's" lair, they found it empty. At Private Titus' burial in Boston soon afterward, Kirkman vowed to bring Baker in at all costs.[45]

The next month, Kirkman and his cavalrymen were escorting DeWitt C. Brown, the Bureau inspector from the Tyler agency, when Baker fired upon them from ambush. Uncertain how many men Baker had with him, Brown spurred his horse, and led the escort out of gunshot range. Kirkman's horse was played out from the long day's journey, however, so he was inadvertently left in the dust, a lone target for the ambushers. Only the escort's corporal returned to cover Kirkman's slow withdrawal with his six-shooter. Kirkman angrily reported Brown's actions to headquarters, and then stated, hopefully, that he thought Baker might have received a wound in the right arm during the fight.[46]

Shortly afterward, Kirkman's supply wagon suffered a Baker-led attack that left a teamster dead. One guard escaped the trap, reached Boston, and returned with Kirkman and four troopers. The attackers had fled with their booty; Kirkman identified the marauders as Baker and Ben Griffith, among others. The Bureau agent suspected that the wagon had been taken to Arkansas for sale, and the mules dyed to conceal their identity. Pursuing cavalry from Mount Pleasant found a blacksmith who remembered shoeing the animals, and some army equipment and a rifle Baker left with a nearby freedman. After a futile search on his own for the outlaws in Arkansas, Kirkman figured that Baker now had somewhere between fifteen to thirty men with him in the Sulphur River bottoms. He said further that the "Yankee Killer" regularly threatened to come into Boston and do him in.[47]

But Baker never made good on his promise that year. On Christmas Day 1867, he and a few friends got rousing drunk and sacked the Howell Smith plantation up in Bright Star, Arkansas, killing the white landowner and several freedmen. During the melee, Baker was accidentally shot in the thigh by one of his own men. The wound incapacitated him for months. During his recuperation Baker set up a school in the swamps to teach others his talents with the handgun and engaged in some able propaganda. The bandit chief spoke of his fight against the Bureau and the army as a "New Rebellion," and collectively labeled his Yankee enemies "abolitionists." Cleverly Baker pledged "that it will not be my purpose to make war upon the good and peaceable citizens or laborers of this section; nor do I intend to interfere with the powers that be." He obviously had heard the muted cheers of bystanders as he made fools of his military pursuers.[48]

Meanwhile Kirkman did not remain idle, either. Working through headquarters, he asked the Texas government to place a price on Baker's head that eventually amounted to $3,000. Wanted posters described

Baker as in his mid-thirties, five feet-eight inches in height, weighing 160 pounds. The outlaw had dark sandy hair, said Kirkman, and appeared to have "little facial hair." He was lean and pale, had a slow walk and talked in a gruff voice. When the Arkansas state executive sweetened the pot by another paltry $1,000, the insulted Baker responded with flyers of his own, offering $5,000 for Governor Powell Clayton, dead or alive. The man obviously had style; the street loungers chuckled admiringly.[49]

Baker's temporary absence from the battlefield allowed Kirkman to focus on other issues. Unlike many subassistant commissioners, Kirkman had had a troop escort from the beginning, probably because of his brother's influence at headquarters and General Griffin's predilection in that course for all agents. In any case, Boston was garrisoned by a corporal and two troopers from the 6th Cavalry out of the Department of Texas, and a sergeant, two corporals, and six privates from the 20th Infantry out of the Department of Louisiana. Even though the soldiers seemed to be sick much of the time, they were healthy enough to give Kirkman the necessary power to compel obedience to his edicts, and protect him from most intimidation by gunmen. Indeed, by November 1867, civil affairs improved so much that Kirkman bragged that if the civil officials would do their duty, he would need no escort at all.[50]

This was an unfortunate admission for any man in the field to make to the bureaucrats at headquarters, especially after General Griffin's death. They specialized in looking for unnecessary expenditures and redefining anomalous lines of authority. General Reynolds soon received all of Texas as his command, which required the recall of Kirkman's infantry detail to Louisiana. Three months later, Reynolds' superior at New Orleans, Maj. Gen. Winfield S. Hancock, a Democrat allied with President Andrew Johnson in opposing the Bureau's independent Reconstruction activities as divisive to the healing of the nation and unfair to white southerners, ordered Reynolds to recall all detached military units, including Kirkman's cavalry detachment.[51]

Kirkman immediately realized the error in his frankness. When the infantry left, the subassistant commissioner's public support dropped markedly. When the cavalry withdrew, the subassistant commissioner began to worry about his own health. "I think it somewhat singular that the small detachment of cavalry should have been so precipitately removed from the district," Kirkman dryly remarked, "rendering an agent liable to be insulted and [to] other possible violence. . . . I will remain here as long as I think I can do so in *safety*," he emphasized, "and if I cannot remain without having to contend with B[ake]r (who is probably not sad), I will remove my office to Jefferson, . . . and discharge the duties of *the 58th Sub-District* from that point." Kirkman then asked that six to eight men be returned to him.

When this proved impossible, Kirkman let off steam by hurling charges of incompetency and neglect of duty against subassistant commissioners Lieutenant Hiram Willis (Rocky Comfort, Arkansas), Bvt. Capt. Charles F. Rand (Clarksville, Texas), Col. DeWitt C. Brown (Paris, Texas), and Bowie County Judge A. G. Haskins and Sheriff W. E. Duke. Haskins and Duke ignored him completely, while Willis was safely in another command area; but Brown and Rand vociferously denied Kirkman's accusations to the satisfaction of headquarters. His handwriting changed dramatically from bold to shaky in the following month's report; it appears that Kirkman was ill, or had acquired a slight drinking problem (his report rambled uncharacteristically), or perhaps a bad case of nerves, undoubtedly intensified by a feeling of abandonment. Kirkman later calmed down and tried to get a transfer from the Bureau to the army's Telegraphic Corps or, failing that, acceptance of his resignation in mid-July 1868. Neither came through, and he struggled on.[52]

The advantage that the soldiers' presence had given the Bureau agent was aptly demonstrated in the Orten's Circus riot, an incident that took place in November 1867, before the troops' withdrawal, and haunted Kirkman for the rest of his stay in Boston. The circus came into town after a lengthy advertising campaign, and all were excited to see it, legitimate entertainment being scarce in Texas towns of that day. The show that first afternoon was heavily attended, and liquor flowed freely all over town. As it developed, the circus performers were from the North, and the drunker, more rowdy patrons began to call them "Yankees," and then, in somewhat vulgar terms, the young "rebs" offered to refight the late war and bragged that they would kill all comers. One man, John Teller (or Tiller, depending on which account one reads), pointed his revolver "and made a good many dangerous motions with it," and openly insulted female performers, whom many "decent" citizens considered generally to be of loose morals, anyway.[53]

The subassistant commissioner suspected early on that "a disturbance or riot" might ensue during the evening performance. He warned the sheriff, and offered himself and his soldiers to preserve the peace. Sheriff Duke preferred to defer action hoping that the drunks, who were riding up and down sidewalks in the business section, waving six-shooters and exchanging insults with passersby, would leave town voluntarily. Duke warned the rowdies that they were to be out of town by dark or face arrest. Most complied with the sheriff's caution, but others stayed on. While this transpired, Kirkman went to dinner with the circus owner, who said his custom was to allow soldiers to attend the shows free. Kirkman accepted the offer and organized the soldiers into shifts, wisely, as it turned out, keeping half the men in reserve.

As Kirkman and his party entered the tent, he noticed a group of rowdies in one corner. John Richardson was entertaining them by marching up and down the aisle with a rifle at "right shoulder shift." All at once the boisterous group got up to leave. Kirkman expected that they might attack the Bureau office or steal the Army's horses. But the young rowdies stopped to cheer as one of their friends rode recklessly into the tent, causing a "general stampede" in the crowd. That was enough for the Bureau agent. Kirkman quickly motioned to the soldiers, and they all left the tent to obtain weapons and reinforcements.

Kirkman brought the soldiers, organized into two groups, back to the tent, where they remained concealed, ready for action. A shot rang out. One of the rowdies had gunned down the show's midget in the center ring. As the thugs roared with laughter, Kirkman ordered his men forward. The soldiers fired a volley, scattering the trouble makers, dropping the boisterous rider from his horse, which also went down, and hitting an innocent freedman in the leg. The horse died at once in the tent, the rider died two hours later. The black man had to have his leg amputated; he died from the effects of that operation a month later.[54]

Outside, as the soldiers rounded up ruffians in the tent, Kirkman saw a figure run toward the Bureau office. Kirkman yelled at him. The man fired his shotgun. Kirkman let him have one barrel from his own scatter gun. The man ran into a dead-end alley from which he emerged a few moments later, dropping to the ground. Kirkman found him to be John Richardson, who had an open wound in his arm, a bruise from a ball on his side, and two holes shot through his pants leg.

The subassistant commissioner arrested Richardson, the revolver-waving John Teller, and E. J. Jansen, the latter of whom had been selling whiskey to the rowdies all day. At the pleading of Judge Haskins and ex-governor Runnels, Kirkman let all of the other young men identified as participants in the riot post bond for their future good behavior, except one, who had fled the county.[55]

The subassistant commissioner also confiscated two horses, which he found grazing near the tent afterward. One of the horses was assessed at $500, a large sum in those days. The horses were eventually claimed by their owners for costs, in a drawn-out process that lasted eight months.

Some of the cost realized from their upkeep went to the doctor who had unsuccessfully amputated the African American's leg. Finally, Kirkman had Sheriff Duke indicted for not dispersing the rioters. Found guilty, Duke was fined a minimal $12.50 by Judge Haskins in county court, but he had to post a $5,000 bond to insure his future good conduct.[56]

Almost a month after the riot, the sheriff and one of the noncommissioned officers under Kirkman's command opened the jail to give the prisoners their breakfasts. To their surprise, both Teller and Richardson covered them with cocked revolvers. The prisoners took off at a run. The corporal drew his six-shooter and fired. Teller and Richardson returned fire. The infantry contingent ran from the courthouse in hot pursuit, but were soon outdistanced by the fleeing prisoners. Kirkman, by chance, already had two horses saddled up for other business.

He and Private W. H. Campbell quickly mounted and caught up to the escapees within a half mile. Campbell, about fifty yards ahead of the Bureau agent, threw down on Richardson and ordered him to give up. Richardson refused and Campbell shot him dead. Teller dropped his gun and surrendered to Kirkman, hands in the air. When questioned about the revolvers, Teller said that someone, he did not know who, had handed the guns through the cell window to Richardson the night before. Teller said the break was Richardson's idea, and Kirkman believed him. But to be safe, the subassistant commissioner took Teller to the military stockade at Mount Pleasant.

Brevet Colonel S. H. Starr, who had replaced Claflin as commandant at Mount Pleasant, recommended that Teller be released on $2,000 bond, which Kirkman acceded to. At the same time, Kirkman cancelled the bond of circus rioter T. A. Shipp, and released E. J. Jansen on $1,500 bond pending his trial. Teller, Jansen, and T. A. Shipp were eventually indicted in the county court, where they asked for a change of venue. Kirkman, however, wanted a military trial on charges he had drawn up earlier. Faced with Kirkman's intransigence, Teller and the others became quite cooperative and followed the conditions of their bonds to the letter, so much so that Kirkman eventually recommended that all their bonds be cancelled. Headquarters agreed, and Kirkman dropped their bonds as one of his last acts in office.[57]

Meanwhile Kirkman had to deal with an outraged community. Judge John A. Talbot and his daughters, in whose yard the prisoners were retaken, testified that Private Campbell had killed Richardson as he tried to surrender, unarmed, with his hands raised. Kirkman was livid. "It has never been my aim to notice what females might say," he sniffed, and he recalled that the Talbot girls cheered "and gave [vent] to their emotions" from the courthouse when Cullen Baker had murdered Private Titus, "all of which ill-becomes a lady." As for Judge Talbot, his response to the rioting at the circus had been a public statement that "he did not see why the citizens did not come together and drive the d----d yankies [*sic*] out of town."[58]

Talbot need not have worried—army headquarters was about to accomplish that very task. Five days after the jailbreak, Kirkman's infantry contingent received orders to return to their regiment in Louisiana. The subassistant protested their removal, especially as the soldiers were key witnesses in the Richardson shooting. He received assurances that the men who could testify would be available when needed. On their way out of town, Sheriff Duke tried to arrest Private Campbell for the "murder" of Richardson. The sergeant in charge told Duke to forget it, and the whole unit marched away to Marshall the day before Christmas, undisturbed, Campbell with them. Kirkman wisely closed all liquor establishments in Boston on both Christmas and New Years' Day to lessen the chance of a new riot.[59]

But Kirkman's enemies would not let the matter rest. In September 1868, the county grand jury indicted the subassistant commissioner for the murder of Richardson, based largely on the testimony of the Talbots. Kirkman was stunned. "I did not shoot the man that was killed," he protested. "I saw him fall." He inquired as to the legal protection he might receive from headquarters, as the act happened in the line of duty. The pressures of his job overwhelmed the harried Bureau agent. It was at this time that his handwriting deteriorated, as noted earlier. Friends thought him "partially deranged, and not capable of realizing what course to pursue." One loyal man, Nathaniel B. Anderson, wrote headquarters that "we are in such a condition here that I don't feel safe, if called upon, to go on his bond." Decrying what he called "malicious prosecution," Anderson related the story of the Richardson jailbreak and shooting in much the same manner as had Kirkman so many months before.[60]

Realizing that Judge Haskins might not render a fair decision, Kirkman managed to gain a hearing in the state district court at Clarksville. There, on September 21, 1868, Judge Winston Banks, a loyal military appointee to office, dismissed the case under the provisions of the Reconstruction Acts. Kirkman returned to Boston to find a letter from headquarters relieving him from duty in Bowie County. General Reynolds did not wish to imperil his life further. Already the Bureau man in Clarksville, Charles Rand, had fled his post secretly at night to save his life from outlaw vengeance after his shooting of Ben Griffith. The agent in Paris, the former Tyler inspector DeWitt C. Brown, had just escaped a Cullen Baker ambush on the Bois D'Arc crossing. Soon he too would have to flee his post just steps ahead of a Ku Klux mob, leaving everything he owned behind.[61]

Reynolds had managed to reinstate the Clarksville agency, but the new man, Bvt. Maj. George W. Shorkley, had to be supported by his full company from the 15th Infantry. Now Cullen Baker was rumored to be on his way to Boston, leading an army he called the "Ku Klux Klan" and looking to install his "New Rebellion" in Bowie County, so Kirkman was to take his books to Clarksville. There Shorkley would assume his responsibilities, and Kirkman could take the stage through Waco to Austin. Reynolds also issued an order exempting Kirkman from further arrest, and told him to ignore any adverse state judicial proceedings. Travel weather was quite poor (it had rained for a week) and Kirkman had some unfinished paperwork to complete before leaving. So he delayed his trip ten days.[62]

In reality, very much to his credit for posterity, Kirkman was very apprehensive in leaving at all despite the personal danger of staying on in Boston. "I am the only protection the negroes in this section have," he explained. "I stand between many of them and death. Ultimately the country will quiet down"—Kirkman never seemed to lose totally his faith in this false hope—"and they will be comparatively safe; but at present my departure would mean their extermination. No matter what the risk," he concluded, " I cannot leave until I have some assurance of their protection." Loyal men urged him to leave his post in haste, while he could still sit astride a horse.[63]

Finally, after days of indecision, Kirkman allowed himself to be persuaded to do the prudent thing. On October 6, he informed certain loyal men of his decision to leave the next morning. That evening, Nathaniel Anderson, the clerk of the county court who allowed Kirkman to board at his house, drew up papers transferring power of attorney from Kirkman to B. T. Ester. Meanwhile William W. Bass consulted with Kirkman in the Bureau office next door on the details of the coming trip. Around midnight, Anderson, who was working in the front room of the house, heard the back door open and close. He assumed both Bass and Kirkman had gone quietly upstairs to bed. He did the same in his downstairs bedroom.[64]

But Anderson was mistaken. Only Bass had come in. Kirkman had remained behind to finish some office paperwork. As nearly as can be pieced together from subsequent investigations, this is what occurred after Bass left Kirkman. About two in the morning, Kirkman must have heard a noise in the street in front of his office. The agent undoubtedly arose from his desk and carefully peered out the window. Outside, he would have seen several heavily armed men dismounting from their lathered horses. Some may have already drawn their revolvers as they stealthily approached the Bureau office's front door. Kirkman was no fool. His life had been threatened too many times before. He had engaged his opponents in gunfights and in Bureau tribunals. He had offended important local citizens. Many had sworn revenge. Kirkman seems to have quietly returned to his desk and picked up his six-shooter. Perhaps he surmised if he could get to Anderson's house, before the gunmen blocked his exit, he could organize a defense and drive them away.

Slowly he opened the rear door to the Bureau office. He crept out into the dank night air. There probably was a commotion. Already someone had tried the locked front door. Kirkman stepped off the back stoop onto the path, watching his back, six-gun cocked and held ready to fire. He silently felt his way down the path. He was a quarter of the distance to safety. All of his senses were alive, as he strained to see any shadow out of place or perceive the slightest movement. But he had been too slow. Without warning, Cullen Baker rose up from behind the board fence that ran parallel to the walkway. Kirkman undoubtedly saw him move out of the corner of his eye. He spun to fire. His revolver discharged harmlessly as Baker hit him at point-blank range with a charge from his Enfield rifle. It was buck and ball, a .57 caliber musket ball topped off with a deadly mixture of number three buckshot. The full blast struck Kirkman in the chest, driving him backward in agony, as he fired his revolver a second time—a reflex action, again to no effect.[65]

The other assailants ran around the office building and opened up with their six-shooters. Kirkman's reeling body was hit again and again. In the side under his right arm, in his right shoulder, the bullets struck home. Pieces of the board fence flew as the bullets ricocheted and buzzed down the street. Explosions echoed through the courthouse square. Twenty shots later, the hated "abolitionist" Bureau agent lay dying on the ground. Coolly and carefully, Cullen Baker aimed his revolver and fired the *coup de grace*. Kirkman's body jumped and kicked as the bullet slammed into his right temple. "Take that, you d--d Yankee son of a b--h," growled Baker—his traditional good-bye to all his victims.[66] Securing their horses, Baker's gang remounted and rode off. Someone stopped at the horse corral and stable and stole Kirkman's horse and equipment. None of the other half dozen animals was touched. Two of the gang rode noisily through the square. The air was pierced with laughing and mock Rebel yells. As they passed Anderson's house, one villain screamed, "Aw right!" in obvious satisfaction.[67]

In his bedroom, Anderson lay awake staring wide-eyed at the ceiling. He was in a state of shock. Kirkman's murder had occurred less than sixty feet from his window. "What happened?" It was Bass calling from his second story room. "I don't know," Anderson retorted. A chill went through him as he suddenly realized the truth. "Did Kirkman come in with you?" Bass replied, "No." It confirmed Anderson's worst fears. "Well, someone is shot," said Anderson. "Come on down." Bass slipped into the room, obviously as shaken as Anderson. Normally weak from asthma, Anderson found that the excitement had brought on another attack. He fought to breathe. Still no one ventured outside. Finally, Anderson saw a curious African American coming up in the shadows of the house. Gasping for breath, he asked him to scout out the scene to the Bureau office.[68]

Reluctantly, the black man set off with a friend. They were back shortly. It was Kirkman, they confirmed. He was lying in the pathway to the Bureau office, his six-shooter clenched in his right hand, still smelling of gunpowder. No one would go back to recover the body until daylight. Everyone was terrified that Baker and his gang would return—perhaps they were still lurking in the shadows! The caution proved wise. A short time later the freedmen saw two men moving in near the Bureau office. "Shoot or get out of the way!" came a menacing cry. The freedmen bolted for their shack and disappeared inside.[69]

The next morning, Anderson, Bass, William A. Payne, and the freedmen went over to the Bureau office. They found Kirkman's body, covered by the morning dew, "dead to all appearances." The agent's pockets had been turned out and his $25 revolver was gone. Payne, who kept Kirkman's accounts at his general store, estimated that the dead agent was missing three twenty-dollar gold pieces, a $100 wad of paper money, and his $150 watch and chain.[70] As county attorney, Anderson sent word to the local justice of the peace, William H. Gibson. The judge arrived with five men in tow, whom, along with Bass, he swore in as a coroner's jury. The verdict on Kirkman's death was that at least two men, unknown, on the morning of October 7, 1868, at two a.m. "did feloniously, voluntarily, and of malice aforethought" make "an assault with certain pistols or guns . . . upon the body of said W. G. Kirkman" which resulted in his "instantaneous death."[71]

Anderson, Payne, and a few others sadly removed Kirkman's body to the cemetery where it was buried. Returning from the solemn service, the mourners were terrified by the appearance of Cullen Baker and four gunhawks. Ever-affable in victory, Baker cockily told them, "Have no fear. We have already accomplished our objective." He went over to the stores facing the square, bought a few items, and rode off with his men toward his Sulphur River hideaway. Soon Baker would kill Kirkman's Arkansas counterpart, Lieutenant Willis, Assistant U.S. Tax Assessor Major Porter J. Andrews, and an African American guide, all shot from ambush later that same month at Walnut Bayou crossing, near Andrews' plantation across the Red River in Little River County.[72]

The news of Kirkman's death spread rapidly. General Reynolds was dismayed. He notified the Bureau command in Washington and promised a full investigation.[73] Bvt. Maj. George W. Shorkley, the subassistant commissioner at Clarksville, who had assumed command of Kirkman's subdistrict a few weeks earlier, received the unenviable task. Because of the danger, he wore civilian clothes. He hired a wagon and a black driver and arrived at Anderson's house a week after the shooting.[74]

Shorkley was disturbed by the pervasive fear that permeated Boston. The mere rumor Baker was coming could clear the streets. No one dared mention Baker by name. Instead, people referred to Baker as "he" or "that man." Everyone suspected his neighbors of being informants or spies for the outlaws. The local black population was panic-stricken. Their only friend and defender, Kirkman, was dead and buried. Some begged their old masters to take them in and protect them. Others slept in the woods, fearing an attack on their homes. The more daring tried to leave the county, traveling little-known roads and trails at night. Authorities refused to act in the matter of Kirkman's death. Even loyal Union men feared retribution and stood by helplessly. Shorkley recommended that General Reynolds send not less than a company of troops, preferably cavalry, under an "active commander." Otherwise, he feared freedmen and loyal whites would be killed off, one by one.

"Mr. Kirkman was esteemed by all good citizens, who knew him as a man of the most unswerving integrity," testified Shorkley in his report to General Reynolds. The dead agent was "earnest, fearless, and faithful in the discharge of every duty. . . . It is hoped," Shorkley concluded, "that the government will be untiring in its efforts to visit upon his murderers the swift vengeance of an outraged law."[75]

Vengeance was on its way. On October 12, Reynolds issued an order to all military and civil officers to arrest persons wearing any disguise or mask, and hold them for the army and military trial. He also noted that so many freedpersons had been killed in eastern Texas that the army could no longer keep track of the numbers. Reynolds then sent the whole 15th

Infantry Regiment to Marshall and Jefferson, the center of outlaw and Klan activity. Kirkman's murder had come at about the same time that the Knights of the Rising Sun, a Ku Klux organization, stormed the Jefferson jail, overpowered the military guards, and assassinated three black politicians and a white carpetbagger, who were being held on assault charges stemming from defending themselves against an earlier Klan-style attack.[76]

In direct response to Kirkman's murder, Reynolds sent an elite squadron from the 6th Cavalry to Sulphur Springs with orders to get tough with the outlaws. Led by Bvt. Maj. Adna R. Chaffee and Capt. Thomas W. Tolman, the troopers swept through the Sulphur River region with heretofore unknown viciousness. Few prisoners were taken. Reports listed suspects "lost in the swamp" or "shot while trying to escape." Local farmers who misled troopers or refused to inform on outlaws were strung up by their thumbs. One column logged over one thousand miles while pursuing brigands. Their tactics in combating outlaws and their sympathizers were so brutal that the column earned the nickname, "Chaffee's Guerrillas." Tolman's counter-intelligence activities in Sulphur Springs, a town surrounded by brigands for weeks on end despite (or because of) the troop presence, led to his eventual court-martial and punishment for undue cruelty toward civilians.[77]

The 6th Cavalry's methodical scourging of northeastern Texas cleaned the area of outlaw gangs within six months. But they never found Kirkman's killer, Cullen Baker. The "Yankee Killer" was murdered by a crippled schoolteacher, who had cheated Baker out of marrying the outlaw's dead wife's sister. Appropriately, Baker was shot from ambush, while he was in a drunken stupor, by Thomas Orr and three compatriots. As befitted a man of action, Baker died carrying four six-shooters, two double-barreled shotguns, three Derringers, and a half-dozen assorted knives.[78]

With Baker's death, the peace that Kirkman had sought to achieve as subassistant commissioner had come to Bowie County at last. But what kind of peace was it? Given the one hundred years that followed until the Second Reconstruction of the 1960s, one is tempted to say the peace was one that offered little real substance for blacks beyond substituting peonage for chattel slavery. Historian Smallwood praises Kirkman for being "scrupulously honest and conscientious"— a man who sympathized with the defeated whites until "he witnessed the daily outrages committed by whites on Negroes."[79]

Crouch is more assertive than Smallwood in his analysis of Kirkman. Agreeing with Smallwood that Kirkman used "common sense and fairness in treating both blacks and whites," Crouch thinks that the know-it-all subassistant commissioner from Illinois "suggests what Reconstruction was all about." Serving alone in an isolated rural area, Crouch admits that Kirkman may not have been "a typical Bureau agent for Texas or for other parts of the South." His critical attribute, according to Crouch, was his refusal to follow "proper Bureau procedure." This meant that "in the field he was precisely the kind of individual who produced results." [80]

But Kirkman was closer to the norm than usually portrayed. No one can deny that Kirkman was sincere in his efforts to bring to fruition the economic and social results of the Civil War. But the key here is both Smallwood and Crouch qualify their assertions too much. Kirkman "tried," "attempted," "could not do all," or acted "as his limits would allow." It is as if these historians want to find a success in Kirkman's efforts that really is not there.

As Randy Finley, an historian of the Freedman's Bureau in Arkansas warns, too often modern historians "decontextualize Reconstruction and judge 1865 and 1866 from the perspective of the New Deal or the Great Society." We forget "that Andrew Johnson was not Lyndon Johnson, that telegraph lines . . . were not television screens to help mobilize public opinion, and that the Holocaust had not yet seared human consciousness with the imprint of racism. . . ." These historians, Finley continues, "are inclined to find angels and demons too readily when, in reality, mixtures of good and evil warred in almost every human during Reconstruction," as they "groped for new understandings of freedom while often subconsciously clinging to old values and patterns of behavior and thought." He concludes that "[t]he struggle over what institutions and values from the past are worth saving is always complicated and angst riddled. . . ." Crouch sees it otherwise. He holds that "with the changed status of Reconstruction historiography, a new examination . . . would seem worth an inquiry"; an inquiry, one suspects, that would emphasize change for the sake of change, regardless of the facts.[81]

But present-day analysis did not contribute to Kirkman's rise or fall. What killed him was the Bureau's performance in light of its organizational structure, its bureaucratic short-comings. One analyst believes that the second Freedmen's Bureau Act of July 28, 1866, passed over President Andrew Johnson's veto, was the culprit. It made the Bureau more independent of the army and expanded the Bureau's responsibilities beyond refugees, freedmen, and abandoned lands to incorporate many other laudable objectives for the newly freed slaves like guaranteed civil rights, improved family structure, contract refereeing, and so on; in short, liberating blacks from their slave past. As a result, the Bureau's effectiveness steadily diminished because its agents in the field could not control the political and economic problems they encountered.[82]

And so it was in Texas. It is here that Crouch's notion that Kirkman cleverly circumvented established procedure falls flat. Far from being wise and effective, it achieved little but headquarters' rebukes and reversals of Kirkman's policies, and the remitting all fines and punishments to his white foes. This did nothing but prove to recalcitrant planters that Kirkman was weak and, in the long run, would be ineffective. As it was, Kirkman affected no labor settlements for 1865, next to nothing for 1866, and as little as fifty cents on the dollar for 1867 (the only year-end settlement he supervised on time). He was denied the chance to make his 1868 program effective because of headquarters' cancellation of his decrees and fines, and, by his death (and the Bureau's demise), left the freedmen at the mercy of the unsympathetic state courts for 1868 and after.[83]

It also indicates that the real place for historians to seek Bureau effectiveness is not in the field agencies, as Crouch maintains, but in the nullifying actions and reprimanding dictates of paper shufflers and bean counters in Galveston and, later, Austin. It was also these men who pulled out the troops critical to any agency's success against violence and non-compliance, only to send them back in a temporary punitive expedition and pull them out again, in the end, leaving the freedpeople to the not-so-tender mercies of whites. Like it or not, higher headquarters, whether in Austin or Washington City, always had the last word, not the local agents.[84]

It has become common to analogize the Bureau's record to a glass—half full, or half empty.[85] William Gilbert Kirkman's brief life and vicious death starkly symbolized so much of the youthful idealism of pre-Civil War America that was compromised by the war-weary cynicism of the postwar Reconstruction era and the Gilded Age that followed. The final result was that the whole struggle for black civil rights and equality before the law remained unsolved to plague the nation all over again, a century later. Hey! There's that glass! Lying at the side of the road to that part of pandemonium paved with good intentions, over in the bar ditch—smashed to pieces.[86]

ENDNOTES:

1. On Boston and Bowie County, see Fred Tarpley, *Place Names of Northeast Texas* (Commerce: East Texas State University Educational Research and Field Services, 1969), 2; Barbara Susan Overton Chandler,

"A History of Bowie County" (M.A. thesis, University of Texas, Austin, 1937); and J. J. Schieffelin, "Bowie County, Texas: Basic Background Book" (Unpublished typescript, N.d., Microfilm No. 1033772, L. D. S. Family History Center, Tucson), 107–10. For population figures, see Walter Louis Buenger, "Stilling the Voice of Reason: Texans and the Union, 1854–1868" (Ph.D. dissertation, Rice University, 1979), 9, 280, which is based on the federal census; and Randolph B. Campbell, *An Empire for Slavery: The Peculiar Institution in Texas, 1821–1865* (Baton Rouge: Louisiana State University Press, 1989), 264, which complements the decennial census figures with five–year calculations based on the county tax rolls. The voter registration figures for all of Texas Reconstruction are in General Orders (GO) No. 73, April 16, 1870, Printed Orders, Record Group (RG) 94, National Archives and Records Administration (NARA).

2. Most of these terms are commonplace. "Scalawag" and "Carpetbagger" served to isolate the Southern loyalists and Yankee interlopers from the ex-Confederate Southern whites. See Ted Tunnell, "Creating 'the Propaganda of History': Southern Editors and the Origins of *Carpetbagger* and *Scalawag*," *Journal of Southern History*, 72 (2006), 789–812. With the publication of William C. Nunn, *Texas under the Carpetbaggers* (Austin: University of Texas Press, 1962), many historians were outraged at the false image created by the book's title, since at no time did Carpetbaggers comprise more than 6 or 7 percent of the Texas Reconstruction civil government. See Randolph B. Campbell, "Carpetbagger Rule in Texas: An Enduring Myth," *Southwestern Historical Quarterly* 97 (1993–94), 587–96. For "blue-coated dogs," see Jennie Chew Young to Louisa Wharton, January 16, 1866, in Edward Clifton Wharton Papers, Department of Archives and Manuscripts, Louisiana State University. The term "Kluckers" is used commonly in army and Bureau reports reflective of local attitudes. See, *e.g.*, William H. Sinclair to Acting Assistant Adjutant General, Headquarters, Texas Freedmen's Bureau (AAAG-TFB), August 18, 1868, Letters Received (LR), Records of the Assistant Commissioner (AC), Texas (T), Records of the Bureau of Refugees, Freedmen, and Abandoned Lands (BRFAL), RG 105, NARA. Hereinafter all documents cited are from the Texas division of this record group unless otherwise noted.

3. The term "drawers of the bureau" is from Samuel Gilmore to AAAG-TFB, May 18, 1866, LR, AC, T. For the organization and activities of the Freedmen's Bureau on the national level, see Paul A. Cimbala, *The Freedmen's Bureau: Reconstructing the American South after the Civil War* (Malabar, FL: Krieger Publishing, 2005); Paul A. Cimbala and

Randall M. Miller, eds., *The Freedmen's Bureau and Reconstruction: Reconsiderations* (New York: Fordham University Press, 1999). See also, George R. Bentley, *A History of the Freedmen's Bureau* (Philadelphia: University of Pennsylvania Press, 1955); Paul Skeels Pierce, *The Freedmen's Bureau: A Chapter in the History of Reconstruction* (Iowa City: University of Iowa Press, 1904); W. E. Burghardt DuBois, "The Freedmen's Bureau," *Atlantic Monthly* 87 (1901): 354–65; Victoria Marcus Olds, "The Freedmen's Bureau as a Social Agency" (Ph.D. dissertation, Columbia University, 1966), 110–54; John and LaWanda Cox, "General Howard and the 'Misrepresented Bureau'," *Journal of Southern History* 19 (1953), 427–56; John A. Carpenter, *Sword and Olive Branch: Oliver Otis Howard* (Pittsburgh: University of Pittsburgh Press, 1964); William S. McFeeley, *Yankee Stepfather: General O. O. Howard and the Freedmen* (New Haven: Yale University Press, 1968); Oliver Otis Howard, *Autobiography*, 2 vols., (New York: The Baker & Taylor Co., 1908).

4. The poignant comparison with Alabama and Mississippi is in Gregg Cantrell, "Racial Violence and Reconstruction Politics in Texas, 1867–1868," *Southwestern Historical Quarterly* 93 (1989–1990): 333–58, especially 339–40. Cantrell asserts that Texas was in effect shortchanged on agents in relation to land area. This may be true but the Bureau seems to have operated on numbers of blacks to be supervised, which totaled around 400,000 in each of the three states at the end of the war. If one leaves out the subdistricts along the frontier (Nos. 42–45, 47–49, 55–57, abutting the Rio Grande or the one hundredth meridian) which have few Reconstruction-oriented problems, the total number of Texas Bureau men (most of whom operated without clerks) compares favorably with those of Alabama or Mississippi (most of whom had a clerk's help). See Mss. Rosters, AC, Alabama, and Mss. Rosters, AC, Mississippi, BFRAL, RG 105, NARA. Texas figures are from "Rosters of Officers and Civilians on Duty . . . ," July 10, 1867, ms. vol. 9, AC, T, BRFAL, RG 105, NARA. Census figures are in Joseph C. G. Kennedy comp., *Population of the United States in 1860 . . .* (Washington, D.C.: Government Printing Office, 1864), 479, 483; Francis A. Walker, comp., *The Statistics of the Population of the United States . . .* (Washington, D.C.: Government Printing Office, 1872), 63–67; U.S., Department of Commerce, *Negro Population, 1790–1915* (Washington, D.C.: Government Printing Office, 1918), 44, 57. Another idea of the increase in the numbers of blacks sent to Texas during the war and the notion of where Bureau interests might cease and the frontier began can be had in Campbell, *An Empire for Slavery*, 2–3, 264–67.

5. For years, the standard study of the Bureau in Texas was Claude Elliott's too-brief article, "The Freedmen's Bureau in Texas," *Southwestern Historical Quarterly* 56 (1952–53), 1–24. More recent comprehensive studies are Robert W. Shook, "Federal Occupation and Administration of Texas, 1865–1870" (Ph.D. dissertation, North Texas State University, 1970), 239–89; James Smallwood, *Time of Hope, Time of Despair: Black Texans During Reconstruction* (Port Washington, NY: National University Publications, 1981); and two newer volumes offering different perspectives of the Bureau's work: Barry A. Crouch, *The Freedmen's Bureau and Black Texans* (Austin: University of Texas, 1992), and William L. Richter, *Overreached on All Sides: The Freedmen's Bureau Administrators in Texas, 1865–1868* (College Station: Texas A&M University Press, 1992). See also, Smallwood's articles "Charles E. Culver, A Reconstruction Agent in Texas: The Work of Local Freedmen's Bureau Agents and the Black Community," *Civil War History* 27 (1981): 350–61, and "G. T. Ruby: Galveston's Black Carpetbagger in Reconstruction," *Houston Review* 6 (1983): 24–33. Some of the better writings on the Texas Bureau come from the pen of Barry A. Crouch. See his "The Freedmen's Bureau and the 30th Sub-district in Texas," *Chronicles of Smith County, Texas* 11 (1972): 15–30; "Black Dreams and White Justice," *Prologue* 6 (1974): 255–65; "Self Determination and Local Black Leaders in Texas," *Phylon* 39 (1978): 344–55; "A Spirit of Lawlessness: White Violence, Texas Blacks, 1865–1868," *Journal of Social History* 18 (1984): 217–32; with L. J. Schultz, "Crisis in Color: Racial Separation in Texas During Reconstruction," *Civil War History* 12 (1970): 34–49; and with Larry Madaras, "Reconstructing Black Families: Perspectives from the Texas Freedmen's Bureau Records," *Prologue* 18 (1986): 109–22. A fine, recent study of one Texas agency is Christopher Bean, "' A Most Singular Attempt': The Freedmen's Bureau at Marshall, Texas," *Southwestern Historical Quarterly* 110 (2006–2007): 464–85. A brief, but excellent, analysis of the state headquarters personnel is in Lonnie Sinclair, "The Freedmen's Bureau in Texas: The Assistant Commissioners and the Negro," unpublished paper submitted to the Institute of Southern History, The Johns Hopkins University, July 22, 1969. The Bureau's opening phases are discussed in Nancy Cohen-Lack, "A Struggle for Sovereignty: National Consolidation, Emancipation, and Free Labor in Texas, 1865," *Journal of Southern History* 58 (1992): 57–88. See also, Diane Neal and Thomas W. Kremm, "'What Shall We Do with the Negro?': The Freedmen's Bureau in Texas," *East Texas Historical Journal* 27, no. 2 (1989): 23–33. The literature and certain Bureau problems are surveyed in Crouch, "Hidden Sources of

Black History: The Texas Freedmen's Bureau Records as a Case Study," *Southwestern Historical Quarterly* 83 (1980), 211–26, and his "Freedmen's Bureau Records: Texas, A Case Study," in *Afro-American History: Sources for Research,* ed. Robert L. Clarke (Washington, D.C.: Howard University Press, 1981), 74–94. Also of interest is Merline Pitre, "A Note on the Historiography of Blacks in the Reconstruction of Texas," *Journal of Negro History* 66 (1981), 340–48; Crouch, "'Unmanacling' Texas Reconstruction: A Twenty Year Perspective," *Southwestern Historical Quarterly* 93 (1989–1990), 275–302; Edgar P. Sneed, "A Historiography of Reconstruction in Texas: Some Myths and Problems," *Southwestern Historical Quarterly* 72 (1968–1969), 435–48.

6. One of the best examples of Crouch lambasting anyone who does not "pose the proper questions" (Crouch's phrase), that is to say, write the book he would have written, is his review (*Societas*, 1 [1971], 317–18) of Howard White's *The Freedmen's Bureau in Louisiana* (Baton Rouge: Louisiana State University Press, 1970). Crouch accused White of giving "us a barely competent work." White supposedly over-emphasized the "overall administration of the Bureau," and ignored "what actually happened in the villages and hamlets. . . ." By relegating the "new outpouring of Reconstruction literature . . . to footnotes" or "simply ignoring it," and overemphasizing the "corruption that seems to have plagued the Bureau in Louisiana," Crouch claims White renders a "distorted picture." Obviously, Crouch has never lived in Louisiana (in what newspaperman A. J. Liebling once called "America's only banana republic" north of the Rio Grande), where monetary and social corruption is an art form. Crouch's review is full of the inconsistencies he accuses White of: White does not "covers all phases of Bureau activity," and Crouch does; White does not cover Louisiana adequately, but fails to cover other states for comparison; he uses some modern literature, but reads it incorrectly; Louisiana cannot be corrupt as White claims, but maybe it is. It was a wonderful beginning to a lengthy career full of more of the same (see his remarks of a similar nature about a short chapter in Richter, *Army in Texas*, 32–46 [Crouch, *Freedmen's Bureau and Black Texans*, 140, 141] that was expanded into the book, *Overreached on All Sides*, which he reviewed as better but not good enough [Crouch, review, *North Carolina Historical Review* 69 [1992], 454]), until he ended such nonsense in his biography of Cullen Baker, co-authored with Donaly Brice, *Cullen Montgomery Baker: Reconstruction Desperado* (Baton Rouge: Louisiana State University Press, 1997), 186, and admitted he just could not stand anyone who disagreed with his view on anything in Texas Reconstruction. This

whole set-up was presaged by Joseph G. Dawson III, comp. and annot., *The Late 19th Century U.S. Army, 1865–1898: A Research Guide* (New York: Greenwood, 1990), 64–65, especially 64, where he calls Richter's interpretation "[m]ore conservative in tone than some later 20th century historians would like," and, horrors of horrors, he "seems at times to support ex-Confederates." Crouch's whole problem was pointed out in James Alex Baggett's review of *Freedmen's Bureau and Black Texans*. Crouch draws his generalities from too small a sample for him to assure us that it is typical for Texas as a whole, *Journal of Southern History* 59 (1993): 571–72.

7. Kirkman was first studied in James Smallwood, "The Freedmen's Bureau Reconsidered: Local Agents and the Black Community" (also subtitled, "The Case of William S. [*sic*] Kirkman," when cited in other of Smallwood's publications), *Texana* 11 (1973): 309–20. Some of the short-comings of his study are noted in Crouch, "'Unmanacling' Texas Reconstruction," 281n12. Unfortunately, after noting Smallwood's inadequacies, Crouch did not do much better. See his *Freedmen's Bureau and Black Texans*, 69–102. The records from the Boston agency are catalogued in the unpublished typescript by Elaine Everly and Wilma Pacheli, eds., "Preliminary Inventory of the Field Offices of the Bureau of Refugees, Freedmen, and Abandoned Lands," 3 parts (Washington, D.C.: NARA, 1974), 3: 457–58. All item numbers refer to listings in this index. Kirkman's letter books were lost for some time after his death, but 1st Lt. James Davidson of the 11th U.S. Infantry found them among various military records at Clarksville and forwarded them to headquarters, which sent them on to Washington. See Davidson to Superintendent of Education, January 5, 1870, LR, ED, T.

8. For a full account of the violence in Bowie County see Register of Complaints, 1867–1868, vol. 70, item 3672, Field Office Records (Boston)-District of Texas, BFRAL, RG 105, NARA. These are itemized in "Record of Criminal Offenses Committed in the State of Texas, 1866–1868," 3 ms. vols., *ibid*., which lists forty-five violent crimes ranging from whippings to murder committed in Bowie County during the Reconstruction era. For those the army tracked independently from the Bureau, see "Register of Felonies Committed in Texas, 1866–1868," 3 ms. vols. (listed by county), and "Abstracts of Crimes Committed in Counties of Texas, 1869–1870," 3 ms. vols. (listed by date), Records of the Fifth Military District, RG 393, NARA, which list forty-two such incidents (the difference usually involves who received which reports).

9. See William G. Kirkman to Joel T. Kirkman, August 10, September 24, 1867, LR, AC, T. William Kirkman was supposedly a brevet

captain in Bureau records (a myth given currency by Smallwood, "The Freedmen's Bureau Reconsidered," 309–10), but he is not listed among the officers of any Northern regiment in U.S., Department of War, Adjutant General's Office, *Official Army Register of the Volunteer Force of the United States Army for the Years 1861–1865*, 8 vols. (Washington, D.C.: Government Printing Office, 1865–1867). His brother is, however, mentioned as captain of Company D, 21st Volunteer Infantry, in *ibid*., VI *(Indiana-Illinois)*, 245–46. See also, *Constitution and By-Laws of the Society of the 21st Illinois Veteran Volunteer Infantry* . . . ([Paris, IL]: J. M. Sheets, Printer, 1882), 16. It is possible that the Bureau records confused the two men's war records by accident or that the Kirkman brothers did it intentionally to make William a more attractive civilian appointee as a former officer rather than an enlisted man. His correct rank of private and an excellent short biography are in Charles D. Clark, *The History of the Thirty-ninth Regiment Illinois Volunteer Veteran Infantry (Yates Phalanx) in the War of the Rebellion, 1861–1865* (Chicago: The Association of the Regiment, 1889), 540–41 (enthusiastic and plucky quote on 540), and a picture of Kirkman appears on p. 527. Another brother, Albert, had been killed by guerrillas near Memphis while returning to his regiment from leave. The fourth Kirkman brother, Marshall, was a comptroller for the Chicago Northwestern Railroad Company. Even though his cited sources do not mention it, Smallwood is probably correct ("The Freedmen's Bureau Reconsidered," 309–10) in attributing William Kirkman's desire to serve to a moral, idealistic motive, common to the Jacksonville area from which he originally came. Crouch too quickly dismisses this notion as an unproven "Congregationalist" philosophy (Crouch, *Freedmen's Bureau and Black Texans*, 140–41, *i.e.* fn 31 from p. 8). See Paul D. Glad, *The Trumpet Soundeth: William Jennings Bryan and His Democracy, 1896–1912* (Lincoln: University of Nebraska Press, 1960), 22–27, for a vivid description of the intellectual environment of the Kirkmans' prewar boyhood home. Griffin's importance to Reconstruction is detailed in William L. Richter, "Tyrant and Reformer: General Griffin Reconstructs Texas, [1866–1867]," *Prologue* 10 (1978): 225–42.

10. The appointment is recommended in Bvt. Maj. Gen. Charles Griffin to Bvt. Maj. Gen. O. O. Howard, June 3, 1867, Letters Sent (LS), AC, T; and approved in AAAG-C (Headquarters, Commissioner, Washington, D.C.) to Kirkman, June 14, 1867, LS, C. The actual appointment was announced in Special Orders (SO) 67, June 22, 1867, Texas Freedmen's Bureau (TFB). Kirkman's trip and arrival in Boston are in Kirkman to AAAG, July 8, 1867, LS, AC, T. Kirkman's complete correspondence is in Register of Letters Sent (vols. 67, and 68, item 3666), and Register

of Letters Received and Endorsements (vol. 66, item 3667), Field Office Records (Boston)-District of Texas, BRFAL, RG 105, NARA. Whenever possible the letters will be cited as received or sent from the office of AC, T, which are also on microfilm from NARA (Microcopy 821 [32 Rolls], Rolls 1, 6, 13, 20–27, *passim*).

11. Very capable (Crouch, *Freedmen's Bureau and Black Texans*, 107–109) Capt. Samuel Sloan, on detached duty from the 116th U.S. Colored Infantry as a subassistant commissioner with the Texas Freedmen's Bureau at Richmond and Millican, estimated that it took an agent about six months to really learn the intricacies of his job and the blacks and whites who made up his subdistrict, Cpt. S. Sloan to AAG-TFB, June 27, 1866, LR, AC, T. Kirkman served in Boston about fifteen months. Of 234 field agents this author has identified, forty-seven served in one subdistrict for an entire growing season (16 percent of 234) or had a total experience of eleven months in a combination of different agencies (or when both are combined, 20 percent of 234).

12. Smallwood, "The Freedmen's Bureau Reconsidered," 311–12, 315–16; Crouch, *Freedmen's Bureau and Black Texans*, 76–77, 88–89.

13. Smallwood, "The Freedmen's Bureau Reconsidered," 312–14; Crouch, *Freedmen's Bureau and Black Texans*, 77–83.

14. Smallwood, "The Freedmen's Bureau Reconsidered," 314–15; Crouch, *Freedmen's Bureau and Black Texans*, 83–87.

15. Smallwood, "The Freedmen's Bureau Reconsidered," 311–12, 314, 315–18; Crouch, *Freedmen's Bureau and Black Texans*, 70–73, 91–101.

16. Kirkman to AAAG-TFB, September 30, 1867, Reports of Operations and Conditions (ROC), AC, T.

17. Kirkman to AAAG-TFB, July 31 1867, LS, AC, T. The Reynolds quotation is from Sinclair,"" The Freedman's Bureau in Texas: The Assistant Commissioners and the Negro," 16. Reynolds' main preoccupation as commander of the army and Bureau was politics, appointing loyal men to office, keeping tabs on the state constitutional convention, and conducting the state and national elections of 1868. William L. Richter,"' We Must Rubb Out and Begin Anew': The Army and the Republican Party in Texas Reconstruction, 1867–1870," *Civil War History* 19 (December 1973): 334–52.

18. Kirkman to AAAG-TFB, October 31, 1867, LS, AC, T. The final quote is from the defendant in *Mrs. Millice Redalson v. Henry Bivins*, September 18, 1867, in Kirkman to AAAG-TFB, October 31, 1867, *ibid.* Bivins, a veteran of Company K, 11th Texas Volunteer Infantry, Bowie

County's contribution to the war effort (Schlieffelin, "Bowie County, Texas: Basic Background Book," 19), fled to Arkansas to avoid prosecution. Another black had complained against Bivins up in Arkansas, claiming that Bivins, who owed him and his wife $100 for labor rendered in 1866, ran them off by threats of violence in breach of contract. The case was never settled, as Bivins fled back to Texas again. See "Register of Complaints, January 1867–July 1868," Records of the Post of Rocky Comfort, Vol. 176, p. 135, Field Office Records (Paraclifta/Rocky Comfort), District of Arkansas, BRFAL, RG 105, NARA (also microfilmed for the Arkansas History Commission in 1976).

19. For the docket of cases heard before agent Kirkman, see any monthly report between July 1867 and September 1868, in ROC, AC, T. Other outrages are in Kirkman to AAAG-TFB, April 11, 24, July 29, 1868, LS, AC, T. The Jones case and the quotes are from Kirkman to AAAG-TFB, November 12, 1867, LR, AC, T. See also, Kirkman to AAAG-TFB, November 25, 1868, *ibid.*, and "Record of Criminal Offenses Committed in the State of Texas" (3 ms. vols., AC, T) vol. I, case # 486, and vol. II, case #1332.

20. Kirkman to AAAG-TFB, July 31, 1867, LR, AC, T (the headquarters clerk misplaced this monthly report [ROC] in the LR file), and AAAG-TFB to Kirkman, October 17, 1867, Endorsements Sent (ES), AC, T. See also, Kirkman to AAAG-TFB, November 25, 1867, April 11, 14, 1868, May 24, 1868, July 29, 1868, LR, AC, T. On Brown's career, see William L. Richter, "'The Revolver Rules the Day': Colonel DeWitt C. Brown and the Freedmen's Bureau in Paris, Texas, 1867–1868," *Southwestern Historical Quarterly* 93 (1989–1990), 303–32.

21. There are numerous cases concerning the apprenticeship of orphan and minor black children. See, e.g., three cases in Kirkman to AAAG-TFB, July 31, 1867, ROC, AC, T; and four cases in Kirkman to AAAG-TFB, November 30, December 3, 1867, LR, AC, T. For more on this topic, see Crouch, "Black Dreams and White Justice," 260–63; Crouch and Madaras, "Reconstructing Black Families," 109–22; Crouch, "' To Enslave the Rising Generation': The Freedmen's Bureau and the Texas Black Code," in *The Freedmen's Bureau and Reconstruction*, ed. Paul A. Cimbala and Randall M. Miller, 261–87.

22. Circ. 9, March 23, 1866, TFB. See also, Kirkman to AAAG-TFB, August 17, 31, November 25, 1867, August 21, 1868, LR, AC, T; Kirkman to AAAG-TFB, July 31, September 30, 1867, ROC, AC, T.

23. For these laws, see N. H. P. Gammel, comp., *The Laws of Texas, 1822–1897*, 10 vols. (Austin: Gammel Book Co., 1898), 5: 994–97. The

background and effect of the laws is in Winnell Albrecht, "The Black Codes of Texas" (M. A. thesis, Southwest Texas State University, 1969), the comparison to Bureau orders is in William L. Richter, "The Army and the Negro during Texas Reconstruction, 1865–1870," *East Texas Historical Journal* 10 (1972): 7–19. See also, Barry A. Crouch,"' All the Vile Passions': The Texas Black Code of 1866," *Southwestern Historical Quarterly* 97 (1993–1994): 12–34, who, conveniently ignoring the army's crucial role, and in"' To enslave the Rising Generation,'" 281n9, 281n10, 282–83n17, sees all other interpretations but his as incorrect. Like many modern, non-Southern intellectuals, he seeks to blame Southerners alone for instituting the Black Codes. For another viewpoint, which sees the only difference between the Black Codes and Bureau orders being that the army and Bureau orders did not emphasize race as did the Southerners' Black Codes, see Amy Dru Stanley, "Beggars Can't Be Choosers: Compulsion and Contract in Postbellum America," *Journal of American History* 78 (1991–1992): 1265–93, especially 1283–88. Laws similar to the Black Codes were common in the North, placed against the poor with no racial emphasis. Bureau orders becoming the basis for the Black Codes holds true for other reconstructed states. See, e.g., Theodore B. Wilson, *The Black Codes of the South* (University: University of Alabama Press, 1965); George A. Wood, "The Black Code of Alabama," *South Atlantic Quarterly* 13 (1914): 350–60; Ronald L. F. Davis, "The U.S. Army and the Origins of Sharecropping in the Natchez District: A Case Study," *Journal of Negro History* 62 (1077): 60–80. But Crouch thinks that any interpretation older than his should conform to his whims,"' To Enslave the Rising Generation,'" 280–81n6, and passes over Stanley with a simple citation, but no comment.

24. See any ROC, AC, T. A good example of one month's operations of Kirkman's office can be garnered from his letter and enclosures, Kirkman to AAAG-TFB, November 30, 1867, LR, AC, T. The Moores case is in Kirkman to AAAG-TFB, September 16, 1867, A. R. Moores to AAAG-TFB, April 7, 1868, with endorsement by Kirkman, April 9, 1868, LR, AC, T; AAAG-TFB to Kirkman, April 24, 1868, LS, AC, T. The case analyses are in Bentley, *History of the Freedmen's Bureau*, 159. He incorrectly calls Bowie County "Borrie County," but Kirkman's hand can be hard to read as he used a very large nib pen point. The flip side of his use of the large-nib pen is that the researcher can go through a roll of microfilm at high speed and pick out every letter and report by the visible blob of black ink used.

25. Kirkman to AAAG-TFB, November 14, 1867, LR, AC, T.

26. Unnumbered Circular, November 5, 1867, in *ibid.* That these men troubled Kirkman can be seen by perusing any of the cases filed by him in "Record of Criminal Offenses Committed in the State of Texas" (3 ms. vols., AC, T). The Jones case is in Kirkman to Wiley Murphy, November 25, 1867 (included with Kirkman to AAAG-TFB, November 30, 1867, LR, AC, T), and Kirkman to AAAG-TFB, December 31, 1867, January 31, 1868, ROC, AC, T. A full listing of Kirkman's issuances are in Orders and Circulars Issued, vol. 69, item 3670, Field Office Records (Boston), District of Texas, BRFAL, RG 105, NARA.

27. Unnumbered Circular, January 27, 1868, in Kirkman to AAAG-TFB, February 6, 1868, LR, AC, T.

28. Unnumbered Circular, March 23, 1868, in Kirkman to AAAG-TFB, March 23, 1868; Kirkman to AAAG-TFB, April 3, 4, 1868, noting several fines assessed and the attempted protest of N. M. Campbell; Unnumbered Circular, April 6, 1868, in Kirkman to AAAG-TFB, April 6, 1868; Kirkman to AAAG-TFB, April 23, 1868, stating that he would, as instructed, suspend the punitive parts of prior circulars and remit all fines. All documents in LR, AC, T. For the Runnels affair, see Kirkman to AAAG-TFB, February 29, March 31, 1868, ROC, AC, T. The addition of Davis County to Kirkman's control is in SO 15, March 2, 1868, TFB; Kirkman's assessment of the contracts is in Kirkman to AAAG-TFB, February 2, 1868, ROC, AC, T.

29. Kirkman to Superintendent of Schools (SS), March 4, 1868 (first quote), Monthly Reports (MR), Records of the Superintendent of Schools (RSS), T, BRFAL, RG 105, NARA; Kirkman to AAAG-TFB, July 31 (all other quotes), August 31, 1867, ROC, AC, T. The standard study of Bureau education efforts in Texas is Alton Hornsby, Jr., "The Freedmen's Schools in Texas, 1865–1870," *Southwestern Historical Quarterly* 76 (1972–73): 397–417. In addition to Hornsby's work, black education in Texas from the freedmen's perspective is studied by Smallwood, "Education and Black Self-Help," in his *Time of Hope, Time of Despair*, 69–95, a shorter summary of which appears as "Early 'Freedom Schools': Black Self-Help and Education in Reconstruction—Texas: A Case Study," *Negro History Bulletin* 41 (1978): 790–93.

30. Kirkman to AAAG-TFB, September 30, October 31, 1867, ROC, AC, T. For the town plot, see Kirkman to AAAG-TFB, March 31, June 30, 1868, *ibid.*; Kirkman to SS, June 23, 30, 1868, MR, RSS, T. On planter support, see Kirkman to AAAG-TFB, May 31, 1868, ROC, AC, T.

31. Kirkman to AAAG-TFB, November 30 (threats), December 31, 1867 (Hooks), ROC, AC, T.

32. The request that Hooks be appointed is in Kirkman to SS, March 4, 1868, LR, RSS, T; Hooks salary is in "Records of Teachers Paid by BRFAL, Texas," p. 41; all quotes are in Forrest Hooks to SS, September 2, 1868, MR, RSS, T, and Kirkman's endorsement of same; Bvt. Maj. George W. Shorkley to AAAG-TFB, October 31, 1868, ROC, AC, T, fears the closing of the schools. See also, Hooks to SS, July 4, 1868 (quoted), MR, RSS, T. A full listing of employees is in Reports of Persons and Articles Hired, ms., item 3671, Field Office Records (Boston)-District of Texas, BFRAL, RG 105, NARA.

33. Kirkman to AAAG-TFB, March 31, 1868, ROC, AC, T.

34. Kirkman to AAAG-TFB, June 30, 1868 (second and third quote), September 30, 1867 (first quote), *ibid.*

35. Kirkman to AAAG-TFB, November 30, 1867 (those who warmly assist), February 29, 1868 (all other quotes), *ibid.*

36. Kirkman to AAAG-TFB, October 31, 1867 (do not feel disposed), February 29 (Moores and Runnels), April 30 (more liberal feeling, aggrieved for being reported), May 31 (generally quiet and peaceful), October 4, 1868 (races getting along well), *ibid.*, and Kirkman to AAAG-TFB, April 11, 1868 (hiring of Griffith), LR, AC, T. On Griffith see, William L. Richter, "'Oh God, Let Us Have Revenge': Ben Griffith and His Family during the Civil War and Reconstruction," *Arkansas Historical Quarterly* 57 (1998): 255–86.

37. It is probably too present-minded to draw this conclusion. Kirkman and all Bureau men faced similar, touchy problems in communication often faced by Peace Corps workers in other countries in the late twentieth century.

38. On Reynolds' policies as commander, see Richter, *The Army in Texas During Reconstruction*, 119–86, *passim*.

39. See, e.g., Kirkman to AAAG-TFB, December 4, 7, 1867, June 13, 1868, LR, AC, T. Kirkman to M. A. McBride, November 26, 1867 in Kirkman to AAAG-TFB, November 30, 1867 (firearms), *ibid.* See W. G. Kirkman to J. T. Kirkman, July 1, 1867 (Finch), LR, AC, T. On the death of Joel Kirkman's wife, see Griffin to 1 Lt. A. H. M. Taylor, August 23, 1867 (telegram), LR, C; SO 130, August 24, 1867, FB, C; Howard to Griffin, August 24, 1867, LR, AC, T.

40. The Duke episode is in Kirkman to AAAG-TFB, September 30, November 22, 1867, February 26, June 13, 1868, *ibid.*; SO 156, July 15, 1868, TFB; Kirkman to AAAG-TFB, October 31, 1867, March 31, October 4, 1868 (quote), ROC, AC, T. Duke's 1866 election and his replacement by Morrow are in Schieffelin, "Bowie County Texas: Basic

Background Book," 20. Finally, after Kirkman's death, U. J. Odell accepted the military appointment as sheriff, SO 44, February 23, 1869, Printed Orders, FMD, RG 94, NARA.

41. Kirkman to AAAG-TFB, September 5 (quote), 12, 16, 1867, February 25, 26, 1868, LR, AC, T; September 30, 1867, ROC, AC, T. See also, "Record of Criminal Offenses Committed in the State of Texas" (3 ms. vols., AC, T) vol. II, case #1193.

42. Kirkman to AAAG-TFB, October 26 (quote), 31, 1867, ROC, AC, T; Kirkman to Willis, October 22, 1867, LR, AC, T. The Rand incident is in Charles Rand to AAAG-TFB, July 21, 1868, LR, AC, T. The career of Willis in Sevier and Little River counties (Arkansas) is treated in William L. Richter, "'A Dear Little Job': Second Lieutenant Hiram F. Willis, Freedmen's Bureau Agent in Southwestern Arkansas, 1866–1868," *Arkansas Historical Quarterly* 50 (1991): 158–200. For Griffith specifically, see Richter, "Ben Griffith and His Family," 255–86. The activities of Rand in Red River County are detailed in Richter, "'This Blood-thirsty Hole': The Freedmen's Bureau Agency at Clarksville, Texas, 1867–1868," *Civil War History* 38 (1992): 51–77.

43. The provisional governor of the state after the war, Andrew J. Hamilton, had warned the federal authorities about this intolerable situation to no avail. See Hamilton to Andrew Johnson, March 1, 1866, Johnson papers, LC. Gang operations in northeastern Texas are described in 2nd Lt. C. S. Roberts to AAAG-TFB, August 12, November 12, 1867, LR, AC, T. Roberts believed that the gangs operated from Kansas to Mexico. The descriptive quote of the terrain is from Kirkman to AAAG-TFB, October 26, 1867, *ibid.* See also, Richter, *Army in Texas During Reconstruction*, 146–52; Crouch and Brice, *Cullen Baker*; James M. Smallwood, Barry A. Crouch, and Larry Peacock, *Murder and Mayhem: The War of Reconstruction in Texas* (College Station: Texas A&M University Press, 2003); Ed Bartholomew, *Cullen Baker: Premier Texas Gunfighter* (Houston: Frontier Press, 1954), which includes a copy of Thomas Orr, *Life of the Notorious Desperado, Cullen Baker, From His Childhood to His Death, With a Full Account of All the Murders He Committed*, first published in Little Rock in 1870; C. L. Sonnichsen, *I'll Die Before I'll Run: The Story of the Great Feuds of Texas* (New York: Harper & Bros., 1951); Gladys Beall Ray, *Murder at the Corners* (San Antonio: Naylor, 1957); Al Eason, "Cullen Baker—Purveyor of Death," *Frontier Times* 40 (August–September 1966): 6–12, 44–47, 67; James Allen Marten, "Drawing the Line: Dissent and Loyalty in Texas, 1856 to 1874" (Ph.D. dissertation, University of Texas, 1986), 264–67; and Boyd W. Johnson,

"Cullen Montgomery Baker: The Arkansas-Texas Desperado," *Arkansas Historical Quarterly* 25 (1966): 229–39.

44. Crouch and Brice, *Cullen Baker*, 1–17, especially 6; Johnson, "Cullen Baker," 229–35; Bartholomew, *Cullen Baker*, 21–52, 111–12, 119.

45. Kirkman to AAAG-TFB, July 31, 1867, ROC, AC, T. For the grave (which Kirkman eventually enclosed with a fence almost like a shrine), see Kirkman to AAAG-TFB, May 26, 1868, LR, AC, T. Kirkman's hearing of "Col. Baker" is in Kirkman to AAAG-TFB, July 9, 1867; and the Davis County connection through Baker's sisters is in Kirkman to AAAG-TFB, August 22, 1867, ibid. See also, Nita Jaynes and Willard Jaynes, "Cass County, Texas: Short Sketches of Its History and People" (Unpublished typescript, 1972, Microfilm No. 0962246, L. D. S. Family History Center, Tucson), 61, for Baker's family in that area. Legend has Baker's lair at a place now called Baker's Slough. See Tarpley, *Place Names of Northeast Texas*, 15. Eason, "Cullen Baker," 10, claims that the fatal shot was really aimed at Kirkman who ducked. Titus, whom he refers to erroneously as a sergeant, was not so lucky and took the whole blast. This might explain Kirkman's unusual reverence over Titus' gravesite. The incident was also reported in "Record of Criminal Offenses Committed in the State of Texas" (3 ms. vols., AC, T) vol. III, case #2154. A citizen of Douglassville, L. M. Rollins, who saw the soldiers crossing the Sulphur River, had spurred his horse ahead to warn Baker. Rollins was later arrested at Jefferson but jumped bail. See 1st Lt. Adam Malloy to Kirkman, September 26, 1867 (including a petition of allegedly trustworthy citizens attesting to Rollins' good reputation and posting bond) and Kirkman to Malloy, October 31, 1867 (endorsement), Kirkman to AAAG-TFB, October 31, 1867, ROC, AC, T. Crouch and Brice, *Cullen Baker*, 75–76, have the most exciting version of the killing of Private Titus. Baker challenged the Yankees to do anything about his presence, Kirkman and his escort attacked Baker in a ten-pin alley and a general gunfight erupted, dozens of shots being fired, as Kirkman and his men retreated to the courthouse and Baker fled, hit in the arm.

46. Kirkman to AAAG-TFB, September 4, 1867, LR, AC, T. See also, Richter, "'The Revolver Rules the Day'," 303–32; Crouch and Brice, *Cullen Baker*, 75. Eason, "Cullen Baker," 9–10, has the attack on Brown and Kirkman made as a prelude to the shooting of Titus in Boston. Kirkman's letters seem to make them unrelated incidents. Worse yet for the Federals, Eason says that Baker ambushed the party alone and that the Yankees panicked and ran. One way or the other, however, Baker blamed Kirkman for the wound in his arm.

47. For the wagon ambush and pursuit, Kirkman to AAAG-TFB, October 8, 14, 1867; Kirkman to 1st. Lt. John S. Allanson, October 8, 1867; and the Arkansas expedition, aided by Lt. Willis from Rocky Comfort, Kirkman to AAAG-TFB, October 26, 1867, another report on Baker is Kirkman to AAAG-TFB, November 13, 1867, all in LR, AC, T. See also, Kirkman to AAAG-TFB, October 31, 1867, ROC, AC, T.

48. Crouch and Brice, *Cullen Baker*, 91–92; Eason, "Cullen Baker," 11–12. Baker's political campaign is in Bartholomew, *Cullen Baker*, 50, 54, 63, 127–28 (quote), 129. The effectiveness of the "New Rebellion" is amply illustrated in recollections of the movement given years later. See I. U. Taylor, "Swamp Fox of the Sulphur, or Life and Times of Cullen Montgomery Baker" (Unpublished undated typescript, UT), *passim*. Taylor got his information by interviewing an old army comrade of Baker in 1926 and passing time may have affected the accuracy of the informant's chronology. Eason sees the Howell Smith murder as the beginning of the end of Baker's popular support, "Cullen Baker," 11.

49. The Texas rewards are in Kirkman to AAAG-TFB, May 24, 27, 1868, LR, AC, T; AAAG-TFB to Kirkman, June 9, 1868, ES, AC, T; Clarksville *Standard*, September 19, 1868, and grew out of the Titus shooting. Baker's description is in Kirkman to AAAG-TFB, September 4, 1867, LR, AC, T. The Arkansas reward is in Powell Clayton, *Aftermath of the Civil War in Arkansas* (New York: Neale Publishing Co., 1915), 115. See also, Johnson, "Cullen Baker," 235; Eason, "Cullen Baker," 10.

50. The troops are ordered to Boston in AAAG-TFB to AAAG-District of Texas (DT), June 10, 23, 1867, LS, AC, T. Their presence and number is reported in Kirkman to AAAG-TFB, July 31, August 31, September 30, October 31, November 30 (could get along without), 1867, ROC, AC, T. There was a quirk in the army district boundaries until 1868 that placed northeastern Texas in the District of Louisiana, that was not mirrored in the Bureau boundaries, which followed the exact state lines. Thus Texas Bureau men in Marshall had to appeal to New Orleans for military support instead of through normal channels to Austin. Evidently no one knew exactly where the boundary was so Kirkman got soldiers from both commands. See 1st Lt. I. M. Beebe to AAAG-DT, May 26, 1866, LR, DT, RG 393, NARA, and Bvt. Maj. Gen. J. B. Kiddoo to Bvt. Maj. Gen. Absalom Baird, June 19, 1866, Kiddoo to Howard, July 20, 1866, ES, AC, T, for complaints about the command system, and SO 217 (December 23, 1867, Printed Orders, FMD, RG 94, NARA) for the combining of the posts of Marshall and Jefferson with the rest of the army's Texas command. The troopers were from Co. H, 6th Cavalry, and

the foot soldiers (including the murdered Private Titus) were from Co. C, 20th Infantry. The rifle company usually served as mounted infantry. See Monthly Roster Reports, Sixth Cavalry Regiment, Returns from Regular Army Cavalry Regiments, 1833–1916, Microcopy 744, Roll 61, NARA, and Monthly Roster Reports, Twentieth Infantry Regiment, Returns from Regular Army Infantry Regiments, 1821–1916, Microcopy 665, Roll 211, NARA, respectively, for the personnel in Kirkman's guard.

51. Kirkman to AAAG-TFB, December 31, 1867 (removal of infantry), January 31, February 29, 1868 (removal of cavalry), ROC, AC, T; medical problems in Kirkman to AAAG-TFB, July 31, ROC, AC, T, and Kirkman to AAAG-TFB, April 17, 1868, LR, AC, T, where the subassistant commissioner forwards as-yet-unpaid doctor bills. Kirkman often had trouble collecting fines and fees from defendants he found guilty, which he used to finance his office. See Kirkman to AAAG-TFB, May 9, 16, 1868, *ibid.* The differences in policy between Hancock and Reynolds are detailed in Richter, *Army in Texas During Reconstruction*, 124–36.

52. Kirkman to AAAG-TFB, December 22, 1867 (loss of support), March 23, 1868 (remain in safety), LR, AC, T; Kirkman to AAAG-TFB, February 29, 1867 (somewhat singular), March 31, 1868 (complaints), April 30, 1868 (slurred handwriting), ROC, AC, T. Rand's and Brown's denials are in AAAG-TFB to Kirkman, May 8, June 15, 1868, ES, AC, T. For the transfer request, see Kirkman to AAAG-TFB, May 16, 1868, LR, AC, T. Kirkman's skill as a telegrapher is a constant theme of his biography in Clark, *History of the Thirty ninth Illinois*, 540–41.

53. The Orten's Circus riot as described in the next few paragraphs, including all quotes, is from Kirkman to AAAG-TFB, November 22, 1867, LR, AC, T. This document also has a copy of the bond required of Sheriff Duke ($5,000), and a lengthy complaint on his inaction.

54. Kirkman to AAAG-TFB, November 22, December 25, 1867, LR, AC, T.

55. Kirkman to AAAG-TFB, November 27, 1867, *ibid.*

56. Kirkman to AAAG-TFB, December 3, 25, 1867, February 4, 5, July 15, 1868, *ibid.* See also, Kirkman to AAAG-TFB, March 31, 1868, ROC, AC, T, and AAAG-TFB to Kirkman, January 6, 1868, ES, AC, T.

57. Kirkman to AAAG-TFB, December 18, 28, 1867, Starr to Kirkman, February 18, 1868, Kirkman to AAAG-TFB, March 18, June 20, August 21, September 26, 29, 1868, LR, AC, T, and AAAG-TFB to Kirkman, September 1, 1868, ES, AC, T. Three years later, Teller was tried before the military commission for assault with intent to kill, and the murder of Kirkman and the robbing of the dead agent's body. The

charges against Kirkman were dropped from lack of evidence, and Teller's assault charge was dropped as the statute of limitations for such a crime in Texas criminal law had been exceeded. See GO No. 26, February 10, 1870, FMD, Printed Orders, RG 94 NARA. The author would like to thank John Nance of Jefferson, Texas, for drawing his attention to this important document.

58. Kirkman to AAAG-TFB, December 25, 1867, LR, AC, T

59. Kirkman to AAAG-TFB, December 22 (troops' orders), 25 (attempted arrest), 1867, *ibid.*; AAAG-TFB to Kirkman, January 3, 1868 (promise of witnesses), ES, AC, T. Unnumbered Circular, December 14, 1867, in Kirkman to AAAG-TFB, December 25, 1867, LR, AC, T.

60. Kirkman to AAAG-TFB, September 18, 1868; N. B. Anderson to AAAG-TFB, September 13, 1868, LR, AC, T.

61. AAAG-TFB to Kirkman, September 22, 1868, LS, AC, T. The order is SO 56, September 22, 1868, TFB. Judge Haskins was finally removed a year later, SO 205, August 31, 1869, Fifth Military District (FMD), RG 94, NARA. For the attack on and flight of Rand, see Rand to AAAG-TFB, August 12, 24, 25, 28, 1868, LR, AC, T; and Richter, "'This Blood-thirsty Hole,'" 68–70. The attack on Brown is in Brown to AAAG-TFB, August 31, September 2, 5, 30, October 28, 31, November 13, 1868, LR, AC, T. Brown's tenure in Lamar County is described in Richter, "'The Revolver Rules the Day,'" 303–32. It had taken Baker nine months to recuperate fully from the wound he suffered during the attack on the Howell Smith Plantation (Crouch and Brice, *Cullen Baker*, 96–97; Eason, "Cullen Baker," 12).

62. AAAG-TFB to Kirkman, September 22, 1868, LS, AC, T. See also, Kirkman to AAAG-TFB, September 24, 1868, LR, AC, T. The outlaws' expropriation of the name, goals, and methods of the Ku Klux is in Brown to AAAG-TFB, August 14, 1868, LR, AC, T. Shorkley's name is misspelled "Shankley" in Smallwood, "The Freedmen's Bureau Reconsidered," 320. On the Ku Klux in Texas see Cantrell, "Racial Violence and Reconstruction Politics in Texas," 333–55; James Smallwood, "When the Klan Rode: White Terror in Reconstruction Texas," *Journal of the West* 25 (1986–1987): 4–13; Christopher Bean, "Death of a Carpetbagger: The George Washington Smith Murder and Stockade Trial in Jefferson, Texas, 1868–1869," *Southwestern Historical Quarterly* 112 (2008–2009): 263–94; Barry A. Crouch, "A Spirit of Lawlessness," 220–21; Barbara Leah Clayton, "The Lone Star Conspiracy: Racial Violence and the Ku Klux Klan Terror in Post-Civil War Texas, 1865–1877" (M.A. thesis, Oklahoma State University, 1979); Douglas Hales, "Violence

Perpetrated against African Americans by Whites in Texas during Reconstruction, 1865–1868" (M.A. thesis, Texas Tech University, 1994); and Rebecca A. Kosary, "Regression to Barbarism in Reconstruction : An Analysis of White Violence against African Americans from the Texas Freedman's Bureau Records, 1865–1868" (M.A. thesis, Southwest Texas State University, 1999).

63. Quoted in Clark, *History of the Thirty-ninth Illinois*, 541.

64. The man who relieved Kirkman, Major Shorkley out of Clarksville, first reported the events of the night of October 6–7, 1868, in a letter to headquarters two days after their occurrence, see Shorkley to AAAG-TFB, October 9, 1868, LR, AC, T. Major Shorkley made a formal report on October 15, which included the first-hand account of N. B. Anderson (Anderson to Shorkley, October 15, 1868), the coroners jury (October 7, 1868), and a map of the scene, Shorkley to AAAG-TFB, October 15, 1868, LR, C. General Reynolds sent these documents to General Howard in Washington at the end of the month. See Reynolds to Howard, October 27, 1868 (Shorkley's letter of 9 Oct.), October 29, 1868 (Shorkley's Report of October 15 and enclosures), LS, AC, T. Material in this paragraph from Anderson to Shorkley, October 15, 1868, included in Shorkley to AAAG-TFB, October 15, 1868, LR, AC, T. The account in Crouch and Brice, *Cullen Baker*, 122–26, is accurate: that in Smallwood, "The Freedmen's Bureau Reconsidered," 317, is not.

65. Ambush was Baker's style, and he would never have allowed Kirkman to escape to find help. Baker's preference for the Enfield rifle and buck and ball charge (which has the effect of a more accurate shotgun) is from Bartholomew, *Cullen Baker*, 50–51. But the charge might well have come from an "enormous shotgun," the explanation favored by Eason, "Cullen Baker," 12. See also, Coroner's Jury Report, October 7, 1868, included in Shorkley to AAAG-TFB, October 15, 1868, LR, C. The buck and ball wound ended all chance for Kirkman to defend himself and, judging from his lack of return fire, was probably the first wound he received.

66. See the Coroner's Jury Report, October 7, 1868, included in Shorkley to AAAG-TFB, October 15, 1868, LR, C. Baker's habit of the bullet in the head is from Bartholomew, *Cullen Baker*, 76. Anderson claims that he heard rifle, revolver, and shotgun fire. Anderson to Shorkley, October 15, 1868, included in Shorkley to AAAG-TFB, October 15, 1868, LR, C. See also, Clark, *History of the Thirty-ninth Illinois*, 541.

67. Anderson to Shorkley, October 15, 1868, included in Shorkley to AAAG-TFB, October 15, 1868, LR, C.

68. Anderson to Shorkley, October 15, 1868, included in *ibid.*

69. Shorkley to AAAG-TFB, October 15, 1868, LR, C.

70. Robbery in *ibid.*, the quote is in Anderson to Shorkley, October 15, 1868 included in *ibid.*

71. Coroner's Jury Report, October 7, 1868, included in *ibid.* See also, GO No. 26, February 10, 1870, FMD, Printed Orders, RG 94 NARA, for the items stolen from Kirkman's body and their assessed value.

72. Shorkley to AAAG-TFB, October 15, 1868, LR, C. See also, Johnson, "Cullen Baker," 236, and Richter, "'A Dear Little Job'," 197.

73. Marshall M. Kirkman in Chicago heard of his brother's death in a local newspaper, and queried Howard about it (AAAG-C to M. M. Kirkman, October 24, 1868, LS, C). Howard immediately telegraphed General Reynolds in Texas (AAAG-C to Reynolds, October 24, 1868, LS, C). Meanwhile, Howard assured Marshall Kirkman that his brother was uninjured according to the latest information available in Washington. Howard also said that General Reynolds would do his best to protect any Bureau agent (AAAG-C to M. M. Kirkman, October 24, 1868, LS, C). But Marshall Kirkman already had an anonymous communique from Shreveport describing his brother's murder (Clark, *History of the Thirty Ninth Illinois*, 541). The next day, however, Howard had received Reynolds' telegram of William G. Kirkman's murder, and notified the family (Reynolds to Howard, October 24, 1868, LS, AC, T; AAAG-C to M. M. Kirkman, October 25, 1868, LS, C; AAAG-TFB to J. T. Kirkman, October 31, 1868, AAAG-TFB to M. M. Kirkman, November 5, 1868, LS, AC, T). Lieutenant Kirkman acknowledged receipt of the relevant papers, nine separate items, a month and a half later from Ringgold Barracks, Texas (J. T. Kirkman to AAAG-TFB, December 15, 1868, LR, AC, T; AAAG-TFB to J. Kirkman, October 31, 1868, LS, AC, T, has a full inventory of the papers). Marshall Kirkman evidently had no idea of Joel Kirkman's exact duty station with the 17th Infantry (M. M. Kirkman to AAAG-TFB, November 4, 1868, LR, AC, T). The Army paid all of Willam G. Kirkman's debts and the funeral expenses (endorsement on Reynolds to Howard, October 27, 1868, LR, C; AAAG-TFB to Shorkley, October 28, 1868, LS, AC, T).

74. Shorkley to AAAG-TFB, October 9, 1868, LS, AC, T.

75. Shorkley to AAAG-TFB, October 15, 1868, LR, C. See also, Crouch and Brice, *Cullen Baker*, 126–27.

76. The Jefferson episode is described in Allen W. Trelease, "Texas: The Knights of the Rising Sun," in his *White Terror: The Ku Klux*

Conspiracy and Southern Reconstruction (New York: Harper & Row, 1971), 137–48. A more recent account is Christopher Bean, "Death of a Carpetbagger," 263–94.

77. The campaign is in Richter, *Army in Texas During Reconstruction*, 146–47; Smallwood, Crouch, and Peacock, *Murder and Mayhem*, 79–81. First Lieutenant Cyrus S. Roberts, a headquarters aide, had called for such a campaign thirteen months previously, when he served as subassistant commissioner at Clarksville, see Roberts to AAAG-TFB, November 12, 1867, LS, AC, T. Kirkman had made a similar proposal in his monthly report, January 1, 1868, as did Shorkley, his successor, later in his report of October 31, 1868, ROC, AC, T. Again, possibly being too present-minded, the Chaffee-Tolman campaign is reminiscent of General David Patraeus' modern "surge" in Iraq, using mobile Striker Battalions.

78. Bartholomew, *Cullen Baker*, 84. Eason, "Cullen Baker," 46–47, 67, says that Baker's own in-laws poisoned him first and Orr and a half-dozen henchmen then came up and shot the body full of holes. Orr's account was dismissed by locals as related by a "Republican Carpetbagger and a liar to boot" (Eason, "Cullen Baker," 67).

79. Smallwood, "The Freedman's Bureau Reconsidered," 317–18.

80. Crouch, *Freedmen's Bureau and Black Texans*, 100–1.

81. Randy Finley, *From Slavery to Uncertain Freedom: The Freedmen's Bureau in Arkansas, 1865–1869* (Fayetteville: University of Arkansas Press, 1996), 167; Crouch,"' To Enslave the Rising Generation,'" 280–81n6. For the change of Reconstruction's heroes of yesteryear into villains and *vice versa*, all of it viewed as progress in historical scholarship, see Thomas J. Pressly, "Racial Attitudes, Scholarship, and Reconstruction: A Review of History," *Journal of Southern History* 32 (1966): 88–93.

82. Robert C. Lieberman, "The Freedmen's Bureau and the Politics of Institutional Structure," *Social Science History* 18 (1994): 405–37.

83. These issues constantly haunted the Bureau at all levels with no real answers, see Richter, *Overreached on All Sides*, 258–561.I BET THIS IS JUST 61

84. Richter, *Overreached on All Sides*, 287–305. Nowhere was the influence of headquarters' desires over local extemporizing better revealed than its rejection of former Lt. Jacob C. DeGress and Capt. Samuel Sloan's policy of seizing all Navasota valley cotton without a stamp of approval from one of them, showing that the freedmen had been fairly paid. Headquarters, in the form of roaming agent, ex-Lt. William H. Sinclair, at first endorsed the seizure policy but quickly reneged

when planters began to complain of delays and dropping prices (*ibid.*, 137–38). Sinclair's influence in this and other headquarters policies from 1866 onward proves Crouch's flippant rejection of William L. Richter, "Who Was the Real Head of the Texas Freedmen's Bureau? The Role of Brevet Colonel William H. Sinclair as Acting Assistant Inspector General," *Military History of the Southwest* 20 (1990), 121–56, as "very strained" (Crouch, *Freedmen's Bureau and Black Texans*, 151, 179) came from pure ignorance as to how the Bureau headquarters in Texas actually functioned, which is explained in another context in Franklin B. Wickwire, *British Subministers and Colonial America, 1763–1783* (New Brunswick: Princeton University Press, 1966), 3–12.

85. For the notion that the Bureau did all it could, see Smallwood, "The Freedman's Bureau Reconsidered," 317–18; Crouch, *Freedmen's Bureau and Black Texans*, 130–31; Bean,"' A Most Singular and Interesting Attempt'," 485; Andrew J. Torget, "Carpetbagger on the Brazos: The Texas Freedmen's Bureau in Robertson County," http:// glasscock.tamu.edu/agora/winter00/torget.html, 12. For the notion that the Bureau left blacks at the mercy of white supremacists, see Walt Bailey, "Missed Opportunity: The Freedmen's Bureau and Black Freedom in Brazoria County, Texas" (unpublished paper in the hands of the author), 61–63. For the notion that the whole program failed because "almost" was not "enough," see Richter, *Overreached on All Sides*, 304–5.

86. The phrase, "hell is paved with good intention," is usually attributed to the medieval Cistercian monk, St. Bernard of Clairvaux, who created the rules followed by the Knights Templar. It was also a favorite aphorism of the English writer and critic, Samuel Johnson. See E. D. Hirsch, Jr., Joseph F. Kett, and James Trefil, eds., *The New Dictionary of Cultural Literacy, Third Edition* (New York: Houghton Mifflin Company, 2002); James Boswell, *Life of Johnson,* ed. R. W. Chapman and J. D. Fleeman (London: Oxford World's Classics paperback, 1998), 624.

CHAPTER 3

The World Turned Upside Down?: The Military Occupation of Victoria and Calhoun Counties, 1865–1867

by

Charles D. Spurlin

The last remnant of formal Confederate military resistance in the Civil War ended on June 2, 1865, with the capitulation of the Trans-Mississippi Department by Maj. Gen. E. Kirby Smith. Soon thereafter, federal forces under Maj. Gen. Gordon Granger, commander of the Thirteenth Army Corps and overall commander of the Union troops in Texas, commenced occupation duty in the state and thus began the first phase of Reconstruction that lasted until 1867. Cavalry units made their way from Louisiana through eastern Texas to reach their assignments in San Antonio and Austin. In addition to the Thirteenth Army Corps and the cavalry regiments, troops from the Twenty-fifth Army Corps were transported by water from City Point, Virginia, to the Texas coast for duty at Indianola and Corpus Christi, but the bulk of the corps was instructed to take positions along the Rio Grande. Meanwhile, the Fourth Army Corps was transported from New Orleans "to Indianola, from thence to Victoria, and ordered to occupy the line from that point to San Antonio." Further organizational refinement of the federal troops occurred on July 20 when the state was divided into the Eastern, Central, and Western districts under General Orders, No. 4 issued in New Orleans by Maj. Gen. Edward R. S. Canby, commander of the Department of Louisiana and Texas.[1]

Under the arrangement, the Eastern District with its headquarters at Houston was comprised of the area "east of the Brazos and Navasota Rivers and the meridian of the town of Springfield, on the Navasota River, except the posts included in the Western District of Louisiana." The Central District was composed of the region "between the Nueces

River and the Eastern District of Texas, as above defined" with temporary headquarters at Victoria whereas the Western District lay "between the Rio Grande and the Nueces River." Brownsville was designated as the headquarters of the latter district. Maj. Gen. Joseph A. Mower was placed in charge of the Eastern District while Maj. Gen. David S. Stanley was given command of the Central District, and Maj. Gen. Frederick Steele took control of the Western District.[2]

Further reorganization of the federal forces in Texas occurred during the summer of 1865. The Department of Texas, which had been in existence since 1853, was omitted when the Department of the Gulf was created on February 23, 1862. However, on November 8, 1862, it was placed in the newly formed department. With the reorganization of the army's military divisions and departments on June 27, 1865, the Department of Texas reappeared and was attached to the Military Division of the Gulf. Maj. Gen. Horatio G. Wright assumed command of the department on

Illustration 4. Maj. Gen. David S. Stanley. (Courtesy of Library of Congress)

August 6 with headquarters at Galveston. Exactly a year later, the Department of Texas was merged into the Department of the Gulf.[3]

After the occupying forces arrived in Texas, military commanders became befuddled as to their proper role within the communities. To clear up the confusion, department headquarters in Galveston issued a series of instructions. Under the rules laid out, military authorities could render civilian officials "assistance as may be necessary to enforce the laws against those who may violate them," but otherwise, military personnel were to limit their efforts "as far as consistent with the good of the service and the protection of the interest of the government, strictly to Military matters." Only when "the United States is a party, as where officers and Soldiers, employee's [*sic*] of the Government and freedmen are concerned," the right to be tried "before a Military tribunal . . . will be exercised." However, freedmen could be tried in a civil court "whenever in the opinion of the Military Commander or the Agent of the Freedman's Bureau, it can be done with a reasonable assurance that justice will be obtained." To do the latter would relieve "the Military from a heavy burden." Military officials were further instructed that even though they might believe justice would not be served in a civil court, the accused should be relinquished to an existing "Court of competent jurisdiction . . . without regard to the probable result of the trial."[4]

Union soldiers were euphoric when the war ended. They looked forward to returning to their homes and renewing their relationships with their wives, children, and extended family members whom many of the troops had not seen for months or years. Consequently, when the soldiers were ordered to Texas to serve occupation duty, they became extremely upset. Members of the 8th Kansas Infantry Regiment considered their enlistment concluded at the end of the conflict, a view that was similarly held by soldiers in other military units. Adding to their frustration was the number of soldiers who were being mustered and discharged from the service and were returning to their home communities. For the most part, the white volunteer troops who were leaving the military belonged to regiments that had entered the service in 1862. On the other hand, those who were required to remain in the service had reenlisted under the 1864 Veteran Volunteer Act. From Maj. Gen. David S. Stanley's perspective, these men "seemed entitled to first favor and the favor the men desired was to be mustered out," but "with sighs and some grumbling, they submitted."Another major contingent retained was the black regiments that composed the Twenty-fifth Army Corps. These units as a component of the Western District were for the most part ordered to the Rio Grande.

However, before the Fourth Army Corps arrived, some of the regiments served within the Central District, for instance Indianola, Victoria, and Corpus Christi.[5]

Black servicemen were just as chagrined over having to remain in the service, holding similar views as their white counterparts, but they were also disturbed over the assignment to Texas out of fear "the officers were going to take them to Cuba and sell them." One black soldier in the 116th Regiment, United States Colored Troops, Sgt. Maj. Thomas Boswell, thought the troops had not been released from military service because they were "' slave State troops.'" He hoped his view was incorrect, and the federal government "will not be guilty of this great wrong toward us, as we have tried to do our duty." Col. James Shaw Jr., commander of the 7th Infantry Regiment, U.S.C.T., theorized that the reason black soldiers disdained going to Texas was because when they were slaves "Texas had been held up to them as a sort of hell to which they would be sold if they misbehaved."[6]

Frightened or not of duty in the Lone Star State, black soldiers were the first to enter Victoria and Calhoun counties. Stanley's Fourth Army Corps comprised the Central District, but shipping delays prevented its arrival until July. Consequently, the Eighth Heavy Artillery, U.S.C.T., an element in the Twenty-fifth Army Corps was evidently the first federal contingent to reach the two counties. A black soldier, "Rufus," after he arrived at Indianola, expressed his disgust for the town in a letter published in the August 12, 1865, edition of *The Anglo-African* newspaper. In his missive, he wrote that Indianola was not much better than Brazos de Santiago, "and the people are not worth speaking of. They are all Germans, of recent importation, and if they are a part of the Texas desperados of whom we have heard, I do not think we will have any trouble in teaching them their true level." Not knowing the reception Union troops might receive from Victorians, the regiment was assigned to occupy the town and to assist the acting provost marshal with "such force as may be needed." To the satisfaction of the troops, they encountered no notable opposition from the local citizens. However, that was not the case elsewhere in the area.[7]

Initially, the landing of troops at Indianola did not go smoothly. Because the port's wharf was completely destroyed, the 7th Infantry Regiment, U.S.C.T., used scows and small schooners over a span of three days, June 25–27, 1865, to disembark. From his headquarters in Indianola, the commander of the foregoing regiment as well as the First Brigade in the Second Division, Twenty-Fifth Army Corps, Col. James Shaw Jr., placed regiments at Old Town and Indianola, four companies at Port Lavaca, and three companies at Matagorda, once all the federal units reached shore. When the units arrived at Matagorda, a young boy witnessed the landing. He was completely surprised by the appearance of the troops, having never before seen federal soldiers. As the men disembarked, the youngster ran home yelling at the top of his voice, "' Mamma, mamma, the Yankees have come and they are just as black as niggers.'" Duty for the soldiers at Port Lavaca went well, but at Indianola, the black troops experienced hostility from the residents who made numerous unspecified complaints to the commanding officer. Shaw maintained that the problems with the local residents came from those who were "stay at homes." He commented there was not an instance where any issue arose from a former Confederate soldier. In a complimentary tone, Shaw stated that these men actually "interfered to prevent the abuse of Union men and freedmen." Victor Rose, an ex-Confederate soldier and author from Victoria, perhaps best stated the prevailing attitude of those who had served in the Confederate military by remarking, "We made a manly fight, and were whipped; and it was just as manly to honestly recognize the fact, and accept the result. To repine, and upbraid fortune was but to 'plead the baby act;' and to nurse—vindictive resolutions was to exchange the high precepts of civilization for the groveling code of the savage."[8]

By July 9, 1865, elements of the Fourth Army Corps unloaded at Indianola. The 59th Illinois Volunteer Infantry Regiment claimed the honor of being the first federal unit to land. As each regiment reached shore, it was instructed to proceed "at once" to Green Lake, some twenty-three miles inland, where there was adequate fresh water and a reasonable amount of timber to accommodate the soldiers. The hasty movement that was perpetuated on the troops caused nightmarish hardships. Some of the men were still feeling the effects of being seasick, sufficient time was not permitted the troops to locate drinking water to replenish their canteens, and an untold number of the soldiers having laid idle for days aboard the ships were simply not in any physical condition to make a sustained march. The men whose canteens were either empty or very low of water resorted to replenishing their containers with water from "cow ponds" that were filled from the summer showers. Even though the water was filthy, the soldiers "had learned by the hardest kind of experience, to take anything, till they could get something better." A compounding problem for the troops was the mid-summer South Texas heat and humidity and an overabundance of mosquitoes that preyed on the soldiers. If there was an upside to the movement, some of the marching was conducted at night, allowing the men to escape the scorching sunrays. Many of the soldiers could not keep pace with their comrades and fell by the wayside. When the lead units arrived at their final destination, water wagons were dispatched to the prostrate soldiers who lay along the route for ten miles or more. By the time the march ended, those who managed to reach Green Lake with their commands were totally exhausted and "[lay] down nearer dead than alive." For hours afterward, the stragglers who still had sufficient energy to complete the journey, having disposed of their equipment, drifted into their respective companies. Whether the criticism was valid or not, troops blamed a drunken guide for their difficulties.[9]

While the various regiments were at Green Lake waiting for orders to move further inland, some of the soldiers amused themselves by shooting alligators and deer. Grapes and pecans were also gathered from which some of the men made wine, pies, cobblers, "and a variety of other very palatable dishes." Other means of passing the time included playing card games and reading novels.[10]

Shortly after the first regiments of the Fourth Army Corps arrived at Green Lake, they were ordered to occupy several communities, including Victoria, Goliad, Clinton, and other locations deemed necessary by the division and brigade commanders to suppress "plundering, robbery, jayhawking, etc., throughout that section of the State." The distribution of the troops in some instances replaced units of the black regiments that were already serving in the area.[11]

Restlessness among the federal soldiers did not abate after they arrived in Texas. Whether stationed in Victoria and Calhoun counties or other sections of the state, they remained very disturbed over having been ordered to the Lone Star State. In addition to their former complaints, a new one arose: comrade deaths. Soldiers became visibly upset whenever they witnessed an acquaintance die of an illness without having the opportunity to visit family members at the conclusion of hostilities. Desertions, or French leave as it was known, lack of discipline, and intoxication among the troops occurred frequently. A variety of tactics were used by the military commands to deal with the dissatisfaction such as roll call three times a day and details sent out every few days whether warranted or not.[12]

Maj. Gen. David S. Stanley, commander of the Fourth Army Corps, arrived at Indianola on July 30, 1865, and immediately made his way to Victoria where he established his headquarters. Shortly afterwards, on August 1, his corps was dissolved and renamed the Army of the Central District of Texas. Stanley remained in Victoria until October when the headquarters was shifted to San Antonio. As more and more troops arrived on the coast and made their way inland by way of Green Lake, a tent encampment, Camp Stanley, was created some four miles northwest of Victoria. From this location, regiments proceeded to the Alamo City and other points. Evidently, Stanley's command in Victoria experienced no serious confrontations with local residents, only the standard declarations condemning the troops for their random shooting of beeves, cutting down pecan trees, and removing wooden fences. Because the area was a prairie with little timber, the federal troops resorted to acquiring firewood in any manner they could. Stanley ultimately suppressed the destruction of the property "but not until several court martials had been called and the men severely punished." After his departure, a series of difficulties arose that created a substantially negative attitude among the townspeople toward the military.[13]

Illustration 5. Col. Thomas E. Rose. (Courtesy of Library of Congress)

One of the federal units assigned for duty in Victoria was the 77th Pennsylvania Infantry Regiment commanded by Col. Thomas E. Rose who possessed a distinguished military career. During the Battle of Chickamauga, he was captured and placed in Libby Prison at Richmond, Virginia. After a few months' confinement, Rose led the largest prisoner escape of the war. Under his supervision, federal officers used a pocket knife, some chisels, a piece of rope, a rubber cloth, and a wooden spittoon to dig a tunnel to the outside in a mere seventeen days. Of the 109 officers who escaped on February 9, 1864, forty-eight were recaptured, including Rose. Rose's re-imprisonment lasted three more months before he was exchanged on April 30 and returned to duty with his regiment.[14]

During October 1865, the Pennsylvania regiment was assigned to Victoria and experienced few notable controversies until November 2. On that date, Henry E. Bradford, an ex-Confederate officer and future city mayor, and Sam A. White, a district judge appointed by Provisional Governor Andrew J. Hamilton and a Whig editor of the *Victoria Advocate*, visited Rose's office. Prior to the meeting, the judge experienced a dispute with the colonel over the closing of the *Advocate* because of a story the newspaper ran on an officer who left the community owing White forty-nine dollars. This earlier encounter may have been a factor in shaping the events that unfolded on November 2.[15]

During the session, White complained to the colonel that federal soldiers "had destroyed his dwelling house and Kitchens etc." and requested the necessary steps he should take to be compensated for the destroyed property. Rose replied that the judge should "make a plain statement in writing of the facts and present it to the Military authorities." In the ongoing conversation, White further accused the troops of cutting "down all his pecan trees and . . . most of the young timber," and he asked the colonel how he should proceed in getting paid for the destruction of the trees. Rose completely rejected the latter charge since the military had issued orders prohibiting such action, surmising that "marauding parties" were to blame, and therefore, he opined there would be no compensation from the government. He further stated there were several similar complaints lodged. However, Rose claimed to have personally checked out the charges and found that "not one tenth one twentieth and not one fortieth Pecan tree[s]" had actually been cut. The judge passionately responded that "he would make no allegation in regard to his timber that he could not prove." Both the colonel and White had by this time become very testy, raising their voices to a high pitch with an abundance of profanity. Rose angrily remarked "that he did not care a Goddam [*sic*] whether . . . White . . . got any pay or not." The judge in a similar vein stated he didn't "Care a damn or God Dam [*sic*] for" Rose. Up until the swearing took place, the three men were seated, but when the heated verbal exchanges were made, they stood up. As they did so, the colonel sternly told the two Victorians to leave. As Bradford and White strolled toward the door to exit the room, the judge for some unknown reason pulled a pocket knife from his pants pocket whereupon Rose made mention of the knife and grabbed a pistol. Seeing the firearm in the colonel's hand, the Victorians hastened their pace. As White was about to make his way through the door, Rose fired his pistol indiscriminately, causing the judge to immediately get "behind the door facing or wall of the room on the out Side." Two additional shots were fired. One of the bullets grazed White's skin in the "right leg just below the cap of the knee . . . and inflicted only a slight wond [*sic*]." As quick as the two Victorians could, they removed themselves from the premises. Fewer than fifteen minutes passed after the episode when White and Bradford were arrested on an order by Rose and placed in the county jail.[16]

In a move to free himself from the county jail, White, being a district judge, issued a writ of habeas corpus on his behalf and presented it to the sheriff. The judge claimed that he was illegally deprived of his liberty. As soon as Rose received the document, the colonel considered White's action foolish and told Sheriff John L. Cunningham if the peace officer didn't want to spend time in jail with the judge, "he'd better keep mum." Unfazed by Rose's action, White issued a writ for the arrest of the colonel. Although the notice was not to be delivered directly to the colonel, the carrier presented it to him nonetheless. When Rose saw the second writ, he became outraged and ordered that "no further communication [was] allowed by citizens except under Survailence [*sic*]." Dejected over the ongoing controversy, White "made a proposition to drop the Matter if turned loose." The judge's incarceration lasted one night and a portion of the next day. However, a contemporary wrote that White actually remained imprisoned until "the bellicose warrior from the state of 'Brotherly Love' became sober."[17]

The confrontation between White and Rose was only one episode between the colonel or his subordinates and Victorians in November 1865. Victoria County Chief Justice Christopher Carsner, an appointee of Governor Hamilton who possessed Unionist proclivities and was a respected individual among the general population in the county, provided the governor with a list of injustices committed by the Union occupiers during the month. Included in his enumeration was a charge that a Robert D.

Tippitt was held in jail without charges for an extended period without food except for what he purchased from the guards. A lawyer who was employed to handle his case was informed by the military authorities that if he "pressed Matters to [*sic*] fast He would himself be placed in jail." Meanwhile, an unidentified person "with a Gold Leaf on his shoulders came forward . . . and offered" to assist in getting the jailed man released for fifty dollars. After Tippett's lawyer paid the man twenty-five dollars, the fellow vanished and was never seen again, leaving the issue unresolved. Another instance of injustice given by Carsner was Colonel Rose's summary removal of William S. Glass, an attorney, from his office building.[18]

Apparently, Rose considered Glass' property an ideal location for the provost marshal and another person especially since the structure had a fireplace that could be used during cold days. The attorney was forced to remove his law books and furniture into an out-of-the-way building that had no means to keep Glass, "a Sickly Man," warm as afforded in the structure he was required to vacate. Consequently, Glass was unable to "attend to any Business except in very pleasant weather."[19]

An edict by Rose that was soundly condemned was an order prohibiting the issuing of permits to sell beer produced in Victoria. Many local citizens resented the colonel's action on the grounds that the community suffered losses of revenue, and their private rights were violated, a cherished commodity by Victorians. One storeowner directly affected by Rose's order was a German merchant who assumed he had good relations with the military. However, the proprietor discovered otherwise when he was accused of violating the restriction. He was forced to stop doing business and ordered to relinquish the key to the building. The merchant vigorously protested the closing of the store to Rose and department officials, maintaining that "he had done nothing to merit this severity." After two months, he was given permission to reopen. When the businessman went into his store, he discovered it had been ransacked. Most of his cigars were gone, "and quantities of the 'old Bourbon' had evaporated." Soldiers were immediately blamed for the destruction since the military possessed the key to the establishment.[20]

Relative calm existed between Victorians and the new occupying force after Colonel Rose and his regiment were mustered out of the service on December 5 and boarded ships at Indianola for the trek to Pennsylvania. However, tranquility lasted only until May 1866 when Benjamin F. Hill was murdered by federal troops when companies from the 7th Regiment, U.S.C.T. were stationed in Victoria. In charge of the occupying force was

Capt. Harlan P. Spaulding, a native of New York who had entered the service as a private in the 44th New York Infantry Regiment in September 1863. Later that year he was commissioned a captain in the black regiment and assumed command of Company E. Before being discharged from the service, Spaulding obtained the rank of lieutenant colonel.[21]

On the afternoon of May 23, 1866, Hill, a pioneer Texan who was a former sheriff of Bexar County and a company commander in the Mexican War, and John Black, a former federal soldier, were in George M. Jackson's Smile Saloon. For some unknown reason, the two men, standing approximately a yard and a half apart and intoxicated, boisterously exchanged heated words. Samuel McDonald, an employee at the saloon, turned toward the commotion. What he saw was a stoneware pitcher in Black's hand, and Hill's derringer pointed at the former Union soldier. Not wishing to have any altercation in the saloon, McDonald told Black to leave. Black responded by remarking "he was not afraid." No sooner did the man utter the words than Hill fired his weapon. Black "staggered forward & said he was shot." He died shortly thereafter. Later, Drs. Sherman Goodwin and James B. P. January examined the body and reported the bullet penetrated Black's "breast bone and probably cutting the aorta." Captain Spaulding took Hill into custody, but very soon afterwards turned him over to Deputy Sheriff Harold Garnett who placed Hill in the county jail.[22]

Sometime in the early evening, a mob of white federal soldiers gathered at the jail, supposedly intoxicated and agitated over Hill killing a person who had served in the Union army. When John W. Abel, who was in the general vicinity, walked toward the jail to find out what was taking place, he was stopped by some of the soldiers and told to leave since he was wearing "citizen's clothes." Heeding their advice, Abel withdrew, but remained close enough to hear yells and to see "a man in light clothes jump out of [the] jail Door & into [the] crowd." As the mob dispersed, Abel went to the jail and "saw Hill . . . hanging under the jail steps apparently dead." At the coroner's inquest, Dr. W. G. Thornton ruled Hill died from a combination of club blows to the head and hanging. During the mob action, neither Spaulding's troops nor local law enforcement officials intervened. The actual culprits in the death of Hill and their precise motive are unknown. But, because the 18th New York Cavalry Regiment and the 3rd Michigan Infantry Regiment were encamped outside the town waiting to be mustered from the service, members of these two units have been blamed. Regardless of who was at fault, Spaulding came under heavy criticism from the local residents for his inaction. Denunciation of the captain became even more intense shortly afterwards when two soldiers in his command killed William Walker.[23]

On July 22, Walker, an employee of a local brewer G. J. Kraft, was instructed by the proprietor to keep men off the property who wanted to visit a black girl who was another employee. He, therefore, armed himself with a pistol loaded with blanks and fired a few shots in the air to keep people away. Nearby were Privates Franklin Smith and William Stanley who were on guard duty but unarmed. Upon hearing the shots, the soldiers immediately went to the guardhouse, some two hundred yards from the brewery, grabbed their muskets with bayonets attached, and proceeded to the location where the shots were fired. They were unaware of why the pistol was discharged. Perhaps, Stanley and Smith thought that the woman, with whom they were acquainted, was being harmed. When the two soldiers arrived at the brewery, they saw Walker "standing outside the yard" and "ordered him to advance." However, Walker was a recent arrival from Germany and possessed a limited English vocabulary. Not understanding the command, he didn't move, "whereupon Franklin Smith rushed upon him and stabed [*sic*] him with his bayonet," penetrating Walker's abdomen some six inches. Not long afterwards the man died. When the news spread around town of Walker's death, some residents called for Spaulding to take punitive action against the two soldiers. This he did not do. Almost a month later, on August 20, a district court grand jury assembled in Victoria and indicted Smith and Stanley for murder.[24]

Troops under Spaulding's command continued to be a source of dissatisfaction in Victoria. After receiving a litany of criticisms on the behavior of the soldiers, Governor James W. Throckmorton sought a remedy from Maj. Gen. Samuel P. Heintzelman, commander of the subdistrict at San Antonio. Of particular importance to the governor was the murder of Walker. Throckmorton insisted that Stanley and Smith be arrested and tried in a civil court. After a review of the charges, Heintzelman informed the governor that he was "satisfied that many illegal & unlawful acts have been committed by Capt. Spaulding's command," and would forward the gathered information to the district commander. Eventually, the issue reached Gen. Phil Sheridan who ordered the two soldiers to be turned over to local officials for trial. But, by this time, Stanley and Smith had been discharged from the service in Maryland and could not be located. Even after the federal volunteer regiments were mustered from service and were replaced by regular units in the latter part of 1866, problems between the military and civilians such as destruction of wooden fences continued, but the issues between the two sides were not at the same high intensity as before.[25]

Unlike Victoria County, Calhoun County's experience with the military was less troublesome. Unquestionably, disagreements existed between members of the federal units and local citizens. Soldiers were accused of "driving off . . . hogs," indiscriminately firing their weapons and endangering people, destroying property, and rudeness toward the residents. During the summer of 1866, a serious difference of opinion emerged between Col. James Shaw Jr. and the editor of the *Indianola Times*, causing the colonel to make a futile attempt to close the newspaper. Whenever issues did arise, the military made serious efforts to resolve the difficulties with local individuals. Intoxication among the soldiers undoubtedly played a role in the problems because when regular troops assumed command of Indianola, an order was issued prohibiting all citizens from "selling or giving Liquor or any Spirituous or Malt Liquor of any kind to the United States Forces stationed" in the port town. Generally, the soldiers, particularly the black troops, found Port Lavaca more hospitable than Indianola in the beginning, but they "learned afterward to like the place much better than . . . at first anticipated or believed possible."[26]

Not all behavior was damnable during the military occupation of Calhoun and Victoria counties from 1865–1867. Without the presence of the army the two counties' rapid economic recovery from the abysmal conditions brought about by the Civil War would not have occurred. Thousands of troops passed through the communities either on their way to duty stations in the interior or while traveling from posts at San Antonio or other locations to board ships at Indianola for their respective homes. When the soldiers paused or were stationed at Victoria, Port Lavaca, or Indianola, they invariably purchased clothing, food, and drinks, mainly beer and lots of it. Capt. Leander A. Poor found the prices at Port Lavaca to be extraordinarily high. In a letter to his girlfriend in Massachusetts, he remarked that a pair of boots cost him twelve dollars and fifty cents, "and one of them went to pieces the first time" he put them on. Poor also bought a hat for six dollars and fifty cents. To his chagrin, he "lost it in the bay one windy night, and the next day paid *seven* dollars for another." Military personnel, particularly officers and their wives, served to boost the profits of the Casimir House in downtown Indianola and the Globe Hotel that was situated on the north side of Victoria's DeLeon Plaza by staying at these two establishments.[27]

Money also flowed into the local coffers when the army purchased food supplies, rented wagons, hired teamsters, and bought forage.

Another source of income from the military was the exorbitant rent paid for billeting soldiers and for office space. Brig. Gen. Charles H. Thompkins, who was headquartered in New Orleans and processed vouchers for payment, maintained rent was frequently 100 percent more than what was charged for the equivalent quarters in the northern cities.[28]

Reconstruction by the army of the San Antonio & Mexican Gulf Railway that extended from Port Lavaca to Victoria and the wharf at Indianola were vital to the economic growth of Victoria and Calhoun counties. In 1863, the wharf and a portion of the railroad were destroyed by Confederate troops to prevent either from being used by federal forces. Because Indianola was the port that was essential on the supply route to the interior posts, and the railroad offered desired land transportation when the "hog wallow" prairie was unreliable during inclement weather, the military placed a high priority on the rebuilding of the wharf and the railroad. If the army had not acted for its own self-interest and given the stagnant economies of the two counties that existed in 1865, the rebuilding of the wharf and the railroad would not have taken place as soon as it did. To illustrate this point, the cost of reconstructing the railway was $45,000, and when its owners were billed that amount, they did not have the funds, so the federal government took complete possession of the line and sold it to Charles Morgan, a steamship and railroad entrepreneur. As events unfolded, the wharf, in particular, and the railroad were vital to reopening "the gates of commerce." At Indianola, building materials, manufactured goods, and machinery that passed through the port "restarted as a dribble [in 1865] and quickly became a flood." A similar occurrence took place in Victoria.[29]

Returning Confederate soldiers and the federal troops in the summer of 1865 viewed Victoria as a dismal town. Dry good stores that were well-stocked with merchandise at the outbreak of the Civil War were barren by the end of the conflict. Victor Rose remarked that he went into Jesse O. Wheeler's store and found "absolutely nothing in abundance but space; and the long lines of shelves like skeletons grinning a welcome to the wanderer's return." Many houses and buildings drifted into dilapidated conditions for lack of lumber and paint. A member of the 51st Indiana Veteran Volunteer Infantry Regiment when he reached Victoria commented that the town "presented a very forbidding appearance, with its dirty streets, rough, unpainted, isolated buildings, broken-down doors and dingy rooms." Within two years, rapid changes took place, and Victoria thrived anew. Victor Rose noted in his history of Victoria there was such a quick transformation he made no effort "to preserve chronological order." Stores were restocked, lumber and building materials were more plentiful, houses were repainted, and new businesses were opened, including J. M. Brownson's bank, a first for the town. Jobs were so plentiful that anyone seeking work could find it.[30]

In assessing the military occupation of Calhoun and Victoria counties during the first phase of Reconstruction, there is no denying that soldiers were involved in physical violence, or that they destroyed property. But, there was a positive side to the military's presence in the counties that is too often overshadowed by stories of ill behavior exercised by soldiers. As previously stated, the military played a significant role in the restoration of the economies. Another positive side of the military occupation was the development of a better understanding among the wartime foes, and the resultant crumbling of stereotypes. Northern soldiers who held ideas that all Texans were uneducated or unsophisticated found the opposite to be true. Victorians and people living in Calhoun County came to acknowledge that northerners possessed social and economic values like themselves. Residents who were initially shocked when federal troops arrived soon discovered the soldiers were "at least part human and that they had many tastes in common." Parties given by federal officers were often attended by non-military personnel, and it was not uncommon for poker parties, horse racing events, and galas to consist of local citizens and federal troops. At a Christmas gathering in Indianola, a regimental band played "Yankee Doodle." While the soldiers cheered, the tune "was received in silence by the citizens." Afterwards, to the surprise of all those in attendance, the band played "Dixie." "For a moment there was not a sound from the multitude. Then a one-armed tall boy in a faded Confederate uniform threw back his head and gave the "Rebel Yell." Soon thereafter, "Home Sweet Home" was played, "and the multitude sank into silence; but each Yankee soldier had as many 'Rebs,' male and females, holding on to him as could lay hands on him." Sparking in some instances between "rebel ladies" and the "Boys in Blue" produced marriages. Many of the Union soldiers decided to remain in the Lone Star State after their enlistments expired. Devaluated land prices and the prospect of good jobs were major incentives to do so, but the camaraderie which emerged made their stay palatable.[31]

Recognition of the good side of the military occupation was seldom expressed by the residents in the two counties. There were, of course, exceptions. At the Masonic Hall in Indianola on the evening of September 30, 1866, those in attendance, many of whom were leading citizens of the community, adopted a resolution, and addressed it to Col. James

Shaw Jr., commanding officer of the 7th Infantry Regiment, U.S.C.T., as his unit prepared to embark for Maryland. In the formal statement, there was an expression of appreciation for the military's presence. The men who affixed their signatures to it acknowledged that discords existed in different parts of Texas "even to the destruction of life and property," but in his "command at this place everything has been smooth and tranquil, even beyond our most sanguine hopes." A similar complimentary comment was made by the *Indianola Times* a short time later. "The conduct of the troops," the newspaper stated, "has been truly praiseworthy, and we rejoice that there has been nothing like a collision between the civil and military authorities." It further remarked that "To the credit of the colored troops here, Indianola has witnessed but little flagrant misconduct." Unfortunately, leading citizens in Victoria and the *Victoria Advocate* did not make similar statements. If they had, Reconstruction might have been viewed differently in the county.[32]

ENDNOTES

1. Philip H. Sheridan to John A. Rawlins, "Report of Maj. Gen. Philip H. Sheridan," November 11, 1866. *War of Rebellion: A Compilation of the Official Records of the Union and Confederate Armies* (hereafter cited as *OR*), comp. Robert N. Scott (Washington, D.C.: U.S. Government Printing Office, 1880–1901), I, 48, pt. 2: 297–98; William L. Richter, *The Army in Texas During Reconstruction, 1865–1870* (College Station: Texas A&M University Press, 1987), 187.

2. "General Orders No. 4," *OR*, I, 48, pt. 2: 1094–95.

3. Frank J. Welcher, *The Union Army 1861–1865*, 2 vols. (Bloomington: Indiana University Press, 1993), 2: 77, 152.

4. Precedent for the action taken by the military was established by Gen. Winfield Scott's General Order 20 that was issued on February 19, 1847, during the Mexican War. Scott did not want to subject civilians to military law unless the civilian committed a crime against military personnel. C. H. Whittelsey to James Shaw Jr., March 23, 1866, *Letters Sent by the Department of Texas and the Fifth Military District*, hereafter cited as *Letters*, RG 393, National Archives; David A. Clary, *Eagles and Empire* (New York: Bantam Books, 2009), 288.

5. Bill McFarland, *Keep the Flag to the Front* (Overland Park, KS: Leathers Publishing, 2008), 299; J. Hill, *A Sketch of the 29th Regiment Connecticut Colored Troops* (Baltimore: Printed by Daughtery, Maguir, 1867), 29; James S. Clark, *History of the Thirty-Fourth Iowa* (Des

Moines: Walters-Talbott Printing, 1892), 32; Sidney H. Herriman, Diary, Bentley Historical Library, University of Michigan; David S. Stanley, *Personal Memoirs of Major-General David S. Stanley, U.S.A.* (Cambridge, MA: Harvard University Press, 1917), 227.

6. *The Anglo-African*, December 23, 1865; James Shaw Jr., *Personal Narratives of Events in the War of Rebellion* (Providence: Rhode Island Soldiers and Sailors Historical Society, 1905), 38.

7. James Shaw Jr. to H. W. Barry, July 18, 1865, *Letters Sent September 1864–February 1866* hereafter cited as *Letters*, RG 393, National Archives.

8. James Shaw Jr. to R. C. Shannor, July 8, 1865, *Letters*; Joseph Mark Califf, *Record of the Services of the Seventh Regiment, U. S. Colored Troops From September, 1863 to November, 1866* (Providence: E. L. Freeman & Co., 1878), 74; Agnes Kane Callum, *Colored Volunteers of Maryland, Civil War, 7th Regiment, United States Colored Troops, 1863–1866* (Baltimore: Mullac Publishers, 1990), 34; Shaw, *Personal Narratives*, 40; J. W. Petty Jr., ed., *Victor Rose's History of Victoria* (Victoria, TX: Book Mart, 1961), 54.

9. William H. Sinclair to Nathan Kimball, July 7, 1865, OR, I, 48, pt.2: 1061–62; McFarland, *Keep the Flag*, 302; Arnold Gates, ed., *The Rough Side of War: The Civil War Journal of Chesley A. Mosman 1st Lieutenant, Company D 59th Illinois Volunteer Infantry Regiment* (Garden City, NY: The Basin Publishing Co., 1987), 369–70; William Hartpence, *History of the Fifty-First Indiana Veteran Voluntary Infantry* (Cincinnati: The Robert Clarke Company, Printers and Binders, 1894), 330–32.

10. Hartpence, *History of the Fifty-First Indiana Veteran Voluntary Infantry*, 332, 334; Gates, *The Rough Side of War*, 370; Stanley, *Personal Memoirs*, 229.

11. Special Orders No. 20, July 13, 1865, *OR*, I, 48, pt. 2: 1075.

12. Samuel H. Fletcher, *The History of Company A, Second Illinois Cavalry* (D. H. Alfred White Stern Collection of Lincolniana, Library of Congress, no date), 166–67; Stanley, *Personal Memoirs*, 231; Fred McDavitt, "The 51st Ohio Volunteer Infantry (OVI): A Regimental History," *Civil War: The Magazine of the Civil War Society* 12 (1988): 34–35; Joseph McCauley to James M. Moore, October 16, 1865, Moore Family Papers, Bentley Historical Library, University of Michigan; Roy Morris Jr., *Sheridan: The Life and Wars of General Phil Sheridan* (New York: Crown Publishers, 1992), 164.

13. James Shaw Jr. to D. D. Wheeler, *Records of the Adjutant General's Office, Records of Volunteer Union Organizations, 7th USCT*

Infantry Regimental Description & Correspondence Book, RG 94, National Archives; Stanley, *Personal Memoirs*, 231.

14. *New York Times*, February 16, 1864; "Tunnel Escape from Libby Prison." http://richmondthenandnow.com/Tunnel-Escape-from-Libby.Prison-html (accessed June 22, 2009).

15. *Galveston Weekly News*, November 29, 1865; H. E. Bradford to A. J. Hamilton, November 21, 1865, Alexander J. Hamilton Papers, Texas State Library, Austin.

16. Ibid.

17. C. Carsner to A. J. Hamilton, November 21, 1865, Hamilton Papers; Petty Jr., ed., *Victor*, 211; Robert W. Shook, "Military Activities in Victoria," *Texana* 3 (Winter, 1965): 350.

18. C. Carsner to A. J. Hamilton, November 21, 1865, Hamilton Papers.

19. Ibid.

20. Ibid.; John J. Linn, *Reminiscences of Fifty Years in Texas* (1883; repr., Austin: State House Press, 1986), 361.

21. Califf, *Record*, 95: Samuel P. Bates, *History of Pennsylvania Volunteers, 1861–65* (Harrisburg: B. Singerly, State Printer, 1869–71), 991–92.

22. Henry Wolff, Jr., "Texas Pioneer Had many Accomplishments," *Victoria Advocate*, May 26, 2002; Petty Jr., *Victor*, 56–57; Roy Grimes, ed., *300 Years in Victoria County* (1968; repr., Austin: Nortex Press, 1985), 278–79; "Coroner's Inquest on Body of John Black," May 24, 1866, "Coroner's Inquest on Body of Ben F. Hill," May 24, 1866, Benjamin F. Hill Collection in possession of David Atmar and Barbara Parsons Smith, Victoria.

23. Ibid.; H. G. Wright to Commanding Officer, June 4, 1866, *Letters*.

24. Charles H. Peters to George C. Potmin, November 29, 1866, "Indictment," August 20, 1866, James W. Throckmorton Papers, Texas State Library; William L. Richter, "It Is Best to Go in Strong-Handed," *Arizona and the West* (Summer, 1985): 131.

25. Robert D. Tippett to J. W. Throckmorton, August 20, 1866, Throckmorton Papers; C. Carsner to J. W. Throckmorton, September 19, 1866, Throckmorton Papers; C. Carsner to J. B. Reid, September 21, 1866, Throckmorton Papers; S. P. Heintzelman to J. W. Throckmorton, September 29, 1866, Throckmorton Papers; San Antonio *Daily Herald*, October 10, 1866; Jerry Thompson, *Civil War to the Bloody End: The Life and Times of Major General Samuel P. Heintzelman* (College Station:

Texas A&M University Press, 2006), 334; Charles William Ramsdell, *Reconstruction in Texas* (paperback, Austin: University of Texas Press, 1970), 131.

26. George French, *Indianola Scrap Book* (Victoria: *The Victoria Advocate*, 1936), 110–13; C. H. Whittelsey to Mary D. Vandevoort, June 19, 1866, *Letters*; Special Order No. 23, August 20, 1866, *Records of the Adjutant General's Office, Book Records of Volunteer Union Organizations*, RG 94, National Archives; General Orders No. 20, February 8, 1867, *Special and General Orders, Indianola, 1866, 1867*, National Archives; Callum, *Colored Volunteers*, 34; Califf, *Record*, 73.

27. Chadwick, Diary; Gates, *Rough Side*, 376; Hartpence, *History*, 342; Herriman, Diary; Thompson, *Civil War*, 326; Leander A. Poor to Mary E. Dore, February 15, 1866, Leander A. Poor Collection, Victoria College/University of Houston-Victoria Library, Victoria.

28. Robert Walker Shook, "Federal Occupation and Administration of Texas, 1865–1870" (Ph. D. diss. North Texas State University, 1970), 479.

29. Sheridan to Rawlins, Report, *OR*, I, 48, pt.1: 299; James Shaw Jr. to R. C. Shannon, July 8, 1865, *Letters;* James Shaw Jr. to H. W. Barry, July 18, 1865, *Letters*; Leander A. Poor to Mary E. Dore, March 10, 1866, Poor Collection; Grimes, *300 Years*, 521–22; Shook, "Federal Occupation and Administration of Texas, 1865–1870," 469; Brownson Malsch, *Indianola: The Mother of Western Ports* (Austin: Shoal Creek Publishers, 1977), 185, 189–90; *Indianola Times*, April 21, 1866.

30. Hartpence, *History*, 336; Petty, *Victor*, 54, 58, 60; *Galveston News*, February 9, 1867; Malsch, *Indianola: The Mother of Western Ports*, 185.

31. French, *Scrap Book*, 51–53; Herriman, Diary; Shook, "Federal Occupation," 465–66; Robert Dunn to A. J. Hamilton, December 8, 1865, Hamilton Papers; Califf, *Record*, 82; Leander A. Poor to Mary E. Dore, March 3, 1866, March 16, 1866, Poor Collection.

32. Shook, "Federal Occupation and Administration of Texas, 1865–1870," 480; Califf, *Record*, 80–82; *Indianola Times*, October 8, 1866.

CHAPTER 4

William Longworth, Republican Villain

by

Richard B. McCaslin

The scholarly effort to retrieve an accurate history of Reconstruction from the intellectual dustbin to which it had been consigned by popular memory has advanced rapidly in the last fifty years or so. Republicans are generally now seen as reformers, local politicians who supported reform are no longer considered scoundrels, and most Freedmen's Bureau agents are considered to have been well-intentioned, if not entirely ready for the tasks to which they were assigned.[1] In fact, the revisionist push has been so effective that historians might well question how the South, and even the nation, was able to embrace a perception of Reconstruction as an era of overzealous or even venal reform. Perhaps even more important, how could Southerners justify violence against such well-intentioned reformers? But if one wants to appreciate the complexity of Reconstruction, one has to accept that, like most myths, there is a kernel of truth in the depiction of it as an era of malice and greed. William Longworth, while he escaped being the target of violence himself, became the evidence for the many in Texas who forgot the promise of progress embedded in Reconstruction, reacted violently against the reformers, and later remembered only the bitterness of the period.

During Reconstruction, county officials, who continued to address the needs of Texas communities more often than any state or national administrators, faced a daunting task. Economically, whites struggled with losses that were difficult to recoup after the emancipation of all slaves, while financial obstacles for the latter often proved impossible to overcome. Prejudices developed by whites toward blacks as slaves did not end with emancipation, contributing to a violent white backlash. Efforts of national agencies to promote change further divided people. Some local leaders did well, but Wilson County seethed under the ambitious hold of Longworth, while the community of Sutherland Springs lost its prominence as the county seat and endured a decade of decline.[2]

Race relations between whites and blacks provided the context for the bitter political battle that ended with the removal of the county seat from Sutherland Springs. Joseph H. Polley had "about twenty slaves" when the Civil War ended, and his actions were typical of those with large numbers of slaves in the region. He told President Andrew Johnson in his application for an executive pardon that he freed his slaves after June 19, 1865, when Gen. Gordon Granger promulgated the Emancipation Proclamation in Texas. He signed labor contracts, the terms of which he described as "fair and liberal," with six former slaves. The agreement with Polley obliged these men to work through December 1865, when Polley purchased forty head of cattle from one of the six, Cato Morgan, who had bought the animals while he was a slave with money earned by hauling goods. Morgan and some older blacks continued to work for Polley for several years.[3]

Many of the freed blacks in Wilson County relocated a short distance from their former owners and organized five colonies. Polley and Gray Jones Houston supported one such group by providing land on Cibolo Creek for a settlement between Sutherland Springs and La Vernia. Called Do-See-Do, it contained stores, a school, and a brush-arbor church where Morgan, although illiterate, delivered a non-denominational sermon every Sunday. Most of the ex-slaves farmed, but some were blacksmiths and mechanics. Whites in the region found that many freedmen did not want to work as employees, no matter what wages were offered. The blacks seemed to prefer the semi-autonomy of sharecropping or independently plying their crafts. At the same time, many black wives and single mothers made some money by washing clothes for white families.[4]

Not all whites accepted emancipation gracefully. John Sutherland, founder and namesake of Sutherland Springs, wrote to his daughter-in-law more than a year after the war that not having slaves was a great hardship. He remarked that "My family is still complaining owing to having all the work to do and not being accustomed to do such." Three years later, his daughter Sarah reported that they had hired "a freedman to cultivate a part of the field but he is too lazy to do much." She noted that her brother Jack—a Confederate veteran who farmed, worked as a carpenter, and operated a store—did better with his black laborers. Economic need may have made him more adaptable: in 1870 he married Mary E. Sutherland, daughter of William Sutherland of Victoria, and they began a family that eventually included eleven children. Other whites continued to agree with the bigoted claim of J. A. Durnand that blacks in Wilson County were "not to be relied upon; they are lazy and worthless."[5]

Racism did lead to violence in Wilson County, as elsewhere in Texas, during Reconstruction. Creed Taylor, remembered by many as a rough character, apparently could not accept defeat or emancipation, and his extended family and other allies joined him in a violent campaign against Union authorities. Among the atrocities committed by Taylor's clan from his ranch east of Sutherland Springs was the murder of a freedman at La Vernia in April 1867. Official protest led to Taylor being questioned, but he provided an alibi for himself and an explanation for those who did the killing. The latter included a claim that they had acted in self-defense, not from racist motives or as hired agents to drive the freedman from his land, as some said. Taylor was repeatedly detained during similar investigations before he moved west in the early 1870s. His son Philip G. Taylor, known as "Doughboy," was less fortunate; months after being arrested in Sutherland Springs in April 1871, he went west like his father but was shot to death in Kerrville.[6]

The struggle for power in Wilson County was more often fought with pens than with guns. The enemy for whites in Sutherland Springs was Longworth, a Canadian-born sheep farmer of modest means who arrived from neighboring Karnes County during the war.[7] Andrew J. Hamilton, the noted Texas Unionist and congressman, during July 1865 transitioned from military to provisional governor of the state under an appointment from President Johnson. His job was to create a new loyal government, for which he accepted nominations from all corners. Upon the recommendation of Thomas A. Stribling, a San Antonio Unionist, Hamilton appointed Longworth as chief justice of Wilson County in September 1865. The commissioners court in each Texas county was the greatest source of power in the nineteenth century, and its presiding officer, known as the chief justice or county judge, wielded much influence. Stribling assured Hamilton that Longworth, who had lived about a year in that county, was "universally known as one of the most reliable Union men" there, for which he has "suffered much." In fact, Longworth's appointment prompted over two hundred voters, including many from Sutherland Springs, to sign a petition calling for his removal within a few weeks.[8]

Longworth provided other names, endorsed by Stribling, for appointments, and Hamilton accepted these as well. But Longworth began to quarrel with his own officers. He wrote on New Year's Day 1866 to Joseph Spence, a Republican clerk in the Texas Secretary of State's office, that several appointees in Wilson County had to be replaced. Daniel H. Bird, a former slaveowner appointed to the county commission, had "failed to qualify," and George Bird "refused to qualify" for his appointment as the district clerk. Longworth especially disliked one man: "I have had some trouble with everything and everyone is now quiet, with the exception of one of the commissioners, John Sutherland, in whom I have been deceived." Longworth wrote that Sutherland "has three separate times laboured [*sic*] to pack the Grand Jury, but thus far I have succeed[ed] in offsetting him." He added, "The effort to pack the Grand Jury was more adroitly made than I can well explain in writing." He asked that Sutherland be suspended from the commissioners court, which apparently was done. Longworth subsequently was appointed justice of the peace for Sutherland Springs to secure his position further against any challenges from Sutherland and others.[9]

Hamilton wanted civil rights for blacks, and Longworth focused on that issue to obtain the governor's support in Wilson County. He wrote to Hamilton in October 1865, "Slavery is as absolute yet in the state as I ever knew it to be." Decisive action had been "imperative," especially in obvious cases of kidnapping, of which there had been more than twenty incidences "almost within my sight since your arrival." As proof, he sent an affidavit recounting the taking of a freedwoman from the home of a white woman by former district clerk, and militia commander, Andrew G. Pickett and three other men on October 6, 1865. This event may have been the source of Longworth's trouble with his commissioners. Pickett's wife Susan contacted Hamilton a few months later, recalling mutual Unionist friends and claiming that Longworth tried to have the commissioners illegally take a black servant from the Picketts. Longworth told the court that Susan J. Pickett was a "severe mistress" and claimed that a black maid had tried to poison her two years earlier. The commissioners refused to support him, and a provost marshal returned the young girl to the Picketts.[10]

The Picketts' alarm was enhanced when Longworth became the local agent for the Freedmen's Bureau in December 1865. Longworth had pressed for the post since June and was finally accepted when he agreed to serve without pay. William Green, an ex-slave, recalled how Longworth argued with former slaveholders who attempted to control the freedmen with unfair contracts. Green commented, "He was a little man but he tole de boss just where matters stand." Whites such as Susan J. Pickett saw matters differently. In her letter to Hamilton, she reported that Longworth had seized black children from white families because he believed no children were truly free until taken from their former masters. She added that he urged blacks to sue for all wages due to them since June 19, when they were freed. Longworth's lack of salary resurfaced as an issue in her claims that he pushed black couples who had lived for years as married to file for a license so he could keep the fee, and that he told blacks to donate money to buy a homestead for him.[11]

Susan J. Pickett asked Hamilton to remove Longworth, or at least restrain him. The governor sent her note to Maj. Gen. Edgar M. Gregory, the assistant commissioner of the Freedmen's Bureau for Texas. Longworth had repeatedly complained about the whites in his district, his lack of supplies, and the number and quality of the troops sent to him. He only received eight or ten soldiers who, as a mixture of Germans, Irish, and Americans, were men "of the lowest order." Now Gregory's query after getting Pickett's letter brought a hostile rebuke from Longworth, who had earlier warned Gregory that someone might "attempt to poison you against me." Gregory could not have been very pleased with Longworth's angry assertion that the word "conciliation" made his "gorge . . . rise," especially when he added, "You might as well try to conciliate a pack of Hyenas by throwing one of four children to them with the hope of saving one." Longworth also claimed that his plans to open a school for blacks had failed because he could not find a teacher, but he still intended to open a hospital for blacks at Sutherland Springs with the aid of a former Navy doctor.[12]

Longworth's frustration led to a confrontation. In April 1866 he arrested James L. Dial, a sixty-year-old former slaveholder. Isaiah A. Paschal, a Unionist acquaintance of Hamilton and the Picketts, had warned the governor about Dial's "peculiar views" on freedmen. When a letter from Dial accusing Longworth of several offenses later arrived in Austin, Longworth in turn hotly accused Dial of kidnapping blacks and making deadly threats. He had soldiers confine Dial at Sutherland Springs "in an old house filled with vermin" for three days. Gregory endorsed Longworth's actions, including Dial's arrest, but outraged residents of Bexar, Wilson, and Guadalupe counties signed another petition demanding Longworth's removal. They declared that he was a "stranger" and "arbitrary, vindictive, and unjust" as well as corrupt. Furthermore, they claimed that his efforts were "calculated to demoralize the freedmen and to prevent the working of crops," while his use of troops was unnecessary.[13]

Longworth responded vigorously to the charges against him. He explained to Gregory, who had warned his agents to expect new resistance after President Johnson's veto of a bill renewing the Freedmen's Bureau, that in regard to Dial he was forced "to make an arrest or acknowledge that I was a useless machine." It was better to press the issue with Dial than to allow the Bureau to "ignominiously expire." About William C. Wiseman, the chief justice of Guadalupe County whom the petitioners had suggested as a replacement agent, Longworth claimed the ex-slaveholder had assaulted him and "sunk the Negro below what he was even as a slave." Continuing in a second note, he added that Wiseman had sold black children into servitude "until their majority for a bite to eat, a little air to breathe, and a horse and saddle." And as for Longworth demoralizing the blacks: "If to send them home elated and buoyant with a knowledge of the fact that they could safely go to work and expand their muscle and intelligence over and on their crops, with a hope of getting paid therefore is demoralization, then I am guilty." He added that the assertion by some that all was peaceful until he arrived was ludicrous. That so-called "peace was all on one side," and it was "peaceable as the volcano smothered up until it got air."[14]

Longworth's verbal attacks on Wiseman were not just intended to undermine a potential rival. During the angry turmoil after Dial's arrest, Longworth moved his office to Seguin, which allowed Wiseman as chief justice of Guadalupe County to arrest him for false imprisonment and financial fraud. Dial was subsequently freed when Wiseman let him post bail, but Longworth appealed to Gregory, who supported him in posting his own bond and then re-arresting Dial. While free on bail, Dial added a civil suit for $20,000 to Longworth's troubles. Seeking more substantial aid, Longworth sent letters to possible sympathizers, including Charles Sumner, the Radical senator in Washington.[15]

Accused of fomenting racial tension, Gregory was replaced in May 1866 with Maj. Gen. Joseph B. Kiddoo, who initially tried to placate the former slaveowners. He removed Longworth, despite his protests, in July 1866. Kiddoo preferred military agents, and he was upset to get a letter from Sumner about Longworth. Matters quickly became worse for Wilson County. Longworth's successor, Lt. James B. Moore, was removed for drunkenness and embezzlement. The next agent, Capt. Samuel A. Craig, came to Seguin after being implicated in the burning of Brenham in September 1866. Under orders from Maj. Gen. Samuel P. Heintzelman, commanding at San Antonio, Craig took the records concerning Longworth's indictment and civil suit, and Moore's indiscretions, from the files of the district court clerk in Guadalupe County in October 1866. The clerk resisted at first, but Craig threatened to arrest him and send him to San Antonio. Concerned about the cholera epidemic ravaging that city, the clerk capitulated. Craig was later arrested by Guadalupe County officials, but Heintzelman rescued him and he mustered out. To add insult to injury, Craig's successor, Maj. George W. Smith, was the officer who allegedly directed the burning of Brenham. Guarded by soldiers, he worked in Seguin from late December 1866 until he was removed for fraud in 1869.[16]

Many Wilson County residents applauded Longworth's removal as a Freedmen's Bureau agent, but he remained their chief justice. This changed after the constitutional convention of 1866, which was dominated by conservatives. In the ensuing elections, James W. Throckmorton, who had opposed secession before he became a Texas Confederate officer, defeated Unionist Elisha M. Pease for the governor's seat. Conservatives swept Wilson County, where Confederate veteran Telemachus S. Wyatt was elected as chief justice and Daniel H. Bird returned as a county commissioner. Wyatt quit in February 1867, but Walker K. Baylor, who was elected to the commission and as a justice of the peace in 1866 and refused to accept either office, took his place as chief justice. John W. Lilly, who had been the captain of the Wilson Guards, a local militia unit during the Civil War, was elected county treasurer.[17]

Longworth tried to reject some of the votes cast against him "from some little irregularity," but he failed. His vindication came during 1867, when Congress passed the Reconstruction Acts in response to conservative triumphs throughout the South. Ten southern states were put in five military districts, each to be administered by a general who could remove any officials deemed to be impediments to Reconstruction. When Maj. Gen. Philip H. Sheridan took charge of the Fifth Military District, which included Texas, the impact was immediate. Chief Justice Baylor wrote to Throckmorton in May 1867, just two months after the first Reconstruction Act, that more than a dozen Wilson County offices were vacant, in part due to Sheridan's ban on elections. That summer, the general replaced Throckmorton with Pease, while Maj. Gen. Charles Griffin, commander of the Department of Texas, and his successor, Maj. Gen. Joseph J. Reynolds, replaced more than 400 Texas officials with Unionists and Republicans. The requirement of a test oath adopted by Congress led to more dismissals because officeholders had to swear that they had never supported the rebellion. Many could not do this and were thus replaced in April 1869 by Maj. Gen. Edward R. S. Canby, who succeeded Reynolds after he was promoted to command the district.[18]

The removal of conservative officials by the military hierarchy, together with a requirement that voters sign a loyalty oath, allowed the Republican Party to take charge in Texas. Longworth did not wait long to make his move. He sent "a list of officials to be decapitated" to Joseph Spence in August 1867. Baylor, Bird, and Lilly were among his targets, and Longworth asked that he succeed Baylor. He warned that the conflict between conservatives and Unionists would become a "life or death grapple, and unless we make it war to the knife we will be defeated, certain." He pledged to do his part, adding, "If Wilson co is lost it wont be my fault [*sic*]." This document was apparently given to Pease, who also received a letter from Baylor and Bird asking him not to be misled by "evil or zealous minded persons" into removing officials who were "competent and worthy." But Baylor went too far. He wrote to Griffin, as he had to Throckmorton, asking what to do about vacant county offices. Apparently annoyed with Baylor's bold inquiries, Griffin agreed with Pease that troublemakers such as Baylor had to go.[19]

Almost every elected official in Wilson County was replaced in accordance with Longworth's suggestions during the fall of 1867. Longworth took Baylor's place as chief justice. He resigned that position in early 1868, shortly before it was abolished statewide, but in 1869 he received appointments as county clerk and as justice of the peace for Sutherland Springs. This made him chair of the new county board under the Constitution of 1869, which was created by a Republican-dominated state convention. Elected as district clerk for Wilson County and justice of the peace for Sutherland Springs in December 1869 and December 1870, he also became county surveyor in January 1871. For much of the time that he held these offices, according to his own reports, he dominated Wilson County. He certainly claimed to be the chief Republican, which was a dubious honor. For example, he was compelled for lack of a better choice to accept George B. Webber as clerk of the county court. A Union veteran, Webber was a "slave to liquor," as Longworth admitted to federal authorities in December 1867. He assured them that Webber would remain in office only as long as he kept his promise to abstain.[20]

Longworth had his fill of Sutherland Springs, where many of his opponents lived, and as chief justice he could settle the county seat question in his own way. In December 1867 he validated the results of an election that designated a new site south of Sutherland Springs as the seat, to be called Floresville. He thus took lawful advantage of the 1860 legislation that created Wilson County, which mandated that the seat should be near its geographical center. The commissioners discussed relocation, but they made no decision. Allegedly Longworth in 1867 asked Lilly for a bribe not to remove the county court from Creed Taylor's building, where the commissioners had met since 1860, but Lilly refused. Longworth and

Webber then hauled the county's records in ox-carts to Lodi, just to the south of Sutherland Springs on the Goliad Road. Older than Sutherland's town, Lodi had never flourished, and it later disappeared. Nevertheless, Longworth settled in rented rooms there until quarters could be constructed at Floresville.[21]

Reshaping the Texas electorate, especially recruiting black voters, was a key part of Republican reforms. Longworth not only removed the county seat from Sutherland Springs, he ensured that the list of Wilson County voters little resembled the group that approved secession in 1861. Under his direction, 407 voters were registered in Wilson County. Of these, almost one-fourth (98) were black, and one-fourth of the white voters (75) were actually born in Mexico. More than one-third (130), black and white alike, had arrived in the area since 1865, though only four newcomers came from the North. Five Union veterans registered, three Irish and two Mexicans, while there were no former Confederates. There remained few early settlers; Daniel H. Bird was the perhaps the best known who was allowed to register, while Walker K. Baylor signed the list but was later removed.[22]

Longworth's efforts reflected the result throughout Texas as almost all eligible blacks but only half of the potential white voters were registered to vote. Two-thirds of the white electorate boycotted the 1868 election for a constitutional convention, thereby hoping to invalidate the result, while 89 percent of black voters cast ballots. Republican reformers thus dominated the 1868 convention. Wilson County, where less than half of the white males registered to vote, elected no delegate. Longworth wrote that those who refused to register did so "out of pure hatred to the Government and laws of the country." He assured Texas Secretary of State D. W. C. Phillips in April 1868 that in all future elections, "Wilson County is safe for Congress and the constitution, should I have the managing as I had last time." Edmund J. Davis, leader of the Radical Republicans in the convention, won the subsequent governor's race in a controversial election that many whites again boycotted while his own party members quarreled among themselves. He took office under a constitution that promised reform, but his enemies included some Republican reformers.[23]

Davis soon ran afoul of Longworth. Before Pease left the governor's office, Longworth asked him for support in the post-convention election. Believing he had been ignored, Longworth declared, "I can do as well without the Republican party as the party can without me." He added, "Of all the Radicals in all the counties in the states I have the smallest party to back me in the County—Collectively the party have not a spoonful of brains. With me out of the way it would be a walk over." His tone did not improve by August 1869, when he wrote to James P. Newcomb, a leading Republican, that he alone had kept the party alive in his county. In January 1870, Longworth wrote to Davis, "I am worth something, and should be upheld . . . If I am allowed to be snuffed out away goes the county. I am the Republican party, in the county."[24]

Longworth's January 1870 declaration was prompted by Davis's decision to find out exactly what was happening in Wilson County. Longworth asked the Army officer assigned to the inquiry to tell him the result, and he triumphantly forwarded the officer's report to Davis in February 1870 with a mocking letter of his own that crowed, "You will easily perceive by the tone of it that I am unsullied in reputation, and as bright as your hopes and wishes could well desire." In fact, the officer had not yet made a decision, and said as much in the note that Longworth sent to Davis. Nevertheless, Longworth added that he needed the governor's "active interference" to be retained as county judge so that he could "maintain the party" and win elections as he had done previously.[25]

After another blast at Davis, Longworth settled for the office of district clerk in 1870, a banner year for the Republicans in Texas as they dominated the legislature and Congress formally readmitted the state to the Union. That summer, Davis signed a hotly debated bill creating a State Guard as the foundation of a new militia. Andrew McClung mustered a company at Sutherland Springs that included some Confederate veterans and other familiar faces. They were intended to work with the State Police, also created in the summer of 1870. The police company organized in Wilson County enrolled several Confederate veterans and other conservatives as well. Often denounced for corruption elsewhere, the Guard and Police in Wilson County helped to keep the peace—McClung's Guards arrested Philip G. "Doughboy" Taylor—but more important they played a role in the removal of Longworth.[26]

Sutherland Springs led the charge against Longworth. Susan J. Pickett wrote in 1860 that if the county seat was not at Sutherland Springs, "I believe after a year or two this place will be only known as having once had an existence." Ten years later she noted that the community had a new school and church as well as new houses, but it was a "dull place." In truth, Sutherland Springs had not expanded much upon its prewar foundations. There were 329 residents, of whom 204 were white (including Mexicans) and 125 were black. Of the heads of households, more than half farmed. There were three grocers and three wagoners, as well as a stonemason, wheelwright, gunsmith, and doctor. Magistrate

Andrew G. Pickett and postmaster Walker K. Baylor represented the government. More troubling to Longworth, sulking at Lodi, was the fact that most of the residents were born in the former Confederacy. Only about three dozen came from states that stayed with the Union, of whom 28 were born in border states. Most of the townspeople were therefore southern in origin and almost certainly more interested in community development than in Republican reform. If they took control of politics, they would not keep Longworth.[27]

Longworth's decline began in 1871. Sutherland Springs officially became the county seat again after an election was held in response to a petition signed by forty men. But the court met in Lodi that fall, so the issue of a seat had obviously not been settled. In October 1871, Longworth also reported to Newcomb that he failed to get satisfactory election results in Wilson County. This may have been due to his lack of control over the Guard and Police, and to his having to serve on the election board with James L. Dial, the man he had arrested, and William T. Sutherland, a Confederate veteran whose late father, John Sutherland, had hotly opposed Longworth. Furthermore, leniency in enforcing the restrictions on voting by ex-Confederates meant that among the 245 voters were more like Sutherland. Significantly, the black electorate was mostly absent, except for a few trusted men such as Cato Morgan. By 1877, in an era characterized by violence and declining black voter turnout, the *Western Chronicle* of Sutherland Springs would ominously remark that local blacks had learned not to vote Radical.[28]

Longworth's Waterloo came in November 1872, when he lost the races for district clerk to Pickett and county surveyor to William T. Sutherland. Longworth served as the registrar for the election, despite protests to Davis, and he tried hard to avoid its obvious conclusion. He refused to allow many voters to register. Then, when electoral judges, led by Dial, asked for the keys to the courthouse in Floresville, which had been endorsed by voters in late 1871 as the county seat, Longworth refused to surrender them. There were no houses in Floresville, but there was a small home in Lodi and the judges held an election there, guarded by the State Police. Longworth demanded to have the results set aside, insisting that the 1869 Constitution required elections to be held in the county seat, even if, as the sheriff admitted in an affidavit, Floresville was "almost as much a place of the imagination as of reality," with only stakes in the ground and piles of lumber for buildings. Matters became stranger when Dial repudiated his own signature on a petition that asserted the election was legal. Instead, Dial insisted he was drunk when he signed the document. Despite the confusion, Davis accepted the election results and Longworth, like many other Texas Republicans that fall, was out. By 1874, he had left the area.[29]

Why did Davis not support Longworth in his fight with conservatives in Wilson County? The governor had received reports about Longworth's negative impact for the Republicans. Records indicate that while electoral support for Davis in Wilson County in 1869 was greater than expected, only 28 percent of the registered whites there voted for him. One local reported to Davis in August 1872 that Mexicans in Wilson County had shifted from the Republicans to the Democrats "entirely [because of] the rascalities, and oppression" of Longworth. A "man without any principal," Longworth used political offices "for oppression, instead of protection to these people." Furthermore, he "publicly proclaims that he has ruled this county for seven years, and will not now lose his power—and goes to all excesses to retain that power." Davis dispatched a State Police lieutenant to investigate Longworth. It has been asserted that Davis "could see nothing good in an opponent." Be that as it may, what he learned from the lieutenant about Longworth did not lead him to ignore other accusations of electoral impropriety, such as a message from Sutherland Springs signed "A True Friend and Allie." When Longworth claimed that his removal would ruin a local black colony, his argument fell on deaf ears in Austin.[30]

Davis was fighting a losing battle for political survival in Texas as well as in Wilson County. Within a year he would be out as conservatives, led by gubernatorial candidate Richard C. Coke, swept the 1873 elections. The Republicans in Texas had divided bitterly over the constitutional convention of 1868, while black and Mexican voter participation was declining in many counties. The loss of grassroots support from local leaders such as Longworth proved fatal to Davis and the Republicans. In 1869, Wilson County gave Davis 59 percent of its total vote. Like elsewhere in Texas, Davis apparently drew strong support from the blacks and Mexicans in the county, while many whites boycotted. By 1873, the composition of Wilson County's electorate shifted, and 78 percent of the county's vote went to Coke. After briefly protesting, Davis angrily surrendered control of the state government one year after refusing to save Longworth.[31]

Longworth was gone, but Sutherland Springs had lost, too. When Chief Justice Telemachus S. Wyatt in the fall of 1866 had raised the issue of a permanent county seat, John Sutherland pushed hard for his town. Instead, the site that became Floresville won in special elections held in 1867 and again in 1871. A courthouse was built in time for Longworth to lock the electoral judges out in the fall of 1872, and in 1873 it officially became the seat of government for Wilson County. Ten years later, when plans were laid for a more substantial courthouse, about 200 people signed a petition asking for it to be in Sutherland Springs, but once more they lost an election. Pickett, formerly of Sutherland Springs, began holding court as the county judge in a new brick courthouse at Floresville in 1885. The San Antonio & Aransas Pass Railroad reached Floresville just a few years later, assuring its economic ascendancy as well.[32]

Sutherland Springs barely survived Reconstruction after it lost the county seat. There would be at least one more period of prosperity for the community, but many who lived there joined with other Wilson County residents in remembering Reconstruction as the time when Longworth ruined everything. While it is not entirely correct that he ruled "with an iron rod," and that "his rulings were always in favor of the Ethiopeans [*sic*]," he did believe the Republicans could provide the only redemption for his jurisdiction, and that he was the savior to deliver their message. It could be argued that many whites in Wilson County were simply being "ornery, unco-operative, and unlaw-abiding."[33] But too many of them, and a Republican governor, were repelled by Longworth's high-handed methods. He proved to be the wrong man for a difficult period, and blacks in the region lost a zealous advocate when he left office. With his egotistical effort, Longworth ironically undermined the significant promise of reform represented by Reconstruction, and he provided at least one kernel of truth for the popular memory of the era as a well-deserved failure. He avoided becoming a victim of the violence that erupted in Texas, but he provided historical justification, albeit misguided, for those who excused it as a necessary reaction against corrupt and venal Republicans.

ENDNOTES

1. For the changing perspectives on Reconstruction in Texas, compare Charles W. Ramsdell, *Reconstruction in Texas* (New York: Columbia University Press, 1910), with Carl W. Moneyhon, *Texas After the Civil War* (College Station: Texas A&M University Press, 2004). On the Freedmen's Bureau, see William L. Richter, *Overreached on All Sides* (College Station: Texas A&M University Press, 1991), and Barry A. Crouch, *The Freedmen's Bureau and Black Texans* (Austin: University of Texas Press, 1992).

2. For an excellent study of county leadership, see Randolph B. Campbell, *Grassroots Reconstruction in Texas* (Baton Rouge: Louisiana State University Press, 1998). Richter, in *Overreached on All Sides*, devotes much attention to Longworth, but only for the period when he was an agent for the Freedmen's Bureau.

3. Joseph H. Polley to Andrew Johnson, Apr. 14, 1866, United States, Department of War, Adjutant General, Case Files of Applications from Former Confederate for Presidential Pardons, 1865–1867, Record Group 94, National Archives, Washington, DC, hereafter cited as NA, microfilm (quotes); Will of Joseph H. Polley, Mar. 30, 1869, Cato Morgan to Joseph H. Polley, Dec. 1865, Joseph H. Polley Family Papers, Dolph Briscoe Center for American History, The University of Texas at Austin, hereafter cited as CAH; Jamie P. M. Frost, "Descendants and Ancestors of Joseph Henry Polley, 1625–1996," Typescript, 1996, in author's collection, 160–64; Josephine Polley Golson, *Bailey's Light* (San Antonio: Naylor Press, 1950), 117, 122; Crouch, *Freedmen's Bureau*, 13.

4. Golson, *Bailey's Light*, 116, 122–24; Sutherland Springs (TX) *Western Chronicle*, Feb. 2, 1877; *Texas Almanac, 1867* (Galveston: Richardson & Company, 1866), 172–76; United States Bureau of the Census, Ninth Census, 1870, Texas, Wilson County, Population Schedule, Record Group 29, NA, online.

5. John Sutherland to Emily E. Sutherland, Nov. 27, 1866 (lst quote), Sarah Sutherland Craighead to Emily E. Sutherland, May 9, 1869 (2nd quote), Sutherland Family Papers, in possession of Elise Kidd, Austin; Vertical File: John Sutherland, CAH; Notes on Sutherland Springs, Historical Marker File, Texas State Historical Commission, Austin; *Texas Almanac, 1867*, 176 (3rd quote).

6. The two most recent works on this conflict are James M. Smallwood, *The Feud That Wasn't* (College Station: Texas A&M University Press, 2008), and Chuck Parsons, *The Sutton-Taylor Feud* (Denton: University of North Texas Press, 2009).

7. Longworth claimed to be a native of New York in Texas Secretary of State, Voter Register, 1867–1869, Texas State Library and Archives, Austin, hereafter cited as TSLA microfilm, and in the 1870 Census, Wilson County, Population Schedule. He correctly identified himself as Canadian in United States Bureau of the Census, Eighth Census, 1860, Texas, Gonzales County, Population Schedule, Record Group 29, NA, online; which is corroborated by the information for his son, Thomas Longworth, in United States Bureau of the Census, Tenth Census, 1880, New Mexico, Lincoln County, Population Schedule, Record Group 29,

NA, online. William Longworth first appears in the Texas tax rolls in 1857, when he was assessed for "hogs & furniture" in Karnes County. Two years later, he owned a horse and fifty hogs. By 1862, he had two horses, sixty hogs, ten cattle and five hundred sheep, and he paid taxes in Karnes County on 683 acres as an "agent." He paid his first Wilson County taxes in 1865, on 640 acres granted in his name, seven horses, and four hundred sheep. He paid on the same in 1866, but not in 1867. See the Wilson County and Karnes County Tax Rolls, TSLA, microfilm.

8. Thomas H. Stribling to Andrew J. Hamilton, Aug. 27, 1865 (quotes), Susan J. Pickett to Hamilton, Jan. 13, 1866, James L. Dial to John Ireland, Feb. 27, 1866, Texas Governor, Records, TSLA; Ron Tyler et al., eds. *The New Handbook of Texas*, 6 vols. (Austin: Texas State Historical Association, 1996), 3: 427–28; William L. Richter, *The Army in Texas During Reconstruction, 1865–1870* (College Station: Texas A&M University Press, 1987), 22, 23.

9. William Longworth to Joseph Spence, Jan. 1, 1866, Governor's Records, TSLA, (1st, 3rd–5th quotes); Texas Secretary of State, Election Returns, TSLA; Texas Secretary of State, Election Register, TSLA, microfilm (2nd quote); Wilson County Tax Rolls, 1860; United States Bureau of the Census, Seventh Census, 1850, Texas, Bexar County, Population and Slave Schedules, TX, Record Group 29, NA, online; 1860 Census, Texas, Wilson County, Population and Slave Schedules; Sutherland Springs (TX) *Western Chronicle*, June 5, 1879; Tyler et al., *New Handbook*, 6: 27.

10. Longworth to Hamilton, Oct. 10, 1865 (1st–3rd quotes), Susan J. Pickett to Hamilton, Jan. 13, 1866 (4th quote), Governor's Records, TSLA. It should be noted that Pickett had trouble with other female slaves whom she hired before and after the Civil War, but she apparently had a good relationship with a freed black man and his wife whom she employed after the war. See S[usan] J. Pickett to "My Dear Friend" [Elizabeth Mary Menefee Riddle Canterbury], June 11, 1860, Sept. 22, 1865, Sept. 16, 1866, Sept. 11, 1868, Jan. 12, 1869, Aline Carter Family Papers, Special Collections, University of Texas at San Antonio.

11. Susan J. Pickett to Hamilton, Jan. 13, 1866, Governor's Records; Longworth to Edgar M. Gregory, Oct. 28, 1865, United States Department of War, Bureau of Refugees, Freedmen and Abandoned Lands, Records of the Assistant Commissioner for the State of Texas, 1865–1869, Letters Received, Record Group 105, NA, microfilm; George Rawick, ed., *The American Slave: A Composite Autobiography, Supplement, Series 2*, 10 vols. (Westwood, CT: Greenwood Press, 1979) 10: 1,596 (quote); Richter, *Overreached on All Sides,* 116, 119.

12. Longworth to William H. Sinclair, Mar. 28, 1866 (1st quote), BRFAL, Asst. Comm., TX, Lets. Recd.; Crouch, *Freedmen's Bureau*, 14; Richter, *Overreached on All Sides*, 117 (2nd quote), 118. The troops sent to assist Longworth and his successors as Freedmen's Bureau agent for the region came from San Antonio, where companies of infantry or cavalry were posted from August 1865 until March 1870. There were never permanent garrisons in Wilson County during Reconstruction, though companies were assigned to neighboring Karnes County. See Richter, *Army in Texas*, 18, 19, 28, 30, 55, 68, 149–53, 163, 185, 186.

13. I[saiah]. A. Paschal to Hamilton, Oct. 4, 1865 (1st quote), Dial to John Ireland, Feb. 27, 1866, Governor's Records; Lemuel P. Hughes et al. to Joseph B. Kiddoo, May 1866 (3rd–5th quotes), Statement of James L. Dial, May 7, 1866 (2nd quote), Statement of R. W. Brahan, May 18, 1866, BRFAL, Asst. Comm., TX, Lets. Recd.; Richter, *Overreached on All Sides*, 117–19.

14. Longworth to Sinclair, May 14 (lst–3rd quotes), 30 (4th–7th quotes), 1866, BRFAL, Asst. Comm., TX, Lets. Recd.; Richter, *Army in Texas*, 39. Longworth need not have bothered with trying to create a test case because the Bureau was renewed over Johnson's veto.

15. Richter, *Overreached on All Sides*, 119–22.

16. James B. Moore to Sinclair, July 29, 1866, BRFAL, Asst. Comm., TX, Lets. Recd.; W. E. Goodrich to Throckmorton, Oct. 8, 1866, Governor's Records; Pat I. Nixon, *The Medical Story of Early Texas* (San Antonio: Mollie Bennett Lupe Memorial Fund, 1946), 298, 299; Crouch, *Freedmen's Bureau*, 21; Richter, *Army in Texas*, 40, 64, 65; Richter, *Overreached on All Sides*, 122–35, 162. William H. Sinclair, sent by Maj. Gen. Joseph B. Kiddoo to investigate the allegations against William Longworth after he was removed, generally confirmed the negative accusations.

17. Telemachus S. Wyatt to Texas Secretary of State, n.d. [July 1866], Nov. 3, 1866, Election Returns; Election Register; Muster Roll of the Wilson Guards, Wilson County, 30th Brigade, Jno. W. Lilly, Capt., Texas Adjutant General, Militia Records, TSLA; J. T. Jaeggli, *The Court House Story* (Privately Published, n.d.), 5; Tyler et al., *New Handbook*, 5: 112, 113, 6: 485, 486; Ramsdell, *Reconstruction*, 87, 89, 90, 108–12, 286; Moneyhon, *Texas After the Civil War*, 43–51.

18. Wyatt to Texas Secretary of State, n.d. [July 1866] (quote), Election Returns; Walker K. Baylor to Throckmorton, May 9, 1867, Governor's Records; Tyler et al., *New Handbook*, 5: 112, 113, 476, 477, 557, 6: 485, 486; Ramsdell, *Reconstruction*, 116, 145–47, 151, 152, 168, 169; Moneyhon, *Texas After the Civil War*, 69–70, 72, 75, 77.

19. Longworth to Spence, Aug. 19, 1867 (1st–3rd quotes), Baylor and Daniel H. Bird to Elisha M. Pease, Aug. 19, 1867 (4th and 5th quotes); Baylor to Charles Griffin, Aug. 31, 1867, Pease to Griffin, Sept. 16, 1867, Governor's Records.

20. Longworth to Pease, Sept. 22, 1867, Governor's Records; Election Register; Longworth to J. P. Richardson, Dec. 9, 1867, Election Returns; *Flake's Bulletin,* Nov. 11 and 14, 1867; *Elections in Second District of Texas*, 41st Congress, 2nd Session, House Executive Document 265, Serial Set 1426; Campbell, *Grassroots Reconstruction*, 45.

21. Notes on Sutherland Springs, Historical Marker File; "Wilson County Commissioners Court Minutes, Volume A," Typescript, undated, Works Progress Administration, Historical Records Survey, CAH, 97; H. P. N. Gammel, comp., *The Laws of Texas, 1822–1897*, 10 vols. (Austin: Gammel Book Company, 1898–1902), 4: 1,462; Louise Stadler, comp., *Wilson County History* (Dallas: Taylor Publishing Company, 1990), 12; Mattie Jackson, comp., *The Rising and Setting of the Lone Star Republic* (Privately Published, 1926), 17, 18; C. L. Patterson, *Wilson County, Texas* (San Antonio: Privately Published, 1939), 8; *Wilson County Centennial, 1860–1960* (Floresville, TX: Wilson County Centennial Association, 1960), n.p.; Jaeggli, *Court House Story*, 2, 5, 6; Tyler et al., *New Handbook*, 4: 260, 6: 1,011.

22. Texas Voter Register, 1867–1869; Moneyhon, *Texas After the Civil War*, 81–82; Ramsdell, *Reconstruction*, 196–98, 252–56. The flood of newcomers in Wilson County is typical of Texas during this period, as is their origin. See Tyler et al., *New Handbook*, 4: 480.

23. Longworth to D. W. C. Phillips, Apr. 21, 1868 (quotes), Governor's Records; Moneyhon, *Texas After the Civil War,* 84–85; Dale Baum, *The Shattering of Texas Unionism* (Baton Rouge: Louisiana State University Press, 1998), 169; Ramsdell, *Reconstruction*, 200–2, 205, 207, 244–46, 280, 286, 287; Tyler et al., *New Handbook*, 2: 525–26, 5: 477, 478.

24. Longworth to Pease, Dec. 12, 1868 (1st and 2nd quotes), Longworth to Edmund J. Davis, Jan. 27, 1870 (3rd quote), Governor's Records; Longworth to James P. Newcomb, Aug. 27, 1869, James P. Newcomb Papers, CAH.

25. A. B. Chamberlain to Longworth, Feb. 3, 1870, Longworth to Davis, Feb. 5, 1870, Governor's Records.

26. Longworth to Davis, n.d., Governor's Records; Muster and Pay Roll of Captain A. McClung's Company of State Guards From the 15th Day of November 1870, to the 1st Day of March 1871, Texas Adjutant General, Muster Roll of County Special Policemen, TSLA; Gammel,

Laws of Texas, 6:185–90; Moneyhon, *Texas After the Civil War*, 135, 136, 139–42; Ramsdell, *Reconstruction*, 296–298, 301, 302; Tyler et al., *New Handbook*, 5:478, 479, 6:75.

27. Susan J. Pickett to "My Dear Friend" [Elizabeth Mary Menefee Riddle Canterbury], June 11, 1860 (first quote), Sept. 20, 1870 (second quote), Carter Family Papers; 1870 Census, TX, Wilson County, Population Schedule; Sutherland Springs Historical Display, Sutherland Springs Museum, Sutherland Springs.

28. Longworth to Davis, Mar. 27, 1871, with attachments, Governor's Records; Longworth to Newcomb, Oct. 8, 1871, Election Returns; Sutherland Springs (TX) *Western Chronicle*, Feb. 2, 1877; "Wilson County Commissioner's Court Minutes, Vol. A," 134, 141; Baum, *Texas Unionism*, 196; Moneyhon, *Texas After the Civil War*, 176–83; Tyler, et al., *New Handbook*, 4: 260, 6: 1,011; Jaeggli, *Court House Story*, 7; *Wilson County Centennial*.

29. Longworth to Board of Returning Officers of Election, Nov. 3, 1872, Affidavit of Nemacio de al Zerda, Jan. 11, 1873 (quote), Affidavit of Haywood W. Brahan, Jan. 21, 1873, Brahan to A. N. Denton, Jan. 21, 1873, Election Returns; H. C. Burke to Davis, Aug. 28, 1872, Brahan to Davis, Sept. 14, 29, 1872, Andrew G. Pickett to Davis, Sept. 17, 1872, R. C. Houston to Davis, Oct. 31, 1872, Longworth to Davis, Nov. 18, Dec. 23, 1872, Governor's Records; Petition of Citizens of Wilson County, Memorials and Petitions File, TSLA; Moneyhon, *Texas After the Civil War*,186–87. Longworth appears in the 1868 tax rolls for Wilson County with 640 acres patented in his name, ten horses, two cattle, and 450 sheep. For 1869 and 1870 he paid for 160 acres, three horses, two cattle and 450 sheep. In 1870, William D. Mayes paid taxes on a grant in Wilson County issued to Longworth, indicating that the latter had sold the land to him. Longworth in the returns for 1871 reported no personal property and that he did not own the 160 acres on which he paid taxes in Wilson County. In 1872 he paid taxes on town lots in Sutherland Springs, three horses and a hundred sheep. In 1873 he paid taxes on two horses, 500 sheep, four lots in Lodi, two acres in Wilson County, 2,300 acres in Bee County, and 80 acres in Menard County. He is not in the 1874 tax rolls for Wilson County or the 1880 census. See the Wilson County Tax Rolls for 1868 to 1874.

30. Burke to Davis, Aug. 28, 1872 (1st–3rd quotes), July 3, 1873, Brahan to Davis, Sept. 14, 29, 1872, Andrew G. Pickett to Davis, Sept. 17, 1872, "A True-Friend and Allie" to Davis, Sept. 17, 1871, Longworth to Davis, Dec. 23, 1872, Governor's Records; Election Register;

Election Returns; Ramsdell, *Reconstruction*, 315–18 (4th quote); Baum, *Texas Unionism*, 198, 208.

31. Election Register; Election Returns; Moneyhon, *Texas After the Civil War*, 191–98; Tyler et al., *New Handbook*, 5: 480. The 1872 elections also mark the first of a string of five Democratic victories in the presidential races in Wilson County, which ended only when unhappy farmers cast their ballots for the Populist ticket in 1892. See W. Dean Burnham, *Presidential Ballots, 1836–1892* (Baltimore: Johns Hopkins Press, 1955), 812, 813.

32. Longworth to Board of Returning Officers of Election, Nov. 1872, Longworth to Newcomb, Oct. 8, 1871, Election Returns; Tyler et al., *New Handbook*, 2: 1,039, 4: 260, 5: 798, 6: 1,011; Stadler, *Wilson County*, 12; Patterson, *Wilson County*, 8; Jackson, *Lone Star Republic*, 17, 18; Jaeggli, *Court House Story*, 7, 9.

33. Cotulla (TX) *Record*, Sept. 25, 1931 (1st quote); Gail W. Shriber to Mrs. D. M. Parmelee, Feb. 18, 1966 (2nd quote), Historical Marker File.

CHAPTER 5

"The Old Hero of Many Cowardly and Bloody Murders": Scalawag Gang Leader Ben Brown

by

Dale Baum

Traditional accounts of Texas history written during the first century after the Civil War portrayed many of the violent desperados of the state's Reconstruction era in the context of family feuds or gun fights in which men would have rather died than backed down from confrontations with their adversaries. Revisionist interpretations more accurately have situated these killers in the arena of the continuation of the war by outlaw guerrilla Klansmen who viciously assaulted ex-slaves and white Unionists. However, the bloody exploits of Benjamin ("Ben") Brown, who in the years immediately after the war became one of the most notorious gang leaders in east central Texas criminal history, are nowhere to be found in either the chronicles of local folklore or published secondary accounts. Ben Brown failed to be romanticized in Reconstruction mythology because he was a southern Unionist who cooperated with the federal army and radical Republican officeholders and even served for a brief period as a hired gun for the Freedmen's Bureau. His disobedience of the law and courts and administering vigilante justice began during the last years of the war and peaked during the early years of Reconstruction. His power and influence waned rapidly after a trial by a military commission in 1869 found him guilty of killing a respected physician in the downtown streets of the newly created railroad town of Calvert (see map 1).[1]

Former wealthy slave owners, with their paternalistic racial ethos and their desire for a dependable supply of cheap labor unimpeded by disruptive white thugs trying to restore slavery in all but name, complied with Ben's acting on their behalf in contravention of the law. Sharing in their complicity in allowing Ben to flout the law were the overburdened and shorthanded military authorities and the men they appointed as local

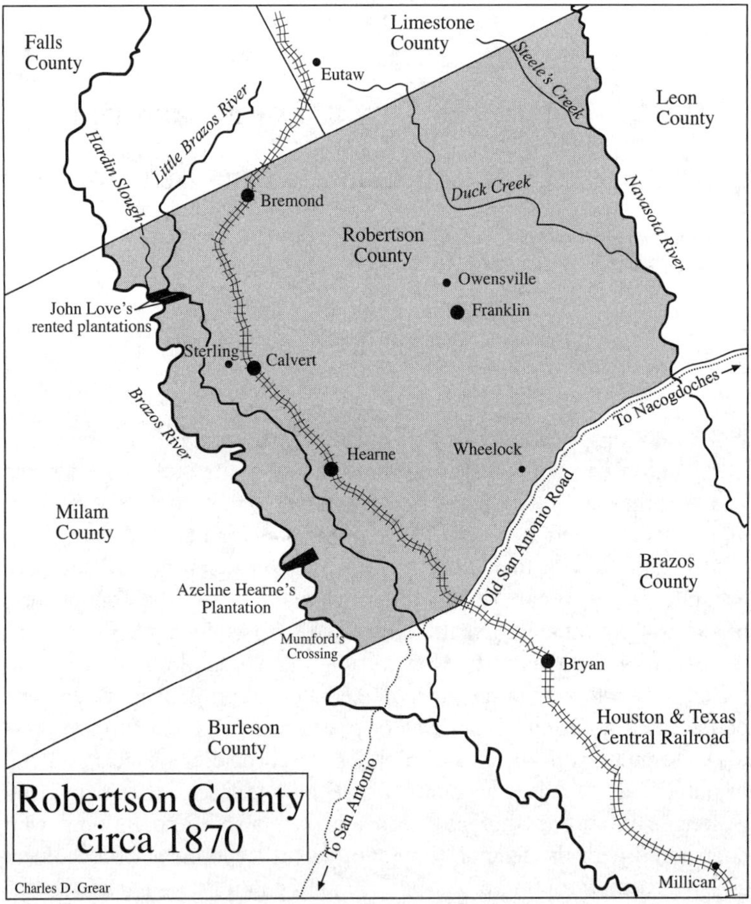

Map 1. Robertson County circa 1870

officeholders: the former were unable to prevent anti-Reconstruction whites from curtailing through violence and intimidation the property rights of blacks as well as their civil and political rights, and the latter were plagued every day by insults and the possibility of physical harm for no other reason than their affiliation with the Republican Party. Any hope of establishing a lasting, exemplary, and genuine biracial democracy upon the ruins of a former slaveholding society would have had to entail many years of federal intervention and supervision far greater than that imposed from 1867 to 1870. In the absence of strict enforcement of the program of Congressional Reconstruction, violence begat violence in

Robertson County at the same time as it frequently did elsewhere in the ex-Confederate South.

In 1841 at age twenty-nine, Ben and his teenage sweetheart Francis ("Fannie") Rogers, who was half his age, left their homes in Jefferson County, Alabama, and emigrated to the Republic of Texas where in the fall of that year they were married. Fannie subsequently bore Ben six children who lived to adulthood. In 1850 they, along with their two young sons and the family's three slaves, resided in rapidly growing Rusk County. Although years later Ben claimed to have moved his family in 1859 to Robertson County, tax records indicate that he, along with his younger brothers, Earle A. ("Early") and Greenwood ("Green") Brown, together with their families, all resided in the county by 1854. From that time until the end of the Civil War, Ben lived on the high prairie, or post oak grassland, in the northeastern corner of the county where he purchased five separate parcels of land. Green Brown settled in the county's southwestern corner on the edge of the large plantation system centering on the extended Hearne and Lewis family's cotton lands on the Brazos River, while Early Brown resided alternately in the vicinity of Green's homestead and on Ben's lands nearest the Limestone County line (see map 1). For the next twenty years the Brown family's imprint on Robertson County history was indelible, and was not fully removed until 1879 when a Hearne city policeman shot and killed Green's third oldest son while he was drinking raucously in his father's saloon.[2]

After arriving in Robertson County, the Brown brothers quickly made their appearance in the folios of courthouse records. In the absence of the case files or surviving newspaper accounts, the full circumstances will never be known surrounding the murder indictment handed down in the spring of 1855 against Early Brown and well-to-do slaveholder Telemachus ("Telephus") A. Johnson, along with two others, for killing William D. Miller, a local notary public and lawyer. Miller, during the previous fall term of the district court, had been indicted for assault with intent to murder Telephus Johnson. Within a month after the botched attempt on his life, Telephus offered a $500 reward for Miller's "arrest and delivery" to the county sheriff to answer for not only having "waited in ambush to assassinate" him, but also, during the surprise attack, for shooting and killing a "[N]egro boy 12 years of age." Present at the courthouse for the beginning of the fall term, Telephus exploded in anger upon learning that the grand jury had refused to indict Miller for "the brutal murder" of his adolescent slave and had advised his filing a civil suit to recoup merely monetary damages for the loss of his chattel property. In regard to the ensuing deadly settling of scores, one of the two others indicted for killing Miller fled to avoid trial. In the spring of 1856, with culpability shifted upon their vanished co-defendant, Early and Telephus, along with the remaining other defendant, were acquitted in the public drama of a district court jury trial of the revenge killing that they had planned and carried out.[3]

The Miller-Johnson case exposed the antebellum ties of comradeship between the Brown brothers and others like them who shared strong loyalties to the so-called Opposition to the Democrats: early on as Whigs, during the mid-1850s as Know-Nothings, and later on as Independents and Union Democrats or followers of Sam Houston, the hero of the Texas Revolution and still "the old lion" of state politics. In local elections during the second half of the 1850s, Robertson County, like many other long-established counties in the interior river valley areas of East Texas, was routinely in the anti-Democratic column. William H. Wheelock, a Houston loyalist and former sheriff, agreed to be one of the underwriters on Early's personal bond. When grand jurors decided amidst Telephus's courtroom outbursts to indict him for unlawfully obstructing an officer of the court, Phagan Brigance, who was the brother of the Know-Nothing clerk of the district court, cosigned Telephus's bond. In the late antebellum years following Telephus and Early's acquittal on murder charges, the Brown brothers and other Houston adherents, including Telephus, were disproportionally among the county's voters called to serve as jurors, culminating with Green serving as a petit juror during the district court's 1859 fall term, Ben serving likewise during the following 1860 spring term, and Early serving on that year's fall term as a member of the grand jury.[4]

At the outbreak of the war all three Brown brothers were over the age limit for the draft. In 1864 when the age limit was expanded to fifty, only Green, the youngest brother who was forty-nine years of age, faced a possible short tour of duty in the Texas Home Guard, but there is no record of his service. Oddly enough, only Ben, the oldest who at the outset of the war was forty-nine years old, served for a few months in a county militia group. Ben was not, however, among those in his unit in the summer of 1861 that authorities merged into the 4th Texas Infantry, which became one of the three regiments in the Texas Brigade of Robert E. Lee's Army of Northern Virginia. For the remainder of the war, Ben, Early, and Green cannot be found on extant lists of men who were liable to the draft, but life on the home front for them was not dull.[5]

In the fall of 1861, Early, who was a landless small slaveholder owning a young mother and her four children and residing on Ben's lands along Duck Creek close to the settlement of Eutaw in neighboring Limestone County, was indicted once again for murder, albeit this time as the sole defendant. Virtually nothing is known about the circumstances surrounding his indictment. The omission of the victim's name in the district court minutes suggests, but does not prove, a lack of commiseration for the person (or persons) that Early allegedly killed. Throughout the Civil War years he remained a fugitive-at-large to evade prosecution—a situation that explains the case's routine continuance devoid of rulings or notations. The case ended in 1867 when the district attorney, then a Radical Republican military appointee, ordered it stricken from the criminal docket due to the technicality that, in his words, "the [original] indictment in this case is lost." Immediately thereafter Early emerged from his six long years as an outlaw-in-hiding.[6]

At some point near the beginning of the war, Green Brown, a non-slaveholder and widower with six children, opened a general merchandise store on the edge of the Brazos River bottomlands where he and his family had resided since their arrival in the county in 1852. From as far as Mumford's Crossing (to the south) to the town of Sterling (to the northwest), Green's customers purchased more than just whips, wire, and whiskey: they took home as loyal patrons assurances of protection of their wellbeing by the Brown brothers. After the war the store became, in spite of Green's inability to read or write, the prominent mercantile firm of Brown & Wilkerson in the newly created railroad town of Hearne situated immediately to the south of Green's former wartime store.[7]

Throughout the war Ben raised cattle, horses, and sheep on his various parcels of post oak grasslands on which two slave houses accommodated his sixteen slaves. Despite being a stockraiser who reported less than $1,400 worth of real property, and despite having a brother on-the-lam, Ben played a major role in county affairs, including participating on two grand juries, being a major surety on the bond for the county treasurer, serving as an administrator of the estates of a few deceased persons, and, far more remarkably, as a law-enforcing citizen who personally punished wrongdoers.[8]

A reference to Ben as a wartime vigilante gang leader is found in J. Allen Myers's unpublished handwritten memoirs. In the 1920s, Myers, who at the time of the Confederate surrender was ten years old and living in Robertson County, recalled that Ben Brown was "a terror to the Jay Hawkers and thieves" during the war. His reference to the former lacks credibility, although it arguably sheds light on the process of historical memory. Not only were Yankee guerrilla fighters as infrequent as hen's teeth in Robertson County and vicinity, but even if Allen's Jayhawkers had been merely draft dodgers who "laid in the bush" in antagonism to Confederate authority, the reference would remain incorrect. Ben's wartime supporters were mostly Union sympathizers or apathetic Confederates whose beliefs or behavior could impose upon one a dicey accusation of being "both a fool and a traitor."[9]

The Brown brothers' ally Telephus Johnson, who remained throughout the war "an out and out Union Man," became such an irritation to the county's "Ultra Secession Men" that they subjected him, in spite of his "shrewdness and unflinching nerve," to considerable harassment. Equally representative of Ben's partisans was New York-born Philip Stonemets, who had reputedly "entered the Confederate Army under a written protest and by compulsion," although no evidence whatsoever of his enlistment can be found. Also among Ben's supporters was the pioneering Louisiana generation of the Hearne and Lewis families who, as ardent prewar Unionists, felt no obligation to fight on the battlefield for the Confederacy. Brothers Horatio ("Rasche") and Ebenezer ("Ebb") Hearne, along with their cousin Alfred Hearne, purchased substitutes, whereas Alfred's brothers Washington ("Wash"), Samuel ("Sam"), and Christopher ("Lum"), respectively, obtained an occupational exemption and positions in a local group of Texas Home Guards—arrangements acquired perhaps through their use of the law exempting slave owners with twenty or more slaves from Confederate military service. Anti-Secessionist State Senator Charles Lewis, who was Rasche and Ebb's brother-in-law, upon the expiration in 1861 of his term in the legislature served in the Texas Home Guards as a private. Shielding the Hearnes and Lewises from verbal abuse and personal injury was more than their wealth and large slaveholder status. Ben's retaliation against anyone who might have harmed them—or their like-minded planter neighbors in the bottomlands such as Telephus Johnson—would have been assured.[10]

A more accurate portrayal of Ben is contained in Allen Myers's remembrances of events in the immediate months after the war. Ben, along "with his followers and his Men with his Dogs," gained a reputation as "constantly hunting the lawless element in central Texas" irrespective of race or political stance. In 1865–1866 when "a sort of dog-eat-dog life" required everyone "to carry six shooters," Ben's posse was the most effective enforcer of the law in Robertson County and nearby Leon, Limestone, Freestone, Houston, and Anderson Counties—a region that conspicuously extended eastward directly toward Ben's previous home in Rusk County (see map 2).[11]

Allen listened to first-hand accounts of Ben's exploits told to him by his father, Robert ("Bob") C. Myers, who throughout the war remained an unapologetic "union sympathizer." Driven away from his plantation in Louisiana by the siege of Vicksburg in 1863, Bob Myers had taken with him to Texas at least fifty of his eighty-plus slaves to prevent them from being liberated by invading Union troops. He relocated in Robertson

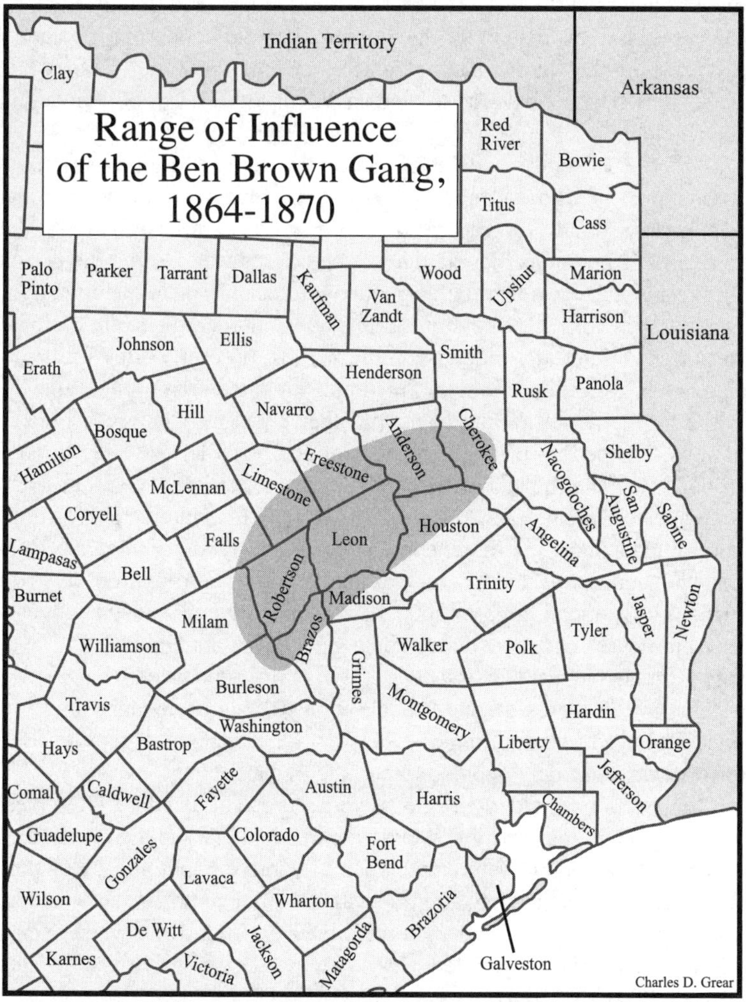

Map 2. Range of Influence of the Ben Brown Gang, 1864–1870

County where his family rented land on Telephus Johnson's plantation. Allen remembered his father and uncle, along with Ben and his hound dogs, in the summer of 1865 chasing down a bunch of thieves led by "a half-breed Indian" who had stolen his father's wagon loaded with goods. To the consternation, if not disgust, of many whites, Ben armed as full-fledged members of his posse some of the ex-slaves of Allen's father and uncle. Upon catching up with the outlaws, who were shocked at the sight of blacks with guns, the Myers brothers convinced Ben to spare the thieves' lives. Fortunately for the outlaws, they did not harm the wagon's driver whom they had kidnapped when they took the wagon. If they had done so, Ben would have, as Allen recalled his father's words, "hung [*sic*] the whole bunch."[12]

Robertson County postwar officeholders were mostly prewar Houston supporters who had chosen to stay in office as Confederates and whom provisional Governor Andrew J. Hamilton, in turn, had allowed to retain the positions they held at the end of the war. During the period of Presidential Reconstruction, Andrew Johnson's undemanding policies allowed former Secessionists and ex-Confederates to be restored to power without any federal commitment to prevent whites from setting harsh restrictions on black freedom. White terrorist groups, such as white brotherhoods, White Caps, or other Ku Klux Klan–type organizations, cropped up throughout the central Brazos River valley to control and regulate the labor and behavior of the ex-slaves. Overburdened Freedmen's Bureau agents reported that appalling numbers of crimes committed against the freedpeople were "an *everyday occurrence*" and that "noncommunicative" witnesses made "getting information" a "great difficulty" if not an impossibility. With an anti-Republican state government in power, county officials "disregarded and abrogated with impunity" Bureau requests for assistance. During this time when whites killed blacks, in the words of one reliable witness, "with the same indifference displayed in the killing of a snake or other venomous reptile," Ben Brown was extremely popular among the freedpeople.[13]

Recollections of elderly former slaves recorded during the 1930s reveal that upon their emancipation "Massa Brown" had assisted them as a labor contractor by finding them employment. Far more importantly, Ben protected their personal safety after they signed labor contracts with planters who patronized Green's store. In the winter of 1865–1866 when annual contracts had been negotiated, Ben's new residence, which was located on the edge of the Brazos River bottomlands in the northwestern corner of the county near the Hardin Slough, provided a safe haven from roaming gangs of irate whites opposed to ex-slaves getting paid for their past year's labors, leaving their places of employment because their employers had not lived up to existing agreements, or switching jobs by signing with new employers offering them better terms. Angry at Ben's excessive concern for the ex-slaves, hooded klansmen "set on fire" his cabin where purportedly "honest freedmen" in need were never "turned away."[14]

Several months after Congress took over control of Reconstruction in March of 1867, Ben, while assisting the local Freedmen's Bureau agent in the arming of a large group of freedmen to hunt down a notorious white criminal, received an on-the-spot appointment as a Bureau agent by a visiting Bureau field agent for the state-at-large who held an extraordinary commission directly from the commander of the Military District of Texas. By the middle of July with the authority of the United States Army behind him and accompanied by the core group of men who always rode with him, Ben brought enthusiasm and effectiveness to his new job, but reports of his activities soon placed him in disfavor with federal authorities.[15]

Ben's career as a Bureau agent was terminated after he filed an eye-opening report at the end of August 1867, detailing his cold-blooded execution orders designed to avoid making prisoners of a couple of white criminals: Bob Leach (alias Robert Locke) who had "*shot down in cold blood*" a freedman for no other reason than his being "a damned nigger" who "should not hold church [services]"; and Robert Savile who, while routinely making it his business to disarm blacks of their weapons, had killed a former slave for merely having questioned a command to surrender his shotgun. Both lawbreakers were proverbial dead men when Ben's men captured them. By summarily taking the life of Savile, who had "showed a disposition to resist" arrest, and by killing Leach after capturing him in accordance with the intention "to arrest and dispose" of him, Ben preempted their all-too-common breakout from jail or all-but-certain acquittal in the civil courts by white jurors determined to ignore both the law and the facts.[16]

Instead of sending his report to the acting adjutant attorney general at Bureau headquarters, Ben leaped up the chain of command by writing directly to Texas's district commander Bvt. Maj. Gen. Charles Griffin—a circumstance guaranteeing that his report would receive considerable scrutiny. Declaring that a few persons were "complaining terribly" of his handling of Leach and Savile, Ben asked for Griffin's authorization "to arrest and put a moderate fine upon [the complainers]," adding that "it would have a good effect" by allowing him to carry out his duties "without expense to the Government": an inopportune phrase often used by self-appointed vigilantes. He boasted that within a little over a month he had made Robertson County "entirely free of lawlessness" and he vowed to keep it "in that desirable condition." He reported that "the best citizens of Freestone County" had begged him to likewise purge their county "of assassins, murderers, and thieves." If Griffin approved, Ben promised to extend his peacekeeping operations. After making a few inquiries, headquarters issued orders for his removal, to be effective on October 1, 1867, after only two months of his service. No responses to the inquiries or explanations for his removal can be found in the records and correspondence of the Freedmen's Bureau or the military district's Office of Civil Affairs. It was not the only time when information about Ben was most likely pulled from the files, warily examined, and never replaced.[17]

Rescinding Ben's appointment did not subtract from his influence and power in Robertson County. Sheriff Thomas G. Logan, who held office from the summer of 1866 until the spring of 1868, was not only a valued member of Ben's posse, but won the highest praise from Ben, in his words, for "firmness & energy in carrying out every order I gave him." When Logan resigned as sheriff, Ben and his wealthy planter allies successfully lobbied provisional Governor Elisha M. Pease to select William Wheelock as Logan's successor, even though it was common knowledge that Wheelock, an antebellum officeholder and anti-Secessionist who during the war had been elected sheriff, would have to perjure himself upon taking the required "iron-clad" oath. Even under these astonishing circumstances, those refusing to support Wheelock hesitated to speak out against his appointment, although one anonymous letter to the governor claimed that all the members of the local bar knew that Wheelock would "pack a jury for $500" from certain bottomland planters. The few who subsequently admitted, albeit guardedly in private conversations, that Ben's corrupt influence over county affairs was "bad," deferentially continued to refer to him as "Capt. Brown"— the title that had been at one time accorded to him as a subassistant commissioner in the employ of the Freedmen's Bureau.[18]

While Ben had been serving as a Bureau agent, a member of his posse, John R. Harlan, shot and killed an unpopular horse trader named John Deveraux during a heated argument. Not only did Ben and Early post a bond amounting to $5,000 to help cover Harlan's bail, but to guarantee his acquittal, Sheriff Wheelock packed the jury not only with Ben, but also with four of Ben's most trustworthy allies: Stonemets, who served as foreman, Richard M. Cage, W. L. Faulkner, and Ebb Hearne. Recently appointed district attorney Phidello ("Fidella") W. Hall, who was supposed to prosecute the case against Harlan, consented to this courtroom charade. With Fidella Hall's recommendation, military authorities subsequently appointed Harlan the county's assessor and collector of taxes. A year later in the pivotal 1869 statewide election, Harlan and Hall, both of whom were Kentucky-born scalawags, successfully ran on the local Radical Republican Party ticket for sheriff and state senator, respectively.[19]

Before the appointments of Hall, Harlan, and other scalawags and carpetbaggers, the freedpeople had no chance of receiving justice and fair play from the previous set of county officials who had been elected during Presidential Reconstruction. After their appointments, indictments and convictions against whites who committed outrages against blacks subsequently became at least within the realm of possibility. However, by 1868 there were other far more revolutionary implications of Congressional Reconstruction that not only altered the electoral map of the entire ex-Confederate South, but also splintered the racial attitudes of Ben's supporters and caused a sharp divergence between political developments in Robertson County on one hand, and neighboring Brazos County (to the south), on the other (see map 1).

Ben Brown's friend and accomplice Bob Myers had moved his family in the fall of 1865 from Telephus Johnson's plantation lands to the town of Millican where he opened a general store, entertained occupying federal troops in his home, and worked to establish a Republican Party Union League, an organization created in the wake of the First Reconstruction Act of March 1867 to register and mobilize black voters. In the military-supervised statewide elections of February 1868, in which Texas voters approved the call for a new state constitutional convention and elected convention delegates, Republican success derived from the addition of blacks to the voting rolls, while at the same time many whites refused to register or, to a lesser extent, were disenfranchised by the Reconstruction Acts. In a number of counties throughout the state, black voters were in the majority. As such, in Brazos County black Republicans successfully elected one of their own race as a convention delegate. However, in Robertson County, where black registered voters also outnumbered their white counterparts, the selection of a freedman to a position of political importance was not acceptable to the overwhelming majority of Ben's planter allies. As a compromise, Ben guaranteed the safety of all blacks who voted and thus allowed them to carry in a racially polarized vote the call for holding a convention, but only on the condition that they accepted voting for an unopposed candidate for delegate whom their former masters selected. This prearrangement made the election precisely the "humbug" that military authorities predicted and, more significantly, accepted in order to preempt white violence directed at the newly enfranchised blacks at the polls.[20]

The year 1868 marked the zenith of Ben's enrichment and fame as a gang leader who imposed his personal brand of law and order upon criminals of both races. In January he broke into the ranks of the large proprietors of cotton land in the Brazos bottoms when he and Early jointly purchased nearly 3,000 acres for $30,000. The tract of land adjoined the river and the plantation lands of former large slaveholder Dr. Benjamin F. Hammond. Although a zealous Secessionist before the war, Dr. Hammond during the postwar years had "accepted [Congressional Reconstruction] in good faith," welcomed the opening of a Freedmen's Bureau school on his plantation, and joined forces with Ben. With support of prominent planter elites, such as Hammond and Rasche Hearne (whose plantation had daringly hosted one of the county's first Bureau schoolhouses for black children), and with the backing of the county's military-appointed officials, Ben and his posse replaced the need for a detachment of the 6th U.S. Cavalry to remain in Sterling. The local Bureau agent requested it be reassigned, due to "their services being no longer necessary in the subdistrict." In such circumstances, Ben had carte blanche. In one notable instance in early June, he tracked down, captured, and lynched in broad daylight a freedman who had allegedly killed a white man.[21]

No more than a single brief statement in the records of criminal offenses compiled by the Freedmen's Bureau reported the lynching:

> [A] freedman killed a white man in Robertson County; the f.m. escaped followed by a party of men who came up with him, arrested and claimed the right to take him back to Robertson County, they conducted the freedman some four or five miles, cut off both ears, and after mistreating him, then hung [*sic*] him by the road side.

Ben and his men's orchestration of this occurrence of vigilante justice was never in doubt. Newspaper accounts described the killing of Robertson County ex-slaveholder Young E. Gray by "a Negro employed on his farm" who fled and was followed by "a number of citizens" to Bryan where the following day he was "captured and executed." A Bryan resident many years later recalled approvingly how the "fearless and tireless" posse led by Ben Brown, along with his brother Green Brown and prominent planter Rasche Hearne, tracked down the fleeing Robertson County freedman and "summarily" hanged him "on a tree limb" on Bryan's North Main Street.[22]

The reference to Bryan's North Main Street, which would have been the western edge of the city's fledgling suburban "Freedmen Town" located a few blocks off the road leading north to Robertson County, is a credible detail. Local blacks would have viewed the victim's mutilated corpse as a demonstration of the power of whites to kill with complete exoneration any African American who committed a shocking crime against a white person. If officers at the post of Bryan, the military-appointed city officials, and the small but influential group of Brazos County white Republicans—all of whom had to have known the particulars of Ben's brazen criminal act—registered any objections about it, they have been lost in the passage of time. Yet their silence was predictable, not only because in the midst of dangerous circumstances they relied on Ben's posse for their own safety, but also for the reason that their energies became during the following month absorbed by a far more deadly outbreak of violence.[23]

In mid-July a group of white men who called themselves the Ku Klux Klan and were annoyed with the success of the Brazos County Union League killed the League's most prominent black leaders. The so-called "Millican riot," in which only blacks died, turned out to be the worst incident of racial violence in Texas during Reconstruction and received considerable attention throughout the nation. Subsequent generations of local whites credited scalawags Bob Myers and Ben Brown with preventing further racial incidents, a sort of backhanded accolade that begs for an explanation because few whites bestowed comparable praise upon occupying federal soldiers and northern carpetbaggers. The vast majority of white Anglo Texans believed that these latter two groups had illegitimately ushered in, as the pro-Democratic Austin *State Gazette* expressed it, "the reign of niggerdom" with its inevitable racial turmoil.[24]

Bob and Ben were among a small group of southern-born slaveholders whose postwar cooperation with the federal army and the Republican Party offered some hope of helping the freedmen reap the rewards of a market-driven economy and gain the benefits of civic and political rights. However, they expected that the ex-slaves would defer to them, rather than to carpetbaggers or their own leaders, for guidance and advice, which often did not mirror precisely the aspirations of the freedmen. Bob's unadulterated radicalism in encouraging black political participation at the polls came to a tragic end in 1871 when a Democratic political opponent assassinated him in the streets of Millican, whereas Ben's personal judgments regarding what was best for the freedpeople, including the extent of their property ownership rights as well as their voting rights, invariably ran afoul of the Republican Party's goal of establishing a new order of things in which the laws applied equally to everyone.[25]

When Robertson County freedwoman Azeline Hearne came abruptly to the precipice of an amount of wealth unimaginable for most whites, her situation necessitated Ben's involvement and protection. During slavery Azeline had been the concubine of her unmarried master Sam Hearne, who was Rasche and Ebb's cousin. Upon Sam's death in 1866 he bequeathed his estate, which included a large Brazos River cotton plantation, to his and Azeline's mulatto son. A blitz of legal maneuvers initiated by his relatives to annul his will in the probate and district courts resulted in military authorities upholding its validity and taking over its administration, which included managing the plantation. When Sam's son died in early 1868, a legatee clause in the will making Azeline her son's solitary heir vested ownership in her. With the Freedmen's Bureau scheduled to shut down its operations by the end of the year, military authorities had no other choice than to beseech Ben to take over as a probate court-appointed administrator of the unfinished business of managing Sam's estate and plantation and to look after Azeline, whom a local attorney described as "an ignorant freedwoman [who] from her status in society is deprived of that physical protection which others possess."[26]

Ben and his men safeguarded the many ex-slaves comprised of hired hands, sharecroppers, and renters who lived in extremely controversial independence from white control on Azeline's 900-plus acre antebellum plantation with its own cotton press. However, by following in the footsteps of the army officials previously placed in charge, Ben made no effort to properly administer Sam's estate, a task admittedly complicated by pending lawsuits challenging the title to the Brazos River plantation with claims based on bogus chains of titles to old Spanish land grants or otherwise laying claims to the estate to satisfy debts that it allegedly secured. Ben, somewhat understandably, did not want to be saddled with a long-drawn-out administration, but he also disapproved of Azeline's exaggerated claim to wealth. At some point during the spring of 1869 Ben fraudulently colluded with false claimants to her plantation's title and allowed their groundless lawsuit to obtain a default judgment against her in the district court. Soon thereafter she and those working on her plantation became easy targets for predatory whites, a situation that Ben could have prevented but for his subsequent elimination from Azeline's affairs as administrator of Sam's estate due to his arrest and incarceration for murder by the United States Army.[27]

On June 25, 1869, Ben and his men killed Dr. J. M. Maxwell, a thirty-three-year-old "high toned and honorable gentleman" whose young wife was related to the well-known Brashear family of Louisiana. Ben and Dr. Maxwell had been on bad terms for over a year because of a dispute growing out of "a personal difficulty" between Maxwell and fellow physician Hammond. Newspaper accounts referred to Ben as "a notorious character" who rode into Calvert, then on the verge of becoming the new northern terminus of the Houston and Texas Central (H&TC) Railroad, with "a posse of about forty desperados" armed "to the teeth" with the sole objective of killing Maxwell. Witnesses to the shooting recounted that, upon seeing Maxwell "with gloves on and without weapons" mount his horse to make a getaway, someone under Ben's leadership had yelled, "Shoot him, kill him." Ben and Hammond, who were at the head of the pursuers, fired the first of successive volleys estimated to be "at least a hundred shots." After falling from his horse and being dragged into a tree, Maxwell was "shot all to pieces," his body "frightfully mangled" by thirty or forty bullets. For added emphasis, as he lay dead, one of Ben's men "more brutal than the rest, stabbed him with a knife."[28]

Because of Dr. Maxwell's social prominence, the appalling cruelty of his murder, and its likely relation to the larger problem of southern Reconstruction-era violence, the *New York Times* reported the incident in its July 7 edition under the headline "Tragedy at Calvert, Texas." Yet no account offered an adequate explanation for it. Conservative Texas newspapers played up the sensational reports from eye witnesses and deprecated the unruly condition of affairs throughout the state, but repeatedly emphasized that "politics had nothing to do with the [Maxwell murder] whatsoever." In point of fact, a dispute had taken place among men whom anti-Reconstruction Democrats disliked: Ben, for having armed ex-slaves and having fawned over their welfare; Hammond, for having enriched an enterprising ex-slave named John C. Love by renting to him two large cotton plantations in the northern part of the county's bottomlands; and Maxwell, for having assisted the local Freedmen's Bureau agent by performing without compensation medical services to blacks. In short, all three had been supportive of the freedpeople, occupying federal troops, and military-appointed officeholders.[29]

Ben and Hammond claimed all responsibility for killing Maxwell and gave themselves up to the sheriff. Tremendous excitement surrounded their arraignment and trial in Calvert before a newly appointed justice of the peace who had never previously tried a criminal case. No one could be found to prosecute the case for the state because Ben and Hammond had hired most of the county's skilled lawyers to handle their defense. When about thirty-five of Ben's men armed with pistols and shotguns filed into the courtroom, witnesses did not dare to talk about what they had seen. The commanding officer at the post of Calvert finally stopped the judicial mockery by clearing the courtroom, filing charges against Ben's men as accessories to murder, issuing summonses for witnesses, and ordering a search for a prosecutor. When Ben and Hammond, who in custody of the sheriff had been allowed to return to their homes, learned that their cases were more serious than they initially believed, they refused to return to Calvert, causing federal authorities to decide that the "safety of society" required a military commission to prosecute all involved in Maxwell's murder. The pro-Democratic press, which previously had denounced all military interference in local civil or criminal proceedings as wrong in principle, expressed exuberant praise for the army's decision to intervene in the prosecution of Maxwell's killers.[30]

Speculation in military circles arose that "startling developments with regard to affairs in Robertson County" would be revealed in the course of the trial. Newspaper accounts, however, pointed out that "for a series of years" Ben Brown, described as an "old hero of many cowardly and bloody murders," and his posse "had bid defiance to all law, overthrowing courts and trampling underfoot the rights of the citizens." Their boldness in killing Maxwell in broad daylight in front of many witnesses had merely confirmed "[t]he strong hold they have in [Robertson County]." Of greater interest were rumors circulating about "a large amount of money having been deposited" for the purpose of bribing local attorneys selected to aid the commission. More informed pundits predicted that "able criminal lawyers" for the defense would not only "prove *alibi*," but also file petitions to the federal courts to get the cases of the prisoners transferred to the civil courts where "no jury could be selected which the gang and its friends could not and would not intimidate."[31]

Federal soldiers stationed in Calvert captured Ben and eight of his men and took them to Bryan for incarceration and trial. The emotional strain of Ben's arrest on his brother Green's family set off a near-deadly "gay old row" on the train station platform in Hearne. Because the combined criminal indictments and reports of atrocities made against Green's four oldest sons were the most for a band of brothers in the county's history, the incident was predictable. Most likely youngest brother Calvin ("Code") Brown, who at age seventeen was already an accused killer, tried to take the life of one of his older brothers. When his father prevented him from doing so, Calvin held a cocked pistol to his father's breast. Repeated blows to the head restrained a third son who injudiciously got between Calvin and his father. That nobody was killed by the brothers' violent conduct—a psychopathic kinship trait that continued in subsequent years to generate deadly confrontations—amazed the terrified onlookers.[32]

Unlike Ben, Hammond escaped military arrest. Rumors circulated that he had fled to Mexico. While the army posted handbills for Hammond's capture, a commission convened in Bryan where many predicted the trial of Ben and the other prisoners would "attract hundreds" of spectators. Of the many attorneys hired as defense counsel, two were exceptionally capable: Charles Stewart who later served five terms in the United States Congress; and Stewart's law partner with the unusual name of Decimus et Ultimus Barziza who later was elected twice to the Texas House of Representatives. From the outset Stewart and Barziza realized that their

ONE THOUSAND DOLLARS REWARD!

HEADQUARTERS POST OF BRYAN,
BRYAN, TEXAS, AUG. 11, 1869.

By the authority of the General Commanding, a REWARD OF ONE THOUSAND DOLLARS is hereby offered for the apprehension and delivery to the Military Authorities, at any Post in Texas, of

B. F. HAMMOND,

charged with implication in the murder of DR. J. M. MAXWELL, at Calvert, Robertson Co., Texas, on the 25TH of June, 1869. The above REWARD OF ONE THOUSAND DOLLARS will be paid upon conviction of the complicity of the said B. F. Hammond in the murder of said Maxwell.

(Official:)
WILLIAM V. WOLFE,
2D LIEUT. U. S. ARMY, Post Adjutant.

THOMAS H. NORTON,
BREVET MAJOR COMMANDING.

DESCRIPTION.—

Illustration 6. "One Thousand Dollars Reward!" [Handbill for arrest of B. F. Hammond], Headquarters Post of Bryan, August 11, 1869, signed by Thomas H. Norton. (Courtesy of Dale Baum) case was "second in importance only to that of Yerger," which was a similar case arising from the stabbing to death in the streets of Jackson, Mississippi, of Maj. Joseph G. Crane, the city's provisional mayor, by ex-Confederate Edward M. Yerger. At stake was the constitutionality of the military's jurisdiction to try these cases under the First Reconstruction Act. In mid-August when the United States Circuit Court for the western district of Texas refused the petition for a writ of habeas corpus for the Brown prisoners, now trimmed down to Ben and six of his posse members, Barziza was in Washington, D. C., lobbying for his clients to get their case placed on the same status as that of Yerger.[33]

Attorney General Ebenezer R. Hoar guaranteed Barziza that any sentences handed down by the military commission would not be executed until the United States Supreme Court rendered its decision in the Yerger case. In a subsequent discussion with President Ulysses S. Grant, Barziza got a similar assurance that the Yerger ruling would be the precedent for the Brown case. On September 6, 1869, Supreme Court Chief Justice Salmon P. Chase ordered accordingly that no sentence by the Bryan commission would be carried out until all the issues raised by the Brown prisoners' petition were resolved by the Yerger decision. Meanwhile back in Brazos County, the military commission trial trudged forward, albeit at the "tedious and protracted" pace predicted by one of its commissioners, and with Ben, who was suffering from an unidentified illness, given permission "to lie down on a pallet in the courtroom." The court summoned over one hundred witnesses to appear and their testimony proved overwhelmingly detrimental against the prisoners.[34]

The commission found Ben guilty of murder and three of the other six prisoners guilty of being accessories to murder. Shortly thereafter on October 25, the same day that federal soldiers escorted Ben and fellow prisoners Granville W. Rose, Eli Wood, and James B. Wharton to the stockade at the post of Calvert to remain imprisoned while awaiting their sentencing, the Supreme Court finally disposed of the Yerger case. In receipt of telegraphic reports from the nation's capital, Barziza relayed to Ben and the others that their petition for a writ of habeas corpus would not be granted, even though the high court ruled that it had the authority to review a denial by a circuit court of a petition for such a writ on behalf of persons imprisoned by the military in the South. More importantly, the crucial issue of Yerger's fate was never reached because it had been resolved by the Grant administration's eleventh-hour compromise decision to turn him over to civil authorities after Mississippi was readmitted to the union: an event on track to occur in February of 1870.[35]

In short, the Supreme Court avoided provoking congressional legislation repealing its authority to issue writs of habeas corpus in cases similar to that of Yerger. Not only were the limits of congressional power under the Constitution not clarified, but there was no more than an assumed assurance that Ben's rights to bail and trial in the civil courts would be guaranteed after Congress restored Texas to the American Union: a tardy event nevertheless on target for the middle of April 1870. Ben, having pinned his hopes during the past four months on Barziza's efforts to have his case transferred to civil authorities, despaired of the prospect of spending at least five more months in military confinement. Moreover, the loathing of him by the officers at the post of Calvert was palpable, and because of his own past callous execution orders he knew how uncomplicated it would be to dispose of a prisoner who supposedly might try to escape.[36]

On the night of November 21, 1869, Ben along with Wood and Rose, broke out of jail by bribing a guard. Standing military orders regarding Ben never changed: No terms were to be negotiated with him and he was to be either taken back into custody or killed. After Ben's nephew Calvin celebrated the jailbreak by shooting "away a portion of the tongue" of "[a] man by the name of Smith," fears arose concerning retaliation by Ben's partisans against those who had had "the temerity to appear as witnesses" at the Bryan commission trial. Equally as disconcerting was the refusal of citizens, with the exception of a few blacks, to volunteer to assist the dozen soldiers billeted at Calvert to organize an effective pursuit of the escapees. In an act of desperation in February 1870, the army allowed Wharton, the remaining prisoner, to escape in order to verify a rumor that Ben was in attendance at a horse race with "a party of 10 or 12 armed men" in an old anti-Secessionist area of Collin County in North Texas. Even though Ben was "always accompanied by others and [made] his home at no place two days" in a row, meetings with him were easily arranged via his brothers Green and Early, if and only if, the men protecting him rendered interviewers incapable of jeopardizing his safety and wellbeing. Ben's message was always the same: having "no enemies to punish and no malice to gratify," he would surrender to "civil tribunels" [*sic*] if set free on bail "no higher than $100,000."[37]

Not until the fall of 1870, five months after the army had officially promulgated President Grant's signing of the act readmitting Texas to congressional representation and after the Robertson County Grand Jury had filed charges of murder against Ben and Hammond, did the two of them come in from "out in the bush" and surrender themselves to stand trial for the killing of Maxwell. Radical Republican Judge James M. Thurmond, in whose district courtroom the trial would be held, set their bail in the amount of $20,000 each. Shortly thereafter while awaiting trial, Hammond became the most important surety on a bond required of Robertson County Sheriff Francis ("Frank") M. Hall, who was the brother of influential State Senator Fidella Hall. Because the Republican Party-dominated commissioners' court controlled, with the assistance of the sheriff, the pool of men selected for jury service, signing as a surety on Frank Hall's new civil commission bond for an amount that had proven an insurmountable obstacle for a couple of previously military-approved candidates represented an investment on Hammond's part in facilitating his and Ben's acquittals.[38]

An indication that Hammond's investment paid off is found in the list of petit jurors drawn for jury duty at the start of the 1871 spring term and just two weeks prior to his and Ben's scheduled trial date. It incredibly included two members of the posse that killed Dr. Maxwell: Granville Rose who had escaped with Ben from the Calvert stockade; and Richard Cage who had been among those the army had initially arrested though subsequently had released. Although Judge Thurmond issued a special summons for new jurors for agreed-upon separate trials for Ben and Hammond, the initial swearing in of Rose and Cage as "good and lawful men" must have made an extraordinary statement to all onlookers present at the district court. In back-to-back trials each lasting only a day, Ben and Hammond were found not guilty of murdering Maxwell. No surviving reports regarding the verdicts claim that any new circumstances or facts had been introduced to show that the killing of Maxwell had been justifiable. The verdicts were not only agreed upon before trial, but were unabashed instances of jury nullification.[39]

Ben and Hammond's support of Sheriff Frank Hall occurred at the outset of bitter factional disputes that disrupted not only Republicans and Democrats, but also the Ben Brown partisans themselves, including brothers Ben and Green. Republican unity was shaken when local blacks bristled over their inability to select the party's nominee for Congress from the Third Congressional District in the fall 1871 election. The resulting disharmony contributed to the white Republican incumbent narrowly losing his bid for reelection to Congress and Robertson County Republicans losing two of the five justice-of-the-peace positions on the commissioners' court. By 1872 the resurgent Democrats fractured when so-called "Straight-Outs," including Green Brown and members of the extended Hearne family, refused to unite with the Liberal Republicans or so-called "Independents" who accepted, at least in theory, the principles contained in the Thirteenth, Fourteenth, and Fifteenth Amendments to the United States Constitution. Because of the machinations of the Independents, including most prominently Ben's allies Hammond and wealthy planter Charles P. Salter, Radical Republican Frank Hall won election as sheriff, and Rasche Hearne, running as an anti–Horace Greeley Democrat, was defeated by Salter for a seat in the state legislature. The Straight-Outs angrily denounced the Independents for having run "fairly and squarely with the [N]egroes" and for being sureties on the required bonds of the "vile crew" of local scalawag and carpetbagger officeholders. A week prior to the election, those supporting Rasche's candidacy had issued a warning to the "Hammond-Salter clique": "[T]he memory of these things will not pass away with the election. . . . nor will retribution fail to be visited on the heads of those who secure the election of [Frank] Hall. . . ."[40]

Many decades would pass before Hammond, Salter, and other homegrown traitors to their own white race in 1872 were completely forgiven by the magnanimity of selective memory in accounts written by latter-day biographers and historians. Rehabilitation of Hammond was far from complete at the time of his death in early 1890 when newspapers tersely reported: "Dr. B. F. Hammond of Calvert is dead." In the twentieth century Robertson County opted to mythologize his legacy into an example of Yankee perfidy during Reconstruction by lauding him as a "[p]rominent physician, planter, industrialist, political leader" who "[a]fter the Civil War gave about 160 acres to each household of his ex-slaves, but carpetbaggers nevertheless put him in Calvert's tree prison." Omitted were Hammond's activities as a murderous vigilante gang member, a financial backer of local radical Republican officeholders, and a miscegenationist slaveholder who had fathered four children with one of his slaves. Lied about was his postwar relationship with over one-hundred ex-slaves whom he formerly had owned as his personal property. Hammond did not give away his land to them, but leased about 900–1000 acres, or appropriately half of his total holdings, to Love who, in turn, subleased to other ex-slaves the remainder of what he himself did not need to cultivate in order to compensate Hammond: a controversial situation requiring Ben's posse to ward off white interlopers demanding to know whose unsupervised freedmen were planting "very indifferent crops" on Hammond's lands. Nor was Hammond, who successfully remained a fugitive-at-large from arrest for his role in the brutal murder of Maxwell, placed at any time in a military stockade, a municipal or county jail, or in a putative "tree prison."[41]

In contrast to Hammond, all collective memory of Ben dissolved in the slow eddies of time. No extant obituary or newspaper reference to his death has been found, although there is a brief typed entry for him in a genealogical record book in the Robertson County Courthouse. Ben died of natural causes on April 9, 1883. He had been a widower since Fannie's death in 1868 and had subsequently through gifts *inter vivos* put most of his real property in his two youngest daughters' names and had transferred the title to his original homestead on Duck Creek to freedwoman America Brown, a light-complexioned "housekeeper" who had lived with his family since emancipation. For "her faithfulness and services" rendered to him, he also made her a primary beneficiary of his will. He appointed Hammond as the executor of his estate, which by then was considerably depleted due to attorney fees and legal expenses as well as payments to cover liabilities that he had incurred as a surety on Sheriff Hall's bond. After being indicted for embezzlement of tax monies in 1875, Hall had resigned and consented to judgments against him greatly surpassing his own net worth and thus devolving upon his bondsmen, who included both Ben and Hammond.[42]

Neither the discredited legends depicting blacks as an incapacitated race victimized by carpetbagger manipulation, nor the revisionist historiographical turning points of the 1960s, provide an interpretative framework to explain Ben's career as a scalawag vigilante gang leader. In the wake of historian Eric Foner's monumental and definitive study of Reconstruction, Ben is perhaps best measured against the hopes and dreams of freedom's first generation of African Texans in Robertson County. Although his desire to help and protect the freedpeople was indisputable, he never embraced the full implications of the egalitarian ideals of the Republican Party. Nor did he share the goals of the former slaves to obtain full political and legal equality and unlimited economic opportunity. Ben and his posse operated primarily in the interest of the planter elites in the Brazos River bottomlands.[43]

When all the facts regarding Ben Brown's career are considered, his place in Texas history will remain situated in the recurrent paroxysms of collective violence that occurred throughout the entire Civil War era—including the panicky murders generated by the 1860 summer fires of misunderstood origins, the extra-legal wartime hangings of Unionist sympathizers, and the Ku Klux Klan postwar assassinations of blacks, scalawags, and carpetbaggers—all of which, along with Ben and his men with their rifles, guns, and hound dogs, in turn perversely prolonged the misrule of law through mob violence as acceptable, necessary, and even honorable, into the early twentieth century. During the sixty years after the end of the Civil War, the area of Robertson County and its immediate vicinity that had been early on dominated by the Ben Brown gang became the heart of an eleven-county region, stretching from Waco to the Gulf of Mexico, that contained the largest concentrations of the lynching of blacks in the Lone Star State.[44]

ENDNOTES

1. For reinterpretations of the older, and often enduring, popular legends regarding Reconstruction-era outlaws, gun fighters, and family feuds, see: Donaly E. Brice and Barry A. Crouch, *Cullen Montgomery Baker: Reconstruction Desperado* (Baton Rouge: Louisiana State University Press, 1997); James M. Smallwood, Barry A. Crouch, and Larry Peacock, *Murder and Mayhem: The War of Reconstruction in Texas* (College Station: Texas A&M University Press, 2003); James M. Smallwood, *The Feud That Wasn't: The Taylor Ring, Bill Sutton, John Wesley Hardin, and Violence in Texas* (College Station: Texas A&M University Press, 2008).

2. ["Benjamin Brown"], Ancestry.com *1850 United States Federal Census*, database on-line (Provo, UT: The Generations Network, Inc., 2005), hereafter cited as *Ancestry.com 1850*, Rusk County, Texas, Microcopy M432, Microfilm Reel #914, Page 242, Image 131; ["B. W. Brown and Francis Rogers"], Oct. 19, 1841, *Marriage Records, 1837–1848*, Vol. "A," Microfilm Reel #1003581, Nacogdoches County Court Records, Family History Library, Microcopy #0025309, Nacogdoches County, Texas; ["Benjn Brown"], Rusk County, Texas, Ancestry.com *1850 U.S. Federal Census—Slave Schedules*, database on-line (Provo, UT: The Generations Network, Inc., 2004) hereafter cited as *Ancestry.com 1850 Slave Schedules*; ["B. Brown"], Registration No. 453, Robertson County, Microfilm Reel #6, *Voter Registration Lists, 1867–1869*, Archives Division, Texas State Library, Austin, Texas, hereafter cited as TSL-AD; ["Benjamin Brown"] Ancestry.com *1860 United States Federal Census*, database on-line (Provo, UT: The Generations Network, Inc., 2004), hereafter cited as *Ancestry.com 1860*, Precinct 1 (Owensville), Robertson County, Texas, Microcopy M653, Microfilm Reel #1303, Page 164, Image 328; ["E A Brown"] *Ancestry.com 1860*, Precinct 5 [Eutaw], Robertson County, Texas, Microcopy M653, Microfilm Reel #1303, Page 183, Image 369; ["Green Brown"], *Ancestry.com 1860*, Precinct 3 (Sterling), Robertson County, Texas, Microcopy M653, Microfilm Reel #1303, Page 178, Image 358; Robertson County Tax Rolls, 1838–1882,

Tax Rolls for 1854 through 1865, Microfilm Reel #119801, TSL-AD; Dallas *Herald*, Jan. 20, 1881, 7. Ben, Early, and Green's older sister, Annie C. Brown Bates, also moved to Robertson County either during or after the Civil War. The criminal careers of Annie's grandsons, Willis and Mack Brooks, are discussed in Edward Herring, *Sam Baker: Winston County's Gunfighter* (Moulton, AL: Frost Printing Company, 1998).

3. ["Teliphus Johnson"], Precinct 3, Robertson County, Texas, Ancestry.com *1860 U.S. Federal Census—Slave Schedules*, database on-line (Provo, UT: The Generations Network, Inc., 2004), hereafter cited as *Ancestry.com 1860 Slave Schedules*; "Arrest the Murderer—$500 Reward." Public Notices. *Texas State Gazette* (Austin), Aug. 19, 1854, (quotations); Citation and fine for being in "contempt of court", Oct. 31, 1854, (Fall Term 1854), Book "I," 292, and *The State of Texas v. William D. Miller*, "Assault with intent to murder," Case No. 211, Fall Term 1854, Book "I," 305, and *The State of Texas v. Lewis Tubbs, Telephus A. Johnson, John Johnson, and Earl A. Brown*, "Murder" Case No. 233, Spring Term 1855, Book "I," 369–370, and renumbered as Case No. 235, Spring Term 1856, Book "J [1–451]," 23–24, and *The State of Texas v. Lewis Tubbs*, "Murder—continued," Case No. 235, Mar. 12, 1856, Spring Term 1856, Book "J[1–451]," 36, Minutes of the District Court, Office of the District Clerk, Robertson County, Texas, hereafter cited as MDC, ODC-RC. Twenty years later the district attorney dismissed the murder charge against Tubbs. See *The State of Texas v. Lewis Tubbs*, "Murder," renumbered as Case No. 234, Feb. 23, 1874, February Term 1874, Book, "L," 466, MDC, ODC-RC.

4. *Southern Intelligencer* (Austin), July 27, 1859 (first quotation); Manuscript Election Returns for 1855, 1857 and 1859, folders for Robertson County, Secretary of State Records, RG 307, TSL-AD; *The State of Texas v. Lewis Tubbs, Telephus A. Johnson, John Johnson, and Earl A. Brown*, "Murder," Case No. 233, Spring Term 1855, Book "I," 369–370, and *The State of Texas v. Telephus A. Johnson*, "Obstructing an officer in the discharge of his duties," Case No. 215, Oct. 9, 1854, Fall Term 1854 , Book "I," 324, and Spring Term 1855, Book "I," 357–358, and Book "J[1–451]," 1, 14, MDC, ODC-RC. For the lists of voters drawn as jurors, see: Spring Term 1856 through Fall Term 1860, Book "J[1–451]," 29, 63, 135, 197, 328, 362 and 364, MDC, ODC-RC.

5. ["Benjamin Brown"], Box 22, Extraction 5, Record 92, United States National Archives, *Civil War Service Records*, database on-line (Provo, UT: The Generations Network, Inc., 1999); *Handbook of Texas Online*, "Fourth Texas Infantry," http://www. tshaonline.org/handbook/

online/articles/FF/qkf1.html (accessed Mar. 9, 2009); "Muster Roll of State Troops of Beat No. 2, 3, & 6 of Robertson County, Tex. for July 1863," Box 3S167, and "A List of names liable to the Draft Beats No. 2, 3, & 6," undated, Box 2J98, Josephus Cavitt Papers, The Dolph Briscoe Center for American History, The University of Texas at Austin, Austin, Texas hereafter cited as CAH-UT.

6. ["E A Brown"], Precinct 3, Robertson County, Texas, *Ancestry.com 1860 Slave Schedules*; Robertson County Tax Rolls, 1838–1882, Tax Rolls for 1861 through 1867, Microfilm Reel #119801, TSL-AD; *The State of Texas vs. E. A. Brown*, "Murder," Case No. 382, Sept. 11, 1861, Fall Term 1861 , Book "J [1–451]," 417, and "*nole prosequi*," Apr. 16, 1867, Spring Term 1867 , Book "J[452–922]," 596 (quotation), MDC, ODC-RC.

7. ["Green Brown"], *Ancestry.com 1860*, Precinct 3 (Sterling), Robertson County, Texas, Microcopy M653, Microfilm Reel #1303, Page 178, Image 358; "[Account of] Mr. S. R. Hearne Bo[ught]t of Greenwood Brown," undated, in Re: Estate of Samuel R. Hearne, Docket #134, Probate Files, County Clerk's Office, Robertson County, Texas, hereafter cited as PF, CCO-RC ; Robertson County Tax Rolls, 1838–1882, Tax Rolls for 1853 through 1861, Microfilm Reel #119801, TSL-AD.

8. ["Benjamin Brown"], Precinct 1, Robertson County, Texas, *Ancestry.com 1860 Slave Schedules*; Robertson County Tax Rolls, 1838–1882, Tax Rolls for 1860 through 1865, Microfilm Reel #119801, TSL-AD; "Petition of Ben Brown," March Term, 1863, February 1856–August 1863, 413, Commissioners Court Minutes, Robertson County, Texas; List of Grand Jurors , Sept. 14, 1863, Fall Term 1863, Book "J [452–922]," 474, and Sept. 12, 1864, Fall Term 1864, Book "J [452-–922]," 500, MDC, ODC-RC; Re: Estate of George W. Jones, Oct. 5, 1864, Vol. "M [1863–1865]," 354, Microfilm Reel #964209, Probate Minutes, County Clerk's Office, Robertson County, Texas, hereafter cited as PM, CCO-RC. In 1860 and 1861 Ben owned 390 acres of land valued for annual county tax purposes at $1,300. Cf: ["Benjamin Brown"], *Ancestry.com 1860*, Precinct 1, Robertson County, Texas, Microcopy M653, Microfilm Reel #1303, Page 164, Image 328, which incorrectly lists the value of Ben's real property at $11,300.

9. Joseph Allen Myers, "Life of Joseph Allen Myers: Written in the Month of November 1927," typescript, taken from a ledger with the handwritten text of Joseph Allen Myers, by William Allen Myers, Nov. 20, 2001, 13–14 (first quotation), Bryan Public Library, Bryan, Texas; Dale Baum, *The Shattering of Texas Unionism: Politics in the Lone Star*

State during the Civil War Era (Baton Rouge: Louisiana State University Press, 1998), 126 (second quotation); "Robertson County Mass Meeting" supplement, *Tri-Weekly Telegraph* (Houston), Oct. 2, 1863 (third quotation).

10. Harvey Mitchell to Governor Hamilton, Aug. 21, 1865 (first, second and third quotations), folder 14, box 49, Governors' Papers: Andrew J. Hamilton, RG 301, TSL-AD; Joshua L. Randall to James P. Richardson, Dec. 24, 1867 (fourth quotation), Microfilm Reel #14, Records of the Assistant Commissioner for the State of Texas, Bureau of Refugees, Freedmen, and Abandoned Lands, hereafter cited as BRFAL (1865–1869), RG 105, M821 (1973), National Archives, Washington, D.C. hereafter cited as NA ; *Texas Confederate Military Service Records,* microform , compiled from muster rolls in the Texas State Archives, 1999, Microfilm Reels #4, #7 and #8, TSL-AD; Janet B. Hewett, ed., *The Roster of Confederate Soldiers, 1861–1865*, 16 vols. (Wilmington, N.C.: Broadfoot Publishing Co., 1995), 7: 396; "Muster Roll of State Troops of Beat No. 2, 3, & 6 of Robertson County, Tex. for July 1863," Box 3S167, and "A List of names liable to the Draft Beats No. 2, 3, & 6," undated, Box 2J98, Josephus Cavitt Papers, CAH-UT; Dale Baum, *Counterfeit Justice: The Judicial Odyssey of Texas Freedwoman Azeline Hearne* (Baton Rouge: Louisiana State University Press, 2009), 41.

11. Myers, "Life of Joseph Allen Myers," 6–8 and 12–14 (first and second quotations); Thomas J. McHugh quoted in J. W. Baker, *A History of Robertson County, Texas* (Waco, TX: Texian Press, 1970), 518 (third and fourth quotations).

12. Dale Baum, "Slaves Taken to Texas for Safekeeping during the Civil War," in *The Fate of Texas: The Civil War and the Lone Star State,* ed. Charles D. Grear (Fayetteville: The University of Arkansas Press, 2008), 93–94 (first quotation); ["R C Myers"], *Ancestry.com 1860*, Madison Parish, Louisiana, Microcopy M653, Microfilm Reel #413, Page 35, Image 316; ["R C Myers"], Madison Parish, Louisiana, *Ancestry.com 1860 Slave Schedules*; Robertson County Tax Rolls, 1838–1882, Tax Rolls for 1864, Microfilm Reel #119801, TSL-AD; Myers, "Life of Joseph Allen Myers," 6–8 and 12–14 (second and third quotations).

13. "Appointment to Office Under Provisional Government," September 1865–July 1866, and "Robertson County Officeholders," in *Registers of Elected and Appointed State and County Officials,* Microfilm Reel #4, 74–75, 143–46, and Microfilm Reel #3, 667–70, TSL-AD; Joshua L. Randall to Joel T. Kirkman, July 10, 1867 (first through fourth quotations), Microfilm Reel #32, and Oscar F. Hunsaker to Joel T.

Kirkman, July 9, 1867 (fifth quotation), Microfilm Reel #6, and George T. Ruby to Joel T. Kirkman, Aug. 12, 1867 (sixth quotation), Microfilm Reel #4, BRFAL (1865–1869), RG 105, M821 (1973), NA; Barry A. Crouch, *The Freedmen's Bureau and Black Texans* (Austin: University of Texas Press, 1992), 108–9.

14. Statements of Louis Young in George P. Rawick, ed., *The American Slave: A Composite Autobiography,* vol. 5, pt. 4 (Westport, CT: Greenwood Press, 1979), 232–234 (first quotation on p. 233); Statements of Hattie (Hearne) Cole in Rawick, ed., *The American Slave,* supp., ser. 2, vol. 3: "Texas Narratives," pt. 2, 780 (second quotation); William L. Richter, *Overreached on All Sides: The Freedmen's Bureau Administrators in Texas, 1865–1868* (College Station: Texas A&M University Press, 1991), 101; "Letter from Brazos County [signed "H.J.J."]," Bryan, Texas, July 18, 1869, quoted in *Flake's Bulletin* (Galveston), July 21, 1869, (third and fourth quotations).

15. Oscar F. Hunsaker to Joel T. Kirkman, July 16, 1867, Microfilm Reel #6, and Charles Griffin to O. O. Howard, Aug. 17, 1867, Microfilm Reel #1, and Benjamin Brown to Charles Garretson, Oct. 28, 1867, Microfilm Reel #10, BRFAL (1865–1869), RG 105, M821 (1973), NA. Cf: William L. Richter, who in his *Overreached on All Sides*, 185 and 257, discusses the controversial arming of around one-hundred Robertson County blacks in mid-July of 1867, but omits mention of Ben Brown's involvement.

16. "Record of Criminal Offenses Committed in Texas," Vol. 2, September 2, 1867, and August 31, 1867, Nos. 1103, "Saville" and 1104, "Locke," 87 (second quotation), Microfilm Reel #32, and Benjamin Brown to Charles Griffin, Aug. 31, 1867 (fourth and fifth quotations), Microfilm Reel #10, and Oscar F. Hunsaker to Joel T. Kirkman, July 16, 1867 (first and third quotations), Microfilm Reel #6, BRFAL (1865–1869), RG 105, M821 (1973), NA.

17. Benjamin Brown to Charles Griffin, Aug. 31, 1867 (quotations), Microfilm Reel #10, BRFAL (1865–1869), RG 105, M821 (1973), NA; "The New Bureau Order," *Flake's Bulletin* (Galveston), Oct. 1, 1867.

18. "Robertson County Officeholders," in *Registers of Elected and Appointed State and County Officials,* Microfilm Reel #2, 390–91, and Microfilm Reel #3, 667–668, TSL-AD; Benjamin Brown to Charles Griffin, August 31, 1867 (first quotation), Microfilm Reel #10, BRFAL (1865–1869), RG 105, M821 (1973), NA; Petition to Governor Pease signed by Joshua L. Randall and 42 others, April 14, 1868, folder 34, Box 57, and "Law and Order" to Governor Pease, April 24, 1868 (second

quotation), folder 36, Box 57, and Isaac B. Ellison to Governor Pease, June 1, 1868, folder 39, Box 57, Governors' Papers: Elisha M. Pease, RG 301, TSL-AD; Special Officer Detective C. H. Bostwick to Charles E. Morse, Sept. 18, 1869 (third and fourth quotations), Microfilm Reel #19, Correspondence of the Office of Civil Affairs of the District of Texas, and the Fifth Military District, and the Department of Texas, 1867–1870, hereafter cited as COCADT, RG 393, M1188 (1981), NA.

19. *The State of Texas v. John R. Harlan*, "Murder," Case No. 494, Spring Term 1868 , Book "J[452–922]," 698, 707, 713, and Oct. 20, 1868, Fall Term 1868, Book "J[452–922]," 754–755, MDC, ODC-RC; "Will of John S. Deveraux," dated May 28, 1864, and filed on Jan. 3, 1868, "Re: Estate of John S. Deveraux," Docket #50, PF, CCO-RC; ["J. R. Harlan"], Registration No. 745, Robertson County, Microfilm Reel VR–10, and ["Phidella W. Hall"], Registration No. 749, Limestone County, Microfilm Reel VR–8, *Voter Registration Lists of 1867–1869*, TSL-AD; Governor Pease to Joseph J. Reynolds, Apr. 14, 1869 (copy), Letterbook, 225, Box 59, Governors' Papers: Elisha M. Pease, RG 301, TSL-AD; William V. Wolfe to Charles E. Morse, Nov. 20, 1869, Microfilm Reel #25, COCADT, RG 393, M1188 (1981), NA; U.S. Army, Fifth Military District, State of Texas, General Orders No. 19, *Tabular Statement, Showing the Number of Votes Cast in Each County For and Against the Constitution, and for State Officers, and Tabular Statement, Showing Number Votes Cast in Each County for Members of Congress,* and *Tabular Statement, Showing the Votes Cast in Each District for Senators and Representatives,* and *Statement, Showing Vote by Counties for Clerks of District Courts, Sheriffs, and Justices of the Peace* (Austin: Feb. 1, 1870), 1–46.

20. Cynthia Skove Nevels, *Lynching to Belong: Claiming Whiteness through Racial Violence* (College Station: Texas A&M University Press, 2007), 23; U.S. Army, Fifth Military District, State of Texas, General Order No. 73, *Tabular Statement of Voters (white and colored) Registered in Texas at Registration in 1867, and at Revision of the Lists in 1867–'68–'69; showing also the number (white and colored) Stricken Off the Lists. Tabular Statement of Votes (white and colored) cast at Election held in the State of Texas, under the authority of the Reconstruction Acts of Congress* (Austin: Apr. 16, 1870), 1–9; Oscar F. Hunsaker to Joel T. Kirkman, July 9, 1867 (quotation), Microfilm Reel #6, BRFAL (1865–1869), RG 105, M821 (1973), NA.

21. Warranty Deed, Joseph S. Ables to Ben Brown and E. A. Brown, Jan. 14, 1868, Book "Q," 12–14, Microfilm Reel #963281, Record of

Deeds, County Clerk's Office, Robertson County, Texas; "Letter from Brazos County" signed "H. J. J." and dated "July 18th, 1860 [*sic*]," quoted in *Flake's Bulletin* (Galveston), July 21, 1869, 8 (first and second quotations); Joshua L. Randall to Joel T. Kirkman, May 27, 1867, Microfilm Reel #4, and Joshua L. Randall to Charles A. Vernon, November 30, 1868, Microfilm Reel #7, Records of the Superintendent of Education for the State of Texas, BRFAL (1865–1870), RG 105, M822 (1973), NA; Joshua L. Randall to William A. Rafferty, Jan. 20, 1868 (third quotation), "Sterling, Tex., Letters sent from Sept. 26/66 to Dec. 15/68," Microfilm Reel #26, Records of the Field Offices for the State of Texas, BRFAL (1865–1870), RG 105, M1912 (2005), NA.

22. "Record of Criminal Offenses Committed in Texas," Vol. 2, June 8, 1868, No. 1787 "A party of men," 142 (first quotation), Microfilm Reel #32, BRFAL (1865–1869), RG 105, M821 (1973), NA; Galveston *Daily News*, May 27, 1868, 2 (second, third and fourth quotations); *The Daily Picayune* (New Orleans, Louisiana), June 2, 1868, 2; "Sam Eaves Tell [*sic*] of His Early Recollections of Bryan," Bryan *Daily Eagle*, July 22, 1926 (fifth, sixth and seventh quotations).

23. Nevels, *Lynching to Belong*, 96–97; Dale Baum, "Burdens of Landholding in a Freed Slave Settlement: The Case of Brazos County's 'Hall's Town'," *Southwestern Historical Quarterly* 113 (Oct. 2009): 185–204, especially map on 191.

24. Crouch, *The Freedmen's Bureau and Black Texans*, (first quotation), 102 –127; "Sam Eaves Tell [*sic*] of His Early Recollections of Bryan"; *Tri-Weekly State Gazette* (Austin), June 29, 1868 (second quotation).

25. Myers, "Life of Joseph Allen Myers," 9; Nevels, *Lynching to Belong*, 23–24.

26. Will of Samuel R. Hearne, Sept. 17, 1866, and filed for record on Nov. 28, 1866, Vol. "O," 302–304, PM, CCO-RC; "B[enjamin] Brown Petition for Administration," June 10, 1868, and filed for record on June 18, 1868, Re: Estate of Samuel R. Hearne, Docket #134, PF, CCO-RC; Harvey D. Prendergast to Thomas H. Norton, undated letter marked as "Exhibit A" (quotation), frames 0628–0632, Microfilm Reel #39, CO-CADT, RG 393, M118 (1981), NA; Baum, *Counterfeit Justice*, 63–99 and 105–8.

27. Baum, *Counterfeit Justice*, 105–8, 114–23 and 263; Baum, "Burdens of Landholding," 199–200.

28. ["Doctor Maxwell"], *Ancestry.com 1860*, Western District (Barwick) St. Mary Parish, Louisiana, Microcopy M653, Reel #425, Page

0, Image 232; Galveston *Daily News,* June 29, 1869, 2 (first, third and fifth quotations); Mordecai S. Boatner quoted in ibid., July 8, 1869, 1 (seventh, ninth and tenth quotations); "Letter from Bryan. Bryan, June 28, 1869. Another Murder," Houston *Union*, June 30, 1869, 3 (second, fourth, sixth, eighth and eleventh quotations).

29. *New York Times,* July 7, 1869, 2 (first quotation); Galveston *Daily News*, June 29, 1869, 2 (second quotation); Houston *Union*, Sept. 21, 1869, 1; Lawrence Ward St. Clair, "History of Robertson County, Texas" (M.A. thesis, University of Texas, 1931), 258; Baum, *Counterfeit Justice*, 123–24.

30. Thomas H. Norton, Commanding Officer Post of Bryan, to Headquarters Fifth Military District, hereafter cited as HFMD, July 29, 1869, "Register of Letters Received," Vol. 3, 74, Microfilm Reel #4, and Thomas H. Norton to Charles E. Morse, July 7, 1869 (quotation), Microfilm Reel #29, COCADT, RG 393, M1188 (1981), NA; Galveston *Tri-Weekly News,* July 23, 1869, 4; Baum, *Counterfeit Justice*, 124.

31. Thomas H. Norton to Charles E. Morse, July 12, 1869, "Register of Letters Received," Vol. 2, #143 (first quotation), Microfilm Reel #3, COCADT, RG 393, M1188 (1981), NA; "Letter from Bryan. Bryan, June 28, 1869. Another Murder," Houston *Union*, June 30, 1869, 3 (second, fourth and fifth quotations); "Letter from Calvert," July 9, 1869, quoted in Galveston *Tri-Weekly News*, July 14, 1869, 2 (third quotation); "Letter from Brazos County" signed "H. J. J." and dated "July 18th, 1860 [*sic*]," quoted in *Flake's Bulletin* (Galveston), July 21, 1869, 8 (sixth quotation); "Editorial Paragraphs.," *Flake's Bulletin* (Galveston), July 24, 1869, 4 (seventh, eighth and ninth quotations).

32. Charles E. Morse to H. Clay Wood, Aug. 2, 1869, "Register of Letters Received," Vol. 2, #415, Benjamin Brown, Eli Wood, John H. Halligan, Granville W. Rose, James B. Wharton, William Andrews, Philip Stonemets, Richard M. Cage, John N. Cage, Microfilm Reel #1, COCADT, RG 393, M1188 (1981), NA; "Letter from Calvert," Galveston *Tri-Weekly News*, July 9, 1869, 2; Bryan *News-Letter* cited in the Galveston *Daily News,* July 11, 1869, 4; and Houston *Daily Times,* July 9, 1869, 2 (quotation). For offenses committed by Calvin ("Code") Brown, see: "June 21st, 1866—Marie Edwards, a freedwoman, was shot and killed by Court [*sic*] Brown," Sam C. Sloan to Lieutenant Maden, Acting Asst. Adj. Gen., "Registered Reports of Murders and Outrages, Sept. 1866–July 1867," Sept. 7, 1866, Microfilm Reel #32, BRFAL (1865–1869), RG 105, M821 (1973) NA; "The wound is not mortal, though the intention of [Calvin]

Brown to kill his victim seems evident," *Flake's Bulletin* (Galveston), Nov. 27, 1869, 4; *The State of Texas v. Calvin Brown*, "Murder [of a state policeman]," Case No. 833, Feb. 29, 1872, February Term 1872, Book "K," 438, MDC, ODC-RC; Chuck Parsons and Marianne E. Hall Little, *Captain L. H. McNelly—Texas Ranger: The Life and Times of a Fighting Man* (Austin: State House Press, 2001), 88–89, and 323n21. For the oldest Brown brother, James C. Brown, who served in the Confederate Army, see: *The State of Texas v. James Brown*, "Aggravated assault and battery," Case No. 362, Spring Term 1860, Book "J [1–451]," 350, MDC, ODC-RC. For the second oldest brother, Samuel C. Brown, see: *The State of Texas v. S. C. Brown and John Roberts*, "Assault & Battery," Case No. 455, Fall Term 1865, and *The State of Texas v. Samuel C. Brown*, "Assault with intent to murder," Case No. 462, Fall Term 1865, Book "J [452–922]," 541–42, MDC, ODC-RC. For the third oldest son, John M. Brown, see: "December 27, 1879: Resisting arrest for disorderly conduct and killed by a pistol shot fired by a Hearne city policeman," Dallas *Weekly Herald*, Jan. 20, 1881, 7.

33. "One Thousand Dollars Reward!" Handbill for arrest of B. F. Hammond, Headquarters Post of Bryan, Aug. 11, 1869, signed by Thomas H. Norton, Microfilm Reel #19, and Thomas H. Norton to Charles E. Morse, July 12, 1869, "Register of Letters Received," Vol. 2, #143, Microfilm Reel #3, COCADT, RG 393, M1188 (1981), NA; "Letter from Bryan. Bryan, July 27, '69," Houston *Union*, July 31, 1869, 3 (first quotation); R. Henderson Shuffler, "Decimus et Ultimus Barziza," *Southwestern Historical Quarterly* 66 (Apr. 1963): 501–12; *Handbook of Texas Online*, "Stewart, Charles," http:// www.tshaonline.org/handbook/online/ articles/SS/ fst52.html (accessed May 8, 2009); *Flake's Bulletin* (Galveston), July 31, 1869, 6 (second quotation); "The Tragedy in Jackson," *New York Times*, June 15, 1869, 1; *In the Matter of Benjamin Brown, et al., Petition*, File Date: Oct. 8, 1869, 11 pages, Term Year: 1869, *U.S. Supreme Court Records and Briefs, 1832–1978*, 9–10, Thomson Gale, Texas A&M University, College Station, http:// galenet.galegroup.com/ servlet/SCRB?uid=0&srchtp=a&ste =14&rcn= DW111215861 (accessed Apr. 3, 2007), hereafter cited as *In the Matter of Benjamin Brown, et al., Petition*; *Ex parte Yerger,* Supreme Court of the United States, 75 U.S. 85, 19 L. Ed. 332, U.S. LEXIS 1085; 8 Wall. 85 (decided Oct. 25, 1869), hereafter cited as *Ex parte Yerger*; Galveston *Tri-Weekly News*, Aug. 2, 1869, 1.

34. *In the Matter of Benjamin Brown, et al., Petition*, 10–11; Galveston *Tri-Weekly News*, Sept. 10, 1869, 4; Thomas H. Norton, Commanding

Officer Post of Bryan, to HFMD, July 29, 1869, "Register of Letters Received," Vol. 3, 74 (first quotation), Microfilm Reel #4, COCADT, RG 393, M1188 (1981), NA; Galveston *Tri-Weekly News*, Aug. 25, 1869, 2 (second quotation) and Sept. 13, 1869, 1.

35. Galveston *Tri-Weekly News*, Oct. 10, 1869, 1; Stanley I. Kutler, "*Ex parte McCardle*: Judicial Impotency? The Supreme Court and Reconstruction Reconsidered," *American Historical Review* 72 (Apr. 1967): 845–48. In March of 1870 the adjutant general of the Fourth Military District transferred Yerger, who had pleaded insanity at his military trial and had afterward remained in confinement awaiting sentencing, to the sheriff of Hinds County, Mississippi. Released from jail on bail, Yerger quickly moved to Maryland where in 1875 he died and thus avoided ever being tried for murder by civil authorities. See: Galveston *Tri-Weekly News*, Aug. 9, 1869, 1; Dallas *Herald*, Mar. 12, 1870, 2; Wikipedia contributors, "Ex parte Yerger," *Wikipedia, The Free Encyclopedia,* http://en.wikipedia.org/w/ index.php? title= Ex_parte_Yerger&oldid=306422241 (accessed Oct. 5, 2009).

36. *Ex parte Yerger*; Frederick J. Blue, *Salmon P. Chase: A Life in Politics* (Kent, OH: Kent State University Press, 1987), 273–74.

37. *Flake's Bulletin* (Galveston), Nov. 27, 1869, 4 (first and second quotations); San Antonio *Express*, Dec. 3, 1869, 5; Calvert *Enterprise* quoted in Galveston *Tri-Weekly News*, June 15, 1870, 1 (third quotation); George K. Sanderson to HFMD, Feb. 25, 1870 (fourth quotation), "Register of Letters Received," Vol. 4, 136, Microfilm Reel #4, and George K. Sanderson to Charles E. Morse, Mar. 30, 1870 (fifth quotation), Microfilm Reel #29, and "Petition of Benjamin Brown" through his attorneys J. L. Bolling and Stephen G. Burton to Thomas H. Norton, Jan. 6, 1870 (sixth, seventh and eighth quotations), Microfilm Reel # 29, COCADT, RG 393, M1188 (1981), NA.

38. Houston *Daily Union*, Sept. 10, 1870, 2, and Sept. 16, 1870, 2; *The State of Texas v. B. F. Hammond and Ben Brown*, "Murder," Case No. 661, Apr. 26, 1870, Spring Term 1870, Book "J[452–922]," 918, MDC, ODC-RC; George K. Sanderson to Charles E. Morse, Mar. 30, 1870 (quotation), Microfilm Reel #29, COCADT, RG 393, M1188 (1981), NA; *Register of Elected and Appointed State and County Officials,* Microfilm Reel #5, 510–511, TSL-AD; "Order of County Court Bonds," Sept. 3, 1870, 236, and Oct. 27, 1870, 241–46, Records of the County Court, County Clerk's Office, Robertson County, Texas, hereafter cited as RCC, CCO-RC. Frank Hall had been selected as the military-appointed

replacement for sheriff-elect John Harlan who died of natural causes during the 1869 statewide election. See: Baum, *Counterfeit Justice*, 145.

39. List of Petit Jurors, Feb. 7, 1871, Spring Term 1871, Book "K," 2, and *The State of Texas v. Ben Brown and B. F. Hammond,* "Murder," Case No. 661, Feb. 24 and 27, 1871, Spring Term 1871, Book "K," 64, 66–68, MDC, ODC-RC.

40. Baum, *Counterfeit Justice*, 174–78 and 182–83; *The Texas Free Press* (Hearne), Oct. 30, 1872, 2 (quotations), in Box 1, Cavitt Family Papers, Texas History Collection, Texas A&M University Archives, College Station, Texas.

41. *Weekly Times Herald* (Dallas), Feb. 2, 1890, 5 (first quotation); "B. F. Hammond," Official Texas Historical Marker (second quotation), No. 5395010928, Calvert Cemetery, Robertson County, Texas; Baum, *Counterfeit Justice*, 241; "Report of W. L. Faulkner," in Re: Estate of John C. Love, Oct. 25, 1869, October Term 1869, Vol. "T," 2–4 (third quotation), Microfilm Reel #964210, PM, CCO-RC. The allusion to a "tree prison" in Calvert was most likely a mistaken reference to the federal stockade built on poles fifteen feet high in downtown Bryan, called the "Yankee Sky Parlor," where Ben and six of his gang members were incarcerated. See: Glenna Fourman Brundidge, *Brazos County History: Rich Past—Bright Future* (Bryan, TX: Family History Foundation, 1986), 29.

42. "Ben Brown," in *Transcript Synopsis of A–P Records Relating to Robertson County "Families" 1838– [?]* (second quotation), Microfilm Reel #964224, County Clerk's Office, Robertson County, Texas; *The State of Texas v. F. M. Hall, B. F. Hammond, Ben Brown, et al.,* Case No. 2195, "Embezzlement," Consent Judgment, Oct. 30, 1875, Book "O," 250–252, MDC, ODC-RC; "Order of County Court Bonds," Nov. 19, 1874, 301–305, RCC, CCO-RC; ["America Brown"], Ancestry.com *1880 United States Federal Census*, database on-line (Provo, UT: The Generations Network, Inc., 2005), Bald Prairie, Robertson County, Texas, Microcopy T9, Microfilm Reel #1324, Page 475, Image 4000, Enumeration District 143 (first quotation); Robertson County Tax Rolls, 1838–1882, Tax Rolls for 1873 through 1883, Microfilm Reel #119801, TSL-AD. Ben's legal defense in a drawn-out trial in federal district court on charges against him and two black Greenback Party leaders for "bulldozing" black Republican voters in the 1878 Texas gubernatorial election had also drained his finances. See: Galveston *Daily News*, Oct. 12, 1879, 1.

43. Eric Foner, *Reconstruction: America's Unfinished Revolution, 1863–1877* (New York: Harper & Row, 1988), xix–xxvii.

44. Nevels, *Lynching to Belong*, 2; William D. Carrigan, *The Making of a Lynching Culture: Violence and Vigilantism in Central Texas, 1836–1916* (Urbana: University of Illinois Press, 2004), 3.

CHAPTER 6

Finding a Solution to Reconstruction Violence: The Texas State Police

by

Donaly Brice

Violence has ever been associated with Texas. The causes for this brutal propensity by its inhabitants, especially after the arrival of immigrants from the United States, have often attracted the attention of writers. Texas violence has been characterized as extensive and the state's "reputation for lawlessness" has been repeatedly chronicled. Charles L. Sonnichsen, a noted scholar of Texas feuds, claimed that the frontier setting, reinforced by a southern and western heritage, "produced a habit of self-redress more deeply ingrained" than anywhere in the country. Perhaps he was right; perhaps the moral code propagated the belief that "' revolvers make all men equal.'"[1]

The Lone Star State has been widely touted for its wayward ways long before the Civil War. After all, the Republic had been born through revolution. The isolation of the frontier and its attendant culture perpetuated the idea of self-defense and "no duty to retreat."[2] The new majority of the inhabitants, many of whom transported slaves, were of a similar cultural background, which tended to be violent, honor-driven, and thus tumultuous. The legacy of the South's defeat in the Civil War and the destruction of slavery added fuel to an already lawless reputation.

The Civil War, emancipation of the slaves, and the subsequent upheaval that characterized Reconstruction, irrevocably altered patterns of violence. Although the Democrats complained that the real necessity was the protection of settlers on the Indian frontier to the north and west—and internal outrages would be disposed of by local authorities—in actuality those inhabitants facing the Native Americans were safer than a black individual living in East Texas. Those who vocalized their unionism in the postwar years also became the subject of dishonorable intentions.

Illustration 7. Edmund J. Davis. (Courtesy of Texas State Library and Archives Commission)

With the cessation of hostilities from the Civil War, mounting evidence from a variety of sources suggested that Texas was a violent place. Writing five weeks after the slaves were emancipated, Provisional Governor Andrew J. Hamilton informed President Andrew Johnson that "we have here" the "most painful accounts of the shooting and hanging of Negroes by the half dozens at a time, for the crime of leaving their former Masters." Hamilton admitted that some of these stories "may be exaggerated as such things generally are, but there is too much evidence that such things have occurred."[3]

In January 1866, after traveling over part of Texas, Brigadier General W. E. Strong described a "fearful state of things" and declared blacks, who had only been free a few months, to be "in a worse condition than they ever were as slaves." Beaten "unmercifully, and shot down like wild beasts, without any provocation," they were "maltreated in every possible way," Strong informed the Commissioner of the Freedmen's Bureau. According to the general, there was more cruelty "in Texas than any southern State" he had visited. He believed that "one campaign of an army through the eastern part of the State, such as was made by General Sherman in South Carolina, would greatly improve the temper and generosity of the people."[4]

This portrayal of Texans' murderous disposition was not unusual or unique. Everywhere one turned, whether visitor, resident, or government official, along with state and national newspapers, all commented upon the quite violent nature of Texas postwar society. Even residents of the region remarked upon what the war and emancipation had wrought. Mrs. L. E. Potts, a native Tennessean who lived in Paris, Texas, implored President Johnson to aid the freedpeople as whites were perpetrating disgusting acts of violence upon them. The goal was "to persecute them back into slavery." Often "run down by blood hounds" and "shot because they do not do precisely as the white man says," Potts contended that killing them was not considered a crime.[5]

When the delegates to the Constitutional Convention of 1868 assembled in Austin on June 1, the majority were Republicans, which included a few carpetbaggers and ten black delegates. Edmund J. Davis, one of the more vociferous Republican delegates at the convention, desired an in-depth investigation into the disorderly nature of the state. A movement soon developed among a few members for the creation of a "loyal militia force" to assist the army in curtailing lawlessness. The Republicans realized quicker than the Democrats/Conservatives that a state-directed organization, with power over local jurisdictions and officials, was a necessity. Clashes over how to control and perhaps limit the violence went to the heart of each party's beliefs.[6]

Heirs to a governmental philosophy that believed centralization of state power was a necessity to bring order to the state's social and economic affairs, the Republican convention agenda was twofold. First, they moved to establish a body of statistics that would irrevocably prove that loyal whites and blacks were being eliminated at an alarming rate. Second, they would then use the compiled numbers to demonstrate the necessity for the establishment of a state constabulary and various other local militia-type units that would assist in enforcing law and order. The participation of citizens in quelling violence throughout the state was essential for the Republican program.[7] However, they would be sorely disappointed, because "Texas was in political chaos during Radical rule and there was an alarming increase in lawlessness."[8]

Delegates at the Constitutional Convention of 1868 established the Committee on Lawlessness and Violence, charging it with the duty of collecting data related to crimes committed in Texas from the records of the Freedmen's Bureau, the state department, district courts and from the testimony of sworn witnesses throughout the state. The committee's initial report revealed that 939 homicides had been recorded in Texas from the end of the Civil War in 1865 to June 1868. Of these homicides, 460 were committed by whites against whites, 373 by whites against blacks, ten by blacks against whites and fifty-eight by blacks against other blacks. A supplementary report issued by the committee raised the total homicide figures to 1,035. These figures were generally accepted as accurate by both Republicans and Democrats alike. However, "conservatives did resent the committee's implication that most of the homicides had been racially or politically" motivated. The conservatives "attributed the lawlessness 'to no other source than the want of an efficient, strong civil government.'"[9] Whether the Democrats wanted to admit it or not, the committee was obviously onto something. Blacks, if calculated from their population percentage or simply the number of murders, were clearly being dispatched at a considerable rate. One percent of all black males between fifteen and forty-five years of age died between 1865 an 1868.[10]

Even with the large numbers of reported homicides in Texas, during the years between 1865 and 1869, there were only 279 indictments and five convictions. This "lax enforcement by local officers can be only partially explained. Some were lethargic, some were intimidated by local conditions, and many were hampered by jurisdictional restraints and inadequate facilities" that could be used as places of incarceration.[11]

The Republicans persevered in their quest for a centralized police organization. As long as the "State government" was "without any militia or police whatever," violence would continue to run amok. The Republicans argued that "either the citizens themselves must keep the peace, or the military must interfere and compel obedience, or there will be no peace." Contrary to the popular belief in Texas Reconstruction history, the Republicans did not yearn for continued army occupation. They desired to transfer these responsibilities to a variety of state forces that would be under the governor's control. In short, the Republicans, unlike the Democrats, did not trust those who wielded power at the local level.[12]

In early October 1869 dates were set for the November gubernatorial election for Texas. A tumultuous campaign ensued betweem Radical Republicans and Conservative Democrats. Although fraud, intimidation, and chicanery characterized the 1869 gubernatorial race, Edmund J. Davis clearly won the election. Moreover, the newly written constitution was approved. Thousands of whites failed to cast ballots. This apathy destroyed any opportunity the conservatives had of winning.[13] By early 1870 the Republicans assumed control of the state government. The army began to formally end its occupation and station troops on the frontier. In fact, fewer than three hundred men, all infantry, remained on duty in the interior of the state, concentrated in Austin, San Antonio, and Jefferson. Although a few soldiers had been stationed at polling places during the 1869 election, they were few and far between.[14] In summary, Davis would have to move quickly to provide some assistance for local and county law enforcement officials to stem the tide of violence and lawlessness. Once officially endowed with gubernatorial powers, he was ready with a comprehensive plan. Davis needed one. In that same year, Texas led the nation in homicides.

In late June 1870, as part of Davis's program for mobilizing the state against internal disturbances, members of the Twelfth Legislature enacted a statute establishing a State Guard and a Reserve Militia, created the office of adjutant general to direct the activities of the new law enforcement agencies, and provided the governor with the authority to declare martial law. All "able-bodied" males between the ages of 18 and 45, with certain exemptions, were subject to military duty. Those individuals liable for service in the Reserve Militia could avoid active service by paying $15 a year, later reduced to $5.00.[15]

On May 10, 1870, Senator P. W. Hall of Robertson County introduced a bill in the state legislature entitled "An Act to establish a State Police, and provide for the regulation and government of the same." After being read, it was referred to the Committee on Militia. The House simultaneously began debating its purpose. According to the Senate and House Journals:

> Both the Militia Act and the State Police Act provoked considerable debate in the legislature. The conservatives, who thought that law enforcement should remain in the hands of local civil authorities exclusively, considered the bills unconstitutional. They feared that the bills vested too much power in the governor and other high state officials—power which rightfully

> belonged to the counties. That both the militia and the police forces would be racially integrated also created much opposition to the bills. In the Senate debates, Negro Senator Matt Gaines charged that the real opposition was not engendered by "the idea of placing such a great power in the hands of the executive," but by the "idea of gentlemen of my color being armed and riding around after desperadoes."[16]

Following several weeks of political infighting, wrangling, charges and counter-charges, the legislature enacted the law creating the State Police in late June. In turn, Governor Davis signed the bill into law on July 1, 1870.[17]

The Twelfth Legislature thus created a State Police organization as well as a state militia system. Its regulation and supervision would be directed by the state's adjutant general, who would be the "Chief of State Police." The force would be comprised of 257 men, including four captains, eight lieutenants, twenty sergeants, and 225 privates. All received four-year appointments, but could be removed by the governor, the chief, or both for "malfeasance, misfeasance, incompetency or disobedience of orders."[18]

Under the law, the governor and the adjutant general wielded considerable power. The chief, with the governor's approval, made "all needful rules and regulations for the government of the State Police." He also formed the rules and regulations for the "government and direction" of the local constabulary "in matters looking to the maintenance of public peace, preventing or suppressing crime, and bringing to justice offenders." If an individual refused to follow these guidelines he would be "removed from office."[19] James Davidson was appointed Adjutant General to act as Chief of State Police. Davidson organized the Adjutant General's Office, sought recommendations for appointments for members of the State Police, and attempted to ascertain just how many criminals inhabited the state.

The Police were "authorized to arrest offenders where local law officers failed to do so." The "police came from all walks of life. They were black, Hispanic, and white, and had fought as both Union and Confederate soldiers. Some were excellent lawmen, some were criminals. Most were Republicans."[20] In the first month of operation the State Police arrested forty-four murderers and felons; five of whom they killed "resisting arrest." By the end of 1870 the number of arrests totaled 978. In 1871 the Police made their largest number of arrests: 3,620. "By 1872 arrests totaled 6,820, and stolen property valued at $200,000 had been recovered. Of these arrests, 581 were for murder, 760 for attempted murder, and 1,748 for other felonies."[21]

Although much of the harsh criticism that was levied on the State Police came because of the racial makeup of the force and because of political partisanship, some of the accusations about the Police were deserved. One example of justified criticism of the State Police was that directed at Capt. John J. "Jack" Helm. Helm's activities in the DeWitt County area would forever taint the reputation of the State Police, often referred to as "the governor's hounds." Jack Helm was well known for aggressively performing his duties as a State Policeman. He also became embroiled in what traditionally has been referred to as the Sutton-Taylor Feud. Helm often ignored the rights of citizens and, on a number of occasions, reported that his prisoners had been killed in attempting to escape. Although he was never convicted of any crime, what finally led to Helm being ousted from the State Police were his heavy-handed and probably illegal activities in his district. The specific incident that raised a storm of protest was the killing of William and Henry Kelly in DeWitt County on August 26, 1870. Four Kelly brothers had shot up a circus performance in Sweet Home, apparently wounding some of the performers and the audience. The brothers were arrested by Helm's men and later released. Several days after this incident, a group of citizens and State Policemen re-arrested Henry and William Kelly under the pretext of taking them to Hallettsville to be interrogated regarding their involvement in the shooting incident. Both men were taken into the brush and were shot. Although no evidence exists that Jack Helm was present at the killing of the Kelly brothers, it is suspected that he had ordered their execution. The political repercussions from the slayings played out in some of the major newspapers of the state. Helm was dismissed from the Police force. He had indeed disgraced the State Police and his obsessive pursuit of either personal or political enemies in the DeWitt County area marred the organization's history forever.[22]

The problems that Governor Davis encountered with Jack Helm and all the detractors of the State Police were only a prelude of what was to come. Texas remained a violent place and blacks, who comprised only 30 percent of the population, were often murdered for no apparent reason. Davis's commitment to protect their lives and property infused his administration and his philosophy. Although the State Police were a mobile force, they could not be everywhere at once. When emergencies arose, personnel had to be co-opted from various districts, in order to form a sizeable contingent. Such an occurrence presented itself in Hill County in December 1870, where two black people were savagely murdered. Davis responded by establishing martial law when local citizens directly interfered with and thwarted the efforts of the State Police in performing their duties.

For a number of years following the close of the Civil War, Hill County had been subjected to increased violence. The county experienced at least twelve murders from 1868 until mid-1870. Half of those murdered were black men. There were also robberies and violent assaults committed upon various individuals, both black and white. Although Hill County blacks composed but a fraction of the total population, they found themselves on the receiving end of most of the criminal acts being committed.

A major reason for the initial State Police presence in Hill County was the desperado Kinch West. West had been a member of William Quantrill's Missouri guerrillas during the Civil War and had participated in their illegal activities over several states. One observer summarized West's life as "daring, reckless," and without remorse.[23] In July 1870 West was accused of killing A. D. Martin in Hill County. In an argument over the ownership of a horse, West pulled a pistol and shot Martin in the temple, killing him instantly. West escaped as several men watched him ride away from the scene of the crime.[24]

In addition to Kinch West and his gang of followers, Hill County was plagued by several other outlaw groups led by William C. Atchison and the Cox brothers, George and William. All these desperadoes were wanted for a number of crimes including the murders of several freedmen in the area. No efforts were made on the part of County Sheriff Evin Beauchamp to arrest any of the lawbreakers. The sheriff and other local officials appeared to be greatly intimidated by the presence of so many criminals who operated openly throughout the county. Even though several State Policemen who operated out of Waco offered their support to restore law and order in Hill County, Sheriff Beauchamp refused to take action against the law breakers.[25]

In August 1870 State Policeman Pierce Nagle was shot and seriously wounded by one of the members of the Kinch West gang. This incident prompted a full-scale intervention by the State Police into Hill County. On September 20 Adjutant General Davidson mobilized the State Police for a Hill County expedition. He informed Sheriff Beauchamp that the police would soon be on their way and they had been ordered to aid him in making the necessary arrests. Earlier, Beauchamp had intimated that he "refused to have anything to do with colored policemen" and would not accompany any unit sent if it included blacks. Davidson reminded Beauchamp that he was a policeman under the law, "and as such you are supposed to give your aid as well as be aided in arresting and securing criminals."[26]

General Davidson selected Lt. Thomas Williams of Lockhart to lead the Police force into Hill County. Williams, one of the best and most versatile men in the Police force, was to consult with the legal and civil officers and then proceed to arrest the desperadoes infesting that section and in adjoining counties. He was given orders "to summon citizens" to assist the Police in tracking down the law offenders.[27]

Lieutenant Williams, along with two sergeants and thirteen privates, arrived in Hillsboro and consulted with the sheriff and other officers of the county, seeking information about the names of the desperadoes and the places to which these outlaws might retreat within the area. Williams received little assistance from the local citizens. Sheriff Beauchamp did provide what information he could regarding the lawless element in the county. The Police then proceeded to Peoria, where the West gang had been seen on the previous day.[28]

On September 29, they located the residences of West and the Cox brothers. While the Police were searching the premises, a number of the outlaws attacked them and then fled, leading the Police force on a four-mile chase across the countryside. West and his gang soon disappeared and the State Police returned to their duty stations empty handed.[29]

Williams contended that the outlaws numbered about fifteen men and they operated in squads of four or five but could "always concentrate when necessary." Well mounted and well armed with guns and revolvers, the desperadoes successfully defied the civil authorities and had "produced a reign of terror in Hill [C]ounty."[30] The State Police force sent into Hill County proved unsuccessful because the citizens either sympathized with or were intimidated by the outlaws. Davis was outraged with the citizens for not offering more support to the Police. He demanded that Sheriff Beauchamp call a meeting of the local citizens and inform them that, unless they "arrested and delivered" the outlaws to the civil officers, he intended to declare martial law in the county and send in a sufficient force of the militia and state guard to secure their apprehension.[31]

Violence in Hill County continued and, in December 1870, a black man and woman were viciously killed in the county. The couple were passing through Clifton on their way to Waco to celebrate Christmas. They had stopped at a grocery store to make a purchase, when the man was whipped by several "drunken men." When their bodies were discovered, the woman, whose corpse was by the roadside, had been shot through the head and heart. The man was found a day later, some three miles down the road. He had been shot several times through the body.[32]

The coroner's inquest concluded that James Gathings and Solloela Nicholson committed the slayings. Both young men were tied to the wealthiest individual in the county, James J. Gathings. After the inquest, a small force of policemen under Lieutenant W. T. Pritchett pursued the accused murderers to the Gathings household in Covington. The Police lieutenant had information that the two killers were concealed in the Gathings home. The officers approached and requested permission to search the premises. Gathings refused and told Lieutenant Pritchett " you cannot search my house with your damned negro police." When Gathings refused to permit the State Police to search his home, except by force of arms, two of the policemen drew their pistols and exclaimed that they intended to do that very thing. Not surprisingly, they found no one. Gathings' stalling tactics had been proven successful.[33]

Lieutenant Pritchett and his men then proceeded about a mile from the Gathings home where they stopped for breakfast. Several of the policemen were sent ahead to continue their search for the fugitives. Shortly after, a party of twelve to fifteen citizens, ostensibly under Gathings' leadership, approached Lieutenant Pritchett and the remaining policemen. Once Gathings' men were close enough, they "leveled their guns [at the lawmen] and demanded their surrender." Pritchett and his men were arrested and charged with forcibly entering the "premises of J. J. Gathings without a search warrant."[34]

The policemen were placed under bond and were released to appear in court in one week. Following their release, local authorities had a change of mind and issued new warrants for the arrest of Pritchett based on the original charges against him. Concerned that a fair trial was impossible, the State Police endeavored to leave the county, but were apprehended by a group of citizen vigilantes. Fortunately, the policemen managed to escape before the vigilantes delivered them to the local sheriff.[35]

After the initial arrest of the State Police, Governor Davis reached the limits of his patience. The total disregard of the law as evinced by Hill County inhabitants induced him to believe that the situation was completely beyond the control of local forces. On January 10, 1871, he proclaimed martial law. Davis announced that there existed a "combination of lawless men, who have been guilty of various outrages against the peace and dignity of said State, and that said combination is too strong to be controlled by the civil authorities of said county."[36] Chief of Police

Davidson prepared to leave Austin for Hill County and ordered a company of the State Guard to proceed to Hillsboro. Davidson found county affairs in complete disarray. The hostility to the presence of Davidson and the governor's men was everywhere evident. James J. Gathings and other local leaders who were responsible for the arrest of Lieutenant Pritchett and his State Policemen were arrested and fined for hindering the apprehension of the murderers of the black man and woman.[37]

Two weeks after the conclusion of martial law, Davidson observed a change in the attitude of Hill County citizens. He was satisfied that the people had decided to "abide by the Laws, and any protection" the state could afford. However, legal fighting between the conservative element and the Radicals in the legislature over Governor Davis's actions in Hill County and his declaration of martial law continued for months. Violence within the county temporarily subsided but continued for years to come.

Governor Davis confronted opposition in other counties that required the intervention of the State Police. In the Piney Woods area in the southern and eastern portion of the state, another test of wills between the administration and local citizens emerged. In a similar scenario, the question was who murdered an elderly black man after his testimony before a grand jury? The response of many Walker County residents to apprehending and protecting the killers of an old freedman was similar to Hill County attitudes. The bitter hatred of the Republicans, the State Police, and black equality, forced Davis to declare martial law in Walker County almost concurrently with the troubles in Hill County.

Sam Jenkins, a sixty-eight year old freedman from Huntsville, had become involved in a dispute over the division of a crop he and Fred Parks had cultivated. Parks ordered Jenkins to leave. Jenkins unsuccessfully attempted to recover his portion of the crop or receive a satisfactory settlement. Jenkins was also an active member of the local Union League. One resident described him as "one of the leaders under 'Carpetbagism' rule," who "made himself obnoxious to white people generally."[38]

Two friends of Parks, John Wright and Nat Outlaw, disgusted at Jenkins' economic demands and political activities, met him several miles outside of Huntsville and gave him a choice of being shot or whipped. The men battered Jenkins with sticks, almost to the point of death. Wright and Outlaw threatened to kill Jenkins if he testified against them before a grand jury.[39]

In December 1870 Jenkins testified before a grand jury on several indictments of assault and battery against Parks, Outlaw, Wright and a fourth man, Jonathan Parrish. For five days the grand jury "gave the matter a very thorough investigation." After exploring "all the sources of information," the panel "refused to find a bill against" the accused men. They argued that the evidence was insufficient for an indictment. When the proceedings finished, Jenkins left the courtroom, followed by four men, three of whom were identified as Outlaw, Parrish and Wright.[40]

About three miles from Huntsville, Jenkins was "cowardly and brutally murdered." The wounds to his head and body suggested he attempted to escape. Although more than a half-dozen witnesses allegedly observed the four white men murder Jenkins, they refused to give any testimony. A reward of $500 was offered for the arrest of Jenkins' killers. District Attorney W. E. Horne, who examined the case, labeled it "a cold-blooded murder and assassination of a poor old freedman."[41]

Writing to District Judge J. P. Burnett, Governor Davis commented that he had heard many unfavorable reports in regard to the county sheriff, William H. Stewart. He had earlier been connected with the killing of several prisoners whom he had attempted to arrest. The murder of Jenkins after his grand jury appearance was a "flagrant affair" in the eyes of Governor Davis, and he would accept no excuse from Sheriff Stewart for not being able to discover the murderer or murderers. "He must find out who did it," Davis emphasized, "or be removed."[42]

Two weeks after the Jenkins murder, Judge Burnett removed Stewart from office and replaced him with Cyrus Hess. In January 1871 a complaint was lodged before Judge Burnett over the unsolved murder of Sam Jenkins prompting Burnett to issue an arrest warrant for the suspected murderers. Captain Leander H. McNelly, of the State Police, was ordered to Huntsville to apprehend the four men and place them in the custody of Sheriff Hess. The men were arraigned before Judge Burnett and charged with killing Jenkins.[43]

As the trial progressed, Judge Burnett became convinced from the testimony that Outlaw, Parrish, and Wright were guilty of the murder. One of the defense attorneys argued that if Burnett committed the men to jail he could not have the "moral support of the community" and that such a course of action was fraught with pitfalls. Burnett perceived this as a threat. Facing the wrath of the majority of the local citizens, Burnett decided to incarcerate Outlaw, Parrish, and Wright until the next term of the district court to answer for the murder of Jenkins.[44]

After announcing the decision, Burnett handed Captain McNelly the warrant and ordered him, along with Sheriff Hess, to escort the prisoners to jail. The judge told Hess that if he expected any difficulties, he could summon as many citizens as necessary to enforce the law. The sheriff anticipated no problems. Judge Burnett exited the courtroom and, as he was walking down the street, pistol shots rang out from the courtroom and gunfire emanated from the streets. One man emptied his six-shooter at the judge and district attorney Horne. Another man discharged a bullet into the ground near Burnett's feet.

As the accused men were being ushered from the courtroom, Captain McNelly discovered that Outlaw had a gun and disarmed him. Sheriff Hess asked Wright if he too had arms. Wright said no, but then drew a revolver and fired at McNelly, as did Parrish. State Policemen McNelly, Tom Keesee, L. E. Dunn, and Joseph Martin returned the gunfire, severely wounding Parrish in the arm and Wright in the leg and the body. Aided by "friends outside and inside the court room," each prisoner had concealed two six-shooters.[45]

McNelly was shot in the leg and Keesee received a ball in the jaw that passed around the neck. Even though wounded, both men continued to fire until Wright and Parrish escaped from the courtroom and down the steps where their friends awaited them. Outlaw was slightly wounded in the gun battle and immediately surrendered and was later taken to the penitentiary for safe-keeping.[46]

Two additional State Policemen were stationed at the base of the courtroom stairs when the shooting began. Preventing the two officers from rendering any assistance, supporters of the prisoners presented pistols and threatened to shoot the officers if either "attempted to move." Wright and Parrish exited the courtroom, bleeding from their wounds. Twenty to thirty ex-Confederates had horses ready and were armed with shotguns. When Wright and Parrish appeared from the building, they were greeted "with cheers." Mounting their horses, shooting and "yelling like savages," the band rode out of Huntsville.[47] McNelly ordered Sheriff Hess to summon a posse, but only two citizens volunteered. It was well known that the fugitives were well-protected and it would be difficult to re-capture them.[48]

When Governor Davis received Judge Burnett's account of the Huntsville clash, he had decided that these outrages would bring upon the residents "severe expense and retribution as well as injury to the reputation and prosperity of the county." On January 20, 1871, Davis placed Walker County under martial law. He felt that the lawless element in the county was too strong to be controlled by the civil authorities and ascertained that they needed outside assistance.[49] After one month martial law was lifted. Walker County returned to a semblance of tranquility, but there was little Davis could do to stem the tide of violence. The area remained hostile to both the State Police and the Republicans.

The Walker County altercation had barely subsided when, within six months, trouble arose again in the blackland prairie section of Central Texas where a congressional election was in the offing. Strained race relations and the appearance of Special Policemen to ensure a fair election led to violence.

For several years Limestone County had endured many racially motivated murders and outrages against the freedpeople and Republicans. In 1871, facing a tumultuous congressional election, Governor Davis felt it necessary to send a number of State and Special Policemen into Limestone County to oversee political activities, to make certain all voters were fairly registered, maintain order at the polls and ensure an honest election.

Amid this politically and racially charged environment, D. C. Applewhite, a white man who had spoken out against the Police and local Republican officials, was killed by several black policemen when they attempted to arrest him for illegally carrying a firearm. On September 30, Applewhite had been drinking at a saloon in the town of Groesbeck. In his drunken condition he announced in the presence of the mayor and several of the Special Policemen that he was armed and boasted that there would be "an insurrection" if they attempted to arrest him. When the Policemen went to arrest him, Applewhite drew a derringer pistol. Mitch Cotton, one of the Policemen, approached Applewhite. Words were exchanged and shots fired, leaving both Applewhite and Cotton wounded. Despite his injuries, Applewhite ran from the saloon with the Policemen firing repeatedly at him. The Policemen followed in pursuit, reaching the door in time to see the hell raiser fall dead in the street. Realizing that locals would not easily accept the fact that the black policemen had shot and killed a white man, the officers proceeded to the mayor's office for protection from the large crowd of local citizens who had already began to congregate in the streets. They refused to be arrested by the mob, but agreed that they would surrender to a detachment of black guardsmen or police. The mayor then sent for a small group of black policemen to take the two Policemen into custody.

Word quickly spread that a large group of armed blacks was heading for Groesbeck to free the two Policemen. Many of the local citizens armed themselves. Policeman Merrick Trammel and four other black citizens were able to make their way into town and remove the two endangered Policemen from harm's way. They made their way to Springfield, the county seat, where the two men were placed in jail. Hostilities and unrest, precipitated by the killing of Applewhite, encompassed the entire county and spilled over into Freestone County. With the situation out of the control of local civil officers, the governor resorted to another declaration of martial law. In addition to bringing a resolution to the violence throughout the county, Governor Davis realized that the increase of troops and policemen provided through martial law would aid greatly in assuring impartial elections in early October. In spite of the imposition of martial law in Limestone and Freestone counties, a large portion of the black population felt the intimidation of the white citizens and refused to vote during the elections. Although this was the last incident in which Governor Davis had to use martial law during his administration, the State Police continued to remain busy. In 1871 the Police made their largest number of arrests for any one year: a total of 3,602. In 1872 the number of arrests dropped to 1,204. This was still more than the total number of arrests reported by local officers for the seven years immediately following the Civil War.[50]

Following the 1872 Texas elections, the Democrats were finally able to regain control of the Thirteenth Legislature and anticipated the termination of the despised State Police. However, incidents of lawlessness and violence in Lampasas County occupied the attention of Governor Davis. For several years Lampasas County had gained a reputation for disturbances and general rowdiness. Between 1871 and 1873 the State Police were in, around, and through Lampasas for a variety of reasons. The town of Lampasas, as the county seat, was prone to trouble whenever courts were in session. Shootings and hollering at night by outcasts disturbed the local residents. Cattle rustling also became prevalent. The county sheriff, S. T. Denson, was unwilling or unable to bring an end to the lawlessness. Disturbances continued until January 14, 1873, when Sheriff Denson was shot in the process of breaking up a fight between several men at one of the local saloons. After a group of local minute men caused a disruption of a session of the district court, a number of citizens of the community felt it their duty to report to Governor Davis and "ask such assistance" as he thought proper to restore order to their community.

Sergeant J. M. Redmon was dispatched to Lampasas to investigate the turbulent state of affairs. On his arrival Redmon found that things were "as bad if not worse than represented" at headquarters. He immediately posted a proclamation issued by Governor Davis prohibiting the carrying of deadly weapons. It was the governor's hopes that such a proclamation would help to alleviate the troubles in the county.

After about a week in Lampasas, Redmon realized that it would require more men than he had to maintain law and order. The sergeant was frustrated in not being able to apprehend the culprits who had been creating most of the disturbances. As the State Policemen were preparing to return to Austin, the people of Lampasas requested that a permanent group of Police be stationed in the town until all the lawbreakers were arrested or driven out of the county.

Local citizens continued to urge the governor to send additional State Police reinforcements. On March 10, 1873, the Adjutant General ordered Captain Thomas Williams and a detachment of seven policemen to proceed to Lampasas without delay and arrest all violators of the law that forbade the wearing of weapons inside the town limits. The Police were well equipped with five Winchester carbines and fifty rounds of ammunition for each weapon. Williams' mission was "to aid the local authorities in quelling" the desperadoes who had been committing outrages and who had attempted to murder Sheriff Denson. The State Police troop was also to prevent these law breakers from "shooting into the citizens' houses" and other illegal acts.[51]

Williams and his men arrived in Lampasas at about one o'clock on March 14. When the Policemen rode into town, Williams saw Bill Bowen, wearing a pistol and entering Scott's Saloon. Williams sent "three of his men to different points," and along with J. M. Daniels, Wesley Cherry, and Andrew Melville, entered the saloon to arrest the man carrying the pistol.[52]

Williams demanded Bowen's surrender. Bowen refused and Williams attempted to wrest his pistol from him. A considerable number of men were in the barroom and stood by watching the affair. At this juncture "a volley was fired into the police from behind, by at least eight or ten men." Williams was hit by three bullets, in the back of the head and "entirely through the face." When he turned the second and third slugs struck him in the chest. His assassins were near him when they fired. Daniels died instantly, receiving several shots in the head and body, one of which passed "from one ear to the other." Cherry suffered a fatal chest wound, as did Melville, but the latter lingered for almost a month before dying.[53]

The desperadoes, led by several brothers named Horrell, exited the barroom and attacked the remaining policemen stationed outside the saloon. In the melee that followed the desperadoes Mart and Thomas Horrell were wounded and the other State Policemen fled Lampasas and returned to Austin.[54]

A number of the desperadoes were later arrested by local officials and others were never found. The Adjutant General, accompanied by twelve State Policemen, was dispatched to Lampasas to investigate the State

Police killings. According to the Adjutant General, the "worst state of affairs possible existed in the town and county. The citizens were panic stricken, had closed their stores," and the policemen discovered that "all business had stopped in anticipation of an attack from the mob party."[55]

In the end, no one was ever convicted for the murders of the State Policemen. A number of these desperadoes did eventually meet violent deaths themselves. The deaths of the four State Policemen in Lampasas signaled the death knell for the entire State Police force. While the Lampasas crisis was in the making, Governor Davis and his adjutant general were at war with the Thirteenth Legislature in a final valiant effort to save the State Police. From its very inception, the Democrats had opposed the organization. Newspapers across the Lone Star State, a majority of the Democratic persuasion, had ceaselessly hammered at the foibles, mistakes, and so-called oppressiveness of the Police. No mistake of the force, no matter how small or large, went unnoticed and, indeed, many were magnified out of proportion to the incident or event. The assassination of the four State Policemen in Lampasas fazed the legislators not at all. On April 22, 1873, the Thirteenth Legislature passed, over the governor's veto, a bill to repeal the State Police Act.

Much of the state rejoiced at the demise of the State Police. In the April 22, 1873, issue of the Dallas *Daily Herald* a flyer was inserted into each paper that read:

> EXTRA
> THE SCEPTER OF THE TYRANT BROKEN!
> THE CHAINS SHATTERED!
> THE PEOPLE FREE!
>
> The people of the State of Texas are to-day delivered of as infernal an engine of oppression as ever crushed any people beneath God's sunlight. The damnable Police Bill is ground beneath the heel of an indignant Legislature. . . . The Police Law is abolished over the Governor's veto. "Glory to God in the highest, and on earth Peace, good will towards men."[56]

ENDNOTES

1. W. Eugene Hollon, *Frontier Violence: Another Look* (New York: Oxford University Press, 1976), 36; C. L. Sonnichsen, *I'll Die Before I'll*

Run: The Story of the Great Feuds of Texas (New York: Harper & Brothers Publishers, 1951), xvi; Stephen Powers, *Afoot and Alone: A Walk From Sea to Sea by the Southern Route: Adventures and Observations in Southern California, New Mexico, Arizona, Texas, Etc.* (Hartford: Columbian Book Company, 1886), 117, 119 (italics mine); Bill O'Neal, "Violence in Texas History," in *Texas: A Sesquicentennial Celebration*, ed., Donald W. Whisenhunt (Austin: Eakin Press, 1984), 353–69. For background, see David J. Weber, *The Spanish Frontier in North America* (New Haven: Yale University Press, 1992), 147–203; Donald E. Chipman, *Spanish Texas, 1519–1821* (Austin: University of Texas Press, 1992); Richard Maxwell Brown, *Strain of Violence: Historical Studies of American Violence and Vigilantism* (New York: Oxford University Press, 1975), 236; Henry P. Lundsgaarde, *Murder in Space City: A Cultural Analysis of Houston Homicide Patterns* (New York: Oxford University Press, 1977), 173–92. In general, see David T. Courtwright, "Violence in America," *American Heritage* 47 (September 1996): 37–51. For the Texas/western/southern connection see Patrick George Williams, "Redeemer Democrats and the Roots of Modern Texas, 1872–1884" (Ph. D. diss., Columbia University, 1996), 1–18; Walter L. Buenger, "Texas and the South," *Southwestern Historical Quarterly* 103 (January 2000): 309–24.

2. Richard Maxwell Brown, *No Duty to Retreat: Violence and Values in American History and Society* (New York: Oxford University Press, 1991); "Violence," in *The Oxford History of the American West*, ed. Clyde A. Milner, II, Carol A. O'Connor, and Martha A. Sandweiss (New York: Oxford University Press, 1994), 393–425; "Historiography of Violence in the American West," in *Historians of the American West,* ed. Michael P. Malone (Lincoln: University of Nebraska Press, 1983), 234–69; Paul D. Lack, *The Texas Revolutionary Experience: A Political and Social History, 1835–1836* (College Station: Texas A&M University Press, 1992); Gary L. Roberts, "Violence and the Frontier Tradition," in *Kansas and the West: Bicentennial essays in Honor of Nyle H. Miller*, ed. Forrest R. Blackburn, Edgar Langsdorf, Robert W. Richmond, Joseph W. Snell, and Homer E. Socolofsky (Topeka: Kansas State Historical Society, 1976), 96–111.

3. A. J. Hamilton to Andrew Johnson, July 24, 1865, Andrew Johnson Papers (Manuscript Division, Library of Congress); Dan T. Carter, *When the War Was Over: The Failure of Self-Reconstruction in the South* (Baton Rouge: Louisiana State University Press, 1985), 25-27, 32, 255-256. Hamilton's response to the violence is down-played in John L. Waller,

Colossal Hamilton of Texas: A Biography of Andrew Jackson Hamilton; Militant Unionist and Reconstruction Governor (El Paso: Texas Western Press, 1968), 59-94. Into 1866 and thereafter, Texas planters still discussed a gradual emancipation of three to five years; Thomas P. Collins (Crockett) to Thaddeus Stevens, February 19, 1866, Cont. 6, Thaddeus Stevens Papers (Manuscript Division, Library of Congress).

4. *Report of the Joint Committee on Reconstruction* (Washington, D.C.: Government Printing Office, 1866), 36–37; Richard Lowe, "The Joint Committee on Reconstruction: Some Clarifications," *Southern Studies*, n.s., 3 (Spring 1992): 55–65; John G. Clark, "Historians and the Joint Committee of Reconstruction," *Historian* 23 (May 1961): 348–361; "Radicals and Moderates on the Joint Committee on Reconstruction," *Mid-America* 45 (April 1963): 79–98. Maj. Gen. David S. Stanley concurred with Strong's perception. Without the presence of the military, blacks would be held in a "bondage more galling than they were ever held before" and in a detestable manner, *Report*, 40. For general military reaction see Robert Shook, "Federal Occupation and Administration of Texas" and William Richter, *The Army in Texas During Reconstruction*; Leon F. Litwack, *Been in the Storm So Long: The Aftermath of Slavery* (New York: Alfred A. Knopf, 1979), 276–77; Charles V Keener, "Racial Turmoil in Texas, 1865–1874" (M. A. thesis, North Texas State University, 1971); James M. Smallwood, *Time of Hope, Time of Despair: Black Texans During Reconstruction* (Port Washington, NY: Kennikat Press, 1981); James Marten,"' What is to Become of the Negro?': White Reaction to Emancipation in Texas," *Mid-America* 73 (April–July 1991): 115–33.

5. Mrs. L. E. Potts (Paris, Tex.), to Mr. President, June ?, 1866, Sheridan Papers, Cont. 4, Manuscript Division, Library of Congress.

6. Ronald N. Gray, "Edmund J. Davis: Radical Republican and Reconstruction Governor of Texas" (Ph. D. diss., Texas Tech University, 1976), 124.

7. Carl H. Moneyhon, *Republicanism in Reconstruction Texas* (Austin: University of Texas Press, 1980), 92–93.

8. Ann Patton Baenziger, "The Texas State Police During Reconstruction: A Reexamination," *Southwestern Historical Quarterly* 72 (April 1969): 471.

9. Ibid., 471–72.

10. Barry A. Crouch, "A Spirit of Lawlessness: White Violence, Texas Blacks, 1865-1868," *Journal of Social History* 18 (December 1984): 218–19.

11. Baenziger, "The Texas State Police," 473.

12. *Report of Special Committee on Lawlessness and Violence in Texas* (Austin: Printed at the Office of the Daily Republican, 1868), 11.

13. Dale Baum, "Chicanery and Intimidation in the 1869 Texas Gubernatorial Race," *Southwestern Historical Quarterly* 97 (July 1993): 37–54; *The Shattering of Texas Unionism: Politics in the Lone Star State During the Civil War Era* (Baton Rouge: Louisiana State University Press, 1998), 180–228; Moneyhon, *Republicanism in Texas*, 104–128; John Pressley Carrier, "A Political History of Texas During the Reconstruction, 1865–1874" (Ph. D. diss., Vanderbilt University, 1971), 389–404; Randolph B. Campbell, *Grass-Roots Reconstruction in Texas, 1865–1880* (Baton Rouge: Louisiana State University Press, 1997), 19, who erroneously claims the Radicals had "working majorities in both houses of the new state legislature, the twelfth."

14. Carrier, "A Political History," 407–8; Richter, *The Army in Texas*, 172–86; Thomas T. Smith, *The Old Army in Texas: A Research Guide to the U.S. Army in Nineteenth-Century Texas* (Austin: Texas State Historical Association, 2000), 110–11; Shook, "The Federal Military in Texas, 1865–1870," *Texas Military History* 6 (Spring 1967): 45–53; "Federal Occupation and Administration of Texas," 486–89; Robert Wooster, "The Army and the Politics of Expansion: Texas and the Southwestern Borderlands, 1870-1886," *Southwestern Historical Quarterly* 93 (October 1989): 151–67.

15. *General Laws of the Twelfth Legislature, Called Session, 1870* (Austin: J. G. Tracy, State Printer, 1870), 11–16; *id., First Session-1871* (Austin: J. G. Tracy, State Printer, 1871), 181, 23–24; Otis A. Singletary, "The Texas Militia During Reconstruction," *Southwestern Historical Quarterly* 60 (July 1956): 25–28; Allan Robert Purcell, "The History of the Texas Militia, 1835–1903" (Ph. D. diss., University of Texas, Austin, 1981), 221–27. It is interesting to note that the law organizing the State Guard/Reserve Militia also mentioned the State Police as part of the military forces of Texas, but the police had yet to be established although they did come into being a week later.

16. Baenziger, "The Texas State Police," 473.

17. Ibid., 473–474; *Senate Journal, First Session*, 85–86; *House Journal, First Session*, 104–105, 154.

18. *General Laws of the Twelfth Legislature, Called Session, 1870*, Ch. XIII, 19. If no adjutant general existed, the governor could appoint, with the Senate's approval, a chief who would receive an annual salary of $2,500.

19. Ibid.

20. Ron Tyler, Douglas E. Barnett, *et al.*, eds. *The New Handbook of Texas* (Austin: Texas State Historical Association, 1996), 6: 75.

21. For all the sheriffs' reports which cover Anderson to Zapata counties, see Reports of Crimes, Arrests, and Fugitives, 1870–1873 and State Police Correspondence, State Police records, Reconstruction records, Adjutant General's Department, Archives and Information Services Division, Texas State Library and Archives Commission (hereafter cited as ARIS/TSLAC); Baenziger, "The Texas State Police," 476.

22. James Davidson to Jack Helm, August 31, 1870, p. 190; September 6, 1870, 216, State Police Letter Press Book, ARIS/TSLAC; *Weekly Austin Republican*, September 14, 1870; November 2, 1870; *Daily State Journal* (Austin), October 19, 1879; Victor Rose, *The Texas Vendetta; or, The Sutton-Taylor Feud* (New York: Printed by J. J. Little & Co., 1880), 40–48.

23. Background on West is courtesy of Dave Johnson, Zionsville, Indiana. See also, F. M. Cross, *A Short Sketch-History from Personal Reminicenses [sic] of Early Days in Central Texas* (Brownwood, TX: Greenwood Printing Company, 1910), 114–16. For a completely unreliable account see A. Y. Kirkpatrick, *The Early Settlers Life in Texas and the Organization of Hill County* (Hillsboro, TX: Privately printed, 1909), 79–82, and Ellis Bailey, *A History of Hill County, Texas, 1838–1865* (Waco: Texian Press, 1966), 119–20, who views West as some kind of "hero"; State of Texas *vs* Kynch West, Bill of Indictment, October 18, 1889, no. 2638, Extradition Papers, Secretary of State, ARIS/TSLAC.

24. *Daily State Journal* (Austin), July 29, 1870, 6.

25. Statement of John J. Gage and H. Harvick to E. J. Davis, November 6, 1870, Governor's Papers (E. J. Davis); also in Executive Record Book (October 10, 1870–May 30, 1871), Vol. II, 82–83, both in ARIS/TSLAC; Bailey, in *A History of Hill County*, 120, claims that Atchison and Beauchamp drank together in Bateman's saloon in Hillsboro where the State Police arrested him. While en route to Waco, Atchison managed to escape. Beauchamp, according to Bailey, carried papers for Atchison's arrest, but did not bother him because the sheriff was "afraid of lead poison," 120; 1870 United States Population Census, Hill County, Texas, Precinct #1, 386, 396; E. J. Davis to Don Campbell (President, State Senate), February 8, 1871, Davis Letter Press Book (January 3, 1871–March 16, 1871), 108-111, ARIS/TSLAC.

26. James Davidson to L. J. Hoffman (Waco), September 20, 1870, 273, State Police Letter Press Book, ARIS/TSLAC; *Daily State Journal*

(Austin), September 23, 1870, p. 1; Hoffman to Davidson, September 2, 1870, in *Message of Gov. Edmund J. Davis, With Documents in Relation to Lawlessness and Crime in Hill and Walker Counties* (Austin: J. G. Tracy, State Printer, 1871), 10, hereafter cited as *Messages and Documents*. Nagle, born in New York City, was a private (later sergeant) for three years in the 3rd US Cavalry and honorably discharged in 1866. B. Rush Plumly, a prominent Galveston politician, wrote that Nagle was "worthy and capable." He was commissioned on July 11, 1870; Pierce Nagle to Davis, July 9, 1870, State Police Correspondence, ARIS/TSLAC.

27. Davidson to Thomas Williams (Lt., State Police), September 23, 1870, 304; November 1, 1870, 465, State Police Letter Press Book, ARIS/TSLAC. On Williams, see Barry A. Crouch, "Captain Thomas Williams: The Path of Duty," in *The Human Tradition in Texas*, ed. Ty Cashion and Jesus F. de la Teja (Wilmington, DE: Scholarly Resources Inc., 2001), 71–86.

28. Williams to Davidson, November 4, 1870, *Messages and Documents*, 15–16. Williams was an excellent officer but often neglected his paperwork. As late as November 1, Davidson ordered Williams to furnish a report of his Hill County activities "giving all particulars," Davidson to Williams, November 1, 1870, 465, State Police Letter Press Book, ARIS/TSLAC.

29. Ibid.; Waco *Register* quoted in *Daily State Journal* (Austin), October 7, 1870.

30. *Weekly Austin Republican*, October 5, 1870; Waco *Register* quoted in *Daily State Journal* (Austin), October 7, 1870.

31. Davis to Campbell, February 8, 1871, 108–11, Letter Press Book, Governor's Papers (E. J. Davis); Davis to Beauchamp, October 3, 1870, 364–65, State Police Letter Press Book, both letters in ARIS/TSLAC; both are reprinted in *Messages and Documents*, 3–4, 12–13.

32. Davis to Yerby and Others, March 3, 1871, 222–27, Letter Press Book, Governor's Papers (E. J. Davis), ARIS/TSLAC; Davidson to Davis, February 1, 1871, *Messages and Documents*, 5; *Tri-Weekly Houston Union*, January 20, 1871, 1; Houston *Daily Union*, January 5, 1871.

33. Davis to Yerby and Others, March 3, 1871, 222–27, Letter Press Book, Governor's Papers (E. J. Davis), ARIS/TSLAC; Davidson to Davis, February 1, 1871, *Messages and Documents*, 5–6; *A Memorial and Biographical History of Johnson and Hill Counties, Texas* (Chicago: Lewis Publishing Company, 1892), 224–25; Houston *Daily Union*, January 5, 1871.

34. Davidson to Davis, February 1, 1871, *Messages and Documents*, 6. According to one writer who garbled the story and the facts: "The officers and the negroes then started toward Covington. Gathings had them arrested before night, for searching his house without legal authority. They gave bonds for their appearance at court, but sent word that they were going to mob Gathings, and the citizens stood guard at his house for eight nights. The mob, however, did not appear. Nor did they appear at court, although Gathings and his friends were on hand," *A Memorial and Biographical History*, 224–25; Houston *Daily Union*, January 5, 1871.

35. *Messages and Documents*, 6–7. Unfortunately, the Hill County courthouse burned in 1874 and thus there is no official account of these proceedings. San Antonio *Daily Herald*, January 5, 1871, citing the "sensational dispatch" of the Houston *Union*, stated that Pritchett, Sergeant Evans, and five State Policemen were "ambushed and captured by twenty-five outlaws," carried to Hillsboro, where they escaped on December 29, and made their way to Waco. The Houston *Daily Union*, January 9, 1871, editorialized that "if the murderers of Christ were Democrats," then the newspapers who supported the party "would attempt to shield them."

36. Davis, Proclamation, January 10, 1871, *Messages and Documents*, 18.

37. Davidson to Davis, February 1, 1871, *Messages and Documents*, 7–8. According to one history, "during reconstruction, Colonel Gathings incurred the displeasure of the carpetbag authorities, and was mulcted of $3,000, which he paid rather than have the county placed under martial law, as the officer threatened to do." The writer believed the "state police and military officers with negro troops were particularly obnoxious in their behavior" in Hill County; T. C. Richardson, *East Texas: Its History and Its Makers*, ed. Dabney White, 4 vols. (New York: Lewis Historical Publishing Company, 1940), 3: 639, 1007. One local aficionado declared that "in the meantime Governor Davis issued writs for the arrest of Gathings and his friends, to be served by Sheriff [John P.] Grace; but when the matter again came up the authorities said they wanted only an amicable adjustment and proposed to release Gathings if he would pay the cost of the proceedings thus far, which amounted to nearly $3,000, and which was readily raised by Gathings and his friends. Afterward, when Coke was elected Governor, the State reimbursed Gathings. James T. Ratcliff, of Hillsboro, was his attorney," *A Memorial and Biographical History*, 225.

38. *1870 Walker County Census*, comp. Anthony Vincent Banes and Dennis Michael Lawlis (Huntsville: Walker County Texas Genealogical

Society, 1993), 17; *Daily State Journal* (Austin), January 27, 1871; Houston *Daily Union*, February 1, 1871; Charles Taylor Rather, "Around the Square in 1862 With a Barefoot Boy," in *Huntsville and Walker County, Texas: A Bicentennial History*, comp. and ed. D'Anne McAdams Crews (Huntsville: Sam Houston State University Press, 1976), 139; J. R. Burnett to Davis, January 12, 1871, 22; W. E. Horne to Davis, January 26, 1871, 21, both in *Messages and Documents*.

39. *Daily State Journal* (Austin), January 27, 1871; Houston *Daily Union*, January 16 and 24, 1871.

40. *The State v. Nat Outlaw, et. al.*, Opinion delivered by Judge [J. R.] Burnett, January 11, 1871, in Houston *Daily Union*, February 9, 1871; *Daily State Journal* (Austin), January 27, 1871; Houston *Daily Union*, January 16, February 1, 1871; Galveston *Daily News*, January 25, February 14, March 9, 1871.

41. Houston *Daily Union*, January 18, 1871; Galveston *Daily News*, January 25, 1871; *The State of Texas Against Hon. James R. Burnett, Judge Thirtieth Judicial District; Evidence Taken Before the Joint Committee of the Fourteenth Legislature Appointed to Investigate Charges Preferred By an Address for Removal From Office* (Austin: J. D. Elliott, State Printer, 1874), 14; Horne to Davis, January 26, 1871, *Messages and Documents*, 21.

42. Davis to Burnett, December 12, 1870, Letter Press Book, 34, Governor's Papers (E. J. Davis), ARIS/TSLAC.

43. Testimony of Burnett, February 24, 1871, Hess Court Martial Proceedings, Reconstruction Records, Adjutant General Records, ARIS/TSLAC; Galveston *Daily News*, February 14 and March 9, 1871; Houston *Daily Union*, January 14, 16, 24, and February 1, 1871; *Daily State Journal* (Austin), January 27, 1871.

44. Testimony of Burnett, February 24, 1871, Hess Court Martial Proceedings, Reconstruction Records, Adjutant General Records, ARIS/TSLAC; *State v. Nat Outlaw, et. al.*, in Houston *Daily Union*, February 9, 1871.

45. Horne to Davis, January 26, 1871, in *Messages and Documents*, 19–20, 22–23; Houston *Daily Union*, January 16 and 24, 1871; *Daily State Journal* (Austin), January 27, 1871; Testimony of Burnett, February 24, 1871, Hess Court Martial Proceedings, Adjutant General Records, ARIS/TSLAC.

46. Horne to Davis, January 26, 1871, 19–20; Burnett to Davis, January 12, 1871, 22, both in *Messages and Documents*; Houston *Daily Union*, January 16 and 24, 1871; *Daily State Journal* (Austin), January 27, 1871; Testimony of William McElroy; Testimony of J. H.

Whitehead; Testimony of Burnett, February 24, 1871, all in Hess Court Martial Proceedings, Adjutant General Records, ARIS/TSLAC. Outlaw had secured a pistol from a black desk occupied by the defense counsel.

47. *Daily State Journal* (Austin), January 27, 1871; The Houston *Daily Union*, January 16, 1871, stated three citizens had been wounded in the altercation. Rather, "Around the Square in 1862," said "horses were saddled and bridled and conveniently placed for the boys to make their getaway," 139.

48. Testimony of Burnett, February 24, 1871. Hess Court Martial Proceedings, ARIS/TSLAC; L. H. McNelly (Captain, State Police) to James Davidson, January 13, 1871, Adjutant General Correspondence, ARIS/TSLAC.

49. Davis to Burnett, January 20, 1871, 58, Letter Press Book, Governor's Papers (E. J. Davis); also in *Messages and Documents*, 25; Proclamation Declaring Martial Law in Walker County, January 20, 1871, Adjutant General Correspondence, all in ARIS/TSLAC; *Flake's Daily Bulletin*, March 4, 1871.

50. Reginald G. Jayne, "Martial Law in Reconstruction Texas" (M. A. thesis, Sam Houston State University, Huntsville, 2005), 59–82; Baenziger, "The Texas State Police," 476.

51. "Statement of S. T. Denson," in *Daily State Journal* (Austin), January 25 and February 4, 1873; "Report on the Condition of Affairs in Lampasas County, March 24, 1873," *Report of the AG For the Year 1873* (Austin: Cardwell & Walker, Printers, 1874), 128.

52. Britton to Davis, March 24, 1873, 196-201, Adjutant General Letter Press Book, ARIS/TSLAC; "Report on the Condition of Affairs in Lampasas County, March 24, 1873," 126–27.

53. *Norton's Union Intelligencer* (Dallas), March 29, 1873; *Daily State Journal* (Austin), March 17 and 19, 1873; "Report on the Condition of Affairs in Lampasas County, March 24, 1873," 126–29.

54. Ibid.

55. *Daily State Journal* (Austin), March 19, 1873; C. L. Douglas, *Famous Texas Feuds* (Dallas: The Turner Co., 1936), contended that when Britton appeared in Lampasas, "he found plenty of help on hand. Even before his arrival two Minute Men companies had mobilized—the Lampasas County group under Lieutenant Lee, and the Burnet County organization under Sergeant W. H. Shelburne. In addition Sheriff S. T. Denson had formed a small posse," 133.

56. Flyer found in Dallas *Daily Herald*, April 22, 1873 (copy from Dolph Briscoe Center for American History, University of Texas, Austin).

Part Two

The Insurgents and Their Allies: Texas Terrorists, Politicians, and Newspaper Editors

CHAPTER 7

When the Klan Rode: Terrorism in Reconstruction Texas

by

James M. Smallwood

In Texas during Reconstruction terrorist groups and outlaw gangs were legion, and they kept the state bathed in blood from 1865 to the mid-1870s. They wrapped themselves in the Confederate flag, bespoke the "Lost Cause," and claimed to be taking the field against Texas's enemies: native white Unionists, who were willing to cooperate with federal authorities; the ex-slaves whose leaders demanded true freedom and wanted all the rights whites enjoyed; and the "Yankee" forces of occupation, including regulars and officers on detached duty as agents for the Freedmen's Bureau. Indeed, for former Confederates in Texas, the war did not end in 1865; rather the "Second Civil War," also called the "War of Reconstruction" was really a holocaust fought in a new guise. Generally in the first phase of Civil War (1861–1865), professional armies fought each other until 1865 when the Northern forces prevailed on the fields of battle. In the second phase (1865–1877), former Confederates, including those living in Texas, were victorious and by 1877 the second phase ended in the South with the region returned to the white supremacist Democratic Party. In the Texas effort, terrorist groups formed in more than sixty counties, and at least a dozen large bands of outlaw guerrilla raiders flourished, all the while claiming to represent the continued fighting spirit of old Dixie. Together the Klan and the outlaw guerrillas (often one in the same) destabilized the Reconstruction process, insuring that the reformist policies of the Republicans would fail. In Northeast Texas alone, Klansmen and outlaws overwhelmed the authorities by using violence extensively in the interest of obtaining plunder. But the groups were discriminate in their attacks. Generally, they left alone Texans who supported the old Confederacy in return for their help. Over time, the violent groups evolved into the paramilitary arm of the Democratic Party: the party of slavery, the party of secession, the party of Civil War. Yes, the Southerners, including ex-Confederate Texans, won the War of Reconstruction and set back their region by at least one hundred years. They turned the South, again Texas included, into a dark and bloody ground.[1] Perhaps a correspondent writing to the *Cincinnati Commercial* said it best:

> You cannot pick up a paper in East Texas without reading of murder, assassinations, and robbery . . . and yet not the fourth part of the truth has been told; not one act in ten is reported. Go where you will, and you will hear of fresh murder and violence . . . The civil authority is powerless—the military insufficient in number, while Hell has transferred its capital from pandemonium to Jefferson, and the devil is holding high carnival in Gilmer, Tyler, Canton, Quitman, Boston, Marshall and other places in Texas.[2]

Not as gifted with words, General Philip Sheridan, who commanded the Fifth Military District (Louisiana and Texas) in 1867, was heard to mutter that if he "owned both Texas and Hell he would rent out Texas and move to Hell."[3] Both the correspondent and the general were, of course, referring to the inordinate amount of violence that accompanied Reconstruction in Texas. Neither missed the mark by much. Indeed, contemporary observers and later historians alike held that Texas was the most lawless of all the states in the Reconstruction South. For instance, Texas was the murder capital of United States in both 1868 and 1869. Louisiana was a distant second place with fewer than half the number of homicides.[4]

In his classic *White Terror: The Ku Klux Klan Conspiracy and Southern Reconstruction*, Allen Trelease offered a view of Klan activities in Dixie, without the usual apologetic rhetoric designed to excuse the violence of the terrorists. He defined the Klan as a pervasive mass conspiracy on the part of Anglos to keep the South a white man's country. Trelease developed a new "blanket" definition of the Klan: According to him, if violent groups—by whatever name—performed Klan work, then they should be considered Klans, or simply terrorists groups.[5]

Trelease's book, however, gave only limited coverage to Texas. For example, he investigated the Lone Star State and found seventeen terrorist groups, when, in fact, Texas was home to more than sixty violence-prone organized groups that went by various names, including the Ku Klux Klan, the Knights of the White Camellia, the Teutonic Knights, the Sons of Washington, the White Brotherhood, the Knights of the Rising Sun, and other such names. During Reconstruction, all fouled Texas by robbing, beating, whipping, and murdering native white Unionists and the new freedpeople. For black women and girls the horrors also included the crime of rape. Indeed, whites in the South, including Texas, engaged in an extended Civil War that did not end with Robert E. Lee's surrender in 1865. Rather, the war continued under a new guise: guerrilla warfare, a war that was ultimately successful.[6]

In Texas, the formation of terrorist organizations pre-dated the historic Ku Klux Klan that was born in Tennessee in 1866. As early as the summer of 1865, George A. Custer—the Civil War hero and the youngest cavalry general to lead federal troops during the war—commanded a cavalry divsiion in the central district of Texas. Testifying before Congress on March 10, 1866, he stated that he had ample proof that secret organizations had formed to resist the policies of the federal government. The terrorists were especially strong in East Texas, and he sent troops to disperse them. As well, it was no secret that whites in Freestone and Limestone counties had organized a Klan group called the "white brotherhood" whose members swore that they would not allow freedpeople to be employed in either of the counties. Making good on their threats, members of the brotherhood whipped blacks who tried to contract for work. If the victims persisted, the terrorist simply killed them. Whites who contracted blacks to work would on the first offense be warned and on second offence be whipped or hanged.[7] Of course, the brotherhood was taking action that defied logic. Their actions threatened to eliminate the cheap labor that ex-slaves provided to planters and merchants. Sober heads objected strenuously to the brotherhood's goals. Ultimately the terrorists in Limestone and Freestone did not prevail, but their actions were supported by many of the "common" people of their region.[8]

Throughout settled Texas in 1865, vigilante groups formed for the purpose of policing the freedpeople, of patrolling them just as whites had always done during the antebellum and wartime eras. Anglos in an effort to ensure that blacks "stayed in their place," sought to impose curfews, and to confiscate all weapons found by searchers who ransacked black homes. All through the latter months of 1865, Provisional Governor of Texas Andrew Jackson Hamilton—a prewar Unionist who went into exile and became a general in the Union army during the war—received reports that former Confederates intended to attack the freedpeople and hold them in a position of semi-slavery. Additionally, the attackers pledged to attack native white Unionists and all federal soldiers stationed in the state. Yet, Hamilton bore some responsibility in causing the conditions he abhorred, for originally he had approved county "supervision" of the ex-slave community. He soon regretted his actions, but damage was done by a policy that foreshadowed the rise of terrorist groups.[9]

In many areas, the "patrolling" led to tragedy. Former slave Susan Merritt remembered that slave owners in Harrison County released their bondsmen before the owners in adjacent Rusk County. Slaves in the latter county naturally tried to escape to freedom in Harrison County. Unfortunately for them, Rusk County officials established patrols whose members shot or lynched blacks who tried to run away. "You could see

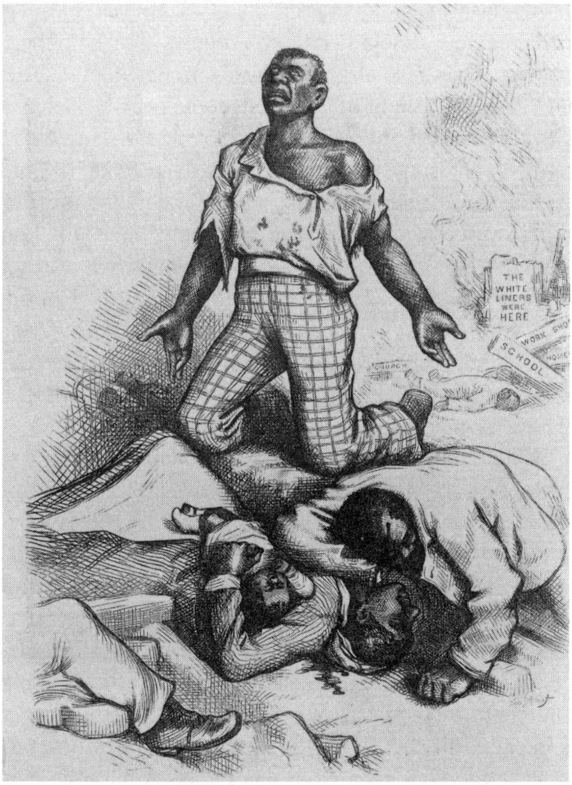

Illustration 8. "Is this a republican form of government? Is this protecting life, liberty, or prosperity? Is this the equal protection of the laws" by Thomas Nast. Illustration first appeared in *Harper's Weekly*, September 2, 1876. (Courtesy of the Library of Congress)

lots of niggers hanging to trees in Sabine bottom right after freedom," said Merritt.[10] When they realized that they were free, many blacks staged jubilees to celebrate, but they had to exercise care and restrain themselves, lest they incur the wrath of whites. Near Hempstead, one jubilee resulted in tragedy when a group of whites rode up and took offense at the celebration. The whites were so disturbed by the festivities that they attacked a freedwoman, disemboweled her, and pitched her body in a wagon and hauled it away.[11]

Violent incidents continued throughout 1866. In April, a white mob in Anderson County attacked a black church group, dispersed the congregation, and warned the pastor not to preach again. Likewise, Lamar County, particularly around Paris (the county seat) went out-of-control as armed bands roamed, attacking church groups to break up the congregations' meetings. They also attacked black families, the goal being plunder. Around Paris, the plight of the freedpeople became so bad that some white residents of the county appealed to President Andrew Johnson for assistance in suppressing the violence. Mrs. L. E. Potts, a Unionist who went into exile in California during the war, wrote the president that "I do not address you as the Chief Magistrate only, but as the father of our beloved country, one to whom we look more or less for protection, but most especially the poor negro [Potts's underlining]." Continuing, she said that "I wish my poor pen could tell you of their persecution here . . . it is not considered a crime to kill a negro. They are often run down by bloodhounds and shot because they do not do precisely as the white man says . . . There have never been any troops here and everything savors of rebellion." Concluding, she said that "for humanity's sake I implore you to send protection in some form to these suffering freedmen."[12] Potts's protest was a rarity because many people who might have spoken out were intimidated by terrorists who were known to beat, shoot, or hang freedmen and their white allies for the slightest complaint to authorities.

Meanwhile, events in Tennessee had an impact on Texas terrorists. The birth of the historic Ku Klux Klan took place in Pulaski, Giles County, Tennessee, in late May or early June of 1866. At first a social club of former Confederates, the Klan quickly evolved into a violent band whose members intended to control the freedpeople, politically, economically, and socially. White Unionists were also targets. Using the model of the Pulaski group, the Klan swept though Tennessee, with many counties having their own autonomous Klaverns by the end of 1866.[13]

Concurrently, similar developments took place in Texas as organized bands continued to coalesce. As far south as Refugio County, terrorists roamed the land, beating and killing a number of freedmen and

Hispanics.[14] By August of 1866, many groups in Texas had heard of the Klan activities in Tennessee. Ominously, the *New Orleans Tribune* reported on September 1 that one of its Texas correspondents had seen evidence that Knights of the Golden Circle (KGC) were banding together again and stockpiling arms and ammunition. The KGC was reappearing, the correspondent warned, and was holding open meetings in "most of the towns in Texas."[15] Undoubtedly the correspondent was mistaken but only to the extent that he/she gave the wrong name to the "concerts" or organizations. The KGC was an antebellum pro-South group who wanted to conquer Mexico, Central America, and various Caribbean islands to found an "empire for slavery." As well, the KGC helped spearhead the drive for secession in the 1850s.[16] The new Klan groups in Texas, however, did not follow the model of the KGC, but, rather, they mimicked Klan organizations in Tennessee.

Later myth-makers ascribed a unity to the Texas Klan that never existed, and they even named a state commander, future Texas Senator Roger Q. Mills. There is little doubt that Mills supported the terrorist movement and might have played a local role, but the Klan groups in Texas, as in most of the South, were completely decentralized, so much so that it is hardly proper to refer to them in the singular number. But, by whatever name and however organized, each group's goals were the same: murder and mayhem and continuing attacks on the freedpeople, native white Unionists, and Yankee soldiers. Klan membership in Texas, as in the rest of the South, was drawn from every rank and class of Anglo society. Indeed, most male Democrats were potential Ku Kluxers. More certain, however, was the age of the members. Most Klansmen were younger men, certainly under fifty year of age, for they had to be physically able to perform their nocturnal deeds.[17]

Although local Klan groups were autonomous, as mentioned above, some Klaverns established ties with organizations in Tennessee. One of the first groups to develop "official" contact with the Volunteer State was a band in Collin County. R. D. Allison—a veteran of both the Mexican War and the Civil War—visited several Tennessee Klaverns in late 1866 and came away with a "charter." Upon returning to Texas, he established his headquarters in McKinney, attracted approximately 200 men, and established a new Klavern. The group held regular meetings, where the men made it clear that they were white supremacists and regarded the freedpeople as an inferior race. Using periodic public displays (such as parades), the members tried to intimidate freedmen but apparently did not engage in overt violence.[18] But, in 1866–1867, Klan organizations in other parts of the state often turned to violence to enforce their will upon local citizens.

Illustration 9. Roger Q. Mills. (Courtesy of Library of Congress)

Reports indicated that by late 1866 Bowie County had descended into complete chaos. The cause centered around one man, known only by the name Captain Tremble. Originally from Illinois, Tremble, who had served in the Union army during the Civil War, moved to Texas after the war. Like many other migrants, he came to the state seeking cheap land. Tremble established a profitable farm and depended on black and white sharecroppers to help him work his land. He was an egalitarian who encouraged the two dozen freedmen who worked for him to press for their rights. Ex-Confederates who lived in the county and who were members of the local Klan, soon learned of Tremble's activities and initiated plans to drive him from the region. One of the Klan's leaders was Cullen Montgomery Baker, a nefarious outlaw who was already wanted by federal authorities.[19] The villains attacked Tremble's farm, wounding him and several freedmen. The next day the captain left for New Orleans—headquarters of the Fifth Military District—to request troops to help him deal with the Klan menace. He succeeded in getting a detachment of twenty men, whom he led back to his property. There, he learned that his farm had been attacked again. The perpetrators had beaten his wife and several freedmen. Moreover, they forced Tremble's wife off the farm. She found her way to Arkansas where she knew people willing to care for her. Meanwhile, the band of ex-Rebels shackled Tremble's black workers and paraded them though the streets of Boston before running them out of the county. Although Tremble had twenty troopers, that small number could take no action against a Klan army of 300 men. Later, care givers took Mrs. Tremble, whose condition had worsened, to a hospital in New Orleans where she soon died from the beating that Klansmen had bestowed on her. Tremble also spent time in the same hospital after the wounds he received in the initial attack became infected. Once he recovered, he sold him farm and left Texas.[20] The local Klan had won a victory. In addition to the trouble in Bowie County, in late 1866, white mobs burned black schools in such diverse locations as Cotton Gin, Waco, and Brenham. In Corsicana, a group of malefactors drove a teacher of freedmen out of town.[21]

Early in 1867, similar events occurred near Marshall, as gangs roamed Harrison County. There, the local Freedmen's Bureau agent, Charles Rand, reported that from January 1 to March 22, he knew of eleven violent acts committed by armed, disguised gangs upon blacks. Rand was powerless, however, because civil authorities refused to take action. He reported a particularly heinous crime that occurred on January 20 when disguised parties lynched three freedmen near Grand Bluff in Panola County. But the distraught agent could only comment to his superior that "I did not deem it necessary to make an investigation as it would have been a waste of time."[22] He was referring to potential white witnesses, who either supported the terrorists or feared them, and refused to give the Bureau any truthful information.

Adding to information about Klansmen, outlaws, and violence, Gov. Elisha Pease, in one of his 1867 reports, discussed 411 separate cases of violence committed by white criminals against blacks and white Unionists. For example, in Sulphur Springs, Hopkins County, a mob hanged several white Unionists in April of the same year. To the northeast, a

Bureau agent reported that Red River County was out-of-control. There was little wonder in this. Hopkins and Red River counties both had pro-Confederate guerrilla raiders led by Ben Bickerstaff and John "Pomp" Duty, both of whom also led Klan groups.[23] At times, it was difficult to know where the Klan left off and pro-Confederate outlaws began. Both worked toward the same goal: the violent subjugation of freedmen, native white Unionists, and occupation troops in their region.

Typical of Klan action was the case of Meshack "Shack" Roberts, a Methodist preacher who served three terms in the Texas Legislature. He had been the faithful slave of O. B. Roberts of Gilmer, Upshur County, taking care of Roberts's family while the man of the family was away at war. Roberts gave Shack a plot of land as a reward for fealty, but Klansmen in the county looked unfavorably on black ownership of land. Thus, masked men from the county "organization" attacked Shack on the road outside Gilmer, whipping him severely and leaving him for dead. Fortunately for him, Shack survived the assault and was able to make his way to his ex-master's home, where O. B. Roberts bandaged his wounds and accompanied him to Marshall. There, protected by a federal garrison, he recovered from his wounds and started life anew.[24]

Bureau agent Rand added another dimension to Klan activities when he reported that, in his district, many so-called outlaw gangs were really Klansmen who rode in the pay of unreconstructed rebels. One of the worst was the Bill Bateman wild bunch, who had a headquarters/hideout at Elysian Fields on the southern border of Harrison County. Bateman was joined by such notables as Phillip Simpson, Charles Hodges, and Bill Parrish. All three were his lieutenants who helped manage the other ruffians who rode with the guerrillas. Counting Bateman, Rand reported that all four "would kill a freedman for 75 cents." Continuing, Rand said that frequently, "for the amusement of high-minded chivalry," the gang terrorized the black community, doing Klan work to keep the freedpeople "in their place." Apparently one of the worst villains was Hodges, who shot and killed a black teenager because the youngster had his hands in his pockets and would not stand at attention when Hodges rode past. Rand learned of the deed but could not go after Hodges because he had no troops.[25]

There were other outlaws performing for the Klan in the northern part of the state. In Titus County, Dave Timmons—who owned a small plantation—hired members of the county Klan to go after and assault blacks who refused to work for him. John Wesley Hardin, a well-known guerrilla, "declared" against Yankees and the freedpeople and apparently took delight in killing them. Also notorious was the aforementioned Cullen Montgomery Baker, who could be hired for a few dollars to kill any freedman that his employer designated. Like Ben Bickerstaff, Baker roamed all of Northeast Texas. Many whites supported him because he claimed to be fighting for the "Lost Cause." They protected him and hid him from the authorities, both civil and military. They told Baker of any new troop movements. They also fed him and other members of his outlaw band, and of course they cared for their horses. Generally, Baker kept blacks in their place, making them fearful, docile workers for white employers. Bureau agent A. G. Malloy said that Baker was "useful to this class [employers of freedpeople] because he controls their freedmen and does not hesitate to shoot them on the slightest complaint."[26] Several times in 1867 Malloy and other agents attempted to capture Baker and break up his raiders, but agents in the field never had enough troops on hand to complete their task.[27]

Despite the harm they caused, outlaw raiders in the pay of planters remained less of a problem when compared to other murder and mayhem that was occurring in the state. Otherwise respectable men continued to join or encourage others to join Klan groups. Members of a "secret organization" murdered several white Unionists who lived in or near Lancaster, yet the culprits could not be caught because former Confederates still controlled the area's law enforcement. Equally, travelers mentioned trouble all over East Texas. Bureau agent David Montgomery frequently rode from his headquarters in Tyler to Austin. He reported that all along the way, on each and every trip, freedpeople begged him for protection of their lives and property, but Montgomery could do nothing. Once again, he was a Bureau man, but he lacked the troops to effectively confront terrorist groups operating in the region.[28]

The Texas Klans reached their zenith in 1868, a pivotal election year. Pursuant to Radical Reconstruction, elections for a new Texas Constitutional Convention were held in February, with elections for a governor to come later. The convention met from June to August, only to adjourn and meet again from December of 1868 to February of 1869. Meanwhile, national voters sent U. S. Grant to the White House in November 1868. These events were harbingers of change. Increasingly, conservative Democrats lost ground to the Republicans. Frustration coupled with an increasing desire to control the black vote influenced many Klansmen to become more active. As well, the Klan had its continuing economic function, just as it had from 1865 to 1867, and its social function to "keep blacks in their place." Influenced by, or in the pay of, wealthy landlords, the terrorists fell upon the freedmen in farming areas after harvests, hoping to drive black sharecroppers from their fields so that landowners could argue that they just ran off and broke their contracts. Owners could, in that way, avoid giving freedmen their fair share of the crops. And those few blacks who owned their own land were constantly harassed by night-riders who wanted landowning freedmen out of their communities.[29]

Beginning in February of 1869, there was a new upsurge of Klan activities. An early focal point was in Jefferson, Marion County. The number of blacks in the county equaled more than 50 percent of the total population, a fact that struck fear among whites living in the county. The Klan tried to intimidate blacks in the area, but for a time no violence resulted. Nevertheless, when blacks began to join the Union League and arm themselves, believing that violence against them would soon come, the stage was set for trouble. The volatile situation was compounded when a new newspaper, the *Ultra Ku Klux*, appeared countywide. It had only a short life, but while it existed, it further inflamed racial hatred. With the emergence of an active Klan group, the presence of armed freedmen, and an antagonistic "Klux" propaganda sheet, conditions were ripe for a racial explosion—one that would erupt later in the year.[30]

Meanwhile, in Limestone County, an individual known to locals as "Dixie" became a scourge, leading a small Klan group and vowing to kill all blacks that he could catch. Dixie was, in reality, Simpson "Simp" Dixon of Northeast Texas who had fled because military authorities were after him. He committed an unknown number of murders, and his effectiveness was attested to by the fact that the freedpeople of the area left their homes at night and hid in the woods for safety. Dixie's murderous career was not ended until Merrit Trammel, a local black leader, brought troops from Waco, surprised Dixie, and shot him dead.[31]

A Klan in Tarrant County, having apparently studied the Klans of Tennessee, wore all the typical Klan paraphernalia—which included hoods and sheets—while terrorizing freedmen in both Tarrant and Dallas counties. They went on night patrols, whipped blacks who were traveling the roads after dark, invaded and searched their homes, and confiscated anything of value. They threatened the life of Unionist Judge B. F. Barkley, who had to have a troop escort at all times to insure his safety. One ex-slave remembered that the "Kluxers" bothered almost all the blacks in the area.[32]

In March of 1868, a Klan group was organized in Bastrop and celebrated by murdering several freedmen. Trinity County also became the scene of Klan violence. A Bureau agent responsible for the county reported that "the whole [white ex-Confederate] community is armed and every man ready to kill his [Unionist] neighbors, or commence a war of extermination . . . The evil disposed to rule by intimidation.[33] By the end of April a new organization also sprang up in Marshall after a local press favorably reported on Klan events in Tennessee. Klaverns spread quickly to other areas such as Paris, Columbus, Palestine, and Navasota by the end of the month. Meanwhile, Democratic presses around the state denied that these terrorist organizations existed. The *Austin Daily State Gazette* "presumed" that Radical Republicans had "imagined" the Klan. The *Denton Monitor* held that talk of secret organizations was a Republican trick to entice freedmen into joining the Union (or Loyal) League.[34]

The Klan made its debut in Clarksville in May by parading in full regalia, after which they attacked a black school, stoning the children and their teacher. By June activity was stepped up in Navasota, while new Klaverns were established in Brazos and Bell counties. Reportedly one freedman went mad with fright after being beaten by Klansmen, and an American Missionary Association teacher, writing from Hempstead, complained of Klan activities in their region, mentioning that she knew one black who was almost beaten to death. Activity soon spread to Anderson County where the Klan drove a one-armed ex-Confederate out of the county because he dared start a school for the freedmen's children. Governor Pease became involved in that particular case, asking the commanding general, Joseph J. Reynolds, for more military assistance. "If such things are permitted," Pease maintained, "there can be no security for any colored man there."[35] But the worst was yet to come.

By June, Harrison, Upshur, Titus, Rusk, and Panola counties were in a state of anarchy. Blacks slept in the woods at night for safety. Armed whites in Kaufman County threatened to "clean out" all black Radicals, and the Bureau man in Kaufman Town claimed to be in a "perilous" condition after Klansmen chased him from his farm. In Hunt County whites carried out their threat, killing white Unionists and blacks, while ordering other freedman to leave the county. In Fannin County black sharecroppers were also driven off the lands where they toiled, forcing them to break their contracts with the landowners. There was also trouble near Waco, where three freedmen were killed in early June. According to Capt. T. M. K. Smith, a Bureau agent, the situation was bad in most of East Texas. Freedmen were, he said, "fleeing for their lives." Kluxers killed many blacks, he continued, saying that in many cases freedmen were "fearfully mutilated." Some whites apparently killed "Negroes for the pure love of killing." Meanwhile, the larger cities in Texas—some even having military garrisons—did not escape Klan activity. S. O. Young, for example, recounted his initiation into the Houston, Harris County, Klan, reporting that his Klavern ultimately numbered at least 300 men.[36]

Some renegades doing Klan work also stepped up their activities during the summer of 1868. Ben Bickerstaff, notorious leader of an East Texas guerrilla group, was also the leader of Klans in both Titus and Hopkins counties. Noted for both his control of a wide-ranging territory and his tendency to shoot first and ask questions later, Bickerstaff robbed six freedmen in Navarro County before Corsicana's Bureau man—with sufficient troop support--caught him and tossed him into the Corsicana jail. However, several of Bickerstaff's men escaped. Then, to the horror of the agent and his Unionist supporters, a local justice of the peace dismissed the case, saying that Bickerstaff only robbed "damned niggers." Upon his release on his way back to Titus County Bickerstaff rejoined his men and then robbed five more Navarro County black families, stole four horses, and hanged two freedmen near Spring Hill. Once home in Titus County, Bickerstaff continued in the pay of local planters and yeomen farmers who wanted freedmen driven from their crops so their harvest could be confiscated.[37]

Ultimately, conditions became so bad for the freedpeople and white Unionists that General Reynolds, although hesitant, finally took action. After Klansmen burned a freedmen's school near Circleville, Williamson County, he offered a $500 reward for information about the culprits. Such action dealing with only one local area was not sufficient; Reynolds began planning for a regional approach. Meanwhile, in July of 1868, he sent twenty troopers to Tyler to quell trouble there, but the countryside around the town remained out-of-control. Soon, Governor Pease again took up the cry for more action. In his correspondence with Reynolds in the summer of 1868, he simply recounted one Klan crime after another. For instance, the governor reported that Klansmen kidnapped A. R. Wilson of Burleson, a freedman and a voter registrar, and murdered him because of his wide-ranging influence in the area's black communities. Pease also reported, apparently randomly, that in such counties as Hunt, Trinity, and Fannin, Klansmen drove many white Unionists and freedpeople to leave the counties, not allowing them to take their possessions with them. In Anderson, Limestone, Young, and Trinity counties atrocities occurred, and Pease seemed to be at the proverbial "end of his rope." And Reynolds could only mutter that the murder of freedmen was so common that it was impossible to keep accurate records of all the incidents.[38]

In North Texas, the *Paris Vindicator* reported that renegades and Klan leaders Bob Lee and Benjamin Bickerstaff intended to kill all blacks between the Red River and Sander's Creek in Lamar County. During a Fourth of July celebration, a riot broke out in the town of Jefferson, where a pro-Confederate mob of 300 men chased the revelers out of town. Much worse, however, was the race war that broke out in Hopkins County, with Bickerstaff, his renegades, and local Klansmen attacking blacks in the area. First, the terrorists invaded black homes, confiscating weapons and anything else of value. Then, they went on an extended rampage. The villains killed or wounded entire black families, including women and children. They also beat or killed white Unionists. The wounded or injured could not get medical help because white physicians were afraid of pro-Rebel retribution should they try to help. Similar events took place in Travis County, and there were new outbreaks of racial violence in Bastrop County.[39]

Meanwhile, in June 1868 in Millican, a small-scale civil war broke out. Trouble there escalated when a newly organized Klan staged a march, hoping to intimidate the freedmen's community. Their maneuvers, however, caused one of the local black leaders, Parson Brooks, to organize a civilian militia made up solely of freedmen. Brooks intended that African Americans should defend themselves if attacked. Approximately 200 men volunteered to protect the black community. Such military maneuvers frightened Anglos, who promised to end the raids if the militia would disband. However, fate intervened to prevent that solution when an unknown, unnumbered group of whites murdered a freedman in the Brazos River bottoms. Brooks called the local militia out to investigate the killing. White Klansmen—seeing that their enemies refused to disband—gathered in force and confronted the black militia. Fighting began. Although the white contingent suffered no fatalities, they killed twenty-five freedmen. Ultimately, the county sheriff and 100 Anglo deputies recruited from Bryan restored "order" by dispersing the blacks, forcing many of them to leave Millican.[40]

Shortly after the incident in Millican, a Klan group from Fayette County invaded Gillespie County in July and rode to Fredericksburg, where they shot and killed white Unionist A. O. Cooley as he sat on his porch. Why? Cooley was a Republican state senator who had much influence in the area black communities. At about the same time, a white mob in Fort Bend County hanged white Unionist Wheelock H. Upton.

Sadly, ex-Confederates in control of the county did not consider the killing a crime because Upton was a Unionist. The Klansmen from Fayette County worked in close cooperation with the Ku Kluxers from adjacent Colorado County, with members of one group performing nocturnal duties for the other. Both units bragged about hanging a Colorado County white Unionist and a "big octoroon from up North," because both men had been preaching racial equality.[41]

In Smith County open warfare broke out on July 19. The "notorious ruffian" and Klan member George Kennedy wantonly assaulted a freedwoman who refused to abandon a downtown sidewalk and get in the street so a group of white women could pass. Freedmen's Bureau agent Lt. Gregory Barrett arrested him, took him to court, and fined him fifty dollars, whereupon Kennedy bolted for the courtroom door while drawing his gun. From a courthouse hallway, he fired at Barrett, two orderlies, and a clerk, all of whom dove for cover. In a maneuver that was likely prearranged, ten Klansmen entered the courthouse and joined Kennedy in the fray. The wild bunch shot up the entire place, critically wounding the two orderlies and the clerk. They also shot Barrett in the leg, but the agent managed to wound Kennedy and thereby ended the battle as the Klansmen joined to help Kennedy get away. Meanwhile, the whole town began to stir. There were threats to "clean out the damned Yankees." Barrett could only appeal to his superiors, asking for troops.[42]

Later, Barrett continued to bemoan his fate, and that of white Unionists and freedmen in his region of the state. He had reports that upper Wood, lower Hunt, and all of Van Zandt counties were in violent turmoil and in the hands of Klansmen and outlaw guerrillas who drove freedmen from their crops. Closer to Tyler, Starville in Smith County was also terrorized by Klansmen led by the "Chauncey brothers," who had already murdered several freedmen but who had been released by civilian pro-Rebel officials. At Starville the brothers and others had already flogged freedmen and freedwomen, giving sometimes as many as 500 lashes and many died as a result. Barrett now had twenty troopers and wanted to help the blacks, but his force was dwarfed by the numbers the Klansmen and the guerrillas could bring to the point of attack. In August he disgustedly wrote headquarters that a Klan party was raiding throughout Smith County and "shooting at any black man they meet." Another county group of six terrorists caught one freedmen on the road, but when he performed his "Sambo" act, they let him go, whereupon, they went straight to another black's cabin, found the owner, and literally "shot him to pieces." It was apparently a "fun" killing.[43]

By September of 1868 Klansmen were terrorizing most counties in eastern Texas, and there was trouble as far south as Corpus Christi. Even in Houston, which was garrisoned, three separate Klan groups formed: one of them was a chapter of the Teutonic Band of Brothers and the other two were circles of the Knights of the White Camellia. Agent Barrett continued to talk of a "reign of terror," mentioning that the sheriff of Van Zandt County had been driven out of his own county because he tried to protect victims. Lieutenant Barrett personally became so discouraged that he resigned as a Bureau agent.[44]

Even as Barrett was being reassigned new duties (his military career extended to the Spanish-American War), trouble continued to occur over a wide-ranging region. A Washington County incident involved the son of a newspaper editor. Seen talking to a freedman who was a friend of the boy's family, the youngster incurred the wrath of the local Klan. A group of disguised men took the boy from his home, robbed him, and then tortured him before murdering him. Hearing from a correspondent, the editor of the *Paris Vindicator* wrote that the lad was "Ku-Kluxed" (beaten) to death.[45] Meanwhile, the Klaverns in Hopkins County, led by Bickerstaff, continued their campaign against white Unionists and the freedpeople. According to several reports, the "Ku Klux Rangers" there included most of the whites in the county. In Trinity County two prominent attorneys and two local judges were known Klan members. These men pressured blacks to join the Democratic Party so they could receive "protection papers" which Klansmen would recognize and would allow those with the papers to live. In Washington County the Klan killed one white Republican and sent threatening letters to others.[46]

The biggest display of all in September was a giant celebration in Jefferson, where the Klan of Marion County staged a big parade, cheered by some 15,000 onlookers. Known as the Knights of the Rising Sun, the group installed George Saufley as grand commander in a move that showed the terrorist groups were a paramilitary arm of the Democratic Party, for Saufley was already the Marion County chairman of the party. Even as he assumed his new post with the Knights, he was wanted for murder in Arkansas. Yet the local press extolled that "we have no better citizen than Colonel Saufley."[47]

There was again trouble near Paris later in September when masked men "Kluxed" (made threats to) a local Bureau agent and several other Republicans. Bureau agent Col. DeWitt Brown had his horse shot out from under him, was driven from his farm, and was forced to seek protection in Paris. The Lamar County Klan also attacked blacks at home and confiscated all arms found. Then the terrorists gave freedmen a choice: If they would join the Democratic Party, they could have precious "protection papers." Much farther south in Georgetown, George Rouser organized four "Democratic clubs," with all four combined growing to a total membership of 192 men. The "clubs" represented a cover for a Klan group, the Knights of the White Camellia.[48]

In October terrorists did not relent. Jefferson again became the site of controversy which stemmed from Klan hatred for George W. Smith, a youthful Union army veteran who became a merchant in Jefferson after the war. Although his business failed, Radical Reconstruction opened a political career for the hated "carpetbagger." Elected to the 1868 Texas Constitution Convention, Smith proved to be an able delegate who firmly supported the rights of the freedmen whom he believed should have the same privileges of citizenship as whites. His friends praised him as being almost austere, never drinking alcohol, never smoking or chewing, nor using profane language. But his enemies said that "he was odious as a Negro leader, as a radical." Further, he alienated many white townspeople by making strenuous efforts to collect debts from white townspeople who owed him money. He was ostracized by area ex-Rebels who threatened his life.[49]

On the night of October 3, 1868, Smith spoke at a Republican meeting where he was joined by freedman Anderson Wright who also addressed the audience. Just as he returned to his cabin, in company with several freedmen, Smith was assailed by four men led by "Colonel" Richard P. Crump. Shooting began. Smith managed to wound two of the attackers and drove the rest away. Then, he went to the army garrison where he hoped to find protection from his assailants. Soon, Crump and other Knights of the Rising Sun showed up with a warrant for Smith's arrest on assault charges. The attackers' intention of murdering Smith now became more urgent because Smith and several freedmen had recognized some of their attackers. Smith protested being taken into "protective" custody, for he knew it was his death warrant, but the military commander on the scene Major James Curtis turned him over to civilian authorities after being assured of the young man's safety. Smith wound up in the local jail, having a small civilian guard to protect him. The next day members of the Knights of the Rising Sun assembled in Jefferson. Knowing that a lynching was possible, Major Curtis sent sixteen men to help guard the lock-up. That night, at about 9 p.m., Saufley mobilized approximately seventy Knights and marched on the jail. All were disguised in Klan garb, and all carried weapons and torches.

The jail was in an enclosed yard, but the Knights easily burst through the fence and overpowered the young guardsmen who were hesitant to shoot. Curtis heard the furor and came to the jail with his few remaining soldiers, but they, too, were quickly overpowered. Saufley and a few other terrorists dragged several freedmen into adjoining woods where they murdered two of them. They had no trouble opening the jail because the city marshal was one of the conspirators, and he had a key. Next, they went to Smith's cell. Smith fought at the door and managed to wound two of his attackers, but holding up their torches to the barred window of the room, the Klansmen were able to shoot into the place, hitting Smith four times. Then they entered the room and one by one filed around Smith, each firing a bullet into the dying man. As one report indicated, "this refinement of barbarity was continued while he writhed and after his limbs had ceased to quiver, that each [Knight] might participate in the triumph."[50]

When the Knights left the jail where Smith lay dead, they broke into squads and began looking for other Republicans, several of whom took refuge with Major Curtis. Because he was a leading Republican and because he had served as the chairman of the Constitutional Convention's committee on violence, Judge Charles Caldwell knew he was in a dangerous position. He fled from his house and disappeared into a nearby forest. Some twenty to thirty terrorists waited in his home for approximately two hours, finally deciding that Caldwell was too savvy to return until the next day. When that day dawned, Major Curtis warned Republicans that the Knights intended to make a "clean sweep" and that he did not have enough men to protect them all. However, he added that he could give them a military escort out of town. Most Republicans took advantage of the major's offer, leaving until law and order could once more be restored in Marion County.[51]

Although federal authorities ultimately cracked down on Jefferson and held the now-famous "Stockade" trials, for many more months Klan groups in other areas around the state remained out-of-control. As well, in mid-October of 1868, the Knights of Marion County, apparently having no fear of legal retribution, struck again. This time, approximately fifty armed, masked men fell on the Willis Whitaker plantation about 12 miles north of Jefferson. Whitaker was another known Unionist who happened to be gone from home when the terrorists struck. They killed seven freedmen, wounded three more, and burned Whitaker's gin and forty bales of cotton. Concurrently, Cullen Baker, called the "Swamp Fox of the Sulphur," continued to terrorize blacks all over Northeast Texas. In early October he and one cohort shot and killed William G. Kirkman, the Bureau agent in Boston, Bowie County. Later, he and his raiders struck a federal supply train going from Jefferson to Boston and killed two of four troopers guarding the wagon train while wounding the other two. Many area whites still protected Baker and his men because they professed to be fighting for the "Lost Cause." Indeed, like other Klansmen and guerrillas, they understood they were engaged in the Second Civil War or the War of Reconstruction. As well, Baker remained in the pay of area planters whose sharecroppers were now running away because they feared the Klan more than ever. Curiously, Baker—who was known for killing freedmen and driving others out the region—now reversed course and attacked them if they tried to leave Northeast Texas, his advice being that he would let them live if they were faithful to their employers.[52]

By November of 1868, conditions had deteriorated further. From Nacogdoches came news of new outrages. Bureau agent Alex Ferguson reported "major activity" against blacks in his district. One night unidentified, disguised masked men killed two freedmen, whipped six more, and stole several horses. Ferguson said he needed troops because similar incidents had occurred in the past, and he believed more violent incidents would occur in the future. He added that many ex-Rebels were openly bragging that "they could easily dispose of a few of the Loyalty Leaguers and then they [could] manage . . . the freedmen . . . as they desired."[53]

Around Marshal, Klansmen continued to harass freedmen and drive them from their farms. In Richmond, one Mr. Martin, a white Unionist—working with the American Missionary Association and the Freedmen's Bureau—had become a teacher for area freedpeople. Masked assailants dragged him from his home and severely assaulted him. Told not to teach again, Martin, for fear of his life, dutifully resigned his position.[54] There was also a reign of horror in Matagorda County. A respected citizen, J. C. McNeill, allowed the terrorists to deposit arms at his place to be used later because he was loyal to the "Lost Cause." Later, the weapons were put to use against white Unionists and the freedpeople. December was like November, with reports of widespread violence in all of eastern Texas. However, events running their course in Jefferson would bring change.[55]

After the murders of Smith and the freedmen in Jefferson, Commanding General Reynolds determined once and for all to bring strong action to limit the violence of Klansmen and guerrilla bands. He recalled Major Curtis and sent Col. H. G. Malloy to Jefferson as provisional mayor with orders to find the murderers. Further, Reynolds gave Malloy a force consisting of nine companies of infantry and four of cavalry, and ordered him to use his forces to bring peace to the area. In December Malloy arrested four of Jefferson's leading citizens who had been implicated in the murders. Saufley would have been arrested too, but he left town the day before "on business," from which he did not return. Ultimately, the "Colonel," still wanted for murder in Arkansas, went first to Indian Territory and then on north all the way to New York, where he disappeared. Authorities never managed to catch him. Meanwhile, on the night of December 5, the Knights of the Rising Sun held an emergency meeting. Immediately thereafter, about twenty men left town for parts unknown, while others prepared to follow.[56]

The number of the incarcerated stood at thirty-seven by April of 1869. Authorities locked up some of the "best, most reputable," men as well as some of the worst citizens of Marion County. Gen. George Buell, whom General Reynolds had recently assigned to Jefferson to restore law and order, sent detectives as far north as New York searching for other suspects (one being Saufley) who scattered to all points of the compass. "General" H. P. Mabry, a former judge and respected citizen of Jefferson, represented the accused, but to his horror, a prisoner admitted that Mabry was a Knight, and in fact had been one of the leaders on the night Smith was murdered. Forewarned by friends, Mabry learned that a detachment of soldiers was coming to arrest him. After quickly packing a few personal items, he escaped to points north. Ultimately, he ended up hiding in Canada. Meanwhile, the defense counsel, made up of eleven attorneys (virtually the whole Jefferson bar), lobbied for a transfer of the cases to civilian courts, but Buell refused. Many delays followed, and the trial continued until September of 1869. By that time Klansmen and guerrillas around the state had committed new atrocities, but violent attacks were becoming less frequent.[57]

While the Jefferson trials plodded along, trouble developed in other areas. On February 7, 1869, near Troup, in Smith County, freedmen met at Hopewell Church to hear a visiting Unionist, a Mr. Lively, deliver a sermon. After the service but before the crowd dispersed, a group of masked men rode up and began firing into the congregation, killing one freedman and wounding others. With guns drawn, some of the Klansmen dismounted and robbed people of all the valuables that they carried on their person. Afterwards, confident of their security, they leisurely rode back to Tyler and ate at a local hotel before going home. However, when investigations began, three freedmen identified one James Gillian as a member of the murderous band. Gillian decided to make an example out of one witness and thereby frighten the other two so they would not testify against him.

He found one of the men working in a nearby field and fired two shotgun blasts, severely wounding the would-be witness. To complete the job, Gillian dismounted, walked to the prone man, put a derringer to his head, and killed him. As Gillian hoped, the brutal act made the other blacks afraid to testify against him. He was free, then, to do more damage to the freedpeople's community. The incident was not an isolated one. Similar stories were heard all across settled Texas. In official testimony, high-ranking officials complained of numerous cases where the perpetrators of violent acts went free for lack of testimony from witnesses.[58]

And the violence continued. In April in Kaufman, the Ku Kluxers burned a freedmen's school and drove the county's blacks away from their crops. Several months later in Panola County, a local Bureau agent stated that the freedmen in his district were also being driven away; the agent sadly concluded that "no civil official [in the county] will do their duty to fight crime wherever found."[59]

Much farther south, in Columbia, Brazoria County, four Klansmen broke up a black church meeting on September 7. As he drew his pistol, ringleader Harry Mason told a Mr. Hardwell to stop preaching. Hardwell grabbed for the weapon and an elderly freedman named Perry tried to help by hitting Mason with his cane. Nevertheless, Mason gained control of his gun after knocking Hardwell to he ground. Then, the renegade shot and killed Perry while the rest of the congregation, Hardwell included, scattered. The sheriff of Brazoria County made a halfhearted investigation but in the end could only report that there were too many Klansmen in the county—some sixty or seventy—for him to bring to justice, as they would all protect each other and would also outnumber his few deputies at the scene should he make attempts to bring in the villains. Thus, another murderer went free.[60]

Meanwhile, the Jefferson trials dragged slowly to a conclusion. Witness after witness was paraded before the military tribunal, all providing alibis for this and that defendant. The Knights had earlier sworn to protect each other, and they too offered testimony, mostly spurious. The prosecution depended on black witnesses and on a few whites who gave evidence to avoid a prison term. The results of the trials were mixed. Fourteen men under arrest never went to trial. The tribunal acquitted seventeen because they had "iron clad" alibis. The court convicted only six, three receiving life prison terms and three receiving four years each in the Huntsville Penitentiary. Even "Colonel" Crump, one of the ringleaders, went free. The arrests and trials, however, did have a pacifying effect on Marion County and adjacent areas. The Knights of the Rising Sun never rode again. New security and freedom from fear was symbolized when Republicans founded a new newspaper in Jefferson.[61]

Other parts of eastern Texas, with some exceptions, tended to become calmer in 1869. Although not many Klansmen were convicted, the Jefferson trials scared many would-be terrorists. Now many sober sorts returned to more peaceful political activities. Moreover, even before Smith's murder, General Reynolds ordered all military and civilian authorities to "arrest on the spot any person wearing a mask or otherwise disguised."[62] Further, he concentrated more troops in eastern Texas, pulling them away from the Indian frontier. Arrests increased, and proportionately the crime rate went down. In one notable action, Reynolds ordered detachments of the 6th Cavalry to move from West Texas to Sulphur Springs, Hopkins County, an area alive with troubles from Klansmen and outlaw guerrillas. In action by October of 1868, the detachment under Major A. R. Chaffee and Capt. Thomas Tolman continued its work through 1869. Harsh tactics earned these troops the name of "Chaffee's Guerrillas," but they reduced Klan activities when they launched a thousand-mile campaign against malefactors. The federal force, for example, broke up several outlaw bands that were doing Klan work. Soldiers killed several of Bickerstaff's gang near Pilot Grove in Northeast Texas and set the stage for his death (at the hands of civilians) in Alvarado. Other federal troops and civilian volunteers ultimately dispersed the Baker guerrillas and killed Baker himself, but not before he murdered another Bureau agent. Likewise, the infamous Bob Lee met his end in early 1869.[63]

In addition to the federal crackdown, some landowners now spoke out about the evils of the Texas Klans and guerrillas. On several occasions some white landowners who were satisfied with their black sharecroppers turned against the various Klan groups and tried to limit their activities. For example, for more than two years the Klan of Tarrant County terrorized the freedpeople. Ultimately, because of frequent raids, blacks became so afraid that they did not work. Instead, they stayed hidden in various wooded areas 24 hours a day. Such conditions spurred two planters in the area (named Harris and Rodgers) into action. One night they armed all their freedmen and had them await the local Klan in ambush. When the terrorists rode through the area, blacks, hiding in a ditch, fired volley after volley. Thereafter, the Klavern discontinued its nightly raids on those plantations.[64]

Further limiting the Klan was the election of, and subsequent actions of, Republican Gov. Edmund J. Davis and his Republican Texas Legislature. The now-in-power Republicans created a state police force that could cut across county lines. They also organized a state militia. The legislature invested the new governor with the power of martial law, a power Davis exercised when necessary. Further, all county sheriffs and deputies and all local constables and marshals were considered part of the state police and thus subject to Davis's orders. Then came a crack-down on lawless elements when the 1871 Republican-controlled legislature passed laws against armed and disguised persons. From July of 1870 to December of 1871, the state police arrested 4,580 people, 829 for murder or attempted murder, crimes usually inflicted by Anglos on blacks. Hundreds of other Klansmen (like Jefferson's Saufley) fled the state to avoid arrest and prosecution.[65]

Police and militia activities, together with Davis's strong actions, diminished lawlessness in Texas; but such activity was not entirely stopped, as Klansmen continued to roam during the early 1870s. In July of 1871 reports from Bastrop County told of widespread Klan activities that included the burning of the freedpeople's school buildings, the whipping teachers and children, and the beating of parents who sent their children to the schools. But an all-white grand jury refused to indict anyone for the crimes although evidence suggested who the culprits were. Near Calvert (Robertson County), Klansmen also burned a schoolhouse as they also did at Towash, Hill County. In Fairfield the local sheriff was the leader of a Klavern that had intimidated all black and white Republicans. In addition, the same bunch murdered at least one freedman. In Polk County the district judge in Beaumont complained that he could not even hold court because of area violence and threats against his life. One irate Unionist from Palestine complained to Texas Secretary of State James Newcomb that all of Cherokee County remained in the hands of the Klan. General Reynolds reported the murders of several black teamsters by terrorists in the Nacogdoches area.[66]

But for a few exceptional incidents such as mentioned above, Klan activities generally ceased to exist in Texas by 1872. Even during the federal and state elections of 1872, wherein the Democrats returned to power, and the gubernatorial elections of 1874, wherein Davis was removed from power, the Klan apparently played only a minor part. The cause is easy to discern. The secret work that Klansmen had done earlier was then being done openly by most Anglos, and "the law" was powerless to oppose a new united majority who intended to return Texas to a white man's country. Many ex-slaves later reported that the Klans had performed their functions all too well, intimidating freedmen and white Unionists all over the state. Particularly in the important political arena, many of the people simply gave up their rights rather than cope with

Klan members, guerrilla gangs, and other terrorist groups. With scattered exceptions, the Ku Klux Klan in Texas lay dormant until the 1920s, successfully fulfilling its heinous mission of restoring white supremacy to the Lone Star State. In essence, they had played a significant role in helping the southern states win the Second Civil War.[67]

ENDNOTES

1. For books, articles, dissertations, and theses stressing violence in Texas during Reconstruction, see, for examples, James M. Smallwood, Barry A. Crouch, and Larry Peacock, *Murder and Mayhem: The War of Reconstruction in Texas* (College Station: Texas A&M University Press, 2003); James M. Smallwood, Kenneth W. Howell, and Carol C. Taylor, *The Devil's Triangle: Ben Bickerstaff, Northeast Texans, and the War of Reconstruction in Texas* (Lufkin: Best of East Texas Publishers, 2007); James M. Smallwood, *The Feud That Wasn't: The Taylor Ring, Bill Sutton, John Wesley Hardin, and Violence in Texas* (College Station: Texas A&M University Press, 2008). For yet more information on Reconstruction violence in Texas, see Gov. Andrew Jackson Hamilton to President Andrew Johnson, March 1, 1866, Andrew Johnson Papers, Archives, Manuscript Division (MD), Library of Congress (LOC); Capt. C. S. Robert to Assistant Adjutant General (AAG), August 12, November 12, 1867, Letters Received (LR), Assistant Commissioner (AC), Texas (T), Bureau of Refugees, Freedmen, and Abandoned Lands (BRFAL), District of Texas (DT), Record Group (RG) 105, National Archives and Records Administration (NARA); Col. S. H. Starr to AAG, February 9, 1868, T, LR, DT, Fifth Military District (FMD), RG 393, NARA; James M. Smallwood, "When the Klan Rode: White Terror in Reconstruction Texas," *Journal of the West* 25 (October, 1986): 4–13; James M. Smallwood, *Time of Hope, Time of Despair* (New York: Kennikat Press, 1981); Barry A. Crouch, *The Freedmen's Bureau and Black Texans* (Austin: University of Texas Press, 1992); Barry A. Crouch and Donaly Brice, *Cullen Montgomery Baker: Reconstruction Desperado* (Baton Rouge: Louisiana State University Press, 1997); William L. Richter, *The Army in Texas During Reconstruction, 1865–1870* (College Station: Texas A&M University Press, 1987); William L. Richter, *Overreached on All Sides: The Freedmen's Bureau Administrators in Texas, 1865–1868* (College Station: Texas A&M University Press, 1991); Charles V. Kenner, "Racial Turmoil in Texas, 1865–1871" (M.A. thesis, North Texas State University, 1971); Rebecca A. Kosary, "Regression to Barbarism in Reconstruction Texas: An Analysis of White Violence against African-Americans from the Texas Freedmen's Bureau Records,

1865–1868" (M. A. thesis, Southwestern Texas State University, 1999); Barry A. Crouch, "A Spirit of Lawlessness: White Violence; Texas Blacks, 1865–1868," *Journal of Social History* 18 (1984): 217–32. A number of studies examine violence across the South during Reconstruction. Two good examples are Allen Trelease, *White Terror: The Ku Klux Klan Conspiracy and Southern Reconstruction* (New York: Harper and Row, 1971) and George C. Rable, *But There Was No Peace: The Role of Violence in the Politics of Reconstruction* (Athens: University of Georgia Press, 1984).

2. *Cincinnati Commercial*, quoted in the *Montgomery Alabama State Journal*, January 30, 1869.

3. Trelease, *White Terror*, 103.

4. See Adjutant General's Reports on Crime, 1868, 1869, LR, Adjutant General (AG), 1861–1870, RG 94, NARA.

5. Trelease, *White Terror*, *passim*.

6. For a general overview of the violence common in Texas, see the sources cited in endnote #1.

7. Custer testified before Congress on March 10, 1866, and his copious report is replete with information and examples of violence in Texas spawned by terrorist groups and renegade raiders (often one in the same). For a transcription of Custer's remarks, see Smallwood, Howell, and Taylor, *The Devil's Triangle*, appendix 1, 191–200. And see, Smallwood, *Time of Hope, Time of Despair*, 29.

8. See Smallwood, Howell, and Taylor, *Devil's Triangle*, 62.

9. A. J. Hamilton, "Proclamation to Freedmen," November 7, 1865, A. J. Hamilton, Governor's Paper (GP), RG 301, Texas State Library and Archives Commission (TSLAC).

10. Statement of Susan Merritt, Federal Writers Project, "A Folk History of Slavery in the United States from Interviews with Former Slaves (Washington, D.C.: National Archives, 1941), Texas Narratives, hereafter cited as Texas Slave Narratives.

11. For "first freedom" in Texas, see Smallwood, *Time of Hope, Time of Despair*, 25–42.

12. "Record of Felonies Committed in Texas, 1866–1868, FMD, RG 393, NARA; see also Charles H. Moore, "Anderson County During Reconstruction, typescript, C. H. Moore, Reminiscences, 1845–1873, Center for American History, University of Texas at Austin Library (CAH-UT); Mrs. L. E. Potts, Lamar County, to the President [Andrew Johnson], June 21, 1866, in "Condition of Affairs in Texas," U.S. House, *Executive Documents*, Doc. No. 61, 1–4. Also see, Smallwood, Crouch, and Peacock, *Murder and Mayhem*, 44, and Smallwood, Howell, and

Taylor, *The Devil's Triangle*, 52, 201–5. *The Devil's Triangle* includes an appendix that contains Potts's entire letter to Johnson and the federal government's reaction to it. The book also has maps showing counties that housed at least one terrorist group.

13. Trelease, *White Terror*, 3–8.

14. Hobart Huson, *Refugio* (Woodsboro, TX: privately published, 1955), 194–95.

15. *New Orleans Tribune*, September 1, 1866.

16. For the KGC, see Roy Sylvan Dunn, "The KGC in Texas, 1860–1861," *Southwestern Historical Quarterly* 70 (April 1967): 543–73.

17. See, Huson, *Refugio*; Dunn, "KGC in Texas"; *New Orleans Tribune*, September 1, 1866.

18. J. Lee Stambaugh and Lillian J. Stambaugh, *A History of Collin County, Texas* (Austin, 1958), 73–74.

19. Capt. Charles F. Rand to AAG, March, 22, 1867, LS, Sub-Assistant Commissioner (SAC), Marshall, Texas, BRFAL, DT, RG 105, NARA; and see Crouch and Brice, *Cullen Montgomery Baker*.

20. Capt. Rand to AAG Lt. J. Kirkman, March 22, 1867, LS, SAC, Marshall, Texas, BRFAL, DT, RG 105, NARA.

21. See Smallwood, "When the Klan Rode," 5.

22. Capt. Rand to AAG, March 22, 1867, LS, SAC, Marshall, Texas, BRFAL, DT, RG 105, NARA.

23. See Smallwood, *Time of Hope, Time of Despair*, 69; United States House of Representatives, *House Miscellaneous Documents*, 40th Cong., 2nd sess., 1868, Doc. No. 127, 7–23 (this document contains Pease's report); Capt. Rand to AAG, April 20, 1867, LS, SAC, Marshall, Texas, BRFAL, DT, RG 105, NARA.

24. See Prentis W. Chumn, Jr., "Education and Politics, a Study of the Negro in Reconstruction Texas" (M.A. thesis, Southwest State Teachers College, 1957), 186; Lawrence D. Rice, *The Negro in Texas, 1874–1900* (Baton Rouge: Louisiana State University Press, 1971), 103; John Mason Brewer, *Negro Legislators of Texas and Their Descendants* (Dallas: Mathis, 1935; repr. Austin: Jenkins Publishing, 1970), 65–67.

25. Capt. Rand to AAG, March 4, 1867, Letters Sent (LS), SAC, Marshall, Texas, BRFAL, DT, RG 105, NARA.

26. Maj. Gorge Malloy to AAG, September 30, 1867, LS, SAC, Marshall, Texas, BRFAL, DT, RG 105, NA.

27. See Winston L. Kinsey, "Negro Labor in Texas, 1865–1876" (M.A. thesis, Baylor University, 1965), 102–3; Maj. Malloy to AAG,

September 30, 1867, LS, SAC, Marshall, Texas, BRFAL, DT, RC 105, NARA; Lt. William Kirkman to Gen. Charles Griffin, July 9, 1867, LS, SAC, Boston, Texas, July 30, 1867, BRFAL, DT, RG 105, NARA.

28. Lt. David Montgomery to AAG, March 26, June 13, 1867, LR, AC, T, BRFAL, DT, RG 105, NARA; and see J. C. Leydce to Governor E. Pease, August 20, 1867, E. M. pease, GP, RG 301, TSLAC.

29. Capt. T. M. K. Smith to AAG, June 28, 1868, LS, SAC, Marshall, Texas, BRFAL, DT, RG 105, NARA; John Mason Brewer, ed., *An Historical Outline of the Negro in Travis County* (Austin: Samuel Huston College, 1940), 18; Ray Marshall, "The Negro in Southern Unions," in *The Negro and the American Labor Movement*, ed. Julius Jacobson (Garden City, NY: Anchor Books, 1968), 129.

30. See Smallwood, "When the Klan Rode," 6–7.

31. Walter F. Cotton, *History of the Negroes of Limestone County from 1860 to 1939* (Mexia, TX: Chatman and Merriwether, 1939), 28. And see Smallwood, Crouch, and Peacock, *Murder and Mayhem*, 121–23, 166; Smallwood, *Time of Hope, Time of Despair*, 126.

32. Statement of Louis Young, Texas Slave Narratives, pt. 4, 232–34; Statement of John Crawford, Texas Slave Narratives, pt. 1, 257–59.

33. Trelease, *White Terror*, 105.

34. *Austin Daily State Gazette*, April 17, 1868; *Denton Monitor*, May 30, September 5, 1868.

35. Gov. Pease to Gen. J. J. Reynolds, June 26, 1868, E. M. Pease, GP, RG 301, TSLAC; also see L. S. Dickinson to George Shepherd, June 5, 1868, American Missionary Association, Texas Correspondence, Archives, American Missionary Association, Dillard University, New Orleans, Louisiana; and Trelease, *White Terror*, 105.

36. Capt. T. M. K. Smith to Texas Assistant Commissioner (TAC), July [?], 1868, LR, TAC, BRFAL, DT, RG 105, NARA; Shook, "Federal Occupation and Administration of Texas, 1865–1870," 435; Smallwood, "When the Klan Rode," 7.

37. Capt. Smith to AAG, June 22, 1868, LS, SAC, Marshall, Texas, BRFAL, DT, RG 105, NARA; H. Sweeney to Mrs. Rogers, October 12, 1868, LS, SAC, Marshall, Texas, BRFAL, DT, RG 105, NARA; *New York Times*, August 31, 1868.

38. See, for example, Gov. Pease to Gen. Reynolds, June 23, 26–27, 30, July 27, August 1, October 8, 1868, E. M. Pease, GP, RG 301, TSLAC.

39. N. A. Randlett to TAC, July [?], 1868, LR, TAC, T, BRFAL, DT, RG 105, NARA; *Houston Weekly Telegraph*, July 17, 1868; *Austin Daily Republican*, August 7, 1868.

40. N. A. Randlett to TAC, July [?], 1868, LR, TAC, BRFAL, DT, RG 105, NARA; *Houston Weekly Telegraph*, July 17, 1868; *Austin Daily Republican*, August 7, 1868.

41. *Austin Daily Republican*, July 14, 1868; Leonie R. Weyland and Houston Wade, *An Early History of Fayette County* (La Grange: privately published, 1936), 265–66.

42. Lt. Gregory Barrett to AAG, July 21, 1868, LS, SAC, Tyler, Texas, BRFAL, DT, RG 105, NARA; *New York Times*, August 31, 1868.

43. Ibid.

44. Smallwood, "When the Klan Rode," 8.

45. *Paris Vindicator*, September 19, 1868; *Austin Daily Republican*, September 21, 1868; *Marshal Texas Republican*, September 25, 1868.

46. *Marshall Texas Republican*, September 25, 1868; *Austin Daily Republican*, September 21, 1868; Smallwood, "When the Klan Rode," 8–9.

47. *Marshal Texas Republican*, September 21, 1868; *Flakes Galveston Daily Bulletin*, August 24, 1868.

48. *Marshal Texas Republican*, September 25, October 9, 1868; Trelease, *White Terror*, 138–39; "Notebook Tally" and "Charter for the Knights of the White Camellia," George Rouser Papers, 1860–1884, TSLAC.

49. *New York Daily Tribune*, July 31, 1868; *Austin Daily Republican*, October 23, 1868; Trelease, *White Terror*, 140–42; *New York Times*, October 25, 1868.

50. *Austin Daily Republican*, October 23, 1868; Trelease, *White Terror*, 140–42; *New York Times*, October 25, 1868; *New York Tribune*, July 31, 1869 (the *Tribune* was flashing back, doing a summary of the killing).

51. D. Campbell to Gov. Pease, November 3, 1868, E. M. Pease, GP, RG 103, Archives, TSLAC; *Austin Daily Republican*, October 23, 1868; *New Orleans Republican*, October 12, 13, 24, 1868.

52. Willis Whitaker to Gen. Reynolds, October 26, 1868, LR, TAC, T, BRFAL, DT, RG 105, NARA; *Marshal Texas Republican*, October 23, 1868.

53. Alex Ferguson to AAG, December 5, 1868, LS, SAC, Nacogdoches, Texas, BRFAL, DT, RG 105, NARA.

54. Mr. [?] Martin to Capt. W. A. Rock, date unknown, LR, SAC, Richmond, Texas, BRFAL, DT, RG 105, NARA; E. C. Henshaw to AAG, November 17, 1868, LS, BRFAL, DT, RG 105, NARA.

55. Smallwood, "When the Klan Rode," 10.

56. Trelease, *White Terror*, 105.

57. Ibid., 145–46.

58. *Tyler Index*, March 20, 1869; "Reports of Scouts, Indian Depredations, and Crimes," FMD, RG 393, NARA.

59. Report of Scouts, Indian Depredations, and Crimes, Gen. Bissell to AAG, August 4, 1869, LS, FMD, RG 393, NARA; Louis Stevenson, American Missionary Association, to Capt. C. S. Roberts, April 26, 1869, BRFAL, DT, RG 105, NARA.

60. Louis Stevenson, American Missionary Association, to Capt. Roberts, April 26, 1869, LS, Assistant Superintendent of Schools (ASS), BRFAL, DT, RG 105, NARA; Gen. Bissell to AAG, August 4, 1869, LS, "Report of Scouts, Indian Depredations, and Crimes," FMD, RG 393, NARA.

61. Smallwood, "When the Klan Rode," 10–11; and see Richter, *The Army in Texas During Reconstruction*, along with Trelease, *White Terror*.

62. Gen. Reynolds, General Order No. 15, October 12, 1868, Special and General Orders, 1865–1869, BRFAL, DT, RG 105, NARA.

63. Ibid.; Letter (author unknown) to Lt. L. V. Caziarc, January 14, 1869, LR, Jefferson Post Records, FMD, RG 393, NARA. For Lee's death, see, Smallwood, Crouch, and Peacock, *Murder and Mayhem*, 109–11.

64. Oliver Knight, *Fort Worth: Outpost on the Trinity* (Norman: University of Oklahoma Press, 1953), 55; Garrett, *Fort Worth: A Frontier Triumph* (Austin: Encino Press, 1972), 278.

65. Trelease, *White Terror*, 147–48.

66. J. C. DeGress to John Eaton, October 28, 1871, LR, BRFAL, DT, RG 105, NARA; W. M. Waddell to James P. Newcomb, July 9, 1870, James P. Newcomb Papers, Archives, University of Texas at Austin Library; *Austin Daily State Journal*, July 29, August, 1871.

67. See, for example, statement of Eli Davison, Texas Slave Narratives, pt. 1, 297, and statement by Tom Holland, Texas Slave Narratives, pt. 2, 147.

CHAPTER 8

The Democratic Party, the Ku Klux Klan, and the Politics of Fear

by

Carl H. Moneyhon

The era of Reconstruction in Texas, as elsewhere in the South, was marked by a wave of violence that revisionist historian Eric Foner has described as lacking a "counterpart in the American experience or in that of the other Western Hemisphere societies that abolished slavery in the nineteenth century." Historians have long recognized that central to the story of this upheaval was the secret organization known as the Ku Klux Klan. Foner, synthesizing Reconstruction scholarship, concluded that while racial, social, and political conflict had been widespread in the South from the end of the Civil War, that strife increased and intensified with the appearance of the Klan. Foner identified the Klan as the embodiment of what he called the "counterrevolutionary terror" that swept over the former Confederate States after 1867. What was this powerful organization? Foner summed up the work of others when he described the Klan movement as a popular uprising by dissatisfied whites who opposed the course of Reconstruction. It served as a "military force" protecting the interests of the planter class, the Democratic party, and all whites who wished to restore as much as possible the white supremacist order of the antebellum South, and ultimately helped undo Reconstruction. Nonetheless, it lacked any real organization and had no clear leadership. Klan violence usually was committed by "local groups on their own initiative."[1]

Historians have long recognized the presence of the Klan in Reconstruction Texas and provided broad generalizations about its purpose and organization, even though little attention has been paid to its actual history. The earliest scholar to comment on the Klan was Charles W. Ramsdell, whose 1910 study of Reconstruction in Texas portrayed it as a unplanned insurgency with no real structure, a conclusion not unlike that of Foner. He differed as to its purpose, however, characterizing it as a response to a legitimate threat to society posed by the actions of freedmen. Klan activity, he believed, focused especially on areas where the "Loyal Union League had produced restlessness among blacks." Ramsdell provided little evidence as a basis for his conclusions, relying on the generalizations provided by contemporary Democratic newspapers and one of the state's only admitted Klansmen, W. D. Wood. In an article published in 1906, Wood had justified the Klan as a reaction to blacks who had become impudent and were prowling on the property of their neighbors. Whites had determined "for the safety of their families" to do something to "regulate the Negroes and curb their insolence."[2]

Revisionist historians have disagreed with Ramsdell on certain points concerning the Texas Klan, although, like his, most of their works have never focused particularly on the movement's history. Alan Trelease's 1971 study of the movement across the South offers a chapter on Texas that is the only scholarly effort aimed specifically at telling the story of the state Klan, but it is based primarily on a detailed look at its activity in Jefferson, Texas, that assumes the story of that group was representative of Klan activity elsewhere. Others have touched on the Klan only tangentially in broader studies of postwar violence that have tried to explain the general upheaval without exploring the story of the Klan itself. In these works, Ramsdell's explanation for the purpose of the Klan has been the principal issue of dispute, with Revisionists attributing it, as does Foner, to a reactionary fury aimed at reversing the revolutionary changes produced by the war and emancipation. On the other hand, they have found themselves in agreement with Ramsdell that the Texas Klan was local in character and lacked central direction. Trelease's explanation is representative of the literature when he described the Jefferson Klan as "a local one, with no apparent relationship outside the area," and generalized that it probably was "typical" of others in the state. "Later mythmakers," he observed, "ascribed a greater organization to the Klan than it ever possessed."[3]

The following essay explores the validity of our views concerning the Ku Klux Klan in Texas by taking a direct look at its post-Civil War history, examining its sources and character. Any understanding of the Klan necessarily begins with uncovering the basic chronology of its story and also recognition that violence against freedmen and the advocates of Reconstruction significantly pre-dated its appearance in Texas. As an organization, the Ku Klux Klan probably originated as early as the spring of 1866, born in Pulaski, Tennessee. By May 1867 the Klan had spread outside of Tennessee and had achieved wider notoriety in the national press. Through these years, however, no Klan dens appeared in Texas despite the fact that military officers in the state found few whites willing to accept black freedom and most whites more than ready to use whatever means possible to keep them subservient. Official reports provided lengthy catalogues of attacks against the freedmen as whites used violence to accomplish everything from depriving them of the fruits of their labor to punishing them for perceived insults. These reports indicated that in parts of the state blacks remained virtually enslaved. Whites had no apparent need for a secret organization to keep blacks in their place.[4]

The absence of a Ku Klux Klan ended in the spring of 1868. Up to this point local newspapers had never mentioned the Klan, even as it gained wider national attention. That spring, however, articles on the Klan suddenly began to appear. Since whites had believed blacks had acted irresponsibly and impudently since freedom and successfully maintained control through violence and other means, what had happened that necessitated a Klan? Answering that question requires a look at state politics. In the spring of 1867 Congress had overturned Presidential Reconstruction, forcing former Confederate states to begin anew the restoration process by holding constitutional conventions, whose delegates were to be chosen by an electorate expanded through the extension of the franchise to the freedmen. In Texas the old Democratic leadership still believed, even in the face of Congressional intervention, that it was possible for them to control government and even avoid permanent black enfranchisement. At Houston on January 20, 1868, those men, styling themselves the "Conservative party," met and advocated organizing like-minded men to carry the election of delegates. Their hopes of reversing the course of Reconstruction were dashed, however, when voters favored a convention and elected a solid Republican majority to go to Austin. In assessing their failure, the Democrats recognized that whites had not responded to their call for a unified turnout, while their Republican opponents successfully organized blacks into Union Leagues and got them to the polls. The old leadership was stunned.[5]

The contest for power, however, was not finished. The Democratic leadership still believed they could avoid permanent black suffrage, relying now on hope that the Constitutional Convention would move quickly to write a new constitution and submit the document to voters during the summer. Approval of a constitution would allow Texas to be restored to the Union, and Texans could then vote in the presidential election to be held that autumn. Texas Democrats would help ensure a national

Democratic victory, a victory that they believed would lead to an abandonment of Congressional Reconstruction and an end of pressure on the South for change. Even if not readmitted by the time of the election, they believed military officials might allow them to vote in the presidential election to achieve their ends.

A strategy for an election victory had begun to take shape prior to the January Conservative conference in Houston. Failure in the election of delegates made it even more imperative, however, to act. Whites had to be mobilized and the black vote counteracted. Democratic political rhetoric became almost hysterical, with leaders warning voters that the white population of the state faced a crisis of catastrophic proportions under Congressional Reconstruction. Unless prevented, blacks would come to dominate Texas society. Whites faced not only subordination but possible annihilation. In calling for the Houston gathering John H. Reagan, former postmaster general of the Confederacy, had declared it had been called to save the "State from Negro supremacy." The delegates in Houston heated up rhetoric even more when they called on whites to act together to prevent black suffrage from being incorporated into state law and stave off the "anarchy and ruin" that would result from "Africanization and war of races" that would be caused by "negro supremacy." As a race whites had to come together and do whatever was necessary to prevent this evil.[6]

To prevent this catastrophe, the Houston delegates urged formation of local Conservative and Democratic clubs. As these developed, they emphasized the Houston theme of race crisis. The local clubs openly declared their intention of keeping government in the hands of whites. Typical of club rhetoric was that of one of the first to be created, in La-Grange, where in March fifteen local politicians called for the creation of a "white man's Democratic Club," warning that black suffrage was just the beginning of a revolution that would lead to the disfranchisement of whites and ultimately black social equality, with racially mixed schools and even miscegenation. At Palestine organizers asked for support from all men who "opposed negro supremacy," while the Democratic club in Freestone County announced its goals as preventing efforts to "Africanize the Southern States, and to destroy civilization in them at the great risk of involving them in a war of races and its consequent horrors and anarchy." Democrats at Greenville echoed the inflammatory rhetoric, calling for unity among those opposing the "illegal Africanization of the State." The language of fear used that spring and summer differed little from the dire warnings issued during the developing sectional crisis in 1860 and 1861, with Democrats demanding racial unity in the face of the social calamity sure to take place if their opponents were not blocked in their purposes.[7]

Democratic newspapers pushed hard the idea that the black threat was not just imagined but real. That enfranchisement had emboldened blacks to a new assertiveness was a recurring theme lifted from the party's national newspapers and supplemented with local reports from across Texas. The editor of the *Galveston News* began running articles that warned of potential black uprisings, including one that charged that freedmen around Holly Springs, Mississippi, were arming themselves and "on every side they are to be seen carrying weapons and talking glibly about using them." The *Houston Telegraph* reported similar events in the vicinity of that city, including an incident in which blacks had proposed to march down Houston's main street, seize arms, "attack the whites," and burn the city. From Harrisburg a correspondent reported that blacks had become "insolent and threatening" and assumed a "hostile demeanor." All this the editor attributed to the white men "who have been the political associates and teachers of the negroes." That political motives for publishing such material may be presumed from that fact that when Bureau agents investigated charges that blacks were arming and intending to wage a war against whites they found most to be baseless rumors.[8]

Even though warning of a race war, Democratic leaders usually committed themselves in public to using only non-violent measures to prevent the threatened catastrophe. Some, however, did not hesitate to advocate white violence for protection. Colonel C. C. Gillespie, one of the men responsible for the Houston convention and the editor of the Democratic *Houston Telegraph*, typified those leaders who believed the time for peaceful political dialogue had passed. In a much publicized speech at the San Jacinto celebration on April 21 Gillespie condemned Texans who supported the revolutionary policies of Congress, saying, "There are grape vines enough on the old battle ground of San Jacinto to hang every one of them, and if I had my way I would have ever damned one of them hung as high as Haman before sundown." The threat of violence was palpable in an editorial in the *Telegraph* that June which warned in any confrontation the "vengance [*sic*] of a ruined, oppressed and enraged people will fall upon them [the white political counselors of blacks] and that without limit or mercy."[9]

Into this volatile situation the state's Democratic newspapers introduced the idea of a Ku Klux Klan, copying news of the Klan elsewhere and suggesting the need to develop a similar organization in Texas. On April 8 the *Galveston News*, in one of its first mentions of the Ku Klux

Klan, published in full an editorial from Virginia's *Richmond Enquirer* that described the Klan movement, declared it to be the "natural result of the condition of things in the South," and vindicated its existence. The editor of the Richmond paper asserted, "The first duty of a people whose liberty and property are menaced as ours are by abandoned apostates, greedy squatters, and insolent negroes, is to organize with such promptitude and stern resolution as to strike terror into the guilty souls of the negroes societies and their delegates to the 'convention,' and the next will be a lesson to these criminals who will teach them that the men who for nearly four years defied the armies of a powerful government will not submit to political outlawry and negro and squatter domination." The *News* subsequently reported that the Klan was spreading across the southern States, attributing its growth to the fact that the southern people were "becoming restive under the military despotism under which they suffer." In the days that followed, the *News* also featured items from the *New York Herald*, the preeminent national newspaper of the Democratic Party, including articles that justified the Klan as a proper response to Republican efforts to "keep in subject the democratic party of the North and Africanize the South." By the end of April the existence of the Klan, its activities, and its practices received prominent newspaper coverage.[10]

Information on the Klan was followed with editorials and the publication of letters to the editor that suggested that it was time for such an organization to appear in the state. One such letter, written from Hempstead in May, declared that the rise of the Klan in Texas should not be unexpected. Alleging corruption by a federal official in that town, the writer asserted that "if the interests and the respectability of our community are to be trampled underfoot by official corruption, perfidy and tyranny, I can see just and reasonable grounds for the organization of *Ku Klux Klans*." Organization was not just reasonable; he went on to call for such a movement. "It is high time," he wrote, "to invoke the *masse* of those brave, chivalrous spirits who laid down their lives as holy offerings on the altar of freedom." The editor of the *Dallas Herald* agreed. While dismissing claims of a Ku Klux organization in northern Texas, he believed that with the South "ground under the iron heel of oppression, . . . 'oppression might beget its *legitimate offspring*.'" A May number of the *Houston Telegraph* published a poem offering a similar invocation:

Come, rally, Brethren, rally!
Come rally one and all:
Democracy's our motto.

By it we'll stand or fall.
So rally, Brethren, rally
And may each Southern man
Who loves his home and country
Join the Ku Klux Klan.

The message, although cautiously avoiding an open call for violence, was clear. A Texas Klan was an appropriate response to the political situation.[11]

Newspapers such as the *News* went from advocating the birth of the Klan to providing interested parties information about the organization. Articles described Klan costumes and terminology. In mid-May the *Galveston News* announced that a local book seller had received Edward H. Dixon's *The Terrible Mysteries of the Ku Klux Klan*. A novel written by the well-known New York medical specialist in sexual problems and Democratic activist under the pseudonym M. D. Scalpel, the book provided graphic information on how the Klan operated and an impressive ritual for those in need of one. "Kurious customers," the paper concluded, "should kall if they want a kopy."[12]

Given the signals sent by Democratic politicians and editors, the subsequent emergence of the Ku Klux in Texas can hardly be called spontaneous. Newspaper editors had begun their attacks upon the freedmen in March and introduced news of the national Klan into their editions in early April. By the end of April they began to report Klan organization around the state. Among the first to receive public attention was one at Navasota in Grimes County, part of the state's important cotton-growing area along the Brazos River. On April 13 the editor of the *Navasota Ranger* published a card that encouraged men to participate in the creation of a local Klan. "This is no humbug," it read, "We know our friends. We know our enemies. We are a white man's society. We will be the saviors of our bleeding and oppressed country." The *Dallas Herald* signaled the Klan's emergence in that area when it reprinted an item, allegedly a command from the local "Great Grand Cyclops," that had appeared in a Republican journal published in nearby McKinney. The Cyclops had called upon the "Shrouded Brothers Dallas Division No. 21" to act, charging that they "on the 11th of this mortal's month, go forth to the harvest of death. Come from the shadow of the Grave and dye your hands red with the blood of your victims. Strike and spare not." In following weeks reports placed Klan dens at Greenville in Hunt County, where Democrats had effected a party club earlier in April, in the Red River country at Clarksville, through eastern Texas at Jefferson in Marion County, Paris, and Tyler, and Columbus in Colorado County.[13]

As the Klan appeared to spread, at least two newspapers that used the Klan's name started publishing. The political connection, once again, was apparent. Both were Democratic newspapers published by party advocates. The first appeared in late May at Jefferson. Upon receiving the first edition of the *Ultra Ku Klux* the editor of the *Galveston News* welcomed and confirmed its political connection, describing it as a "large and well-filled Conservative paper." At Houston C. C. Gillespie left the Democratic *Telegraph* and started publishing the *Ku Klux Vedette*. The first issue proclaimed that it did not propose to "advocate rapine and violence," but it would be an "organ of truth." Gillespie's stated intention was to throw light on the corruption of the men who had become the South's principal radicals, to expose the leaders of the South's Republican Party. Neither newspaper provided a uniquely Klan view point on issues. They pushed Democratic causes. Neither newspaper proved long-lived. The reason for their existence would disappear by the end of the summer of 1868.[14]

Democratic newspapers generally did not report Klan violence, but by mid-May Bureau and military officials began to report widespread Klan activity. Initially such incidents seemed relatively non-violent, involving efforts at intimidating the freedmen by preying upon their alleged superstitions. At Clarksville a "party dressed in white" appeared at a party given at the freedmen's school, throwing rocks at the participants, and then dancing among the graves outside of the school singing "Ku Klux, Ku Klux." The local Bureau agent initially thought the organization consisted of nothing more than "wild boys who wished to frighten the freedmen." He later came to see its activities as much more sinister. In Leon County, Klansmen decided to intimidate two local black political leaders by scaring them. They intercepted them on the road while dressed in costumes that made them appear twelve or fourteen feet high, "with fiery eyes and red-hot teeth, some with their heads dangling on their breasts and some with hideous masks." Klansman W. D. Wood remembered the costumes had been modeled after those reported in the newspapers. In eastern Texas Klan activities were widespread. After touring the area, William Sinclair of the Freedmen's Bureau found that almost everywhere whites gathered at night, disguised themselves and their horses in sheets, and rode across the countryside. Sinclair did not doubt that their purpose was to intimidate blacks and especially black voters by scaring them. "Munchausen stories are told them of the prowess of this wonderful organization," he wrote, "and with the inclination ignorant people have to believe all things of a supernatural character nothing is now necessary over there but to say Ku Klux and almost anything might be accomplished."[15]

Klan activities often turned into much more than simple costumed efforts at intimidating the freedmen by suggesting that ghosts of dead Confederates prowled the countryside. In many cases the Klan openly threatened violence against individual freedmen, especially those believed to be Republican leaders. When a black speaker appeared at a Republican meeting at Victoria locals threatened him with lynching, shouted "nigger" at him as he walked the streets, and warned him that the town was "not a healthy place for my sort." At Paris a white Republican suffered a visit from the Klan when a group of some forty men rode into town "arrayed in the ghostly habiliments of their favorite secret society, the Ku Klux." Their object was the editor of the local Republican newspaper. Halting outside his home, they yelled "O Radical, show yourself!" "Come out here, Vindicator man!" "O little man, come out." They subsequently rode over, "screeching: 'Hunt your hole and pull your hole in after you,'' then headed for other parts of town demanding the whereabouts of blacks and the local Bureau agent, DeWitt C. Brown. In Washington County, blacks known to be members of the Union League received warnings to quit the organization. The warning to one, Luke Gentry, charged, "You were once known as a good slave who would do right, but you have become notorious—a regular he devil, doing all you can against white men and yourself in connection with the black hearted devilish loyal league." Warned that he would be watched, he was counseled to quit the league or leave the country. "Look sharp and act, or you will suffer," it concluded, "Very respectfully, C. M. D. C. Official: K. K. K."[16]

In some cases threats turned into actual violence. At Gilmer a group of men dressed in white disguises and calling themselves "dead men or Ku Klux" rode up to the home of a politically active freedman demanding that he come out. When he left his home they took him away, stripped him, blindfolded him, and then whipped him, telling him he was being punished because he was a member of the "Loyal league." After the whipping they issued an ultimatum giving him three days to leave Gilmer or be killed. Near Jefferson, two white men attacked Peter Hill, a blacksmith and prominent leader of black Republicans in that area, cutting off his beard. Hill managed to escape, secured his gun, and chased them off before more violence could be done. A white planter who had leased land to Hill observed that despite the fact that the blacksmith was "most gentlemanly" he had "rendered himself obnoxious by voting the radical ticket for delegates to the convention and influencing other negroes to do likewise." Reports indicated that across the state whites were whipping freedmen and taking their guns away, and when a Bureau agent arrived at Jefferson at the end of the summer he found that these efforts had been so successful that many blacks were "now pretty well defenceless [*sic*]."[17]

Murder ultimately became an inevitable part of the political terror of the Klan that summer. On June 7, alleged Klansmen surrounded the home of the black registrar for Hopkins County, Charles Grimes, and shot him down. Later, in the same county a deputy sheriff was gunned down. His wife attributed his murder to men who hated him because of his "being a southern man and so mean as to be a unionist loyal leaguer." At Jefferson the local Bureau agent reported that black voting rights there were a "farce," that many blacks had been killed "for daring to be Radicals." The black voting registrar at San Augustine was luckier, escaping assassination when assailants shot at him through a window. He understood the intended message, however, and abandoned his post. When asked to meet a visiting inspector from the Bureau, the registrar came with "trepidation, fearing that the fact of having been closeted with me would bring down upon him again the wrath of the white people." The registrar had been a preacher, but was compelled to give up his pulpit and even refrain from attending church after having been charged with "dabbling in politics."[18]

Klan activities in the summer of 1868 unquestionably were political in their aims. The goal was to drive blacks out of the Union League and the Republican party. The effort meshed well with a less secretive effort by the Democratic Party to enroll blacks in Democratic clubs. Democrats usually denied that the Klan really existed, but they commonly offered freedmen protection from this non-existent organization if they would join local Democratic groups. As early as May 16 the editor of the *Galveston News* had recommended that Democrats impose economic sanctions on those who opposed them politically and reward those who were with them. Those who voted for Democratic enemies "should be treated accordingly," the editor insisted. "They should be made to know that we will distinguish between our friends and our enemies and that we will systematically reward, encourage and patronage the former and withhold all patronage from the former." Afterwards, Democratic clubs tacitly admitted the violence directed at blacks in their efforts at creating the black clubs. Threatening blacks who did not join with unemployment, they also promised protection. A "Certificate of Membership" distributed by Marion County Democrats offered preference in employment and favors, but more critically "guaranteed protection," and a Democratic newspaper at Nacogdoches assured blacks that if they joined Democratic clubs they would have "such full and ample protection as they cannot get by relying on the Loyal League conspirators." Providing an explicit definition of the meaning of protection, the editor went on to assure potential members they would be insured "against the lawlessness of the midnight assassin and murderer."[19]

The use of the Klan as a political tool always presented risks for Democrats, and party newspapers, while reporting on the Klan's existence, underplayed the whippings and murder. They well understood that news of widespread violence could work to their disadvantage in the national political arena and strengthen their enemies. If conditions became too bad they understood that it could even lead to military intervention by the federal troops stationed within the state. They had chosen to encourage it, however, and the potential for a political disaster always loomed over them. That it might precipitate intervention appeared a distinct possibility as Klan activity produced a major racial confrontation in the plantation counties along the lower Brazos and Colorado river valleys that summer.[20]

Austin, Burleson, Brazos, Fort Bend, Grimes, and Washington counties along the Brazos and Colorado and Wharton counties on the Colorado were the heart of the state's cotton economy and the place where Klan activities possibly best reflected the group's purposes and the dangers of its tactics. These counties contained much of the black population. Located close to Houston, they had seen a military presence earlier than other parts of the state. They also had been the location of the earliest Republican efforts in 1867 at organizing Union Leagues to mobilize black voters and these voters had given Republicans decisive victories in the January 1868, convention election. In the wake of that election Bureau officials assigned to these counties found racial tension on the increase. From Brazos County agent Captain N. H. Randlett reported "a general feeling of hostility is expressed towards the freed people especially those who took an active part in the late election." The agent in nearby Harris County agreed, concluding that relations between whites and the freedmen was "imbittered [*sic*] by political complications and the influence upon the blacks of political organizations and the dread thereof on the part of whites." At Brenham, F. P. Wood reported that the Leagues in Washington County had produced "much bitterness towards the Freed people."[21]

Such communities were inevitable Klan targets and by April Freedmen's Bureau agents reported that the Klan had appeared in many of them. In April the Klan arrived in Colorado County, although the agent dismissed its impact, indicating that while a Klan had organized it had not as yet "frightened nor hurt anyone." He later would change his views. Costumed Klansmen also made their appearance at Millican in Brazos County, showing up at a church during a Union League meeting, declaring that they would break up the League, and ultimately firing into the building. Whites also disrupted a meeting of freedmen at Brenham. Wild rumors spread among blacks. One freedman later testified that he had been told that the "whites purpose [was] to murder all the male adult freedmen and put the women & children back in bondage." Others heard that blacks were being beaten and lynched to keep them from joining the Union League. T. P. Wood, agent at Brenham, worried that a major confrontation was possible, concluding that the Klan there consisted of "*bitter rebels*" who were trying to "frighten the Freedmen from league Meetings" and even hoping to "bring on a war of races." The terror was felt also at Wharton, where the local agent indicated the freedmen remained in a "constant state of alarm and excitement," as whites threatened them because "they will not vote for the Democratic party. They hate the freedman for his constant loyalty." A letter from Millican, signed by the town mayor and others, attributed the attack upon the League meeting near that town to a "party of boys . . . who had read of the Ku Klux, concluded that they would have some fun; dressed themselves for the occasion" and did not fire upon the church but were fired upon by the blacks who were being drilled in the manual of arms by a white.[22]

The political terror in the river counties that summer included murders attributed to the Klan that increased fear among blacks. The particularly brutal murder of A. R. Wilson, the black registrar in Burleson County, received widespread publicity. Wilson was taken from his home in mid-June, killed, and his body dumped into the Brazos River. When officials recovered his body they found it mutilated, stabbed repeatedly, and possibly scalped. His assailants were never identified, but local freedmen believed that they were, in the words of the local Bureau agent, part of "an organization known as the Ku Klux." In keeping with their practice of denying Klan terror Democratic newspapers charged that Wilson actually had been murdered by members of the Union League. The *Austin Republican* saw this accusation as disingenuous, since Wilson had been active member of the League and voted the Republican ticket. The *Republican's* editor believed the registrar had been assassinated only because of his "loyalty, intelligence and influence." Later that June another freedman, Clinton Fort, was murdered. Again, no one could identify his killers, but word spread among the freedmen that the deed had been carried out by men hostile to Fort's membership in the Union League.[23]

The attacks on politically active freedmen in the river counties produced what one Bureau agent described as "intense excitement" in the area, but it did not overawe blacks as the perpetrators hoped. Blacks armed themselves to resist the Klan incursion, rather than be intimidated. Many freedmen began taking weapons with them to the fields. At Millican George Brooks, a black Methodist minister and the voter registrar, began organizing men in the freedmen's village into military companies and drilling them in order that they could protect themselves. Whites believed the freedmen also were forming military companies around Hempstead after one white citizen encountered a large group of freedmen outside the town. They were mounted and riding in military order, singing "Rally arround [*sic*] the Flag boys." Townspeople also heard that freedmen were drilling on the nearby Rock Island plantation and a witness reported he had seen at least four hundred freedmen in that vicinity, armed and carrying out drills "with surprising facility." A freedman had told the man that "if a fus should start the determination was to exterminate the 'reb's' from the cradle up and if the Rebs thought the Yanks were hard on them they intended to be ten times with them, they would not leave them a spot to sleep."[24]

Even though the Klan had appeared prior to black efforts at self protection, Democratic editors denied that the freedmen had any reason to arm themselves. In fact they now used what clearly was growing black militancy as proof that all the charges they had made about a potential uprising among the freedmen were true. The conditions, according to them, provided an immediate need for whites to organize into groups like the Klan to defend themselves. The editor of the *Texas Ranger* at Navasota insisted that the Ku Klux Klan in the community had been organized all along to provide a response to the long-threatened uprising and that whites in the Klan were taking "prudent steps to prevent mischief."[25]

Ironically, white attacks had produced a real threat from the black community and while white leaders used the situation to encourage the Klan, they ultimately did not see the organization as their sole salvation. In a remarkable change of direction, local leaders who had long criticized the presence of the Freedmen's Bureau and federal troops found themselves appealing to their antagonists for protection. Officials from Brazoria County called for Bureau assistance in resisting what they believed was a force of a thousand freedmen that threatened a "wholesale slaughter of the whites." At Columbia officials also wanted troops to fight against an anticipated "uprising of the freedmen." No aid was sent immediately and Bureau agents who went into the river counties did find blacks armed and organizing, but only to defend themselves. The agents could find nothing to justify white fears. Given the circumstances, however, they worried that some sort of conflict was inevitable. Their concerns proved true.[26]

The feared explosion nearly took place at Hempstead on June 26. The murder of the Union League member Clinton Fort had produced considerable tension there and authorities finally arrested a white man for the deed. The officials, however, immediately released him on bail. The release outraged local blacks and convinced them that they could not count on public officials to protect them. Subsequent events indicated they even may have concluded that county officers were part of the Ku Klux. A clash between blacks and whites finally occurred when a deputy sheriff arrested two freedmen on the Rock Island plantation. Rather than taking them back to Hempstead, he placed them in irons and rode for his home. He later said that he did not take them to town because of the inadequacy of the jail there, but his actions created concern among the plantation's freedmen who were convinced that the arrests had been made without cause and that the victims "had been Ku Kluxed." A party of freedmen armed themselves and rode to catch up with the deputy. Confronting him, they forced the release of his charges and took them back to the plantation.[27]

Officials in Hempstead were convinced that the incident marked the beginning of a black attack upon the town and immediately called on the Bureau and military to send troops for protection. On June 27, T. P. Wood from the Freedmen's Bureau arrived and immediately sent couriers into the countryside to demand the prisoners be returned to authorities. Tension increased when one of the couriers rode back immediately, reporting that he had encountered a large party of armed blacks on their way to Hempstead. In fact, the men were coming to the regular meeting of the Union League and they left their weapons outside of town before entering. That evening Wood addressed them, promising to hear their grievances, and insisting they return the prisoners. They later surrendered the men taken from the deputy, but at least one freedmen present that evening believed that if Wood had not intervened there would "have been blood shed."[28]

The following morning large crowds of whites and blacks met at the Hempstead town hall where Wood urged both sides to back down and insisted that they obey the laws forbidding unlawful assemblies, carrying arms in town, and discharging weapons in any city or town. In addition, he informed them that an order had been issued forbidding military drilling. Something of a stalemate had been reached, but both parties remained wary. One believed that blacks would "remain quiet and lay aside their arms," but only "if the white people will do the same thing." After the meeting town officials remained fearful of a collision and still insisted that Wood send for soldiers. Recognizing that "excitement had become intense and on both sides serious fears of an outbreak [were] entertained," Wood brought a squad of soldiers in from Brenham. Rumors of a black uprising continued to circulate, fueled by the gathering of a large crowd attending a funeral outside the town, but by the afternoon Wood's intervention appeared to have calmed the situation. Wood having prevented the much-feared conflict boarded the train to return to his headquarters at Brenham.[29]

When Wood got off the train at Brenham he found himself confronting another crisis. Blacks there had been outraged by an attack by whites on a freedman. The situation had worsened when another white was accused of trespassing on a black woman's property. After Wood's arrival he counseled all to remain calm, but on July 4 the situation worsened when two white men appeared at a gathering of freedmen and threatened to "break up the meeting, kill freedmen, &c. &c." The intruders fired their weapons. Blacks took out their own arms and fired back. Wood acted immediately to calm things down, but informed military headquarters that he believed whites and the Klan were doing all they could to frighten the freedmen away from League meetings and he feared that "an outbreak between the races." Wood moved quickly, meeting with representatives of the freedmen and assuring them that they would be protected. His intervention averted an expansion of open hostilities once again, but the potential for violence in the river plantation area was far from over.[30]

Given Klan attacks and the black response, avoiding a violent confrontation was not likely. Neither side appeared willing to back down. The almost inevitable encounter finally took place at Millican on July 15. As elsewhere in the region, tensions had steadily increased after the first appearance of the Klan. In June, Captain Randlett, the Bureau agent at Bryan, had come to Millican after local whites had complained of George Brooks's efforts at creating black military companies. Randlett met with Brooks and white leaders and thought he had secured an agreement that the blacks would stop drilling if the Klan would stop its incursions. The agent had ordered that "no *armed* band, organization or secret society not authorized by law" would operate in the county. Apparently neither side abided by the agreement and both continued their activities.

On July 15, word spread that a white had killed a freedman and Brooks sent a party of armed men under one of his lieutenants, Harry Thomas, to look for the victim's body. As they searched, Thomas and his men encountered the man supposed responsible for the murder and chased him to his home. There they surrounded the house and threatened to take the suspect and hang him. When word the situation reached Millican the mayor and a deputy sheriff organized a party of armed whites and the group rode to the surrounded house. The mayor talked with Thomas and encouraged him to take his men and leave. Testimony concerning subsequent events was conflicting, but both sides were uneasy. Someone fired a gun. Both sides drew their weapons and engaged in a general exchange of gunfire. Thomas, the freedmen's leader, fell. Differing accounts placed the casualty rate among his men as between four and fifteen killed. No whites died, a fact that inevitably raises unanswerable questions about the nature of the confrontation.[31] Randlett initially believed that whites had initiated the gunfire, but later concluded that a freedman had fired the first shot.

The whites involved in the incident returned to Millican, and the mayor and deputy sheriff immediately rode to the nearby freedmen's village where they talked with Reverend Brooks. They asked Brooks to disarm his men, but he replied that his men had been killed, that his men would not lay down their weapons, nor would they agree to any peace terms. He did promise to meet with them again the next morning. The officials feared that Brooks actually intended to attack Millican and on their return they telegraphed county officials at Bryan for help. That evening a train arrived bringing the sheriff, a posse of one hundred and fifty men, and Captain Randlett. The sheriff's men placed sentinels around the town that evening to prevent anyone from entering. Through the night the guards shot several blacks who approached.[32]

On the morning of July 16 Randlett accompanied local officials when they returned to the freedmen's village for the planned meeting. They found the village virtually abandoned and Brooks gone. Brooks's disappearance encouraged rumors that the preacher had gathered thousands of men in the vicinity and was prepared to attack and burn Millican to the ground. Through the day more armed whites arrived by train. These rode out of the town looking for Brooks and intending to disarm the freedmen. Randlett, now concerned that if these parties encountered large numbers of blacks a real uprising might take place, sent word to the nearest telegraph station with a request for troops to be sent to Millican from Brenham. Randlett remained in town and at the end of the afternoon optimistically reported, "no freedmen were found with arms and much less damage was done than I had anticipated." That evening United States troops arrived.[33]

Randlett's hopeful assessment of the situation was premature. The soldiers kept the peace in Millican, remaining in the town and protecting it. Randlett also remained in town and with the sheriff sent representatives into the countryside to find Brooks. Randlett wanted him to know that if he surrendered the Bureau would protect him and ensure that he received a fair trial. Brooks did not reply. As the agent sought peace, whites continued to ride through the countryside, as later information indicated, unrestrained in carrying out attacks upon the freedmen. Exactly what happened is unclear, but the men seeking Brooks appear to have found plenty of blacks to kill. Randlett later could verify the deaths of only five men, but many more simply disappeared. Republican newspapers would speculate that as many as fifty or sixty freedmen had been killed in the countryside around Millican. On June 18 Randlett found out why he had received no answer to his messages to Brooks: parties found the preacher's body. He had been lynched. The much-feared confrontation between the races had taken place, with whites protected by the United States Army and blacks massacred.[34]

The violence at Millican for all practical purposes brought an end to the Ku Klux Klan as a statewide movement. The Klan had not produced good political results. Federal troops had been dispatched into local communities, although ironically to protect whites and not the black victims of Klan violence. Further, Klan activity convinced Texas Republican leaders at Austin that a safe election could not be held. Republicans in the constitutional convention that assembled in June drafted a report detailing the extent to which violence prevailed in the state and finally sent a delegation to Washington to lobby against an election. The delegates also took their own steps to ensure Texans would not vote that fall when they adjourned the convention and set a date for it to reconvene after the national election. Texas Republicans wanted no part of that fall's presidential vote.[35]

Democrats retained some hope and continued to prepare for a possible election. Democrats kept up their organizational efforts through the late summer, but party newspapers stopped mentioning the Klan and instead increased their coverage of efforts at placing economic pressure on blacks to join Democratic clubs. The Klan may have been seen as producing more trouble than good by this time. Their optimistic view that they could participate in an election remained intact until it was dashed in late September. On September 28 the chairman of the Democratic Central Executive Committee urged Gen. Joseph J. Reynolds, commander of the Fifth Military District, to call an election for presidential electors, arguing that the Reconstruction Act of March 2, 1867, gave him the authority to hold such an election. Three days later, however, Reynolds brought an end to the Democratic campaign. The general replied that he stood by his earlier Special Order No. 44 prohibiting an election. Citing a Joint Resolution passed by Congress on July 20, 1868, Reynolds noted that the votes of unorganized states would not be counted in the electoral college. He believed the resolution implicitly forbade the holding of a presidential election in Texas and he would not allow one to be held. For all of its efforts the Klan had done little but heat up tension between whites and blacks that summer.[36]

After 1868 the Texas Democratic Party evidenced no further need to use the Ku Klux Klan as a political tool. That did not mean that elections were free of violence, however, and the Republican opposition often charged that the Klan was responsible. In April 1870, for example, the county clerk in Freestone County informed Republican governor Edmund J. Davis that the Ku Klux Klan was present and murdering politically active blacks. That same year, with a special election in process, a group of fifty horsemen dressed as Klansmen rode into Bastrop. Governor Davis also believed that a Klan operated in Tarrant County at about the same time. While such incidents may have been Klan-like, investigations by the State Police and federal authorities could never prove a broad conspiracy and no prosecutions resulted from their efforts. Local politicians may have resurrected Klan tactics at times, but the state's Democratic leaders apparently found no use for the secret organization.[37]

This examination focusing solely on the Klan suggests that the movement in Texas has been misunderstood by past scholars. Clearly there was no structured organization to the Klan in the state, but that does not mean that it was a spontaneous uprising against the course of Reconstruction nor that it was local in character. Rather it appears largely to have been the creature of the state's Democratic Party. Party leaders and the party press paved the way for its existence in 1868. They created the reasons it should exist, promoted and encouraged its formation, and established its basic identity. The Klan, in the end, was used to effect the party's principal political goal: restoration of the Democrats to power at both the state and national level in what was perceived a critical election year.

As to its accomplishments, the Klan of 1868 contributed to the legacy of violence that helped to define the history of Reconstruction in Texas. It existed, however, only for a short time and achieved none of the political goals that its creators sought; in fact its existence helped ensure Texans would not get to vote in the presidential elections. Its suppression of black voters lasted, if at all, for only a short time, as the 1869 state election saw blacks turn out in large numbers. It did not end Reconstruction, which would continue in Texas for four more years. Its celebration would take place only decades later when, possibly to justify a renewed attack upon the democratic political process in the South, new Democrat leaders created a mythical Reconstruction, when brave whites had taken violent but necessary measures to keep blacks from destroying southern society. That was the story told by W. D. Wood when he celebrated the Texas Klan as "aiding her people to rid themselves from Negro rule and domination." Insisting that the Klan deserved a prominent place in history, he believed that it made possible the "miraculous deliverance of the Confederate people from the dangers and troubles that threatened to destroy them." Indeed, the Klan deserves a place in history, but more properly as an example of how a political elite such as the leaders of the state's Democratic Party preyed upon the fears of whites and blacks and replaced the political process with violence and intimidation in their efforts at regaining power.

ENDNOTES

1. Eric Foner, *Reconstruction: America's Unfinished Revolution, 1863–1877* (New York: Harper & Row, 1988), 425.

2. W. D. Wood, "The Ku Klux Klan," *Quarterly of the Texas Historical Association* 9 (April, 1906): 266; Charles W. Ramsdell, *Reconstruction in Texas* (New York: Columbia University Press, 1910), 232–33, 232 (second quotation); see also W. C. Nunn, *Texas Under the Carpetbaggers* (Austin: University of Texas Press, 1962), 247–53.

3. Allen Trelease, *White Terror: The Ku Klux Klan Conspiracy and Southern Reconstruction* (New York: Harper & Row, 1971; repr. Baton Rouge: Lousiana State University Press, 1999), 108–9 (quotes); James M. Smallwood, *Time of Hope, Time of Despair: Black Texans during Reconstruction* (Port Washington, NY: Kennikat Press, 1981), 132; William

L. Richter, *The Army in Texas during Reconstruction, 1865–1870* (College Station: Texas A&M University Press, 1987), 143–45.

4. Trelease, *White Terror*, 3–27.

5. David G. Burnet to Editor, April 5, 1867, in *Galveston Daily News*, April 5, 1867, James W. Throckmorton to Ashbel Smith, April 5, 1867, in ibid., April 13, 1867; ibid., April 25, 1867; Registrar's statement in Baum, *Shattering of Texas Unionism*, 172.

6. *Flake's Daily Bulletin*, January 23, 1868 (Reagan quote); "Address to the People of Texas," January 23, 1868, in *Galveston Daily News*, January 24, 1868.

7. *Galveston Daily News*, March 15 (first quotation), 18, 21, (third quotation), April 7 (second quotation), 14, 15, June 18, 26, July 2, 1868; *Greenville Independent* in *Galveston Daily News*, April 6, 1868 (fourth quotation).

8. *Galveston Daily News*, May 6, 1868 (first quotation); *Houston Weekly Telegraph*, June 18, (second and third quotations), June 25.

9. *Galveston Daily News*, April 25 (first quotation), 1868; *Houston Weekly Telegraph*, June 18, 1861 (second quotation); *Flake's Daily Bulletin*, April 23, 1868.

10. *Richmond Enquirer*, in *Galveston Daily News*, April 8 (first quote), 15 (second quote), 1868; Washington Correspondent, in *Galveston Daiy News*, April 12, 1868; *New York Herald*, in *Galveston Daily News*, April 26, 1868.

11. S. T. S. to *News*, May 6, 1868, in *Galveston Daily News*, May 6, 1868 (first quotation); *Weekly Dallas Herald*, May 23, 1868 (second quotation); *Houston Weekly Telegraph*, May 21, 1868 (third quotation).

12. *Galveston Daily News*, May 14, 1868.

13. Navasota *Ranger*, in *Galveston Daily News*, April 22, 1868 (first quotation); *Dallas Weekly Herald*, May 9, 1868 (second quotation); Gregory Barrett, Jr. to George A. Vernou, June 6, 1868, "Letters Received," Records of the Assistant Commissioner, Bureau of Refugees, Freedmen, and Abandoned Lands, Record Group 105, National Archives, Microfilm Series 821, Roll 10, hereafter referred to as RAC, BRFAL, RG, NA, M; James Curtis to J. J. Reynolds, Sept. 19, 1868, "Letters Received," ibid; Charles F. Rand to J. P. Richardson, May 10, 1868, "Letters Received," ibid.; Roll 14; Report of DeWitt C. Brown, April 30, 1868, Reports of Operations and Conditions, ibid., Roll 25; Report of Louis W. Stevenson, April 30, 1868, Reports of Operations and Conditions, ibid., Roll 25.

14. *Galveston Daily News*, May 6 (first quote), 27, 28 (second quote), 1868

15. Charles F. Rand to J. P. Richardson, May 10, 1868 (first quotation), "Letters Received," RAC, BRFAL, RG105, NA, M821, Roll 14; Gregory Barrett, Jr. to George A. Vernou, June 6, 1868, "Letters Received," ibid., Roll 10; W. D. Wood, "The Ku Klux Klan," *Southwestern Historical Quarterly* 9 (April 1906): 267 (second quotation); William Sinclair to C. S. Roberts, August 18, 1868 (third quotation), "Letters Received," RAC, BRFAL, RG105, NA, M821, Roll 15.

16. George Jackson to Editor *Guard*, July 11, 1868 (first quotation), in *Daily Austin Republican*, July 25, 1868; *Paris Vindicator*, in *Daily Austin Republican*, September 21, 1868 (second quotation); *Daily Austin Republican*, September 21, 1868 (third quotation).

17. Affidavit of Gabriel Floy, June 27, 1868, in T. M. K. Smith to Charles A. Vernou, June 28, 1868 (first quotation), "Letters Received," RAC, BRFAL, RG 105, NA, M821, Reel 15; Ben F. Whitaker to J. J. Reynolds, Oct. 26, 1868 (second quotation), attached to H. Sweeney to C. S. Roberts, October 26, 1868, in "Letters Received," ibid.; James Curtis to J. J. Reynolds, Sept. 19, 1868 (third quotation), "Letters Received," ibid., Roll 10.

18. W. H. Howard to Charles Vernou, Aug. 6, 1868 (first quotation), "Letters Received," RAC, BRFAL, RG105, NA, M821, Roll 12; James Curtis to J. J. Reynolds, Sept. 19, 1868 (second quotation), "Letters Received," ibid., Roll 10; William Sinclair to C. S. Roberts, August 18, 1868 (third quotation), "Letters Received," ibid., Roll 15.

19. *Galveston Daily News*, May 16, 1868 (first quotation); Report for the Month Ending June 30, 1868, T. M. K. Smith, RAC, BRFAL, RG90, NA, M821, Roll 26; H. C. Pedigo to E. M. Pease, September 11, 1868, Elisha M. Pease Gubernatorial Papers, Texas State Library and Archives; "Certificate of Membership," in *Daily Austin Republican*, July 7, 1868 (second quotation); *Nacogdoches Register*, July 14, 1868, in *Daily Austin Republican*, July 30, 1868 (third quotation); *Galveston Daily News*, July 16, 1868; see also *Daily Austin Republican*, August 26, 1868.

20. For evidence of Democratic awareness of the potential backlash that might be generated by the Klan see *Weekly Houston Telegraph*, June 4, 1868; *Weekly Dallas Herald*, May 9, 23, 1868.

21. "Report of N. H. Randlett, Bryan, for the month ending June 30, 1868," RAC, BRFAL, RG105, NA, M821, Reel 26; Report of M. E. Davis, July 31, 1868, ibid.; Report of Louis W. Stevenson, August 31, 1868, ibid.; Report of F. P. Wood, August 31, 1868, ibid.

22. Report of Louis W. Stevenson, Columbus, April 30, 1868 (first quotation), Reports of Operations and Conditions, RAC, BRFAL, RG

105, NA, M821, Reel 25; Affidavit of Bram Gorden, June 27, 1868 (second quotation), in "Letters Received," ibid., Reel 16; T. P. Wood to J. J. Reynolds, July 6, 1868 (third quotation), "Letters Received," ibid.; Report of Nesbit B. Jenkins, Wharton, July 31, 1868 (fourth quotation), "Reports of Operations and Conditions," ibid., Reel 26; also Report of N. H. Randlett, Bryan, May 31, 1868, "Reports of Operations and Conditions," ibid., Reel 25; Report of N. H. Randlett, Bryan, June 30, 1868, ibid., Report of A. B. Horner, Columbia, July 31, 1868, ibid.; Report of T. P. Wood, Brenham, June 30, 1868, ibid.; *Houston Weekly Telegraph*, August 6, 1868; . R. C. Meyers and others to Editor of the Telegraph, *Houston Weekly Telegraph*, August 6, 1868

23. Report of N. H. Randlett, June 30, 1868, (first quotation), "Reports of Operations and Conditions," RAC, BRFAL, RG90, NA, M821, Roll 26; *Austin Daily Republican*, June 30, 1868 (second quote); L. Shoemaker to E. M. Pease, June 23, 1868, "Misc. Reports Relating to Murder and Other Criminal Offences," RAC Texas, BRFAL, RG90, NA, M821, Roll 32; T. P. Wood to J. J. Reynolds, June 30, 1868, Affidavit of Bram Gorden, June 27, 1868, Affidavit of Eric Love, June 29, 1868, "Letters Received," ibid., Reel 16.

24. N. H. Randlett to Charles A. Vernou, July 22, 1868 (first quotation), "Letters Received," RAC, BRFAL, RG105, NA, M821, Roll 14; Affidavit of Reuben Loggins, June 27, 1868 (second quote), Affidavit of R. Mebus, June 27, 1868 (third and fourth quote), ibid.; T. P. Wood to J. J. Reynolds, June 30, 1868, Affidavit of Bram Gorden, June 27, 1868, Affidavit of Eric Love, June 29, 1868, Affidavit of T. W. Rodgers, June 27, 1868, ibid., Reel 16; Report of N. H. Randlett, Bryan, "Reports of Operations and Conditions," ibid., Reel 26; Letter of Mayor G. A. Wheat, July 17, 1868, Millican, in *Houston Weekly Telegraph*, July 23, 1868.

25. *Texas Ranger*, April 13, 1868, quoted in *Galveston Daily News*, April 19, 1868; see also *Galveston Daily News*, July 18, 1868.

26. George H. Cram to C. A. Vernou, June 13, 1868 (first quote), Galveston, "Letters Sent," Subordinate Field Offices, BRFAL, RG105, NA, M1912, Roll 19; A. B. Honer to C. A. Vernou, June 25, 1868 (second quote), Columbia, ibid.

27. T. P. Wood to J. J. Reynolds, June 30, 1868 (quotation), Affidavit of Bram Gorden, June 27, 1868, Affidavit of Eric Love, June 29, 1868, "Letters Received," RAC, BRFAL, RG105, NA, M821, Reel 16.

28. T. P. Wood to J. J. Reynolds, June 30, 1868, Affidavit of Eric Love, June 29, 1868 (quotation), "Letters Received," RAC, BRFAL, RG105, NA, M821, Reel 16.

29. Affidavit of Eric Love, June 29, 1868 (first quotation); T. P. Wood to J. J. Reynolds, June 30, 1868 (second quotation), Affidavit of Bram Gorden, June 27, 1868, "Letters Received," RAC, BRFAL, RG105, NA, M821, Reel 16; *Houston Weekly Telegraph*, July 2, 1868.

30. T. P. Wood to J. J. Reynolds, July 6, 1868, RAC, BRFAL, RG105, NA, M821, Reel 16.

31. N. H. Randlett to Charles A. Vernou, July 22, 1868 (quotation), July 23, 1868, "Letters Received," RAC, BRFAL, RG105, NA, M821, Roll 14; Report of N. H. Randlett, Bryan, July 31, 1868, ibid., Roll 26; *Houston Weekly Telegraph*, July 23, 1868.

32. N. H. Randlett to Charles A. Vernou, July 23, 1868, "Letters Received," RAC, BRFAL, RG105, NA, M821, Roll 14, *Galveston Daily News*, July 27, 1868.

33. Ibid.

34. Ibid.; *Daily Austin Republican*, July 28, 1868.

35. Carl H. Moneyhon, *Texas After the Civil War: The Struggle of Reconstruction* (College Station: Texas A&M University Press, 2004), 96–97.

36. W. M. Walton to J. J. Reynolds, September 28, 1868, in *Galveston Daily News*, October 23, 1868; J. J. Reynolds to George J. Durham and others, Oct. 1, 1868, in *Galveston Daily News*, October 23, 1868.

37. James King to E. J. Davis, Apr. 10, 1870, F. P. Wood to E. J. Davis, Dec. 6, 1870, E. J. Davis Governor's Papers, Texas State Library and Archives, hereafter TSLA; *Daily State Journal*, July 3, 1870; E. J. Davis to Thomas Williams, July 19, 1871, Davis to J. B. McFarland, July 31, 1871, Letters Press Book, E. J. Davis Governor's Papers, TSLA; *Daily State Journal*, June 6, July 8, 1871; E. J. Davis to U. S. Grant, Feb. 1, 1872, in John Y. Simon, ed., *The Papers of Ulysses S. Grant* (Carbondale: Southern Illinois University Press, 1998), 23: 169; E. J. Davis to George H. Williams, Feb. 13 (quote), 1872, Davis to Williams, Feb. 13, 1873, Letter Book, Records of the Governor, Edmund J. Davis, TSLA; E. J. Davis to W. T. Clark, Mar. 13, 1872, Appointments, Justice Department, RG 90, NA; A. J. Evans to George H. Williams, Apr. 10, 1873 (quote), David Boaz to U. S. Grant, Feb. 8, 1873, in Simon, *Papers of Ulysses S. Grant*, 24: 336 (quote), 335–36; *Galveston Daily News*, Mar. 9, 1873.

CHAPTER 9

"A Free and Outspoken Press": Coverage of Reconstruction Violence and Turmoil in Texas Newspapers, 1866–1868

by

Mary Jo O'Rear[1]

In early February of 1861 virtually every publisher in Texas printed the Declaration of Causes of Secession in his newspaper. Two items stood out within its last paragraph. One, that "the servitude of the African race is mutually beneficial to both bond and free," became a clarion call for many as the Confederacy moved into war. The other, that "the destruction of the existing relations between the two races . . . [will] bring inevitable calamities upon both," served as a warning for the future; Southern loss meant cultural chaos.[2] Secession's failure made the first concept moot and the second real. With no value as property and little as citizens in the eyes of many, Texas freedmen became human targets. Their persecution between April 1865 and November 1868 would not only create unparalleled records of abuse but also underscore the overt bias of the state press.

Periodicals had been influential in Texas beginning in 1813, but it was not until the founding of the *Telegraph and Texas Register* twenty-two years later that a sustained commercial newspaper system began in the state. Subject to the vicissitudes of poor roads, bad weather, incomplete supplies, and inadequate help, publishers printed news from every source available. If an issue of any kind were to be espoused, it would be the literate, opinionated, "often remarkable" pressmen of Texas who would do it.[3] But by 1865, they were few. A majority of editors closed their offices due to war.[4] Those newspapers that did survive roared into peace with a vengeance. Rarely objective in the best of times, most had supported secession and saw no reason to conceal their horror at its collapse. Despising the idea of federal Reconstruction in any form, even the mild program initiated by Abraham Lincoln and carried on by his successor, Andrew Johnson, they remained staunch supporters of the Democratic Party. Publisher David Richardson of the *Texas Almanac* characterized over 90 percent of the state's sixty-one secular newspapers as Conservative, a label easily interchanged with unrepentant rebel.[5] Such publications reflected the mood of most white citizenry in Texas, who generally supported Conservative Democrats in local and state political contests.

The opposition called themselves "Unionists" or "Loyalists," but most people termed them Radicals, a term laden with negative implications. They encompassed all those in favor of Reconstruction—Republicans, Unionists, carpetbaggers, scalawags, northern immigrants, and anyone else who supported federal authority.[6] Radicals were everywhere in Texas, but their numbers paled in comparison with that of their rivals. The overwhelming majority of secular newspaper editors were conservative in their opinions.

Chief among conservative editors was Willard Richardson, whose presses produced both *The Texas Almanac* and the *Galveston Daily News*. Before the war, Richardson was a strong advocate of slavery; afterwards, he continued to promote the advantages of bondage labor although admitting that "the South would not reestablish slavery . . . unless she could change or control the mind of the country on the subject." He regretted emancipation and felt it would not be long before the freedmen "will look back on their former condition with a favor which will make them feel kindly toward their masters."[7] Although a long-standing Galveston citizen, Richardson began his career as a newspaper editor with the Houston *Telegraph and Texas Register*. Even after Richardson left the Houston-based newspaper, subsequent editors maintained the former editor's conservative biases, especially in the post-Civil War years. In May 1867, the new editor, C. C. Gillespie, summed up his attitude toward Reconstruction, stating that "a more damnable notoriety of villainry never encompassed a people than that woven for the South by the leaders of the Radical Party."[8]

No less rabid in his contempt for the North was John Walker of the *Austin State Gazette*. It was his partner, John Marshall, who hounded Sam Houston out of the governorship in 1857, and it was Marshall and Walker who first called on the state to secede in 1860. The war saw Marshall's death at the Battle of Gaines' Mill, but Walker continued publishing, taking particular aim in 1867 at "the violent tirades and bloody revolutionary schemes of the Radicals."[9]

Less combative was the *Harrison Flag's* William Barrett. His father, John Barrett, began publishing in 1848 and by 1856 was circulating the *Flag*, headquartered in Marshall. An ardent opponent of secession, the elder Barrett considered Lincoln a moderate and saw in his election no reason to break up the Union. With John Barrett's death in 1862, the paper ceased publication.[10] Three years later, William Barrett revived the *Flag*. However, William was more favorable to the South than his father. Soon after the press became operational, William mourned the Lost Cause, "A people's hope . . . sanctified by tears!"[11] Although classified as a Conservative, the younger Barrett generally avoided the rancor characteristic of Richardson and Walker.

John Osterhout of the *Texas Countryman* (Bellville) was also more amenable. True to his motto of being "Independent in All Things—Neutral in None," Osterhout supported secession and the subsequent war that followed. Once the war was over, however, he was willing to make concessions to the federal government and hoped for a speedy reconstruction of the South.[12] In an early 1866 editorial, he stressed the reality of the Confederate defeat, stating that "events have shown that the triumph of the South, if it ever takes place, must be in the Union and not out of it." He then called upon his readers to "let the past pass away."[13] Though considered a Conservative during the early years of Reconstruction, Osterhout tried to make his paper an instrument of conciliation.

Publishing was far more confrontational for John D. Logan. In 1856, Logan moved to San Antonio and invested in the *San Antonio Herald*, partnering with James P. Newcomb. Their periodical became a staple in South Texas, reflecting Logan's own irascible style. By 1860, he had driven away the more liberal Newcomb over the issue of secession, hired a new editor, and sanctioned the secession movement.[14] The Union victory in the Civil War merely exacerbated Logan's ire. Initially following Osterhout's example, in January of 1866 he called on his readers to demonstrate a "spirit of forgiveness." However, less than six months later, Logan had completely changed positions, characterizing the war as a "bloody . . . relentless" ordeal primarily instigated by the North. Unlike Osterhout, Logan had no hope for the future of the South and dreaded the day that "Radicals get the upper hand, as they have in West Virginia."[15]

Hoping that Radicals would indeed "get the upper hand" was Logan's former colleague and leading Unionist publisher, James P. Newcomb. Determined to advance his position, he founded the pro-Union *Alamo Express* almost immediately after leaving Logan, only to have it destroyed a year later by angry Confederates.[16] At war's end, Newcomb joined with

August Siemering and Major W. Moore to establish the *San Antonio Express*, becoming "a bold, fearless supporter of the [federal] government, denouncing treason in every shape."[17] Unfazed by past attacks, Newcomb supported Unionists both black and white, and in 1868 became the agent for the *Weekly Freedman's Press*, the only paper published specifically for freedpeople at that time. In its first issue, he promised to support the "fight for freedom [which] has just begun" but warned that the power of "the enemies of equal rights" would not be easy to defeat.[18]

Like Newcomb in his allegiance to the Union but different in that he owned slaves, Ferdinand Flake was controversial even among Radical newsmen. Immigrating to Texas in the 1840s, he earned enough money to purchase Galveston's *Die Union* in 1855. His opposition to secession was so strong that a mob destroyed his press in 1860; undaunted, he initiated an English-language counterpart, *Flake's Daily Bulletin*, the next year.[19] By 1867 he was distributing both papers to an ever-increasing readership despite criticism from colleagues for not being "outspoken and clear enough on the vital question of politics." His response was succinct: "We are for the Federal Union . . . and opposed to all those which militate against it." Then he went one step further: "As for the Negro he is, and of right, ought to be perfectly and absolutely free. He should have every social and political opportunity for advancement . . . and it is right for the Government . . . to protect his interests."[20]

It was typical that in their statements of principles, both Flake and Newcomb sided with the freedmen. Newly liberated and struggling to survive, blacks represented a significant percentage of the population in the areas where the *Daily Bulletin* and the *Express* circulated. Between 10 and 15 percent of the population in Bexar and Harris counties were black, over 20 percent in Galveston and Travis counties, and between 40 to 50 percent in Harrison, Austin, and Washington counties.[21] Laborers, ministers, carpenters, teachers, laundrywomen, doctors, sharecroppers, and stablemen—they were as eager to work as whites, and it was this characteristic that Conservative publishers noted. In the February 1866, John Logan wrote in the *Herald* about the "many signs of industry and good conduct on the part of the freedman... that certainly speak . . . well for them."[22] No less impressed was Osterhout in the *Texas Countryman:* "As a general rule, we believe the freedmen are complying with their contracts in this county, and are doing very good work."[23] Similarly pleased was Gillespie in the *Houston Telegraph:* "[F]reedmen have nearly all entered into contracts, found employment and gone to work . . . . This was unexpected to nearly every person . . . . The freedmen have welcomely [*sic*] deceived us this time."[24] Beneath the Conservatives' grudging praise was the unspoken assumption that freedmen were little more than field hands. Radicals like Newcomb and Flake, however, saw them as citizens. These drastic differences would trail Texas newspapers for the next three years as editors reported events both within and outside the state, their accounts inevitably shaded by personal viewpoints. Most revealing was coverage of one of the first violent episodes of Reconstruction, the Memphis riots.

Long-standing antipathy between urban blacks and whites living in Memphis, Tennessee, came to a head May 2, 1866, when two teamsters, one white and one black, collided on a South Memphis street. Impatient and angry, the men attacked each other with words, then with horsewhips as a crowd gathered. Soon police, soldiers, and the fire brigade converged, shots were fired, and the melee became a riot. By nightfall, armed vigilantes roamed deathly still streets, taking potshots at wandering blacks and other pedestrians. Wednesday morning brought more disturbances near the railroad depot until federal troops restored calm. It was that night, though, that saw the greatest damage as irate mobs set fire to black neighborhoods in the area. Unable or unwilling to douse the flames, the fire brigades watched whole blocks disintegrate into ashes as more people died.[25]

Texas coverage of the event differed according to the mind-set of each editor. For William Barrett, despite his Conservative leanings, the Memphis riot was a catastrophe. In the *Harrison Flag*, he described two days and nights of bloodshed and carnage, ending early on Thursday. "Before the morning's sun rose," he wrote, "no less than three colored churches, four colored schools, and about thirty cabins had fallen . . . . The number killed [included] Henry Dunn . . . and officer Stephens . . . . Twelve negroes, in all, were killed." As was common with conservatives, Negroes went nameless, except for "a woman named Rachel."[26] Willard Richardson of the *Galveston Daily News* revealed how she died, writing that Rachel, "sick and unable to escape . . . burned to death."[27]

While Conservatives showed some remorse for slain freedpeople, they were quick to defend whites involved in the riot. Attempting to shift blame away from southern sympathizers, Richardson's account focused upon ethnic differences. The original altercation, he maintained, had been between a policeman and a liquor dealer. "The antipathy of the Irish to the negroes is well known," he continued. As there were "a large number of Irish in the Police . . . the riots were simply an onslaught upon the negroes by the Police and fire companies . . . . Neither civilians, rebels, or returned rebels," he roundly concluded, "had anything to do with the outbreak."[28]

Ferdinand Flake disagreed with Richardson's assessment. The conflict began between two teamsters, he insisted, and started out as a "trifling street quarrel that a judicious policeman ought to have settled in five minutes." Not missing a chance to praise troops that were stationed in Galveston, Flake wrote that Conservatives "who are seized with a sudden retching at the sight of a blue jacket," should now realize that "these jackets are here for their protection."[29] His message was clear: Texas cities might reenact the scenes of Memphis if it were not for the federal soldiers garrisoned in the state. Finally, Flake warned his readers of the impact such riots had on the economy. "The disturbances in Memphis have damaged the business of that city to the extent of millions," he penned. "They have retarded her advancement and hindered her progress . . . . That riots have not occurred in Galveston," he stated, "is simply because our inhabitants, both white and black, are more law-abiding and have their passions under better control."[30]

Far more serious, and bloodier, was the New Orleans riot two months later. Incensed that blacks did not gain suffrage rights under Louisiana's provisional constitution of 1864, freedmen and their white supporters decided to rewrite the document. Acting with the guarded approval of Governor Wells, they publicized their intent to meet in New Orleans in late July 1866. These plans, however, had not been approved by Washington, and soon the governor began down-playing his support. In addition, city authorities saw the convocation as disruptive and requested the local Union commander for help in suppressing the event. His refusal, on the grounds of peaceable assembly, left Mayor Monroe on his own, and when the meeting convened in the Mechanics Institute near Canal Street on July 30, the police were out in force—only to be met head-on by a group of black Army veterans marching to the Mechanic's Institute to ensure that the convention approved Negro suffrage. Alarmed and angered by the presence of armed whites, the African Americans fell back momentarily only to resume their trek to the Institute. But by this time shots had been fired by both sides, and within minutes, a bloody turmoil erupted on the street. Brutally disposing of the marchers, the police and mob turned their attention to conventioneers inside the Mechanic's Institute.[31]

As the rioters made their way to the front of the building, those inside decided to barricade the doors, but they were too late. Policemen were inside. The next few minutes saw desperate delegates attempting to escape, some jumping out of the second floor windows, only to be captured, beaten, and killed. Some lawmen defended their own against attack, while others simply watched the mêlée unfold. By sunset federal forces had arrived on the scene and regained control of the city. In the sullen quiet of evening, the 81st U. S. Colored Infantry entered the Institute and discovered "the entrance slippery with blood, the halls horribly besmeared . . . hats, caps, and . . . clothing strewn . . . dead bodies and a number of wounded lying about."[32] Included among the dead were three white supporters of Negro suffrage, including former state auditor, Anthony Dostie, and thirty-seven African Americans. Only one attacker died.

Conservatives castigated the organizers. "The riot was the practical fruit of Radicalism in the South," fumed Logan in the *Daily Herald* on August 8. "The real and controlling motive of these reckless and unprincipled men was to regain offices. . . . It should not be believed for a moment that they had . . . any honest sympathy or concern for the freedmen." Willard Richardson of the *Daily News* was no less incensed, writing that "the riot at New Orleans resulted . . . from the assembling of the convention, which even Thaddeus Stevens denounced as unworthy."[33] Flying in the face of every fact, the *Flag's* Barrett insisted the event was "proof . . . that civil authorities were equal to the emergency without the aid of the military."[34]

Publisher Flake instead eulogized the victims, stating that "the men who were shot were in almost every case incapable of making a fight." He continued, "[One] is a cripple and walks with a crutch . . . . Dr. Dostie was a weak, frail man." Furthermore, he reported, "The Negrocs suffered most severely, the victims of repeated and wanton cruelty." He made only one comment on the convention itself: "As a body, it was one of the least capable of offering resistance that can be imagined . . . . No power on earth had a right to forbid its sessions."[35]

It was an incident in Brenham, Texas, however, that stretched Flake's equanimity to its limits. By September of that year relations between townsmen and Union soldiers there had grown tense, exacerbated by the fiery editorials of the *Brenham Banner* editor, D. L. McGary. One of McGary's favorite targets was Freedman's Bureau commander Samuel A. Craig. Thin-skinned and intense, Craig took as much abuse as he could, then arrested and imprisoned McGary. Turning the action to his advantage, the publisher refused bail and continued his invectives against the military and the Bureau from his cell. Less than a month later, two soldiers got into a fight with civilians at a freedman's ball, carried it to a white gathering, and ended up being shot. Within a few hours, troopers set two of the town's main stores afire; by dawn an entire city block had burned down.[36]

Flake was of two minds about the affair. It was his account that revealed a mob attack upon several freedmen on the same night as the fire. It was also he who reported a pre-fire conspiracy among residents to "send couriers into the country to raise a force and 'wipe out the soldiers.'"[37] But the arrest of a fellow newsman rankled him, so he took pains to print a second version of the incident placing complete blame upon the military.[38]

Publisher Logan wasted no space on objectivity. His headline on Brenham said it all: "The Town Fired by Federal Soldiers." Inflammatory terms like "outrage" and "wicked soldiers" appeared in subsequent articles, along with a suggestion that "the destruction of [McGary's] printing office was the object of the burning."[39] But it was his comment, occasioned by national coverage of the violence, that merited notice. "*The New York Tribune*, on hearing of the affair at Brenham, at once pronounced it an 'insurrection,'" he reported. "If the burning of a town by . . . soldiers sent to protect the people, constitutes an 'insurrection' we can imagine no sort of a fracas that the radicals would not be able to turn to political profit."[40]

His concern reflected the mood of his readers specifically and of many Southerners in general. Congressional elections came just months after the Memphis, New Orleans, and Brenham riots. The furor of the Conservatives grew as Radicals began to spotlight statutes that Texas and other southern states had enacted to deny freedpeople equality before the law. Republicans across the nation had little need to exaggerate the difficulties faced by southern blacks; they just needed to report what was taking place throughout the South—and they did. Logan's observation after the mid-term 1866 elections was a masterpiece of Conservative understatement, "The result of the elections are anything but encouraging."[41] Voters, especially in the northern states, had overwhelmingly rejected President Johnson's plan of Reconstruction which most viewed as too lenient. Radicals would now have control of the federal government.

In 1867 Congress took measures to renovate the South, including a strengthened Freedman's Bureau, a broadened suffrage plan, and plans for each state to write a new constitution. Perhaps the most stringent, however, was the imposition of martial law. By March, the old Confederacy (with the exception of Tennessee) had been fragmented into five military districts, each headed by its own military commander, garrisoned with additional troops, and subordinate to Washington directives. Logan's fear had become a reality: Texas had become "Radicalized."[42]

But despite increased federal intervention, violence against the state's freedmen did not cease. In fact, white-on-black assaults increased throughout the summer, according to Freedman's Bureau records as well as Radical newspapers.[43] Finally even Conservative publishers began to acknowledge strife: weeklong riots in Marshall, trouble in Bryan, problems in Hempstead, near-riots in Navasota, and mêlées throughout the other southern states.[44] But ferocity peaked in July 1868, with a confrontation in Millican, Texas, over the rumored lynching of a freedman.

Blacks in Millican were often targets of white racists in the years following emancipation. Like freedpeople in other parts of the state, they had seen teachers beaten, preachers attacked, sisters raped, families murdered, and property destroyed or stolen. They also learned that they would receive little to no help from civil and federal authorities. By summer of 1868, some blacks in the Central Texas town decided to assert themselves, and when a band of masked ruffians rode shooting into their enclave that June, several of the men shot back.

No one was killed, but leaders of the white community demanded Bureau commander Nathan Randlett forcibly disarm the freedmen. Refusing to cooperate, Randlett instead issued an order forbidding the existence of any armed band; he then initiated more patrols around the region. Tensions escalated during the next few weeks, and when Miles Brown, a well-known black, appeared to have suddenly disappeared in July, his comrades assumed he had been murdered. In their upheaval, they took Brown's boss, plantation owner Anthony Holiday, hostage.

The idea of a white landowner held by a few armed blacks enraged townsfolk. It took several violent confrontations, numerous negotiated parleys, a trainload of over one hundred citizens from Bryan, three days of rampant rumors, and the final arrival of the cavalry from Brenham to quell the riots, and the death count was telling. Six blacks from Millican had been killed by gunplay, and one, the minister who organized the freedmen in the first place, hanged. Miles Brown, the feared victim, was never in danger; he had simply left town.[45]

Texas editors' coverage of the event generally aligned with their political beliefs. Radical James Newcomb saw Millican as one more example of secessionist hatred. "Another Negro Massacre," the *Express* editor headlined, "Twenty-five Negroes Murdered!" Under a subtopic sardonically labeled, "More Universal Peace in Texas," he predicted the Conservatives would call "this, the 'war of races." He mocked them, "We have had one war of races, as the whole rebel press in the South used to say the 'Yankee nation' was a different race." Newcomb concluded on a sarcastic note, "It can't be possible the negroes had any cause for fortifying, to protect themselves! Oh no, it was done just for fun!"[46] Ferdinand Flake was far more objective in his assessment: "It would have been wiser for [the freedmen] not to have taken arms when they went to look for the supposed dead man."[47] Conservatives were predictably indignant. "Every circumstance about the unfortunate affair," snorted Logan in the *Daily Herald,* "goes to show that the negroes brought upon themselves the severe chastisement they received."[48] Willard Richardson in his *Galveston News* was more succinct: "It is all the work of the infernal carpetbaggers."[49]

But blaming carpetbaggers or scalawags for burgeoning violence in Texas lost its effectiveness as new types of killers began to appear. "On or about the night of April 15, 1868," *Flake's Daily Bulletin* reported, "the mob, or the Ku Klux as they are called . . . came to the house of . . . Benjamin Crouch. [They] . . . forced his wife to open the door . . . and threatened to shoot him. They also said they would kill him if he ever fed or harbored any of his friends . . . . Mrs. Julia Ellington [testified] that on the night of the 23rd of April . . . several men came to her house . . . and shot Mr. Ellington through the head." Earlier on the same night, "a crowd of men came to . . . Bell county . . . and called Mr. Benjamin Schoonover and his sons . . . out of [their] house . . . after which they . . . fired several shots . . . killing the old man and his son George."[50]

Ex-Confederates in Texas had taken on a new identity, that of the Ku Klux Klan. Considered by many to be "the madcap fancy of schoolboys in Pulaski, Tennessee," the organization, under the leadership of former Confederate general Nathan Forrest, had grown into "a species of Regulator organization" that spread throughout the Reconstruction South. Incensed by Negro suffrage and threatened by new state constitutional conventions convening in 1868, the Klan determined to undermine Radicals by wreaking havoc. Thus they "occupied themselves by destroying Union League councils, breaking up bands of roving Negroes, whipping Negro militiamen, forcing victims to pledge non-support of . . . Radical politicians, and coercing individual carpetbaggers and scalawags."[51]

Characterized by hooded, painted, or blackened faces, Klansmen were about as organized as the ragtag mobs they had displaced. Especially in Texas, they seemed to form independently, "having no official connection with any other Klan." Yet their mystical aura, their placards with skull, crossbones, and arcane writing, their secret oaths and promises to protect "the men, women, and children of the white race against the brutality, rapacity, and ferocity of the black barbarians," ennobled them to most.[52]

Unwilling to take their existence seriously at first, Conservative newsmen soon extolled them as "snow white spirits," determined to destroy "carpetbaggers . . . scalawags, and . . . the L.U.L. [Loyal Union League] and G. A. of the R [Grand Army of the Republic]."[53] Some publishers endorsed the Klansmen and their activities: "We believed the Ku Klux organization to be entirely innocent, and intended only for convivial purposes," asserted John Logan. He continued, "But should it turn out . . . to be a secret combination . . . against the dangers of negro supremacy, we are prepared to defend the organization . . . until the day of judgment."[54] The *Houston Democrat* went even further: "We firmly and honestly believe that the Klan should be encouraged and fostered by all true Southern men."[55] This horrified the *Daily Bulletin's* Ferdinand Flake, who contended that "Not only should the military break [the organization] up and scatter its members, but the ringleaders should be tried by military commission and hung as conspirators against good order."[56]

Flake was correct about the destructive force of the Klan. By late summer of 1868, accounts of Klan outrages in the *Daily Bulletin* abounded. In an August issue, a correspondent wrote that on July 9, "a party of horsemen, with masked faces, forced the door of a blacksmith, dragged him out of bed, took him out into the bushes . . . beat him unmercifully, and then . . . shot into his house . . . . The mob of Ku Kluxers go the rounds every night," the writer continued. "They visited a shop last evening and killed one negro and beat another almost to death . . . . The morning question now is, 'What did the Ku Kluxers do last night?' . . . . The killing goes bravely on.'" The letter finally ended, "Last night two white men were killed at the same place where the negroes were the night before."[57] In another incident, Flake reported that "a negro man [was found] . . .hanging to a tree, about one mile east of Bryan . . . . The murdered negro's wife says that a party of white men, with painted faces, came to his house on Monday night and took him away."[58] The *Daily Bulletin* reported another atrocity, this one on the edge of Cass County; "Above Jefferson . . . a plantation was attacked at night and seven negroes were found dead this morning."[59]

The actions of the terrorists spread fear throughout the black community. Flake emphasized this in his report of the murder of George Smith, a Waco delegate to the 1868 Constitutional Convention. According to the *Daily Bulletin*, Smith was assaulted as he returned home from the convention. "It seems that for safe keeping he was placed in the jail," the paper stated, "as were also several freedmen who were objects of popular vengeance. . . . On the next night, a mob of disguised men . . . broke open the jail [and] took out Smith and the freedmen. Smith . . . died fighting . . . . A volley was fired into the freedmen, two of whom were killed, while a third was badly wounded. It is now evident," Flake concluded, "that the fear of [convention] delegates to go home was well founded."[60]

Fear trumped everything. "There can be little doubt the same party is doing it all," one correspondent admitted; "they can be identified, but those who knew them are afraid to testify."[61] A federal officer, in a report from Bell County, stated the same: "With everybody with whom I conversed . . . they are in such dread of this mob that it was with greatest difficulty I could get any facts whatsoever . . . . The families . . . have fled from that part of the state."[62] In desperation, Union commander Joseph J. Reynolds issued General Order #14 prohibiting "the future wearing of masks or other disguises, under penalty of being arrested on the spot," an order roundly mocked by the Conservative press.[63] General Reynolds, however, was serious, as was his November report to Washington on Freedmen's Affairs. In it he listed 761 officially reported murders since war's end.[64] His numbers came fairly close to those already released to the public in a report compiled by the state Committee on Lawlessness and Crime. Although the first attempt of Radicals to write a new constitution failed, it had given birth to a documented record of violence in Texas. Admitting to inadequacies and the "difficulty of getting gentlemen to testify before us," committeemen had accessed the files of district courts and the Freedman's Bureau between April 1865 and the first half of 1868 to arrive at a total of 938 homicides. Of those, whites had killed 460 other whites and 373 blacks, while freedmen had killed ten whites and 48 blacks. "This great disparity between the numbers of the two races killed, the one by the other," the committee agreed, "shows conclusively that the 'war of the races,' is all on the part of the whites against the blacks."[65]

Conservatives denigrated the July report in the ugliest of terms. "Villainous," "atrocious," "maliciously false," roared the *Herald's* Logan; committee members' determination to present the report to Congress "cannot fail to stir up strife and set one class of people in deadly hostility against the other," he added.[66] Richardson of the *Galveston News* disparaged the sources. "The . . . convention report is made up from reports of county clerks, some of whom took a very radical view of their duties; from the . . . Freedman's Bureau, which are utterly unreliable . . . and from . . . 'reliable witnesses' . . . most of whom . . . were anxious to see the subject in the light required by the committee. Our Austin correspondent," he concluded, "has shown it to be the lamest affair that was ever sent abroad with such a flourish of trumpets."[67]

But the *San Antonio Express* calmly disagreed. "The report of the committee on Lawlessness and Crime," wrote James Newcomb, "we commend to the attention of every thoughtful man, of every good citizen. The 938 homicides committed in this State since the conclusion of the war . . . is but the shadow of the great bulk of crime which has stalked through our land . . . . [It is] a terrible verdict against the peace and quiet of our State."[68] The *Daily Bulletin* concurred. Securing a synopsis of the committee report weeks before its official publication, Ferdinand Flake previewed part of it for his readers. "Our correspondent in Austin has sent us a document such as it seldom falls to the lot of journalists to publish," he warned; "The revelations that he makes of crime are enough to harrow the soul of man." Flake concluded by listing 411 specific murders and assaults with intent to kill that occurred within just the previous year.[69]

The first three years of Reconstruction had proved tumultuous. Whether the number of homicides was 938 or 761 or somewhere in between, and whether the instigators were individuals, mobs, or the Klan, emancipated Texans had endured unimaginable suffering. Securing safety and the ability to vote remained a primary objective of freedmen and their white allies. Many Radicals called upon Washington to sanction a state armed militia.[70] Others believed that the federals would have to completely take over the state in order to establish law and order. James Newcomb espoused this view, stating that "crime [in the state] is due to the remissness of the [United States] government in not taking complete charge of our State . . . and suspending all civil authority."[71] However, greater federal intervention was far more than Conservatives desired. Logan termed such ideas as "revolutionary," and threatened that, "in place of punishing lawlessness and crime, the violent action proposed will increase it tenfold, and . . . introduce a 'reign of terror' throughout this State."[72]

But Texas as described in late November, "demoralized . . . intolerant . . . [with a] total disregard for law and order, and [a] light value . . . [for] human life," merited such action.[73] As the state careened toward a second constitutional convention at the end of 1868, three things were certain. First, a militia would be created to combat internal lawlessness and crime. Second, the actions of this militia would be closely scrutinized by the press. Finally, each publisher would present his reports to the public in the flamboyant wordage of Radical or Conservative thought. Maybe the only thing Texans had not destroyed in their three blood-ridden years since war's end was an opinionated, "free, and outspoken press."[74]

ENDNOTES

1. The author wishes to thank the historians and archivists—Gary McKee, Linda Wolff, Bill Page, Jan Weaver, Grace Charles, and Sandra Rexroat—who helped so much with the research for this work.

2. Ernest Wallace, David M. Vigness, and George B. Ward, eds., *Documents of Texas History* (Austin: State House Press, 1994), 194.

3. Marilyn McAdams Sibley, *Lone Stars and State Gazettes: Texas Newspapers before the Civil War* (College Station: Texas A&M University Press, 1973), 4–9, 14–15, 65.

4. J. M. Day, *Texas Almanac: 1857–1873: A Compendium of Texas History* (Waco, TX: Texian Press, 1967), 515; Sibley, *Lone Stars and State Gazettes*, 302.

5. Day, *Texas Almanac*, 515; Randolph Campbell, *Gone to Texas: A History of the Lone Star State* (New York: Oxford University Press, 2003), 276; W. L. Richter, *The Army in Texas during Reconstruction, 1866–1870* (College Station: Texas A&M University Press, 1987), xi.

6. "Carpetbaggers" referred to Northern Republicans who moved to the South after the War; "Scalawags" denoted the Southerners who worked with them. For information on "Conservatives," see Campbell, *Gone to Texas,* 276, and Richter, *The Army in Texas during Reconstruction*, xi.

7. *Galveston Daily News*, August 16, 1866.

8. "The Riot in Mobile," *Houston Tri-Weekly Telegram*, May 17, 1867.

9. "Telegraphic," *(Austin) Tri-Weekly State Gazette*, November 4, 1867; *Handbook of Texas Online*, "Austin *State Gazette,*" http://www.tshaonline.org/handbook/online/articles/AA/eeayy.html (accessed January 5, 2010).

10. *Handbook of Texas Online,* "John W. Barrett," http://www.tshaonline.org/handbook/online/articles/BB/fbabp.html (accessed January 5, 2010); Sibley, *Lone Stars and State Gazettes*, 274, 349–50.

11. "The Confederate Flag," *Harrison (Marshall) Flag*, May 24, 1866.

12. Sibley, *Lone Stars and State Gazettes*, 308; *Handbook of Texas Online,* "John Patterson Osterhout," http://www.tshaonline.org/handbook/online/articles/OO/fos10_print..html (accessed January 5, 2010).

13. "Once More," *(Bellville) Texas Countryman*, January 26, 1866.

14. Sibley, *Lone Stars and State Gazettes*, 274, 288, 361; *Handbook of Texas Online,* "John Davis Logan," http://www.tshaonline.org/handbook/online/articles/LL/flo43_print.html (accessed January 5, 2010); *Handbook of Texas Online,* "San Antonio *Herald*," http://www.tshaonline.org/handbook/online/articles/SS/ees4_print.html (accessed January 5, 2010).

15. "Texas Items," *The Daily (San Antonio) Herald*, June 21, 1866.

16. Sibley, *Lone Stars and State Gazettes*, 296–98, 359–60; *Handbook of Texas Online,* "James Pearson Newcomb," http://www.tshaonline.org/handbook/online/articles/NN/fne19_print.html (accessed January 5, 2010).

17. "Close of the Second Volume," *San Antonio Express*, September 26, 1867.

18. "The Freedman's Press," *Weekly Freedman's Press*, July 18, 1868.

19. Sibley, *Lone Stars and State Gazettes*, 226–28, 272–73; *Handbook of Texas Online,* "Ferdinand Flake," http://www.tshaonline.org/handbook/online/articles/FF/ff12_print.html (accessed January 5, 2010).

20. "Our Sentiments," *Flake's Daily Galveston Bulletin*, January 10, 1866.

21. The census count from each county for both years was averaged to arrive at these estimates. U. S. Department of Commerce, Bureau of the Census, *Eight Census of the United States—1860, Ninth Census of the United States—1870.*

22. "The Freedmen," *The Daily (San Antonio) Herald*, February 7, 1866.

23. "The Freedmen," *(Bellville) Texas Countryman*, March 2, 1866.

24. "Eastern Texas," *Houston Tri-Weekly Telegram*, Janurary 17, 1866.

25. J. G. Randall and David Donald, *The Civil War and Reconstruction* (Boston: D.D. Heath and Company, 1961), 587. For newspaper coverage of the Memphis riots, see *Flake's Galveston Daily Bulletin*, May 8–19, August 15, 1866; *Harrison (Marshall) Flag*, May 24, 1866; *Galveston Daily News*, May 9, June 9, 1866.

26. "The Late Riots," *Harrison (Marshall) Flag*, May 24, 1866.

27. The Memphis Riot," *Galveston Daily News*, June 6, 1866.

28. Ibid.

29. "The Memphis Riot," "The Great Memphis Riot," *Flake's Daily Galveston Bulletin*, May 8, 1866.

30. "The Memphis Riot," *Flake's Daily Galveston Bulletin*, May 18, 1866.

31. Randall and Donald, *The Civil War and Reconstruction*, 587; "New Orleans Race Riot of 1866," http://chnm.gmu.edu/courses/122/carr/riottext.html (accessed January 10, 2010). For newspaper coverage of the New Orleans riots, see Flake's *Galveston Daily Bulletin*, August 1–August 12, September 1–November 22, 1866; *Harrison (Marshall) Flag*, August 1–August 16, 1866; *San Antonio Herald*, August 5–August 21, September 19, 1866; *Galveston Daily News*, August 1–August 14, 1866; Richter, *The Army in Texas during Reconstruction*, 54–56; James Alex Baggett, *The Scalawags: Southern Dissenters in the Civil War and Reconstruction* (Baton Rouge: Louisiana State University Press, 2003), 140, 144–46. For more information about the New Orleans Riots, see *Aftershock: Beyond the Civil War*. DVD, directed by David W. Padrusch (2006; The History Channel, A&E Television Network), and *Reconstruction: The Second Civil War,* DVD, directed by Llewellyn Smith (2004; American Experience, WGBH Boston Educational Foundation).

32. "The New Orleans Riots," *Flake's Daily Galveston Bulletin*, August 4, 1866.

33. *Galveston Daily News*, August 1, 1866.

34. "New Orleans," *Harrison (Marshall) Flag*, August 16, 1866.

35. "The New Orleans Riots," *Flake's Daily Galveston Bulletin*, August 4, 1866; "Local Intelligence," *Flake's Daily Galveston Bulletin*, August 9, 1866.

36. Richter, *The Army in Texas,* 64–65; Carl H. Moneyhon, *Texas after the Civil War: The Struggle for Reconstruction* (College Station: Texas A&M University Press, 2004) , 63–64; Charles William Ramsdell, *Reconstruction in Texas* (1910; repr., Austin: University of Texas Press, 1970), 127–29. For newspaper coverage of the Brenham riots, see *Flake's Daily Galveston Bulletin*, September 9–October 4, 1866; *San Antonio Herald,* September 16-October 11, 1866; *San Antonio Express*, October 16, 1866.

37. "Serious Disturbance at Brenham," *Flake's Daily Galveston Bulletin*, September 9,1866.

38. "Another Version of the Brenham Disturbance," *Flake's Daily Galveston Bulletin*, September 11, 1866.

39. "Riot at Brenham," *The Daily (San Antonio) Herald*, September 16, 1866.

40. *The Daily (San Antonio) Herald*, October 10, 1866.

41. "The Elections," *The Daily (San Antonio) Herald,* November 11, 1866.

42. Randall and Donald, *The Civil War and Reconstruction,* 595–600; Gregg Cantrell, "Racial Violence and Reconstruction Politics in Texas, 1867–1868, *Southwestern Historical Quarterly (*January 1990), 355.

43. Cantrell, "Racial Violence and Reconstruction," 342. For specific incidents, see *Flake's Daily Galveston Bulletin*, July 4, July 20, August 8, 1867; *San Antonio Express,* September 13, 1867.

44. For specific incidents, see *(Austin) Tri-Weekly State Gazette,* January 15–22, 1868; *Houston Tri-Weekly Telegram,* January 14, 1868; *The Daily (San Antonio) Herald*, April 29, September 26, September 30, October 9, 1868; *Galveston Daily News*, July 2, September 10, September 16, 1868.

45. Barry Crouch, *The Freedman's Bureau and Black Texans* (Austin: University of Texas Press, 1992), 115–22; Bill Page, "Millican, Texas, 1821–1889: A Sourcebook," (February 21, 2007), 147–57. See articles in *The (San Antonio) Daily Herald,* July 20, 1868; *Galveston Daily News,* July 17–18, 1868; *San Antonio Express,* July 19, 1868; *Flake's Daily Galveston Bulletin*, July 18-August 25, 1868; also, "Brazos County," *Handbook of Texas Online:* http://wwwa.tshaonline.org/handbook/online/articles (accessed September 5, 2009).

46. "Another Negro Massacre!" *San Antonio Express*, July 19, 1868.

47. *Flake's Daily Galveston Bulletin*, August 4, 1868.

48. "The Millican Riot," *The Daily (San Antonio) Herald*, July 20, 1868.

49. *Galveston Daily News*, July 18, 1868.

50. "Official Statement," *Flake's Daily Galveston Bulletin,* June 18, 1868.

51. W. D. Wood, "The Ku Klux Klan," *Southwestern Historical Quarterly Online* 9 (accessed March 12, 2008); "The Ku Klux Klan," *The Daily (San Antonio) Herald*, April 16, 1868; Randall and Donald, *The Civil War and Reconstruction*, 682–83.

52. Wood, "Ku Klux Klan," *The Daily (San Antonio) Herald*, May 9, 1868.

53. "The Ku Klux Klan," April 17, 1868, "Editorial Brevities," April 7, 1868, *The Daily (San Antonio) Herald*. "L.U.L." and "G.A. of the R." were Conservative euphemisms for two groups, the Loyal or Union League and the Grand Army of the Republic, organized to support Republicanism

and black suffrage in the South. See Claude Elliot, "Loyal Union League," in *The Handbook of Texas,* ed. W. P. Webb (Austin: Texas State Historical Association, 1952) , and Moneyhon, *Texas after the Civil War,* 178.

54. "Ku Klux Klan," *The Daily (San Antonio) Herald*, May 9, 1868.

55. *Houston Democrat*, April 26, 1868, as quoted in "Local Intelligence," *Flake's Daily Galveston Bulletin*, May 29, 1868.

56. "Secret Political Societies," *Flake's Daily Galveston Bulletin,* April 30, 1868.

57. "The Situation at Jefferson," *Flake's Daily Galveston Bulletin,* August 5, 1868.

58. "Local Intelligence," *Flake's Daily Galveston Bulletin*, October 4, 1868.

59. *Flake's Daily Galveston Bulletin*, October 30, 1868.

60. "More Murder," *Flake's Daily Galveston Bulletin*, October 11, 1868.

61. "The Situation at Jefferson," *Flake's Daily Galveston Bulletin,* August 5, 1868.

62. "Official Statement," *Flake's Daily Galveston Bulletin,* June 18, 1868.

63. *Houston Telegraph,* quoted in "What's Next?" *Flake's Daily Galveston Bulletin,* October 24, 1868.

64. "Texas," *Flake's Daily Galveston Bulletin*, November 14, 1868.

65. "Report of the Committee on Lawlessness and Crime," *Flake's Daily Galveston Bulletin*, July 5, 1868.

66. "The Reign of Terror," July 7, "Lawlessness and Crime," July 8, "Report of the Committee on Lawlessness and Violence," July 9, 1868, *The Daily (San Antonio) Herald.*

67. "Crime and the Convention," *Galveston Daily News*, July 10, 1868.

68. "Lawlessness and Crime," *San Antonio Express*, July 10, 1868.

69. "Crime," June 19, "The Bloody Record," June 23, 1868, *Flake's Daily Galveston Bulletin.*

70. Moneyhon, *Texas after the Civil War*, 96.

71. "Lawlessness and Crime," *San Antonio Express*, July 19, 1868.

72. "The Reign of Terror," *The (San Antonio) Daily Herald*, July 7, 1868.

73. "Texas," *Flake's Daily Galveston Bulletin*, November 18, 1868.

74. "Letter from Houston," *Flake's Daily (Galveston) Bulletin*, June 5, 1868.

Part Three

The Victims: Minorities and Women

CHAPTER 10

Into Freedom's Abyss: Reflections of Reconstruction Violence in Texas

by

Ronald E. Goodwin

During the past four decades, scholars have convincingly argued that violence was commonplace in Texas during the post-Civil War years. These scholars have examined various aspects of Reconstruction violence, including political, racial, and socio-economic factors. Unfortunately, few researchers have discussed the intense atmosphere of violence from the perspective of the freedmen themselves. Many black Texans, whether they were enslaved elsewhere throughout the old Confederacy or not, found themselves mired in the abyss of a theoretical freedom, a freedom where they faced racism as intense and violent as any experienced during the antebellum years. Nonetheless, these former slaves attempted to transform their promised freedoms into a tangible reality. They faced the daunting task of altering their own mind-sets from thinking and acting as dependent chattel slaves to succeeding in a free society as independent freed men and women.

Unfortunately, violence was used all too often to retard this transformation. In this chapter, the vile acts of violence are retold from the unique vantage point of the former slaves. Such a vantage point illustrates how a formerly enslaved people adapted to the challenges of the responsibilities of freedom, and perhaps most importantly, being confronted daily with the constant threat of violence from their white neighbors who devoted themselves to the ideals of white supremacy.

Fortunately, the Slaves Narratives, a New Deal-era WPA project, documents the experiences of the former bondsmen as they struggled to survive the new era of violence in the years immediately following the Civil War. Admittedly, many of the former slaves interviewed in Texas during the 1930s were originally enslaved elsewhere throughout the Confederacy. They arrived in Texas either in the waning years of the

Civil War or soon after emancipation. Nonetheless, the myriad acts of violence and terror they conveyed to their WPA interviewer demonstrate how commonplace it was to live in a state of fear and anxiousness.

No other primary source conveys the paradoxical sense of fear and hopefulness as does the Slave Narratives. However, scholars throughout the decades have worried about the validity of the Slave Narratives since those interviewed were recalling events that occurred decades earlier. Nonetheless, with the emergence of the modern Civil Rights movement scholars began not only a reevaluation of slavery, but the roles of black slaves as well, based on the information provided by the Slave Narratives.

Research prior to the modern Civil Rights-era relied almost exclusively on records left by white Southerners, so blacks were often seen as dependent wards of southern charity, unable to govern or manage their own families or personal affairs. However, with the Slave Narratives scholars were allowed inside the black community as those interviewed elaborated on their familial relationships, the clothes they wore and the food they ate, their relationships with whites, and the expectations of work on the antebellum plantation. They also told of the violent repercussions of emancipation. Granted, these events took place decades earlier, but such limitations of the Slave Narratives are the same as might be found with any oral interviews of elderly people. Therefore, the Slave Narratives remain a valid source for understanding the experiences of freedpeople in the Reconstruction era.

* * * * *

In Texas, the origins of violence against blacks in the years following emancipation can be found in the sudden change in the relationships between whites and blacks. During the Civil War, most white Texans recognized a Union victory would mean the end of slavery. Their premonitions became a reality when Gen. Gordon Granger arrived in Galveston on June 19, 1865, announcing that the Emancipation Proclamation was the law of the land and would be enforced in Texas from that day forth. White Texans, especially slaveholders, were unsure of what would become of them now that nearly 250,000 slaves were suddenly freed.

During the antebellum years whites were able to use force and intimidation to control slaves. However, Granger's arrival implied an end to white domination and the emergence of equality between blacks and whites.[1] But too many white Texans clung to the principles of white supremacy and remained unapologetic for what they believed was the natural order of society. Even though the Civil War was officially over, they initiated a new wave of terror primarily aimed at their former slaves. Such acts of violence were justified as the only means to maintain antebellum race relations—no matter how many innocent people had to perish.

Although historian Alwyn Barr is correct in stating that "Slavery died with the Confederacy," too many whites were unprepared to let their control of the black population end in Texas.[2] Accustomed to forcing

Illustration 10. Gen. Gordon Granger. (Courtesy of Library of Congress)

their will upon the former slaves, often at the crack of the whip, many former masters still expected local blacks to practice the same deference to whites that they had in the years prior to the war. Other former slave owners were less resolute. Cato Carter, who arrived in Texas shortly after the end of the war, remembered his owner tearfully announcing to his newly freed slaves, "You are free to do as you like, 'cause the damned Yankees done 'creed you are. They ain't a nigger on my place what was born here or ever lived here who can't stay here and work and eat to the end of his days, as long as this old place will raise peas and goobers. Go if you wants, and stay if you wants."[3] J. W. Terrill also remembered the reaction of his former slave owner who was obviously unsettled about a future without slaves and wished ill will on her former chattel. Terrill, who was born in Louisiana and brought to Texas by his owner around 1850, said, "Missy, she cries and cries, and tells us we is free and she hopes we starve to death and she'd be glad, 'cause it ruin her to lose us."[4]

Whereas Terrill's former owner released her slaves, albeit reluctantly, others only did so by force. Those who were forced to release their slaves eventually lashed out against them, attempting to scare and intimidate blacks into remaining subservient to whites. Those who did not comply became victims of violent crimes, including murder. Susan Merritt remembered, "Lots of niggers was kilt after freedom, 'cause the slaves in Harrison County turn loose right at freedom and them in Rusk County wasn't. But they hears 'bout it and runs away to freedom in Harrison County they owners have 'em bushwhacked, that shot down. You could see lots of niggers hangin' to trees in Sabine bottom right after freedom, 'cause they cotch 'em swimming 'cross Sabine River and shoot 'em."[5]

Admittedly, like their former owners, many blacks in Texas were not prepared for the sudden end of slavery or the responsibilities of exercising their first freedoms. Their uncertainties only intensified those of white Texans who were faced with new labor and social systems where blacks were supposed to be equal. The concentration of a majority of Texas' black populace on the former cotton plantations in the rural eastern region of the state made it easier to intimidate blacks into staying on, or near, the cotton fields. Even though the reactions after learning of their freedom were generally the same (some danced and sang songs about John Brown and hoped to reunite with displaced family members), many blacks were just not prepared emotionally to leave their former owners.[6] Some black families made the decision to remain with their former owners even though they only received food and shelter, "but no money."[7]

Sadly, this was also a period when some black families were torn apart. Andrew Columbus recalled his owner as "one white man that 'sho took care of his niggers." His former master graciously allowed male slaves to leave his property with a wagon and a team of horses after emancipation. Columbus's father accepted the offer and left the plantation. However, he not only left the plantation, but he also left his family. Columbus said his mother remained on the plantation with her children and worked for their former owner for fifteen years.[8]

This indicates that blacks who chose to remain on or near the plantations posed little threat to what white Texans perceived to be the normal social order where blacks were subordinate to whites. However, those who dared venture away from the plantation after emancipation presented a greater threat to white supremacy by exercising perhaps the basic tenet of their new constitutional rights: the freedom to make their own decisions. For example, Susan Ross remembered the excitement expressed by her family when they were told of their freedom. She especially remembered the reaction of her brother. She said that he "whoop, run and jump a high fence and told mammy goodbye. Den he grab me up and hug and kiss me and say, 'brother gone, don't 'spect you ever see me no more.' I don't know where he go, but I never did se him 'gain." Ross also stated that she and the rest of her family left the plantation a short time after her brother.[9] Even though her family was now free it was never the same again as her brother made a decision for his own life for perhaps the first time. Such independent thought and action was surely a threat to white supremacy in the state.

In Texas, members of the black community soon became victims of terroristic violence. For example, Galveston's George T. Ruby, perhaps the most influential black leader of the Reconstruction era, was nearly beaten to death while trying to establish a school for blacks.[10] While Ruby served as a model for future black politicians, political power within the black population in Reconstruction Texas was more an illusion than a reality. Similar to other Southerners, ex-Confederates and Conservative Democrats in Texas perceived that black political influence derived from southern scalawags and northern carpetbaggers instead of originating from the political acumen of the freedmen.[11] As such, blacks as well as their white allies became the victims of violence and terror.

The veil of violence and terror that covered the black community during the Reconstruction era was generally rooted in white supremacy. In part, white Texans adhered to the idea of white supremacy because they feared black equality would result from the apparent coalition forged between blacks, Radical Republicans, and federal authorities (for example, Freedmen's Bureau agents and U.S. military personnel). However, evidence suggests that these fears were exaggerated, especially since Republicans and federal authorities were committed to black equality only to the extent that the black vote could be used to punish white Southerners. In return, Republicans established many paternalistic policies and programs designed to aid blacks in the tenuous transformation from slaves to freed people. Official records and oral interviews acknowledged that the brutality exercised against blacks because of their political associations served two purposes. First, brutal acts punished those blacks who dared to exercise their new rights as freed people. Second, brutality stymied the Republican political agenda designed to transform Southern culture away from its antebellum ancestral roots.[12]

White Texans viewed the presence of carpetbaggers and federal agents, especially those assigned to the Freedmen's Bureau, as an occupying force. As such, these federal officials were a constant reminder of the failure of the Confederacy and the humiliation of having outsiders dominate state and local affairs. Whites in Texas were further agitated by the rampant rumors that Republican policies intended to turn southern society upside down by placing blacks in a superior social position over whites. Though these rumors were unfounded, white Texans sought ways, mostly violent, to protect their social standing and the continued enforcement of black servitude.

The Freedmen's Bureau operated in Texas from September 1865 until January 1869. During these three years, the Bureau served as a perfect case study of government-sponsored paternalism. In Texas, as in other southern states, the Bureau's primary responsibility was to aid the former slaves in their transition to freedom. Integral to this responsibility was the restructuring of southern agriculture and the establishment of schools for the children of the former slaves. Regrettably, the fierce opposition to the Bureau's agenda severely minimized their efforts to reconstruct society in Texas during the postwar years. Too many white Texans remained loyal to the fading memory of the failed Confederacy and routinely engaged in acts of terror against Bureau agents and the blacks who benefitted from their initiatives.[13] As a result, by December 1868, the lack of funds and federal support led to the closing of Freedmen's Bureau offices throughout the state and the cessation of all its programs except those involving education.[14]

Even though the educational initiatives enjoyed a modicum of success, federal paternalism nonetheless failed to protect the freedmen from the increasing brutality of vigilante violence. For example, from June 1865 to December 1866, there were over twelve homicides and thirty-nine physical assaults in the Houston, Texas, area alone.[15] Furthermore, Bureau agents reported that black males were sometimes killed because they did not remove their hats when greeting whites, or because they did not move off the sidewalk when a white female approached.[16] Whites also frequently victimized black females for various social offenses. For example, one black woman was stripped of her clothes and given 200 lashes with leather strap because she supposedly made insulting noises when a white female passed her on the street, while during a separate incident, a woman, who was pregnant at the time of her assault, reported receiving 150 blows from the cane of her attacker for no apparent reason. One couple, a man and his wife, were tied, beaten, and kicked because their sons left the plantation without permission. Unfortunately, Bureau agents were often unable to prosecute offenders. [17]

As a way of preserving what they believed was their diminishing respect and social status, white vigilantes sometimes publicly bragged about murdering blacks, including a number of blacks who worked for the Freedmen's Bureau. Thus, they exhibited an arrogance derived from the belief that whites would most likely never be punished for any offense against blacks. These attacks were clearly designed to intimidate other blacks from supporting any federal initiative or policy.[18]

Many blacks also felt caught in the middle of the ongoing conflict between ex-Confederates and Republicans. A few blacks even believed that leaders of the Republican Party were guilty of malevolent, or perhaps misguided, acts themselves. When interviewed as part of Texas' Slave Narratives project, Will Adams candidly stated that it was the relationship between blacks and the Republican Party that led to the rampant brutality against the former slaves. He remembered it was the carpetbaggers and Republicans that encouraged blacks to stand up against the racism of the postwar years. However, Adams did not believe the motives of the Republicans were in the best interest of blacks or the establishment of social equality. He believed Northerners encouraged blacks to "sass the white folks what done fed them," and used their newfound political suffrage as a means of degrading and humiliating white Southerners.[19]

Not all of the interviewees agreed with Will Adams. Some of the former slaves interviewed during the Great Depression placed blame for the violence squarely at the feet of white Southerners. Several of the WPA interviews indicated that brutality was used as a means to control those blacks who dared agitate for their rights. Throughout the Slave

Illustration 11. Will Adams. (Courtesy of Library of Congress)

Narratives, blacks commented that whites warned local freedpeople that any noncompliant behavior would ultimately result in violence from either individuals or groups. Born into slavery in Georgia, Pauline Grice, for example, remembered that her family decided to remain with their former owner after emancipation, and he cautioned them to stay away from those who were causing "trouble." She also said that she believed some hate groups only "bothered" those blacks considered troublemakers by whites. Grice said, "Massa say not to mix with dat crowd what lose de head, jus' stay to home and work. Some dem niggers on other plantations ain't keep de head and dey gits whipped and some gits kilt, but us does what massa say and has no trouble with dem Klux."[20]

Likewise, John Crawford agreed with Grice in that hate groups operating in Texas and throughout the South typically targeted only those blacks who tried to defiantly shed the image of the compliant slave. He also acknowledged that since many of the newly freed slaves openly disobeyed existing social norms they especially became the object of white retaliation. Crawford remembered, "When dey gits free, dey gits wild.

Illustration 12. Pauline Grice. (Courtesy of Library of Congress)

Dey won't work or do nothing and thinks they don't have to. We didn't have no trouble 'cause we stays on de farm and works and don't have no truck with dem wild niggers."[21]

One hate group in particular, the Ku Klux Klan (KKK), became a fierce enforcer of southern values, particularly those that required the complete subordination of blacks. Organized in Tennessee shortly after the conclusion of the Civil War, the group was not initially concerned with the actions of the newly freed slaves, but in continuing the camaraderie of Confederate soldiers formed during the Civil War.[22] However, the appearance of outsiders wielding political power, while simultaneously manipulating blacks into defying long-established racial customs of southern civility, soon led the Ku Klux Klan to become so-called defenders of the proper God-sanctioned order of civilization, in other words, the complete subjugation of blacks to white authority.[23]

Numerous former slaves remembered how members of the KKK sought to physically intimidate blacks. Dressed in attire meant to elicit fear by reinforcing the supposed superstitious beliefs held in the black community of ghosts, Klansmen felt little restraint in physically brutalizing any black found in their sights. William Hamilton recalled that it was common for members of the KKK to appear at night and randomly murder blacks without fear of any reprisals. He said, "It am allus after dark when dey comes to the house and catches the men whups him for nuttin. Dey has de power and it am done for to show dey has de power."[24]

Andy Anderson's recollection of the KKK was also vivid in that he remembered how its members were a visible presence in the Texas countryside and how they would punish any black whom they perceived to be acting inappropriately. Sadly, he said blacks were already accustomed to such social controls since bands of whites patrolled the same areas before emancipation, maintaining control over the movements of slaves. As a result, Anderson believed there was little change in the violence committed against blacks as a result of emancipation. However, he did recall how the pre-emancipation support for "patter rollers" became explicit and obvious after blacks were granted their freedom. Anderson commented, "Den surrender am 'nounced and massa tells us we's free. What dat takes place, it am 'bout one hour by sun. I says to myself, 'I won't be here long.' But I's not realize what I's in for till after I's started, but I couldn't turn back." Anderson continued, "For dat means de whippin' or danger from de patter rollers. Dere I was and I kep' on gwine. No nigger an supposed to be off massa's place without de pass, so I travels at night and hides durin' de daylight."[25]

Anderson's memories of those first moments of freedom indicate how difficult it was for blacks to rid their minds of their antebellum conditioning. The Emancipation Proclamation physically freed black slaves, but the generations of emotional conditioning and servile way of thinking were still evident decades after black slaves gained their freedom. There is no accurate way to determine if, or how many, bands of whites were still stopping blacks throughout the old Confederate states and asking for their passes in the years following the war. However, Ellen Betts, enslaved in Louisiana but arrived in Texas after the end of the war, assured her interviewer that the patrol did indeed continued to exist during the Reconstruction-era. As a consequence, Betts indicated that she feared traveling too far from home.[26] Likewise, Anderson also recognized the dangers of moving about the Texas landscape in the years following the war. After making the decision to move away from his former master and the life he knew as a slave, Anderson survived by hiding in the woods during the day and traveling only at night.[27]

While Anderson found the cover of night a safer time to move about, other freedpeople feared the nightfall. Even though she and her family remained on their former owner's land, Scott Hooper remembered that it was at night when the KKK would most likely appear. She recalled how her former owner agreed to let them work as sharecroppers and that her family might have even remained there indefinitely if it were not for the viciousness of the KKK in Shelby County, Texas, after emancipation. Hooper said, "When surrender come mass calls all us in de yard and makes de talk. He tells us we's free and am awful sorry and show great worriment. He say he hate to part with us and us been good to him, but it am de law. He say us can stay and work de land on shares, but mostest left. Course, mamy go to Massa Hooper's place to pappy and he rents land from Massa Hooper and us live there seven years and might yet, but dem Klu Klux causes so much troublement. All us niggers 'fraid to sleep in de house and goes to de woods at night."[28]

Like Hooper, Cato Carter also remembered fearing the night as he said bands of whites, "was allus skullduggering 'round at night." Carter said he carried a gun to protect his house and family, but their best defense against violent reprisals was to pretend they were not at home after sunset. He commented that "We didn't use torches any more when we went 'round at night, 'cause we was afeared. We put out all the fires 'round the house at nighttime."[29]

While the perceived coalition of blacks and Republicans leading to vicious acts designed to socially control blacks was a foundation of white supremacy, another foundation was the control of the new black electorate. Many of those participating in Texas' Slave Narratives recalled how blacks were frequently discouraged from exercising perhaps the most cherished of our American freedoms—the right to vote. Though they encouraged blacks to exercise this right, Republicans were often unable to prevent the torture and murders of blacks who attempted to go the polls. Members of the Klan and other similar terrorist groups routinely disrupted Republican meetings, terrorized black potential voters, and threatened anyone involved in organizing the black electorate.[30] Former slaves Will Adams, Eli Davison, Tom Holland, James W. Smith, and Agatha Babino all remembered how blacks were often brutalized for attempting to participate in the electoral processes.

Adams indicated that he was well aware of the activities of those who committed acts of violence against blacks and believed it was a result of the animosities toward the newly arrived carpetbaggers who were encouraging blacks to vote in local elections. He further stated that, "I 'members when the Ku Klux business starts up. Smart niggers caused that. The carpet-baggers ruint the niggers and the white men couldn't do a thing with them, so they got up the Ku Klux and stirs up the world. Them carpet-baggers come 'round larnin' niggers to sass the white folks what done fed them." He continued to disparage Northerners in Texas when he said, "Them carpet-baggers starts all the trouble at 'lections in Reconstruction. Niggers didn't know anythin' 'bout politics."[31]

Davison and Holland both said the "Klu Kluxers" would routinely be present at the voting polls on election days and openly intimidate blacks. In fact, Holland recalled how members of the KKK had the audacity to murder blacks in front of witnesses. He said, "they'd ride up by a Negro and shoot him jus' like a wild hawg and never a word said or done 'bout it."[32]

Likewise, Smith and Babino recalled how members of the KKK oftentimes physically intimidated those freedmen who attempted to politically organize others and who petitioned the Republicans to protect their civil liberties. Smith said there were occasions when there were federal troops stationed near the voting polls, providing some semblance of security for black voters. Unfortunately, such appearances merely supported the illusion that Republicans could protect the freedpeople. In reality, leaders in the Republican Party could not guarantee the safety of black Texans. As a result, ex-Confederates and conservative Democrats continued to victimize the black community. Smith shared with his interviewer that "Plenty gits whipped round our place and some what wasn't 'titled to it."[33]

Born into slavery in Louisiana, Babino was very forthright in claiming that the KKK discouraged the freedmen from voting and from specifically supporting the Republican Party during Reconstruction. Babino frankly stated, "De Ku Klux kill niggers. Dey come to take my uncle. He open de door. Dey don't take him but tell him to vote Democrat next day or dey will. Dey kilt some niggers what wouldn't vote Democrat. Dey kill my old uncle Davis. He won't vote Democrat. Dey shoot him. Den dey stand him up and let him fall down. Dey tie him by de feet. Dey drag him through de brush. Dey dare his wife to cry."[34]

Babino's recollections not only support the idea that much of the post-Civil War violence involved politics, but that many of the newly freed slaves did not feel safe in their own homes. William Hamilton further stated that members of the KKK would frequently attack at night and drag individuals out of their homes and then brutalize them, thus reinforcing the idea that fear was associated with sundown. Furthermore, he said, "No one knowed when de Klux comin'. All a-sudden up dey gallops on hosses, all covered with hoods, and bust right into de house." Such attacks were so pervasive that Hamilton indicated that it was his responsibility to keep a "look-out" and alert other family members of the impending arrival of Klan members. "I'd hear dem comin' when dey hit de lane and I'd holler, 'De Klux am comin'.' It was my job, after dark, listenin' for dem Klux, den I gits under de bed."[35] Continuing, Hamilton was blunt in his assessment that blacks had little official recourse in protecting themselves, their family members, or their property. However, he did recall an instance when an individual succeeded in defending herself. Unfortunately, this resulted in increased visits by Klan members.

> Why they comes so many times round dere, am 'cause de second time dey comes, Jane Bensom am dere. Jane am lots of woman, wide as de door and tall, and weighs 'bout three hunder pounds. I calls, "Here comes de Klux." And makes for under de bed. There am embers in de fireplace and she fills a pail with dem and when de Klux busts in de door she lets dem have de embers in de face, and den out de back door she goes. Two of dem am burnt purty bad. De nex' night back dey comes and asks where jane am. She 'long to Massa John Ditto and am so big everybody knows her, but de niggers won't tell on her. She leaves de country fin'ly, but dey comes lookin' for her every night for two months.[36]

Even though the woman in Hamilton's story experienced a momentary victory in defending herself and her home, in the long run the Klansmen succeeded in displacing her from that home and her family. Everyone was aware that her life was in danger because of her actions and she ultimately made the decision to flee.

During slavery, black families were often ripped apart because of the auction block. Having survived that, black families were still nonetheless vulnerable because of violence. The heroine in Hamilton's story fled because members of the Ku Klux Klan relentlessly pursued her for two months. However, there were instances when whites forced blacks out of their homes and off lands that they had legally purchased. In these cases, the motivations of whites were simple: they wanted the property for themselves.[37]

John Moore, who came to Texas in 1876 from Louisiana, bluntly stated that if members of the KKK wanted the homes and lands of former slaves, it was in the best interest of those individual to simply pack up their families and their belongings and move . . . quickly. "I heared lots about de Ku Klux. Sometimes dey want a nigger's place and dey put up a notice he better sell out and leave. Iffen he go see a lawyer, de lawyer wouldn' take de case, 'cause mos' dem in with de Klux. He tell de nigger he better sell."[38]

Moore's memories illustrate well that terrorist organizations such as the Klan often sought to keep their identities and nighttime activities hidden from blacks by wearing costumes and masks. Moore implied that many white men in positions of authority were most likely members of local terrorist groups, or at the very least, supportive of their murderous activities. Nonetheless, despite attempting to keep their identity a secret, the freedmen often knew the men who hid behind the costumes and mask. For example, Lorenza Ezell stated that "De funny thing, I knowed all dem Klu Klux. Spite dey sheets and things, I knowed dey voices and dey saddle hosses."[39]

Understanding that the KKK originally used robes and disguises to exploit the perceived superstitious nature of blacks, it is unclear from the oral narratives if their members were really attempting to hide their identities at all. As illustrated, many conducted their reign of terror without fear of official reprisals from federal authorities in Texas and throughout the rest of the old Confederacy.

While the implicit cause of Reconstruction violence was the preservation of white supremacy, from the freedmen's point of view, the violence that occurred was a constant reminder of their previous status as slaves. Sadly, the mind-set that enslaved them during the antebellum years continued to dictate how they would conduct themselves for the rest of their lives. Lu Perkins and Bud Jones were cautious in their interviews not to blame anyone for the violence they witnessed. After all the years that had past, they still feared reprisal. Unlike Will Adams, who candidly said any Reconstruction violence was a result of blacks challenging the authority of southern whites buoyed by what he now believed were false Republican promises of lawful equality, Perkins and Jones merely shared their memories of violence in those first fateful moments of freedom. However, both individuals still suffered from the psychological effects of living in an age when they were never secure in their persons, let alone their own homes; an age when they could be murdered, or witness the murder of a loved one, and be forced to accept that the perpetrators would most likely never be brought to trial, let alone convicted. Perkins said she was grateful to have survived the violence of the Klan and prayed for "a wall of the Lord 'round me so they couldn't get at me. The turrible things they did ain't worth tellin'. I wouldn't want to make no recollection of them."[40] Likewise, Jones also indicated during his interview that he still remembered seeing blacks hanging from trees, and said, "The Ku Klux was strong in the country. I seen niggers hanging on trees and they cut their ears off."[41]

The end of slavery was supposed to be the catalyst for a new America, one in which racism and violence would eventually fade from the national consciousness. Not only did the racism of the antebellum years remain a constant in the South, it was strengthened by the irrational belief that the Republican Party was going to subjugate white Southerners to black rule. White Southerners often argued that the South was changed forever following the war, and in many ways they were right: the South had entered a period of change and where there was uncertainty many whites clung to the belief of white supremacy and black inferiority.

However, for most of the former slaves in Texas, and throughout the former Confederate states, freedom seemed like a leap into a dark and unfamiliar abyss. In many regards, their first experiences with freedom did not seem very different from their antebellum experiences in slavery, especially in regards to the forced subjugation of blacks to whites. Upon learning of their emancipation many former slaves remembered the exuberance and hopefulness that they would finally be recognized as free Americans with the same rights and opportunities as any other group in the United States.

Sadly, for too many of the freedmen, those initial feelings of excitement gave way to the realization that emancipation would not end the torture and violence that had suppressed them and their ancestors since the earliest history of the United States. Acts of violence, like murder, rape, and robbery, sadly became commonplace; furthermore, the lynching of black men seared forever into the national consciousness the image of "strange fruit" hanging from trees throughout Texas and the South.[42] In freedom's abyss such violence and oppression were commonplace for nearly a century. Only after the Civil Rights Movement of the 1960s did blacks in Texas, as well as the rest of the South, emerge from freedom's chasm to enjoy the first true taste of liberty.

ENDNOTES

1. Robin D. G. Kelley and Earl Lewis, *To Make Our Own World Anew: A History of African Americans* (New York: Oxford University Press, 2000), 236; Randolph B. Campbell, *An Empire for Slavery: The Peculiar Institution in Texas, 1821–1865* (Baton Rouge: Louisiana State University Press, 1989), 231, 233.

2. Alwyn Barr, "Change and Continuity in Texas during the Civil War and Reconstruction," in *Texas Heritage* (Arlington Heights, IL: Harlan Davidson, 1992), 97.

3. Cato Carter, *Slave Narratives*, The Center for American History, The University of Texas at Austin, hereafter cited as CAHUT-Austin.

4. J. W. Terrell, *Slave Narratives*, CAHUT-Austin.

5. Susan Merritt, *Slave Narratives*, CAHUT-Austin.

6. Federal Writer's Program, "The Negro in Texas," Box 4H350, CAHUT-Austin.

7. Emma Watson, *Slave Narratives*, CAHUT-Austin.

8. Andrew Columbus, *Slave Narratives*, CAHUT-Austin.

9. Susan Ross, *Slave Narratives*, CAHUT-Austin.

10. Barry Crouch, "Self-Determination and Local Black Leaders in Texas," *Phylon* 39, no. 4 (1978): 346.

11. James Smallwood, *Time of Hope, Time of Despair: Black Texans During the Reconstruction* (Port Washington, NY: Kennikat Press, 1981); Merline Pitre, *Through Many Dangers, Toils and Snares: The Black Leadership of Texas, 1868–1900* (Austin: Eakin Press, 1985).

12. Smallwood, *Time of Hope, Time of Despair*; Pitre, *Through Many Dangers, Toils and Snares*.

13. William Richter, *Overreached on All Sides: The Freedmen's Bureau Administrators in Texas, 1865–1868* (College Station: Texas A&M University Press, 1991); Barry Crouch, *The Freedmen's Bureau and Black Texans* (Austin: University of Texas Press, 1999). Richter's findings indicate that the bureaucratic nature of the Freedmen's Bureau

kept it from making real or significant contributions to Texas' postwar society. He also found that those Texans who remained loyal to the Confederate cause were the ones responsible for terrorizing blacks, Bureau agents, and Union army soldiers.

14. Bureau of Refugees, Freedmen and Abandoned Lands, 1865–1869, National Archives M821, roll 32, Miscellaneous Records Relating to Murders and other Criminal Offenses Committed in Texas 1865–1868; James Johnson, *Slave Narratives*, CAHUT-Austin. In his narrative, James Johnson recalled how local whites disapproved of the education programs established by the Freedmen's Bureau and would often harass the white northern teachers for helping educate blacks.

15. Bureau of Refugees, Freedmen and Abandoned Lands, 1865–1869, National Archives M821, roll 32, Miscellaneous Records Relating to Murders and other Criminal Offenses Committed in Texas 1865–1868.

16. Ibid.

17. Ibid.; Letter from ME Davis to HA Ellis, October 13, 1866, Bureau of Refugees, Freedmen and Abandoned Lands, 1865–1869, National Archives M821, roll 32.

18. Letter from L. Shoemaker to E. M. Pease, June 23, 1868, Bureau of Refugees, Freedmen and Abandoned Lands, 1865–1869, National Archives M821, roll 32.

19. Will Adams, *Slave Narratives*, CAHUT-Austin.

20. Pauline Grice, *Slave Narratives*, CAHUT-Austin.

21. John Crawford, *Slave Narratives*, CAHUT-Austin. Also see the narratives of Betty Bormer and Philles Thomas.

22. Gladys Marie Fry, *Night Riders in Black Folk History* (Chapel Hill: University of North Carolina Press, 2000), 110.

23. Ibid., 146.

24. William Hamilton, *Slave Narratives*, CAHUT-Austin.

25. Andy Anderson, *Slave Narratives*, CAHUT-Austin.

26. Ellen Betts, *Slave Narratives*, CAHUT-Austin.

27. Andy Anderson, *Slave Narratives*, CAHUT-Austin.

28. Scott Hooper, *Slave Narratives*, CAHUT-Austin.

29. Cato Carter, *Slave Narratives*, CAHUT-Austin.

30. Elliott J. Gorn, "Black Spirits: The Ghostlore of Afro American Slaves," *American Quarterly* 36 (1984): 551.

31. Will Adams, *Slave Narratives*, CAHUT-Austin.

32. Eli Davison, *Slave Narratives*, CAHUT-Austin; Tom Holland, *Slave Narratives*, CAHUT-Austin.

33. James W. Smith, *Slave Narratives*, CAHUT-Austin.

34. Agatha Babino, *Slave Narratives*, CAHUT-Austin.

35. William Hamilton, *Slave Narratives*, CAHUT-Austin.

36. Ibid.

37. Kenneth Stampp, *The Era of Reconstruction, 1865–1877* (New York: Vantage Books, 1965), 199–201; John Hope Franklin and Alfred Moss, Jr., *From Slavery to Freedom* (New York: Knopf, 2000), 275.

38. John Moore, *Slave Narratives*, CAHUT-Austin.

39. Lorenza Ezell, *Slave Narratives*, CAHUT-Austin.

40. Lu Perkins, *Slave Narratives*, CAHUT-Austin.

41. Bud Jones, *Slave Narratives*, CAHUT-Austin.

42. "Strange Fruit" was recorded by famed blues singer Billie Holliday and describes the lynching of two black men in Marion, Indiana. The following are the lyrics: Southern trees bear strange fruit/Blood on the leaves/Blood at the root/Black bodies swinging in the southern breeze/ Strange fruit hanging from the poplar trees/Pastoral scene of the gallant south/The bulging eyes and the twisted mouth/The scent of magnolia sweet and fresh/Then the sudden smell of burning flesh/Here is a fruit for the crows to pluck/for the rain to gather/for the wind to suck/for the sun to rot/for the tree to drop/Here is a strange and bitter crop.

CHAPTER 11

Foreigners in Their Native Land: The Violent Struggle between Anglos and Tejanos for Land Titles in South Texas during Reconstruction

by

Andrés Tijerina

"We were really a vigilante committee." In these words, a raider admitted that though they acted under the color of law as "rangers" or "Minutemen Militia," scores of Anglo-Texan vigilantes in the 1870s raided Tejano homes and ranches, killing, lynching, and driving them out of Texas. The Tejanos who survived fled sometimes to Mexico, sometimes to neighboring counties, but always out of prime lands coveted by Anglo ranchers, land speculators, and squatters. The raids occurred in different parts of the state and varied according to circumstances, but the attacks had a few basic commonalities: The raiders often acted in cooperation with lawmen and used terror tactics to acquire Tejano lands. As such, the violence waged against the Tejanos represented a continuation of a struggle that predated the Civil War by more than twenty-five years—a dispute between Hispanics and Anglos over land titles in Texas.

The story of Tejanos during the Reconstruction era is a tale of continued violence that was a pervasive and constant phenomenon beginning in 1836, when Anglo-Americans seized control of Texas government. Despite the large population of Tejanos living in Texas, Anglo control of the state was expanded after the United States defeated Mexico in the U.S.-Mexico War of 1846–1848. The traumatic manner in which Mexican Texans were forced to become U.S. citizens through conquest created inequalities between them and Anglos. For the next three decades and beyond, Tejanos endured economic, social, legal, and political hardships. They were denied access to law enforcement, economic power, and government protection from their assailants. Thus, racial violence and discriminatory treatment became a central characteristic and a constant thread in the relationship between Mexican Americans and Anglo-Americans especially during the Reconstruction era. Anglo-Americans consistently used their advantages to disenfranchise Hispanics, steal their lands, exploit their labors, and destroy their cultural heritage. Just as Anglo Texans used violence to assert their political dominance over blacks and Radical Republicans in the state government, their objective vis-à -vis Tejanos was clearly directed at ethnic cleansing and the forced acquisition of valuable Tejano land grants.

This chapter examines a few of the violent episodes that Tejanos experienced during the Reconstruction era in Texas. This brief narrative does not pretend to provide a broad history of the Tejano community, for Tejanos were engaged in major demographic changes, migratory shifts, commercial expansion, and land acquisition from El Paso to Houston during this same time. Those constructive trends are not described herein, though they do provide a major argument for a rebounding agency of Tejanos toward the turn of the century. The major thesis of this chapter is that Anglos accelerated their efforts to steal vast landholdings from Tejanos during the Reconstruction years, a process that began shortly after the conclusion of the Texas Revolution. To understand this point, it is necessary to examine briefly the history of the conflict between Anglos and Tejanos between 1836 and 1866.

Tejanos founded Texas under a European style of government. They had initially settled the territories north of the Rio Grande under the flag of Spain. Later, following independence from Spain, they came to the region as Mexican citizens. Throughout the Spanish and Mexican eras, Tejanos acquired land not so much for financial gain, but rather as a way of providing their families a title to legitimacy. In other words, land was a symbol of wealth and power—the more land one owned, the more power and wealth they possessed. During the latter nineteenth century, transfer of Tejano titles to Anglos occurred with such frequency that Tejanos soon lost possession of the bulk of their original land grants. Not surprisingly, the loss of their ancestral lands meant the loss of their political, social, and economic influence in Texas.

Historians have debated the manner in which Tejanos were dispossessed of their lands. Some early historians like Walter Prescott Webb, Paul S. Taylor, and Hobart Huson comment that Tejano lands and cattle were stolen.[1] They cited the racism of incoming Anglo-Americans after the Texas Revolution as a major factor contributing to the ill treatment of Hispanic Texans. Indeed, the history of that period caused the political decline of Tejanos. Even those Tejanos who had fought for Texas Independence from Mexico in 1836 were subjected to harassment. Juan N. Seguin, one of the most celebrated battle heroes of the Texas Revolution, found himself a "foreigner in [his] native land." With a hundred other Bexareños (residents of San Antonio), Seguin hid on his ranch, before he was eventually driven out of Texas altogether. In addition, Anglos robbed and plundered the town of Goliad in 1836, forcing many Tejano families out of the region. In another incident, Anglos arrested Fernando de Leon of Victoria, who had contributed generously to the Texas forces, in 1837, ostensibly for conspiring with the enemies of Texas who desired to reverse the outcome of the Texas Revolution. The citizens of Nacogdoches had a similar experience when Tejano families were robbed of their livestock, their grain, and their personal belongings. Furthermore, Anglo troops conducted what was called "a piratical and predatory war."

As Tejano leaders were forced to defend themselves against Anglo attacks, Hispanic families began to leave Texas. Hundreds of Bexareño families went into hiding on their ranches, before finally leaving Texas and moving to the northern state of Coahuila in Mexico. At the same time, Tejanos living near Nacogdoches attempted to protect their families by fleeing to Louisiana. Likewise, most of the Goliad families fled across the Rio Grande into Tamaulipas and Nuevo Leon, while others fled to Louisiana. Contemporaries often described Goliad as being in a "virtual state of abandonment." As the 1840s progressed, Anglo immigrants continued to trespass on Tejano lands, and they continued to take their ranches and livestock, stripping the Hispanic population of its livelihood, especially those living in the vicinity of Bexar, Goliad, and Nacogdoches. By 1845, for example, forty of the forty-five Goliad Tejano ranches had passed into Anglo hands for a pittance of their value.[2] While many of these émigré Tejanos returned to reclaim their lands during the 1840s, others did not.

After the U.S.-Mexico War, the Treaty of Guadalupe Hidalgo in 1848 incorporated the trans-Nueces region to Texas, and ushered in another wave of land transfers. Historians like David Montejano in his award-winning book, *Anglos and Mexicans in the Making of Texas*, suggest that a great number of the Tejano lands were transferred during this period and throughout the Civil War and Reconstruction. South Texas counties like Nueces, Kleberg, Cameron, and Hidalgo experienced a major pattern of Tejano land dispossession, which Montejano has characterized as one-way and irreversible. That is, the land exchange went from Tejano possession into Anglo hands, and rarely from Anglos to Tejanos. While

Anglos did buy and sell among themselves, Tejanos rarely bought land from either Anglo or Tejano sellers. In addition, Walter Prescott Webb's book, *The Texas Rangers*, which can hardly be accused of being pro-Mexican, also stated that as Tejano families fled the turmoil of the 1860s and 1870s and that many of them lost their lands to "fictitious suits," sheriff's auctions, and dubious transfers of title. During the Reconstruction years, Anglo newcomers like Stephen Powers, Charles Stillman, Richard King, and Mifflin Kenedy, to use Webb's expression, "bamboozled" the Mexicans in South Texas. Webb added, "The old landholding Mexican families found their titles in jeopardy and if they did not lose in the courts they lost to their American lawyers." But Montejano's study has argued that Tejano land dispossession was directly related to economic, rather than racial, motives. Furthermore, Montejano asserts that the wealthy Anglo ranchers like Richard King were "color blind" regarding their land deals, purchasing property from both Anglos as well as from Tejanos. After the Civil War, Tejanos became increasingly isolated from Anglo sources of capital as the Texas economic infrastructure tended to favor white citizens over minorities toward the end of the nineteenth century. Thus, in "The Play of the Market," Montejano maintained that Tejanos generally sold their land in depressed economic times for lower prices. Significantly, Montejano draws a strong correlation between the years of drought and the increased sales of Tejano lands to white South Texas barons, especially to well-capitalized operations like those of King and Kenedy.[3]

Throughout Reconstruction, racism played a larger role in the dispossession of Tejano lands. Bigotry was characteristic of many newly arriving Anglo-Americans, particularly those who came from other southern states. Southerners, who possessed a deep-seated prejudice against people of color, used legal and extralegal means to terrorize "the Mexicans of the Rio Grande Valley." In his award-winning book, *The White Scourge*, Neil Foley provides a wealth of literature to affirm conclusively that "with few exceptions, Anglo Texan constructions of whiteness rarely included people of Mexican descent. . . . When Anglo Texans married Mexicans, they often juggled the nomenclature to whiten their spouses by calling them Spanish Americans or simply Spanish." And in the *Southwestern Historical Quarterly*, distinguished southern historian Walter L. Buenger states that "Texans escaped from the defeated, isolated, impoverished, brutally bigoted South" to segregate Tejanos, and to recreate a history of the Alamo and Texas with themselves at the crest of society. The price for this racist construct, according to Buenger, was to sink Texas history "to the level of comic books." But the real price of racism in Texas has been much more than a few racial slurs and a distorted history. The price for Tejanos, after the Civil War, has been in the dispossession of their lands along with their legitimate place in Texas history.[4]

As Abel Rubio indicated in his book title, the dispossession of his family's land was "The Stolen Heritage." Racial prejudice itself may not be germane to the present study, but when a well-defined sense of racial superiority was directed specifically to justifying land theft, it is no longer simply a matter of prejudice. Historian Paul S. Taylor described one method in the Anglo-Texan use of terror and intimidation as a subterfuge to legitimize land theft. He states, "Among the traditions still whispered among Mexicans and Americans in the entire region between the Nueces and lower Rio Grande are the stories that in one way or another—by chicane, by creating alarm for their personal safety, or by even stronger measures—many of the Mexican property owners were 'run out' of the country and their lands obtained cheaply." This was explicitly articulated during the Texas Revolution when Edward Dwyer, an Irish merchant in San Antonio, encouraged Texas Army Gen. Thomas Jefferson Green to expedite the army into Bexar. Stating that "the people [of San Antonio de Bexar] . . . are not sufficiently scared to make an advantigius [*sic*] sale of their Lands. In case two or three hundred of our troops should be stationed there, I have no doubt but a man could make some good speculations with Gold and Silver. Bank notes will not do to purchase Land from Mexicans," Dwyer was clearly promoting what historian Paul S. Taylor calls "chicane" to "run out" Tejanos specifically to obtain their lands cheaply. John Linn of Victoria described a similar situation during the same period: "Fernando de Leon was subsequently persecuted by the presentation of unjust claims against him, and, owing to the prejudice then existing against the Mexicans, many illegal and unfair judgments were rendered against him. Thus was a princely landed estate dissipated, and its owner died in comparative poverty." This was verified by historian Carolina Castillo Crimm who used the Victoria land abstracts to reveal that de Leon was able to reclaim 50,000 acres upon his return from Louisiana, but that he lost 58,000 acres to those judgments. During the U.S.-Mexico War, a U.S. Army officer, Gen. William North, boasted "our Anglo-Saxon race [have] been land stealers from time immemorial, and why shouldn't they [be]?" In this regard, racism was not simply an emotion, but was often used as a motive and a justification for land theft. Thus, the forced acquisition of Tejano lands during Reconstruction simply reflected the racist rationale already in place after the Texas Revolution and the Civil War.[5]

Another method used to drive Tejanos off their lands was land squatting by migrant Anglos who used fictitious lawsuits with the rationale that Tejanos were simply Mexicans who had no right to Texas land. The squatters used persistent threats and brutal atrocities against many of the Tejano families. One specific case in 1843 was recorded in Karnes County, where the ranches on the Spanish land grant of Carlos Martinez were raided. According to the *The Kennedy Times*, the Tejano extended families on the ranches were attacked by "companies of white people, who came to the rancho from the Guadalupe and Colorado rivers, and killed the people at the rancho and stole their stock." The predatory warfare reportedly continued against the surviving family members until the Reconstruction period. Descendants of Martinez were able to win a court case held in Helena in 1871, divesting the "white settlers on the Carlos Martinez grant." The court gave title of fifteen leagues back to the descendants, and declared all of the Anglo squatter claims to be annulled. The Martinez heirs eventually moved out of the county, selling the land for fifty cents an acre. Another murder on the nearby Becerra land grant also drove the Tejano families off their lands. Juan Elias Lozano, a Confederate veteran, and his wife, Trinidad, were the last of the de la Garza heirs living on the Becerra grant when Juan Elias was ambushed and shot in the back in Refugio in 1877. Trinidad, now a widow, was forced to abandon the ranch when mounted Anglo riders repeatedly threatened her as well. Antonio de la Garza and his wife, Ponposa, had already abandoned the Rancho Alamito on the same Becerra grant in Refugio County. They fled to Goliad after their livestock had been killed and their barns burned by mounted Anglo marauders who gave Antonio a twenty-four-hour ultimatum. Ponposa's brother, Gregorio Esparza Bontan, had been lynched earlier by an Anglo mounted mob who dragged his body through the streets of Refugio. Antonio and Ponposa de la Garza survived the threats, but they lost their relatives, and they lost their legitimate land heritage forever. A rare example of the personal terror directed at Tejano widows and their surviving families is reflected in the following letter of testimonial left by Paula Lozano de Martinez, niece of Trinidad and the murdered Juan Elias Lozano.

Letter Date of 1955

I, Paula L. Martinez, remember that an American man named Jack Gaines used to come from a nearby town 2 or 3 times he came to tell my aunt to vacate the ranch because the land was not theirs. He would not dismount; he would just sit on his horse

> outside the fence and tell my aunt that they had already killed Uncle Elias Lozano and that my aunt should leave the ranch in the year 1878. That was when they told her to leave the ranch because it was not theirs and she had two nephews about 18 years old to help her on the ranch, and they had great fear because at night they could hear voices talking around the house and they had great fear because they could hear them talking at night around the Ranch and once they saw them mounted on horseback. And they would go sleep out in the brush for fear that they were going to be killed. And because the ranch was in a very isolated place. This is what I remember because I was born in the year 1871 and I remember where the house was and the distance to the cemetery about 100 yards from the house of my Uncle Elias.[6]

The Reconstruction period in Texas was so violent that government officials and committees at the state and even federal levels were alarmed. Texas Governor E. J. Davis issued a statement to the state legislature on April 19, 1873, deploring the critical state of violence. According to the statistics that he cited for the state, "More murders had been committed in it during three months with a population of little more than 800,000 than in the State of New York excluding the city of New York with more than three million souls."[7]

On the federal level, in 1872 President U. S. Grant responded to complaints of depredations on the Texas frontiers by Indians and Mexicans accused of marauding, capturing citizens or livestock, and damaging property. He sent three commissioners to investigate and submit a formal report on "Depredations on the Frontiers of the State of Texas," commonly referred to as the Robb Report. The commissioners were Thomas P. Robb, F. J. Mead, and Richard H. Savage. Their method of investigation was to go to Texas, and to travel from Point Isabel up the Rio Grande to El Paso, but they received such a volume of complaints and testimony from victims that they did not complete their trek past Rio Grande City. They issued public notices in the newspapers, announcing that they planned to hold fact-finding hearings and sessions between July and October 1872. During these sessions, the committee took the sworn testimony of local citizens regarding the conditions of the frontier. Later, they compiled a government report of their findings. Their report described the vast region of the frontier between the Nueces and the Rio Grande rivers, noting the large ranches of between 10,000 and 200,000 acres with many cattle in "countless" herds. They indicated that most of the cattle frontier was open range as of 1870 with few exceptions such as the ranch of Mifflin Kenedy. And they were alarmed to report that even these large herds were reportedly only a fraction of the size they had been in 1866 "at the close of the war of the rebellion."[8]

The thrust of their report was that the depredations of cattle rustling were primarily committed by armed bands of Mexicans who used the proximity of the Rio Grande and adjoining Mexico to plunder the herds of Texas "rancheros." Exacerbating the problem was the fact that "corrupt officials" of neighboring Mexican cities and states not only condoned the plunder, but openly engaged in support and profit from it. The report continued, "That the action of the local Mexican authorities, has been characterized by duplicity, connivance at fraud, or a complete subserviency [*sic*] to a corrupt military rule, there seems to be little room left for doubt," citing the Mexican government's "inability" to control crime on either bank of the Rio Grande. An extract from the official report quoted cavalry Col. Ranald S. Mackenzie in 1867 summarizing the situation at the end of the Civil War, saying that "Cattle-stealing is practiced to an outrageous extent."[9]

The same type of statistics and testimonies were taken on the murders committed by Mexicans in Texas, to the point that the commissioners generalized with the statement that "the mortality among American officials on the Rio Grande frontier has been alarming," blaming most of the murders on Mexicans. It concluded by stating that "the testimony of all witnesses questioned is unanimous as to the fact of life being unsafe, even within the corporate limits of Brownsville." The commissioners recommended that a force of cavalry be assigned to guard the frontier, and barring that, a large force of trained volunteers. The report took testimony from Thaddeus M. Rhodes, justice of the peace of Hidalgo County, who reported that he had personally pursued Mexican cattle rustlers into Mexico, and Adolphus Glaevecke who reported that he had personally filed his complaints with the Mexican authorities in Matamoros, to no avail. Most of the citizens who were interviewed and who filled grievances against Mexican offenses were Tejano rancheros, such as Severiano Hinojosa, Abbato Longoria, Antonio Tigerina [*sic*], and Pedro Vela, well-known South Texas rancheros.[10]

In an indignant response to the American report, the Republic of Mexico commissioned its own investigation known as *El Informe de la Comisión Pesquisidora* or *Report of the Investigative Committee*. The Mexican Congress sent their four commissioners, Emilio Velasco,

Illustration 13. Col. Ranald S. Mackenzie. (Courtesy of Library of Congress)

Ygnacto Galindo, Antonio Garcia Carrillo, and Augustin Silicio as secretary. They conducted their interviews of 300 witnesses, scanned thousands of pages of newspaper and government reports, and submitted their report in 1873. The Mexican report found that the "complaints of the Texans are groundless" and that their claims of the number of cattle stolen was an "enormous exaggeration." Indeed, the Texans claimed to have "lost much more than they ever could possess." Worse, the actual cattle thefts were often conducted by Texans and "consented by the American authorities."

Of the Anglo-American witnesses who had submitted grievances to the Robb Report, the Mexican *Comisión Pesquisidora* specifically accused Adolfo Glaevecke and Thadeus Rhodes "as cases of peculiar notoriety and because they are so well established by the public voice . . . also because these men hold or have held positions of public trust." The report indicated that Glaevecke was the self-same horse thief that the Robb Report cited as being a Mexican thief. According to witnesses, the *Comisión Pesquisidora* stated, "Glaevecke owns a horse pen on the Texas shore of the river which used to bear the name of Santa Rita but is now called Lineno. On one side of this enclosure was the ford known as Tia Morales. Here the thieves in the employ of Glaevecke congregate and to this pen or enclosure are the animals stolen in Mexico carried driven for the most part across the ford Tia Morales. . . . From here the animals were taken to Palo Alto and in that district the number necessary to complete the drove was furnished and from thence driven into Texas." What was worse, added the *Comisión Pesquisidora*, "He is a juror in the county of Cameron was elected alderman of the municipal corporation of Brownsville in 1866 and reelected in 1873." As for "Thadeus Rhodes commonly known among Mexicans as Teodoro. He is a resident of Rosario in the county of Hidalgo, Texas and under his authority and protection especially in former years a band of robbers dwelt who pillaged the farms of Reynosa and the villages of Nuevo Leon." Rhodes was an Hidalgo County judge, and the *Comisión Pesquisidora* Mexican commissioners lamented that "a judge like Rhodes charged with the carrying out of the laws and the pursuit of criminals are themselves the chief instigators abetting the criminals and enjoying the proceeds of the crime."[11]

The Mexican commissioners indicated that the murders and cattle rustling were only a continuation of the raids by Texas Confederate armies during the Civil War. It was ironic, they said, that the Mexicans were the real victims. Sparing no sympathy for Anglo-Texans, the commissioners stated, "A great number of Texans some of them officers in the Confederate army took large droves of cattle to Matamoros as a market . . . The armed forces of Texas disorderly and insubordinate never hesitated to commit any act of plunder . . . Those who really suffer are Mexican stock owners against whom the greatest indignation would be manifested if they dared to act in like manner. They are really therefore the principal victims and some of them have preferred to abandon Texas."[12]

According to South Texas historian Jerry Thompson, both reports, the Robb Report and the *Comisión Pesquisidora*, were "less than objective in their conclusions." They differed on the reasons and the blame for the violence. No one disputed, however, that both commissions had amassed a great volume of evidence to demonstrate that South Texas was a hostile environment during Reconstruction, and that Tejanos were often the victims of criminal acts.[13] Other investigative reports by the U.S. federal government provided strong testimony on volatility of the Tejano community in Texas during Reconstruction. U.S. Army officers and government officials in Texas testified to the U.S. Congress that "Mexicans" on the U.S. side of the Rio Grande were often victims of not only the Mexicans from across the border, but Americans as well.

One federal government report prepared by the House of Representatives "Special Committee on Texas Frontier Troubles" provided not only evidence on the violence but a primary account of the cultural characteristics of Mexican Americans in 1876. The report cited the 1870 U.S. Census as indicating a population of 27,000 living south of the Nueces River in Texas, with 16,478 being "foreign-born, all but a few hundred being Mexican; white or Americans no more than 3,000." It described their language as Spanish, saying that almost all the Tejanos spoke Spanish and no English, adding that Anglo Texans refused to learn Spanish. "The result is that this people generally have retained their ancient manners, customs, and traditions, and continue their intercourse with the people from whom they sprang, with whom their relations are more intimate than with the people of this State to whom they have become territorially and politically attached." It recorded the complaints of the Anglo courts and officers that Tejanos would not testify against Mexican thieves and robbers, but would simply shrug and say "*quien sabe.*" And with regard to the Tejano character, the report stated, "In justice to our preponderating population of Mexican origin we cheerfully bear testimony that the great majority of them are honest industrious, and laborious people, and they own a greater part of the soil in this section of the State, upon which they graze thousands upon thousands of head of stock—cattle, horses, mules, and sheep, and they suffer very greatly from the operations of the cattle-thieves."[14]

The government report added a review of "Wrongs Perpetrated Against Mexicans." It readily admitted that many wrongs had been "committed against Mexicans by Americans in their individual capacity," but denied that any were done by officials, federal or state. Ninety percent of the population south of the Nueces were voting Tejano citizens, the report conceded, and that political reality alone would make it obvious that a "lean minority can never so oppress a preponderating majority."[15] Another contemporary source strongly implied that Tejanos were not only a law-abiding majority, but that they held an undeniable voting strength. The Brownsville *American Flag* reported in an editorial on August 20, 1856, that Tejanos were good American citizens. It stated that, "Our population is as is well known divided into two classes Americans and Mexicans the latter are unquestionably more exposed to wrong than the former their natural timidity makes them inoffensive and by reason of the difference of language they cannot well understand our laws or fully enjoy their rights. We have heard one of our highest officers state that it would be difficult to find a class of people more obedient to the laws." The editor of the *American Flag* continued, "It is true that among them there are bad characters and these should be severely punished, but this fact at times gives rise to their all being classed in the same category and ill used. We do not address any one in particular our remarks are general. Americans have at times committed offenses which in them have been overlooked but which if committed by Mexicans would have been severely punished." In conclusion, the editor wrote that "promises of all kinds are made to them but scarcely are the promises made when they are broken. An hour before the election they are fast friends, 'Mexicans my very good friends'— an hour after the election they are a 'crowd of greasers.'"[16]

After the Civil War, European and Anglo-American immigrants began to pour deeper into South Texas ranch lands previously conceded to the original Tejano ranch families. Across the state of Texas, Tejanos found themselves pressured into subordinate racial status, but nowhere was the suppression more violent than in the ranch country of South Texas and far West Texas. There, the violence seemed to take on the classic characteristics of twentieth-century ethnic cleansing: raids, mass murders, systematic rape, and a callous dehumanization. In the mid-1870s, three major waves of violence were sparked by incidents that were different in circumstances but similar in objective: to drive Tejanos from strategic lands. Two of these waves were vigilante raids in South Texas and the third was a raid on a group of villages in West Texas. They combined to disintegrate the last major concentrations of large Tejano ranch possessions, while creating some of the strongest Anglo ranch empires in Texas.

The South Texas vigilante raids swept from Victoria down to Refugio and from Corpus Christi down to present-day Raymondville. The Refugio raid in 1874 was ostensibly in reaction to the murder of a prominent Anglo rancher and wife, but local county historian Hobart Huson posited a more realistic explanation for the violence waged against the largest Tejanos landowning families. "A distinct minority" of prominent Tejano families had still held on to their lands since the Texas Revolution and throughout the Civil War. Rafael Aldrete, Carlos and Rafael de la Garza, and Pedro Curbello had survived not only in large ranches, but operated a successful cattle trading company and a profitable river ferry known as Carols Crossing on the San Antonio River. During the Reconstruction period, the Ku Klux Klan was rumored to have been active, but most importantly, the county had organized a vigilante company. The state legislature had authorized the formation of "Minute Men" companies in 1874. But even after the state authorization law had expired, local vigilantes and Regulators rode when called out under the command of stalwart leaders like Henry Scott, Edward Fennessy, and Coon Dunham to persecute "hostile Indians, Mexicans, or other marauding or thieving parties."[17] These were the groups who reported for posse duty when word spread that Thadeus Swift and his wife had been robbed, murdered, and horribly mutilated on June 7, 1874, at their ranch in Refugio County. According to the notes of Refugio County Judge William Louis Rea, "Then began the greatest manhunt that has ever taken place in Refugio County." The judge conceded that "No one knew who the guilty persons were, so practically every Mexican of the laboring class in the surrounding country was regarded as a likely suspect."[18] And just as the ethnicity of the perpetrators was predetermined, so was the identity of the prime suspect—Antonio Moya, the nearest prominent landowning Tejano.

According to John Young, J. Frank Dobie's "Vaquero of the Brush Country," the Refugio County Sheriff Jephtha Williams ordered his posse to apprehend the Moya family patriarch and his two sons, Marcelo and Antonio Moya, saying only "Go get him." There was no warrant, no investigation, and no summons. Twelve Anglo-Texan posse riders approached the Moya ranch house at sunrise. The house was a typical Mexican *jacal* or log cabin with vertical logs and a thatched roof. One rider later recalled, "As our horses clattered up on the hard-baked ground in front of the house, a voice in Spanish asked what we wanted— '*Que quieren*?' "In English, "What do you want?" When a vigilante rider rode up to a porthole in the cabin wall, he was shot and killed, and "the fight was on."[19]

Meanwhile, another posse led by Goliad County Sheriff Phil Fulcrod found the elder Moya working out in a field, and arrested him. When they brought him to the ranch house around 11 a.m., his sons surrendered to the sheriff "under promise of protection." By this time, over 100 armed vigilantes had surrounded the Moya ranch house, and were closing in on the sheriff and his prisoners. The rider's account proceeded as follows:

> Antonio Moyer [Moya] was placed on a horse, Marcelo Moyer and his father were placed in a hack, and thus the three prisoners,

> guarded by Fulcrod and eight or ten deputies, were started for Goliad. A lot us, however, did not propose to put off a punishment that we knew the Mexicans deserved. The guard and prisoners had gone only about three miles when we surrounded them. The guard offered practically no interference, and in the melée that followed Marcelo was shot dead. Old Moyer was wounded and down on the ground. A maddened ranch boy rode his plunging horse over him, at the same time emptying his six-shooter at him without effect. Another man dismounted and cut the Mexican's throat with a butcher knife. Antonio Moyer, who it will be remembered, was on a horse, made an attempt to run but had his arm shot off and was soon dispatched.[20]

Meanwhile, in town, two other Tejanos were nabbed by other vigilantes in the countywide raids and taken to the jail. They were taken out of the jail by a mob, and transported to the Swift ranch house where they were lynched, hanging "from a pole that was fixed over a gate. The house was no longer inhabited, and the bodies swung there, in full view of the public road, for a week before they were cut down."[21]

The aftermath of the Refugio vigilante raid initially was a clean sweep of Tejanos in the fertile prairies of traditional Tejano land grants from Victoria to Beeville. Coon Dunham's Regulators went out on a frenzied rampage, with their avowed purpose being "to make every Mexican who could not give an account of himself either leave the country or take his chances of kicking at Texas soil with nothing to stand on." A young recruit of the vigilantes later admitted that although they claimed to be Minute Men or Regulators, "We were really a vigilante committee." Other county vigilantes continued to attack Tejanos in the region, "killing every Mexican" in Goliad or "demanding passports from all Mexicans." Some vindictive Anglo Texans "offered fifty dollars for every pair of Mexican ears brought" to them like the Rabb family whose "famous Bow and Arrow brand is among the thirty-six representative Texas brands that decorate the walls of Garrison Hall on the University of Texas campus." The vigilantes rode as far away as San Antonio, where vigilante Asa Mitchell kept "a tidy rope" in his pocket. Following the murder of a member of the powerful Welder ranch family, Anglos engaged in additional vigilante activities, hanging more Tejano suspects without due process of the law. In the words of Hobart Huson, "Most of the remaining Mexicans then began an exodus into Mexico. The roads were lined with ox-carts and wagons . . . being driven by women, and not a man was to be seen . . . The aftermath of the Swift and Welder murders was that practically all of the old colonial Mexican families of Refugio County, including the Aldretes, sold their lands and moved to the safety of Mexico." A jury later convicted Juan Flores, who had been arrested by authorities in Mexico and confessed to the Swift murders. He was hanged as the guilty party, but as mentioned above, these vigilante raids were more representative of Anglo sentiments against the Tejanos than a posse seeking justice. By the end of 1874, the Regulators were still admittedly "desperate for revenge." When they later heard that Mexicans had committed a murder at a small Anglo community on the Nueces River, they were so excited that they rode sixty miles non-stop overnight to the Nueces River to enroll in the posse being formed.[22]

The devastating vigilante raid in Nueces County was the Peñascal Raid of 1875. This episode revealed how white vigilantes and acquisitive Anglo ranchers targeted Tejano families on lands long coveted by Anglo ranchers. On March 26, 1875, a raid known as "the Corpus Christi raid" or the "Nuecestown Raid" was perpetrated by about twenty Mexican citizens known to have been followers of the notorious Juan Cortina. These raiders swept along the Nueces River near Corpus Christi, and assaulted several Anglos at Frank's Store on the Sais Ranch, about twenty miles from Corpus Christi. They robbed "a number of Mexican women and children" and took some of them along as they left. On leaving Frank's Store, "One of the robbers asked a Mexican to join the party in their raid. He refused, when a [pistol] was placed to his head, the trigger pulled, and his soul sent to eternity," according to accounts of the robbery. The Mexican raiders proceeded south through San Diego to Laredo with two wagons of plunder, killing Mexican-American vaqueros and Anglo ranchers along the way. They were arrested and jailed in Camargo, Mexico, by those authorities.[23]

A vigilante committee of about one hundred Anglos from Corpus Christi set out ostensibly to avenge the murder of several Anglos by Mexicans at Frank's Store near Corpus Christi. But for several months prior to the raids, Richard King had stirred passions against the old Tejano ranches, such as the Atravesada, La Parra, El Corral de Piedra, and El Mesquite, as well as the Peñascal Ranch in present-day Kenedy County, about sixty miles south of Corpus Christi. These ranches were home to hundreds of Tejano men, women, and children. According to the testimony of U.S. Army Captain J. W. Clous to the U.S. House Committee on Military Affairs in 1877, "Some ranches probably number as many as five or six hundred souls."[24]

King and others accused vaqueros from the Tejano ranches of stealing cattle, but it was the murder of the Anglos at the store that ostensibly sparked the raid. A vigilante posse from Corpus Christi gathered at King's ranch for his guidance. King instructed them to elect leaders—about twenty men—who should go first to Brownsville to be deputized. After being deputized, the posse returned to King "to receive instructions." If there were killings, they asked, "Would King stand by the deputies? "He replied, "He would see them justified." With their instructions, and acting under the color of law, the vigilantes then masked and painted themselves, took up arms, and set out at around midnight, "full of mescal and drunk." They threw coal oil on the thatched roofs of the houses and stores at the ranches and systematically killed all of the Tejano patriarchs and "every adult male that was present." As the raiders swept through one ranch after another, the women and children fled into the chaparral and hid throughout the night. At daylight, only the chimneys of the ranch houses remained standing amid smoldering ashes. Many of the men's bodies were never found and were presumed to have been "dumped in the bay."[25]

On April 18, 1875, the Corpus Christi sheriff wired a telegram to Austin. His message read: "IS CAPT [Ranger L. H.] MCNELLY COMING. WE ARE IN TROUBLE. FIVE RANCHES BURNED BY DISGUISED MEN NEAR LAPARRA LAST WEEK. ANSWER." When Texas Ranger Capt. L. H. McNelly arrived to investigate the raids, he wrote back to Austin, "The acts committed by Americans are horrible to relate; many ranches have been plundered and burned, and the people murdered or driven away; one of these parties confessed to me in Corpus Christi as having killed eleven men on their last raid." According to Texas Ranger N. A. Jennings, the Tejano victims were "peaceful Mexican farmers and stockmen who had lived all their lives in Texas."[26]

Testimony in the U.S. Congress Special Committee on Texas Frontier Troubles admitted that the Tejanos were victims of vindictive Anglos, saying, "As we have stated above, the recent raid of Mexican banditti near Corpus Christi brought about a retaliatory raid on the part of a few unthinking Americans living near the Nueces River. These men came down to the Encinal country among the squatter Mexicans, and found them, it is said, with stolen hides buried in their yards or concealed about their premises, when they burned down the jacales and killed some three men, according to the best information we can gather. There is no defense for such lawless acts." The irony of the attacks on Tejanos is that Richard King, Thadeus Rhodes, and other Anglo ranchers had long coveted these lands, and directed violence against the innocent Tejano families. The Mexican *Informe de la Comisión Pesquisidora* specifically identified them as *"robavacas*," or "cattle rustlers." King also kept a band of hired guns on his ranch, whom the Tejano ranchers called "*los rinches de la kineña*," to insulate him personally from his rustling operation. The Mexican investigative report added that "Ricardo King had a large band who ran constantly in all directions of the country marking calves though they did not belong to him."[27]

Many of the Tejano lands involved in the Peñascal Raid were incorporated into the King and Kenedy ranch empires, as the women and children and other Tejano rancheros fled across the border to Mexico. According to one account, "They departed taking their money and personal possessions with them, and often they were found dead along the way with their money missing." Later, Army Captain Clous testified that, "The land has been depopulated . . . I have . . . found many abandoned ranches (as they are called), in consequence of insecurity of life and property." He stated that the livestock were stolen and "lives endangered." He later asserted, "I went there a month or two afterward. I went up there on the heels of the Corpus raid, and shortly afterward I found the ranches abandoned." When asked if the ranches were viable ranching operations, he admitted that "half a dozen on the route on which I traveled to Kings ranch" between Brownsville and Corpus Christi would have continued to profit except for the raids. [28]

The third major conflict in the 1870s was the Salt War of El Paso, where an Anglo-American capitalist Charles Howard attempted to appropriate surface salt deposits that Tejanos had traditionally used as a communal resource. In October 1877, Howard attempted to enforce a restraining order against Tejano leaders José María Juárez and Macedonio Gandara. When hundreds of Tejanos from El Paso, known as Pasenos, and Mexicans from south of the Rio Grande gathered in protest, the incident quickly became violent. Texas Rangers and local Anglo vigilantes killed an estimated five to fifteen Pasenos and wounded forty to fifty of them while two Rangers were killed and several were wounded. Howard himself was killed during the mêlée, and the U.S. Army threatened to take military action. Notorious among the vigilantes was John Kinney, who led a vigilante raid of seventy "Rangers" into the Tejano community. The members of Kinney's vigilantes were later accused of being nothing more than "hardened criminals masquerading as peace officers and Texas troops. They were a gang with badges." Indeed, they committed systematic rape among Tejana women, specifically Salome Telles, the wife of one of the Tejano leaders. A U.S. Army colonel reprimanded the head of the El Paso law enforcement officials, saying "the State troops under your command have been committing outrages of greater or less magnitude on the peaceable people of the valley, including women and children, who, for fear of your men, have fled from their homes, and are now perishing for want of food and from exposure to cold" in the mountains of Mexico.

After the so-called Salt War was over, the Tejano villages were left "deserted" and their crops and ranches abandoned. Kinney, on the other hand, became saloonkeeper and later sheriff of El Paso, reportedly allowing his men to continue raids and use his saloon as an exchange house for stolen property.[29] Although this incident has received only passing treatment in the textbooks of Texas history, fuller research and analysis has begun to reveal that it was an integral element of the violence against Tejanos during Reconstruction. Moreover, the Salt War appears to have all the markers of the ethnic cleansing seen in the other major raids of the 1870s—the raids, mass murders, systematic rape, and the same callous dehumanization of Tejanos.

In summary, the actual cases recorded in county and state land records verify the historical interpretations that the violence waged against Tejanos during Reconstruction was primarily used by Anglos in an effort to steal their lands. It cannot be characterized—and it should not be trivialized—as one short period of unfortunate but legal transfer of title from unwitting victims. It involved mass murder of whole families, whole ranch settlements, and titled patriarchs of landholding families who were citizens of Texas. In its various forms, the violence was perpetrated by the Army of the Republic of Texas, it was condoned by the Confederate State of Texas, it was actively promoted by the State of Texas, and it was knowingly permitted, contrived, and facilitated by the local governments. And when the sheriffs' auctions, and the vigilante raids, and the legal trials covered up the atrocities, the theft of Hispanic lands was legitimized and shielded under the sanctity of the courts and the Texas General Land Office.

When Anglo Texan citizens met in mass meetings in Brownsville and Corpus Christi in December of 1875, they not only demanded a troop of Texas Rangers, but they specifically requested Captain L. H. McNelly by name. They used coded words to identify his use of torture and summary executions, which they considered critical to Anglo law enforcement in Texas. The testimony of U.S. Army commissioned officers under oath to the U.S. Congress, explicitly acknowledged McNelly's reputation for torture and execution. Captain J. W. Clous stated, "Well, I understand they went to work and choked a few individuals and made them tell where the raiders were coming from and where they were going to. I understand that is the way they got their information." Captain H. C. Corbin of the 24th Infantry Regiment, testified in December 1877 that "Captain McNelly applied treatment which officers of the regular Army are not allowed to do. He found some suspicious characters, and under torture he made them confess . . . He caught them in the chaparral, and under torture got their confession."[30] Not only did the people of Texas support McNelly's method, but the governor of Texas—above all others—fully embraced violence in his official correspondence with the Texas Delegation in Congress on December 24, 1875. Governor Richard Coke demanded federal compensation for Texas expenses in defending the border, asking for 350 men for McNelly because, "They will do service such as the officers of the United States Army *cannot or will not do* [his italics]. They never have done any good against the predatory bands of robbers who are devastating that country, and never will. None but Texas troops have ever checked their operations at all."[31]

Unfortunately, the Reconstruction era in Texas history was characterized by violence, and Tejanos were not its only victims, to be sure. Nevertheless, the story of how Tejanos became dispossessed of their landed heritage has been irreversibly tainted by the violence against them by Anglo bandits and Texas Rangers. This conflict, uniquely combined with their proud Spanish-Mexican heritage, had become a distinctive element in the formation of the modern Tejano identity by the mid-1880s, and inevitably, it brushed its indelible mark on the character of Texas as well. Throughout Reconstruction, Texas was a dynamic zone of exchange where the contest of power remained constant, and Tejanos made frequent and consistent adjustments in order to ensure that their community remained viable for future generations of Mexican Americans.

ENDNOTES

1. Hobart Huson, *Refugio: A Comprehensive History of Refugio County from Aboriginal Times to 1953*, 2 vols. (Woodsboro: The Rooke Foundation, 1953), 1: 471; Walter Prescott Webb, *The Texas Rangers: A Century of Frontier Defense*, 2nd ed. (Austin: University of Texas Press, 1991); Paul Schuster Taylor, *An American-Mexican Frontier: Nueces County, Texas* (Chapel Hill: The University of North Carolina Press, 1934), 108.

2. Huson, *Refugio*, 1:471; Goliad County, Records; Ana Carolina Castillo Crimm, "The Community: The Mexican Americans of Victoria County, Texas, 1800–1880." (Unpublished MS. Sam Houston State University, 1998), 177–78.

3. David Montejano, *Anglos and Mexicans in the Making of Texas, 1836–1886* (Austin: University of Texas Press, 1987), 72; Webb, *The Texas Rangers*.

4. James Ernest Crisp, "Anglo-Texan Attitudes toward the Mexican, 1821–1845" (Ph.D. dissertation, Yale University, 1976), 343; Neil Foley, *The White Scourge: Mexicans, Blacks, and Poor Whites in Texas Cotton Culture* (Berkeley: University of California Press, 1997), 21; Castillo Crimm, "The Community," 170; Taylor, *American-Mexican Frontier*, 108; Walter L. Buenger, "Texas and the South" *Southwestern Historical Quarterly* 103, no. 3 (January 2000): 324.

5. Hidalgo County, Court Record Book A:149; Castillo Crimm, "The Community," 175; Arthur J. Rubel, *Across the Tracks: Mexican-Americans in a Texas City* (Austin: University of Texas Press, 1966), 36; Taylor, *American-Mexican Frontier*, 184.

6. Castillo Crimm, "The Community," 141; *The Kennedy Times*, October 31, 1963, Sect. 10; Abel G. Rubio, *Stolen Heritage: A Mexican-American's Rediscovery of His Family's Lost Land Grant* (Austin: Eakin Press, 1986), 136.

7. Mexico, *Reports of the Committee of Investigation Sent in 1873 by the Mexican Government to the Frontier of Texas: Translated from the Official Edition Made in Mexico* (New York: Baker & Godwin, 1875), iv.

8. U.S. Congress, Report of the United States to Texas, Appointed under Joint Resolution of Congress, approved May 7 1872, Washington, D.C., December 10, 1872, pp. 1–7; U.S. Congress, 45th Congress, 2d Session, House of Representatives, Report No 701. *Report and Accompanying Documents of the Committee on Foreign Affairs on the Relations of the United States with Mexico* (Washington: Government Printing Office, 1878), Appendix B, 97–99.

9. Ibid., 99.

10. Ibid., 105.

11. Mexico, *Reports of the Committee of Investigation*, 29.

12. Ibid., 55.

13. Jerry Thompson, *Cortina: Defending the Mexican Name in Texas* (College Station: Texas A&M University Press, 2007), 218.

14. U.S. Congress, 44th Cong., 1st sess., House of Representatives, Report No. 343, *Texas Frontier Troubles* (Washington, 1876), 56.

15. Ibid., 54.

16. Mexico, *Reports of the Committee of Investigation*, 131 and 132.

17. Huson, *Refugio*, 2: 206–8.

18. Ibid.

19. J. Frank Dobie, *A Vaquero of the Brush Country: Partly from the Reminiscences of John Young* (Dallas: The Southwest Press, 1929), 74.

20. Ibid, 75.

21. Ibid.

22. Dobie, *Vaquero*[0], 73–80, 125; Huson, *Refugio*, 2: 214; U.S. Congress, Report No. 343, *Texas Frontier Troubles*, xviii.

23. U.S. Congress, Report No. 343, *Texas Frontier Troubles*, xix, xx.

24. U.S. Congress, Mis. doc. No. 64, *Texas Border Troubles*, 104.

25. J. B. (Red) Dunn, *Perilous Trails of Texas,* ed. Lilith Lorraine (Dallas: Southwest Press, 1932), 9, 36, 41, 63; Roberto M. Villareal, "The Mexican-American Vaqueros of the Kenedy Ranch: A Social History" (Master's thesis, Texas A&I University, 1972), 16–19.

26. John C. Rayburn and Virginia Kemp Rayburn, eds., with the assistance of Ethel Neale Fry, *Century of Conflict, 1821–1913: Incidents in the Lives of William Neale and William A. Neale, Early Settlers in South Texas* (Waco: Texian Press, 1966), 103–6; Montejano, *Anglos and Mexicans,* 53; Webb, *Texas Rangers*, 238.

27. Webb, *Texas Rangers*, 176n; Mexico, *Reports of the Committee of Investigation*, 105; U.S. Congress, 44th Cong., 1st sess. House of Representatives, Report No. 343, *Texas Frontier Troubles. Testimony Taken by the Special Committee on Texas Frontier Troubles* (Washington, January 6, 1876), 56.

28. U.S. Congress, Mis. doc. No. 64, *Texas Border Troubles*, pp. 131–33; Villareal, "Vaqueros," 16–19.

29. Paul Cool, *Salt Warriors: Insurgency on the Rio Grand* (College Station: Texas A&M University Press, 2008), 197, 234, 264.

30. U.S. Congress, Misc. Doc. No. 64, *Texas Border Troubles*, 131–33, 151.

31. U.S. Congress, 44th Congress, 2d session, House, Ex. Doc. No. 14, *Accounts of the State of Texas: Letter from the Secretary of War, concerning accounts of the State of Texas* (Washington, D.C.: G.P.O., 1876), 5.

CHAPTER 12

"To Punish and Humiliate the Entire Community": White Violence Perpetrated Against African-American Women in Texas, 1865–1868

by

Rebecca A. Kosary

Immediately following the Civil War, many former slaves in Texas found themselves at the mercy of whites—in their homes, their places of work and recreation, their churches, and even in the courts. For them, the "freedom" granted in the Thirteenth and Fourteenth Amendments to the U.S. Constitution was a far cry from reality. Although nominal rights for African Americans had increased since 1865, violence of against them increased as well. This was particularly true for black women, whose ambiguous legal status (ironically, now equal to that of white women) left them particularly vulnerable to racist violence that was often perpetrated against them with impunity.

Freedwomen were subjected to verbal, physical, and sexual assaults, torture, and murder during Reconstruction and they received little or no protection from local and state authorities. In addition, as mothers and wives, black women endured the trauma of separated families, the forcible apprenticeship of their children, and the injury and death of family members at the hands of resentful, bitter whites. While black men certainly suffered vicious and deadly attacks by whites during the period, black women were, by virtue of their gender, peculiarly susceptible to racist violence, and doubly victimized—once as blacks and again as women. As victims of both racism and sexism, black women in Texas faced incredible obstacles in the transition from slavery to freedom.

Brutal physical coercion had been used during the antebellum period by whites, whether slave owners or not, to exert mastery and control over human chattel. During Reconstruction in Texas whites continued and even increased the violence in an effort to hold onto their dominant place in society and to control and undermine the resolve of the newly freed black community. Black women were especially vulnerable to attacks, and although records reveal fewer incidents perpetrated against them than against their male counterparts, women frequently endured brutality that was most often implicitly or explicitly sexual in nature. Unfortunately, statistics from the period related to violence against women are limited, but the records of the Freedmen's Bureau point to the fact that brutality against black women was intense during Reconstruction in Texas.[1]

Between 1865 and 1868, Bureau agents recorded over 2,200 violent incidents throughout Texas. Of these incidents, 13 percent involved black women as the victims.[2] At first glance, Bureau records depict these incidents as mere violations of the law, but the listing of criminal acts alone obscures the motives behind the acts. Fortunately, Bureau entries also describe conditions and circumstances in many cases. From a careful reading of these circumstances, it is possible to glean insight into the extent of violence suffered by black women, and make some generalizations about the impact of this violence on the Texas black community as a whole.[3]

When emancipation officially made its way to Texas in June 1865, black men and women entered a period of social, political, and economic uncertainty. It became clear very quickly that a large proportion of white Texans had no intention of accepting black freedom and were determined to use every means available—both legal and extralegal – to restore white hegemony in the state. This had dire consequences for black women who were particularly vulnerable to physical and sexual threats with little legal recourse. While race alone established the perimeters of behavior and rights for freedmen, black women were constrained within limitations of both race and gender through law and social custom, and as a result, their lives were permeated with violence.[4]

Such seemingly senseless violence against women existed because, although newly freed black men clearly represented a potential political and economic threat, black women also represented a threat to the social order, albeit a more elusive one. In one sense, they were now equal to white women; both were virtually excluded from the political and juridical domains, while their male counterparts had such access. Physical and sexual violence against black women, thus, served a multiple purpose: it was used to reaffirm white dominance and control over black women, and to undermine their legal equality with white women, further preventing the formation of relationships based on gender solidarity. The victimization of black women by whites also served to perpetuate the oppression of all black Texans by preventing freedmen from defending "their own" women.[5]

Black women suffered indignities, humiliation, and brutal violence at the hands of whites during the postwar years. This continual threat was compounded by the inaction of civil authorities, and even Bureau officials in many instances, demonstrating the insignificant place black women held in the eyes of the law. Civil authorities implicitly condoned the violence against black women by their outright failure to protect them in many cases. For example, Davis County freedwoman Susan Goosely was for no stated reason, dragged out of bed by a group of men who raped and pistol-whipped her, knocked her teeth out, strung her up by the thumbs, and choked her by placing a halter around her neck. Afterward, Ms. Goosely was forced to flee the county for her life because local authorities failed to take action against the perpetrators of this crime, even though she identified her attackers. Law enforcement officers, as well,

Illustration 14. "Visit of the Ku-Klux" by Frank Bellew. Illustration first appeared in *Harper's Weekly*, February 24, 1872. (Courtesy of Library of Congress)

frequently participated in atrocities committed against black women. In Harrison County, Deputy Sheriff Warnell took Rose Campbell from her home claiming that she was being arrested; he then raped her. Because Warnell was "the law" in that county, he submitted to no legal action. The sheriff of Panola County led an attack on a group of freedpeople who were "innocently enjoying themselves dancing." A black woman suffered serious injury as a result of the mêlée that left three men dead.[6]

Unlike many civil authorities, most Texas Freedmen's Bureau agents apparently endeavored to protect black women from exploitation and violence. The language they used in their official records, however, demonstrates that many agents probably shared the views of their white southern counterparts and, likewise placed a limited value on black women's lives and bodies. For example, very few black female victims named in the "Record of Criminal Offenses" are listed by their full names; neither were any designated with the honorific title of either Miss or Mrs. In stark contrast, white females who perpetrated violence against blacks were, at the least, listed by their full names, and most were accorded their marital honorific titles as well.[7] While this may be due in part to the fact that Texas did not officially recognize marriages between black men and women until 1869, it also stems from the disrespect shown to black women by white men generally, which in turn stemmed from the widespread social and legal practices that reinforced the myth of the "bad black woman."[8] According to historian Gerda Lerner, the "myth" arose after emancipation to sanction the continued assault and exploitation of black women by white men. These alleged naturally "loose" women, of low moral character and greater sexual desires, were considered undeserving of the same respect or "chivalry" granted to white women. So while white female perpetrators—criminals, in fact—were given nominal respect in the records because of their gender, black female victims were not because of their race, and as such, were further de-feminized.[9] Although it appears that most Freedmen's Bureau agents, then, tried to protect black women from white violence, their records demonstrate that the white male agents' personal philosophies on race and gender colored policies and procedures, at least to some degree, at the local level.[10]

White civilians also rarely gave reasons for even the most brutal attacks on freedpeople and were almost never convicted, regardless of the degree of barbarity the incident entailed. This was particularly true when the violence was perpetrated against women. For example, James Wise whipped and gouged out the eye of Emily Granes. Wise gave no reason for the crime that could very well have cost the victim her life. In

Limestone, John Fogarty cut Minerva Ward's ears off and burned her arms "to a crisp." Astonishingly, Bureau officials recorded no explanation for this brutality and it appears that civil authorities chose not to act.[11] Whites in Texas, thus, exercised considerable control over freedwomen, in large part, because authorities failed to control the racialized violence against them that pervaded the state.

Violence took many forms during Reconstruction and physical assault, especially whipping, was a common outlet. Whipping not only served as a psychological reminder of slavery, but also demonstrated the fact that many whites viewed blacks merely as animals.[12] White males frequently strapped up and whipped black women, or struck them with implements ranging from pistols, chairs, hammers, saws, and bricks, to metal whip handles, animal bones, and clubs. In most cases, the justifications for such abuses reflected ingrained antebellum ideas of what had previously constituted appropriate disciplinary action against slaves. For example, after Julie Gardner disagreed with her white employer, R. H. Wren, he whipped her "almost to death" with a handsaw. Two black women in Upshur County were given one hundred lashes each; one for not hoeing fast enough and the other for hoeing up a single cotton stalk. This was not the first time complaints were lodged against this perpetrator for similar offenses. Frank Waller whipped an unnamed freedwoman after knocking her to the ground, because he considered the bread she baked for one of his meals unsuitable, while a woman in Harris County was brutally beaten across the face with a paddle for being "lazy." For no reported reason, a woman in Grimes County was taken into the woods with her hands tied and then given a hundred lashes.[13]

Whipping and similar physical abuse were instruments of coercion used by whites of both genders. The Bureau listed white women as perpetrators of whippings and beatings in 5 percent of cases involving black women. In half of these incidents, no explanation or details are given and the weapons used unknown. In the other crimes, white women used shovels, lead whip handles, tree branches, and other large objects in their rampages. Often the women's stated reasons for committing these violent acts were similar to those of their male counterparts. White women, it seems, had a unique stake in preserving the social order. For many, assaulting black women may have been their only opportunity to express authority in a male-dominated society. White women, like African Americans, were marginalized and therefore struck back at the only people they could: black women. For example, Mrs. America Sherrell bloodied a black woman's head by beating her with a large animal bone. Bureau officials recorded Sherrell's explanation for the beating was that the woman disobeyed her in "some household matter." A white woman in Houston "whipped and pounded" a young girl with a stick and a shovel on two different occasions for no apparent reason. In Bexar County, a white woman tied a black woman to a tree before whipping her severely for no reported reason. Similar to circumstances involving white men accused of crimes against black women, civil authorities did not take immediate action against the white women who were accused of abusing freedwomen. In fact, in over 50 percent of the 131 cases of whipping and similar physical assaults reported to the Bureau, agents recorded no explanation for the crimes and described civil authorities as refusing to act, even when given evidence by the Bureau. It appears that many white Texans, civilians and local officials alike, believed that the physical assault of black women, clearly reminiscent of the days of slavery, was their prerogative and certainly not a crime. On the contrary, when a black woman in Walker County reported a white woman for assaulting her, local authorities heard the case but fined the injured woman for court costs totaling $23. This, no doubt, reassured the white populace that the physical assault of black women was acceptable social behavior in the eyes of the law.[14]

Because many Bureau officials rightly associated whipping with the institution of slavery, agents in Northeast Texas specifically ordered landowners not to whip their former slaves after emancipation. Unfortunately, however, those few who complied simply found other ways of violently disciplining their workforce. William Sinclair, the state inspector for Texas, reported that a "new method of correcting evils on the plantation" was tying former slaves "by the thumbs with only their toes touching the ground." Bureau officials recorded this form of punishment being used frequently during Reconstruction, and women suffered as often as men.[15]

Age was no deterrent to physical abuse, as even elderly African-American women fell victim to brutal whippings and beatings perpetrated by whites. An unnamed "old woman" in Anderson County was beaten with rocks and stones, and "shamefully" treated by a group of white men who barged into her house and threw all of her belongings outside. In Freestone County, after a seventy-year-old woman named Lucy was brutally beaten with a club for no stated reason, the local Bureau agent, Charles Culver, in utter disgust, wrote only one word in his record of the event: "Chivalry!!!" Similarly, in McLennan County, after seventy-five-year-old Lotta Brown was pistol whipped by a group of white men and robbed of seventy-five cents, Bureau agent Charles Haughn commented "so much for chivalry."[16]

Black economic independence reflected the ultimate detachment from slavery, an institution that intimately entwined labor with power and violence. Many white Texans were, thus, virulently resistant to any expression of economic freedom by their former chattel and used various methods to intimidate and control black women by keeping them economically dependent. Bureau records include many cases of black women being victimized for exercising the most basic of freedoms: expressing a desire to quit their jobs or change employers. For example, a woman named Margaret was "knocked down and treated inhumanely" for wishing to leave the employ of E. Morse, who, on a separate occasion, whipped another black woman for the same reason. Unfortunately, for some white employers, physical assault was not enough. A particularly senseless tragedy occurred in Rusk County, when a mother and her newborn died after being shot to death by a white man for leaving his employ. It seems that the perpetrator in this case cared more about maintaining power and control over black people than keeping employees working on his property.[17]

Many black women, such as Caroline Wallace, worked diligently for their new "employers" but were driven from their homes just prior to receiving their promised earnings. After signing a contract with W. C. McDowell, Wallace and her daughter were beaten and driven from the farm after the crops were harvested. When a group of men in Walker County, armed with clubs and guns, decided an unnamed black woman should be driven off the plantation without her years' earnings, they did so with impunity. A similar incident happened to a woman in Bowie County who was beaten with clubs and chains and then run off the property after asking to be paid for her work.[18]

White "employers" resorted to other more subtle forms of abuse such as withholding food or providing inadequate shelter, and many physically assaulted those who would dare complain about their situation or attempt to leave. A woman in Bowie County was beaten severely by her employer for stating that she did not have enough to eat, while another reported her boss for starving her and repeatedly beating her over the head. Even women in poor health were not immune from this type of brutal treatment, as evidenced by one official's report of a sick woman being thrown out to "die of starvation and exposure" by her employer, Mr. Dewalt. Records are unclear as to whether or not this particular woman survived.[19]

Such maltreatment forced many women to steal in order to survive, even though such "crimes" could likely result in lengthy prison sentences. Of the fourteen black women incarcerated at the Texas State Penitentiary at Huntsville in 1867, thirteen had been convicted of stealing from their employers and were serving sentences ranging from two to five years.[20] Landowners did not always report theft to the authorities, however, as it seems many preferred to take the law into their own hands. A white man in Bastrop shot his employee through the thigh for stealing peaches, and a woman in Bowie County was whipped severely, pounded with a stick, and then tied up by one thumb for allegedly taking some flour. May Oglesby planned to report Mr. Shaw to the Bureau for "detaining her forcibly" in his service and keeping her in deplorable living conditions. In retaliation, Shaw shot at Oglesby four times. Likewise, a woman in Dallas County was "whipped and kicked" for "trying to procure her freedom" from her employer. Many black women, thus, found themselves in a state of virtual slavery as their "employers" controlled not only their labor, but their movements as well.[21]

After the Civil War, many whites sought to sustain antebellum racial deference and used violence to do so. Not only did white men and women of every social class expect humble obedience from blacks, they regularly responded with brutality when confronted with what they observed to be insolence, disrespectful language, or acting out of place. Bureau records indicate that such "crimes" by black women, especially if committed in the presence of white women, resulted in severe retaliation. For example, a black woman in Brazoria County was beaten on her shoulders and face and was threatened with her life by a man who claimed she spoke disrespectfully to his wife. Likewise, in McLennan County, James shot and severely injured Fanny, a black woman who worked in his home, for giving "some saucy words" to his wife.[22] For a similar offense, a group of white men severely beat a woman in Brazoria County, inflicting blows on her head with the iron butt of a whip. After the beating, they tied her hands together, "bucked" her, and then gave her nearly 200 lashes. "Bucking" was a form of corporal punishment used primarily during the antebellum period, but continued throughout Reconstruction in Texas. After being totally or partially stripped, a victim was forced into a squatting position with both hands tied together in front of the shins; a log or sturdy branch would then be placed through the opening above the elbows and below the knees, serving to hold the victim in the squatting position bent over forward, while being whipped or beaten over the bare back.[23] For this particular woman, the bucking was in retaliation for the insulting noises she allegedly made as the wife of one of the group passed. In contrast, when a black woman scolded a white man for using vulgar language in her presence, she was brutally beaten for her insolence. The Bureau reported that civil authorities failed to take action in these cases. Their inaction not only reinforced the notion that whites dictated acceptable behavior for both races; more significantly, it suggests the unwillingness of Southern white society to expand its prewar definition of womanhood to include former slaves.[24]

Very few freedwomen fit white ideas of the "true" woman, an ideal within which domesticity, piety, purity, and submissiveness were central. Women who worked outside the home, in particular, were viewed as unnatural and unfeminine. The fact that the overwhelming number of black women in Texas performed "double duty in both home and field," weakened their role in white eyes as mothers and wives and came to symbolize "the low esteem in which she was held in society." Like white women, black women suffered the same restrictions of their male-enforced gender roles; unlike their white counterparts, however, black women were denied its protections and, as such, were vulnerable to white violence with little recourse.[25]

While nineteenth-century ideals of womanhood and femininity typically subjected white pregnant women to chivalry and special protection, it seems that black women in the same condition faced the opposite circumstances and were, in fact, more harshly abused. White Texans showed very little restraint in dealing with pregnant black women and in some cases, seem to have accelerated the brutality against them specifically because of the pregnancy. During the antebellum period, some slaveholders probably gave slave women the benefit of the doubt when they claimed to have pregnancy-related aches and pains, if only because they realized the economic benefit of a full-term pregnancy and birth. But in just as many cases, it seems, pregnant slaves were not only forced to continue carrying their normal work load in the fields, they often found themselves beaten or otherwise harshly treated for failing to meet their quotas.[26]

One common punishment for such offenses entailed beating a woman's entire backside with a whip or other implement while she lay flat on the ground, her protruding stomach shoved into a hole. While this type of beating would certainly be excessively painful for the mother and dangerous to the pregnancy, the practice of lying over a hole may have actually been a means of protecting the fetus and thus the slave owners' investment, while allowing the offending slave to be punished accordingly. Circumstances seem to have been worse for freedwomen in Texas when they became pregnant, however, as they and their unborn children were no longer seen as investments to be protected. Like the pregnant woman in Fort Bend County who was seriously injured when a white man gave her 150 lashes for no reported reason, black women throughout the Reconstruction period were whipped, raped, shot, and brutally murdered with little regard or respect for their physical or maternal state.[27]

Commonly viewed by whites as carriers of the "despised" race, pregnant black women faced violence specifically directed against their wombs. This type of abuse further served as a weapon of terror aimed at the black population as a whole. Inspector William H. Sinclair recorded such an incident perpetrated by Eli Guest, a known desperado in Northeast Texas. After shooting a freedwoman who was "in a family way, [he] cut out her womb with its living content [still inside] and exhibited [the fetus to others] in his drunken glee." Another brutal violent act was perpetrated against a pregnant woman in Upshur county, when one Anderson shot and killed a woman named Mary, reported to be "in the last stages" of her pregnancy. Apparently her child was born alive minutes after her death and the perpetrators buried both mother and infant "so near the surface that buzzards ate them." It is unclear whether or not the baby was buried alive.[28]

The amount of physical violence inflicted upon freedwomen in Texas indicates that whites were bitterly opposed to the notion of black freedom and were determined, by any means necessary, to maintain social, economic, political, and sexual control of their former chattel. Both white men and women perpetrated heinous acts upon black women, most often with impunity. Black women, of course, were not passive victims. On the contrary, many risked their lives resisting their own physical abuse, and especially protecting their children from cruelty. For some, the Freedmen's Bureau served as a beacon in this difficult transition from slavery to freedom. Not only did agents oversee contract negotiations between landowners and freedpeople, but they also kept records of offenses perpetrated upon former slaves and, it seems, tried to make the transition as smooth as possible. But Bureau agents, like local authorities, seem to have placed little value on black women's lives. Of the 281 incidents of violence against black women reported to the Bureau between 1865 and 1868, local authorities acted in a mere 14 percent (38) of the cases. The Bureau's track record is hardly better for the period, having only acted in 19 percent (54) of the cases.[29] To be sure, the hands of Bureau officials were tied in many ways, as local citizens and civil authorities for the most part did not support them, and the agency itself was severely under-staffed and under-funded. But their inaction also raises the question of whether the white male agents' own philosophies on race and gender dictated their responses to some of these crimes. Under such conditions, black women found themselves particularly susceptible to rape and other forms of sexualized violence and left with virtually no protection.

Violence against black women was intense and pervasive during Reconstruction in Texas, with sexual violence in particular serving as an essential feature of the period. Black women faced rape and other forms of sexual abuse frequently, as they had during the antebellum period. Rape and other forms of sexualized violence—including whipping, mutilation, forced nakedness, and sexual humiliation—served to create a climate of fear and to further demonstrate white hegemony and control over the entire black community.[30] While many individuals were direct victims of such abuses during Reconstruction, this horrific strain of violence did not have to be witnessed directly by the black community for white Texans to make their point. Simply knowing that these abuses happened frequently, and often with impunity, burned it "indelibly into the mind" of the larger African American community in Texas.[31]

The rape of black women and girls, and the related lynching of black men for the alleged rape of white women, were more than acts of violence against individuals; both represented methods of racial subordination.[32] "Splitting a nigger woman," a repugnant euphemism used to describe the rape of black women, was considered not only "a white man's prerogative" but was also "a way to express his anger and contempt" toward all blacks during the period.[33] Although first and foremost a crime against a woman's body, rape can also be viewed as an indirect assault on all black Texans because it served the additional purpose, intentional or not, of communicating defeat to black men. Throughout history, the rape of women has been recognized as a predictable part of military conflict, serving additionally as a "consequence of defeat" in war.[34] From the perspective of white Southerners, while they may not have had the ability to overturn their own military defeat by the U.S. Army, many refused to be doubly defeated by accepting the equality of their former chattel. Therefore, the rape of black women by whites during Reconstruction could certainly have served as an instrument to drive into the black community—literally and figuratively—the idea that they were, in fact, the defeated people, regardless of the war's military outcome. Through the abuse of black women, then, white Texans attempted to ensure what they failed to accomplish in the Civil War: the continued subjugation of African Americans.[35]

The sexual exploitation and rape of black women and girls, considered one of the most significant bases of white male power during slavery, was just as widespread, if not more so, after emancipation.[36] Because freedom from slavery meant that black women were no longer the legal property of a particular white man, they became, to a great degree, "sexually available to all white men."[37] Most white Southerners, both civilians and law enforcement officials, forcefully rejected the idea that a black woman could actually be raped. As was the case in most of the violent incidents perpetrated against black women, white perpetrators were not likely to be charged with nor convicted of rape or sexual assault when their victims were black; neither were black men likely to be charged with or convicted of raping black women.[38] For example, three black women in McLennan County were raped, beaten, and robbed by William Killum, J. Tubbs, and Parish Johnson. These same three white men continued their rampage the following day, sexually assaulting seven-year-old Dolla Jackson and robbing her of twenty-five cents. None of these men were questioned or charged with these atrocities, even though they were reported by name to authorities. A Bureau agent commenting on the Jackson assault merely wrote "Chivalry???" in his record of the event, implicitly acknowledging that black women and girls did not enjoy the same basic protections granted to whites of the same gender, or perhaps indicating disdain at southern concepts of chivalry. When Mr. Narrymore of Harrison County raped a young girl before driving her father off his land without his earned portion of the crop, Bureau authorities reported that civil authorities took no action against the perpetrator.[39]

Charges were seldom levied for the rape of black women, but when they were charged, white men were typically acquitted and their black victims blamed for provoking the act. On the very rare occasion that a white man was actually convicted of sexually assaulting a black woman, the racist stereotype of black female promiscuity was likely the main justification for the relatively lighter punishments they normally received. Texas Bureau agents recorded only one case of a white man charged and convicted of a crime involving the rape of a black woman. E. A. Bingham of Red River County was fined $200 for the "assault and battery" of Emily Reed, an assault that, according to Bureau agents, included rape. Because he claimed to be financially unable to make this court-ordered payment, however, Bingham's fine was subsequently reduced to a mere thirty-five dollars. That the perpetrator in this case received a fine in the first place is highly notable, perhaps speaking either to the singular violence of his crime or to his general unpopularity among his peers, as Texas statutes provided specific penalties for rape that did not include monetary fines.[40] The records are unclear, however, as to whether or not the rape was actually recognized as part of the formal charge. If Bingham was not charged with raping a black woman, it would certainly reflect nineteenth-century gender conventions as to who could and could not be raped. It is also likely that Ms. Reed, being black and female, was unable to furnish corroborating evidence and witness testimony to the court's liking (by an upstanding white, preferably male witness), resulting in less than a preponderance of the evidence necessary to sustain such a charge. Nonetheless, and despite the rarity of both the conviction and the punishment, the court devalued the victim in this case by reducing the fine to an amount agreeable to the criminal, rather than imposing the sanctioned jail time for the assault.[41]

Black women were often victimized further for defending themselves against the unwelcome sexual advances of white men. For example, in Bowie County, Tilman Curloo threatened and then murdered Virginia Harrison, because "she wouldn't yield to his desires." Similarly, in Anderson, John Cautly shot and killed an unnamed black woman because she refused to engage in "adultery" with him. A white man, Mr. Moore, attempted to rape a young black girl named Millie who successfully resisted him the first time. Unfortunately, Moore returned the following day, took Millie into the woods and sexually assaulted her, beating her "on her bare parts twenty times with a stick."[42]

Black women not only had to fear the threat of rape itself and retaliation for reporting such abuses, but they additionally had to deal with their accusations likely being met with disbelief—by civil authorities and, unfortunately, by Bureau officials in many instances. Although most Bureau agents probably did their best to protect black Texans from violence, their records indicate that they, like whites generally, did not recognize the rape of black women as a serious crime. Descriptions of circumstances in the records are rife with euphemisms, such as "ravishing" or "maltreatment," but agents then seem to move on to emphasize what they apparently believe to be crimes of a more serious nature.[43] For example, when a black woman was brutally beaten, raped, and hanged by a group of white men, the Bureau described the crime as "hanging by thumbs and striking over the head with a pistol," yet being "ravished" was part of a litany of abuses suffered by the woman. Likewise, when a young girl successfully resisted an attempted rape by a group of white men and reported the incident to the Harrison County Bureau office, the agent listed the offense as "whipping and threatening to kill."[44] Although "attempted rape" is mentioned as part of the lengthier offense description, it is clear that the agent in this case, like many others, did not view this type of violation as severe enough to be predominant in the record. This fact is especially disturbing when one considers that in 34 percent (96) of all cases of violence perpetrated against black women, agents failed to describe incidents at all, aside from listing the crime that was alleged to have been committed or the law that was violated ("homicide" or "assault and battery," for example). This certainly begs the question as to whether at least some of these crimes perpetrated against black women were not also sexual assaults.

In complete contrast to the experience of black women, alleged black rapists inspired white supremacy in its extreme.[45] In response to white fears of innate black male lustfulness, the Texas Legislature in 1866 amended the Penal Code so that black men could be easily incarcerated, while white criminals who violated blacks remained free. Of particular importance was Article 529, which was amended to ensure that rapists, insinuated to all be black, were given the severest punishments. The amended article read:

> Whoever shall be guilty of rape, shall be punished by death, or by confinement in the penitentiary for life, or for any term of years not less than five, in the discretion of the jury.[46]

Although the wording appears nondiscriminatory, Bureau records indicate that this outwardly color-blind law was not applied equally when the rape victim was black. According to historian Victoria Bynum, throughout the nineteenth century, rape was regarded as "the theft of a woman's prized possession—a body reserved exclusively for her future or present husband." The selective application of Texas law demonstrates that, in cases of rape, the law was designed strictly for the protection of a white woman's "prized possession."[47]

In their quest to maintain racial dominance, many white Texans also relied heavily on other forms of sexual and sexualized violence besides rape and, unfortunately, former slaves—women as well as men—became regular objects of these types of abuses. As used here and in its broadest context, sexual violence is more than rape. Medical scholars Inge Lunde and Jørgen Ortmann define "sexual torture" as including: "(1) violence against the sexual organs; (2) physical assault—i.e., sexual acts involving direct physical contact; (3) mental sexual assault—i.e., forced nakedness, sexual humiliations, sexual threats, and witnessing others being sexually tortured; and (4) a combination of these."[48] Freedmen's Bureau records indicate that this kind of abuse was endemic in Texas, as whites used it in varying forms to dehumanize and demoralize the black community and thus, exert further domination and control over them.

Often Bureau agents only allude to sexualized forms of abuse in their records, using terms such as "unmercifully" or "shamefully" to describe physical violence that is implicitly sexual. According to one historian, it is this implied sexuality, rather than the violent act itself, that is thought of as shameful by agents. This same implicit sexual undertone is evident in the many cases where partially or totally naked victims are further degraded by "bucking" or being whipped on their "private" or "bare" parts.[49]

Whipping had been a central feature of slavery, one that white Texans were clearly unwilling to relinquish simply because the shackles of the institution were removed by law. While many whites may have used the lash during Reconstruction because it was a familiar instrument of corporeal punishment, others used it deliberately in a form that bore implicit, if not explicit, sexual overtones. While these sexualized whippings varied in form and intensity, they served the additional purpose of shaming victims and inducing further humiliation by forcing them to be partially or totally naked, in addition to purposefully inflicting pain on the genitals. Black women, as well as men, were frequent victims of this kind of violence.[50] In Brazoria County, after a young black woman was beaten over the head with a whip handle, the perpetrators "pulled her clothes over her hips, bucked her and gave her about 200 lashes on her bare parts." Likewise, a woman in Harrison County reported having been struck on her "bare parts" with a stick. The agent recording this incident failed to mention the number of times she was beaten with the stick or if the implement was used in a more explicitly sexualized way. A woman named Lucinda was taken into the woods in Panola County by a group of white men who forced her to "lie on her stomach . . .[they] threw up her clothes," and held a pistol to her head while beating her "on her bare parts."[51]

It is important to note that every incident of sexualized violence as defined here and recorded in the Texas Bureau's official records, regardless of the gender of the victims, was perpetrated by groups of white men, rather than individuals. Perhaps, as psychologists have concluded with regard to gang rape, whipping on the genitals and similar sexualized abuse of naked victims, including castration, provided a certain homoerotic outlet for the perpetrators.[52] Whether or not individuals within a group were sexually aroused by their collective abuse of black victims cannot be determined from the extant sources. At the most basic level, in performing these violent acts the group of perpetrators was sending a message to the victim directly and to the black community indirectly. It cannot be ruled out, however, that in sexually abusing and humiliating their victims, individual white male perpetrators within a group setting were also demonstrating their manhood to their cohorts. As in gang rape, these perpetrators were, in effect, using black bodies as "verbs with which to communicate with one another."[53]

During the early years of Reconstruction in Texas, African American men and women frequently suffered sexualized violence at the hands of white men. Black women not only had to suffer through their own experience of rape, but many endured the additional trauma of knowing their own daughters were similarly abused. As if to add insult to injury, laws regarding rape were not equally applied when rape victims were black, regardless of the race of the perpetrator. Black women and girls were not the only victims of rape and sexualized violence during Reconstruction, but they were certainly the most vulnerable, as they had few legal protections from this most vicious and invasive of crimes prior to Congressional Reconstruction. While black men could be lynched for even the slightest social indiscretion, black women who had been sexually assaulted suffered the additional indignity of having to prove their chastity to authorities who, like white men generally, based their presumption of guilt on stereotypes about black women's innate lasciviousness. In addition to rape, black women suffered other forms of sexualized violence including whipping and torture of the "bare parts," forced nakedness, and genital mutilation. Groups of white men castrated and otherwise mutilated black men and boys, seemingly with impunity, throughout the state. In cutting off a black man's penis, white men sought not only to emasculate and subjugate the individual victim (in addition to causing his death), but also to consolidate white hegemony and control over all African Americans. Similarly, the rape of black women, while first and foremost a crime against a woman's body, also served the purpose of driving defeat into the black community. By assaulting the bodies of African Americans in this way, whites sought to inflict additional injury on their psyches by creating a climate of fear that would virtually re-enslave all black Texans before they had a chance to taste freedom.

ENDNOTES

1. To date there is no full-length scholarly study of violence against black women during Reconstruction in Texas. There are, however, many important works that cover more generally violence against women during the postwar period in the former Confederacy, especially Jacquelyn Dowd Hall, "The Mind That Burns in Each Body: Women, Rape, and Racial Violence," *Southern Exposure* 12 (1984): 61–71, and Catherine Clinton, "Bloody Terrain: Freedwomen, Sexuality, and Violence During Reconstruction," in *Half Sisters of History: Southern Women and the American Past*, ed. Catherine Clinton (Durham: Duke University Press, 1994). For more general studies of nineteenth-century violence against women see, for example, Elizabeth Pleck, "Wife Beating in Nineteenth-Century America," *Victimology* 4 (1979): 60–74; and "Feminist Responses to 'Crimes Against Women,' 1868–1896," *Signs* 8 (Spring 1983): 451–70.

2. Texas Freedmen's Bureau agents recorded a total of 1681 incidents of violence against blacks; 281 perpetrated against black women and 25 against children. The "Report of Outrages," however, does not specifically categorize either gender or age for either perpetrators or victims. The statistics used here with regard to violence against black women, thus represent only those incidents where the gender of the victim can be accurately determined. This is an especially difficult task, as many entries omit victims' names and any explanation or circumstances surrounding the incident. These omissions, together with the fact that obviously not every case of abuse of black women made its way to the Bureau offices, suggests that the number of black women victims is probably higher. Further, of the 281 incidents of violence perpetrated against black women, the majority (92 percent) were perpetrated by individuals; of the 21 incidents perpetrated by groups of 2 or more, one-third were crimes of a sexual nature. All tabulations by the author from "Records of Criminal Offenses Committed in the State of Texas," Assistant Commissioner (AC), Texas, Vols. 11–13 (T), Bureau of Refugees, Freedmen, and Abandoned Lands (BRFAL), Record Group (RG) 105, roll 32, National Archives (NA). Hereafter cited as "CO no." followed by incident numbers.

3. See for example CO no. 406. The offense is listed simply as "homicide" and, therefore, the context of the crime is not immediately apparent. The circumstances, however, explain that the victim was shot and killed "because she would not commit adultery with him," making this a crime of a sexual nature. This is just one example out of many in the records where the context is only apparent after a review of the

circumstances. Many of the letters written by local Bureau agents to headquarters contain more descriptive language and have, therefore, been additionally useful in determining the context surrounding some of the violent incidents.

4. For the Bureau's perspective on state-sanctioned legal protections for freed people, see W. G. Kirkman to J. P. Richardson (AAAG), 31 January 1868, LS, Vol. 68, pp. 20–24; L. H. Warren to Henry North, 16 Jun 1867, LS, Vol. 102, 30; AC, T, BRFAL, RG 105, NA.

5. Although women could not vote, both black and white women in some instances could sue and be sued in the state of Texas after the Civil War. This was hardly the rule, however, as women were generally excluded from the judicial system based on their gender and black women faced additional restrictions based on race—particularly in the early years of Reconstruction. See Hall, "The Mind That Burns in Each Body," 62; Gerda Lerner, ed., *Black Women in White America: A Documentary History* (New York: Vintage Books, 1992), 149.

6. CO nos. 308, 1653, 1660.

7. Every white female perpetrator in the "Record of Criminal Offenses" is listed by her first and last name, or by the title of "Mrs." or "Miss" followed by her full name or surname only. The overwhelming majority of black women victims in the records, if listed by name at all, are listed by first name only; none are given the title of "Mrs." or "Miss." This follows similar Southern gender conventions as witnessed by J. S. Buckingham and described in his travel accounts. "A female negro is called a 'wench' or 'woman'; and it is this, perhaps, which makes the term 'woman' so offensive to American ears, when applied to white females, who must be called 'ladies.'" J. S. Buckingham, *The Slave States of America* (1842; repr. New York: Negro Universities Press, 1968), 2: 29–30.

8. The Civil Rights Act of 1866 granted African Americans the right to "make and enforce contracts," which presumably included the right to make marital contracts. As such, all blacks living together as married were considered to be so by the Freedmen's Bureau. The state legislature of Texas, however, refused to officially recognize black marriages and most county clerks' offices throughout the state regularly declined to grant marriage licenses to freedmen, until the Republican-dominated legislature of 1870. See for example, B. F. McFarland (County Clerk, Rusk County) to A. J. Hamilton, December 1, 1865; James D. Campbell (County Clerk, Karnes County) to Hamilton, February 5, 1866,

Governor's Papers (Hamilton), Texas State Library, Austin; James W. Throckmorton to Gentlemen of the House of Representatives, August 14, 1866, and "Throckmorton Recommendations to the Legislature, 1866" in James W. Throckmorton Papers, Center for American History, University of Texas, Austin. See also Barry A. Crouch, "The 'Chords of Love': Legalizing Black Marital and Family Rights in Postwar Texas," *Journal of Negro History* 79, Issue 4 (Autumn, 1994): 334–51; Margaret Burnham, "An Impossible Marriage: Slave Law and Family Law," *Law and Inequality: A Journal of Theory and Practice* 5 (July 1987): 187–225; Katherine M. Franke, "Becoming a Citizen: Reconstruction Era Regulation of African American Marriages," *Yale Journal of Law and the Humanities* 11 (1999): 251–309.

9. See Lerner, *Black Women in White America*, 163–64. For a thorough discussion of antebellum southern gender conventions and their relationship to violence, see Elizabeth Fox-Genovese, *Within the Plantation Household: Black and White Women of the Old South* (Chapel Hill: University of North Carolina Press, 1988), 200–3.

10. For Freedmen's Bureau agents specifically protecting black women from violence, see James Smallwood, "Emancipation and the Black Family: A Case Study in Texas," *Social Science Quarterly* (1977): 551–52; and "Black Freedwomen after Emancipation: The Texas Experience," *Prologue* 27 (1995): 315. Although there is limited, if any, evidence of agents' direct complicity in the abuse of black women in Texas, one historian has shown compelling evidence that agents in other states felt they deserved equal access to black women. This is a topic that should be further examined for Texas specifically. Randy Finley, *From Slavery to Uncertain Freedom: The Freedmen's Bureau in Arkansas, 1865–1869* (Fayetteville: University of Arkansas Press, 1996), 20.

11. CO nos. 107, 838.

12. Frequently the whipping of black women and men amounted to a form of sexualized violence, wherein women were whipped on their "bare parts" or otherwise "shamefully" beaten. In addition, it was quite common for victims to be partially or even totally stripped of their clothing prior to whippings.

13. CO nos. 474, 476, 141, 319, 570.

14. CO nos. 1721, 108, 109, 14, 163. White women participated in other forms of brutality against black women. See for example, CO nos. 1639, 372, 1846, 743. As stated previously, it is difficult to determine the gender of perpetrators, as there is not a specific category in the records.

15. W. H. Sinclair to H. A. Ellis, December 23, 1866, Inspection Tour Report, BRFAL, RG 105, NA. See for example, CO nos. 276, 308, 487.

16. CO nos. 159, 1130, 2076. Bureau agents typically used terms such as "shameful" to describe abuses of a sexual nature. Like the elderly, the very young were also victims of racial violence.

17. CO nos. 373, 377, 295. One of the problems in trying to determine the number of black children who suffered at the hands of whites is evident in CO no. 295. This newborn, like so many other children injured or killed along with a parent, is not listed separately in the records as an individual victim, making an accurate accounting of young victims impossible.

18. CO nos. 1825, 2278, 484. It should be noted that the daughter of Caroline Wallace, who was obviously a victim in this particular case, is not listed separately in the "Report of Outrages."

19. CO nos. 488, 490, 219.

20. William H. Sinclair (inspector) to J.T. Kirkman Acting Assistant Adjutant General (AAAG), Feb. 26, 1867, box 21, AC, T, BRFAL, RG 105, NA. One woman was convicted of helping her husband escape from jail with a pick axe. See also *List of Freedmen and Women Confined in the Texas Penitentiary, Nov. 6, 1866*, Penitentiary Papers, Texas State Library, Austin, Texas.

21. CO nos. 1975, 901, 366.

22. CO nos. 241, 2044.

23. CO no. 199. "Bucking" was a common form of punishment used during the antebellum and Reconstruction periods. For first-hand accounts see for example Henry Bibb, *The Life and Adventures of Henry Bibb: An American Slave* (1849; reprint with an introduction by Charles J. Heglar, Madison: University of Wisconsin Press, 2001), 103–5; and George P. Rawick, *The American Slave: A Composite Autobiography* (Westport: Greenwood Press, 1972), 61–62, 142–43, 202.

24. CO no. 902; Catherine Clinton, "Reconstructing Freedwomen," in *Divided Houses: Gender and the Civil War*, ed. Catherine Clinton and Nina Silber (New York: Oxford University Press, 1992), 310.

25. Paula Giddings, *When and Where I Enter: The Impact of Black Women on Race and Sex in America* (New York: Bantam Books, 1984), 47–48, 62; Fox-Genovese, *Within the Plantation Household*, 49–50, 64–65, 202–3, 290.

26. Angela Y. Davis, *Women, Race and Class* (New York: Random House, 1981), 9–10; Fox-Genovese, *Within the Plantation Household*,

322; Deborah Gray White, *Ar'n't I a Woman?: Female Slaves in the Plantation South* (New York: W.W. Norton & Company, 1985), 98–99. Fox-Genovese and White posit that slave women often used pregnancy, real or feigned, as a negotiating tool to get better treatment and lighten the work load while Davis describes slave owners' complete disregard for slave women even in the later months of pregnancy. See also Thelma Jennings, "' Us Colored Women Had to Go Through a Plenty': Sexual Exploitation of African-American Slave Women," *Journal of Women's History* 1 (1991): 54.

27. Davis, *Women, Race and Class*, 10; CO no. 204; Jennings, "' Us Colored Women Had to Go Through a Plenty,'" 56–57.

28. Sinclair to AAAG J. Kirkman, July 2, 1867, LR, AC, T, BRFAL, RG 105, NA; CO no. 1133.

29. All tabulations by author from the "Record of Criminal Offenses." Civil "action" includes arresting, filing charges against, trying, and assessing fines. Bureau "action" includes the same, although agents also frequently turned perpetrators over immediately to civil authorities, as they had limited jurisdiction in many cases. It is possible that some of these cases may have been prosecuted after agents filed reports. With the widespread practice of jury nullification, however, it is doubtful that any significant number would have resulted in convictions. For limitations and constraints on the Freedmen's Bureau generally, see James Oakes, "A Failure of Vision: The Collapse of the Freedmen's Bureau Courts," *Civil War History* 25 (1979): 66–76.

30. John D'Emilio and Estelle B. Freedman, *Intimate Matters: A History of Sexuality in America*, 2nd ed. (Chicago: University of Chicago Press, 1997), 104. See also Cardyn, "Sexualized Racism/Gendered Violence," 10, 11, 13. Because Cardyn's work relies heavily on the thirteen-volume *Klan Report* to analyze sexual violence in the former Confederacy, she all but ignores Texas. One purpose of this essay is to fill that void in the literature.

31. Hall, "The Mind that Burns," 62.

32. Jacquelyn Dowd Hall discusses the rape of black women as the counterpart to the lynching of black men in "The Mind that Burns," 62, a theme that runs throughout her biography of white anti-lynching crusader, Jessie Daniel Ames. See Hall, *Revolt Against Chivalry: Jessie Daniel Ames and the Women's Campaign against Lynching* (New York: Columbia University Press, 1979), 131. For further discussion of lynching used specifically as a tool to reinforce the status quo for all whites and all blacks, see Angela Y. Davis, *Women, Race, and Class*,

185; Laura F. Edwards, "Sexual Violence, Gender, Reconstruction, and the Extension of Patriarchy in Granville County, North Carolina," *North Carolina Historical Review* 68 (1991): 237–60; Martha Hodes, "The Sexualization of Reconstruction Politics: White Women and Black Men in the South after the Civil War," *Journal of the History of Sexuality* 3 (1993): 402–17; Robyn Wiegman, "The Anatomy of Lynching," *Journal of the History of Sexuality* 3 (1993):445–67. General accounts of lynching include W. Fitzhugh Brundage, *Lynching in the New South: Georgia and Virginia, 1880–1930* (Urbana: University of Illinois Press, 1997) and *Under Sentence of Death: Lynching in the South*, ed. W. Fitzhugh Brundage (Chapel Hill: University of North Carolina Press, 1997); Philip Dray, *At the Hands of Persons Unknown: The Lynching of Black America* (New York: Random House, 2002).

33. Sterling, *We Are Your Sisters*, 353 (quoting an unnamed Alabama doctor); Hall, "The Mind that Burns," 63.

34. Ronald Littlewood, "Military Rape," *Anthropology Today* 13, no. 2 (April 1997): 8. The use of rape specifically as an instrument of warfare, especially in recent conflicts, has been documented in a number of scholarly works. In this context, rape during the Reconstruction conflict may be seen as a systematic effort of white men to inflict defeat on blacks. James Smallwood's recent work on the Lee-Peacock feud in Texas looks at Reconstruction in the context of a continuation of the Civil War. Smallwood, *Murder and Mayhem*. For a general history of rape as social control, see Merril D. Smith, ed., *Sex Without Consent: Rape and Sexual Coercion in America* (New York: New York University Press, 2001).

35. Beverly Greene Bond, "' Till Fair Aurora Rise': African American Women in Memphis, Tennessee 1840–1915" (Ph.D. diss., University of Memphis, 1996), 98. See also Lerner, *Black Women in White America*, 172–73.

36. Many historians have posited that black women were, in fact, more vulnerable to rape and other forms of sexual abuse after emancipation. According to Laura Edwards, "emancipation heightened the vulnerability of African-American women to violence at the hands of white men, who used rape and other ritualized forms of sexual abuse to limit black women's freedom and to reinscribe antebellum racial hierarchies." Edwards, *Gendered Strife and Confusion*, 199. See also Hazel V. Carby, *Reconstructing Womanhood: The Emergence of the Afro-American Woman Novelist* (New York: Oxford University Press, 1987), 39; Clinton,

"Bloody Terrain," 331; Davis, *Women, Race and Class*, 175–76; Hall, "The Mind That Burns in Each Body," 63; Smallwood, "Black Freedwomen after Emancipation," 313.

37. D'Emilio, *Intimate Matters*, 107.

38. The Bureau's "Record of Criminal Offenses" does not list black men as perpetrators of rape or attempted rape on black women—although one incident describes the "constant ravishing of a favorite black man" (CO no. 497). This is a surprising oversight in the Bureau's violence compilation, as some black women did report such crimes to agents who then alerted civil authorities in many cases. See for example, L. H. Warren (Agent, Houston) to Mayor De Daligethy, June 13, 1867, Vol. 102, p. 27; Warren to Judge B.P. Fuller, June 27, 1867, Vol. 102, p. 57–58, AC, T, BRFAL, RG 105, NA. Unfortunately, there is no record of charges being filed in these specific cases. Jacquelyn Dowd Hall speaks to the prevalence of black on black rape and its near inevitability during the period: "In a society that defines manhood in terms of power and possessions, black men are denied the resources to fulfill their expected roles . . . inevitably, they turn to domination of women, the one means of asserting traditional manhood within their control." Hall, "The Mind that Burns," 70.

39. CO nos. 2073, 2074, 2075, 2077, 1252.

40. H. P. N. Gammel, *The Laws of Texas, 1822–1897* (Austin: The Gammel Book Company, 1898), 5: 161.

41. Lerner, *Black Women in White America*, 164; CO no. 1893; see also Gammel, *The Laws of Texas*, 161; D'Emilio, *Intimate Matters*, 104–8.

42. CO nos. 1331, 406, 1587.

43. All calculations by author from "Record of Criminal Offenses." Of the 281 incidents of violence against black women recorded in the Bureau records, 2.5 percent (7) are noted specifically as rape or attempted rape in the "Offense Nature" or crime column. In that same number of cases, 2.5 percent (7), rape is not noted specifically, but instead "assault and battery" or some other generic description is noted in the crime column, while rape or "shameful treatment" is described in the circumstances surrounding the attack.

44. CO nos. 308, 1587.

45. The myth of the black rapist not only led to numerous lynchings, but it also became deeply ingrained in the interpretation of law and in trial procedure for decades into the twentieth century. The foundation of

this myth rested on the belief that consensual sex between a black man and a white woman was impossible; any sexual activity between them constituted rape.

46. Gammel, *The Laws of Texas*, 161.

47. Victoria Bynum, *Unruly Women: The Politics of Social and Sexual Control in the Old South* (Chapel Hill: University of North Carolina Press, 1992), 109.

48. Inge Lunde and Jørgen Ortmann, "Prevalence and Sequelae of Sexual Torture," *Lancet* 336 (1991): 289. Lisa Cardyn has examined sexualized violence perpetrated by the Ku Klux Klan during the later years of Reconstruction in this context. See Cardyn, "Sexualized Racism/Gendered Violence: Trauma and the Body Politic in the Reconstruction South" (Ph.D. diss., Yale University, 2003). For rape as sexualized racism, see Coramae Richey Mann and Lance H. Selva, "The Sexualization of Racism: The Black as Rapist and White Justice," *Western Journal of Black Studies* 3 (1979): 168–177. For an analysis of the use of sexualized violence in the context of war and defeat, see Ronald Littlewood, "Military Rape," *Anthropology Today* 13, no. 2 (April 1997): 8. Littlewood explains how violence against women's bodies in particular translates into violence against the defeated society, although his explanation can certainly be applied to men's bodies as well.

49. Cardyn, 62.

50. Deborah Gray White has posited that many whippings during the post-bellum period were indeed "sexually suggestive." See White, *Ar'n't I a Woman?*, 33. For whippings by Klan members specifically serving a sexual purpose see Cardyn, "Sexualized Racism/Gendered Violence," 60–79. Cardyn also suggests that lynchings—even those that did not include castration or other genital mutilation—could be seen as sexual in nature: "These blood-drenched spectacles, with their defilement, desecration, and display of the oppositional body, are at times as suffused with sexual meaning as was their sustaining logic" (Cardyn, 130). For lynchings as metaphorical rapes, see also Trudier Harris-Lopez, *Exorcising Blackness: Historical and Literary Lynching and Burning Rituals* (Bloomington: Indiana University Press, 1984), 23.

51. CO nos. 199, 1587, 1588. Black men were often stripped and abused in the same sexualized fashion as their female counterparts. For elaboration see Rebecca A. Kosary, "To Degrade and Control: White Violence and the Maintenance of Racial and Gender Boundaries in Reconstruction Texas, 1865–1868" (Ph.D. diss., Texas A&M University, 2006).

52. On the psychology of gang rape, see for example W. H. Blanchard, "The Group Process in Gang Rape," *Journal of Social Psychology* 49 (1959): 259; A. Nicholas Groth, *Men Who Rape: The Psychology of the Offender* (New York: Plenum Press, 1979), 115; Susan Brownmiller, *Against Our Will: Men, Women, and Rape* (New York: Simon & Schuster, 1975), 125.

53. Hall, "Mind that Burns," 63. For rape as communication between men, see for example Robin Morgan, "Theory and Practice: Pornography and Rape" in *Take Back the Night: Women on Pornography*, ed. Laura Lederer (New York: William Morrow and Company, 1980), 140. Cardyn, "Sexualized Racism/Gendered Violence," 101.

PART FOUR

Regional Perspectives: The Frontier, the Interior, and Places in Between

CHAPTER 13

Governor James Throckmorton and the Question of Frontier Violence in Reconstruction Texas, 1866–1867

by

Kenneth W. Howell

At the close of the Civil War, Kiowa and Comanche warriors increased their raids against Anglo settlers living along the Texas frontier. The line of settlements, which were fairly stable during the war, retreated more than a hundred miles eastward as settlers abandoned their homes and moved to the safety of more populated regions. The population of Wise County alone decreased from 3,160 in 1860 to 1,450 in 1870. Those families who refused to leave their homes often moved in close proximity of their neighbors and created fortifications to guard against Indian raiders. Many settlers hoped that the end of the war would prompt the return of the U.S. Army. In fact, in 1865, approximately 4,000 federal troops were stationed in Texas, but instead of serving on the frontier, they were located in the interior of the state. General Philip H. Sheridan, Commander of the Department of the Gulf, ordered them to remain in the interior where they could protect freedmen and white Unionists from ex-Confederates, organized terrorist groups, and outlaw gangs.[1] Conditions continued to deteriorate in the western counties for almost a year before the state and federal government began to seriously consider the need to send troops westward. During this time, one of the principal voices calling on the government to protect the western settlers was James Webb Throckmorton, a North Texas politician who had forged his career on defending the frontier.

When he was sixteen years old, Throckmorton moved with his family to the wilds of North Texas, settling lands in an area northeast of the present-day town of McKinney.[2] Less than a year after his arrival, young James learned his first lesson about frontier violence. On Christmas Day

Illustration 15. Gov. James Webb Throckmorton. (Courtesy of Library of Congress)

1842, the families of Wesley Clements and Peg Whistler started to build a small settlement approximately eight miles north of the Throckmorton family home. As Clements and his neighbor were cutting logs to finish work on their cabins, an unidentified group of Indians attacked and killed them. The wives and children of the men watched the brutal attack from the Clements family cabin. During the attack, Mrs. Clements attempted to take a gun to her husband, but the assailants forced her to retreat back to the safety of her home. Their attackers then moved toward the settlers' house but were turned away when the women fired several shots in their direction. The female defenders remained in the cabin until nightfall. Realizing that their attackers had apparently left the area, the women quietly moved to the side of their fallen men, hoping that they might still be alive. They were not. After assessing their circumstances, the women decided that Catherine Clements and her children would remain with the slain bodies to keep wild animals from devouring the corpses during the night, while Mrs. Whistler walked to the Throckmorton settlement and sought help from other white inhabitants in the area. The following day, Throckmorton's father, with the aid of other settlers, rescued Mrs. Clements and recovered the bodies of the two men. The families interred the slain men in a cemetery near the Throckmorton family home.[3]

The Indian raid was undoubtedly etched into the future governor's memory, especially considering that Wesley Clements was his stepmother's brother. The attack strengthened young Throckmorton's resolve to protect settlers from future raids. Between 1842 and 1843, he served as a member of Capt. Jesse Stiff's ranger company that patrolled North Texas guarding against Indian depredations. James eventually became a sergeant of a company of sixteen men from Fannin County. Perhaps because of his family's personal loss or maybe as a result of his experiences as a frontier ranger, Throckmorton dedicated the remainder of his life to protecting the settlers.[4] At no time was this more evident than during his brief tenure as governor of Texas, when he pushed the federal government to protect the frontier. In fact, Throckmorton pursued frontier defense with such vigor that he strained relations and created an environment of distrust between his office and the authorities who were charged with enforcing federal Reconstruction policies in the state. This breach of trust would ultimately contribute to Throckmorton's political downfall.

Prior to his inauguration, Throckmorton wrote to a group of citizens living on the frontier assuring them that adequate protection would soon be forthcoming. He stated that "every exertion within my reach shall be exhausted—the frontier shall be protected. We must first look to the General Government. If that fails, then [we will] take the burden upon ourselves." He continued, "I shall urge upon the Legislature the passage of such measures as will give me the power to defend the border, in the event of failure on the part of the General Government to afford adequate and permanent protection." Throckmorton then asked the people on the frontier to send him as much information as possible on the condition of their area.[5]

In his inaugural address on August 9, 1866, the governor reiterated these themes and made sure that the legislature understood his position. In his opening paragraph, Throckmorton informed those present at the inaugural ceremonies that the frontier settlers were "being desolated by a murderous and powerful enemy" and that "their property [was] given to the flames, or carried off as booty." Additionally, he revealed that "their little ones [were being] murdered, and their wives and daughters carried into a captivity more terrible than death, and reserved for tortures such as savage cruelty and lust can alone inflict." And in the face of such dangers, Throckmorton reminded his audience that the settlers remained "unprotected by the [federal] government we support, with troops quartered in the interior, where there is peace and quiet; unwilling to send armed citizens to defend the suffering border, for fear of arousing unjust suspicions as to the motive."[6]

Having stated the facts as he understood them, Throckmorton then revealed his determination to help the settlers at all cost, echoing his letter to the settlers before his inauguration. He stated that "the conditions of the frontier shall receive my serious attention. At the earliest moment, I shall endeavor to secure from the General Government adequate and permanent protection, and will, at the same time, make every exertion to have such treaties, made by the proper authorities, as will insure future security to the people." Furthermore, Throckmorton announced that he would push for frontier protection even if the federal government refused to send troops. He said, "In the event, a sufficient number of troops cannot be procured from the Government, for the protection of the frontier, I shall not hesitate to urge expenditures by the State for this purpose." Continuing, the governor revealed his affinity for the settlers by telling his audience that "the people of that region, have already suffered with a patience and fortitude truly commendable. They are a bulwark to the older settled portions of the country, and if they give way, and are broken up in their homes, the loss of life and property, so long borne by them, will fall upon sections now enjoying peace and prosperity."[7] As if to put an exclamation point on his inaugural address, frontier settlers began to inundate the governor's office with letters that described the intensity and horror of the Indian raids on white settlements: Each correspondent ended their letters with the same plea—send troops to help protect the white settlements until the Native Americans could be removed or exterminated.[8]

On August 14, the governor received a report from the Cherokee Nation that "a party of thirty Osage Indians on their return from Texas with a large number of [stolen] horses passed" nearby Washita "about a week ago and thence came two miles in the direction of this place where they turned north towards the Osage Country."[9] Another report of stock theft detailed that four white men ran across two different groups of Indians near the "mouth of the Concho [River]" and that the Indians were in possession of a large number of stolen horses and cattle. According to this report, "cattle in that section of country were nearly all driven out," and "many settlers have left the country" because "a general feeling of uncertainty prevails."[10] Numerous letters such as these crossed the governor's desk, and financial loss due to theft was a commonly reported occurrence. However, these accounts were not as terrifying as the reports of violent acts committed against the pioneers.

Two days after receiving the report on Osage activities, the governor received a letter from T. Smiley, a trader in the Cherokee Nation. Smiley reported that a potential Indian war against Texas seemed evident. Relaying information he had obtained from Major R. Miller, a former United States Indian agent in the Indian Territories, the correspondent stated that "the Indians of the prairie (Kiowas & Comanches) have had their usual annual council and being represented by the Arapahos and others. They have determined to make war on the state of Texas with renewed vigor." Smiley continued, "I need not explain to you the small amount of interest that the agents and other officials on this side of Red River take in the welfare of the state of Texas, and it would appear from the slow movement of the Government troops that the protection of the frontier is almost lost sight of." The Indian trader then warned Throckmorton that "unless there is some active measures taken, the people of the border counties [of Texas] are bound to suffer."[11] Undoubtedly, this report as well as other accounts of Indian depredations strengthened the governor's resolve to protect settlers living on the Texas frontier.

Believing that one of the primary responsibilities of government was to protect and to aid the people it served, Throckmorton turned to the federal military for a solution to the frontier problems. Apparently, he was not bothered by the crimes being committed against the freedmen and their white allies in the interior of the state.[12] However, most of the correspondence reaching the governor's desk during his early months in office was from frontier settlers. As a result, the governor called on the U. S. Army to move its troops to frontier counties, leaving the freedmen to fend for themselves.

Throckmorton's appeal to the federal government for frontier protection faced two major obstacles. First, U. S. Army commanders believed that reports of hostile activities on the Texas frontier were exaggerated. Second, the occupation forces distrusted the loyalty of the Texas government, inferring that the state officials were only trying to move the U. S. forces from the interior where soldiers were protecting freedmen and white radical Unionists from ex-Confederates and former Secessionists. Throckmorton quickly realized that he would need to gain the trust of the occupying forces if the frontier was to be rid of Native Americans.[13]

Throckmorton sent a request for frontier troops to Maj. Gen. Horatio G. Wright, who had replaced Gen. Gordon Granger as commander of the District of Texas a year earlier. General Wright replied to Throckmorton that he had no authority to send troops to the western region of the state but that he would send the governor's request to his superior, Commander of the Department of the Gulf Gen. Philip Sheridan. Wright also informed Throckmorton that there were few available troops for the frontier service and that current hostility in Texas against the freedmen and Unionists warranted keeping all available forces in the interior of the state.[14]

The governor was disappointed in Wright's reply, believing that federal troops were no longer needed within the interior of the state. Throckmorton undoubtedly weighed the evidence that crossed his desk, the majority of which was concerned with Indian depredations on the frontier, while reports of the injustices perpetrated against freedmen and Unionists were primarily limited to a few military reports.[15] Thus, while waiting for General Sheridan to respond to Wright's message, the governor wrote to President Andrew Johnson on August 25, informing him of the conditions on the frontier.

Throckmorton's decision to write the president was a logical move considering that the governor had earlier pledged support for his plan of reconstruction and the president's views of the freedmen were closely aligned with his own: Neither man was willing to afford the ex-slaves more than freedom from slavery. Thus, the governor may have entertained the idea that Johnson would order the military from the interior. In his letter to the president, Throckmorton strongly suggested that the settlers' safety hinged on troop deployment to the frontier, especially in the northern part of the state. He voiced his opinion that only a show of force could prevent future Indian raids on white settlements.[16]

Meanwhile, Wright forwarded Throckmorton's request to General Sheridan with an endorsement of the governor's petition for frontier troops.[17] Sheridan was not convinced by his subordinate's assessment of frontier conditions in Texas, believing that Throckmorton was purposely exaggerating the severity and number of Indian depredations in an effort to obstruct the military's effort to protect blacks and Unionists from their ex-Confederate neighbors. Nevertheless, the general promptly informed the governor that he had "directed the District [of Texas] commander to send a cavalry force to Fredericksburg or [in the] vicinity, from thence to operate against such Indians and white men as are committing depredations on this portion of the frontier." Sheridan also noted that "as soon as additional troops are sent me to establish forts on the frontier, it will be done."[18]

While Throckmorton was trying to secure a federal presence in West Texas, the state legislature attempted to provide relief to the settlers by creating three mounted volunteer regiments for service on the frontier. In an effort to win federal approval for their actions, the legislators placed the newly formed regiments under the direction of the federal military with the stipulation that the volunteers could not be removed from the state for detached service. The Texas Legislature justified the creation of the frontier troops by arguing that a majority of the federal soldiers were posted along the Rio Grande due to political unrest in Mexico: At the instigation of Napoleon III of France, Maximilian was attempting to establish himself as emperor of Mexico, and federal authorities were concerned that Maximilian might contemplate an invasion of Texas if he were successful in seizing the reins of power. Therefore, the legislature deemed it necessary to authorize the enlistment of the Texas frontier troops for use in the unprotected northern and western regions of the state.[19]

The legislature's debates regarding the formation of frontier regiments were published in various newspapers throughout the state, and even before the legislature officially passed the act, the governor received numerous letters recommending various men to command ranging companies that might be raised in their region of the state. Typical of these letters was the one from John Baylor on September 1, 1866, recommending Capt. John Pulliam for command of one of the proposed Frontier Regiments. "Capt Pulliam was with me during the late war and was a most efficient and excellent officer," Baylor wrote. "Should you think proper to authorize him to raise a Company, I have no hesitation in saying that he will prove in every way worthy of your confidence."[20]

Throckmorton continued to receive reports throughout September from settlers outlining new Indian depredations and letters from frontiersmen requesting that he provide immediate and adequate protection of their homes. In one such letter, Jack J. Cureton, a noted Indian fighter, wrote that people "in all parts of the country" were continually asking him what he thought the governor would do to protect them. "I answer them as I did when talking about the election," Cureton explained. "Throckmorton will do all in his power to protect us. I assured the frontier people if we elect Throckmorton we will have a friend on whom we can depend." Cureton then moved to the central point of his letter, stating that "I have been solicited time and again to [write] to you on this subject. We want some organization of a military character to compel men to there [*sic*] duty . . . all eyes are directed towards Austin for relief. They hope to hear of our own countrymen being called out in addition to the troops sent by the Federal Government." The frontiersman concluded by stating that "the sentiments of [the] frontier people who are willing to shoulder their arms to protect their property, wives, children, fathers & mothers if they are permitted to take part in the work and they think that there are no men in the world so capable of doing justice to the service as those who have lived and battled with the enemy for the last eight years."[21]

Throckmorton replied to Cureton on September 8 and reaffirmed his determination to help the people of the frontier, but he also revealed the obstacles that confronted him in providing relief. "I can assure you that I will give every exertion in my power to the protection of the frontier," Throckmorton declared that "the legislature is now considering a bill for this purpose, and I hope they will do something. But unless they provide the means to pay for it, it is useless to give me the power to raise men." The governor prophetically concluded that "after the legislature does all it can, it may be that the General Government will not permit us to call out men for this purpose. I have already called upon the President and Military authorities for protection, and shall continue to press it in every conceivable way until it is accomplished."[22]

At about the same time Cureton's letter arrived, Throckmorton began receiving reports of depredations in Montague and Cooke counties. According to J. T. Mosby, "a man by the name of Box was killed and his family consisting of a wife & four daughters were carried off." Mosby stated that "immediate action in reference to frontier protection" was necessary. "Something must be done," proclaimed the frontiersman, because "the settlements on the frontier will be abandoned."[23] After receiving numerous letters like those mentioned above and reading the many newspaper accounts of the same stripe, Throckmorton strengthened his resolve to provide relief to the people living in the northwestern counties.

At the end of September, Throckmorton informed both Secretary of War Edwin M. Stanton and General Sheridan of the legislature's act that authorized him to raise state troops for the frontier. The governor urged Sheridan to accept the regiments as part of his command and stressed the need for troops on the frontier. In his letter to Stanton, Throckmorton was more forward. He stated that if the federal government failed to adequately protect the frontier settlers then the "state will be compelled to undertake it." The governor expressed his opinion that "the troops stationed in the interior of the state are of no service whatever. The laws can be enforced, and every class of our population can be protected in all their rights, without the aid of the military, and I most respectfully ask that the troops be withdrawn."[24] He requested again that federal troops, especially black soldiers, be removed from the interior of the state, blaming them for inciting unnecessary violence. The governor's appraisal of the troops in the interior seemed to reflect his own racist views. He unfairly blamed black troops for the atrocities occurring in the interior of the state, rather than properly faulting unreconstructed white Texans.[25]

Also in late September, Maj. Gen. George W. Getty replaced Wright as the commander of the District of Texas. Still waiting to hear from federal authorities in Washington, Throckmorton immediately wrote to Getty apprising him of the situation and requested that he use his influence to ensure the protection of the settlers. Additionally, the governor wrote to Gen. Ulysses S. Grant requesting that the Texas be allowed to raise state troops to protect the frontier. By early October, Throckmorton's campaign to procure troops was being closely scrutinized by federal officials and military commanders.[26]

The governor soon received ironically disappointing news. On October 11, Secretary of War Stanton wrote to him that the president had considered the circumstances in Texas in a recent cabinet meeting and was disposed to provide the Texas settlers all possible aid. Stanton continued, however, by informing the governor that the president believed that the United States military would be able to provide adequate protection to the settlers without the help of the Texas volunteers. Stanton's letter to Throckmorton reaffirmed an earlier telegram that General Sheridan had sent the governor on October 9, 1866. Sheridan informed the state's chief executive that he would not accept the Texas volunteers as part of his command. However, despite his suspicion that the Texas Legislature was conspiring to remove the federal troops from the interior, General Sheridan stated that "I have the pleasure of informing you that additional troops have been ordered to your state; that an inspector will be at once sent to the northern frontier of Texas and that as much protection as we possibly can give to the frontier will be cheerfully given, and also, that in the early spring the frontier posts will be established."[27]

The federal authorities' refusal to allow the state to raise frontier troops created an embarrassing situation for the governor because he had already issued an order to begin organizing these companies on October 6.[28] In many of the frontier counties, the inhabitants enthusiastically responded to the governor's call for troops and immediately began to volunteer for service. In early November with federal troops on their way to the frontier, Throckmorton was forced to rescind his earlier order. In writing to the frontiersmen, Throckmorton put the best possible interpretation on his predicament. For example, the governor wrote to Thomas F. Mosby that "I do not contemplate at this time, being forced to the necessity of using them [state troops]. Yet, I desired very much that the company should be organized so that should the absolute necessity occur I could order them out." Throckmorton then updated Mosby on the federal army's efforts, stating that "eleven companies [of] regular cavalry, under Lt. Col. Oats, an old experienced frontier officer, are ordered to concentrate immediately at Jacksboro. I have asked and believe I will succeed in the request, to have four companies stationed in Montague, one or two in Cook [*sic;* County]. . . . Finally, the governor stated that he had "such hints from Sheridan that I am satisfied it would not do for me to order out the frontier reg's at this juncture. This will explain the reason of my not rushing them in the field."[29] Despite his awkward situation, Throckmorton had reasons to be optimistic about the federal government's protection of the frontier.

In mid-October, Sheridan initiated a plan to provide protection to the western and northern counties of the state. The commanding officer wrote to Bvt. Maj. Gen. Samuel P. Heintzelman authorizing him to post troops under his command on the frontier if he deemed it necessary. Sheridan also informed Heintzelman that additional infantry troops were en route to Texas. On October 16, General Sheridan informed Throckmorton that he had transferred command of the District of Texas to General Heintzelman and that he had authorized the new commander to concentrate his entire cavalry force, approximately 2,000 men, on the frontier.[30]

Furthermore, Sheridan ordered Major G. A. Forsythe to the northwestern part of the state to ascertain the true nature of the Indian threat.[31] Throckmorton sent a dispatch to Major Forsythe after learning of his mission. The governor urged the army scout to closely examine the circumstances in Montague, Jack, Palo Pinto, Erath, Comanche, Brown,

San Saba, Llano, and Mason counties, which seemed to be the counties most devastated by Indian raids. The governor wrote to J. P. Dumas of Sherman informing him that Forsythe was en route to the area to examine possible locations for additional fortifications. In essence, Throckmorton asked Dumas to function as a guide for Major Forsythe and to inform him of the Indians' devastating effect on the northern frontier. Naturally, it took time for Forsythe to complete his task. As a result, the deployment of troops was delayed several weeks.[32]

Desiring that troops be deployed to the frontier as quickly as possible, Throckmorton wrote to the commander of the 6th U.S. Cavalry on November 5, 1866, and inquired as to why federal forces had not started their march to the frontier region. The governor warned the commander that additional delays and continued raids would force him to muster the Texas volunteers into service.[33] Throckmorton's impatience was unfounded. Even as he wrote to the commander of the 6th Cavalry, General Sheridan ordered troops deployed to the frontier. On November 6, he instructed General Heintzelman to post the second battalion of the 17th U. S. Infantry at Austin and to send the 4th and 6th U. S. Cavalry units to the northern and western counties of the state. Sheridan ordered Heintzelman to move troops without orders from the headquarters in cases of emergency.[34] After receiving these instructions, the Texas commander ordered eleven companies of the 6th Cavalry to take winter quarters in Jacksboro while he sent five companies of 4th Cavalry to Fort Mason. Of the companies sent to Fort Mason, one was to remain there while three were to proceed to Camp Verde and one to Fort Clark. While Heintzelman relocated troops, he left some soldiers in the southern part of the state: One company remained at Fort Inge, while two others relocated in the subdistrict of the Rio Grande border. Additionally, the general sent troops to reinforce interior posts. Ten companies in the first battalion of the 17th Infantry were sent to major points in southeast Texas: Two companies were sent to Hempstead; two to Brenham; two to Houston; and four to Galveston.[35]

The deployment of troops slowly proceeded, but it appears that the U. S. Army reacted in good faith to protect the citizens on the Texas frontier. By the end of December 1866, the northern and western counties had been adequately supplied with U. S. soldiers, and the troops seemed to have been effective in curbing Indian raids. The number of the reports of new depredations declined in 1867. As a result, the frontier ceased to be a major issue of concern for the Throckmorton administration. The governor could boast that he had been the driving force behind protecting the settlers. However, the governor's threat to use Texas volunteers obviously produced distrust between his administration and the military authorities. It seems certain that Throckmorton's persistence in demanding that the troops be removed from the interior of the state to frontier fortifications and the tactics of appealing to General Sheridan's superiors in Washington were two contributing factors that eventually led to the governor's removal from office in August 1867.[36]

Furthermore, the conflicts between Governor Throckmorton and the federal government reveal how difficult it was for the federal government to carry out its Reconstruction policies in Texas, especially considering that the state had to contend with violence on multiple fronts. In the Lone Star State, the military not only had to protect blacks and their white allies from ex-Confederates and former Secessionists, but they also had to provide troops to defend frontier settlers from Indian and bandito raids, and during the early months of Reconstruction, they had to maintain a military presence on the border as events unfolded in Mexico. Ultimately, violence on the Texas frontier and elsewhere in the state contributed significantly to the failure of federal Reconstruction policies in the state. As such, scholars can no longer ignore the impact that frontier violence had on Texas politics during the Reconstruction era.

ENDNOTES

1. Ernest Wallace, *Ranald S. Mackenzie on the Texas Frontier* (College Station: Texas A&M University Press, 1993), 23; Allen Lee Hamilton, *Sentinel of the Southern Plains: Fort Richardson and the Northwest Texas Frontier, 1866–1878* (Fort Worth: Texas Christian University Press, 1988), 5–6.

2. Claude Elliott, *Leathercoat: The Life of James W. Throckmorton* (San Antonio: Standard Printing Co, 1938), 5–7; *McKinney Examiner*, October 3, 1940; Ruby Crawford Holbert, "The Public Career of James Webb Throckmorton, 1851–1867" (M.A. thesis, University of Texas, 1932), 3–4; Lee J. Strambaugh and Lillian J. Strambaugh, *A History of Collin County, Texas* (Austin: The Texas State Historical Association, 1958), 206; Harold E. Massey, "A History of Collin County" (M.A. thesis, Southwestern University, 1948), 1–2; Z. T. Fulmore, *The History and Geography of Texas As Told in County Names* (Austin: Press of E. L. Stech, 1915), 97–98.

3. J. W. Wilbarger, *Indian Depredations in Texas* (Austin: Hutchinson Printing House, 1889; repr., Austin: The Pemberton Press, 1967),

436–37; W. A. Carter, *History of Fannin County, Texas* (Bonham, TX: privately printed, 1885), 30–31; Alice Ellison Pitts and Minnie Pitts Champ, *Collin County, Texas, Families* (Fort Worth: Landmark Publishing, 1998), 2: 55; Massey, "A History of Collin County," 24. Massey reveals that few Indian attacks occurred in Collin County and that most of them were the result of Anglo encroachment upon their lands and the natives' need for horses. For other examples of Indian raids occurring in Fannin County in 1842 see Dorman H. Winfrey and James M. Day, eds., *The Indian Papers of Texas and the Southwest, 1825–1916* (Austin: The Pemberton Press, 1966), 1: 125, 127, 129, 131, 134.

4. Elliott, *Leathercoat*, 7–8.

5. Throckmorton to Col. W. W. Cochran, E. Stewart, and others, August 8, 1866, Throckmorton (J. W.) Letter Book, CAH; Bruce Logan Parker, "Indian Affairs and the Frontier of Texas" (M.A. Thesis, University of Texas, 1925), 33–34.

6. Bruce Logan Parker, "Indian Affairs and the Frontier of Texas" (M.A. Thesis, University of Texas, 1925), 23–24; Charles W. Ramsdell, *Reconstruction in Texas* (Austin: University of Texas Press, 1910; repr. 1970), 136–37; Holbert, "The Public Career of James Webb Throckmorton," 83–84; Elliott, *Leathercoat*, 133–34; *Dallas Herald*, August 18, 1866; Transcription of Inaugural Ceremonies of James W. Throckmorton, August 13, 1866, James W. Throckmorton Collection, 1838–1888. Center of American History, Austin, Texas, hereafter cited as CAH.

7. Transcription of Inaugural Ceremonies of James W. Throckmorton, August 13, 1866, James W. Throckmorton Collection, 1838–1888, CAH.

8. Elliott, *Leathercoat*, 134.

9. T. Smiley to Hon. J. W. Throckmorton, August 14, 1866, Records of James Throckmorton, Texas Office of the Governor, Archives Division, Texas State Library, hereafter cited as TOG/AD/TSL.

10. T. L. Jackson and others to Governor J. W. Throckmorton, August 15, 1866, Records of James Throckmorton, TOG/AD/TSL.

11. T. Smiley to Governor J. W. Throckmorton, August 16, 1866, Records of James Throckmorton, TOG/AD/TSL.

12. For a statistical analysis of the violence perpetrated against the freedmen and white Unionists see Gregg Cantrell, "Racial Violence and Reconstruction Politics in Texas," *Southwestern Historical Quarterly* 93 (January 1990): 333–55.

13. Parker, "Indian Affairs and the Frontier of Texas," 15 and 29–30; Walter Tribble Chapin, "Presidential Reconstruction in Texas,

1865–1867" (M.A. thesis, North Texas State University, 1979), 121; Elliott, *Leathercoat*, 135.

14. Major General Wright to Throckmorton, August 14, 1866, Records of James Throckmorton, TOG/AD/TSL; William Richter, *The Army in Texas During Reconstruction, 1865–1870* (College Station: Texas A&M University, 1987), 54.

15. *Dallas Herald*, October 6, 1866. This issue of the *Herald* contains extracts from letters received by Governor Throckmorton. The governor apparently allowed the correspondent to view a letter sent to General Sheridan that contained copies of letters that the governor had received since the beginning of his administration, regarding Indian depredations on the frontier.

16. Throckmorton to President Johnson, August 25, 1866, James W. Throckmorton Collection, 1838–1888, CAH; Ramsdell, *Reconstruction in Texas*, 137–38; Chapin, "Presidential Reconstruction in Texas," 119–20; Holbert, "The Public Career of James Webb Throckmorton," 101; Elliott, *Leathercoat*, 136–37.

17. Major General Wright to Throckmorton, August 21, 1866, Records of James Throckmorton, TOG/AD/TSL.

18. Major General Sheridan to Throckmorton, September 3, 1866, Records of James Throckmorton, TOG/AD/TSL; Richter, *The Army in Texas During Reconstruction*, 67; Roy Morris, Jr, *Sheridan: The Life and Wars of General Phil Sheridan* (New York: Crown Publishers, Inc., 1992), 276–77.

19. *New York Times*, January 17, 1867; Patsy McDonald Spaw, *The Texas Senate: Civil War to the Eve of Reform, 1861–1889* (College Station: Texas A&M University Press, 1999), 67.

20. Baylor to Throckmorton, September 1, 1866, Records of James Throckmorton, TOG/AD/TSL; Elliott, *Leathercoat*, 138–39.

21. J. J. Cureton to Throckmorton, September 2, 1866, Records of James Throckmorton, TOG/AD/TSL.

22. Throckmorton to Capt. J. J. Cureton, September 8, 1866, James W. Throckmorton Collection, 1838–1888, CAH.

23. J. F. Mosby to T. F. Barrets, September 2, 1866, Records of James Throckmorton, TOG/AD/TSL. This letter was undoubtedly forwarded to the governor's office by the recipient.

24. Throckmorton to Major General Sheridan, September 27, 1866, James W. Throckmorton Collection, 1838–1888, CAH; Throckmorton to E. M. Stanton, September 29, 1866, James W. Throckmorton Collection, 1838–1888, CAH.

25. General Sheridan to Throckmorton, October 16, 1866, Records of James Throckmorton, TOG/AD/TSL; Elliott, *Leathercoat*, 138–39. Sheridan's letter to Throckmorton makes reference to the governor's request that colored troops be removed from the interior of the state. The general informed Throckmorton that federal troops would be placed in Texas wherever they were needed without discrimination between colored and white troops.

26. Throckmorton to General Getty, October 3, 1866. James W. Throckmorton Collection, 1838–1888, CAH; Throckmorton to U. S. Grant, October 6, 1866, James W. Throckmorton Collection, 1838–1888, CAH; Elliott, *Leathercoat*, 139–40. Also, see Grant to Throckmorton, October 20, 1866, Records of James Throckmorton, TOG/AD/TSL. Grant advised against raising state troops and promised more U. S. troops would be sent to the state if circumstances warranted their deployment.

27. General Phil Sheridan to Throckmorton, October 1, 1866, Records of James Throckmorton, TOG/AD/TSL; General Sheridan to Throckmorton, October 9, 1866, Records of James Throckmorton, TOG/AD/TSL; Parker, "Indian Affairs and the Frontier of Texas," 29–31; Holbert, "The Public Career of James Webb Throckmorton," 102–3; Elliott, *Leathercoat*, 140–42.

28. See various letters from Throckmorton to George B. Pickett, Jack Cureton, J. B. Barry, J. B. Davis, C. R. Perry, W. C. Durand, J. W. Sansome, T. P. C. Hambrick, W. H. Harris, J. B. Earhart, and others, located in James W. Throckmorton Collection, 1838–1888, CAH and in the Records of James Throckmorton, TOG/AD/TSL. Letters from Throckmorton are dated October 6, 1866. Letters received by the governor are found between October 9, 1866 and throughout November 1866.

29. Throckmorton to Thos. F. Mosby, November 26, 1866. James W. Throckmorton Collection, 1838–1888, CAH.

30. Sheridan to Throckmorton, October 16, 1866, Records of James Throckmorton, TOG/AD/TSL; Parker, "Indian Affairs and the Frontier of Texas," 29–31; Holbert, "The Public Career of James Webb Throckmorton," 102–3; Elliott, *Leathercoat*, 140–42; Jerry Thompson, *Civil War to the Bloody End: The Life and Times of Major General Samuel P. Heintzelman* (College Station: Texas A&M University Press, 2006), 332–33.

31. Major General Sheridan to Throckmorton, October 25, 1866, Records of James Throckmorton, TOG/AD/TSL; Major General Sheridan to Throckmorton, November 3, 1866, Records of James Throckmorton, TOG/AD/TSL.

32. Morris, *Sheridan: The Life and Wars of General Phil Sheridan*, 280; Elliott, *Leathercoat*, 142.

33. Elliott, *Leathercoat*, 142.

34. General Sheridan to General Heintzelman, November 6, 1866, Records of James Throckmorton, TOG/AD/TSL.

35. General Heintzelman to Throckmorton, November 13, 1866. Records of James Throckmorton. TOG/AD/TSL; Elliott, *Leathercoat*, 142–43.

36. Elliott, *Leathercoat*, 144–46.

CHAPTER 14

An Uncompromising Line between Yankee Rule and Rebel Rowdies: Reconstruction Violence in Lavaca County

by

Douglas Kubicek and Carroll Scogin-Brincefield

Lavaca County was one of the many counties in Texas that continued to resist federal intervention in state and local politics following the Civil War. Corrupt politicians, outlaw gangs, and horse rustlers were commonplace in the region. Murders, lynchings, raids, and the destruction of private property made Lavaca County unsafe for all living within its borders, especially blacks and their white allies. What made the county such a violent place? Primarily, ex-Confederates and conservative Democrats refused to accept federal control in the county, detesting what they termed "Yankee rule." Violence basically divided the county into three areas: Tiger Bend in the southwest part of the county; Mixon Creek in the northeast part of the county in the bend of the Lavaca River; and the Navidad Nation located on the Navidad River east of Hallettsville. The latter became the favored haunt of the most violent citizens in the area. Criminals often met in the Navidad Nation to divvy up the spoils of their crimes.

The abuse of law and order in Lavaca County began on May 26, 1865, when an armed mob of over thirty former Confederate soldiers and southern sympathizers ransacked a leading merchant store and "former Confederate government warehouse" owned by John W. Kelly of Hallettsville. In plain sight with over twenty witnesses standing in the streets of the town square the mob destroyed property and stole over $9,000 in goods from the store. When arrests were made and the men were brought to trial, the twenty-plus witnesses who were summoned before the court refused to testify, stating that they did not see anything. The case was dismissed. This was just the beginning of the era known as Reconstruction in Lavaca County.

The Lavaca County Criminal Court records reveal that the case involving destruction of Kelly's warehouse was not an isolated incident. For example, the following month, on June 11, 1865, Theodore Johnson, a teamster in charge of a "wagon train, carrying goods from Corpus Christi via Bee County then north to Hallettsville was assaulted on successive days. James Fatheree and nine others were the first to attack the wagon train, taking with them what they could of Johnson's $2,000.00 in merchandise." The next day the wagon train was "attacked again by two different gangs both from Lavaca County. Early in the day the first gang of men led by William and Henry Kelly attacked the wagon train, followed later that afternoon by a small gang led by Henry Boatwright." By the time Johnson reached Hallettsville he had been "threatened with death . . . [and] pistol whipped three times and severely beaten up with his clothes nearly ripped off."[1] In his Grand Jury testimony, Johnson acknowledged that he feared losing his life, and that he allowed the men to have their way and dispense the "chattel among themselves."[2] The members of all three gangs were former Confederate soldiers, taking what they felt belonged to them as payment for their services in the Confederate military and keeping Confederate goods out of the clutches of the Union authorities.

Unionists in the county looked to the federal government for protection against the ex-Confederates and outlaw gangs in the region. Their prayers were answered when Capt. Daniel Harvey of the U.S. Volunteers and Capt. Frank Kress with a detachment of men from the 77th Pennsylvania Volunteers arrived in the county. The 77th Pennsylvania Volunteers had been sent to Texas to aid in the protection of the frontier. Moving by rail throughout the South, the 77th proceeded to New Orleans, where they bivouacked for three weeks and thence traveled by steamer, to Indianola, Texas, arriving on July 27. From here they marched to Green Lake, before proceeding to Camp Stanley, four miles above Victoria, on the Guadalupe River.[3] Unionists in Hallettsville were hopeful that the troopers would stay and give some direction to the county's Reconstruction program. Unfortunately, this was not to be. The detachment was recalled home after recording the amnesty oaths of the citizens in the county. On the December 5, the 77th Pennsylvania Volunteers broke camp, marched back to Indianola, embarked on transport ships, and arrived in Philadelphia where they were mustered out of service on January 6, 1866.[4]

Following Captain Kress's departure, Republican authorities in Austin sent directives to Abner Keeling Foster, the most prominent Unionist in Lavaca County. His task was relatively unobtrusive: He was to send a list of local citizens who would make viable Republican appointees to county office, especially election registers. Writing to Governor Andrew J. Hamilton on August 22, 1865, Foster observed, "Loyal material [here] is rather scarce."[5] Instead, Foster reported that the vast majority of the citizens still pledged their loyalty to the southern cause in public meetings. One citizen of Lavaca County, William M. Harper, even pledged loyalty to the Confederacy from the grave, stating in his probated will "that any person against Yankee Rule should do battle for our liberties against an unholy fanatical horde of the Federal Union of North America."[6] Harper was not alone in his sentiments, as many of the people in Lavaca County expressed the same hatred of Unionists.

Foster's claim that few loyal men remained in the county was true. Even before the war, Unionists had found the county inhospitable. During the referendum on secession in 1861, 592 county residents voted in favor of leaving the Union, while only thirty-six voted against it.[7] Many of those citizens voting against secession soon fled the county, fearing for their lives. Some took flight south to Mexico, while a few fled the state and enrolled in the Union Army. Those Unionists who stayed in the county remained silent in their support of Republican policies during and after the war. Of the Unionists in the area, a few attempted to correspond with Republican leaders, including H. M. Crabb, John Simms, and Abner Keeling Foster. Others, such as A. M. Clare, Dr. M. B. Bennett, A. B. McDonald, and Lee Green, seemed more ready to let past transgression go and move forward, making the most of Reconstruction.[8]

Of the Unionists in the county, H. M. Crabb was the only one to ask Governor Hamilton for political favors. Crabb had become acquainted with Hamilton before the war when both lived in Madison County, Texas. The war had been difficult for Crabb, and when he arrived in Lavaca County in 1865, economic hardships continued to plague him. He wrote to his friend Hamilton that ever since the war, he had been met head-on "with death" and acknowledged that "the people stole nearly everything he owned." He was asking for a position in county or state government by which he could make an "honest living." He also inquired "if under the current civil law, could a person be sued on debts contracted before and during the war."[9] Governor Hamilton had gradually accepted the policy of recognizing as valid those acts and laws that were not in conflict with the laws of the United States. It was known that under the acts of the provisional government "no person was to be sued or prosecuted for any action done in compliance with superior orders under Confederate authority." Furthermore, "Persons absent from Texas during the war, against whom any judgment was rendered in a civil suit during such absence, were allowed two years from April 1, 1866, in which to reopen and set aside such judgment, with the effect to set aside any sale or disposition of any property affected."[10] No evidence exists as to whether or not Hamilton answered Crabb's letters, but it seems probable that the citizens of Lavaca County already knew the governor's policy toward collecting debts incurred during the war.

With an uncompromising line between themselves and Republicans, ex-Confederates and conservative Democrats, or as one Lavaca County Unionist began calling them "rebel rowdies," tried to maintain political control of the county. Between August 9 to August 18, 1865, ten men, all former supporters of the Confederacy, wrote letters to Governor Hamilton soliciting appointments to almost every office in the county. Abner Keeling Foster warned Hamilton that "Rebel rascality is here in full blast . . . Regard everything coming to you through such sources as a lie." [11]

In their efforts to secure control of the local government, ex-Confederates knew that they also would need to gain control of the legal system. As such, they began to target local judges and lawmen. On March 26, 1866, County Judge Isham Sims, an appointee of Hamilton, wrote the governor that "during the recent session of District Court, the Sheriff resigned followed by the appointment and resignation of another, followed by the resignation of still another." He went on to say, "since that time we have had no Sheriff and it is impossible for the County Court to get along without a Sheriff."[12] In 1866 alone, the county office of sheriff was a revolving door with four serving before the end of the year.

With law enforcement at bay, whites began to attack local blacks. W. H. Heistead, the Freedmen's Bureau agent assigned to Hallettsville, summed up the disorderly activities shortly after his arrival on October 16, 1866, stating that "Free men in many cases are still ruled by revolver and bowie knife, leading a much worse life and being more cruelly treated than when slaves." He continued by explaining that Unionist and free men are afraid to complain as they had been "threatened with instant death if found out."[13] One of Heistead's first reports to Assistant Comissioner of the Freedmen's Bureau General Kiddoo, referred to gangs operating in the county as "a migratory class commonly called cowboys."[14] The southwestern part of the county was held by the gang known as the "Tiger Benders" led by Thomas Hodge.[15]

The gang's headquarters was located in an area that was a natural bend (Tiger Bend) in the Lavaca River about twelve miles southwest of Hallettsville. Within its ranks, the loose band of men numbered over thirty, including the infamous Kelly boys (Wiley, Eugene, and Franklin, and William and Henry who were later killed by Captain Jack Helm). Another gang, the Mixon Creekers, operated in the northeast part of Lavaca County. Their headquarters were located in an area between Mixon Creek and the Lavaca-Colorado County line.

As the violence broadened and following numerous attacks on freedmen who were pistol whipped and beaten, members of the two gangs were brought before the local courts. Because jurors were often sympathetic toward the gangs, victims found little, if any, justice in the county. The wrongdoers were usually issued a minor fine or acquitted of all charges against them.[16] For example, in the case against William Thurmond, a member of the Tiger Benders, who assaulted Newton Anderson, a farmer from the southern part of the county near Mossy Grove, Judge Burkhart of the 20th District listened to testimony against Thurmond. In court, a freedman named Cass North testified on behalf Newton Anderson, while two known members of the Tiger Benders, James Kindred and Walter Jones, testified for the accused. After hearing both sides, Judge Burkhart ruled that "drunkenness cannot be pleaded as excuses or justification for an assault," but then he dismissed the case.[17] What is interesting about this case was that Newton Anderson was a member of the Tiger Benders, the very gang that had assaulted him. It is possible, even probable, that this incident was spurred by personal motivations. Regardless, this case reveals how the Lavaca County gangs operated and protected their members from prosecution in the courts.

Other gang members were not even brought to trial, or given such a ridiculous sentence as to make a mockery of the court. Such was the case involving a group of desperados who came into town, got drunk, and rode their horses into the residence of Mr. Farrentholt. Afterwards, the gang went on a shooting spree in town and proceeded "cussing, defying and abusing the US government in a most shameful manner."[18] These men were not apprehended or indicted for their crimes. Likewise, Heistead noted, "most trials were conducted in accordance of the law" but "ended in a farce" when the accused were fined "one cent," such as in the case involving the assault of John Robinson, a local freedman. According to court records, William Millburn beat Robinson with a revolver. Though Millburn was arrested and tried the next day, the court dismissed the testimony of the principal witness, a freeman. The court objected to his testimony on the "grounds they did not recognize Negro equality." Millburn was found guilty, and County Judge Joel Ponton fined him one cent, a meaningless sentence.[19]

In March of 1867, Heistead reported that the "county is quieter than it has been for a long time" but recognized that "a great majority of the persons living in the county are a wild low and wandering set, having no respect for man or God and bitterly opposed to the United States Government."[20] It did not remain quiet for long. In early July 1867, eight Unionists representing concerned citizens from both DeWitt and Lavaca counties addressed a letter to Maj. Gen. Charles Griffin, commander of the District of Texas. They stated that "upon the most positive evidence that organized bands of thieves and desperadoes exist in out midst, we request and petition that you authorize and empower Mr. J. J. Helm, as the Deputy Sheriff of Lavaca County to arrest and bring to justice such offenders against the law"[21] Soon afterward, Jack Helm arrived, and by late July 1867, he became the acting deputy sheriff. It did not take much detective work to uncover what the law-abiding citizens were clamoring for. Helm had set up his residence in the community of Sweet Home, which enabled him to be, for the most part, right in the middle of the most lawless areas in the county, the home of the Tiger Benders. While in the area, the new deputy sheriff seemed to restore order, but he soon left the county to aid Capt. Charles Bell in Dewitt County with the Taylor–Sutton Feud. Later, Gov. Edmund Davis would make Helm a captain in the state police. While serving with the state law enforcement agency, Helm suffered a violent death when he was gunned down by the notorious John Wesley Hardin and Jim Taylor in the summer of 1873.

Following additional reports of violence in September 1867 from Heistead, a detachment of troops led by Lt. Phinias Stevens of the 35th Infantry arrived in Lavaca County.[22] Lieutenant Stevens immediately came to detest County Judge Joel Ponton and reported to his commander Brigadier General J. A. Potter that "the county Court as conducted by Joel Ponton is a ridiculous farce." Within the month, Major General Griffin approved the appointment of Abner Foster as county judge.[23] Foster began serving in November 1867 and held the position until February 1870. He immediately began to purge the county government. In a letter to Maj. Gen. Joseph J. Reynolds, who had succeeded General Griffin as commander of the District of Texas, Foster wrote that numerous local officials needed to be removed from office, because of their "disloyalty and for using their official influence to hinder, obstruct and delay Reconstruction."[24]

By the later part of 1867 and early 1868 the county was besieged with horse thieves, cattle rustling, and the beginning of what could be considered an organized crime ring. The Criminal and Civil Docket of District Court in the county became overloaded as the court began handing out a mixed bag of indictments that ranged from stealing cattle and horses to unlawfully slaughtering or removing hides. Jack Helm as deputy of Lavaca County reported to Brig. Gen. James Oakes on the well-thought-out course of action by which the "organized bands of robbers and desperados" were able to move cattle and horses out from under the eyes of the law. In the letter to Oakes, Helm located one of the cattle herds being moved out of Lavaca, Gonzales, and DeWitt counties and up the trail towards McLennan, Bell, and Bosque counties. Following one such group, Helm acknowledged he was "a day or so behind them but was never able to make any arrests."[25]

According to the number of indictments issued for his arrest, the leading criminal in the county was Jabez Franks, one of the Franks brothers, whose family's homestead was located in the southwestern part of the county near Sweet Home. Acting alone or with members of the Tiger Benders, his name appears in sixty-six cases of stealing cattle in one year. Samuel Magee, another member of the Tiger Benders, was constantly in trouble with the law. In less than a year, he was wanted on five indictments with an assortment of charges, including "driving not less than twenty five cattle out of the county to a market and moving cattle to DeWitt County and Bee County" by way of Gonzales County "not covered by a bill of sale."[26] In other words, he was a noted cattle thief. There was very little honor even among this group of cattle thieves, or as they were called in the indictments, "cattle rustlers." Other members of the Tiger Benders wanted for stealing cattle included J. W. Mangum and Lews McClanahan.[27]

While trying to restore and keep order as deputy of Lavaca County, Deputy Helm assisted in bringing criminals to justice in over fifty-five cases. Those individuals who were arrested were turned over to the sheriff, but in most cases the legal counsel in the county found ways to have the charges dropped, or they had their sentences reduced, or they were simply released on bond. The gangs by this time had learned to use the legal system to their advantage and to play off the sympathies of the court officials. Many criminals were released because of minor technicalities that otherwise would not have warranted a dismissal of the case.[28] Additionally, the court docket included a growing number of indictments (examples listed below) for assault, rape, attempted rape, murder, attempted murder, gambling, aggravated assault, and four cases of attempted murder at a place of worship. For example, W. C. Jones and Henry Bradberry, both members of the Tiger Benders, were arrested for pointing pistols at Glen Foster, a local freedman, after which the two gang members hit the defenseless man in the head, leaving a serious wound. At least in this case the two outlaws were found guilty of assault and fined $100.00. James Kindred, another member of the Tiger Benders, was found guilty of disrupting a religious service, but the court dismissed charges against him in a case involving the attempted murder of H. H. Shoemaker, a local Unionist. In another case where Kindred used a knife to assault another local Unionist, Bernard Schwartz, the criminal was charged a fine of $20.00.[29]

By February of 1869, the gangs changed tactics and began random assaults on various freedpeople in the county. Stewart Campbell and Tucker Campbell, who were associated with the Mixon Creek gang, were two of the worst offenders. The Campbell boys in less than two years had been indicted in over forty-one cases involving a wide range of felony and misdemeanor charges. The final mark of brutality came when they murdered a young teenage girl, Sarah Curry, near Peach Creek on the Lavaca-Gonzales county line. After their capture in Hallettsville by Sheriff Jim Bennett, the Campbell boys were being returned to Gonzales County to stand trial when they were intercepted, reportedly by a mob of over 100 men, They were taken from the lawmen under gunpoint and lynched.[30]

The Campbell brothers were not the only terrorists operating in the county. Marshall Mathews and Lev Blakely, often described as "most desperate outlaws," committed a crime that baffled many of the local citizens. Apparently, the pair murdered a "whole family, consisting of a man, his wife and their infant child as well as a small black girl." To hide the crime, they placed the bodies in the murdered family's home and burned it to the ground. Shortly afterwards, the two were apprehended and charged with murder. At the hearing, threats were made by the men against the "citizens of the neighborhood" and anyone who "had any hand in bringing them to justice." To the relief of the town, the two outlaws were shot to death while attempting to escape from their jail cell.[31]

County Judge A. K. Foster reported to the adjutant general in Austin that several incidents during February had most of the county's freedmen unwilling to leave their houses. In a second letter to the adjutant general, Foster reported that the condition of the freedpeople in Lavaca County had deteriorated even further and he had advised them "to arm and defend themselves as best they can until military protection can be had."[32] The citizens of Lavaca County were troubled by the fact that freemen were arming themselves. John Folwell and Sam McGown (Mixon Creekers) broke into the homes of Prairie Point, David Shelton, Manuel Thompson, and Isaac Thompson—all freemen—and stole their weapons, which included three revolvers and an Enfield rifle. The thefts did not stop there. Thomas Hodge and members of the Tiger Benders confiscated weapons when they raided the homes of freedmen Stephen Porter, Martin Cunningham, and Jacob Oakman.[33] Foster stated, "I have confidence in the fidelity of our Sheriff W. H. Coleman and feel that he will faithfully discharge his duty under any circumstance to break up these rowdy gangs by civil process." However, the county's law enforcement proved ineffective in maintaining order, and Foster feared that Coleman's efforts to end the violence would "jeopardize his [the sheriff's] life and that of other good men."[34]

Responding to Foster's letter, the adjutant general sent 2nd Lt. James W. Tanfield from the 17th Infantry stationed at Wharton, Texas, on a fact-finding mission to Hallettsville. Taking a stagecoach from Columbus, he arrived in Hallettsville on March 19, 1869. Upon his arrival, he immediately met with Judge Foster, Sheriff Coleman, and "some of the principal citizens of the town."[35] The focus of Tanfield's investigation was the attacks on the freedmen Stephen Porter and Martin Cunningham, who lived on the W. G. L. Foley Plantation in the northern part of the county.[36] Tanfield's investigation uncovered that the three freedmen had been assaulted at night by members of the Mixon Creek gang who busted in the front door and ransacked the houses. Finding guns in the house, they beat the freedmen as well as their wives and children. As the Mixon Creekers mounted their horses and prepared to ride off, they riddled the freedmen's homes with bullets. After completing his investigation, Tanfield examined the attempted murder of Foster. He noted, "the outrage was perpetrated by 25 to 30 masked men of a gang known as the Tiger Benders," who surrounded Foster's house and "commenced firing into it." During the raid, the outlaws wounded the judge in the thigh. If it had not been for several armed freedmen coming to his rescue, the attackers might have succeeded in killing Foster. Once the freedmen arrived, a gun battle ensued in which one of the assailants shouted, "By God the nigger has shot me." At that point, Tiger Benders decided to withdraw into the darkness. Shortly after this incident, Foster and his family left their farmhouse, taking up residence in the safety of town. Tanfield's final remarks in his report acknowledged that "these two parties of desperadoes do not appear to be actuated by any political motives or prompted by any other partisan feeling than that of mere lawlessness, nor is there any concert between them; on the contrary they exhibit a feeling of dislike and opposition toward each other."[37]

Whether it was the attack on his life or the lure of a state political office, Foster allowed his name to be submitted as a candidate for the state senate from the 25th District, which was comprised of Lavaca and Colorado counties. The year 1870 marked a turning point for Unionists in the county, when officials were able to restore a semblance of law and order. Prior to the senate election, Foster campaigned vigorously throughout the 25th District. His efforts were not lost on the Republican papers in the state capital. The *Daily State Journal* described him as a "gentleman of fine presence" and as being on "the right side of Chickahominy." The editor of the *Weekly Austin Republican*, A. H. Longly, remembered meeting Foster for the first time. He stated that they "were both political exiles because of our devotion to the Union of our fathers."[38]

Judge Foster was elected by an overwhelming majority and took the oath as state senator on February 8, 1870. The Provisional Session of the legislature was a short one, lasting only between February 8 and 24. The principal work was the adoption of the Fifteenth Amendment which stated that "the right of citizens of the United States to vote shall not be denied or abridged . . . on account of race, color, or previous condition of servitude." Foster was one of twenty-three senators voting "aye" with only two opposed. At the close of the Provisional Session and with the Regular Session slated to start in April, Foster returned to Lavaca County on horseback. En route he was caught in a rainstorm that soaked him. Within days, a high fever and pneumonia ravaged his body, and Abner Keeling Foster died on March 9, 1870. He was survived by his daughter Fanny from his first marriage and his second wife Elizabeth Ann and their five children.

Following Foster's death, G. Welworth, a member of the State Police, visited Lavaca County. He acknowledged, "We will have a hard fight here." In one of his last letters as county judge before leaving for the provisional legislative session in Austin, Foster made the same conclusion, stating that "Rebel rascality" would "continue and would never really end as long as the so called carpet bag rule drew a breath."[39] The "rebel rascality" that Foster identified took on a new facade when M. B. Bennett and approximately forty pro-Unionists in Hallettsville petitioned the county government to incorporate the town of Hallettsville. The Lavaca County Court received the request and forwarded it to General Reynolds, commander of the Fifth Military District, for his approval.[40] On August 13, 1870, Hallettsville was finally incorporated by a special act of the Legislature. An *ad interim* city government was followed by the first city election in 1871. Robert M. Tevis, an attorney in Hallettsville who had been a major in the Confederate Army and who provided legal counsel to many of the apprehended gang members in the county, was elected as the first mayor. However, he did not remain in office long. Since the act of incorporation fell under federal supervision, Tevis was removed from office because he was a traitor to the Republican Party. Soon after, Francis Richartts was named as the new mayor. In an outburst of letters addressed to the governor, local Unionists praised the decision to remove Tevis from office, stating that it "would be a signal to Rebel Democracy" that they were no longer in control of the city. Several of Richartts' supporters, freedmen William Washington and Clark Moore, Lee Green, and H. M. Shoemaker, a white Unionist, praised Richartts as being a man with "good practical common sense" and who was "honest and fearless." Nevertheless, they also acknowledged that Richartts as mayor would have "more than ordinary difficulties to contend" as the "rowdies and Democrats" retaliated against his authority."[41]

Within two weeks of R. M. Trevis' removal, agitators from both the Mixon Creekers and Tiger Benders started promoting a series of illegal acts and mayhem. Those outside the law tried to discredit Richartts as mayor as well as his allies who served on the city council. Richartts was publicly accused of neglecting his duty and he responded by asking the city council to hire a city marshal to maintain law and order in the city. They responded by hiring James H. Rice. With a new marshal in town, it was only a matter of time before ex-Confederates tested his authority.

Mayhem arrived in Hallettsville when a group of Tiger Benders, led by Thomas Hodge and James Kindred, entered the town "heavily armed." According to witnesses, the group rode their horses "at full speed . . . yelling like Indians, around and on the courthouse yard." The group discharged their pistols in the air, shouted insults at town residents, and swore to enact vengeance against Sheriff Coleman and the mayor. The ncar riot finally diffused itself as Coleman called for his deputies "armed with double barrel shotguns to halt the desperadoes and if necessary shoot them."[42] Sheriff Coleman later remarked at the court hearing that he "could not find any law, necessary to stop such conduct other than disturbing the peace." Hodge and Kindred were taken into custody, but they quickly made bail and were released. Other gang members who were arrested were not as fortunate. Apparently, they could not make bail. As a result, Thomas Hodge and other Tiger Benders successfully carried out two different jail breaks. During the first attack on the jail, John Turner aided Wiley Neal to escape by slipping him a wood auger to cut his way out of the wooden cell. The second escape was more violent. According to witnesses, James Goodson slipped James Barry Holland a gun that he used against his guards. Shortly after these occurrences, unknown assailants burned the jail to the ground, causing the county sheriff to purchase several sets of "trace chains" with shackles. The chains were designed to bind prisoners to trees near the courthouse during the day while moving them (still wearing their shackles) inside private homes at night.[43]

The criminals became even more vindictive when they attempted to burn down the Lavaca County courthouse in the hope of destroying some 75 to 100 pending indictments involving members of both gangs. The courthouse was set afire by torches that the outlaws threw through the windows of the building. Much to the chagrin of the terrorists, local citizens were able to save the county's records. Despite the fact that the fire was discovered in time, the building suffered significant damage, which was not completely discovered until 1876, when during a United States centennial celebration, a portion of the second floor of the courthouse collapsed under the weight of a crowd who were holding a dance.[44]

Eventually, the violence in the county did subside. What had caused the gangs to dissolve? Why did they end their reign of terror? Did the rebel rowdies finally run out of clout with the local populace? Evidence suggests that most of the gang members were either killed or they left the county. It also seems probable that many of the locals were ready to move beyond the violence of the period, especially after ex-Confederates gained control of the county in the mid-1870s. Once conservative Democrats recaptured local political offices, the actions of former gang members were dismissed. Often the courts listed the accused as deceased. After all, dead men cannot be brought to justice. In the cases of Jabez Franks and Sam Magee, members of the Tiger Bender Gang, both men never stood trial. Instead, they were dropped from the docket of the District Court with the explanation "Defendant Dead" written beside their case numbers. All told, more than twenty-seven felony cases in the Criminal Court Index (1866–1871) listed the "Defendant as Dead." There were other cases in which the accused or the fugitive died before or after he was in formal custody. Very few if any of the gang members who were arrested ever came to trial for felony crimes during this time era. The few that did went to trial on lesser charges, paid their fine, and sometimes lived the rest of their life in the county in obscurity, while others disappeared and were never to be found again.

Of the many gang members, only Dan Merritt made something of himself. He became a lawman, serving as the town marshal. During a gun fight on the street in Hallettsville he killed Jim Buckley, one of the last members of the Tiger Benders. Other gang members were less successful and often left their family destitute. In fact, one of the forgotten causalities of the "Second Civil War" in Lavaca County were the non-combatants: the family members of both gangs. Noted Tiger Bender James Kindred died at age thirty-two, leaving his widow Kate destitute. A sale was ordered by the court to settle Kindred's estate. After being forced to sell her home and the thirty-seven acres that it sat upon, Kate was left homeless. The court did, however, allow her to keep "one bed, the kitchen wares and one milk cow."[45] William McElroy, another Tiger Bender, left his widow, Malvinia, and children in a little better shape. According to probate records, the family received 200 acres to maintain themselves, but the rest of the McElroy estate, including a large

Illustration 16. Confederate Veterans Monument Dedication, Hallettsville, Lavaca, County, Texas. Photo taken on the grounds of the Lavaca County Courthouse.

number of cattle and horses, were sold to pay off debts that William had incurred.[46]

One of the final acts of the ex-Confederates in Lavaca County played out in January 1913. The remnants of the "Rebel Rowdies" gathered on the courthouse lawn to dedicate a monument commemorating the 50th anniversary of the Battle of Galveston. The *Hallettsville Herald* reported that "a large assemblage gathered at the Opera House," with music provided by the "Ideal Band." As soon as the first bars of "Dixie" were played, "the Confederate yell" was followed by the "throwing of their hats in the air." The reporter for the *Herald* noted that "though becoming feeble in years, the veterans still recognized and appreciated Dixie."

ENDNOTES

1. Lavaca County Criminal Court Docket 1865, Criminal Case Docket 590.

2. Ibid.

3. Frederick H. Dyer, *A Compendium of the War of the Rebellion Compiled and Arranged from Official Records of the Federal and Confederate Armies, Reports of the Adjutant Generals of the Several States, the Army Registers, and Other Reliable Documents and Sources* (Des Moines, IA: The Dyer Publishing Company, 1908).

4. Ibid.

5. A. K. Foster to A. J. Hamilton, Provisional Governor of Texas, August 22, 1865, Barry Crouch Collection, Box 3-B, Victoria College/UHV Library, hereafter cited as BCC.

6. Probate Record of Estate Book A Page 620 Harper, William, Lavaca County Clerk Records, Hallettsville, TX.

7. County Convention for Secession, Lavaca County.

8. Ibid.

9. H. M. Crabb to A. J. Hamilton,Provisional Governor, September 29, 1865, Governor's Letters, State Archives, Austin, TX.

10. See H. P. N. Gammel, comp. *The Laws of Texas, 1822–1897* (Austin: The Gammel Book Co., 1898), 5: 895–98.

11. A. K. Foster to A. J. Hamilton, Provisional Governor, July 16, 1865, Governor's Letters, State Archives, Austin, TX.

12. Isham Sims to Provisional Governor A. J. Hamilton, March 26, 1866, BCC, Box 3-B.

13. W. H. Hiestand, Sub-Assistant Commission Hallettsville to Kiddo January 24, 1867, BCC, Box 4-B.

14. W. H. Hiestand, Sub-Assistant Commission Hallettsville, to Kiddo January 24, 1867 BCC, Box 4-B.

15. Letter, 2nd Lt. J. W. Tanfield of the 17th Infantry to 1st Lieutenant W. H. W. Krebbs 17th Infantry Command Post, Post of Wharton Texas, March 1869, BCC.

16. Criminal and Civil Court Docket, Minute Books District Court Records. Various examples are listed, such as Case Number 1107 involving Stewart Campbell, who was found guilty of altering a brand. He was sentenced to only ten minutes in jail.

17. Civil Court Docket, Minute Book District Court Records.

18. W. H. Heistead (Hallettsville) to J. P. Kirkman, February 1867, Victoria College/UHV Library, BCC, Box 4-B.

19. Ibid.

20. W. H. Heistead (Hallettsville) to J. P. Kirkman March 1867, BCC, Box 4-B

21. M. Jacobs, N. L. Newton, Augustine Douglass, Charles Coleman, Jorden Morris, J. T. J. Culpepper, S. M. Guthrie to Major General Griffin Commander Military District 1867, BCC, Box 4-B.

22. "Official Roster of Officers and Civilians on Duty in the Bureau Refugees, Freedmen and Abandoned Land State of Texas February 1868," BCC, Box 4-B. Lieutenant Stevens was listed as a Sub-assistant Commissioner. His sub-district included Lavaca and Jackson counties, and north of Texana, exclusive.

23. Phinias Stevens to A. J. Hamilton September 7, 1867, BCC, Box 4-B.

24. Letter from Abner K. Foster to Major General J. J. Reynolds, Commander, District of Texas, November 1867, BCC, Box 4-B. Besides A. K. Foster's signature, Unionists Lee Green, H. M. Shoemaker, P. H. Stokes, J. R. Conner and W. H. Posey (F.M.C.) signed.

25. J. J. Helm, Deputy Sheriff Lavaca County, to Brig. Gen. James A. Oakes, Commander Post, Austin, July 1867, BCC, Box 4-B.

26. Criminal Court Docket Index, Lavaca County District Court Records, Case numbers 828, 829, 830, 831, 835.

27. Ibid. Case Number 495.

28. Criminal and Civil Docket, Index Books D and E, Lavaca County District Court Records.

29. Ibid.

30. *Galveston News*, June 28, 1876, and July 1, 5, 6, 1876.

31. *Galveston Daily News*, January 15, 1867.

32. A. K. Foster, Lavaca County Judge, to 5th Military District, Austin, Texas, February 1869, BCC, Box 4-B.

33. BCC, Box 4-B.

34. A. K. Foster, Lavaca County Judge, to 5th Military District, Austin, Texas, February 1869, BCC, Box 4-B.

35. 2nd Lt. J. W. Tanfield, 17th Infantry, to 1st Lieutenant W. H. W. Krebbs, 17th Infantry Command Post, Post of Wharton, TX, 1869, BCC, Box 4-B.

36. A. K. Foster to Adjunct General 5th Military District February 1869, BCC, Box 4-B.

37. 2nd Lt. J. W. Tanfield, 17th Infantry to 1st Lieutenant W. H. W. Krebbs, 17th Infantry Command Post, Post of Wharton, TX, 1869, BCC, Box 4-B.

38. Texas State Archives, *Austin Texas Daily State Journal*, February 4, 1870 and *Weekly Austin Republican*, March 16, 1870.

39. A. K. Foster, Lavaca County Judge, to 5th Military District, Austin, Texas, 1869, BCC, Box 4-B.

40. Lavaca County Police Court Minutes, 1870, Book C, p. 343.

41. W. Washington, C. Moore, L. Green, M. H. Shoemaker, Letters of Correspondence to Governor 1870, BCC.

42. Letter from Lavaca County Sheriff W. B. Coleman to the Adjunct General, 5th Military District, Referred to Commanding Office, Post of Wharton, Texas, November 1869, BCC, Box 3-B.

43. Lavaca County Police Court Minutes, Book C, p. 365, July 1870. Louis Turner was reimbursed $40.25 for repairing the jail and making five pairs of shackles for prisoners.

44. Private Collection of Douglas Kubicek, Lavaca County Historian.

45. Lavaca County Probate Minutes, 1866–67, Book D, pp. 99, 131, 149, 199; Book E pages 22, 27, 34, 46, 184.

46. Ibid.

Chapter 15

Reconstruction Violence in the Lower Brazos River Valley

by

John Gorman

The end of the Civil War offered a new beginning for race relations in the United States. The passage of the Thirteenth and Fourteenth Amendments, which guaranteed freedom, citizenship, and political equality, offered hope to millions of freed slaves throughout the South. However, changes to southern political and economic institutions led white Southerners to use intimidation, violence, and outright murder in an attempt to maintain as much of their antebellum way of life as possible. As a result, former slaves and their families soon discovered that their ability to exercise their new-found civil rights was blocked by new legal restraints and outright violence. Newspaper articles and the Freedmen's Bureau records provide insight into the horrors that the freedpeople living in the Brazos River Valley were confronted with on a daily basis as they struggled to assert their new political and economic freedom.

From 1865 to 1868 there were a total of 939 murders committed in Texas and of that total, 429 (or roughly 1 percent of the adult black population ages 15–49), were blacks murdered by whites, while only ten were whites murdered by blacks (see table 1).[1] This statistic led the Committee on Lawlessness and Violence to conclude that a race war was raging in Texas, a one-sided conflict that African Americans were losing.[2] Freedpeople were not the only victims of this race war. Organizations of ex-Confederates and conservative Democrats were also targeting prominent Unionists within the state, including many Republican judges.[3] However, the committee's most striking findings were in the revelations of the degree to which the freedpeople of Texas were being persecuted, abused, and murdered.[4] The Texas Freedmen's Bureau further reported a staggering 2,225 physical acts of violence committed against the black population of Texas.[5] One of the most striking characteristics of violence reported between 1865 and 1869 was the complete inability of the local authorities to do anything to prosecute and convict those persons responsible. The Bureau reported that between 1865 and 1867 there were only 249 indictments for murder found in the district courts and only five convictions, roughly 2 percent (see table 2). In all, for the approximately 900 reported murders committed in the state, there was only one capital execution. Taken together, these figures conclusively indicate that in many areas of Texas there was a complete breakdown in the civilian authority and a general lack of respect for human life.[6]

Violence in Texas tended to followed three major patterns: social violence, political violence, and labor violence. Social violence is an often overlooked dynamic in the study of race relations. There were no discernible patterns to incidents of violence for violations of accepted social norms. But, a small list of the social etiquette Texas blacks were supposed to follow included: not making insulting noises, speaking disrespectfully or out of turn, disputing the word of whites, standing at attention when a white passed by, and stepping aside when white women were on the sidewalk. Failure to comply with any of the expected social behaviors resulted in retaliation that included verbal threats and physical violence.[7]

Political violence was often directed at blacks who were involved in local politics, were members of civic organizations, or were leaders in their community. Once blacks organized politically they became a serious threat to the established political and social mores. Many times these acts of violence were perpetrated by small groups of whites, as was witnessed in the Millican race riot. The death rate of Texas blacks between 1866 and 1867 rose 50 percent and correlates with the rise of local blacks as they began to exercise their political rights (see table 3).[8] In the immediate postwar years, a few blacks did become involved in politics, enjoying their greatest degree of participation at the local level, but even at the state level nine blacks participated in the constitutional convention of 1868–69, and eleven were elected to the legislature in 1871.[9] However, in the post-Reconstruction years in Texas, black political participation steadily declined. It is significant to note that of all the southern states, Texas was the only one not to have a single black occupy an important executive or judicial post during the Reconstruction period.[10]

Planters, ex-Confederate soldiers, and small groups of whites appear to have been primarily responsible for acts of violence committed against the freedpeople. Planters routinely resorted to violence to coerce a specific response from individual blacks regarding their performance of requested tasks. Texas blacks were frequently beaten or whipped for just being late to work. The Freedmen's Bureau recorded that freedpeople were often beaten or whipped with a variety of instruments including pistols, belts, tools, and chains. In many instances, if a freed person attempted to leave the plantations where they were employed, their employers would resort to intimidation and physical violence to keep them bound to the land.[11]

Serving as inspector general for the Freedmen's Bureau, Brigadier General W. E. Strong traveled throughout the southern states in 1865 and noted that the incidence of cruelty and violence against the freedpeople in Texas exceeded that of any other southern state. During his travels through Texas in the fall of 1865 he went as far north as Huntsville and as far west as Millican and he testified that cases of violence were everywhere, noting that the freedpeople were "frequently beaten unmercifully, and shot down like wild beasts, without any provocation, followed with hounds, and maltreated in every possible way."[12] Strong pointed out that in the larger cities of Austin, Galveston, and, especially Houston, whites were decidedly more favorable towards emancipation and treated the freedpeople with a greater degree of dignity and respect.[13] A possible reason for this difference in tone was a strong federal troop presence in those cities. Additionally, slavery had not been as predominant in the urban centers as it was in the more rural regions of the Old South where slavery was more important to the economic success of planter. Furthermore, the black population in the larger cities was substantially lower. Thus, the white population had less to fear from a politically active black electorate.

What is clear is that in the larger cities and the few areas where there was a sufficient federal troop presence, whites were more accommodating toward blacks, but in the interior of the state, where the federal footprint was minimal or nonexistent, the treatment of the black population was considerably more brutal and violent. It was the planters' belief that the system of free labor was untenable and that the only way to get work out of the freedmen was to resort to the overseer, the whip, and the hounds.[14] However, General Strong observed something quite different from the white stereotype of the freedmen, noting that if there was any work done, it was done by the freedmen, though they rarely received payment for their labor. Strong estimated that two-thirds of the freedmen in the areas of Texas had never received "one cent in wages since they were declared free."[15]

There were a few dissenting opinions on the condition of the freedmen population in Texas. Benjamin C. Truman, a correspondent for the *New York Times*, stated that freedpeople were in far better condition today than they were when they were slaves and, in fact, the freedmen in Texas were doing better than in any of the other southern states. In the Brazos River Valley he noticed that a great many planters were giving the freedmen two-thirds of the crops and at no time did he witness abuse or maltreatment of any freedmen. He concluded "that free labor is a success in Texas. Most of the former slaves are with their former masters everywhere in the interior."[16] However, it should be noted Truman was a committed Unionist who supported the efforts of Presidential Reconstruction, and any negative view of the Reconstruction efforts would indicate that President Andrew Johnson was not effectively rehabilitating the southern states.

Truman's perception of race relations in Texas, however, was not based in reality. Planters in the Brazos River Valley had to contend with vast and far-reaching economic changes after the Civil War and some were forced to file for bankruptcy.[17] Labor in postwar Texas was an extremely valuable commodity, and the freedmen tended to accept work more readily from planters who had treated them honorably and fairly during times of slavery. However, with the continual talk among the planters regarding the inability to adapt free-labor principles to their economic needs, freedmen were naturally apprehensive about working for their former masters.[18] The freedmen learned very quickly which planters treated them fairly and there was a noted shift in the voluntary employment patterns after the Civil War in the Lower Brazos River Valley as freedmen in increasing frequency worked for those planters who were honest and fair in dealing with them.[19] The resultant labor shortage experienced by abusive landowners allowed them to return to practicing the methods they had used in the antebellum era to effectively control the freedmen population.[20]

Texas also possessed a strong tradition of vigilante justice. During the late 1850s, with secession rhetoric at a feverish pitch, and with the belief that abolitionists were operating within the state, fear of slave uprisings began to manifest itself throughout the Brazos River Valley. Vigilante organizations and various types of armed safety committees, which were already in existence, became more active. Texans' fears seemed to be justified after four planned slave rebellions were uncovered and thwarted. During the panic of 1860, vigilante groups lynched an untold number of suspected abolitionists in and around the upper Brazos River

Valley. These fears prompted the *State Gazette* to urge local communities to form vigilante associations.[21] As the fabric of their communities broke down, white Texans began to draw on this vigilante tradition to try and stall, and in some cases prevent, the loss of both their economic and political supremacy.

At the end of the Civil War there were approximately 200,000 slaves in Texas. The great majority resided on the rich plantations situated on the Sabine, Neches, Trinity, Brazos, and Colorado rivers. There were only a few freedmen who lived north of Waco on the Brazos or north of Austin on the Colorado. Western and northwestern Texas were wild and uncultivated regions where Indian raids still posed a significant threat to settlers.[22] The freedpeople who lived in areas that contained a high concentration of slaves during the antebellum era faced tremendous hardships as they attempted to cope with their changed political and economic status. They were routinely assaulted and there were frequent murders, especially in counties where the federal presence was minimal.

The murder of Lucy Grimes in Marshall, Texas, was a typical example of the type of violence that freedpeople experienced throughout the state. In December of 1865, Lt. Col. H. S. Hall, sub-assistant commissioner in the northeastern district of Texas, reported that Grimes was taken into the woods by two men, stripped from the waist down, beaten severely with a whip or strap, and then struck on the back of the head with a club, which the local physician determined was the cause of death. The chief justice for the county, D. B. Bonnefoy, refused to issue an arrest warrant based upon the "evidence of a negro."[23] Colonel Hall recalled that in another instance a black woman was seriously injured when she was fired upon by her employer for language he considered offensive. The person responsible for this act was arrested by the military and fined $100.00.[24] These same types of incidents were commonplace in the Lower Brazos River Valley. For example, in Brazos County a freedman named Upton, who was accused of cattle stealing, was forcibly removed from the jail by a vigilante mob and promptly hanged.[25] In another incident in Bryan, two federal soldiers attempted to rob a freedman in the freedpeople's part of town and cut him severely on the neck and face.[26] Finally, the *Houston Daily Times* reported that a "Negro" man was found hanging from a tree, about one mile east of Bryan. The murdered victim's wife said that a party of white men with painted faces came to the house the night before, tied him up, and took him away.[27] These types of incidents were reported in the local newspapers with alarming frequency. Overall, of the estimated 373 black murders by whites between 1865 and

1868, approximately 120 occurred in the Lower Brazos River Valley (see tables 1 and 4). These acts of violence were indicative of the problems in Texas during Reconstruction. The military lacked the power or the authority to pursue and adequately punish violence inflicted upon the black population.[28]

The task of protecting the rights of the freedmen in the years immediately after the Civil War fell upon the newly created Bureau of Refugees, Freedmen, and Abandoned Lands, a federal agency that was established March 3, 1865. The Bureau was designed to assist freedmen in their transition from slaves to freedmen and to ensure that they had an economic "fair chance."[29] The Bureau proved not only to be an invaluable instrument in providing educational activities, but it was also indispensable in providing an avenue through which the freedmen could redress their grievances against the white population, especially regarding lost wages and acts of violence. Indeed, the greatest benefit of the Bureau to the freedmen was that it did manage, with varying degrees of success, to provide a semblance of protection against exploitation, abuse, and outright violence. Lieutenant Wilson Miller, who was with the U.S. Colored Troops stationed in Corpus Christi, asserted that the Bureau was an absolute necessity in Texas. He believed that in the absence of the Bureau, and some armed force to back it up, the freedmen's chance for justice was limited and their lives would not be "worth a cent."[30] General Christopher Andrews went even further by pointing out that he had seen copies of contracts entered into between freedmen and planters that contained "so many deductions for loss of time, and charges for medical attendance, and care of children, etc..." that if enforced strictly, would barely be sufficient for the freedmen's room and board.[31] Andrews concluded by stating that if the government failed to protect the freedpeople, they would be worse off than they were as slaves.[32]

The Freedmen's Bureau operated in Texas from September 1865 through December 31, 1868. All of the assistant commissioners for Texas insisted that the court system accord the freedmen the same legal rights that whites enjoyed. They also supervised labor contracts entered into by freedmen, aided blacks in organizing schools, and provided safety for the teachers in those schools. However, in Texas, the Bureau faced some challenges that severely hampered the agency's efforts, including the sheer size of the state, the hostility of the local white population, and an archaic transportation and communication network. Additionally, the Bureau suffered from a lack of funding and manpower throughout its entire existence. Even with the aid of federal troops, there were never enough agents to adequately complete the Bureau's mission.[33] The one area in which the Bureau apparently enjoyed considerable success was in education. There were just 16 schools serving 1,000 black students at the end of 1865 and by the end of 1868, at the time of the Bureau's closing, there were 150 schools serving 9,806 black students.[34]

The election of a conservative government in Texas in 1866 provided a source of continual irritation to the senior commander of the Department of the Gulf, Philip H. Sheridan, who had little time to be distracted by developments in Texas because the situation in Louisiana required his immediate attention.[35] In an effort to effectively maintain control of both states, Sheridan appointed Bvt. Maj. Gen. George W. Getty to supervise military affairs in Texas.[36] Unfortunately Getty, who was still recovering from an injury sustained in 1864, soon collapsed from the rigors of the Texas command. The result was a void in command and control within the District of Texas. Governor Throckmorton and the state legislature eagerly exploited this situation and started to exert greater control over the state's internal affairs. They attempted to raise volunteers for the purpose of defending the frontier counties; passed the "black codes"; verbally attacked the Freedmen's Bureau; and rejected both the Thirteenth and Fourteenth Amendments.[37] The cumulative effect of these events within the state government and the citizenry at large was to foster a strong independent streak and a belief that Reconstruction was effectively over within the state. State officials began the process of reasserting state sovereignty.[38] The local white population began to reassert their control over the freedmen who were themselves trying to assert their own independence. The result was an atmosphere conducive to conflict and violence.

In order to gain a greater understanding of the motivating forces behind the violence in Reconstruction Texas, this study will focus on six counties in the Lower Brazos River Valley: Brazos, Grimes, Washington, Austin, Fort Bend, and Brazoria counties. These counties were selected because each contained significant black populations during the Reconstruction era. To quantify the violence that took place in the Lower Brazos River Valley, two data sets were compiled. In the first data set all incidents of violence reported to the Freedmen's Bureau for the six counties were extracted from the Freedmen's Bureau records for the years between 1865 and 1868. The data was organized by the year in which the act occurred; the type of violence; and if known, the name, age, and race of the accused and victim. This data set is not without its limitations. There is a statistical bias inherent in the data set because

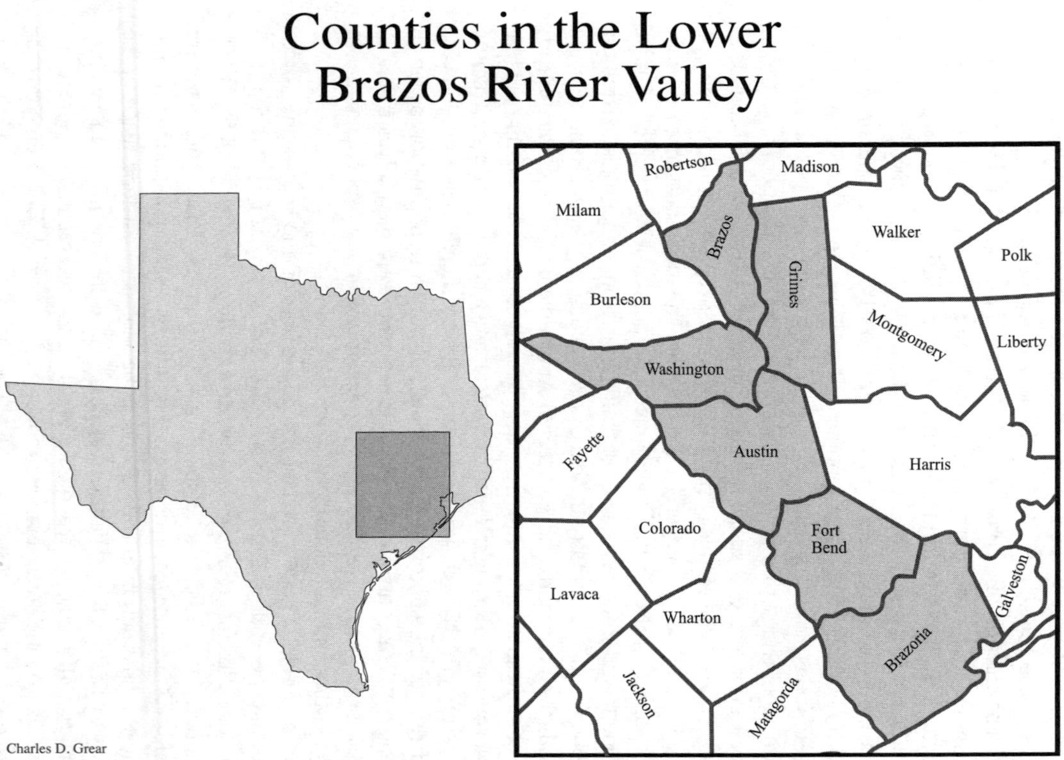

Map 3. Countries in the Lower Brazos River Valley

many of the names could not be positively matched to a specific county and an untold number of violent crimes went unreported out of fear, intimidation, and violence. However, while the relatively small size of the sample population does make drawing linear conclusions difficult, it does illustrate important trends in race relations in the Lower Brazos River Valley.

The second data set was created in order to illustrate demographic trends over time within the six counties of this study. Population totals for the six counties were extracted from the U. S. Census records for the years 1850, 1860, and 1870 and organized by total population and ethnicity for each of the six counties.[39] The resulting data sets allow for an examination of the demographics of population shift and growth in correlation with the incidence of violence over time. In each of these counties there existed large African American populations that were close to or exceeded the county's white population. Historian Dale Baum estimates that during the Civil War the state's slave population increased by approximately 32,000, as planters from other southern states left their war-torn homes with their slaves in tow, and travelled to Texas where they hoped to find refuge from the Union armies. The majority of these individuals and their slaves filtered into ten counties, only one of which, Hopkins, does not border the Sabine, Trinity, or Brazos rivers. Four of the ten counties that witnessed a growth of over 1,000 refugee slaves were located in the lower Brazos River Valley.[40]

Prior to the outbreak of the Civil War, Brazos County was one of the fastest growing counties in Texas, due in large part to the arrival of the Houston & Texas Central Railroad, with Millican as its terminus. In 1860 the county's population was composed of 1,713 whites and 1,063 slaves, with 118 slaveholders. Among the slaveholders, seventy-seven of them owned fewer than five slaves and four owned more than fifty. There were 14,509 cultivated acres, composed mostly of small farms and a few large plantations.[41] The county also demonstrated strong support for the Confederate cause, voting 215 to 44 for secession and the men of the county formed several companies in the 21st and 25th Texas Cavalry regiments. The war's end brought new labor and political struggles in the county. The result was a sharp and often violent struggle between the two groups as they attempted to come to terms with the changing social and economic landscape.

Racial violence reached an apex in 1868 with the appearance of the Ku Klux Klan in the county. In part the emergence of the Klan coincided with the rise of black participation in local and state politics.

Additionally, demographics of the county were further destabilized during the period by the extension of the Houston & Texas Central Railroad from Millican to Bryan with the latter becoming the new county seat. Other towns, including Millican and Boonville, witnessed a sharp population decline as their inhabitants moved their businesses and their homes to Bryan, which by 1870 would see its population increase 297 percent to 9,205 during the decade (see table 5).[42]

The awakening of black political consciousness in Brazos County led directly to one of the worst incidents of violence in Texas during Reconstruction: the Millican race riot. Before the war, Millican's slave population was almost equal to the white population, and the increase in refugee slaves that occurred during the war further increased the slave population. By 1868 Millican's black community was becoming more politically active, especially after George E. Brooks organized the Millican Union League. The impact of the Union League was evident when voters sent freedman Stephen Curtis to the State Constitutional Convention in 1868. Curtis's election was significant because it represented a direct challenge to the white community's traditional control.[43]

Violence was a way of life for the black community in Millican and civil authorities had no interest in investigating criminal offensives committed against blacks. However, in Millican, as in other places throughout the South, the black community was developing a group consciousness that led them to band together for their own protection. Klan activities in and around Millican appear to have intensified the black community's fear, but it was the murder of a black man just five miles from the sheriff's house and his refusal to hold the accused murderer in jail that caused the black community to raise and train a militia. [44] The confrontation that ensued, which became known as the "Millican race riot," was reported in newspapers throughout the country, including the *New York Times*.[45] The riot would leave Brooks and six other Millican blacks dead with two more wounded.[46] It was not by accident that the two most prominent leaders of Millican's black community were killed during the riot, and with their primary organizers out of the way, the blacks of Millican struggled to maintain a semblance of community organization and structure.[47]

The Millican riot was the most famous of conflicts between whites and blacks in Brazos County; however, it was not an isolated incident. Area newspapers reported numerous violent attacks against the county's black population. A sampling of the various newspaper accounts paints a striking picture of violence in and around Brazos County. *Flake's*

Bulletin out of Galveston reported the following incident in 1867: "A colored man was found dead in the streets of Bryan on Sunday morning, and that a white man was killed in a gambling saloon at that place on Saturday evening. Another colored man was also found dead on Monday morning. A Pleasant place that Bryan to live in?"[48] However, the newspapers also reveal that there was a significant degree of black on black violence as well. *The Galveston Daily News* tells of a "black man, Brigham Young, who shot and killed another black man, Wild Oats, on the plantation of James M. Wilson, ten miles west of Bryan." Originally appearing in the *Bryan Appeal*, the *Houston Times* reprinted "Murder seems to be on the rampage among the freedmen of our county. Since Christmas, no less than 6 Negroes have been killed. The fusses all seem to be among themselves. If they keep up at this rate, by next election the whites will be largely in the majority in the county."[49]

Overall, Brazos county ranked first among the six counties in total incidents of violence reported to the Freedmen's Bureau (see table 6), but also it also had the smallest African American population among the counties included in this study. In Brazos County, blacks composed just 24 percent of the population in 1850, 34 percent in 1860, and only 39 percent in 1870. This is critical in understanding the high incidence of violence within the county. In the majority, whites were able maintain a greater degree of freedom in their actions toward the black population than their counterparts in counties that had large black majorities. Furthermore, the black population was significantly increasing each decade, a fact that would have concerned the local white population, especially given that blacks were increasingly gaining civil rights. Undoubtedly, due to the Millican race riot and its aftermath, there was a significant difference in the reported incidence of violence between 1866 and 1868. The peak years for violence were 1867 with twenty-four total offenses reported, second only to Grimes County, and 1868 with twenty-two total offenses reported (see table 3). An examination of violence in Brazos County illustrates that Bryan and Millican were the county's two most violent towns and accounted for all the reported violent acts inflicted upon the black population in the county (see table 7). These statistics, along with the regional newspapers accounts suggests that Brazos County was by far the most violent of any of the counties studied in the Lower Brazos Valley.

Grimes County, located forty miles northwest of Houston, was an emerging agricultural region within the state, and remained one of its fastest growing counties during the 1850s. The arrival of the railroad in

Navasota in 1859 further accelerated the county's growth. The 1850 census reported that the county had a population of 4,008, of which 1,680 were slaves, representing 42 percent of the total population for Grimes County. Over the next decade Grimes County continued to experience rapid population growth. But the growth in the number of slaves in the county significantly outpaced the white population. By 1860, the county's 10,320 in total population consisted of 5,468 slaves, representing 53 percent of the total. [50] Fueled by the large influx of refugees from the Lower South during the war, the county's black population increased dramatically during the war years, by 2,173. By 1870, another 916 blacks had migrated into Grimes County for a total of 7,921 freedpeople residing in the county, or 60 percent of the total population (see tables 5 and 8).

Like Brazos County, Grimes County overwhelmingly supported the Confederate cause, voting 916 to 9 in favor of secession. During the war the county made significant contributions to the war effort with its men serving in the 2nd, 4th, 8th, and 14th Texas Infantry and the 21st Texas Calvary.[51] Following the Confederate defeat there was a general feeling of resentment towards the Union and this feeling was intensified by economic turmoil and outbreaks of cholera and yellow fever. However, in May 1865 an event in Navasota would play an important role in framing the nature of the federal response to the increase in lawlessness and violence in the Brazos River Valley. Dissatisfied ex-Confederate soldiers looted a warehouse in Navasota filled with cotton and munitions and during the process the structure caught fire. The fire produced a violent explosion that destroyed several nearby buildings, and by the time the fire had run its course, much of the town's commercial district had been destroyed.[52]

The Navasota fire was indicative of a growing spirit of lawlessness that would soon engulf Grimes County, as well as the majority of the Lower Brazos River Valley. The Freedmen's Bureau's Twentieth Sub-district, which included most of Grimes and Brazos counties, reported that immediately following the Confederate surrender there was a general breakdown of law and order in the area. In 1867 alone twelve freedmen were murdered in Grimes County, another twenty-one were assaulted, and in May of 1868 the Ku Klux Klan made its first appearance in the county (see table 4). The freedmen reacted to intimidation and violence by organizing militias for their own protection. Additionally, with the assistance of prominent Republicans, black leaders formed Union Leagues, an organization designed to unite white and black Republicans into a group that could effectively exercise political power. In a scene that was to be repeated throughout the Brazos River Valley, whites met this challenge to their supremacy in the same manner they always had, by coercion, intimidation, and violence. Regarding incidents of reported violence, Grimes County ranked third among the six counties included in this study.[53] However, for the year 1867 the thirty-one reported incidents of violence was the highest of all the counties studied (see table 3). These outright acts of murder and violence were effective in the short term of suppressing the freedmen's new political rights, but due to growing Republican control, blacks' participation in local and state elections continued to grow and reached a zenith between 1870 and 1873.

Named for George Washington, Washington County is located in southeast central Texas bordered by Brazos County to the north, Grimes County to the east, and Austin County to the south. By 1850 Washington County had emerged as one of the region's largest agricultural centers ranking second, only behind Brazoria County, with 2,817 total slaves (see table 8).

During the 1850s the county enjoyed tremendous growth and its population increased by 9,232 and its slave population increased twofold to 7,268 total slaves. By the time of the Civil War farms covered 365,000 acres, an increase of 101,083 acres, and the total acres of improved land had risen from 19,535 in 1850 to 76,000 in 1860. The county voted 95 percent in favor of secession, and its people enthusiastically support the Confederate cause with its men serving in the 5th Texas Cavalry and Hood's Texas Brigade.[54] During the war, southern refugees, slave and white, continued to add significantly to the county's population. County tax records from 1864 indicate that the slave population had increased by 16 percent to 8,663 in just 4 years of war.[55] This growth continued after the war, and by 1870, the county's population increased to 23,104 with a total black population of 12,241 (see tables 6 and 8).

In the immediate aftermath of the war, people of the Lower Brazos River Valley refused to accept the idea that their way of life had forever been changed by the South's defeat. This is possibly due to the fact that there had not been the kind of upheaval during the war that was experienced in the other areas of the South. The election of James W. Throckmorton as governor in 1866 could only serve to enhance this mentality. After the war, Brenham especially had a reputation of possessing an "unreconstructed" population.[56]

Brenham, located about halfway between Houston and Austin in Washington County, had emerged as an important commercial junction between Houston and the surrounding areas.[57] In the immediate postwar years, the town experienced a significant increase in violence. The town averaged two violent crimes per month and ranked ninth out of 129 counties in frequency of crime. Observers who passed through Brenham during this period made specific references to the violent nature of the town.[58] Bvt. Maj. Gen. Christopher C. Andrews, who had visited Beaumont, Liberty, Brenham, and Columbus at the end of 1865, made a specific point to mention the fact that the large majority of white people there were still disloyal and entertained a hope of reestablishing slavery. Andrews also pointed out that there was a disdain for Northerners, and a specific aversion to federal authority.[59]

Federal troops arrived in Brenham at the end of 1865 and the Freedmen's Bureau established an office in Brenham shortly afterwards. What ensued was an escalation of tensions that reached their breaking point on September 7, 1866, in what became known as the Brenham fire, an incident that left two federal soldiers dead and more than a block of the town in flames.[60]

However, the Brenham fire would set in motion a chain of events that would culminate in the removal of Throckmorton as governor on July 30, 1867, a greater federal footprint in the area, and the Freedmen's Bureau receiving extra resources as it endeavored to protect the rights of the freedpeople of Texas. [61] The Klan also made an appearance in the county almost immediately upon the escalation of federal control within the county and the first black murder attributed to the Klan occurred within a year in 1868.[62]

Washington County ranked second in total incidents of violence for the years 1865–1868 and led the six counties examined with a total number of forty capital crimes committed against blacks (see tables 4 and 6). The black and white populations of the county remained relatively equal between 1850 and 1870 with blacks constituting only a slight majority of 53 percent of the total population in 1870 (see table 8). It is important to note that the two counties with the greatest incidence of violence were also the counties in which whites were either close to or in the majority of the county's population. An examination of the yearly trends indicates that 1866 and 1868 were the peak years for violence within the county. In 1866 and 1868 the county ranked first in total acts of violence and overall was just five short of Brazos County's high water mark of fifty-three. The high rate of violent incidents in 1866 can be attributed to the arrival of federal troops and the rise of the Union League and subsequent awakening of black political consciousness. The low rate of violence for 1867 might be due to the fact that, at least in the short term, the whites had been successful in eliminating key black leaders who were inspiring their brethren to become more assertive. Another factor that might account for the decrease was an increased presence of military personnel following the Brenham fire. However, by 1868, violence once again increased. The Klan was gaining strength in the county, Throckmorton had been removed from office, and there was increasing resistance to the efforts of the Bureau and a more politically assertive freedpeople population. What followed in 1868 was the highest number of violent acts found for any of the six counties with a total of twenty-five incidents of violence reported against blacks. Second only to Grimes County, this was the highest number of acts reported for any of the three years that followed the end of the war (see table 3).

Named after Stephen F. Austin, Austin County is located thirty-five miles west of Houston and is bordered to the north by Washington County and on the east by Fort Bend County. Most of the county's early immigrants migrated from the South and brought their slaves with them. By the time of the Texas Revolution, the county already had a population of just over 1,000, of which 350 were slaves. In 1850 the county's population increased to 3,841 of which 40 percent, or 1,549, were slaves. During the 1850 the population of the county exploded by 270 percent to 10,398 and the slave population experienced a similar growth rate of 237 percent to 3,668, comprising 35 percent of the total population. During the next decade, the county grew an additional 68 percent. The census of 1870 reports a total population of 15,087, of which 44 percent were black (see tables 5 and 8).

The largest number of people moving into the county came from the Upper South states of Tennessee, Virginia, and North Carolina and accompanying them were large numbers of slaves. The county very rapidly developed a plantation system primarily based on cotton, but other crops included corn, tobacco, and sweet potatoes. By 1850 there were more than thirty planters in the county, and by 1860 that number had grown to forty-six with a total of 346 slaveholders.[63]

The South was not the only contributor to the population growth of the county. Beginning in the 1830s and 1840s and continuing through the beginning of the Civil War, Germans began to immigrate into the county in substantial numbers. By 1850 there were 750 German-born residents in the county making up close to one-third of the total white population, and by 1860 German residents owned more farms than native-born whites. The Census of 1870 reports that a total of 2,111 German-born residents lived in Austin County, which was only seventeen behind Fayetteville's 2,128, which possessed the largest concentration of German-born immigrants in the state. The census of 1870 further illustrates that there were 5,481 people living in Austin County with at least one foreign-born parent. [64] With a total white population of 8,513, it would be safe to assume, since at least some of these were the children of German-born immigrants, that Germans as an ethnic group constituted a significant percentage of Austin County's total white population.

Unlike other areas in the Lower Brazos River Valley, the secession vote of 825 to 212 illustrated that a significant minority opposed leaving the Union. This was in large part due to the heavy population of Germans in the six precincts that voted decisively against secession.[65] However, during the war, the county did make significant contributes to the Confederate cause with its men serving in the 2nd, 8th, 21st, 24th, and 25th Texas Cavalry regiments, and the 1st and 20th Texas Infantry, but many others within the county, especially Germans, openly refused to serve.[66] By late 1862 events in the county were moving towards a climax. Approximately 150 Germans within the county refused to present themselves for conscription, and shortly thereafter, formed something resembling the Union Loyalty League that had appeared around Fredericksburg and New Braunfels in late 1861 and early 1862. German citizens even began forming militia and cavalry units to oppose the Confederates. On January 8, 1863, martial law was declared and over the next two weeks the state sent in several army units and the rebellion was suppressed.[67] The incident created animosity between the local German community and native-born whites in the county, which extended into the postwar years.

During Reconstruction, Austin County experienced its share of violence. During the war the county's black population increased by 47 percent to 4,702, and by 1870 it had reached 6,574, approximately 44 percent of the county's total population. Union troops arrived in the county in the fall of 1865 and the Freedmen's Bureau set up operations out of Hempstead. With the African American population hovering around 44 percent in the later part of the decade, Austin was one of only two counties in the Lower Brazos River Valley, the other being Brazos County, that maintained a white majority in its population (see tables 6 and 8). While Austin County ranked fifth out of the six counties studied in total incidents of violence, the Bureau still reported four murders for the year 1866 and ten in 1867. No records were found for 1868. However, these results for Austin County were atypical. Based on the percentage of blacks within the population, the county should have ranked near the top in total violence. The most likely explanation for this is that the high concentration of Germans in the county, with their pro-Union attitudes, played a substantial role in the depressed incidence of violence. However, others were not so inclined to accept a federal presence within the county.[68] With an active Bureau and federal troops, Republicans were successful in getting several blacks elected to political office, and this no doubt antagonized the more conservative elements within the county. The approximately 400 slaveholders in Austin County, as well as those who had supported the Confederacy, resented federal occupation and the loss of their slave labor and they did everything in their power to recreate a semblance of the antebellum labor system. The result was that 1867 was the deadliest year for freedpeople living in Austin County with fourteen reported acts of violence (see table 3).

Situated just twenty-eight miles southwest of Houston, Fort Bend County is bordered by Austin County to the north, Houston County to the east, and Brazoria County to the south. The Brazos River runs diagonally through the county and Richmond, the county seat, quickly developed into a vital trade center for the region as barges and steamboats navigated the Brazos carrying cotton and other products grown in the region to market. Fort Bend had developed a plantation system very early and by 1840 there were already 572 slaves in the county. By 1850 that number had increased to 1,172, placing Fort Bend among only six Texas counties in which slaves constituted the majority of the population in 1850.[69] The county's rapid growth continued and by 1860 it had a total of 159 farms covering 18,000 acres. The number of slaves residing within the county continued to escalate as well, and by 1860, there were a total of 4,127 slaves, constituting 67 percent of the county's total population (see table 8). The county vote for secession was 486 to 0 and the people of Fort Bend, like others throughout the Lower Brazos River Valley, enthusiastically supported the Confederate cause with many of its men serving in the Confederate army, including the famous 8th Texas Cavalry (Terry's Texas Rangers).[70]

During Reconstruction, with freedpeople outnumbering whites by more than two to one, Republicans had a distinct political advantage. As one would expect with such an overwhelming percentage of blacks in the county, the rate of violence was significantly lower than in those counties where the population differences were less favorable to freedmen. Of the six counties in this study, Fort Bend, at 78 percent, ranked first in the percentage of blacks within the population, but only fourth in the number of reported acts of violence (see table 6). However, with the Freedmen's Bureau reporting a total of thirty-three violent acts, including fourteen murders, the black population of Fort Bend still paid a heavy price for their freedom (see table 4).

Brazoria County covers 1,407 square miles of territory and is situated at the mouth of the Brazos River. The county is bordered by Fort Bend County to the northwest, Harris County to the northeast and Galveston County to east. Growing mostly sugar and cotton, the county developed a more complete plantation system based on slavery, and its society more closely resembled that of the Lower South than did other counties in Texas. By 1850 Brazoria possessed the largest slave population in the state, constituting 72 percent of the county's total population.[71] During the 1850s the county continued to enjoy success and by the end of the decade had emerged as the wealthiest county in Texas.[72] By 1860 the county's population had increased 70 percent, and its slave population had increased to 5,110, or 75 percent of the county's total population (see table 5).

Typical of other counties in the Lower Brazos River Valley, Brazoria demonstrated overwhelming support for secession and the Confederate cause. The people of Brazoria voted 527 to 4 in favor of leaving the Union, and during the war, its men saw service in a variety of Confederate units, including Hood's Texas Brigade. The county also manufactured weapons for the Confederacy and its harbor protected Confederate blockade runners. However, with the onset of Reconstruction, the county's fortunes changed dramatically. Total property value fell over 33 percent by 1866 and many of the large plantations were broken up.[73] With a strong federal troop presence in the area and an active Freedmen's Bureau, the county voted Republican throughout the Reconstruction era, primarily the result of the county's overwhelming black majority that was now voting in local and state elections.

Reconstruction also brought new hardships to the newly freed slaves of Brazoria, but perhaps due to a strong federal troop presence, and the fact that blacks constituted a two to one majority of the county's population, the incidence of reported violence was relatively low for the period 1866 through 1868, with only eight murders and eleven assaults (see table 4). The county's nineteen total number of reported incidents was the lowest of all the counties studied (see table 6). However, it is also important to note that the county was trending upward slightly each year, peaking in 1868 with nine reported violent acts directed at its black population (see table 3). Organizations like the Klan began to appear in the county by the end of the Reconstruction era and, ultimately, as was the case throughout the South after the federal troop presence was withdrawn and the Freedmen's Bureau was shut down, they were successful in disenfranchising the blacks of the county.[74]

Overall, the newly freed blacks of Texas discovered that the cost of freedom was extremely high. In the immediate postwar years they had to contend with an inordinate amount of abuse and violence directed at them by the white population. By 1870, blacks made up 31 percent of the population in Texas, and yet 40 percent of the known murders in the state were blacks murdered by whites, while only ten whites were murdered by blacks during the same period (see table 1). This clearly illustrates the degree of violence to which the black population of Texas had to contend. Of the known murders in Texas, blacks were disproportionately overrepresented possessing an index of representation of 129.[75] Even more striking is that, of the 373 known blacks murdered by whites between 1865 and 1868, 32 percent occurred in the six counties of the Lower Brazos River Valley.

This study does provide strong evidence that the Lower Brazos River Valley was one of the most violent regions in Texas. In 1870, there were 253,475 African Americans living in Texas, representing 31 percent of the state's total population. The six counties of the Lower Brazos River Valley contained 41,741 blacks, who accounted for 16 percent of the state's total black population. However, the 120 known blacks murdered by whites that occurred in these counties account for 13 percent of all reported murders in Texas, and 32 percent of all blacks murdered by whites occurred in the Lower Brazos Valley, which results in a 169 index of representation. While blacks statewide experienced a disproportionate amount of violence, as the index of 129 indicates, the black population that resided in the Lower Brazos River Valley had to contend with an even greater degree of violence than their counterparts living in other regions of Texas.

As one would expect, the frequency of violence is directly related to the percentage of African Americans within the population. The two counties that possessed black populations over 70 percent displayed a significantly lower tendency toward violence than those counties in which the white population was either in the majority or approximately equal to the black population (see table 7). Brazos County, which had the smallest black population at 39 percent, displayed the greatest tendency toward violent acts committed against its black inhabitants. Austin County was the only county that deviated significantly from the norm.

Next to Brazos County, Austin County possessed the second largest percentage of whites at 56 percent, and yet the county had the second fewest reported acts of violence. However, this is most likely explained by the presence of large numbers of Germans living within the county. Reinforcing this is the fact that Austin County was the only county that had any substantial opposition to secession.

Bvt. Maj. Gen. George A. Custer, stationed in Austin, succinctly described the situation in the Lower Brazos River Valley in his testimony before the Joint Committee on Reconstruction. Planters, he observed, were able to use the indebtedness of tenants to landlords as a means of controlling the freedmen labor force. While freedmen did possess the right to seek employment elsewhere, it was more illusory than reality because they had few real choices available to them other than to labor on some other person's land, but this option was limited as well, because their level of indebtedness kept them tied to land in much the same way that they had been when they were slaves.[76] Custer also noted that the activities of the Freedmen's Bureau alarmed the white population, especially its attempt to educate the black population, but also its circumventing due process and trial by jury, essentially acting as a military tribunal. Custer correctly saw that the courts by themselves provided inadequate protection for the freedmen and, like the Bureau, only served to provoke whites to even greater opposition.[77] However, foreshadowing the development of Jim Crow laws in the South, there was one answer in Custer's testimony that stood out above the rest: When asked "what would be the condition of the colored population in Texas, if the people were left to do with them as they pleased?" Custer responded "I think a system of laws would be passed, which, while it would not give the former owners the right to transfer freedmen without their consent to another owner, they would still have as much control over their labor as they had before slavery was abolished. And I think, too, that it would inaugurate a system of oppression that would be equally as bad as slavery itself."[78]

Violence in the Lower Brazos River Valley was motivated by a variety of reasons. The Brenham riot was less about race and more about a general atmosphere of lawlessness. The citizens of Brenham showed a complete lack of respect for authority and federal soldiers possessed none of the usual restraints of American military units. It was inevitable that these two elements would clash in Brenham. It was somewhat ironic that soldiers sent to Brenham, in part to assist in the protection of the freedpeople, were the ones who were inflicting violence upon them and it was the local citizens who wanted the soldiers to act appropriately. In Millican, race was the determinate factor in the riot. The white citizenry of Millican grew increasingly alarmed as the black population organized Loyal Union Leagues and became politically active, which served as a direct threat to whites' control of the political process. Whites' fear was further enhanced by the fact that Millican blacks were raising and training a militia. Combined with a low federal troop presence, Millican became a virtual powder keg waiting for the right spark to ignite it.

There were other reasons for racial violence in the Lower Brazos River Valley during Reconstruction. A significant number of local officials believed in the necessity of undermining and removing the Republican Party from the region. There was deep anger generated by the Confederate defeat and the economic collapse that followed. Also, there was the historical memory of violence used not only against slaves, but also Indians and Unionists. But ultimately, racial violence in Texas was primarily motivated by one of two main themes, one political, the other economic. Politically, whites resorted to violence to prevent newly enfranchised African Americans from asserting their new civil rights. As the freedpeople of the Lower Brazos River Valley and members of the Republican Party organized Union Leagues with the express purpose of asserting political power, whites reverted to using violence as a means of answering what they perceived to be a direct challenge to their political control.

Economically, the introduction of the free labor system combined with the arrival of the Freedmen's Bureau to ensure that the freedmen received adequate protection was more than the white community in the Lower Brazos River Valley could tolerate. Whites resented efforts to enforce a free-labor system, and they resorted to intimidation and violence in an attempt to maintain the central precepts their economic system. The supreme irony is that once the Freedmen's Bureau closed down and federal troops left the South, the advancements made during Reconstruction quickly eroded away. By the beginning the twentieth century the basic foundations of Jim Crow had been established and the system of subjugation through intimidation and violence would remain a staple of race relations in the United States for another sixty years. It would take what C. Vann Woodard termed a "Second Reconstruction," to complete what was left unfinished by the first.[79]

Table 1: Murders in State of Texas, 1865–1868

Blacks murdered by whites	373 (40%)
Blacks murdered by Blacks	48 (5%)
Whites murdered by blacks	10 (1.06%)
Whites murdered by whites	464 (49%)
unknown	48 (5%)
Total	939

Statistics drawn from the *Journal of the Reconstruction Convention*, Report of the Special Committee of Lawlessness and Violence in Texas (Austin, 1868).

Table 2: Freedmen's Bureau: Total Reported Acts of Violence, 1866–1868

Acts of Violence	2225
Murders	900
Indictments	249 (11.19%)
Convictions	5 (2.01%)
Capital Executions	1

Numbers drawn from Barry A. Crouch, "A Spirit of Lawlessness: White Violence; Texas Blacks, 1865–1868" *Journal of Social History* 18, no 2 (Winter, 1984).

Table 3: Freedmen's Bureau Records: Total incidents of violence in the Lower Brazos River Valley, 1866–1868

County	*Year*			*Total*
	1866	*1867*	*1868*	
Austin	4	14	4	22
Brazoria	4	6	9	19
Brazos	7	24	22	53
Fort Bend	11	8	14	33
Grimes	5	31	6	42
Washington	15	9	25	49
Total	46	92	80	218

Dale Baum has estimated that there were a staggering 2,225 physical acts of violence. While these figures are not exact, the roughly 218 known acts of violence in the six counties of the Lower Brazos Valley constituted 10.54 percent of the total acts of violence inflicted upon the African American population of Texas in the three years following the Civil War.

Table 4: Freedmen's Bureau Records: Total incidents recorded by County

County	*Offense*		*Total*
	Murder	*Assault*	
Austin	14	8	22
Brazoria	8	11	19
Brazos	29	24	53
Fort Bend	14	19	33
Grimes	15	27	42
Washington	40	9	49
Total	120	98	218

"Records of the Assistant Commissioner for the State of Texas," Bureau of Refugees, Freedmen, and Abandoned Lands, 1865–1869 [microform]. Washington : National Archives and Records Service, General Services Administration, 1973.

Table 5: Population Totals for Texas by County 1860 and 1870

	1860			*1870*		
	Total Population	*White*	*Slave*	*Total Population*	*White*	*Black*
Statewide	604, 215	420,891 (70%)	182,566 (30%)	818,579	564,700 (69%)	253,475 (31%)
Austin	10,398	6730 (65%)	3668 (35%)	15,087	8513 (56%)	6574 (44%)
Brazoria	6832	2027 (30%)	5110 (70%)	7527	1791 (24%)	5736 (76%)
Brazos	3096	1713 (55%)	1063 (35%)	9205	5466 (59%)	3759 (39%)
Fort Bend	6143	2001 (33%)	4127 (67%)	7114	1604 (23%)	5510 (77%)
Grimes	10,307	4832 (46%)	5468 (53%)	13,218	4748 (35%)	7921 (60%)
Washington	15,215	7268 (48%)	7941 (52%)	23,104	10,863 (47%)	12,241 (53%)

Population data extracted from the Virginia Library Historical Census Browser. http://mapserver.lib.virginia.edu/

Table 6: Comparison: County Population Density and Incidents of Violence.

	Percent African American		*Pop. Rank*	*Incidents*			*Total incidents*	*Violence Rank*	*White Population +/– 50%*
	1860	*1870*		*1866*	*1867*	*1868*			
Austin	35%	44%	5	4	14	4	22	5	+6%
Brazoria	70%	76%	2	4	6	9	19	6	–26%
Brazos	34%	39%	6	7	24	22	53	1	+9%
Fort Bend	67%	77%	1	11	8	14	33	4	–27%
Grimes	53%	60%	3	5	31	6	42	3	–15%
Washington	52%	53%	4	15	9	25	49	2	–3%

1. Population data extracted from the Virginia Library Historical Census Browser. http://mapserver.lib.virginia.edu/
2. Numbers for the incidents of violence were extracted from the Records of the Assistant Commissioner for the State of Texas," Bureau of Refugees, Freedmen, and Abandoned Lands, 1865–1869 [microform].
3. Population rank—highest % African American population to total population = 1, lowest = 6
4. Violence rank—highest total incidence = 1, lowest = 6

Table 7: Freedmen's Bureau Records Total incidents of Violence, 1866–1868

Town	*Offense*		*Total*
	Murder	*Assault*	
Anderson	5	18	23
Austin	4	2	6
Brenham	41	8	49
Bryan	14	13	27
Columbia	8	7	15
Courtney	2	0	2
Hempstead	10	7	17
Houston	2	7	9
Millican	13	13	26
Navasota	3	4	7
Richmond	12	17	29
Unknown Town	5	3	8
Total	114	99	218

Numbers for incidences of violence obtained from the "Records of the Assistant Commissioner for the State of Texas," Bureau of Refugees, Freedmen, and Abandoned Lands, 1865–1869 [microform]. Texas A & M University.

Table 8: Growth of Total African American population, 1850–1870

	Percent of Total Population with County			*Percent of Total Population within Region*		
	1850	*1860*	*1870*	*1850*	*1860*	*1870*
Statewide	11,255	27,377	41,741			
Austin	1549 (40%)	3668 (36%)	6574 (44%)	14%	10%	16%
Brazoria	3507 (72%)	5110 (75%	5736 (76%)	31%	19%	14%
Brazos	148 (24%)	1063 (34%)	3759 (41%)	1.3%	14%	9%
Fort Bend	1554 (61%)	4127 (67%)	5510 (78%)	14%	15%	13%
Grimes	1680 (42%)	5468 (53%)	7921 (60%)	15%	19%	19%
Washington	2817 (47%)	7940 (52%)	12,241 (53%	25%	29%	29%

1. Region as defined to include the six counties within this study
2. Population data extracted from the Virginia Library Historical Census Browser. http://mapserver.lib.virginia.edu/

ENDNOTES

1. United States Congress, *Report of the Joint Committee on Reconstruction: Florida, Louisiana, Texas* (Washington, D.C. Government Printing Office, 1866). Hereafter *Report of the Joint Committee on Reconstruction, 1866*. Testimony of John T. Allen, 88. There were roughly 260 blacks murdered in the states as of January 1866 and their bodies were found in creeks, floating down streams, and simply lying along the roadside.

2. *Journal of the Reconstruction Convention, Which met in Austin, Texas June 1, A.D., 1868* (Austin, 1870) July 20, 1868, 194; Report of the Special Committee on Lawlessness and Violence in Texas (Austin, 1868), 2. The report also notes that a large number of the murdered whites were Union men. For a detailed examination of the demographics of violence in the state, see Barry A. Crouch, "A Spirit of Lawlessness: White Violence; Texas Blacks, 1865–1868," *Journal of Social History* 18, no 2 (Winter 1984): 218–19.

3. *Journal of the Reconstruction Convention*, July 20, 1868, 194; Report of the Special Committee on Lawlessness and Violence, 3. Judge Black, a Republican in Uvalde County, Milton Biggs, a Unionist appointed county judge of Blanco County, and Judge Christian, a Unionist in Bell County, were all murdered in 1867. In 1868, four Unionists were murdered in Hunt County and six more in Bell County.

4. Report of Special Committee on Lawlessness and Violence, 3.

5. Crouch, "A Spirit of Lawlessness," 218–19.

6. Report of Special Committee on Lawlessness and Violence, 5. The findings of the Special Committee of Lawlessness and the Violence Registrar compiled by the Texas Freedman's Bureau allow a detailed examination of racial conflict and violence in the state between 1865 and 1870.

7. Ibid.

8. Ibid., 2. The number of blacks murdered between 1865 and 1867 rose 171 percent, from 38 in 1865 to 166 in 1867.

9. Barry A. Crouch, "Self-Determination and Local Black Leaders in Texas" *Phylon* 39, no. 4 (1978): 344.

10. Ibid.

11. *Report of the Joint Committee on Reconstruction, 1866*, 39. Testimony of Major General David S. Stanley, January 1, 1866.

12. *Report of the Joint Committee on Reconstruction, 1866*, 35. Testimony of Brigadier General W. E. Strong. January 1, 1866.

13. *Report of the Joint Committee on Reconstruction, 1866*, 36. It should be noted that the federal troop presence in those cities was more substantial than elsewhere and their black populations were not close to 50 percent so the white population had less to fear from a politically active black electorate and there was not the strong need for labor as there was in the more agricultural regions.

14. The reality is that the planters did not want to pay for labor when they used to own the labor supply, so in the absence of federal authority they resorted to coercion and violence in an attempt to maintain the status quo as it had existed prior to the Civil War.

15. *Report of the Joint Committee on Reconstruction, 1866*, 35. Testimony of Brigadier General W. E. Strong, January 1, 1866. Strong pointed out that he had been informed that there were freedmen east of the Trinity River who did not know they were free and in the area around Mount Jordan and Jasper, on the Neches River and San Augustine the freedmen were still held in a state of slavery and that along the Trinity River the freedmen did not even know they were free.

16. *Report of the Joint Committee on Reconstruction, 1866*, 137–38. Testimony of Benjamin C. Truman, Washington, April 5, 1866. It must be pointed out that this was one of the only individuals to testify that the freedmen were doing remarkably well in the state and that, in his opinion, the Freedmen's Bureau was no longer necessary in Texas.

17. Dale Baum, "Slaves Taken to Texas for Safekeeping during the Civil War," in *The Fate of Texas: The Civil War in the Lone Star State*, ed. Charles W. Greer (Fayetteville: University of Arkansas Press, 2008), 99.

18. *Report of the Joint Committee on Reconstruction, 1866*, 125. Testimony of Bvt. Maj. Gen. Christopher C. Andrews, March 14, 1866.

19. For the purpose of this study, any reference to the "Lower Brazos Valley" or to "region" will be defined as the six counties that are the subject of this study.

20. *Report of the Joint Committee on Reconstruction, 1866*, 125. Testimony of Bvt. Maj. Gen. Christopher C. Andrews, March 14. Andrews concludes his testimony by asserting that the freedmen are naturally unfriendly towards whites because they are treated as an abject and inferior race and whites are unwilling to concede to them any of the merits they possess.

21. William D. Carrigan, *The Making of a Lynching Culture: Violence and Vigilantism in Central Texas, 1836–1916* (Champaign: University of Illinois Press, 2004), 75. Moreover, it is important to remember that Texas had been in a state of continual conflict with hostile Native

Americans, recently embroiled in a conflict with Mexico, and possessed a strong tradition of vigilantism.

22. *Report of the Joint Committee on Reconstruction, 1866*, 38. Testimony of Brigadier General W. E. Strong, January 1, 1866.

23. *Report of the Joint Committee on Reconstruction, 1866*, 46–47. Testimony of Lieutenant Colonel H. S. Hall, January 1, 1866.

24. Ibid.

25. *Daily Austin Republican*, 11 July 1868, 2. See also *San Antonio Express* July 17, 1868, 2. The *Mobile Daily Register*, August 7, 1868, 4, reprinted from the *Texas Ranger* reports that W. H. Upton, "who was recently hung, as the *Austin Republican* says, because he was well known for his loyalty, came to his death because he was better known for cow stealing."

26. *Galveston Tri-Weekly News*, June 14, 1869, 2.

27. *Houston Daily Times*, 9 October 1868, 1, col.6.

28. *Report of the Joint Committee on Reconstruction, 1866*, 46–47. Testimony of Lieutenant Colonel H. S. Hall, January 1, 1866. Colonel Hall further illustrates this problem by pointing out that General Camby refused to allow any citizen to be punished by a military commission.

29. Barry A. Crouch, *The Freedmen's Bureau and Black Texans* (Austin: University of Texas Press, 1992), xiii.

30. *Report of the Joint Committee on Reconstruction, 1866*, 45 and 89. Testimony of Lt. Wilson Miller. Also see testimony of John T. Allen.

31. *Report of the Joint Committee on Reconstruction, 1866*, 123–24. Testimony of Bvt. Maj. Gen. Christopher C. Andrews, Washington, March 14, 1866.

32. *Report of the Joint Committee on Reconstruction, 1866*, 124. Testimony of Bvt. Maj. Gen. Christopher C. Andrews, Washington, March 14, 1866. Andrews went on to say that, in the areas with which he was familiar, the majority of white people attempted to obtain the labor of the freedmen at the cheapest possible rates and they would force them to accept these rates through coercion and violence if necessary.

33. Cecil Harper, Jr., "Freedmen's Bureau," *Handbook of Texas Online* (http://www.tshaonline.org/handbook/online/articles/ncf01), accessed July 29, 2011. The number of sub-assistant commissioners went from a low of twenty-seven to a high of fifty-nine.

34. Ibid. Harper attempts to underscore the one success of the Bureau in Texas by mentioning that at the time of the Bureau's closing its assistant superintendent noted that the burning of school houses and the harassment of teachers, which was so common in 1865, had virtually disappeared by 1870.

35. On July 30, 1866, the New Orleans race riot broke out as a result of the passage of "black codes" in the state. Former Confederates, aided by the police, attacked a gathering of about 200 blacks and 25 Republican delegates who were attempting the reconvene the constitutional convention. Close to 100 people were injured in the riot, and thirty-four blacks and three white Republicans were killed.

36. See William L. Richter, "The Brenham Fire of 1866: A Texas Reconstruction Atrocity," *Louisiana Studies* 14 (Fall 1975): 291. Richter states that Sheridan's problem was that the New Orleans race riots had just occurred and these developments in Louisiana required his full attention.

37. Ibid., 292.

38. *Report of the Joint Committee on Reconstruction, 1866*, 39. Testimony of Maj. Gen. David S. Stanley, January 1, 1866. Stanley also testified that there was a widespread belief among the people of Texas that the state had not been surrendered by Lee. He also pointed out that the largest support for the Union came from Germans in the densely populated western counties.

39. Historical Census Browser. Retrieved June 16, 2011, from the University of Virginia, Geospatial and Statistical Data Center: http://fisher.lib.virginia.edu/collections/stats/histcensus/index.html.

40. Baum, "Slaves Taken to Texas," 88–89. Baum also found that the actual number of refugee slaves for each county was 2,155 (Grimes), 2,047 (Washington), 1,503 (Austin), and 1,278 (Brazos). It should also be noted that Brazos County had the second largest increase in percentage of slaves taxed, at 174 percent; Van Zandt was first with a 402 percent increase.

41. Mark Odintz, "Brazos County," *Handbook of Texas Online* (http://www.tshaonline.org/handbook/online/articles/hcb13), accessed July 29, 2011.

42. Ibid.

43. See *Texas State Library Archives Commission: The 1860s: Freedom at Last* (http://www.tsl.state.tx.us/exhibits/forever/freedom/page6.html) for further details on the ten African Americans who were elected to the ninety-delegate convention, including Charles W. Bryant, James McWashington, Stephen Curtis, Sheppard Mullens, Wiley Johnson, George Ruby, Mitchell Kendal, Benjamin Watrous, Ralph Long, and Benjamin Williams.

44. Crouch, "Self Determination and Local Black Leaders in Texas," 350. Crouch speculates that on some level the white community's fear

of armed blacks had its roots in some of the more notorious armed slave rebellions throughout the South prior to the Civil War and, if you are trying to manipulate and control a specific part of the population, you do not want them to organize, vote, or to arm themselves. These things could create a serious challenge to white supremacy and control if left unchecked.

45. *New York Times*, August 6, 1868. (Reprint from *Flake's Bulletin*, July 29, 1868)

46. Odintz, "Brazos County." The Millican riot reverberated throughout the country and was even reported in the *New York Times*.

47. Throughout the South during the Reconstruction period black leaders who attempted to organize the black community routinely disappeared, leaving the organizational efforts floundering as a result. This was a very effective means of controlling the black population that the white community often employed.

48. *Flake's Bulletin*, Galveston, January 16, 1868, 6.

49. *Houston Times*, January 19, 1870, 1. (reprint from the *Bryan Appeal*)

50. Charles Christopher Jackson, "Grimes County," *Handbook of Texas Online* (http://www.tshaonline.org/handbook/online/articles/hcg11), accessed July 29, 2011.

51. Ibid.

52. Ibid.

53. It is hard to believe that the Freedmen's Bureau had only five recorded incidents of violence in Grimes County for the year 1866. This is possibly due to a loss of records or that, when a name could not be matched to a specific county it was deleted from the data set. It was difficult to determine either the place or year for an act of violence, or whether it was white on white, black on black, or white on black violence. In such instances the names were removed from the data set.

54. James L. Hailey and John Leffler, "Washington County," *Handbook of Texas Online* (http://www.tshaonline.org/handbook/online/articles/hcw04), accessed July 16, 2011.

55. Ibid.

56. Ibid.

57. Richter, "The Brenham Fire of 1866," 294. A rail line was being constructed to link Houston and Austin, but the endeavor collapsed with the onset of the Civil War when the rail line had only made it as far as Brenham.

58. Ibid., 294–95. Among the people commenting on the violent nature of the town was Mrs. Custer, who noted when she and her husband passed through the town, that the streets were filled with people looking for a fight.

59. *Report of the Joint Committee on Reconstruction, 1866*, 1866, 124. Testimony of Bvt. Maj. Gen. Christopher C. Andrews, March 14, 1866. By contrast Andrews notes that Union sentiment was good in Austin and very good in New Braunfels, which is not surprising considering its large German population.

60. Texas Senate, Senate Journal of the Eleventh Legislature, "Report of the Joint Select Committee to Investigate Facts in Regard to the Burning of Brenham" (Austin: Office of the State Gazette, I866), 1–54. Testimony of Susan Walker, September, 28, 1866, 7. Estimates for the losses incurred by the fire were set at $131,026.

61. Richter, "The Brenham Fire of 1866," 313.

62. Hailey and Leffler, "Washington County."

63. Jackson, "Austin County." "Planter" as defined to mean a person owning 20 or more slaves.

64. Historical Census Browser. Retrieved July 17, 2011, from the University of Virginia, Geospatial and Statistical Data Center: http://fisher.lib.virginia.edu/collections/stats/histcensus/index.html.

65. Jackson, "Austin County."

66. John Gorman, "Frontier Defense: Enlistment Patterns for the Texas Frontier Regiments in the Civil War," in *Seventh Star of the Confederacy: Texas During the Civil War*, ed. Ken Howell (Denton: University of North Texas Press, 2009), 76. German immigrants around Fredericksburg and New Braunfels formed a Union Loyalty League (ULL) in late 1860 or early 1861 and took an oath "never to betray the United States of America." Texas considered the ULL a threat to its sovereignty and over the next year two leaders of the ULL were executed, another German settler was beaten to death, and there were several armed confrontations between German militia and Texas State Troops. And it was Texas' harsh treatment of the ULL and German settlers in the area that convinced many other Germans to support the Union.

67. Jackson, "Austin County."

68. Ibid.

69. Virginia Laird Ott, "Fort Bend County," *Handbook of Texas Online* (http://www.tshaonline.org/handbook/online/articles/hcf07), accessed July 17, 2011.

70. Ibid.

71. Historical Census Browser. Retrieved July 18, 2011, from the University of Virginia, Geospatial and Statistical Data Center: http://fisher.lib.virginia.edu/collections/stats/histcensus/index.html.

72. Diana J. Kleiner, "Brazoria County," *Handbook of Texas Online* (http://www.tshaonline.org/handbook/online/articles/hcb12), accessed July 19, 2011.

73. Ibid.

74. Ibid.

75. To highlight the degree to which a specific group is represented within a given population, the use of an index of representation is useful in allowing for comparisons between the various groups. The index of representation was arrived at by dividing the percent of blacks murdered statewide with their percent of the total population and then multiplying that number by 100 to arrive at an index value. A value of 100 represents a perfect relationship between the percent of a particular group within the total population and their relationship to the murder rate. Values that are over 100 represent overrepresentation while values less than 100 represent underrepresentation.

76. *Report of the Joint Committee on Reconstruction, 1866*, 75. Testimony of Bvt. Maj. Gen. George A. Custer, Washington, March, 16, 1866. Also see the Testimony of Maj. Gen. David S. Stanley.

77. Carl H. Moneyhon, "Reconstruction," *Handbook of Texas Online* (http://www.tshaonline.org/handbook/online/articles/mzr01), accessed July 16, 2011.

78. *Report of the Joint Committee on Reconstruction, 1866*, 76. Testimony of Bvt. Maj. Gen. George A. Custer, Washington, March, 16, 1866.

79. C. Vann Woodard, *The Strange Career of Jim Crow,* 3rd. ed. (1955; repr., New York: Oxford University Press, 1974).

List of Contributors

Dale Baum is a Professor of History at Texas A&M University. He is the author of *Counterfeit Justice: The Judicial Odyssey of Texas Freedwoman Azeline Hearne* (2009), *The Shattering of Texas Unionism: Politics in the Lone Star State during the Civil War Era* (1998), and *The Civil War Party System: The Case of Massachusetts, 1848–1876* (1984).

Christopher Bean is an Assistant Professor of History at East Central University. He is the author of several articles on Reconstruction, including his "Death of a Carpetbagger: The George Washington Smith Murder and Stockade Trial in Jefferson, Texas, 1868–1869," which won the H. Bailey Carroll Award in 2010. This award is presented annually by the Texas State Historical Association for the best article published in the *Southwestern Historical Quarterly*.

Donaly Brice is an archivist at the Texas State Library in Austin. He is the author of *The Great Comanche Raid: Boldest Indian Attack of the Texas Republic* (1987). Brice has also co-authored several books, including *Cullen Montgomery Baker: Reconstruction Desperado* (1997) and *The Governor's Hounds: The Texas State Police, 1870–1873* (2011).

Ronald E. Goodwin is an Adjunct Assistant Professor of History at Prairie View A&M University. His research focuses on urban history, the impact of planning decisions on neighborhood development, and the historical development of black community in Texas. His most recent article is "Control after Dark: Slave Owners and their Control of Slaves' Intimate Relationships OR Who's your Daddy?" in the *Journal of Texas History and Culture*. Goodwin is also the co-author of "On the Edge of First Freedoms: Black Texans and the Civil War" in *The Seventh Star of the Confederacy: Texas during the Civil War* (2009).

John Gorman is an Instructor of History at Blinn College in Bryan, Texas. At present he is working on a Ph.D. in history at Texas A&M University. Gorman specializes in late nineteenth and twentieth-century United States history with a focus on Civil War enlistment patterns. His most recent publication is "Frontier Defense: Enlistment Patterns for the Texas Frontier Regiments in the Civil War" in *The Seventh Star of the Confederacy: Texas during the Civil War* (2009).

Kenneth W. Howell is an Associate Professor of History at Prairie View A&M University. Howell has several publications that focus on the history of Texas and the Old South, including *Henderson County, Texas, 1846–1861: An Antebellum History* (1999); *The Devil's Triangle: Ben Bickerstaff, Northeast Texans, and the War of Reconstruction* (2007); *Texas Confederate, Reconstruction Governor: James Webb Throckmorton* (2008), *Beyond Myth and Legend: A Narrative History of Texas* (2008). He is also the editor of *The Seventh Star of the Confederacy: Texas during the Civil War* (2009).

Rebecca A. Kosary is an Assistant Professor of History and the Director of the African American Studies Program at Texas Lutheran University. Kosary's research focuses on the plight of freewomen during the Reconstruction era. Her most recent publication is "Wantonly Maltreated and Slain, Simply Because They Are Free: Racial Violence during Reconstruction in South Texas" in *African Americans in South Texas History* (2011).

Douglas Kubicek is the chairman of the Lavaca County Historical Commission and has served as a professional educator in the Texas public school system for more than 22 years. For most of those years, Kubicek has taught in the Hallettsville Independent School District, but he has also taught at Moulton and Cuero. He was also a photographer and columnist for the *Hallettsville Tribune-Herald* from 1979 to 1992. Specializing in Lavaca County History and Cultural Geography, his publications include *Grand, Complete and Perfect: The Lavaca County Courthouse 1897–1899*. He has also had articles printed in various genealogical publications.

Richard B. McCaslin is a Professor of History at the University of North Texas. He is the author of *Tainted Breeze: The Great Hanging at Gainesville, Texas, October 1862* (1994) which won the Coral H. Tullis Prize awarded by the Texas State Historical Association. He also wrote *Lee in the Shadow of Washington* (2001) which was nominated for the Pulitzer Prize and won the Slatten Award and the Laney Prize. His most recent publication is *Fighting Stock: John S. "Rip" Ford of Texas* (2011).

Carl H. Moneyhon is a Professor of History at the University of Arkansas in Little Rock. He is a specialist on the Civil War and Reconstruction, with much of his work focusing on the Texas experience. His Texas related works include *Republicanism in Reconstruction Texas* (1980), *Texas After the Civil War: The Struggle of Reconstruction* (2004), and *Portraits of Conflict: A Photographic History* *of the Civil War in Texas* (1998). His most recent publication is *Edmund J. Davis: Civil War General, Republican Leader, Reconstruction Governor* (2010).

Mary Jo O'Rear has served in regional and local history groups and as an Adjunct Professor of History at Del Mar College in Corpus Christi and Texas A&M University-Kingsville. She is a former instructor in history, economics, and geography for the Corpus Christi Independent School District. Her most recent publications include the award-winning *Storm Over the Bay: The People of Corpus Christi and Their Port* (2009).

William L. Richter is a noted historian who has researched, written, and published almost two dozen articles emphasizing military-civil affairs, race relations, constitutional issues, and Spanish colonial efforts in North America. In addition to his numerous articles, Richter's most influential work on Reconstruction Texas is *The Army in Texas during Reconstruction, 1865–1870* (1987) and *Overreached on All Sides: The Freedmen's Bureau Administrators in Texas, 1865–1868* (1991).

Carroll Scogin-Brincefield has served as an instructor of World History, World Geography, and American Government and Economics for Corpus Christi Independent School District. She lectures throughout Texas on numerous historical topics and has served as the director of the Oral History program in Lavaca. Her published works include a wide range of topics from Native American history and culture to women and children of the Civil War. Her most recent publications and research have brought her into the 20th century with studies focusing on military topics, including World War II internment and prisoner of war camps in Texas.

James M. Smallwood is an Emeritus Professor of History at Oklahoma State University. He is the author of seventeen books, most of which focus on Texas history. His *Time of Hope, Time of Despair: Black Texans during Reconstruction* won the Texas State Historical Association's Coral H. Tullis Award in 1982 for the best book of the year on Texas history. His most recent publication, *The Feud That Wasn't: The Taylor Ring, Bill Sutton, John Wesley Hardin, and Violence in Texas* (2008) also won the Tullis Award in 2008, the Ottis Lock Award for Superior Publication in East Texas History in 2008, presented by the East Texas Historical Association, and the Most Significant Scholarly Book Award in 2009, presented by the Texas Institute of Letters.

Charles D. Spurlin is an Emeritus Professor of History at Victoria College. He is the author of numerous professional articles focusing on Texas history. His publications include *West of the Mississippi with Waller's 13th Texas Cavalry Battalion* (1971), *The Civil War Diary of Charles A. Leuschner* (1992), and *Texas Volunteers in the Mexican War* (1998).

Andrés Tijerina is a Professor of History at the Pinnacle Campus. He is the author of *Tejanos and Texas Under the Mexican Flag, 1821–1836* (1994) and *Tejano Empire: Life on the South Texas Ranchos* (2008). He edited Andrés Saenz's *Early Tejano Ranching in Duval County* (1998) and co-edited Elena Zamora O'Shea's novel entitled *El Mesquite* (2000). Organizations such as the Sons of the Republic of Texas, the Texas State Historical Association, and the Texas Historical Commission have officially recognized the significance of such works with the Presidio La Bahía Award, the Kate Broocks Bates Award, and the T. R. Fehrenbach Award.

Index